WIREGRASS TO APPOMATTOX

The Untold Story of the
50th Georgia Infantry Regiment, C.S.A.

JAMES W. PARRISH

D1711722

Angle Valley Press
Winchester, Virginia

www.AngleValleyPress.com

Printed in the United States of America

First Edition, First Printing
12 11 10 09   4 3 2 1

ISBN 13: 978-0-9711950-7-3

ISBN 10: 0-9711950-7-2

Publisher's Cataloging-in-Publication
(Provided by Quality Books, Inc.)

Parrish, James W. (James William)
Wiregrass to Appomattox : the untold story of the
50th Georgia Infantry Regiment, C.S.A. / James W. Parrish. — 1st ed.
p. cm.
Includes bibliographical references and index.
LCCN 2008922715
ISBN-13: 978-0-9711950-7-3
ISBN-10: 0-9711950-7-2

1. Confederate States of America. Army. Georgia
Infantry Regiment, 50th. 2. Georgia—History—Civil
War, 1861-1865—Regimental histories. 3. Georgia—
History—Civil War, 1861-1865—Registers. 4. United
States—History—Civil War, 1861-1865—Regimental
histories. 5. United States—History—Civil War,
1861-1865—Registers. 6. Soldiers—Georgia—History—
19th century.   I. Title.

E559.5 50th.P37 2008   973.7'458
                              QBI08-600240

This book is dedicated to the memory of my two great-great-grandfathers,
Sergeant George Washington Chitty and
Captain Quarterman Baker Staten,
and to all the Wiregrass men who served in the
50th Georgia Volunteer Infantry Regiment, C.S.A.

"My country; I love thee better than life. There is no sacrifice but what I would willingly take for thee."

"Confederate Diary," Capt. William F. Pendleton, February 6, 1865.

TABLE OF
CONTENTS

ILLUSTRATIONS

MAPS

PHOTOGRAPHS

PHOTOGRAPHS IN REAR OF BOOK

PREFACE

My Wiregrass roots run deep as a result of the migration of my ancestors from Virginia, North Carolina and South Carolina into southern Georgia between the late 1700's and mid-1800's. Born in Quitman, Georgia, I grew up just across the border in rural Madison County, Florida. I spent much of my early childhood wandering through the longleaf pine forests that grew on my grandfather's farm. Although my specific interest in the War Between the States would not emerge until later, I vaguely remember older relatives talking about the war. They uttered the name of Robert E. Lee with the utmost reverence. However, I recall one of my great aunts referring to General William Tecumseh Sherman as, "that damned old Yankee heathen." The scars brought about by Sherman's historic march through Georgia and the "Yankee occupation" after the "War of Northern Aggression" remained fresh in this area almost one hundred years after the war.

Genealogy became a serious interest in my adult life. While researching the Chitty, Moore, Parrish and Staten branches of my family tree, I became aware that some of my ancestors had links to the Confederacy. Two of my maternal great-great grandfathers, George Washington Chitty and Quarterman Baker Staten, served in the 50th Georgia Volunteer Infantry Regiment. Chitty owned a small farm in Echols County, while Staten came from a very prosperous Clinch County family.

While I initially focused on the military backgrounds of my ancestors, I soon discovered information about other members of the regiment. I became fascinated with the personal accounts of many other 50th Georgia soldiers through their letters, diaries and post-war remembrances. More information on the regiment began to come in and like pieces of a puzzle, the story of the regiment waited to be put together. Unfortunately, I found no single comprehensive source that followed the men of the 50th Georgia Regiment from initial organization to final surrender. This decade-long quest became an obsession, and I became determined to compile the history of the regiment.

The 50th Georgia Regiment was organized in March 1862. The majority of men who made up the regiment were simple rural farmers between the ages of 18 and 29. Few owned large landholdings or slaves. Most had never ventured far from their home county. The 50th Georgia initially consisted of ten companies that totaled approximately nine hundred volunteers. During the conflict, a total of over fourteen hundred men served in the regiment at one time or another. Of that number, more than one of every three died from battle or illness.

The material used in this work came from soldier's compiled service and pension records, archives data, books, articles, individual diaries, letters, memoirs, and private collections. Descendants of the soldiers have been exceptionally generous in sharing priceless mementos of their ancestors. Letters and diaries from soldiers and their families have been liberally utilized complete with misspelled words and punctuation errors. Limited punctuation has been added in some instances to help the reader, but for the most part the words are printed as originally written by the soldier.

My research has also allowed me to walk the hallowed ground of many battlefields where this regiment fought. I felt an eerie, almost spiritual feeling as I walked the path of my ancestors at places like Gettysburg's Rose Farm and the Old Sharpsburg Road at Fox's Gap. These battles are now no longer just names in a book to me, but they have become part of my family history.

The complete history of the 50th Georgia Infantry Regiment may never be known as certain records are missing or do not exist. I hope this book will motivate others who are interested in their Wiregrass roots to search for clues and to help fill in the blanks wherever possible. Anyone with additional information is encouraged to contact me.

ACKNOWLEDGMENTS

It is impossible to complete a project of this magnitude without the generous assistance of scores of relatives, friends, descendants of soldiers, and others interested in Civil War history. Several times I thought I was finished with my research and someone would provide me with another photo, or letter, or diary. The generosity of the descendants of the men who served in the 50th Georgia is amazing and truly appreciated. Although official reports and documents provide a picture of a military unit, the story of the individual soldier can only be told from personal accounts.

There are many others who helped this project come to fruition. I am more than a little awed by the time many distinguished historians and battlefield authorities gave in reviewing portions of this work. Included in this group are Brandon H. Beck, Keith A. Bohannon, Chip L. Bragg, Chris M. Calkins, Robert K. Krick, Frank A. O'Reilly, Al Preston, J. Michael Priest, Jeffry D. Wert and Mac Wyckoff. Their insightful comments and suggestions for style and historic accuracy were invaluable and greatly appreciated.

A host of individuals provided resource materials, research assistance, and encouragement. In 2000, John A. Griffin authored *Warriors of the Wiregrass*, a book that highlighted several South Georgia Confederate regiments, including the 50th Georgia. His excellent research provided me with the framework from which to create a comprehensive history of the 50th Georgia. Charlotte Ray, retired senior archivist at the Georgia Division of Archives and History, provided valuable help and advice early in my quest for 50th Georgia material. Keith Bohannon provided valuable resource material from his extensive collection. Chris L. Ferguson, author of *Southerners at Rest: Confederate Dead at Hollywood Cemetery*, shared information that helped identify numerous Wiregrass Georgia soldiers who now rest at Hollywood and Oakwood Cemeteries in Richmond, Virginia. Kurt Graham opened his files and shared extensive information for the Fox's Gap and Gettysburg chapters. He was always available to entertain theories and ideas about unit location during these battles. Frank O'Reilly allowed the use of his sketch depicting the 50th Georgia overrunning Monk's Battery at Cedar Creek. Greg Biggs and Greg White enthusiastically offered ongoing resource material and encouragement. David L. Richards, a Gettysburg battlefield guide, guided my son-in-law, Gregg Becker, and me on a detailed walking tour of the Rose Farm area of the battlefield where the 50th Georgia fought on day two; Al Preston, assistant manager of the South Mountain Recreation Area, provided an interesting tour of the Fox's Gap battlefield. Mark F. Farrell gave permission to use the diary entry of his great grandfather, Sergeant Henry W. Tisdale, 35th Massachusetts Volunteers, to help view the Fox's Gap carnage through the eyes of a Union soldier.

John Coski permitted me the use of research materials in the Museum of the Confederacy's research library. Timothy Frilingos took me on a guided tour of the Georgia Capitol Museum archives and allowed me to photograph the 50th Georgia Battle Flag. The museum also gave permission for their photo of the 50th Georgia battle flag from *Hallowed Banners* to be placed on this book cover. Donald O. Davis and Renate K. Miller, Valdosta/Lowndes County Museum, provided research assistance and several photos of Wiregrass Georgia soldiers. Ann R. Harrison, Thomas County Historical Society, and her staff supplied valuable photos and aid at the Thomas County Museum of History; Kathryn Lillethun, Decatur County Historical Society, assisted in researching the letters of Major Duncan Curry. Sylvia Frank Rodrigue furnished important editorial assistance. Blake A. Magner helped transfer text into detailed maps. J. B. Bechtol added her magic with the graphic and book design work. Publisher John J. Fox, owner of Angle Valley Press and author of the acclaimed *Red Clay to Richmond,* exhibited ongoing patience and guidance throughout the project.

The staffs from the following places provided invaluable assistance: Georgia Division of Archives and History, Morrow, Georgia; Reference Library, Georgia Historical Society, Savannah, Georgia; Hargrett Rare Book and Manuscript Library, University of Georgia, Athens, Georgia; Manuscript, Archives, and Rare Book Library, Robert W. Woodruff Library, Emory University, Atlanta, Georgia; Kenan Research Center, Atlanta History Center, Atlanta, Georgia; Huxford Genealogy Library, Homerville, Georgia; Southwest Georgia Regional Library, Bainbridge, Georgia; Roddenbery Memorial Library, Cairo, Georgia; Ellen Payne Odom Genealogy Library, Moultrie, Georgia; Museum of Colquitt County History, Moultrie, Georgia; Satilla Regional Library, Douglas, Georgia; Three Rivers Regional Library, Brunswick, Georgia; Quitman/Brooks County Historical Museum and Cultural Center, Quitman, Georgia; U.S. Army Military

Institute, Carlisle, Pennsylvania; Stewart Bell Jr. Archives Room, Handley Regional Library, Winchester, Virginia; Special Collections Library, University of Tennessee, Knoxville, Tennessee; State Library and Archives of Florida, Tallahassee, Florida; and Elmer's Genealogical Library, Madison, Florida.

I would like to thank the many descendants of 50th Georgia soldiers who graciously shared stories and provided personal mementos. Glenn Hodges of Nashville, Georgia provided photocopies of letters from his great-great grandfather, Lieutenant Francis L. Mobley, a photo of his ancestor and photos of Lieutenant Mobley's sword, blood spattered trousers, and other treasured memorabilia; Mr. and Mrs. William L. Fleming Sr. of Bainbridge, Georgia furnished a portrait of William's great-grandfather, Lieutenant Colonel William O. Fleming, and a photo of Colonel Fleming's sword; Mrs. Ermon (Marilee) Butler of Calvary, Georgia shared a photo and reminiscences of her husband's ancestor, Lewis Fennell Butler, and information on Lewis Fennell Butler's brother, Lucian; Carolyn Herring Chason of Cairo, Georgia provided the photo of her great grandfather, Joseph Rawls, who graces the cover of this book; Ben Pendleton, Carroll Odhner and Aubrey Odhner shared information on their mutual ancestor, William F. Pendleton; Robert L. and Annette C. Harrell of Cairo, Georgia supplied the photo of Robert Harrell's great-great grandfather, Sergeant John Wade King; Dorothy E. Neisen of Lake Park, Georgia furnished information on her great uncle, Cornelius Peterson; and Paul C. Bunce, Sr., of Winterville, Georgia submitted a photo of his great grandfather, Captain James A. Waters.

I also want to thank my cousin, George R. Pridgeon, for accompanying me on research trips to area genealogy libraries and museums over the years. Although research remained the primary motivation, the excuse to sample the quality of local barbeque establishments throughout the Wiregrass Georgia area was a close second. Finally, I give unqualified thanks to my wife Margaret, who accompanied me on numerous battlefield tours and visits to museums and archives throughout Georgia, Maryland, Pennsylvania, Tennessee and Virginia. Without her unending patience and willingness to allow vacations to be scheduled around battlefield tours and archival visits, this project would never have gotten off the ground.

James W. Parrish
Tallahassee, Florida
September 4, 2008

Chapter One
Defending the Homeland:
Organization and Early Camp Life
March 4–July 19, 1862

Most of the men who would make up the companies of the 50th Georgia Infantry Regiment lived in the Wiregrass Region of south Georgia, which extends along the Florida border from Alabama to Savannah. Its name comes from a type of plant growing in the region that has long, thin, wiry leaves. Wiregrass (*Aristida stricta*) is a very hardy and fast-growing species found from Mississippi to Florida and as far north as South Carolina. It is common in the pine flatwoods and upland sandhills of Georgia. The land was made up primarily of pinewood forests, scattered oak hammocks, and wiregrass. In cleared areas, the soil was generally good for growing crops, such as tobacco, corn, and cotton. There was an abundance of wild game throughout the area. At the time of the Civil War, the region was still sparsely populated. Settlers had wrestled it from local Native Americans only a few years earlier, and many future soldiers had been born during or just after the last Seminole War, which ended in the late 1830s. These hardy Georgians spent much of their lives in the outdoors, farming, hunting, and fishing. Most knew how to handle a musket and were crack shots. Their individualism and toughness, much like that of the wiregrass plant, were strengths they would need to help carry them through the difficult times ahead.

Organization of the Companies
Within one year after the Civil War began, both sides realized that the bloody conflict would require many more men than had first been thought necessary. The Confederacy desperately needed new recruits to feed the war machine fighting against the vastly superior numbers of the Union. Patriotism ran high throughout the Wiregrass Region in early 1862, and companies were quickly organized in response to the calls by President Jefferson Davis and Georgia Governor Joe E. Brown for additional volunteers to protect the homeland.

The Wiregrass recruits who would initially make up the 50th Georgia Regiment were mustered into service in their respective counties on March 4, 1862. Although the majority of these new volunteers worked as farmers, they came from all walks of life, including merchants, lawyers, politicians, teachers, and craftsmen. Most volunteers were young and single, and many were related

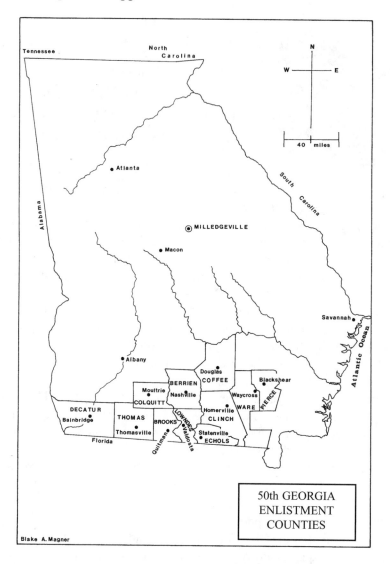

Tennessee

North Carolina

N

W ———— E

40 miles

• Atlanta

Alabama

South Carolina

⊚ MILLEDGEVILLE

• Macon

Savannah •

Atlantic Ocean

• Albany

Douglas

COFFEE

Blackshear

BERRIEN

Moultrie • Nashville

Waycross

COLQUITT

WARE

PIERCE

DECATUR

Homerville

Bainbridge •

THOMAS

BROOKS

CLINCH

Thomasville •

Quitman

Valdosta

Statenville

LOWNDES

• ECHOLS

Florida

**50th GEORGIA
ENLISTMENT
COUNTIES**

Blake A. Magner

as brothers, cousins, or by marriage. It was not uncommon for several members of the same family to enlist together in the same unit. The term of enlistment was for three years or the war. When the companies formed, members of the units elected their own officers. In many instances, a wealthy and powerful member of the local community had organized the company, and the men usually elected this organizer as captain to lead the company. Most other officers came from well-known families and had made their mark in the community. Some had previous military experience, which would become a critical asset later in the war. A few were elected purely through their popularity or family connections. Many who did not possess the necessary leadership skills would falter early, and the common soldier quickly learned his chance of survival was enhanced by the quality of the officer leading his company. Popularity was soon replaced by the cold hard facts of survival.

The 50th Georgia was composed of ten companies, each from a different county.

Company A – Satilla Rangers (Pierce County)

The Satilla Rangers mustered into service at Blackshear with approximately eighty-four men. Most of the men were from Pierce County. Captain John T. Wilson, commissioned in May 1861, became company commander. Members of the company elected James A. Waters as first lieutenant, Aaron Dowling as second lieutenant, and John M. Dowling as ensign. The company soon left for Camp Davis, near Savannah.[1]

Lieutenant James A. Waters, Company A. Pierce County native James A. Waters was elected first lieutenant when the Satilla Rangers were formed on March 4, 1862. On January 1, 1863, Waters was appointed captain of Company A to replace John Wilson, who had been mortally wounded at Fox's Gap. Captain Waters resigned his commission in May 1863 but remained in the company. The February 28, 1865, Muster Roll listed him as absent with leave. The war ended as Waters attempted to return to his regiment. Courtesy of Paul C. Bunce Sr., Winterville, Georgia.

Company B – Ware Volunteers (Ware County)

The Ware Volunteers entered service at Waycross with approximately eighty-nine men. Officers included Captain Philip Coleman Pendleton, First Lieutenant Peter B. Bedford, Second Lieutenant William T. Whiteford, Second Lieutenant Daniel J. Jeffords, and First Sergeant William J. Shone. Captain Pendleton, an Indian War veteran, would soon be elected as major of the new regiment, and Lieutenant Bedford would be promoted to captain and commander of Company B.[2]

Captain John Middleton Spence, Company C. A respected farmer before the war, John Spence organized the Coffee Guards, and the men elected him captain when the company was mustered into service on March 4, 1862. Spence earned a promotion to major on December 21, 1863, and he served with the regiment until he received a leave of absence in February 1865. John Spence was at home in Coffee County at the close of the war. From *Ward's History of Coffee County.*

Company C – Coffee Guards (Coffee County)

The Coffee Guards enlisted at Douglas with approximately ninety men, who elected Captain John Middleton Spence, First Lieutenant Alfred A. Smith, Second Lieutenant James Kinchen Hilliard, Second Lieutenant Thomas George White Jr., and First Sergeant Edward H. Moore.[3]

Company D – Valdosta Guards (Lowndes County)

The Valdosta Guards mustered into service at Valdosta with approximately eighty-nine men. The company officers were Captain James T. Bevill, First Lieutenant William D. Howell, Second Lieutenant Augustus Harding Lane, Second Lieutenant S. W. Baker Jr., and First Sergeant Reuben Thomason "Tompy" Roberds.[4]

Shortly after being organized, the company received a flag from the local ladies of Lowndes County. The stirring event, typical of the fervor and excitement of the day, was reported in the April 14, 1862, edition of the *Savannah Republican.*[5]

Second Lieutenant Augustus Harding Lane, Company D. Augustus Harding Lane was elected second lieutenant when the Valdosta Guards were mustered into service on March 4, 1862. Promoted to first lieutenant on June 9, 1863, Lane rose to captain shortly thereafter. He resigned his commission on December 30, 1863. Courtesy of Lowndes County Historical Society and Museum, Valdosta, Georgia.

Rueben Thomason "Tompy" Roberds, Company D, as a Citadel cadet. Born the son of a prosperous South Carolina planter and state legislator in 1834, Reuben T. Roberds attended the Citadel as a young man. He moved to Lowndes County in 1859 and opened a successful mercantile business. The voters elected Roberds as the first mayor of Valdosta in late 1860. When the Valdosta Guards were formed on March 4, 1862, the men elected the popular figure as first sergeant. He received a promotion to adjutant of the regiment in early 1863. Courtesy of Lowndes County Historical Society and Museum, Valdosta, Georgia.

Company E – Thomas County Rangers (Thomas County)

The Thomas County Rangers enlisted at the county court house in Thomasville with a total of 107 men, including four officers, ten non-commissioned officers, and ninety-three privates. Officers included Captain Cicero Holt Young, First Lieutenant Peter Alexander Selkirk McGlashan, Second Lieutenant John N. McKinnon, Second Lieutenant Richard J. McLean Jr., and First Sergeant John C. Reynolds. The company soon boarded the train to Camp Davis near Savannah.

Peter Alexander Selkirk McGlashan. Peter A. S. McGlashan was born in Edinburgh, Scotland. In 1848, at age seventeen, he came to America with his parents and settled in Savannah, Georgia. After spending time in the California goldfields and with William Walker's military expedition to Nicaragua in the late 1850s, McGlashan owned a Thomasville saddle and manufactory business, selling saddles, bridles, and leather goods. The Thomas County Rangers were organized on March 4, 1862, and the men elected McGlashan first lieutenant. Military experience and excellent leadership skills ultimately carried the Scotsman to command of the regiment. The veteran commander suffered serious wounds in both thighs at the Battle of Cedar Creek on October 19, 1864. He was later captured at the Battle of Sailor's Creek on April 6, 1865, and spent the rest of the war as a Union prisoner. He was released from the Johnson's Island, Ohio, Prison in July 1865. Courtesy of Thomas County Historical Society and Museum, Thomasville, Georgia.

Company F – Decatur Infantry (Decatur County)

The Decatur Infantry organized at Bainbridge with approximately 104 men from Decatur County and the immediate area. On March 3, 1862, Governor Joseph E. Brown appointed Duncan Curry, a well-known and prosperous planter, as captain of the company. Other officers included First Lieutenant William Oliver Fleming, Second Lieutenant William Powell, Second Lieutenant William G. Dekle Jr., and First Sergeant Henry W. McTyre. Shortly after being organized, the company left for Camp Davis.[7]

The son of a circuit judge, William Oliver Fleming was born in Liberty County, Georgia. Fleming later moved to Decatur County and became a successful lawyer and planter prior to the war. When the hostilities first began, Fleming was elected lieutenant in the Bainbridge Independents, 1st Georgia Regiment. When the Decatur Infantry was formed on March 4, 1862, the men elected twenty-seven-year-old Fleming as first lieutenant of the new company. When Captain Duncan Curry received a promotion to major on October 8, 1862, Fleming replaced him as captain of Company F. On August 18, 1863, Fleming rose to major. In September of that year he received a promotion to lieutenant colonel, effective July 31. Fleming resigned his commission on December 21, 1863, to serve in the Georgia State Legislature. He returned to military duty in 1864, when Union forces threatened Georgia. Courtesy of William L. Fleming Sr., great-grandson of William O. Fleming, Bainbridge, Georgia.

Company G – Clinch Volunteers (Clinch & Echols Counties)
The Clinch Volunteers mustered into service at Homerville with approximately eighty-six men. The company consisted primarily of volunteers from Clinch and Echols Counties. The men elected thirty-seven-year-old John Riley O'Steen, a large landowner in the area, as captain. Other officers were First Lieutenant Quarterman Baker Staten, Second Lieutenant Isaac Burkhalter, Second Lieutenant Jacob S. Lightsey Jr., and First Sergeant James Douglass.[8]

Thirty-year-old Clinch County native Quarterman Staten was a well-respected planter. His lineage went back to the late 1660s, when his ancestors immigrated to America from England. Staten's great-great-grandfather served in the Revolutionary War and received a land grant in Georgia. His father moved to the area in 1830 and had been an early settler and Indian fighter, amassing huge landholdings that were divided among the children upon his death. Staten served as first lieutenant in the Clinch Invincibles, a home guard unit, and he retained that rank upon enlistment into the Clinch Volunteers.[9]

Thirty-one year old Isaac Burkhalter had moved to Clinch County with his father around 1845. He grew up in the area and served as justice of the peace from 1857 until 1861.[10]

Company H – Colquitt Marksmen (Colquitt County)
The Colquitt Marksmen, originally called the Colquitt Volunteers, joined at Moultrie. Officers included Captain Jeremiah Wesley Wells, First Lieutenant Jonathan J. Johnson, Second Lieutenant Elijah Tillman, Junior Second Lieutenant John Tucker Sr., Junior Second Lieutenant William C. Dodd, and First Sergeant James R. Algier.[11]

Shortly after being mustered into service, "92 young men representing fifty-three Colquitt County families" departed for induction and orientation in Macon. The men "left from the west side of the Courthouse, marching two abreast with the unforgettable sounds of wailing and weeping women." After spending several weeks in Macon, the company left for Fort Brown near Savannah.[12]

Company I –Berrien Light Infantry (Berrien County)
The Berrien Light Infantry entered into service at Nashville with approximately ninety-four men. Officers elected were Captain Elijah C. Morgan, First Lieutenant John C. McMillan, Second Lieutenant David Perry Luke, Junior Second Lieutenant Francis Lawton Mobley, and First Sergeant Lemuel P. Goodwin.[13]

Company K – Brooks Volunteers (Brooks County)

The Brooks Volunteers formed at Quitman with approximately eighty-seven men. The company had been raised by Pliny Sheffield, a well-to-do landowner in the county, who was elected captain. Other officers included First Lieutenant John G. McCall, Second Lieutenant James B. Finch, Junior Second Lieutenant Eben J. Wood, and First Sergeant William H. McMurray. On March 11, the unit left for Camp Davis.[14]

Early Camp Life

After the individual companies were organized in their home counties, each eventually reported to camp near Savannah. The Wiregrass volunteers began arriving in early March 1862 and were stationed at newly created Camp Davis, near Guyton (also known as Whitesville) in Effingham County. Camp Davis was described as: "three or four successive elevated ridges of land interspersed with a plentiful growth of oak and pine with the prospect of an abundant supply of wood and water. There are two flush branches of water—one below and the other just above this Site and the grounds are so that the 4 Regiments can all be encamped within a 1/4 of a mile of each other. Convenient to the whole is an open old field large enough for 5,000 men to drill on."[15]

On March 20, the ten companies comprising 898 men from the Wiregrass area formed the newly created 50th Georgia Volunteer Infantry Regiment. The regiment became part of the Second Brigade, District of Georgia, Department of South Carolina and Georgia, commanded by fifty-four-year-old Brigadier General Hugh Weedon Mercer. Born in Fredericksburg, Virginia, Mercer graduated from West Point in 1828. In 1835, he resigned from the U.S. Army and moved to Savannah, Georgia. Mercer worked in a Savannah bank before joining the Confederate forces in 1861.[16]

On March 21, 1862, the men elected field officers for the new regiment. Native Georgian William R. Manning, a wealthy forty-five-year-old landowner in Lowndes County, became colonel. Prior to the war, Manning served as justice of the peace in nearby Telfair County from 1843 to 1845. He also served as colonel of the 58th Regiment, Georgia Militia, from 1846 to 1852. By the time Coffee County was cut from Telfair County in 1854, Manning had become a large landowner and slaveholder. When war broke out in 1861, Manning helped organize the first company from Coffee County. Later that year, he moved to Lowndes County and purchased several hundred acres near the town of Valdosta.[17]

In a unique twist, Francis Kearse, who had recently moved to Thomas County and was only a private in Company E, was elected lieutenant colonel. Kearse, originally from the Barnwell District of South Carolina, graduated from the Kentucky Military Institute and moved to Georgia to study law. Kearse's military schooling at KMI was most likely a primary reason for his election as the regiment's lieutenant colonel.[18]

The men elected forty-nine-year-old Philip Coleman Pendleton, captain of Company B, as the regiment's major. At age thirteen, Pendleton had moved with his family from Putnam County to Butts County. He later moved to nearby Macon to study and practice law, but instead decided to join the army and fight in the Indian Wars. After service in the Second Seminole War, Pendleton moved back to Macon and started a weekly newspaper. His publishing career took him to Savannah, Charleston, and later to Ware County.[19]

Philip Coleman Pendleton was elected captain of the Ware County Volunteers when the company was organized in March 1862. Later that month he was elected major in the 50th Georgia Regiment and served in that capacity until chronic illness forced him to resign his commission on October 8, 1862. He returned home and ran his farm until the end of the war. After the war, Pendleton began a publishing business in Lowndes County, Georgia, but was killed in 1869, when he was accidentally thrown from his horse. Courtesy of Lowndes County Historical Society and Museum, Valdosta, Georgia.

After initially settling in and drawing clothing and equipment, the soldiers' first few months of camp life involved organizational activities and military drill. This must have been a challenge for many south Georgians, who were generally used to a much more independent lifestyle away from crowds of people. Most of these men had probably never traveled far from home.

Exuberance was evident in early letters home, such as the one from Private John G. F. McCall of Company K, Brooks Volunteers, to his father shortly after arriving at Camp Davis:

Camp Davis Geo. March 20th 1862

Dear Father,
I seat myself this eavening to rite you a few lines to let you no how I am getting along this leaves me enjoying good health & hope this may reach you enjoying the same blessing. We arrived on Sunday after we left Quitman. I have enjoyed myself finely ever since I have been here & the boys are all well pleased. we have not been mustard in yet but I think we will be tomorrow. there is about six thousand men stationed here. I don't know how long we will stay here. I am well pleased with our officer & I think Capt. Sheffield a world beater. I have no news to write though I no you are anxious to hear from me. Tom is well pleased and I assure you I am pleased to have him here. I think we will be stationed at the Alapaha Bridge on the Gulf road after we drill here a few weeks. we have not had anything to do yet. we have got our tents and cooking utensils. we get plenty to eat such as beef bacon coffee flour sugar and corn meal. I would not quit this company to go to any other that ever could be made up. Tell [Uncle] Moses that I will write to him as soon as I can. I have not paper. I thought I would get paper in Savannah but the stores were all shut up when we got there and we did not stay there long no how. we are living as fine as you ever saw. I have found several relations here. John Fletcher is here from Eckles [Echols County] some of the Fletchers from Tatnall. I must close for the want of something to rite. it looks like I mite have more news to rite but I can't think of anything worth riting. you must all rite. tell Beck [sister Rebecca] to rite to me. I would be glad to hear how she has got. don't be uneasy about me. I will take care of myself. I have nothing more at present. I remain as ever your son
J. G. F. McCall
Direct your letters to Camp Davis Effingham Co. in care of Capt. Sheffield[20]

Early camp life soon began to take a terrible physical toll on the men, most of whom were living together in large groups for the first time. Shortly after arriving at Camp Davis, the soldiers were exposed to a variety of highly communicable diseases, including measles, mumps, and chicken pox. In a March 22 letter to his wife, Captain Duncan Curry of Company F, Decatur Infantry, reported that some 4,634 men were crammed into the camp, and "measles are thick." Lieutenant Francis L. Mobley of Company I, Berrien Light Infantry, wrote to his wife, "I am well my Self though there is 25 of the boyes that are sick with the measles."[21]

A letter from Corporal William A. Studstill of Company K, Brooks Volunteers, is positive but also mentions the sickness that raged throughout his company:

> Dear Father Mother & Sisters
> I seat myself this morning to let you know that I am still in the land of the living. We are all tolerably well at present. There is not a half a dozen men in the company but what has been sick already. I have not myself. Flavius has been very sick but is now well. I hope you are well also & doing well. I have not got homesick yet. We have plenty to eat such as flour pork sugar coffee molasses beef. I have found more kin folks here than you ever saw. Uncle Joe Cousin Jonathon Studstill and Cousin [?] Marchant Cousin John Fletcher & Cousin Duncan Curry Captains of the Decator company. As for my part—I am very well satisfied. I sent mother a three dollar bill also you must excuse my scribbling as I do it in a hurry. I have nothing more of interest at present. Flavius is fifth sergeant—I am first—corporal myself. J. N. Stephens commissary. You must write me all the knews.
> Yours truly
> W A Studstill
> A Soldier of the Highest degree[22]

Less than a week after writing this letter, Studstill fell critically ill. Private John G. F. McCall described the corporal's deteriorating health in an April 1 letter to his sister Becky. The tone of McCall's letter remained positive but less enthusiastic than the one he sent his father a few weeks earlier:

> Dear Sister,
> I take my seat this morning to drop you a few lines to let you no that I am well and have been very well all the time and

hope this may reach you all the same. I have no good news to rite you there is a good deal of sickness in camp. I reckon you have heard of the death of Wm. Alderman, Daniel Alderman's brother. He died on Sunday last about one oclock and Wm. Studstill is very low I don't think he can live more than three hours longer, the rest is all getting along very well. I and Tom stands it finely. it is a kind of life that suits, agrees with me. I did not tell you about our trip down here. we had a fine trip, there was about six thousand men a part of the way. in Valdosta there was some speaking and then some young ladies sang songs for us that beat anything I ever heard about. What I am doing is most nothing but lying about camp, we have not drilled much yet and have not had out any guard on account of bad health and our little officres—McMurrey is first Sergt. Young and two Yate's Wm. Studstill J. Blair the two Alderman boys corpol. I don't know how long we will stay here or where we will go to, I think now that we will stay here long – this a very pretty and health looking place. I must close. you must be a good girl and be all the comfort to Pa and mother you can. Excuse my poor letter. rite me often give my love to all give my respects to all enquiring friends. it will be about 80 days before I can get a furlow then I will come home.
I remain your brother J. G. F. McCall[23]

First Corporal William Studstill died the next evening. The Brooks County soldier was only nineteen years old.[24]

Excitement ran high in the regiment on the morning of April 2. The Wiregrass soldiers received orders to "sirke [strike] our tents and prepare for marching to Goldsborough, N.C." Lieutenant Frances Mobley, however, was concerned about the terrible physical condition of the men in his company: "We are in a bad fix to move fore there is but 28 of our men that is able to go." The order was countermanded later that same day because of the rampant sickness throughout the regiment.[25]

Lieutenant Mobley continued his description of the conditions in a letter to his wife a few days later: "Times is hard here[.] provision is hie though it dose not take mutch to eat here for all of the men is sick[.] out of ten companies I do not think that there is more than three hundred men able to do duty and a new case every day. The malada is the measles and the Brain fevor." The Berrien County officer added, "there is but thirty six of our men able to muster and they are not all well able."[26]

Even as they endured the horrid camp conditions, the Wiregrass men spent much of their time worrying about loved ones and friends back home. In a letter to his father-in-law, Mobley asked, "You will please let Samuel Fords wife have sum corn if I have enough to spare any for she has wrote to Sam that She is starveing and can not any thing to eat[.] if you can spare it let her have Eight bushels and if you can get it let her have some meet."[27]

In addition to battling disease throughout the regiment, the initial thrill of enlistment began to wear off for many young Wiregrass volunteers. Private Jesse A. Hardee of Company D, Valdosta Guards, tried to remain positive in an April 14 letter as he fought homesickness and monotony:

> Dear Sir,
> I seat myself to rite you a few lines to let you no that I am well at this time hoping that these few lines may find you well. I have ritten back home several times and have got no answer yet. I want you to rite to me and let me no how you are getting along with your crop and rite me the news. generally, every body can get letters from home but me. you can tell mary ann that joel has been rite sick but he is better. he and all the rest of sick of this regiment was sent to macon to the hospittle. we have not got our uniform yet nor guns. Lieut guss lane wil start Friday next after our uniforms. I bet by george it wont be long before we will give the Yankees hell and I don't care how soon for I am tired of camp life. I don't feel rite. I don't like to cook and wash. These is squally times about savannah. the[y] will be an end to many a poor soldier. I have nothing to rite that will interest you at al. you no more about war news than I do and we will drop the conversation. The last thing that joel said to me was to rite to mary ann and tell her to tell peat that he must put a musle [muzzle] on floyd when he goes to plowing corn for it wil not do to whip him for biting the corn. I will close by saying I remain yours as ever.[28]

Letters from home—the link between the lonely soldier and the loved ones he missed so desperately—were critical to a soldier's morale. In early April, a homesick and despondent Francis Mobley pleaded with his wife for a letter:

> Rodey [Rhoda] I am siting in my tent by my lone self by my candle thinking about you and writing to you. I have been here four or five weeks and have not got but one short letter from you and that is all that I have heard from you and I think hard of it [.] the letter you wrote you wrote that you was sick

and I am uneasy about you. I fear that you or Marquies [their
young son] is verry sick and not write it to me and if so
please write to me for I shall get the truth of it when D. P. [Lt.
David Perry) Luke gets back. I am informed that the mail
goes to Nashville [Georgia] twice a week and if so you could
write as often as once a week and if you would it would give
me some satisfaction. I wrote as often as twice a week ever
since I have been here. I want you to write me how Marquies
is getting along and wither he can taulk or not. I would give a
round sum to see you and him though I expect it will be six
months first if we all live for it is ordered by Adjutant and
Insector General that no more furloughs be granted untill
times get better and I do not think that times will by any
better untill warm wether. So I will close for the present and I
will not write a gain until I get a letter from you let it be long
or short [.] I do not write this in anger but with regret [.] it
seams to me that I have not got any friends at home I think
they must have all come with me. I can write and shed tears
but no one noes it but me. I know your hand is bad but I think
if you have practiceed since I left you can write so I can read
it and I want you to practice for I think shurly you have not
for got me a readey and if you have not write to me or I shall
think that you have. [29]

By the middle of April, illness had decimated the 50th Georgia.
Almost two-thirds of the men in this nine-hundred-man regiment were unfit
for duty. By April 21, only Company E had not suffered the death of a
soldier by disease. Captain Duncan Curry of Company F related the terrible
conditions to his wife in an April 14 letter. Battling sickness himself, Curry
reported, "I have had a tedious time in nursing the sick in camp. Last night
I had a good nights rest. The sick of our Company having been sent to the
hospital in Macon leaving here about three oclock yesterday evening on
the cars: We sent 36 from this Company nearly all measles cases. The
Camp is a bad place for a sick man agreeable to my experience, as a man is
much exposed in camp and doesn't get well. All the three men we have had
to get well yet we sent to a private house." Captain Curry also reported that
ten of the men in the regiment had died from disease, "the last one today."[30]

While at Camp Davis, the men received word that the Yankees had
taken Fort Pulaski on the Savannah River, and that nearby Savannah was
thought to be in jeopardy. Although Fort Pulaski fell, the immediate danger
to the city passed, and it remained under Confederate control. As the Federal
presence along the South Carolina and Georgia coasts increased, camp
rumors abounded, most of which proved unreliable.

The 50th Georgia moved a few miles south of Savannah in early May to assist in the construction of Camp Brown (also known as Fort Brown and Fort Boggs). During its time at Camp Brown, the regiment assisted in blockading the Savannah River to obstruct Federal vessels. The work included sinking old ships as well as felling trees and placing them in the river. The duty of defending the Georgia coast around Savannah did not expose the new regiment to extensive combat. That good fortune allowed the men to train and become more accustomed to army life. Unfortunately, many Wiregrass soldiers continued to succumb to illness from exposure to disease.[31]

In a May report, Colonel William R. Manning glumly described the poor condition of his men as follows: "This regiment is still unable to turn out a very large number of effective men owing to the prevalence of measles, mumps and the effect of vaccination. Quite a large number, too, who have had measles, pneumonia, rheumatism, and other diseases incident to camp and to new regiments are yet invalids and unfit for duty."[32]

Federal activities along the Georgia and South Carolina coast created a flurry of activity in the regiment. Units were rushed toward the threatened port cities of Savannah and Charleston as the Confederates sought to respond by shoring up their defenses. In a May 26 letter to his wife, Captain Duncan Curry of Company F reported, "A detachment of one hundred men left this reg. this morning at five oclock for detached service somewhere. . . . The soldiers have been going towards Charleston with a rush for two days that means something in that direction. . . . The 50th reg. is now divided. Four comp. being detached and I fear we shall have to stay here or here abouts." During the next several weeks, portions of the regiment would be detached for various duties.[33]

The detachment Captain Curry referenced included men from Companies I and K. A soldier in Company K explained their mission in a letter home: "I am about six or eight miles from camps rite up the river a cutting liveoak to blockade the river [.] their is one hundred men here at work from our regiment, we are getting the river pretty well blockaded though it will take some time yet to get it completed."[34]

In late May or early June, Company E moved to Cedar Hill Battery near Camp Brown. In late June, Company F headed to Battery Walker, located south of Savannah. Captain Curry reported the move to his wife in a June 23 letter: "Saturday we moved down here and it was a busy day for me as most of the officers of the Comp. were unfit for duty. Powell [Second Lieutenant William] has been sick but is now up and better Dekle [Second Lieutenant William G.] is sick and gone home. We have eight men sick in the hospital one in camp quite sick and a number complaining. We are situated about three miles South of Savannah nobody being with us except our own Comp."[35]

The assignment apparently provided some improvement over conditions at Fort Brown. According to Captain Curry, "We were placed here to guard and learn to drill on the cannon in Battery Walker. The Battery is an earth work with two eight inch guns in position. It is in a very large level old field. Our camp is on a slight elevation near the Battery with some very large shady live oak trees near by that protects us from the sun in the heat of the day all round is swamp and low country. The Comp. that left here when we came had better health than we had at Fort Boggs."[36]

As the temperature and humidity rose in June and July, disease continued to plague the 50th Georgia. In early June, Francis Mobley became quite ill. Fever and chills racked the young officer for weeks. On June 16, Captain Cicero Holt Young tendered his resignation as Company E commander due to lingering illness. On June 30, Captain Curry reported in a letter to his wife that he again felt sick due to "my throat a little sore and my bowels a little troubled to day." Many of his men were sick. Curry recalled, "Say twenty or thirty in Camp and eight at the hospitals." Most suffered from the mumps, chills, fever, and diarrhea. The Decatur County commander mentioned, "Riley Brown died yesterday morning and his body was sent off this morning in the cars for home by John Brown."[37]

A July 3 letter from Private Simeon L. Morton of nearby Company B, 18th Georgia Battalion, to his sister underscored the terrible camp conditions. In his letter Morton described the situation, "This is a very nonhealthy place where we are camped now. The fiftieth Regiment is camped about a quarter of a mile from our camp. Out of nine hundred they have only two hundred on duty. Mr. Turner and myself get sick by alternations. As soon as I get well he gets sick."[38]

Illness also visited both Private George Washington Chitty of Company D and Lieutenant Quarterman Baker Staten of Company G early in their service. Twenty-four-year-old George Chitty's great-great-grandfather had emigrated from England to America in the early 1700s, settling in South Carolina. At age three, Chitty had moved with his family from Barnwell, South Carolina, to Lowndes County. The married father of two young sons owned a modest farm and, like most Confederate soldiers, had no slaves. When the call for volunteers went out in March, Chitty joined the Valdosta Guards to protect his homeland and his family. By May 1862, Chitty was in a hospital at Macon, and the next month he took thirty days' sick leave. He was not well enough to return to the regiment until August. A July regimental return listed Lieutenant Staten as "absent sick at convalescent camp near Springfield, GA." Staten sufficiently recovered to join his company later that month near Chaffin's Farm, Virginia.[39]

On July 18, after some four months of training and defensive duties in the hellholes of Camp Davis and Camp Brown, the regiment finally received marching orders. Many of the men, perhaps up to two-thirds of the original number of enlistees, were still too ill to join the regiment as it left Savannah.

Duncan Curry contracted the mumps in early July. In a July 19 letter to his wife, Curry described his condition, "It is now eight oclock on Saturday morning. The mumps have proved so painful that I could not eat up to this time but am now a little better and can begin to eat a little and walk about a little. . . . I am now left at Battery Walker with eleven other sick men. Our Comp. and Reg. having recd marching orders last night at eight oclock to leave the depot in cars this morning." Lieutenant William O. Fleming assumed temporary command of Company F until Captain Curry recovered his health.[40]

Still too weak to travel, Lieutenant Francis Mobley also remained behind. Another member of the regiment who did not leave with the regiment was Major Philip Pendleton. Pendleton, who had been joined earlier in camp by his seventeen-year-old son, Billy, was on a two-week furlough back to Ware County due to illness. The elder Pendleton received a letter from Lieutenant Colonel Kearse, advising that the regiment had been ordered to Virginia.[41]

Most all the Wiregrass men became ill during their first four months of service. Of the 898 enlistees in the 50th Georgia Regiment, at least eighty-one (9 percent) died from disease during this period. The hardest hit was Company H. Sixteen of the initial ninety-two Colquitt Marksmen enlistees (seventeen percent) died. Disease claimed the lives of at least four men from every company in the regiment during this period. All these young men died for the Confederacy without ever setting foot on a battlefield or leaving their home state of Georgia. Sadly, the combined effects of disease, weather, poor rations, and unsanitary living conditions would kill more Civil War soldiers than actual combat.[42]

On the morning of July 19, the remaining able-bodied men of the 50th Georgia Volunteer Infantry Regiment boarded rail cars and left their home state of Georgia. Their destination was Richmond, Virginia, the Confederate capital, where they would join up with Brigadier General Thomas Fenwick Drayton's Brigade. Excitement ran high as the boys from the Wiregrass Region were about to have their chance to shoot some Yankees. They would not have to wait for long.[43]

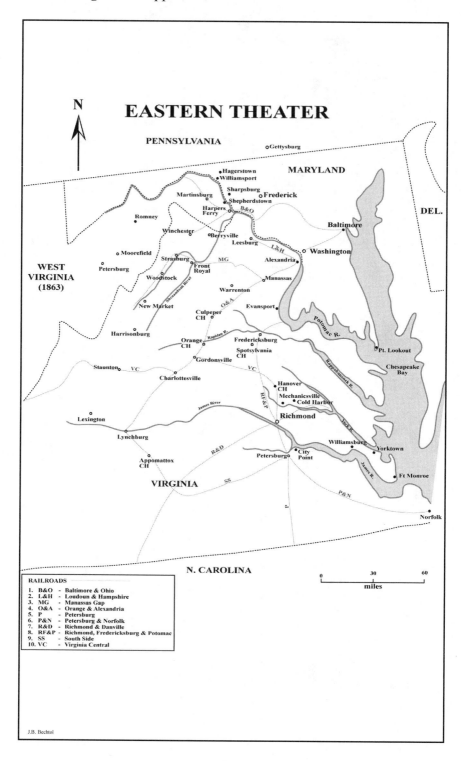

EASTERN THEATER

N

PENNSYLVANIA

Gettysburg

MARYLAND

Hagerstown
Williamsport
Sharpsburg
Martinsburg   Frederick
Shepherdstown
Harpers   B&O
Ferry

Romney   DEL.

Winchester
Berryville   Baltimore
Leesburg   L&H
Moorefield   Washington
Strasburg   MG   Alexandria
WEST   Petersburg   Front
VIRGINIA   Royal
(1863)   Woodstock   Manassas

Warrenton
New Market
Culpeper   Evansport
CH
Harrisonburg   Potomac R.

Orange   Rapidan R.   Fredericksburg   Pt. Lookout
CH   Spotsylvania
Gordonsville   CH   Chesapeake
Staunton   VC   Bay
VC
Charlottesville   Rappahannock R.

Hanover
CH
Lexington   James River   Mechanicsville
Cold Harbor
Richmond
Lynchburg
Williamsburg   Yorktown
R&D   City
Appomattox   Petersburg   Point
CH
James R.
VIRGINIA   SS   Ft Monroe

P&N

Norfolk

N. CAROLINA   0   30   60

miles

RAILROADS
1. B&O   - Baltimore & Ohio
2. L&H   - Loudoun & Hampshire
3. MG   - Manassas Gap
4. O&A   - Orange & Alexandria
5. P   - Petersburg
6. P&N   - Petersburg & Norfolk
7. R&D   - Richmond & Danville
8. RF&P - Richmond, Fredericksburg & Potomac
9. SS   - South Side
10. VC   - Virginia Central

J.B. Bechtol

Chapter Two
Second Manassas Campaign
August 16–September 1, 1862

O n July 17, Brigadier General Thomas Fenwick Drayton received orders to report to Richmond, Virginia, to take command of a brigade that included the 50th and 51st Georgia Infantry Regiments, the 15th South Carolina Infantry Regiment, the Phillip's Georgia Legion, and the 3rd South Carolina Infantry Battalion. The brigade was assigned to Major General David Rumph Jones' division, which was part of Major General James Longstreet's command, Army of Northern Virginia.[1]

Major General James Longstreet, Commander, First Corps, Army of Northern Virginia. U.S. Army Military History Institute, Carlisle, Pennsylvania.

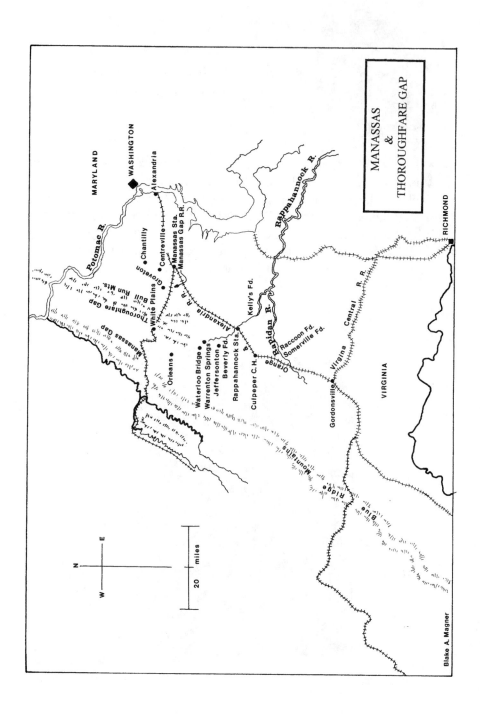

Blake A. Magner

A native of Charleston, South Carolina, Thomas Drayton graduated from West Point in 1823 and served in the U.S. Army until resigning in 1838 to become a planter and railroad president in South Carolina. Drayton also served in the South Carolina legislature before joining the Confederacy. Questions would soon surface about his leadership during the Second Manassas and Maryland Campaigns.

The 50th Georgia reached Richmond on the evening of July 24 and bivouacked at Camp Lee, about two miles north of the city. The regiment remained at the camp until July 29, when it moved to Chaffin's Farm near Cornelius Creek, just east of Richmond. The Georgians remained at Chaffin's Farm for the next two weeks. During that time, many of the previously sick and furloughed soldiers, including Private George Chitty and Lieutenant Quarterman Staten, recovered and rejoined their companies. One regimental report noted, "Since August 1, twenty-five of the absentees from this company [H] have reported for duty, also a great many absentees from each of the companies have reported and having no room to put down all the names and the paper upon which this report is made being very poor, will simply copy the number of noncommissioned officers and privates absent from Companies H, I and K."[2]

Major Philip C. Pendleton and his seventeen-year-old son, William F. "Billy" Pendleton, also rejoined the regiment. Major Pendleton had been on furlough in Ware County when the 50th Georgia left Savannah for Richmond. Billy Pendleton, who had served as his father's orderly, officially enlisted in Company B and was soon promoted to second sergeant. [3]

Shortly before Drayton's Brigade assembled in Richmond, the newly appointed Confederate commander, General Robert Edward Lee, defeated General George B. McClellan's Army of the Potomac in the Seven Days' Battles. Although McClellan's defeat removed the immediate Federal threat to the Confederate capital, General Lee soon learned of a new menace. Major General John Pope had led his Army of Virginia south from Washington, D.C., toward the Rappahannock River in the central part of the state. If Pope's men were joined by McClellan from the Peninsula and by Major General Ambrose Burnside's corps moving up from North Carolina, Richmond would again be in jeopardy. Realizing the dire consequences, Lee decided to confront Pope's army before it could be reinforced. On August 9, Major General Thomas J. "Stonewall" Jackson defeated Pope's army south of Culpeper at the Battle of Cedar Mountain.[4]

Three days later, the men of the 50th Georgia received new Enfield rifles with bayonets, cartridge boxes and belts, and ammunition. Although the regimental strength swelled as men returned from sick leave, the 50th Georgia could only muster around five hundred soldiers, slightly over one-

General Robert Edward Lee, Commander, Army of Northern Virginia. Photo by
Julian Vannerson, 1863. Library of Congress.

half of the original 898 Wiregrass men who had enlisted a little more than
five months earlier on March 4, 1862.[5]

On August 13, Lee ordered Longstreet's command, including
Drayton's Brigade, to "proceed without delay by cars of Virginia Central
Railroad to Gordonsville." The men of the 50th Georgia marched to the
railroad depot and boarded the cars, taking with them only the belongings
they could carry. The next evening, the regiment reached Gordonsville and
camped about six miles away.[6]

During the next few days, the air was electric as more troops
continued to arrive into camp. The Wiregrass men sensed that they would
soon be seeing action. First Lieutenant William O. Fleming of Company F,
Decatur Infantry, described his living conditions and the feeling of an
impending battle in an August 16 letter to his wife:

> My dear Georgia,
>   We reached Gordonsville the evening of the 14th inst by
> R-Road. We rested about 1/2 hour & took up the line of
> march to where we are now encamped. I am once in sight of

the mountains of this State—a spur of the Blue Ridge being over a few miles distant & in full view. Our army is swelling to a considerable size on the line of the Rapidan though if reports be true the enemy are in greatly superior force. Genl Jackson has issued an order to the troops to fight against any odds & be victorious at any cost. This is the ring of the right metal. If we will only carry out the order, placing a firm reliance in the God of battle, we must be victorious. There is no telling how long the terrible conflict will be postponed, but come it must & that soon. The rapid movement of troops from one point to another augurs a battle near at hand. It is thought that we will attack the enemy notwithstanding our inferiority in numbers

In my opinion the advantages are greatly in favor of the attacking party.

We left all our baggage in Richmond to be brought around in wagons so that we are here with nothing but what we could carry on our backs. I have my overcoat & a small single blanket. Dr. McTyer has nothing but an overcoat so my little blanket has to serve as covering for us both. We lie in our overcoats and cover with the blanket. The bed is very hard but I sleep soundly. The Dr. stands the life finely. He is a splendid companion for me in camps. I would not be without him for a great deal. Our company has improved a great deal since he has been with us & the men are delighted with him, he is so kind and attentive to their every want.

Yr Aff husband

W. O. Fleming[7]

General Lee hoped to catch General Pope's army in a trap between the Rappahannock and Rapidan Rivers. Lee planned for the Confederate cavalry to destroy the bridge over the Rappahannock River in the Federal rear at Rappahannock Station on August 17, cutting off the enemy's retreat route. The next day Generals Longstreet and Jackson planned to cross the Rapidan River and turn the enemy's left flank. Unfortunately, due to delays in coordination, the movement was delayed until August 20. In the meantime, Pope became aware of Lee's intention and hastily moved his army back to the north side of the Rappahannock.[8]

On the evening of August 19, the men of the 50th Georgia received orders to cook three days' rations and be ready to move out early the next morning. At dawn on August 20, Longstreet and Jackson hurriedly marched their commands toward the Rapidan River. Longstreet, who commanded the right wing of Lee's army, moved his men across the river at Raccoon Ford and headed toward Culpeper Court House. Jackson, commanding the left wing, crossed at Somerville Ford and moved in the same direction on Longstreet's left flank.[9]

Acting Company E Commander Lieutenant Peter McGlashan noted the 50th Georgia marched "some thirty odd miles" in twenty hot, dusty hours. Sergeant Pendleton recalled, "It was my first march. There was a strong odor of dead horses, left by General Pope's retreating army. We marched all night and all the next day. I fell asleep while walking until my knees gave out. On this march the soldiers were ordered to leave their knapsacks, I never used one again." Longstreet's exhausted command arrived near Kelly's Ford on the south side of the Rappahannock River by late afternoon. They found the Federal army had already retired across to the other side.[10]

With his initial plan spoiled, General Lee next decided to concentrate on turning General Pope's right flank. The Confederate commander wanted Longstreet to threaten the Federal left while General Jackson moved farther up the river to get around the enemy right. Between August 21 and 22, Longstreet's men marched from Kelly's Ford up the river to Rappahannock Station, finally reaching their destination in the pre-dawn darkness of Saturday, August 23. Longstreet's men took their position in front of the Federal force near Beverly Ford and the Orange and Alexandria Railroad bridge.[11]

Shortly after reaching the area, Drayton's footsore brigade shuffled along the road leading to Beverly Ford in support of Colonel John B. Walton's Washington (Louisiana) Artillery. Colonel Walton had been ordered to place his long-range guns into position and drive back a Federal force that had crossed to the south bank of the river. Walton's artillery barrage opened at 6:00 a.m. and received a quick response from the Union guns. The two-hour artillery exchange pushed the enemy back across the river, but not before the Federals torched the railroad bridge. Drayton's men could not ford the swollen river, due to heavy rains on the previous day, and they suffered only minimal casualties from enemy artillery shelling. Billy Pendleton recalled that this was the first time the 50th Georgia came under fire. "It was not a battle, just some shelling, but it continued off and on all day."[12]

Captain Duncan Curry, Company F, who had gained enough strength to make his way from Savannah to resume command of his company, was slightly wounded when struck in the chest by a spent shell fragment. Captain Curry described his wound in a letter to his wife written later that day, "I was struck by a fragment of a shell this morning in a battle but it was so far spent that it did not break the skin. It struck me in the left breast and bruised me some what but I recovered from the shock in a minute or two and did not leave the field but continued in command of the Comp." A canister fragment struck Second Lieutenant Henry S. Reeves in the foot, but he was also able to remain with the company. Private Elijah Howell of Company B was not as fortunate. Howell fell out sick on the march, and Federal troops captured him at Manassas Gap. The Ware County soldier later died of disease at Point Lookout Prison, Maryland, on October 16.[13]

In the late afternoon of August 24, General Longstreet moved up the river and bivouacked at Jeffersonton. He relieved a portion of Jackson's command early the next morning. Before daybreak on the 25th, Jackson crossed the Rappahannock at Hinson's Mill and moved undetected behind the Federal right flank. In the meantime, David Jones' division took a position in the Federal front at Waterloo Bridge to divert the enemy's attention away from Jackson's movement. A regiment of sharpshooters from Drayton's Brigade crossed the river to engage the enemy, resulting in only slight loss to the brigade.[14]

Longstreet's men succeeded in distracting the enemy while Jackson quietly slipped around the enemy right. By late afternoon on the 26th, Longstreet's wing followed in Jackson's wake. They camped that night near Orleans, and the following night they bivouacked at White Plains.[15]

Lieutenant McGlashan reported that the 50th Georgia participated in engagements at three different fords of the Rappahannock. Although it came under heavy artillery fire, the regiment saw little action and suffered few casualties.[16]

Thoroughfare Gap - August 28, 1862

When the Georgians broke camp on August 28, they could clearly see the outline of the Bull Run Mountains to the east. The road snaked up the west side of the mountain, and by early afternoon, the troops reached the west side of Thoroughfare Gap. The tired soldiers drained their canteens and sought shade, but they found the gap occupied by enemy cavalry and infantry. Jones' division received orders to push out the Federal force and occupy the passage. As Colonel George T. "Tige" Anderson's lead brigade reached the gap, General James Ricketts' division greeted them with heavy artillery and infantry fire. General Jones immediately brought up more troops to help Anderson's Georgians.[17]

Heavy fighting broke out on the Confederate left flank while skirmishers traded shots on the right. The 50th Georgia received orders to charge through the pass and storm the heights on the left. As Lieutenant

McGlashan reported, "The Fiftieth went through at the double quick in splendid style, but by some misunderstanding we were thrown on the right instead of the left. The mistake was soon rectified, however, the regiment dashing across the Gap again and scaling the heights in magnificent style, getting there just in time to see the discomfited foe flying before Anderson's Brigade in utter confusion."[18]

The Federal troops kept up a heavy artillery fire until dark, when they retreated. Jones' command advanced and bivouacked east of the gap for the night. Total losses to the division were estimated at not more than twenty-five. The 50th Georgia suffered only one known casualty. Private James Ricketson, Company C, fell behind during the march and was captured. Federal authorities paroled him with other Confederate prisoners at Leesburg, Virginia, on October 2.[19]

Battle of Second Manassas (Bull Run) - August 29-30, 1862
The rumble of heavy firing to the east greeted the Georgians early on August 29, and Longstreet hurriedly marched his command toward the old Manassas battlefield. The hot sun beat down on the men as they marched. The unfortunate troops bringing up the rear were covered by the choking dust left by thousands of plodding feet before them. Sergeant Billy Pendleton recalled, "I was suffering from thirst and drank warm muddy water from a puddle, and filled my canteen." Jones' division entered the turnpike near Gainesville and moved toward Groveton, arriving before noon. Longstreet's men moved into position to the right of Stonewall Jackson's troops, who had defended the spot in bloody fighting during the previous day.[20]

Drayton's Brigade relieved Colonel M. D. Corse's Brigade of Brigadier James L. Kemper's division and formed along Longstreet's extreme right on the Manassas Gap Railroad. Although subjected to shelling during the rest of the day, Jones' division suffered minimal casualties. The fighting lasted until about 9 p.m., with the Federals taking their artillery and retreating to a strong position. Later that evening, Longstreet withdrew his men to their original lines and into better defensive positions.[21]

The next morning, Jones readjusted his lines. The heaviest fighting during the day continued to Jones' left along General Jackson's front. Jackson's veterans threw back several fierce Federal assaults, with heavy losses on both sides. Near the end of the day, Jackson's men pressed the enemy right while Longstreet made an all-out assault on the Federal center and left. At about 5:00 p.m., most of Jones' division moved up into line of battle and took position near the Chinn house.[22]

Drayton delayed in joining the final assault until dusk due to his concern over a mistaken cavalry report of enemy movement on the right

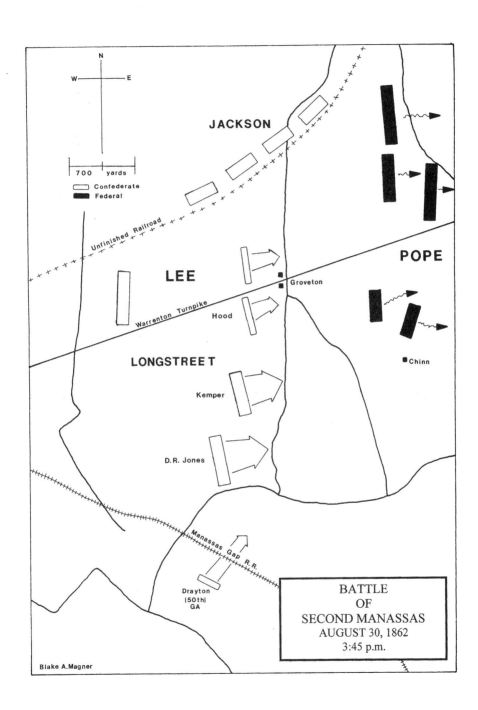

N
W———E

700 yards
□ Confederate
■ Federal

JACKSON

Unfinished Railroad

LEE

POPE

Groveton

Warrenton Turnpike

Hood

LONGSTREET

Chinn

Kemper

D. R. Jones

Manassas Gap R. R.

Drayton
(50th)
GA

BATTLE
OF
SECOND MANASSAS
AUGUST 30, 1862
3:45 p.m.

Blake A.Magner

flank. The 50th Georgia did not take part in the fighting; instead, they remained behind on picket duty.[23]

The Battle of Second Manassas finally ended by 10:00 p.m. with the enemy decisively driven from the field. That evening, Pope withdrew to Centreville, about six miles east of Groveton.[24]

In a subsequent report, Jones questioned Drayton's tardiness. The brigades of Brigadier General Robert Toombs and Colonel George T. "Tige" Anderson "went in most gallantly, suffering severe loss." Jones stated, "Again and again did I send for Drayton, who, after delaying till he heard the unfounded nature of the report on which he acted, hurried up at speed and went in on the right only a few moments before firing ceased at dusk, too late to accomplish the results contemplated."[25]

Lieutenant McGlashan showed support for his brigade commander when he wrote:

> Arriving there [Manassas] we were placed on the extreme
> right of the line, and remained there two days under artillery
> fire, but not immediately engaged until the evening of the
> 30th, when we were ordered, by mistake, I believe, instead of
> Kemper's brigade, to advance on the enemy's line at the
> double quick. A more welcome order could not have come to
> us, for the men in hearing of the terrible struggle for over
> thirty-six hours, were chafing a good deal. They dashed off
> with a shout that made everything ring around; but ere we
> had gone six hundred yards we were ordered back again, and
> on returning were ordered to leave our regiment on picket
> and carry the remainder of the brigade into action at the
> double quick. The Fiftieth was left, greatly to our chagrin, but
> it mattered little, as the rest of the brigade got into action too
> late to do the service required. Whose fault that was, I cannot
> pretend to say. I kept a bright look out during the time, and all
> orders received by Gen. Drayton seemed to me to be
> promptly obeyed. I say this much, as some strictures have
> been passed on his management of his brigade on that day.[26]

That night, as a heavy rain began falling, General Longstreet's men remained on the battlefield to bury the dead and remove the wounded. Jackson prepared to move out and cut off Pope's retreating army before it reached Washington. Jones' division suffered heavy casualties in the fierce struggle, with the exception of Drayton's Brigade. The only reported casualty for the 50th Georgia on the day was Private Samuel W. Register, Company G. An artillery blast seriously wounded Private Register in the hand, requiring the amputation of three fingers.[27]

The next morning, the 50th Georgia Commander, Colonel William R. Manning, ordered a detail to capture some of the enemy that remained in a nearby farmhouse. Billy Pendleton recalled the situation: "Colonel Manning detailed Sergeant Bailey [James S.] and me with six or seven men to capture them, but when we got there they had left, and the house was deserted." On their return, Pendleton noted the terrible effects of the battle. "We marched across the battlefield. It was an awful sight to see the dead covering the ground. There was a company of enemy soldiers, under a flag of truce, burying their dead."[28]

As rain continued to fall in the early darkness of August 31, Jackson's men marched east in pursuit of the enemy. Longstreet moved out in the afternoon to catch up with Jackson, but his men found the going slow due to the muddy roads. Jones' division crossed Bull Run at Sudley Ford and turned onto the Little River Turnpike. They reached the Chantilly area the following day as the rain continued. Jones sent Toombs' and Anderson's Brigades ahead to support Jackson's command, which had engaged the Federals at Ox Hill.[29]

The rest of Jones' division remained behind near Chantilly and bivouacked for the night. The next morning, the surprised Confederates found that the enemy had silently withdrawn from their Ox Hill position under the cover of darkness. Pope's battered army succeeded in escaping to fortified positions near Alexandria and Washington, and General Lee abandoned any attempts at further pursuit.[30]

Robert E. Lee's army won a decisive victory at Second Manassas, defeating Pope for the second time in the month and eliminating any immediate threat to Richmond. General Longstreet heaped praise on the gallant men: "In one month these troops had marched over 200 miles upon little more than half rations and fought nine battles and skirmishes; killed, wounded, and captured nearly as many men as we had in our ranks, besides taking arms and other munitions of war in large quantities. I would that I could do justice to all of these gallant officers and men in this report."[31]

Both armies suffered heavily in the battle, although Drayton's Brigade only reported a total of ninety-three killed and wounded by virtue of its supporting role. The 50th Georgia received eight casualties during the Second Manassas Campaign.[32]

Shortly after the battle, a citizen committee from Washington arrived under a flag of truce with doctors and ambulances to help care for the wounded Yankees, many of whom still remained on the battlefield next to their dead comrades. An unarmed Federal cavalry unit accompanied the committee to help bury the dead. Rebel cavalrymen escorted this group on their unpleasant mission.[33]

One small party of the group went into Centreville to do their work. A company from the 50th Georgia, serving as provost guard, met the party. According to one northern gentleman, the Georgians exhibited good spirits. "They were making themselves happy with the liquors and other medical steres [stores] left in the place; and were a lank, lean, hard looking set of half starved fellows, in light flannel colored dress. Their Captain gave us passes to the Union lines. He looked a cunning fellow enough, and bad [had] more whiskey in him than appeared at first sight; still he was decidedly in good temper with himself, his position, his dirty gang, and all the world."[34]

The company referenced by the gentleman may have been Company A, the Satilla Rangers. According to Lieutenant McGlashan, "a portion of the Fiftieth under command of Capt. Wilson, of Company A, captured 175 prisoners and considerable stores at Centreville."[35]

The inexperienced men of the 50th Georgia had tasted limited combat for the first time and escaped relatively unscathed. The Wiregrass soldiers would not be as fortunate in the near future.

Chapter Three
Into Maryland: Fox's Gap
September 2–14, 1862

G eneral Robert E. Lee faced a major decision after his overwhelming victory at Second Manassas. The Army of Northern Virginia was on the offensive, and the Union army appeared demoralized after the crushing defeat of General John Pope. Should the Confederate commander continue to press the war into the North, or should he stop and resupply his troops? Although victorious, Lee's exhausted command desperately needed rations, supplies, and munitions. Much of central and northern Virginia had been picked clean, and the army needed to leave the area in order to resupply itself for the next campaign.

Buoyed by his success at Second Manassas, General Lee decided on a bold move: he would take the war to the North. He had several good reasons for his gamble. Confederate success on Northern soil could elicit recognition from England and France. A victory might impact the fall elections in the North and put more pressure on the Federal government to negotiate a peace with the South. A foray into the North would also keep the Federal army occupied and unable to attack Richmond. Additionally, Lee's hungry army needed the rich farmlands of Maryland and Pennsylvania. The capture of Federal arsenals at Martinsburg and Harper's Ferry, Virginia, would also provide ammunition, weapons, and supplies. Lee hoped both Federal garrisons would abandon their posts when his army approached.

This decision was not without significant risks. The Army of Northern Virginia had just endured a punishing campaign. The tired and hungry Southern soldiers lacked shoes, proper clothing, and sufficient ammunition. Lee would need to ask his men to perform another improbable task, but it was one most were eager to take for "Marse Robert."

Once Lee made his decision, the army wasted little time in beginning its trek to Maryland. On September 3, the Army of Northern Virginia moved northward from the Bull Run/Chantilly area toward Leesburg, Virginia. Brigadier General David R. Jones' division left the Ox Hill area in the morning. The men marched by the Dranesville Road, crossed Goose Creek, and reached Leesburg the next evening.[1]

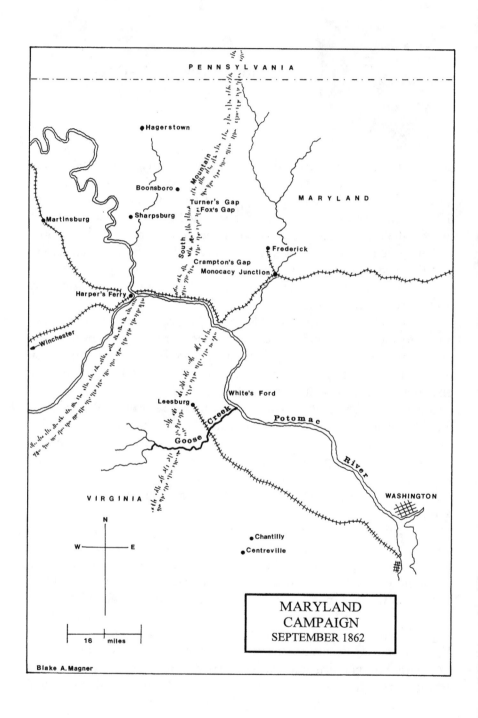

PENNSYLVANIA

● Hagerstown

Boonsboro ●

● Martinsburg   ● Sharpsburg

MARYLAND

Turner's Gap
Fox's Gap

● Frederick

Crampton's Gap
Monocacy Junction ●

Harper's Ferry ●

● Winchester

White's Ford

Leesburg ●

Potomac

Goose Creek

River

WASHINGTON

VIRGINIA

N
W — E

● Chantilly
● Centreville

MARYLAND
CAMPAIGN
SEPTEMBER 1862

16   miles

Blake A. Magner

General Lee had chosen to leave a sizable portion of his army behind at Leesburg. Those who would not be crossing the Potomac River into Maryland included many men who were too ill or poorly equipped to make the hard march. Lee also excused all barefooted soldiers from marching. Many took the opportunity to remain in Virginia, but others opted to stay with their comrades and continue the trek. A number of men who refused to march into Maryland because they had enlisted as defenders of their homeland and not as invaders of the North were also allowed to remain behind.[2]

In an article for the *Savannah Republican*, soldier/correspondent Virgil A. S. Parks reported, "Here [Leesburg] all our sick and barefooted men were left. When they marched in they looked as large as a brigade."[3]

Illness remained a constant companion to the 50th Georgia. Seventeen year-old Sergeant Billy Pendleton recalled the worsening condition of his father, Major Philip C. Pendleton: "By this time my father was so ill that he could hardly ride his horse. . . . That afternoon [September 3] we marched up the Potomac and camped in the road for the night. I went to the fire where my father was. He felt so ill that he had decided to resign and go home."[4]

Nevertheless, Major Pendleton became senior officer of an estimated thirty-five hundred soldiers left behind at Leesburg. Pendleton, along with a small cavalry escort, marched the ragged band of Southerners, including his son, across the Blue Ridge Mountains to Winchester, Virginia. After turning over his command in Winchester, Pendleton, who was still very sick, applied for a furlough home to recuperate. His son, who had also become ill, received a discharge for being underage. The Pendletons made their way back to Ware County together. Philip Pendleton never fully recovered, and he resigned from the army one month later. Billy Pendleton would rejoin his company in March 1863, upon reaching age eighteen.[5]

By the time the Army of Northern Virginia reached the Potomac River, the effective strength of many companies had already been reduced by one-half or more. Lieutenant Peter McGlashan, Company E, estimated that some fifteen thousand to twenty thousand men had remained behind in Leesburg or had fallen out along the route. The loss of so many soldiers reduced the effectiveness of Lee's command as it undertook another brutal campaign. After the war, Major General Daniel Harvey Hill confirmed the weakened condition of Lee's army in an address before an 1885 Confederate veterans' reunion, stating, "The campaigns against McClellan and Pope had greatly reduced Lee's army. The order issued on crossing the Potomac excusing all barefooted men from marching had reduced it still more. So, at Sharpsburg [and at South Mountain] General Lee had only the hardiest, strongest and bravest of his

Rebel boys. The straggling had been enormous. The chaff had been blown off and only the sound, solid wheat had been left."[6]

Rations were poor at best; many men ate apples and green corn, which created digestive troubles. At times water was scarce. The constant marching took a severe toll on the relatively green troops in Drayton's Brigade. Lieutenant McGlashan reported, "I have seen the poor fellows drop dead out of the ranks when toiling along in quick time under the hot broiling sun. Others would stagger off under a tree, lay their blankets under their heads, and die there amid the dust and with the tramps of the rapidly passing host ringing in their ears. The Fiftieth, at Hagerstown [Md.], showed only some 250 out of 500 that left Gordonsville. A large proportion were stragglers, but quite a number were literally marched down and left sick on the road."[7]

Brigade Adjutant J. Evans Edings listed the regimental numbers for the 50th Georgia on September 11 as "16 officers and 288 enlisted men," an effective fighting force of just over three hundred men. The roster of the 50th Georgia, therefore, had been reduced by two-thirds during the six-month period after the ten companies formed the regiment. The remaining Wiregrass men who marched into Maryland were ill prepared for the desperate struggle they would soon face.[8]

On the morning of September 6, the men of the 50th Georgia held their rifles and equipment belts over their heads as they sloshed across the Potomac River into Maryland at White's Ford. They marched through Buckeystown and camped on the banks of the Monocacy River later that night. The next day the Georgians marched to Monocacy Junction and camped near Frederick, less than fifty miles from Washington. Lee rested his tired army for a few days. During this time, the men bathed their filthy bodies and scrubbed their tattered clothes. After mail call, many caught up on the news from home.[9]

A familiar face rejoined Company I on the evening of September 7. Lieutenant Francis L. Mobley had been ill and remained behind when the 50th Georgia left Savannah for Richmond on July 19. By late August, Mobley had gained enough strength to travel. The young lieutenant dutifully made an exhausting, sixteen-day journey to catch up with the regiment. During the trek, Mobley commanded twenty-six other Wiregrass men who had also been left behind or had recently been conscripted into service. Mobley wrote his wife the following day to let her know that he had finally rejoined his company.

> I reached my company last knight[.] I was 16 days coming
> and I am worn out[.] my feet blistered the worst kind. . . . I

had to march from the Rappadan river witch is 15 miles from
Gordinsville to Federicksburg [Frederick, Md.]. I croused the
Patomic River Saturday night about three o'clock. . . . You
must excuse a bad written letter for am seting on my carpet
sack writing. I have got to be in a hurry for we are at a minute
warning and we do not know when we will have to Start and
I do not know when I can get a chance to write you a gain for
there is no chance to get a letter to the mail. I can not write
only when I can find a friend going there. I am at the least
twelve 1200 miles from home[.] You must not be uneasy
about me for I will come as soon as I can and would if it was
twelve hundred times twelve hundred. I would walk it to
come.[10]

General Lee faced a significant problem as his army entered
Maryland: the Federal troops at Martinsburg and Harper's Ferry did not
abandon their posts. The Confederate commander could not afford to have
a large Federal force between his army and the critical Shenandoah Valley
supply line. After deliberating, Lee decided to split his force. A portion of
the army would be sent to handle the Martinsburg and Harper's Ferry
problems, while the remainder would continue on as planned. This bold
move later had near disastrous consequences for the Army of Northern
Virginia.[11]

On the morning of September 10, General Stonewall Jackson
marched west with three divisions. Major General Lafayette McLaws moved
with his division toward Maryland Heights while Brigadier General John
G. Walker's division marched toward Loudoun Heights. Both of these
precipices overlooked Harper's Ferry. The combined total of these three
groups came to some twenty-four thousand men - the majority of Lee's
army. Jackson planned to capture the small Federal garrison at Martinsburg
and then take the larger Federal stronghold at Harper's Ferry.[12]

Longstreet's two divisions, led by Brigadier Generals David R.
Jones and John B. Hood (with Brigadier General Nathan G. Evans
temporarily in command), marched northwest over South Mountain to
Boonsboro, some fifteen miles north of Harper's Ferry, and waited for
Jackson to return. Lee knew that the Federal army would eventually learn
of his movements, but he assumed that newly reinstated commander Major
General George B. McClellan would act very cautiously before taking
action, thereby allowing Jackson to complete his mission and rejoin the
rest of the army.[13]

General Lee felt that the rugged terrain and limited access points
at South Mountain would make a good buffer between his army on the

west and McClellan's army on the east. After being resupplied, the Confederate commander hoped to draw McClellan out of Washington and defeat him on a battlefield of Lee's choosing. The more than eighty thousand Federal troops greatly outnumbered the much smaller effective fighting force of the Confederates, estimated at between forty thousand and fifty thousand. Lee was confident his plan would work. He had faced disparity in numbers in previous battles and had been successful. Implementation of the plan was complex and depended on swift action by Jackson and caution by McClellan. This time, however, events would not go quite as planned.

Lee had originally intended to wait for General Jackson's return at Boonsboro, near the western base of South Mountain. However, a report that Federal troops were approaching from Chambersburg, which later proved to be unfounded, caused Lee to move farther northwest to Hagerstown. He took with him Longstreet's two divisions led by Jones and Hood while leaving Major General Daniel Harvey Hill's infantry division at Boonsboro to catch anticipated Federal troops fleeing from Harper's Ferry and to guard Turner's Gap on South Mountain against an enemy attack from the east.[14]

Generals Lee and Longstreet entered Hagerstown on the afternoon of September 11 to wait until Jackson's force could rejoin the army. At about the same time, General McClellan tentatively began moving his army from the Washington area toward Frederick. The Federal commander still did not know of Lee's plan or his strength. Through a stroke of luck, however, that was about to change.

The lead elements of General McClellan's army entered Frederick on September 12. Union troops captured at least six ill men from the 50th Georgia who had fallen out on the march and been left behind. These unfortunate Wiregrass men included Sergeant Edmund Thomas and Private David L. Dowling of Company A, Sergeant James S. Bailey and Private David L. Brewton of Company B, Private Simeon B. Lester of Company D, and Private William E. Hurst of Company E. All but one of the men were exchanged before the end of the year. The last of those captured at Frederick, Sergeant Thomas, died in Fort Delaware Prison on September 25.[15]

On September 13, the majority of the Federal troops entered Frederick, and one of the soldiers found a copy of Lee's operational orders lying on the ground near the city. McClellan now knew the Confederate commander's plans and could smash the divided Southern army. The Federal commander ordered one part of his army toward Crampton's Gap to reinforce Harper's Ferry, while the main force moved toward Turner's Gap to meet and destroy the much smaller Confederate force near Boonsboro.

The stage was now set for brutal collisions at South Mountain, and again a few days later at Sharpsburg. As the green troops of the 50th Georgia camped that Saturday night near Hagerstown, little did they know that one of the most horrible days of the war awaited them in only a few hours. Some of the Wiregrass boys cleaned their new Enfield rifles. A few wrote letters home to friends and loved ones, while others read or just tried to steal some sleep. For many, it would be their last night in this world. Tomorrow they would really "see the elephant."

Battle of Fox's Gap - September 14, 1862

Major General Daniel Harvey Hill learned on September 13 that a large Federal force was headed toward him from the east. That evening, Lee ordered Longstreet to march the divisions of Jones and Hood back from Hagerstown to Boonsboro to reinforce Hill on South Mountain. Unfortunately for the Confederates, however, Longstreet did not leave Hagerstown until mid-morning of September 14. The men of the 50th Georgia labored under the warm September sun as they hurriedly marched toward Boonsboro. That same morning, McClellan's much larger force would make contact with Hill's tiny body of defenders at Fox's Gap.[16]

Earlier that morning, General Hill looked out to the east through his field glass and saw a vast sea of blue-clad soldiers moving in his direction. Hill had been informed the day before that only two brigades of Federal infantry were approaching. Instead, McClellan's magnificent army spread out before him. Hill later recalled, "The marching columns extended back as far as eye could see. It was a grand and glorious spectacle. It was impossible to look at it without admiration. I had never seen so tremendous an army before, and I did not see one like it afterward."[17]

Hill knew he had no time to admire the Federal display as he maneuvered his small force to defend the unprotected gaps at South Mountain. He sent Brigadier General Alfred Colquitt's Georgia brigade to defend the area where the National Road passed through Turner's Gap, and he ordered Brigadier General Samuel Garland's North Carolina brigade to hold the area where Old Sharpsburg Road passed through Fox's Gap, about one mile farther south. Hill had no more than five thousand men to defend against an army five to six times his size.[18]

The terrain of South Mountain was uneven and rugged, with deep ravines and steep peaks. The slopes included heavily wooded areas that made cohesive movements difficult. Some of the hilltops had been cleared for farming. In general, it was a very difficult place to attack, but it was equally difficult to defend. General Hill could only hope that his small force could stave off the Federals until reinforcements arrived.

The fighting for South Mountain erupted at about 9:00 a.m. around Fox's Gap, when approximately three thousand Federal troops from Brigadier General Jacob Cox's all-Ohio Kanawha Division of Major General Jesse Reno's IX Corps encountered Garland's much smaller North Carolina Brigade. Colonel Eliakim P. Scammon's 1st Brigade and Colonel George Crook's 2nd Brigade comprised Cox's division.

Samuel Garland formed his men into a line of battle behind a stone wall and offered an initial fierce defense against the Ohioans. The struggle raged on property owned by elderly farmer Daniel Wise, who hustled his family out of the area. About mid-morning, Garland fell with a mortal wound while gallantly leading his men. Without their leader, the North Carolina lines gave way against the overwhelming Federal force. A discouraged D. H. Hill now anticipated the full impact of the Federal onslaught against his small force at Turner's Gap. However, Cox's troops halted to regroup, and the Federal reinforcements were slow to arrive.[19]

Hill awaited the inevitable attack and hoped for reinforcements. Brigadier General George B. Anderson's Brigade, from Hill's own division, appeared first. Anderson's men helped provide enough resistance to delay Cox's advance. Brigadier General Roswell Ripley, who commanded another brigade of Hill's, arrived and formed to the left of Anderson. Both had rushed up from Boonsboro. Later in the afternoon, Longstreet's troops arrived to help fill the positions at Turner's and Fox's Gaps. Longstreet's men had hustled eleven miles from Hagerstown and received no time to rest upon reaching South Mountain. As General Hill would later recall, "Then three very small brigades of Longstreet's command, in an exhausted condition from their hot and hurried march, came to our assistance."[20]

David R. Jones' weary division rushed through Boonsboro to the western base of South Mountain. Longstreet immediately detached Thomas Drayton's 1,300-man brigade and George T. "Tige" Anderson's much smaller brigade directly under D. H. Hill's command. Both exhausted brigades began the hot climb up South Mountain and arrived at Turner's Gap at about 3 p.m. Hill hurriedly called the commanders together and directed them to follow the narrow Wood Road south about a mile to Fox's Gap. The two brigades, along with the brigades of George B. Anderson and Roswell Ripley, would help man Hill's southern (right) flank.[21]

A four-way intersection reflected the military importance of Fox's Gap. Old Sharpsburg Road, the main transportation route, ran east to west over the crest. Wood Road was a narrow road running south along the crest from Turner's Gap to Old Sharpsburg Road. Ridge Road continued south along the crest from Old Sharpsburg Road.

Wood Road leading south from Turner's Gap. From his headquarters near Turner's Gap, General D. H. Hill directed Drayton's Brigade down this narrow trail (Wood Road) south approximately one mile to Fox's Gap. Photo by author.

Tige Anderson's Brigade took a position along Old Sharpsburg Road to the west of the intersection and generally faced south. The brigades of Roswell Ripley and George B. Anderson extended farther west along the road.

A portion of Drayton's Brigade filed onto the Old Sharpsburg Road east of the intersection, and the rest went into a field north of the road. The 50th Georgians scampered across the field to a stone wall about two hundred yards east of the Wood Road. The men looked with anticipation across the wall at a steep ravine. They anchored Drayton's left flank. Troops from the 51st Georgia and Phillips Legion fell in on the right. The right flank of Phillips Legion connected with the Old Sharpsburg Road. At this point Drayton's line made a ninety-degree turn to the west. The small 3rd South Carolina Battalion and much larger 15th South Carolina extended west up the road to the intersection. Captain J. W. Bondurant's artillery battery rolled up in the northeast corner of Old Sharpsburg Road and the Wood Road and deployed behind the Georgians facing east.

D. H. Hill ordered a counterattack shortly after the Confederate reinforcements arrived at Fox's Gap. Hill intended for the brigades to perform a left-wheel sweeping movement that would drive the Federals from the fields and woods south of the gap and down the east side of the mountain. Drayton's Brigade was to be the hinge of the movement;

Drayton's men were to hold their position while the other three brigades swept the enemy off the mountain. Hill placed General Roswell Ripley, who was senior commander, in charge of the operation. The plan immediately fell apart, with disastrous results.[22]

Facing north from Old Sharpsburg Road. The 50th and 51st Georgia Regiments, along with the Phillips Legion, initially formed along a stone wall facing east (right) in the area where the current tree line to the right now stands. The 17th Michigan would later turn the 50th Georgia's left flank, move across this field, and fire into the rear of the Georgians. Photo by author.

Hill's other three brigades extended too far west up Old Sharpsburg Road and lost contact with the right of General Drayton's Brigade at the gap. The movement quickly disintegrated in confusion. Tige Anderson's Brigade, which was supposed to extend Drayton's right, drifted at least three hundred yards too far to the west. This resulted in a large hole between the two commands and left Drayton's right flank dangerously exposed. George B. Anderson's Brigade, which was supposed to lead the sweeping movement, had trouble moving south into position. Roswell Ripley's Brigade moved too far southwest and drifted off the mountain, effectively taking itself completely out of the battle.[23]

Drayton attempted to fill the large hole between his right flank and that of Tige Anderson by shifting the two South Carolina units farther west up Old Sharpsburg Road and moving the Phillips Legion from the field into the road. After completing this movement at about 4:00 p.m., he ordered the three units to attack southward across Wise's Field against the enemy positioned in the woods beyond. They ran directly into Brigadier General Orlando B. Willcox's 3,600-man Federal division spearheading a IX Corps attack along the mountain ridge.

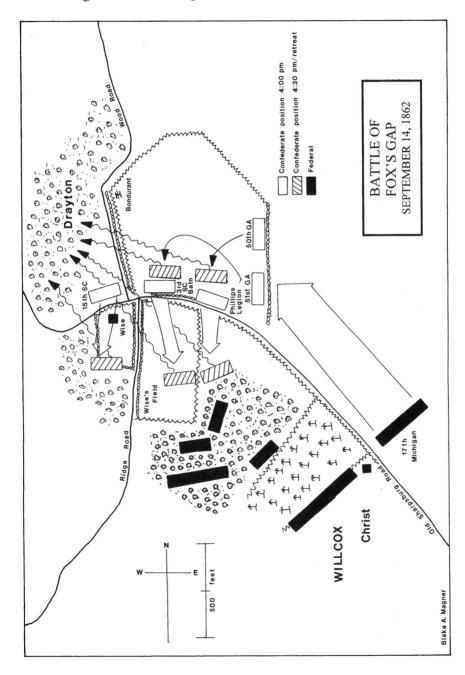

BATTLE OF
FOX'S GAP
SEPTEMBER 14, 1862

Confederate position 4:00 pm
Confederate position 4:30 pm / retreat
Federal

Blake A. Magner

Facing east down Old Sharpsburg Road from the intersection of Wood Road. Old Sharpsburg Road slopes down the mountain from the Wood Road intersection. Drayton attempted to fill the gap between his brigade and Tige Anderson's Brigade by shifting the two South Carolina units west along this portion of Old Sharpsburg Road facing right (south). When Drayton attacked to the south, the 51st Georgia would have moved up to this position. The 50th Georgia would have probably been a little farther east around the curve. Photo by author.

As his other units vacated the Old Sharpsburg Road, Drayton ordered the 50th and 51st Georgia regiments to leave the protection of the stone wall and redeploy into the road. As the Georgians were in the process of executing the movement, they came under heavy fire from a portion of Willcox's division moving up from the south and east.

Old Sharpsburg Road sloped from west to east. Years of wagon traffic had cut a deep swath in the mountain. An eight-foot embankment ran along the south side of the road. A stone wall on top of a four-foot embankment ran along the north side. The road leveled out as it extended farther east and south, causing the embankments to gradually decline and eventually flatten out.[24]

Elements of Union colonel Benjamin C. Christ's 1st Brigade and Colonel Thomas Welsh's 2nd Brigade fired into the Rebels from across a small field, protected by a stone wall and rail fence that stood on the edge of the woods. This murderous oblique fire ripped into the 50th Georgia and 51st Georgia regiments. Some of the men of the 51st Georgia Regiment were able to move up the western portion of the road and were protected

Facing east down Old Sharpsburg Road from the 50th Georgia's approximate position. The 50th Georgia filed into the road from the area to the middle left of the photo. The eight-foot embankment would be on the right (south) and the four-foot embankment on the left (north). The banks gradually leveled out beyond the curve (east and south). Photo by author.

relatively well by the steep embankments. Unfortunately, the 50th Georgia was last in executing the movement into the road. Most of the Wiregrass men were exposed to enemy fire, by virtue of the regiment's position at the bottom of the slope.

Company F received the most destructive fire. Lieutenant William O. Fleming recalled:

> While forming in the line of battle, so as to be in position to make the assault, we were exposed to the most dreadful rifle and musket fire from the enemy. . . . Our company [F] was the last that could take its position in line, and this took some of the men entirely from under cover. It was painful to see our men shot down while taking their positions. O. Trawick, near me on the right of the company, was shot down when about to file into his place. He was shot in reach of me. The enemy was posted behind a fence and trees, not over sixty or seventy yards from us, pouring their deadly volleys into us in comparative security. Some of the bolder of the enemy would come out into the road and fire down it.[25]

Private Orthenald Trawick would be the first of many Decatur County soldiers to fall. Most of the company would be lost before the end of the day.

As the two inexperienced Georgia regiments were locked in a fierce struggle for survival in Old Sharpsburg Road, Willcox's Federal troops easily repulsed the attack by Drayton's other three units, forcing the men of the 15th and 3rd South Carolina and the Phillips Legion into a desperate defensive position. Federal troops maneuvered into the exposed gap between Tige Anderson's Brigade and Drayton's right as the battle raged, and both Drayton's flanks stood in danger of being turned. Drayton's men found themselves facing an overwhelming Federal force from the east and south. The brigade took heavy casualties as the embattled Confederates scrambled to defend themselves from enemy attack on three sides.

In the sunken road, the dead and wounded piled up as volley after volley of enemy fire continued to rake the huddled Georgians. Although the Battle of Sharpsburg, still three days in the future, would became widely known for its "Bloody Lane," the men of the 50th and 51st Georgia regiments experienced their own "Bloody Lane" in Old Sharpsburg Road at Fox's Gap.

Company A Commander, Captain John Wilson, and Company B Commander, Captain John Riley O'Steen, fell with mortal wounds. Popular thirty-two-year-old Second Lieutenant William G. Dekle of Company F was also killed. Before the end of the day, almost all commissioned officers in the 50th Georgia would be either killed or wounded.[26]

Lieutenant Peter McGlashan recounted the desperate situation: "The Fiftieth were posted in a narrow path washed out into a regular gully, and were fired into by the enemy from the front, rear and left flank. The men stood their ground nobly, returning the fire until nearly two-thirds of their number lay dead or wounded in that lane. Out of 210 carried into the fight over 125 were killed and wounded in less than twenty minutes. The slaughter was horrible." One Company I officer called the carnage "a slaughter pen to our regiment."[27]

After the 50th Georgia endured about twenty minutes of heavy enemy fire, the eight-hundred-man 17th Michigan Regiment of Christ's Brigade suddenly appeared about eighty yards in the undefended rear and on the left flank of the Confederate regiment. Lieutenant Fleming reported, "The command was given them to charge, and they came toward us at the charge bayonet about 20 or 30 yards when they stopped. I directed my men to fire at them, which the few that were left did, with some effect, I know." The Michigan men moved forward and raked the embattled Georgians with a murderous fire. Coincidentally the 17th Michigan was seeing its first real action of the war, having been mustered into service only one month earlier.[28]

The appearance of the Michigan troops on the 50th Georgia's left flank and rear finally broke the Georgians' resistance. Just before the final enemy assault, Lieutenant Fleming recalled asking Colonel William R. Manning, "why we were left in such a place–that I thought we should either advance on the enemy or return. He said he could not understand it." Colonel Manning valiantly tried to keep the regiment from breaking, but the intensity of the enemy fire eventually took its toll. Manning went down with a flesh wound in the thigh as he tried to rally his Wiregrass soldiers. The wounded commander had to be helped from the field and narrowly escaped capture.[29]

The Georgia survivors retreated out of the road to the west through the gauntlet of 17th Michigan rifles. Lieutenant McGlashan described the carnage: "When ordered to retreat I could scarce extricate myself from the dead and wounded around me. A man could have walked from the head of our line to the foot on their bodies."[30]

One final tragic insult was heaped upon the many seriously wounded and dead from the 50th Georgia and 51st Georgia regiments as they lay in the Old Sharpsburg Road. Private George Hitchcock of the 21st Massachusetts described the horrible scene: "The sunken road is literally packed with dead and dying rebels who had held so stubbornly the pass against our troops who have resistlessly swept up over the hill. Here the horrors of war were revealed as [we] see our heavy ammunition wagons go tearing up, right over the dead and dying, mangling many in their terrible course. The shrieks of the poor fellows were heartrending."[31]

Sergeant Henry W. Tisdale, 35th Massachusetts Infantry Regiment, took part in the general Federal assault on Drayton's Brigade during the afternoon. Tisdale's regiment was "drawn up in the line of battle in a cornfield and then advanced through a sort of wooden field to a thick wood where we met the rebels or a few scattering ones for their main body was on the retreat. In entering the wood [we] came upon a large number of rebel dead lying in a ravine, presenting a sad and sickening sight. They were making an advance upon our lines, but when crossing the ravine, were met by a volley from the 17th Michigan which so thinned their ranks that on that part of their line they made a precipitate retreat." Some of these dead probably belonged to the 50th and 51st Georgia regiments lying in Old Sharpsburg Road.[32]

Just after entering the woods, Sergeant Tisdale received a flesh wound "by a rifle ball passing through my left leg just opposite the

Standing in the road facing the embankment along the northern portion of Old Sharpsburg Road. Those Wiregrass troops fortunate to have the protection of the four-foot embankment and a stone wall on top received some protection to their rear. However, the 17th Michigan Regiment turned the 50th Georgia's left flank and came across the field from the east, firing into the rear of the regiment. At that point, the Georgians were surrounded on three sides: south, east, and north. Photo by author.

thighbone." Tisdale bound his wound to stop the bleeding and hobbled his way back to the rear. He recalled an encounter he had with a Georgia soldier:

> a wounded rebel who was sitting against a tree called me and asked me if I did not have something to eat. Exhibiting a loaf and going to him I opened my knife to cut off a slice when he placed his hands before his face exclaiming 'Don't kill me' and begging me to put up the knife and not to hurt him. Assuring him I had no intention of hurting him I spoke with him a little. Found he had a family in Ga. that he was badly wounded and was anxious to have me remain with him and help him off. But found I was growing weaker from loss of blood and that the surging to and fro the troops about us made it a dangerous place so limping and crawling was obliged to leave him and move for the rear.[33]

Sergeant Tisdale made it to the rear and recovered from his wound. He never learned the fate of the wounded Georgian. This random act of kindness was not unusual during the war. At one moment men tried desperately to kill one another, and the next moment they would stop to comfort a dying foe.

One Wiregrass solider who narrowly escaped death was Sergeant George E. Fahm of Company E, Thomas County Rangers. Sergeant Fahm served as the regimental color bearer, one of the most honorable but most dangerous positions a soldier could hold. The Thomas County soldier recalled his miraculous escape:

> One of the most notable features of that fight is, that the day before we crossed the Potomac River, in the first Maryland Campaign, the 50th Georgia Regiment was placed on Dress Parade. The Colonel of the Regiment selected eight of the most soldierly members of the Regiment and placed them as Color Bearers [Guards], four on each side of the flag, or colors of the Regiment. in that fearful battle, seven of these eight men were killed where they stood; the eighth man was wounded; the flag, flag-staff, clothing, cap and blanket of the color bearer (myself) showed thirty-two bullet holes, and yet most strangly to relate, I did not receive a scratch in that battle. Surely God was with me in that fearful struggle.[34]

Severe fighting continued around Turner's and Fox's Gaps all afternoon. Charges and countercharges by both sides left the mountain littered with dead and wounded. Men fired pointblank into one another, and some used the bayonet and rifle butt in fierce hand-to-hand struggles. The killing continued after nightfall until it was too dark to see. The much larger Federal force had almost pushed the Confederates off the mountain. As the fighting finally stopped, the pitiful sounds of the wounded took over the night.

As the battles at Fox's and Turner's Gaps raged, the enemy also attacked and pushed back the outgunned Rebels at Crampton's Gap, about six miles to the south and closer to Harper's Ferry. This gave total control of South Mountain to the Yankees.

General Lee took time to assess his position after the fighting on South Mountain ended for the day. Jackson still had not captured Harper's Ferry and General McClellan knew that Lee had divided his force. The Confederate army faced potential disaster. That night, Lee reluctantly decided to abandon his position on South Mountain and withdraw his troops before daylight the next morning. He would move west across Antietam Creek to a better defensive position along the heights around Sharpsburg. The Confederate commander could wait there for Jackson's force to return from Harper's Ferry and reinforce his wounded army. The position would also give his army a quicker retreat route should Jackson not be able to rejoin him in time. The fate of the Army of Northern Virginia was still very much in question.[35]

Although the Confederates had been beaten on South Mountain, their fierce defense bought precious time for General Jackson to complete the capture of Harper's Ferry. By 8:00 a.m. on September 15, the Federal garrison there surrendered. The night before, General Lee seriously considered retreating back across the Potomac into Virginia, but Jackson's success gave him renewed hope for a successful campaign. He would wait for Jackson to return from Harper's Ferry in time to rejoin the rest of the army.[36]

The day after the horrible battle at Fox's Gap, Federal soldiers captured at least six Wiregrass soldiers at Williamsport, Maryland. They could have been too sick to continue on the initial march north, or they might have been part of a wagon train sent back from South Mountain by General Longstreet after the battle. Federal cavalry attacked the wagon train as it waited to cross the Potomac River to safety and captured numerous men and wagons. The unfortunate Georgians were Sergeant William H. Briggs of Company D, Sergeant Henry W. McTyre of Company F, Private Mark F. Henderson of Company G, Privates Hugh C. Chambers and Josiah McCranie of Company I, and Private George S. Edwards of Company K. All the men were exchanged before the end of the year.[37]

During the battle for South Mountain, the Federals suffered around twenty-three hundred casualties. The Confederates lost about thirty-three hundred men, including several hundred taken prisoner. Lee's divided army might have been destroyed had the Confederate defenders not held the mountain gaps for most of the day against overwhelming odds. Many historians considered the battle for South Mountain as just a prelude to the much bloodier Battle of Sharpsburg (Antietam) three days later. The battered survivors of the 50th Georgia, however, certainly did not consider their fight at Fox's Gap a prelude. They had almost been annihilated in their first real battle.

Although no post-battle report by Drayton has been found, it is estimated that the brigade suffered more than 50 percent casualties at the Battle of Fox's Gap. The actual losses for the 50th Georgia at Fox's Gap vary depending upon the source and may never be known. The official medical report for the entire Maryland Campaign (September 3–20) listed twenty-nine killed and ninety-seven wounded for the regiment. General Drayton's adjutant, J. Evans Edings, recorded "16 officers & 288 enlisted men" as of September 11, three days before Fox's Gap. As of September 17, Edings showed the number as having been reduced to only "8 officers & 90 enlisted men." Lieutenant McGlashan reported, "Out of 210 carried into the fight over

125 were killed and wounded in less than twenty minutes. The slaughter was horrible." Although McGlashan's number of 210 probably did not include officers, the total effective force for the 50th Georgia on September 14 was likely no more than 225, due to attrition from sickness and considerable straggling.[38]

Almost no one in the 50th Georgia who fought that day survived unscathed. The regiment suffered at least 194 casualties at Fox's Gap, an astonishing 86 percent casualty rate, and more than it would experience in any other single battle of the war. Of these losses, forty-seven were killed in action, twenty-two were mortally wounded, fifty-eight were wounded and escaped, thirty-two were wounded and captured, thirty-three were captured, and two were reported missing. Many men who had initially been reported missing during the confusion of battle were actually killed or mortally wounded and died shortly thereafter. Individual company casualties are as follows:

Regimental Staff (1) – 1 wounded
Company A (17) – 3 killed, 2 mortally wounded, 6 wounded, 4 wounded/captured, 2 captured
Company B (10) – 5 wounded, 3 wounded/captured, 2 captured
Company C (27) – 7 killed, 1 mortally wounded, 5 wounded, 9 wounded/captured, 4 captured, 1 missing
Company D (17) – 4 killed, 2 mortally wounded, 6 wounded, 2 wounded/captured, 3 captured
Company E (24) – 8 killed, 2 mortally wounded, 3 wounded, 6 wounded/captured, 4 captured, 1 missing
Company F (36) – 11 killed, 6 mortally wounded, 7 wounded, 4 wounded/ captured, 8 captured
Company G (25) – 4 killed, 6 mortally wounded, 12 wounded, 2 wounded/captured, 1 captured
Company H (13) – 5 killed, 1 mortally wounded, 6 wounded, 1 captured
Company I (13) – 6 killed, 1 mortally wounded, 4 wounded, 2 captured
Company K (12) – 1 mortally wounded, 4 wounded, 2 wounded/ captured, 5 captured[39]

All of the dead and many of the seriously wounded Confederates from South Mountain had to be left on the battlefield when Lee withdrew back to Sharpsburg. Those wounded who could not escape were captured and taken to Federal hospitals in the area. The hard and rocky soil made the gruesome job of disposing of Confederate dead a difficult one for Union burial details. In one instance, Federals unceremoniously dumped the bodies of fifty-eight Rebels into an unfinished well on Daniel Wise's property. In 1874, the remains of 2,240 Southern soldiers were relocated to the Confederate Section of Rose Hill Cemetery at Hagerstown, Maryland. A plaque lists the names of those few soldiers who could be identified, but the vast majority are unknown. The remains of several Wiregrass soldiers are likely buried at Rose Hill Cemetery.

Monument to Confederate dead at Rose Hill Cemetery in Hagerstown, Maryland. Photo Courtesy of Al Preston, Hagerstown, Maryland.

In Frederick, Maryland, a long, solemn row of Confederate headstones sits on the western edge of Mount Olivet Cemetery. Included in the row are headstones of 50th Georgia soldiers who were wounded at Fox's Gap, captured, and later died in a Frederick hospital. These Wiregrass men never made it back to their homes or loved ones in Georgia. (The spelling of some of the names and dates of death on the headstones are incorrect):

Captain:	John Riley O'Steen, Co G, Sep 23 1862
Privates:	Manning Corbert, Co G, Oct 1 1862
	R. P. Hughs, Co D, Nov 5 1862
	Wyat H. McPherson, Co E, Oct 27 1862
	John T. Nix, Co F, Oct 4 1862
	Andrew Shuman, Co E, Sep 25 1862
	Emanuel Shuman, Co E, Sep 24 1862
	David Sloan, Co F, Sep 27 1862
	M. T. Strickland, Co G, Dec 4 1862
	J. M. Summerall, Co G, Sep 19 1862
	Orthnold Trawick, Co F, Sep 28 1862
	Charles Trulock, Co F, Sep 27 1862
	William Wiley, Co F, Sep 23 1862

Twenty-year-old William W. Douglass had been badly wounded but managed to escape and eventually return to his regiment. Young Douglass was the fourth son of George and Mary Ann Douglass of Thomas County, Georgia. William, a "very delicate and frail boy" by his mother's account, had followed the path of his three brothers in defending his homeland. The three brothers joined the Thomasville Guards, a company in the 29th Georgia Infantry Regiment, several months before William's enlistment in the 50th Georgia.[40]

Even after her three older sons had joined the army, Mary Ann Douglass still felt a need to offer her services in some meaningful way. She became a nurse, in part to follow her older sons, whose regiment had left for Savannah. Before she departed for Savannah, however, another call went out for soldiers, and it was then that William signed up.[41]

Several days after learning of William's wounding at Fox's Gap, Mary Ann Douglass heard he was in the hospital in Savannah. She left her nursing post at Guyton, located in Effingham County near Savannah, and arrived at her son's bedside late that night. Although she witnessed terrible suffering as a nurse in Guyton, Mrs. Douglass had never seen a wounded soldier. Incredibly, the first one she saw was her young son, fifteen days after his wounding.[42]

Mrs. Douglass recorded William's condition in her diary:

When I saw him he was tearbille to look at. it was a horrible sight to me his head was swollen so bad. No shape and he was as yellow as a pumpkin and had a large hole through his hip. the doctors said it just graised the bone. The ball went

Clear through. a large hole Where the ball entered and one
Where it came out. . . . Next morning through the kindness of
one Dr. Cummings I got a furlough to take him home for I
knew his poor old Father was suffering all the agoney of a
terrible suspense. he suffered so from the Jolting of the cars I
was fearful he would never Live to reach home with. I had
pillows and bolstered him up so as to be as easy as possible
but still he suffered terribly.[43]

By June 1863, William Douglass felt well enough to be assigned
to work on the commissary wagons. He never returned to the field. Mary
Ann Douglass continued to serve as a nurse for much of the war.[44]

Fox's Gap had been a terrible baptism under fire for the 50th
Georgia and one that would stand as the regiment's most desperate
engagement. All companies suffered heavy casualties and some were almost
obliterated. There would be little time to rest for the surviving Wiregrass
Georgians. As these men slowly trudged west from South Mountain toward
Sharpsburg, the bloodiest single day of the entire war soon awaited them.

Chapter Four
Sharpsburg and Operations in Virginia
September 15–November 20, 1862

After the battle of Fox's Gap, the remnants of Thomas Drayton's shattered brigade returned to Brigadier General David R. Jones' command. On the morning of September 15, Jones' division reached Sharpsburg and took its position on the heights overlooking Antietam Creek, just southeast of town. Later in the day, Drayton's Brigade moved farther southwest and formed on the left of Brigadier General James L. Kemper's Virginia brigade. At this point, Jones' entire six-brigade command numbered only 2,430 men.[1]

With Jones' division positioned at the extreme right, the entire Confederate battle line stretched some four miles long. The line paralleled the Hagerstown Turnpike north of Sharpsburg and extended south past the town. The right flank continued along the bluffs overlooking Antietam Creek to a spot just west of Snavely's Ford, a mile below the Rohrbach Bridge, also called the Lower Bridge. Less than a mile farther to the west was Colonel Thomas T. Munford's Cavalry Brigade, which guarded the southern approach into town along Harper's Ferry Road.[2]

Jones ordered Brigadier General Robert A. Toombs to defend the Rohrbach Bridge across Antietam Creek in the division's forefront. General Toombs in turn ordered Colonel Henry L. Benning to place the 20th Georgia Infantry Regiment and 2nd Georgia Infantry Regiment, "both together numbering but a little over 400 muskets," along the west bank of the creek. The 20th Georgia deployed on the high, wooded bank immediately opposite the bridge. The 2nd Georgia deployed farther south and east. The Georgians, therefore, held a commanding view from the bluff overlooking the narrow structure; the stone bridge was approximately 125 feet long and only 12 feet wide. Their strong defensive position ensured that anyone who attempted to cross the bridge would suffer greatly.[3]

On Tuesday, September 16, General Jones detached the 50th Georgia Regiment from Drayton's Brigade and sent it to support Toombs' Brigade at the Rohrbach Bridge. Lieutenant Colonel Francis L. Kearse temporarily replaced Colonel William R. Manning as commander of the 50th Georgia, due to Manning's wounding at Fox's Gap.

The exhausted Wiregrass soldiers, "some ninety strong," took up positions to the right of the 2nd Georgia Regiment. In a report to General Jones, Toombs later stated: "I ordered this regiment on the right of the 2nd Georgia, extending it in open order, so as to guard a blind plantation road leading to a ford between the lower ford before referred to and the right of the Second Georgia Volunteers."[4]

The ragged little band of 50th Georgians secured a razor-thin defensive line above the creek bank to the right of the 2nd Georgia. The line snaked westerly, following a bend in the creek all the way to Snavely's Ford, almost a mile southwest of the Rohrbach Bridge. This position represented another

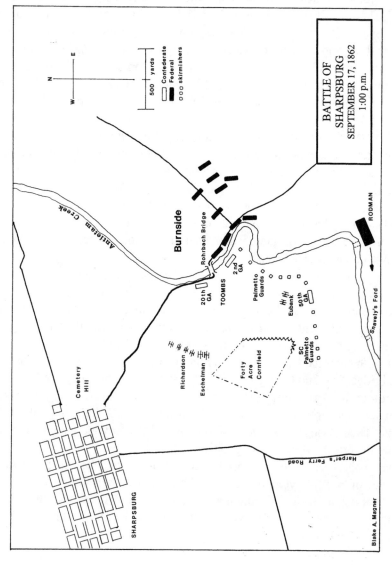

difficult assignment for the men of the 50th Georgia. The regiment's right wing anchored Toombs' right flank. It was critical that Federal troops not be allowed to cross the creek and move behind the Georgians. This would prove to be a tall order for Kearse's determined but over-extended Wiregrass men.

Battle of Sharpsburg (Antietam) – September 17, 1862

At daybreak on Wednesday, September 17, the deadliest single day of the war began when Federal forces attacked the Confederate left flank north of Sharpsburg. Later that morning, the 50th Georgia received some welcome reinforcements when a small company of skirmishers from the Palmetto Sharpshooters Regiment of Brigadier General Micah Jenkins' South Carolina brigade arrived. Toombs deployed half of the company between the 50th and 2nd Georgia regiments. He sent the rest of the company to the right of the 50th Georgia to help guard Snavely's Ford. Toombs pleaded for additional reinforcements from Jones and Longstreet to help fortify the weak defenses guarding these two important creek crossings, but he was told that none were available.[5]

To Toombs' rear stood Captain John B. Richardson's Battery of the Washington (Louisiana) Artillery, which held the high ground about five hundred yards northwest of the bridge. The Georgia commander also placed Captain John L. Eubank's Virginia Battery farther south on the bluff overlooking the bridge, about halfway between Richardson's Battery and the creek. The

Burnside (Rohrbach/Lower) Bridge. View from the west bank overlooking the bridge. Toombs' Georgians occupied this strong position. Photo by author.

main line of Confederate artillery on Cemetery Hill also commanded the bridge and the road to Sharpsburg. The determined Georgians and South Carolinians settled into their thin defensive line. They would soon need more than just determination.[6]

During the morning, as the battle raged to the north, General McClellan ordered Major General Ambrose Burnside's 12,500-man IX Corps to cross the Antietam Creek and attack the Confederate right flank. "At between 9 and 10 o'clock," the 11th Connecticut Regiment made the initial attempt at crossing the Rohrbach Bridge but failed under a withering fire from the rifles of the 20th and 2nd Georgia Regiments. During that ill-fated assault, the 11th Connecticut Commander, Colonel Henry W. Kingsbury, received a mortal wound. In a tragic twist of fate, Kingsbury happened to be a close friend and brother-in-law of Confederate division commander David R. Jones, whose troops defended the bridge. Kingsbury and Jones had married sisters before the war. Jones learned of his friend's mortal wounding by the hands of his own men after the battle. The grief-stricken Jones would die of a heart attack four months later.[7]

After the 11th Connecticut's disastrous attempt to cross the bridge, the 11th Ohio made a gallant charge. The withering fire from Toombs' entrenched Georgians beat them back. Soon afterward, the 2nd Maryland and the 6th New Hampshire charged ahead with the same result. As wave after wave of Burnside's men vainly attempted to cross the bridge, elements of Brigadier General Isaac P. Rodman's 3rd Division searched southward for another location to cross the creek. As these blue-clad troops slowly moved south along the creek's eastern bank, the Wiregrass soldiers and Palmetto Sharpshooters peppered them with a deadly fire from behind the protection of trees and a stone wall.[8]

The rapid fire from the 50th Georgians and Palmetto Sharpshooters attracted the attention of Union artillery. Company E Commander, Lieutenant Peter McGlashan recalled the 50th Georgia's determined attempt to hold the ford against the Yankee tide: "Three brigades passed along in plain view of our pickets to our right to attempt crossing. I having command of the right wing of the regiment, strung out my pickets. In obedience to orders from Gen. Drayton, as far to the right as the men could be placed, greatly weakening my line of skirmishers. The enemy having succeeded in silencing our supporting battery, commenced pouring in a tremendous fire of grape and canister on us while their skirmishers engaged ours."[9]

Despite their efforts, the company-size group of Georgians and South Carolinians could not hold back Rodman's division. Shortly before 1:00 p.m., the Yankees reached Snavely's Ford. Led by Colonel Harrison S. Fairchild's 1st Brigade and Colonel Edward Harland's 2nd Brigade, the blue-clad enemy poured across the creek against the blistering Southern fire.[10]

Looking south across Antietam Creek near Snavely's Ford. Rodman's division poured down the hill from the far banks and splashed northward across the shallow creek. The 50th Georgia and the Palmetto Sharpshooters were on a hill above the crossing, firing into the Yankees as they forded the creek. Photo by author.

Enemy troops swarmed up the slippery western banks and headed north toward the crest of a hill overlooking the Rohrbach Bridge. They drove a wedge between the 50th Georgia's right and left wings. Lieutenant McGlashan described the desperate situation facing the Confederate regiment: "Lieut. Col. Kearse, of the Fiftieth, finding his position untenable, and ascertaining that the enemy in strong force were passing the river on our right, and having no support on that side, drew his line of pickets back some three hundred yards from the river, just in time, as it proved, as our right was flanked and fired on by the enemy's skirmishers as we fell back."[11]

Toombs' men at the Rohrbach Bridge now faced immediate jeopardy. Not only was he flanked on the far right, but the enemy threatened his rear. From the crest of the hill, the Yankees had a commanding view of the 20th and 2nd Georgia's Rohrbach Bridge defenses.[12]

As Rodman's men streamed across the creek to the south, an all-out assault led by the 51st New York and 51st Pennsylvania regiments of Brigadier General Edward Ferrero's 2nd Brigade finally carried the bridge against the depleted ranks of the Georgians. With their cartridge boxes almost empty, General Toombs withdrew his men from the Rohrbach Bridge. Toombs now faced the threat of being cut off as Federal troops rushed into his rear.[13]

The exhausted survivors fell back from the bridge. After firing a final volley from behind a stone wall, the 50th Georgia men raced from their positions and joined the other retreating Georgians. While under intense fire from Burnside's onrushing men, the defenders scrambled westward toward the outskirts of Sharpsburg. Robert Toombs reported, "This change of position was made to my entire satisfaction, and with but small loss, in the face of greatly superior numbers."[14]

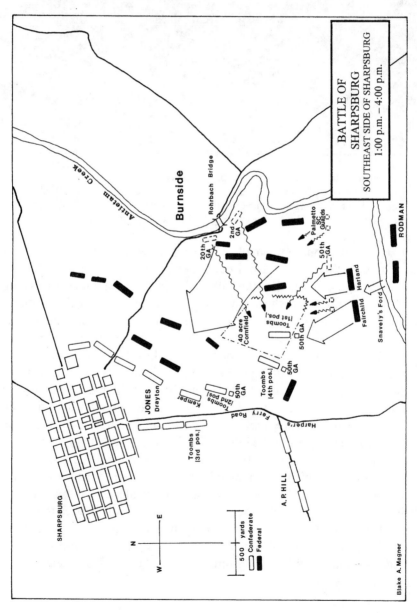

Approximately 500 Federal and 120 Confederate casualties fell near the bridge that morning and early afternoon. However, the small number of Georgians and South Carolinians managed to hold Burnside's IX Corps at bay for more than three brutal hours.

Toombs' men took up new defensive positions approximately one-half mile to the right and in front of General Jones' line of battle. Running low on ammunition, they awaited the inevitable assault of Burnside's IX Corps. Fortunately, Toombs' other two regiments, the 15th and 17th Georgia, and five companies from the 11th Georgia Regiment of Colonel George T. "Tige" Anderson's Brigade rushed to their aid. As the reinforcements arrived, the 20th Georgia and 2nd Georgia pulled back toward Harper's Ferry Road to replenish their cartridge boxes.[15]

Shortly after 4 p.m., the IX Corps began their assault to take Sharpsburg and the heights south of the town. Lieutenant William O. Fleming and about a dozen men stood on a picket line in a cornfield to the left of the 50th Georgia Regiment when the enemy began advancing on the heights. Lieutenant Fleming climbed to the top of an apple tree in the field to get a better view of the approaching enemy. He described the sight as "a beautiful view of the advancing columns of the enemy." Fleming continued, "Considering the rough plowed ground they had to pass over, their line of battle was kept admirably. Besides, not infrequently, a shell from one of our guns would burst in their midst, and for a moment create confusion, but soon they would close up again and move on."[16]

As Fleming looked toward the 50th Georgia Regiment, he saw them quickly marching off with Toombs' Brigade to meet the enemy. He slid down the tree and called in his small group of men. They raced off after the regiment, but it had already disappeared. Separated from the rest of the 50th Georgia, Fleming and his men joined another brigade that was crouched behind a stone wall.[17]

The Federal advance steadily pushed the smaller Confederate force to the outskirts of Sharpsburg. The situation became desperate. To help meet the attack, General Jones ordered Toombs to move forward from his position. With full cartridge boxes, the 20th Georgia raced back to the western portion of what is now called the Forty-Acre Cornfield. The 15th, 17th, and 11th Georgia Regiments, along with "a small number of Kearse's [50th Georgia] regiment," followed closely.[18]

As the enemy threatened to break the Southerners' right flank, reinforcements from Major General A. P. Hill's division smashed into the IX Corps' unsuspecting left flank. Hill's men had marched at the double-quick for seventeen grueling miles from Harper's Ferry, and they arrived just in time to help turn the tide of battle.[19]

As Hill's men reinforced the Confederate right, Toombs' command, including the 50th Georgia, quickly formed a line of battle within one hundred yards of the advancing enemy. When elements of the IX Corps got within sixty to eighty yards, the greatly outnumbered Georgians released a torrential hail of musketry into the startled Yankees. The fiery Georgia commander then ordered a charge into the disordered Union ranks. "Shouting like wild Indians," the newly energized Confederates slammed into the enemy troops in the Forty-Acre Cornfield.[20]

The Confederate counterattack rolled back the left flank of Burnside's IX Corps. In minutes, the enemy changed from attackers to defenders as they fled in confusion back toward Antietam Creek and the Rohrbach Bridge. By late afternoon, Rebel troops had chased the IX Corps back across the bridge. Robert Toombs wanted to pursue the retreating Yankees, but exhaustion and nightfall put an end to his plan.[21]

Lieutenant McGlashan described the 50th Georgia's role in the Confederate counterattack:

> We were quickly formed in the rear of the guns [Richardson's Battery], the Fiftieth Georgia on the left, and as soon as formed we saw the Yankee line, in splendid order advance on the guns. We let them get within sixty or seventy yards of us, and poured in a withering volley, that made their whole line reel and stagger under the dreadful effect of the fire, as if they were drunk. Again and again, with murderous aim, we poured into them volley after volley, until, utterly unable to face such terrible punishment, their whole line broke and sought the shelter of the hill. The Fiftieth leaped a wood fence in front, charged to the edge of the hill and pursued the flying foe for nearly a mile towards the river. The gunners, running back to their guns, opened a terrible fire with shell on their already thinned ranks. I never saw guns served quicker or with more fearful effect. I have no idea that one third of that splendid column got back to tell the tale; it was a wholesale slaughter.[22]

The 50th Georgia lost two color bearers during the day. When the second went down, Lieutenant Colonel Kearse grabbed up the colors and personally carried them until he could place them in the hands of another man. The brave commander and other officers also grabbed weapons from fallen comrades and fired on the enemy during the desperate struggle.[23]

The success of the 50th Georgia was bittersweet. Many Wiregrass soldiers fell, including Lieutenant Francis L. Mobley. The young officer had received a grazing head wound from a minie ball during the horrible carnage at Fox's Gap a few days earlier, and during the fierce afternoon fighting, he was struck by an enemy bullet in the right breast that pierced his lung. Litter bearers carried him from the field. The Berrien County soldier was later transported to a makeshift hospital in Winchester, Virginia.[24]

By the end of the day, Jones' command had recaptured all the ground it had held that morning, with the exception of the Rohrbach Bridge. By early evening, the Confederate counterattack slowed and the Battle of Sharpsburg ended. As General Lee reported, "The repulse on the right ended the engagement, and, after a protracted and sanguinary conflict, every effort of the enemy to dislodge us from our position had been defeated with severe loss."[25]

Lieutenant McGlashan recalled trying to find Drayton's Brigade in the darkness. "It was now night, and we gathered together what remained of our sorely shattered regiment, only 55 men, and started out over the hard fought field to find our proper brigade. We were over forty-eight hours without anything to eat, and the men were utterly exhausted. We found the brigade about midnight, and receiving some cooked provisions from our indefatigable commissary, who was looking out for us, we lay down on the battle field surrounded by dead and wounded men and horses, and slept as only tired and weary soldiers can sleep."[26]

Lee's army remained entrenched the following day, expecting another Federal attack. Although considerable picket firing took place between the lines, there was no active engagement. At 9 p.m., Jones' division joined the Confederate withdrawal to Virginia. During the night of September 18, the 50th Georgia crossed the Potomac River back into Virginia at Boteler's Ford, about a mile and a half downstream from Shepherdstown, en route to Martinsburg. The regiment camped near Shepherdstown the next morning.[27]

Sharpsburg had been the second desperate struggle within a three-day period for the 50th Georgia. The regiment lost at least twenty-four men during this recent battle. Of these losses, three were killed, one was mortally wounded, fifteen were wounded, one was wounded and captured, and four were captured. Individual company casualties are as follows:

Company A (0) – No casualties reported
Company B (0) – No casualties reported
Company C (3) – 1 wounded, 2 captured
Company D (4) – 3 wounded, 1 captured
Company E (4) – 4 wounded

Company F (0) – No casualties reported
Company G (1) – 1 killed
Company H (2) – 2 wounded
Company I (3) – 1 killed, 1 mortally wounded, 1 wounded
Company K (7) – 1 killed, 4 wounded, 1 wounded/captured, 2 captured [28]

After the battle, an article surprisingly critical of the 50th Georgia's performance at Sharpsburg appeared in the October 8, 1862, *Savannah Republican.* Correspondent P. W. A. (Peter Wellington Alexander) wrote, "It is said that the Fiftieth Georgia regiment, Col. Manning, did not maintain their ground as steadily at Sharpsburg as they might have done, but with this exception our troops conducted themselves with a gallantry and heroism which have not been excelled during the war."[29]

Colonel William R. Manning, who did not command the 50th Georgia at Sharpsburg due to a wound suffered at Fox's Gap, took strong exception to the article. Manning responded in a letter to the editor on October 15, 1862, pointing out that another *Savannah Republican* correspondent, Virgil A. Parks, had praised the efforts of the regiment and its leader, Lieutenant Colonel Francis Kearse. Parks reported in the October 1, 1862, *Savannah Republican,* "In the affair of Wednesday, (Battle of Sharpsburg) I witnessed the part taken in the closing fight by the 50th. They followed our brigade into the fight, and took position next to the 15th. In the charge they, led by Col. Kearse, acted most nobly. They charged over the hill, and took position behind the same stone fence behind which the Fifteenth fought with much effect. The regiment did not number more than sixty or seventy men."[30]

Colonel Manning also quoted a letter received from Lieutenant Colonel Kearse concerning the role of the 50th Georgia during the conflict. Kearse wrote the following:

> We were placed in position Tuesday morning to guard a
> bridge over the river, and remained on post, without being
> relieved, until Wednesday, two o'clock, without food, water
> or sleep, under the heaviest fire ever witnessed. Some six or
> eight thousand men, with muskets and rifles, fronted the
> bridge in opposition to our little force; at the same time six or
> seven batteries were playing upon us with grape, canister and
> shell. At two o'clock we left the bridge to engage the enemy
> in the open field, where our boys had an opportunity of
> exhibiting their bravery. I am pleased to be able to state that
> they fought well. I lost two color bearers during the day.[31]

Manning closed his letter to the editor by chiding the correspondent, "It appears from the testimony of these two gentlemen that the regiment did very well, and that P. W. A.'s informant was in error. A correspondent should never brand regiments or individuals with cowardice, without better evidence than camp rumor. As an act of justice you will please publish this note, and oblige."[32]

The fierce defense of the Rohrbach Bridge and Snavely's Ford by the small but determined force of Georgia riflemen helped save Lee's army, because it allowed time for A. P. Hill's Light Division to march from Harper's Ferry and bolster the Confederate right flank. The Georgians also distinguished themselves in the afternoon counterattack that routed Burnside's men. The Wiregrass men had proven their courage, but now the regiment was decimated. The 50th Georgia needed time to regroup.

The Army Regroups and Conducts Operations in Northern Virginia: September 20 - November 20, 1862

Indeed, the entire Army of Northern Virginia would need the next couple months to recover. As General Lee stated, "The condition of our troops now demanded repose." The 50th Georgia Regiment had been almost destroyed. Drayton's Brigade adjutant, J. Evans Edings, reported the effective strength of the regiment as of September 18, the day after the Battle of Sharpsburg, to be "6 officers & 50 enlisted men." This represented a fraction of the "16 officers & 288 enlisted men" present on September 11, a few days before Fox's Gap. It is also consistent with Lieutenant McGlashan's report of "only 55 men," remaining in the regiment after the battle. Although the ranks of the 50th Georgia would gradually be replenished by returning soldiers and new conscripts, the regiment would never regain its original strength.[33]

The 50th Georgia marched with Drayton's Brigade to Martinsburg and remained there until September 26. After a few days of rest, the regiment marched to Brucetown, near Winchester, on the 29th. They would remain in the area, many of them in critical condition at local hospitals, for about one month.[34]

One seriously wounded soldier, Lieutenant Francis Mobley, recuperated in a Winchester hospital and appeared to be improving. In a September 25 letter to his wife, the Berrien County officer described the recent battle and his condition:

> During this fight I received a wound the bullet passing
> through my right breast just below the nipple. It was God's
> mercy that saved me from instant death, as there is not one in

a thousand that could live after receiving such a wound. It is
now the next day and though I am feeble yet I feel like I am
getting much better every day. I am in good comfortable
quarters in Winchester and have Mr. Jno T. Weakly [Private
John T. Weekly, Co. I] to nurse me. He gives me any thing I
canever desire. You must not be uneasy about me as I will
have everything done for me that is necessary. I have no
doubt that I will get a furlough to go home as soon as I can
travel not being able to now I have got Dr. McLynn [?] to
write this to you for me-
I remain as ever
Your affectionate Husband

F L Mobley[35]

Other 50th Georgia soldiers struggled with illness, and their deaths
often led to promotion for others. Captain Cicero Holt Young of Company
E succumbed to typhoid pneumonia in a Winchester hospital on October 1.
That same day, Young was replaced by First Lieutenant Peter McGlashan,
who received a promotion to captain. The men of the company elected
Second Lieutenant John N. McKinnon as first lieutenant to fill the vacancy
created by McGlashan's promotion and elected Junior Second Lieutenant
Richard J. McLean as second lieutenant.[36]

On October 5, Captain McGlashan reported that the regiment had
swelled back to a strength of 350, and that "stragglers and conscripts are
coming in very fast."[37] The Confederate government had begun conscripting
men to replenish the army in April 1862. In many instances, the physical
and emotional qualities of the recruits were poor. William J. Evers was one
such recruit. He wrote a letter from Savannah on August 11, 1862, to his
wife Margaret, in which he shared his fate and encouraged his wife to
persevere:

Dear wife, I drop you a few lines to let you know that I am
received into the servis. Doctor Tucker did not give us any
chance atall. He takes anything that can walk or nearly, so I
will state to you that I am about like I have bin. I am sick but
I am bad of [off] with my back and misery through my
stomac. Wee will leave for Camp Randolph some time today I
exspect. I will write to you when I get there as soon as I can
do so. I want you to write to me. I want to hear from you all. I
wish you to be as well composed as you can and get along the
best you can. So I must come to close by saying I remain
your loveing husband until death.[38]

Later in the month William Evers left Camp Randolph with other conscripts for Richmond. On September 29, after missing the Battles of Fox's Gap and Sharpsburg, Evers reached the 50th Georgia Regiment and was assigned to Company E. Although he did his duty, Evers suffered several physical ailments throughout his service, as he reported to his wife in numerous letters. He would be seriously wounded ten months later at the Battle of Gettysburg.[39]

By early October, the cool winds signaled the approach of winter weather in Virginia. The drop in temperature made many of the Wiregrass soldiers uncomfortable because of their inadequate clothing. Lieutenant William O. Fleming described the conditions in an October 7 letter to his wife: "The weather is getting very cold here. Yesterday morning we had a considerable frost. Johnny [brother and Adjutant John M. Fleming] & myself slept together but we have not blankets enough together to keep warm. We have two small ones together—one we lay on the ground to lie on & [cover?] with the other."[40]

On October 8, Captain Duncan Curry, Company F, received a promotion to major. He replaced Phillip Pendleton, who had resigned due to illness. That same day, Lieutenant William O. Fleming became captain of Company F to fill the vacancy created by Curry's promotion, and Henry S. Reeves moved up to first lieutenant.[41]

Lieutenant Francis L. Mobley succumbed to the wound suffered at Sharpsburg on October 9. Shortly before his death, Mobley asked to see his best friend, Lieutenant David Perry Luke. Luke received a brief leave of absence and rushed to his friend's bedside. In a letter to Francis Mobley's wife, David Luke described the meeting with his dying friend:

Camp near Bruiceville
Oct. 14th 1862
Mrs. F. L. Mobley
Heighly Esteemed friend it is with deep
regret that I now enter on the painful duty of writing you this
letter, though it is at the dying request of your brave and noble
hearted husband. When I arrived to my company to my sorrow
and grief I learned that he was mortally wounded lying at
Winchester and wanted to see me and I got a short leave of
absense and Walked Eight mile as feeble as I was and when I
found him I saw that he was subject to die at any moment,
though he was perfectly cool and resigned to his fate the
physician has informed him that morning that he must die but it
did not seem to affect him. I set over him all night and talked
with him as much as he could bare to talk for his voice was

very week and faint he told me how he wanted his business
fixed he requested ne [me] that when I knew he was dead that I
would write three letters for him one to you and one to his
father in law and one to his father and to say to you all that it
was his dying request that his child should be raised up in the
right manner and to live and fear the Lord and at all Hazards
have it well educated and that his fatherin Law and father
should assist you in so doing. he requested me to send you the
ball that Killed him which I have done by Mr. Sutton all his
clothing and I now send you by F. Gaskins his Sachel with his
vests, Sash and some little paper in his vest pocket he told me
he threw away his sword on the battle ground his pistol I sold
to Lt. Gaskins and sent you the note by Mr. Sutton which I
hope will all arrive safe to you.

My Dear friend I can say to you that you have been
bereaved of a noble hearted and as brave a Husband as ever
steped on the soil of Maryland according to his age and
practice. I wished to God that he could have lived to have
fought many Battles unhurt and returned to you again
So I will come to a close for want of time.
Your most humble
And obt Svt
D. P. Luke[42]

The 50th Georgia remained at Brucetown until October 18, when
the regiment marched toward Harper's Ferry and participated in a three-
day raid to destroy part of the Baltimore and Ohio Railroad. The men then
marched back to Brucetown, a roundtrip of some thirty-eight miles, and
remained in the area for the rest of the month.[43]

Major Duncan Curry described the frustrations of the three-day
march in an October 23 letter to his wife:

My health is pretty good this morning considering what I have
under went the last three days. Last Monday . . . we were
marched out of our camp and then back again and held until four
oclock and then marched out in another direction and . . .
marched about twelve miles that night and quartered in an open
old field. Tuesday we marched up in the vicinity of Harper's
Ferry and are camped in an old field again. Wednesday we were
marched six miles on the rail road and put to tearing it up which
we done by riping the iron and piling up the crossties, laying the
iron rails on top and seting fire to the whole. About sunset we
were marched six miles back to our night before camp where we
arrived about ten oclock, and here we are.[44]

Lieutenant Francis Lawton Mobley, Company I, Berrien Light Infantry. Mobley enlisted in the Berrien Light Infantry on March 4, 1862, at Nashville and soon became second lieutenant. In June 1862, Mobley received a promotion to senior second lieutenant. Ill at the time the regiment left Savannah for Richmond, Lieutenant Mobley later rejoined the regiment at Frederick, Maryland, on September 7. The Berrien County native received a slight wound on September 14 at the Battle of Fox's Gap and received a mortal wound three days later at the Battle of Sharpsburg. He died in a Winchester, Virginia, hospital on October 9. Mobley is buried at Stonewall Confederate Cemetery (Mount Hebron) in Winchester. Courtesy of Glenn Hodges, great-great grandson of Francis L. Mobley, Nashville, Georgia.

The next morning, Major Curry continued the letter and expressed his strong feelings about brigade commander Thomas Drayton:

> We were interrupted at nine oclock yesterday by marching orders and were marched fifteen miles to this Camp in sight of our old camp six miles from Winchester. Our men that is our Camp is in very bad condition a number sick footsore barefooted and etc. We have had frost every morning for sometime and our Gen Drayton has not got since [sense] enough to pitch a camp in a wood, but will stick us out in an old field to be frosted on and suffer from the cold. The soldiers that are use to this climate get along much better than we do.[45]

Despite Captain McGlashan's optimism over the increased ranks, illness continued to plague the 50th Georgia. At least thirty men died from disease between August 1 and October 31, 1862. Many more were newly hospitalized, including Private George W. Chitty of Company D, who became seriously ill for the second time in two months. On October 31, he was admitted to General Hospital #16 in Richmond, and on November 17 he was moved to Winder Division #3 Hospital. Chitty remained hospitalized for about six weeks, finally returning to duty on December 16, just after the Battle of Fredericksburg.[46]

More men were promoted on October 25. The soldiers of Company G elected First Lieutenant Quarterman B. Staten as captain, replacing John Riley O'Steen, who had been mortally wounded at Fox's Gap. Company G also elected Second Lieutenant Isaac Burkhalter as first lieutenant to fill the vacancy created by Staten's promotion and elected Junior Second Lieutenant Jacob S. Lightsey as second lieutenant.[47]

On November 1, a rested and replenished 50th Georgia left Brucetown and marched toward Culpeper Court House. The men made the grueling eighty-five mile journey in only four days, arriving on November 5. In a letter to his wife, footsore Major Duncan Curry described the march and again revealed his feelings about General Drayton:

> On last Fryday we took up the line of march at daybreak in the direction of Culpeper Courthouse and marched twenty three miles before sunset. The next morning we started before sunrise and marched about ten miles wading two rivers. Sunday we marched about twenty miles and yesterday we marched about twenty three miles badly jaded as we were marched all day being on our feet all day long, except about twenty minutes but I am ready for it again this morning if it was necessary. The marches are unreasonable and managed by our drunken Gen Drayton. He is a sorry [word illegible] in my opinion.[48]

The 50th Georgia remained at Culpeper Court House until November 20, when Drayton's Brigade marched to Fredericksburg. These Wiregrass men would soon be called upon again, this time to defend Fredericksburg against an overwhelming Federal force. The Georgia veterans would also face a bitter winter and their first Christmas away from home.

Chapter Five
Fredericksburg: The Battle
and the Harsh Winter
November 1862–April 1863

P resident Abraham Lincoln's patience with General George B. McClellan finally ran out. The "Young Napoleon's" failure to pursue Lee's retreating army after Sharpsburg was the last straw. On November 7, Lincoln replaced the cautious McClellan with affable Major General Ambrose E. Burnside. In response to pressure to show some progress in the war, the new Federal commander decided on a bold move to capture the Confederate capital. Burnside planned to swiftly march his army to Fredericksburg, cross the Rappahannock River, and reach Richmond before General Robert E. Lee's much smaller force could block his advance.

Thousands of new recruits, conscripts, and men returning to duty from wounds or illness over the previous two months swelled the ranks of the Army of Northern Virginia to more than seventy thousand. Although the army had grown, it was not yet strong enough to mount an offensive against the much larger Army of the Potomac, which numbered one hundred thousand men. The Southerners still desperately needed food and supplies. Surprisingly, however, some legislators in the Confederate capital considered reducing military rations. Lee expressed extreme concern over that idea in a November 17 letter to Secretary of War George W. Randolph:

> The future supply of subsistence for the army is to me a
> source of great anxiety. I have endeavored all in my power to
> economize that now exists, and to provide for our future
> wants. While in the valley, the complaint from the officers of
> an insufficient quantity of food for the troops became so
> general that, after consultation with the chief commissary of
> the army, I determined to increase the ration of flour to 1 1/8
> pounds and of beef to 1 1/4 pounds. It was stated that one
> great cause of straggling from the ranks was the insufficiency
> of the ration to appease the hunger of the men. At that time
> we were using the flour ground from the wheat in the valley,
> and collecting a quantity of meat on the hoof. No other part
> of the ration could be furnished to the men, except salt, nor
> could the men increase their fare by the purchase of bread, &

vegetables, &c. Their whole ration consisted of bread and
meat. From my examination into the matter, I do not think
this allowance is too great, and complaints are even now
received that the bread ration is too small. The same
condition of things now exists. The daily diet of the men is
bread and meat, without any addition of vegetables, &c., and,
in view of the labor before them, I do not think it can be
reduced to advantage. If this amount cannot be furnished,
necessity will oblige its reduction; but if it can, I recommend
it be continued.[1]

The gracious commander closed by expressing appreciation for recent
supplies and gently pointing out the need for more: "We have received in the
last few days about 5,000 pairs of shoes, and clothing and blankets in
proportion, which has added very much to the comfort of the army. There
are still about 2,000 men barefooted, and about 3,000 more whose shoes are
in such a condition that they will not last another march." Lee understated
the severity of the problem. Before the recent shipment, an inventory of
Longstreet's Corps indicated that approximately seven thousand men were
barefoot. Of that number, almost fifteen hundred were in McLaws' division.[2]

On November 16, Rebel cavalry scouts reported a large Federal force
moving toward the Richmond, Fredericksburg, and Potomac Railroad. Lee
sensed Fredericksburg was their destination, but he had no firm evidence to
confirm his hunch. Early on the morning of November 18, James Longstreet
sent the divisions of Major General Lafayette McLaws and Brigadier General
Robert Ransom toward Fredericksburg to delay a possible Federal attempt
to cross the Rappahannock River. Later that day, reports confirmed that the
Army of the Potomac was marching toward the city. Lee's hunch had been
correct.[3]

The next day, the rest of Longstreet's Corps began moving from
Culpeper Court House to Fredericksburg. At dawn on the morning of
November 20, the 50th Georgia Regiment packed their knapsacks and headed
in the direction of Fredericksburg. Recent rains muddied the road and made
for tough conditions as the men slipped and sloshed along in the muck and
the cold. The Confederates were also slowed by congestion from scores of
refugees, who had fled the city in fear of an impending battle. On November
23, after four days of hard marching, the exhausted Wiregrass men finally
arrived near the city and immediately set up camp.[4]

The two armies concentrated their forces near Fredericksburg over
the next several days. Federal troops massed on the east side of the
Rappahannock River along Stafford Heights. An exasperated Burnside waited
for pontoon bridges to arrive by wagon so his army could cross the icy

river. While the Union commander fumed, Lee's men hurriedly constructed strong entrenchments west of the river and along the heights overlooking the city.

General Lee conducted some distasteful business as he awaited the inevitable battle. He reluctantly relieved General Thomas Drayton of command on November 25. Frequent complaints from division commanders, and more recently from General Longstreet, concerning Drayton's lack of leadership gave the Confederate commander no choice. Lee reported in a letter to President Jefferson Davis: "General Drayton's brigade has been a source of delay and embarrassment from the time the army left Richmond. At Manassas it could not get into battle. At South Mountain and Sharpsburg it broke to pieces. I do not mean to charge this as a fault of General Drayton; but, in addition, he does not seem able to keep up the organization of his brigade." Lee went on, "He is a gentleman, and in his own person a soldier, but seems to lack the capacity to command."[5]

The following day, the 50th Georgia and 51st Georgia Infantry Regiments were transferred from Drayton's Brigade to Brigadier General Paul Jones Semmes' Brigade. The Georgians joined Semmes' two other battle-tested regiments, the 10th Georgia and 53rd Georgia Infantry Regiments.[6]

Brigadier General Paul Jones Semmes. When Thomas Drayton was relieved from brigade command in November 1862, the 50th Georgia moved to Semmes' Brigade. The hard-fighting Semmes would be mortally wounded leading his men near the Rose Woods at Gettysburg on July 2, 1863. Courtesy U.S. Army Military History Institute, Carlisle, Pennsylvania.

Paul J. Semmes had been a prosperous planter and banker near Columbus, Georgia, before the war, and he was elected colonel of the 2nd Georgia Infantry Regiment in May 1861. Semmes received a promotion to brigadier general in March 1862 and distinguished himself in battle during the Peninsula and Maryland Campaigns. Now in his late forties, the native Georgian cut a tall, imposing figure. Admired by his men for his personal bravery, he looked and acted the part of a leader and would be an ideal fit for his fellow Georgians during the upcoming hard campaigns.

One of the admiring soldiers in Semmes' 10th Georgia Regiment provided the following glowing description of the general:

> I doubt that there was ever a better brigade commander in either army than Paul J. Semmes; tall, well proportioned, handsome, ruddy complexioned, piercing eyes, aquiline nose, his auburn hair just tingeing with gray, scrupulously neat in his dress, he was a striking figure and would command attention and respect on any assembly. He was a humble, devoted Christian. When a battle was imminent, General Semmes dressed with extraordinary care, carefully polished boots, spotless linen, elegant uniform, a brilliant red sash around his waist and shoulders and a red turban on his head. When a fight began, he took his position in front of his brigade, so as to be seen by every man in it if possible. Pelides did not shine brighter in his martial array or inspire more courage in his followers or terrors to his enemies.[7]

The 50th Georgia also moved to a different division commanded by forty-one-year-old Major General Lafayette McLaws. The Augusta, Georgia, native and Mexican War veteran had graduated in the same 1842 West Point class as James Longstreet. McLaws previously distinguished himself as commander of the 10th Georgia Regiment before being promoted to major general and division commander in May 1862. Unlike Semmes, the stocky McLaws resembled a bear, with his dark thick curly hair and full beard. He was also known to have some mastery of profanity. In addition to General Semmes' all-Georgia brigade, McLaws' division included Brigadier General Joseph B. Kershaw's South Carolina brigade, Brigadier General William Barksdale's Mississippi brigade, and Brigadier General Thomas R. R. Cobb's Georgia brigade.[8]

Upon reaching Fredericksburg, James Longstreet's First Corps moved to anchor the Confederate left, a six-mile stretch overlooking the city and ending at a bend in the Rappahannock River. On Longstreet's right, Stonewall Jackson's Second Corps occupied an additional two-mile line of entrenchments that stood west of the Richmond, Fredericksburg, and Potomac Railroad and stretched from just south of the city to Prospect Hill.

McLaws' division occupied the ridge behind Fredericksburg that ran south from Hazel Run to Howison Hill. The 50th Georgia Regiment and the rest of Semmes' Brigade held a reserve position south of Telegraph Road about two miles to the rear of Marye's Heights. George Pickett's division stood on McLaws' immediate right. Richard H. Anderson's and Robert Ransom's divisions guarded McLaws' left and defended the Confederate line north to the Rappahannock.[9]

As the Confederate army moved into position, General Lee took the opportunity before the battle to implore new Secretary of War James A. Seddon for shoes to shod his barefoot men. Lee explained, "I have the honor to represent to you that there is still a great want of shoes in the army, between 2,000 and 3,000 men being at present barefooted. Many have lost their shoes in the long marches over rough roads recently made, and the number forwarded was insufficient to meet the necessities of the troops. I am informed that there is a large number of shoes now in Richmond, in the hands of extortioners, who hold them at an extravagant price." The Confederate commander continued, "I earnestly hope that some effectual means may be adopted to supply the wants of the army as speedily as possible, and avert the sufferings that threaten the troops during the approaching cold and wet weather."[10]

Private John G. F. McCall, Company K, took advantage of a lull in preparations to express his thoughts of the impending clash and the increasingly harsh winter conditions to his sister, Becky:

> I haven't anything of a cheering nature to communicate to you, only times are very dull and hard here at the present. We are daily expecting a fight here, as we are in a mile & a half of the Yankees, supposed to be about two hundred thousand. Our pickets stand on one side of the river & the Yankees on the other, not more than one hundred yards a part. We also have a very large force at this place. It is getting very cold in this part of the country now & continues to get colder. I don't know what we will all do here this winter. The boys have nearly all drawn shoes, & are drawing some clothing occationally but not nearly enough to supply their wants. I am proud to know that the people of Brooks Co. have not forgotten the suffering soldiers who have rallied here in their defence as well as our own. I want to come home very bad but I don't know when I will ever get the chance to come. As I am in a Hurry I must close. This leaves me well, hoping these few lines may reach you all the same. Give

my love to all & except this for yourself. I remain as ever your affectionate Bro. until death,

J. G. F. McCall[11]

The weather worsened, and winter's signs became unmistakable. The morning of December 6 began cold and miserable. Rain turned to sleet, and then more than four inches of snow carpeted the Fredericksburg area. These conditions signaled a harsh first winter far from home for the Wiregrass men.[12]

Battle of Fredericksburg: December 11 – 15

Just before daylight on December 11, General Burnside's army finally attempted to cross the river against Lee's much smaller force. Confederate guns announced the enemy advance. The Rebel troops hurriedly formed up and moved to their positions. The men of Semmes' Brigade, including the 50th Georgia, took up positions in support of the Confederate batteries along the heights. William Barksdale's Mississippi sharpshooters played havoc with Federal engineers as they struggled against the river current to secure their pontoon bridges together.[13]

Despite stiff opposition from Barksdale's men, the overwhelming Federal force eventually moved enough troops across the river to drive the Mississippians from Fredericksburg. During the night and into the next day, the occupying Yankees sacked the abandoned city. The invaders pillaged and destroyed homes and property while Lee's men angrily watched from the heights. Heavy skirmishing occurred during the day, but the enemy made no move to attack as they continued to pour across the river and fill the streets of the town.[14]

The Georgians in Semmes' Brigade received a lively shelling from the enemy guns. A soldier in the 53rd Georgia Regiment recalled, "The shells fell and busted around us in all directions, but fortunately, hurt none of us, though they fell very close sometimes to us."[15]

At early dawn on December 13, a thunderous enemy artillery barrage announced the impending infantry assault against General Stonewall Jackson's position along the Confederate right. Although not subjected to the initial shelling, the men of the 50th Georgia rushed toward their support positions behind the heights with the rest of Semmes' Brigade. A dense fog made it impossible to see the enemy movements, but the sounds were clear.

Burnside's men boldly stepped out against the Rebel defenses as the fog burned off. Andrew J. McBride of the 10th Georgia described the scene: "About 10 o'clock the fog began to disappear and in a short time the bright sun had revealed to our view a splendid scene; a line of battle several miles

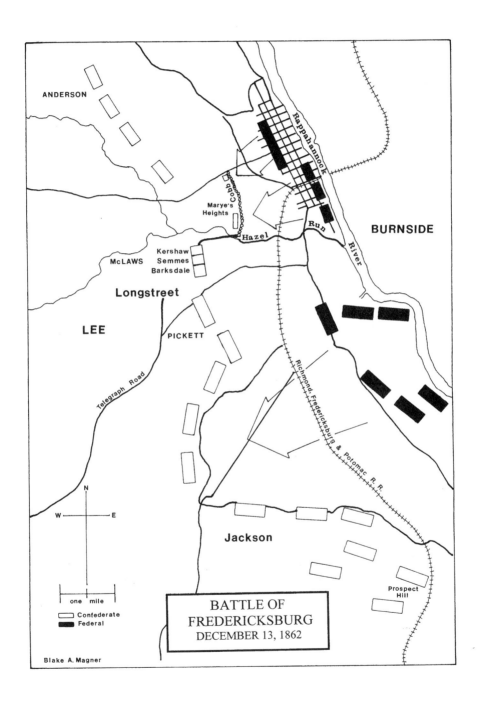

ANDERSON

Rappahannock

Marye's
Heights

Cobb

Hazel   Run   River   BURNSIDE

Kershaw
McLAWS   Semmes
Barksdale

Longstreet

LEE   PICKETT

Telegraph Road

Richmond, Fredericksburg & Potomac R.R.

N

W ——— E

Jackson

Prospect
Hill

one mile

☐ Confederate
■ Federal

BATTLE OF
FREDERICKSBURG
DECEMBER 13, 1862

Blake A. Magner

long was plainly in view and rapidly advancing. The music of a hundred bands encouraged the troops; banners streaming, neighing horses, shouting captains, rattling musketry, roaring cannon told that a mighty struggle was on between the contending hosts; the beautiful Rappahannock flowed peacefully on to the sea, its lovely valleys being drenched with fraternal blood."[16]

After attacking the Confederate right, Burnside launched numerous massive assaults against Longstreet's position on the Rebel left. About 11:00 a.m., a large force attacked across an open field against the impenetrable Rebel defenses atop Marye's Heights. At least six blue-clad waves of men advanced uphill against Longstreet's veterans during the day, but Confederate artillery and rifle fire ravaged the Federal attackers as they repeatedly charged the stone wall below Marye's Heights. Not one enemy soldier breached the wall that day.[17]

Sergeant William Moore Jones, Company K, 50th Georgia, proudly recorded in his diary, "In this engagement my brigade (Paul J. Semmes') supported the Johnson Siege Artillery, which occupied a position that did greater damage to the enemy's lines that day than any other battery in the engagement."[18]

Burnside called off further futile assaults by nightfall. The day had been a disaster for the Federals, and that evening the temperature dropped near freezing. Some survivors slowly dragged themselves back to the city. Others froze to death. Thousands of Union dead and wounded littered this killing field.

The Confederates maintained their defensive positions throughout the next day in expectation of further Federal assaults. Burnside, however, made no attacks that day or the next, although sharpshooters skirmished along the lines. During the late afternoon and evening of December 14, the 50th Georgia and the rest of Semmes' Brigade relieved Cobb's exhausted men in the sunken road at the foot of Marye's Heights.[19]

Andrew J. McBride recalled, "About 4 o'clock Sunday evening, December 14th, the Tenth Georgia marched from Lee's Hill to the stone fence and relieved the Twenty-fourth Georgia regiment which had covered itself with glory in the banner battle of the war." Private Andrew Wood, 53rd Georgia, also reported: "Sunday. [,] about 10 o'clock P.M. we were ordered to relieve the 18th Ga. Regt. which was stationed at the lower edge of town in line of battle, and had been partially engaged the preceding day."[20]

The brigade endured heavy skirmishing that night and the next day. "The enemy fired at our brigade pickets about one o'clock A.M.," reported Private Wood, "but as good luck would have it, hurt none of them. Monday there was skirmishing all day among the pickets and sharpshooters along the line. We were visited all day off and on by shells. Our pickets were fired upon again by the enemy about midnight. Monday night several balls passed over us."[21]

A fierce rainstorm blew through the area during the evening of December 15. When the fog lifted the next morning, the astonished Confederates found that the Federal army had withdrawn across the river. General Lee's men immediately reoccupied the city. Although the Confederates did not fully appreciate the extent of their success at the time, the battle had been a crushing and demoralizing defeat for General Burnside and his men.

Robert E. Lee expressed surprise at the relatively easy victory, stating in his post-battle report:

> The attack on the 13th had been so easily repulsed, and by so small a part of our army, that it was not supposed the enemy would limit his efforts to an attempt, which, in view of the magnitude of his preparations and the extent of his force, seemed to be comparatively insignificant. Believing, therefore, that he would attack us, it was not deemed expedient to lose the advantages of our position and expose the troops to the fire of his inaccessible batteries beyond the river, by advancing against him; but we were necessarily ignorant of the extent to which he had suffered, and only became aware of it when, on the morning of the 16th, it was discovered that he had availed himself of the darkness of night, and the prevalence of a violent storm of wind and rain, to recross the river. The town was immediately reoccupied and our position on the river bank resumed.[22]

The Federal casualties numbered about 12,600, while the Confederates losses came to about 5,300. McLaws' division suffered 100 killed, 686 wounded, and 67 missing. The heavy artillery fire that rained among Semmes' men caused the majority of casualties in the brigade. Although the official medical report listed only one man in the 50th Georgia as being wounded during the battle, the regiment suffered at least three casualties: Private William N. Smith, Company B, received a mortal wound; an artillery round fragment struck Private Matthew Knight, Company F, in the arm; and Private John P. Bennett, Company G, went down with an artillery fragment in his left arm, causing permanent loss of use.[23]

Private John P. Bennett, Company G. Bennett enlisted in the Clinch Volunteers at Homerville on March 4, 1862. He was wounded in the left arm by artillery shell fragments during the Battle of Fredericksburg on December 13. Bennett lost the use of his left arm and received a disability discharge on April 27, 1863. Courtesy U.S. Army Military History Institute, Carlisle, Pennsylvania.

Although the brigade served a supporting role, General McLaws nevertheless praised General Semmes, stating: "The brigade of General Semmes was not actually engaged, but under his supervision the position he commanded was strongly fortified, and his men were well prepared and eager for the fight under his leadership."[24]

After the battle, Lee's army remained encamped on the west side of the Rappahannock River. The demoralized Federal army remained on the east bank opposite Fredericksburg.

The Harsh Winter: December 1862 – April 1863

Along with the rest of Lee's army, the 50th Georgians built winter quarters and camped near Fredericksburg through February 1863, "performing some fatigue duty and discipline." The bitterly cold Virginia weather made life hard for these Wiregrass boys. Snow fell frequently as the soldiers dug in for the winter. Obtaining adequate food and clothing continued to be a problem for the Confederate army, and illness took a toll on the men. The men of the 50th Georgia endured a difficult first Christmas away from home.[25]

The proximity of the Union lines kept Lee's army on alert. From time to time, the men were ordered to be ready to march immediately. Captain William O. Fleming, Company F, described one such occasion in a January 22 letter to his wife:

> Yesterday afternoon an order was recd to be in readiness to march at a moments summoning as information obtained led to the belief that the enemy would make an immediate advance upon our lines. It has been raining for the last two days & the weather very severe, so that I thought it would be madness for the enemy to make an advance & consequently did not expect an alarm notwithstanding the order, but sure enough about 2 hours before day this morning the alarm gun was fired & we were all up in the cold rain ready to march to the front. Daylight came & no order to march was recd. It is now Nine o'clock & we have just been notified by a courier from Hd Qtrs that it was a false alarm, but to hold ourselves in readiness.[26]

The incident Fleming described was the infamous "Mud March" of General Burnside's army. On January 20, Burnside made an attempt to cross the river and flank Lee's left. Unfortunately for the Federals, torrential rains had turned the roads into a quagmire, causing men and equipment to sink into sucking mud. The frustrated Union commander finally called off the movement two days later and returned to camp amid the taunts of amused Confederates from across the river. After the fiasco, the embattled Burnside offered his resignation. President Lincoln accepted it on January 26 and appointed Major General Joseph Hooker as the new Federal commander.

During the long winter, the men of the 50th Georgia made several leadership changes. Major Duncan Curry, who had been beset with illness for most of his time in service, finally offered his resignation on February 24, returning home to Decatur County to convalesce. Captain Peter McGlashan, Company E, temporarily replaced Curry as major.[27]

A few days later, the men of Company A elected First Lieutenant James A. Waters as captain to replace John T. Wilson, who had been mortally wounded at Fox's Gap. Waters' rank was made retroactive to January 1, 1863. On March 2, Second Lieutenant Jacob S. Lightsy of Company G resigned, and the men elected First Sergeant James Douglass as second lieutenant.[28]

On March 23, Adjutant John M. Fleming, brother of Company F captain William O. Fleming, died from illness in a hospital in Mechanicsville, Virginia. Another Wiregrass soldier who succumbed to illness, Private Daniel

McMillan of Company I, had been weakened by bouts of measles and mumps since his enlistment the previous August, and he was admitted to a hospital with typhoid fever on February 22. Unfortunately, McMillan's condition worsened, and he died at a Farmville hospital on April 1, shortly after the birth of his second son.[29]

Colonel William R. Manning, who really never recovered after his wound at Fox's Gap, became quite ill from chronic hepatitis and had to be hospitalized in Richmond on February 26. When Manning submitted his resignation due to the continuing seriousness of his illness, Lieutenant Colonel Francis Kearse again took temporary command of the 50th Georgia.[30]

A serious bout of typhoid fever in late January required the Company G commander, Captain Quarterman B. Staten, to be admitted to a Richmond hospital. On March 3, while still hospitalized, Staten submitted his resignation as company commander. Although the particulars are unknown, the resignation apparently involved more than his being incapacitated by illness. Staten's letter read:

> Richmond, Va
> March 3rd 1863
> Genrl Samuel Cooper
> Adj & Inspt Genrl CSA
>
> Genrl
> Having been suspended from duty by Genrl R E Lee on
> account of report of Board of Examiners for McLaws Division
> before whom I appeared for examination as to my capacity as
> an officer in the army. I hereby tender my resignation of office
> of Captain Company "G", 50th Geo Regt to take effect
> immediately.
>   I have the honor to be Genrl
>   Your Obed Servt
>   Quarterman B. Staten[31]

The men of Company G elected First Lieutenant Isaac Burkhalter as captain on March 20, filling the vacancy created by Staten's resignation. Staten felt well enough by April 4 to rejoin his company and, whatever the cause for his resignation, it apparently had little effect on his popularity with his men. They quickly elected the Clinch County soldier to second lieutenant on April 9.[32]

Shortly after the death of John M. Fleming, Rueben Thomason "Tompy" Roberds, Company D, received a promotion to adjutant. Roberds related the harsh conditions in an April 1 letter to his wife, but he brought out a lighter side of winter encampment by describing a snowball fight:

Yesterday morning when I woke every little corner of my tent
was closed up and at first waking I did not know what was to
pay and to my astonishment the earth was again covered in
snow about six inches deep, which even now is not thawed. on
yesterday the adjoining Reg; The 53rd came out and gave us
battle. we sent out skirmishers and after getting their position
our boys charged them gallantly. I was in the scrape myself and
selected a huge orderly of the 53rd to combat with. I balled
him well and we charged them, whereupon a truce was called.
I then went forward and met this officer and we agreed to turn
upon the spectators. our Company Officers were among the
lookers on and if we did not give them a snow balling sure.
Well such are the diversions we enjoy but amind [amid] all this
our joys are often saddened by the departure to that Land from
whence no traveller returns. of some noble comrade[s] during
the past week our loss in the Regt was (8) eight. one of Berrien
died a few moments since–his name was Langdale [Private
John R.]; in our Company we have eight down sick and sent
Sego [Private John T.] to the Hospital in Richmond this
morning spitting blood which is of common occurrence here.[33]

The difficult winter conditions affected the soldiers' livestock as
well. Roberds noted, "nearly all of the mules are dedd and in all my life you
never saw such poor horses. Ah, I cannot but feel for the poor brutes that
they should thus suffer and die for want of food. Col K [50th Georgia
commander Kearse] had a forager out as far as eight miles & could get but
200 pounds hay. think of that and all the fields and fences laid waste &
barren."[34]

During the winter of 1862-1863, a total of eighty-four Wiregrass
soldiers died of illness from November through the end of March. Their
afflictions included a variety of illnesses common to the troops, such as
pneumonia, bronchitis, typhoid fever, measles, small pox, and chronic
diarrhea.[35]

The lack of sufficient nutrition contributed to the rampant illness,
and General Lee continued to express his concern over the issue. In a March
27 letter to Secretary of War James A. Seddon, Lee reported:

The troops of this portion of the army have for some time
been confined the reduced rations, consisting of 18 ounces of
flour, 4 ounces of bacon of indifferent quality, with
occasionally supplies of rice, sugar, or molasses. The men are
cheerful, and I receive but few complaints; still, I do not think
it is enough to continue them in health and vigor, and I fear

they will be unable to endure the hardships of the
approaching campaign. Symptoms of scurvy are appearing
among them, and to supply the place of vegetables each
regiment is directed to send a daily detail to gather sassafras
buds, wild onions, garlic, lamb's quarter, and poke sprouts,
but for so large an army the supply obtained is very small.[36]

As the winter started to draw to a close, a happy surprise occurred
for the men of Company B. On March 25, William F. "Billy" Pendleton
rejoined the company on his eighteenth birthday. The popular young
Pendleton had been discharged the previous September for being under
age. He received a warm welcome from his comrades.[37]

A flurry of organizational activity occurred in April. On April 3,
the men in Company E elected First Lieutenant Richard McLean as captain
and Kenneth McDonald as first lieutenant. Company I commander, Captain
Elijah C. Morgan, resigned on April 14, and the men elected David Perry
Luke as captain.[38]

On April 27, the men of Company H elected Hiram Gay as first
lieutenant and Lott Townsend as second lieutenant. That same day,
Quarterman B. Staten of Company G became first lieutenant, and Billy
Pendleton of Company B became second lieutenant. Pendleton recalled
his election: "Third Lieutenant Shone had resigned and Captain Bedford
and Lieutenant Whiteford wanted me to run for his place. In the Confederate
Army company officers were elected by the men. I won by a majority of
one."[39]

The signs of spring popped up all around as April turned into May.
The snow melted, and the flowers bloomed while the birds flitted about.
Like bears coming out of hibernation, the two great armies slowly came to
life. The men of the 50th Georgia welcomed the end of the harsh winter of
1862-1863. These Wiregrass veterans, however, also knew that the arrival
of spring meant more hard marching, more fighting, and more dying, with
no end in sight.

Chapter Six
The Chancellorsville Campaign
April 27–May 6, 1863

Union major general Joseph Hooker replaced Ambrose Burnside in January 1863 after Burnside's crushing defeat at Fredericksburg. General Hooker reorganized the Army of the Potomac and began making detailed plans to take the war to the Southerners. Hooker intended to make a surprise crossing of the Rappahannock and Rapidan Rivers west of Fredericksburg and flank the Confederate position, forcing the Army of Northern Virginia to move away from its fortified positions near the city and fight on grounds more favorable to the superior Federal numbers. Hooker's army exceeded one hundred and thirty thousand men, while Robert E. Lee had less than half that number, just over sixty thousand troops.

Throughout the harsh winter and early spring, most of the Army of Northern Virginia remained in winter quarters near Fredericksburg. In February approximately twenty thousand men led by General James Longstreet, including the divisions of Major General George E. Pickett and Major General John Bell Hood, were detached for service south of Richmond. Longstreet's command would not rejoin General Lee until later in May, after the battle of Chancellorsville.

Lieutenant General Stonewall Jackson's entire Second Corps remained with Lee. Longstreet's other two divisions, commanded by Major General Lafayette McLaws and Major General Richard H. Anderson, also remained behind. Brigadier General William T. Wofford became the new commander of Thomas R. Cobb's Georgia Brigade after Cobb's death at the Battle of Fredericksburg.

A weapons report of Semmes' Brigade, probably prepared in early-1863, provided an estimate of the individual regimental strengths: 50th Georgia Regiment, 335; 10th Georgia Regiment, 299; 51st Georgia Regiment, 336; 53rd Georgia Regiment, 354. Based on these numbers, the brigade's fighting force available for the coming spring campaign likely stood between 1,300 and 1,400 men.[1]

After three months of preparation, Hooker's army finally began its march on Monday, April 27. The new Union commander ordered Major General George G. Meade's V Corps, Major General Oliver Otis Howard's

XI Corps, and Major General Henry W. Slocum's XII Corps to make a flanking movement to the west. The large Federal force crossed the Rappahannock River at Kelly's Ford then circled back to the southeast.

The XI and XII Corps then crossed the Rapidan River at Germanna Ford while the V Corps crossed the river farther east at Ely's Ford. Major General John Sedgwick's VI Corps and Major General John F. Reynolds' I Corps crossed the Rappahannock River south of Fredericksburg during the evening of April 28 and early the next morning. Hooker left Major General Daniel E. Sickles' III Corps in Falmouth, across the river, in view of the Confederates. Hooker hoped that the III Corps' position and the movements of the I Corps and VI Corps would occupy the Southerners' attention and mask the Federal flanking movement to the west.

General Lee became aware of the flurry of Federal activities early on April 29, but he could not be sure of their ultimate intent. Fearing the possibility of an assault against Fredericksburg, Lee visited McLaws' headquarters and ordered the division commander to tell his men to hold their position at all costs. McLaws' division guarded the section of the line at Fredericksburg where Burnside's heaviest force had assaulted Marye's Heights the previous December.

As Sedgwick's and Reynolds' troops crossed to the south side of the river, McLaws ordered General Semmes to prepare his brigade for action. Semmes reported: "the Fiftieth Georgia Volunteers, Lieutenant-Colonel Kearse, and the Fifty-third Georgia Volunteers, Colonel Simms, were moved [from camp] forward to the designated position of the brigade in reserve, with their left resting on the Telegraph road half a mile in rear of the heights overlooking Howison's house. The Tenth Georgia Volunteers, Lieutenant-Colonel Holt, and Fifty-first Georgia Volunteers, Colonel Slaughter, being on picket opposite Falmouth, were ordered at night to rejoin the brigade."[2]

At the end of the day Lee finally became certain of Hooker's flanking movement. He ordered General Richard H. Anderson to immediately march his division to Chancellorsville, some ten miles to the west, along the Orange Plank Road. The Confederate commander also ordered General McLaws to prepare to follow Anderson.

From Fredericksburg, the Orange Plank Road ran west to a fork in the road about one mile east of Zoan Church. The left branch, still called Orange Plank Road, meandered south and west about five miles before turning north toward Chancellorsville. The right branch, the Orange Turnpike, ran directly west through Chancellorsville, converging with Orange Plank Road at the town's crossroads. Ely's Ford Road ran southeast from the Rapidan River to Chancellorsville. A large rambling brick structure and a few outbuildings occupied the northwest corner of the crossroads junction.

The building had earlier been used as a tavern, but for years the Chancellor family had used it as a residence.[3]

General Anderson reached Chancellorsville about midnight. He found the brigades of Brigadier General Carnot Posey and Brigadier General William Mahone already there. Posey and Mahone had withdrawn from their positions on the Rappahannock River at United States Ford in the face of Major General Darius N. Couch's II Corps. After evaluating the much stronger oncoming Federal force, Anderson decided to fall back from Chancellorsville to the east along the Orange Turnpike and a better defensive position near Zoan Church, located about half way between the Chancellorsville junction and Fredericksburg.

Anderson chose a good location on a ridge just east of the tangled growth of forest known as the Wilderness. Shortly after arriving, the division commander received further reinforcements from Brigadier General Ambrose R. Wright's Brigade. The Rebels feverishly dug rifle pits and threw up fortifications in the darkness. On April 30, the exhausted defenders waited for the inevitable Federal assault and hoped for reinforcements.

The Federal V, XI, and XII corps reached the Chancellorsville crossroads from the northwest during the afternoon of April 30. To the dismay of some officers, General Hooker ordered the men to bivouac for the rest of the day instead of pressing Anderson's heavily outnumbered force. The Federal commander preferred to wait for additional troops and advance the next morning. This critical decision would allow Confederate reinforcements to reach Anderson's tenuous defensive position near the Zoan Church early on May 1. Hooker's lack of aggressiveness would have severe implications on the outcome of the impending battle.

General Semmes recalled the 10th Georgia and 51st Georgia Regiments from picket duty at Fredericksburg during the evening of April 29. The men rejoined the rest of the brigade and caught some sleep. At 3:00 the next morning, McLaws ordered Semmes to move his brigade forward and occupy a line of battle in the rifle pits on the heights near Fredericksburg. The brigade remained in position until later that afternoon, when the men were told to cook two day's rations and be ready to march at a moment's notice.[4]

At sunset on April 30, Semmes' Brigade marched west along the Orange Plank Road in the vanguard of McLaws' division toward Anderson's position. The Georgians quickly covered the five-mile distance. Semmes' men hustled into position behind the fortifications on the right of Mahone's Brigade as darkness fell. The Wiregrass soldiers sensed something big was about to happen.[5]

The brigades of Kershaw and Wofford followed Semmes' Brigade shortly after midnight on May 1. A bright moonlit sky illuminated the way as the men silently shuffled along the road. Stonewall Jackson departed

Fredericksburg at first light with the divisions of A. P. Hill and Robert E. Rodes as ground fog covered the area. About ten thousand men from General Jubal A. Early's division and General William Barksdale's Brigade of McLaws' division remained behind at Fredericksburg to defend against any advance by Sedgwick's troops upon the city. General Lee had committed almost his entire army to doing battle with Hooker at the little crossroads known as Chancellorsville.[6]

Kershaw and Wofford reached Anderson and took position in the line by about 6 a.m. The exhausted Confederates anticipated a Federal attack at any moment. The Rebels anxiously waited, but the enemy still had not attacked by 8 a.m. This stroke of good luck allowed General Jackson to arrive shortly thereafter with additional reinforcements. Stonewall Jackson seized the offensive. After sizing up the situation, the aggressive commander ordered McLaws to march his division and Mahone's Brigade westward along the Orange Turnpike toward the Federal positions four miles away at Chancellorsville. The brigades of Cadmus Wilcox and W. A. Perry from Anderson's division supported the advance.[7]

Jackson ordered Anderson's other two brigades of Carnot Posey and Ransom Wright to lead the advance along the Orange Plank Road. Most of Jackson's troops were still arriving as he led the column west.

The morning fog burned off as the sun rose higher on that beautiful warm Virginia day. At about 10:30, General Hooker confidently ordered his troops to advance east along the Orange Turnpike toward Fredericksburg. The two armies were now on a collision course. Before noon, the rattle of musketry signaled the initial contact between the advancing skirmishers. This was followed by much heavier rifle fire and the unmistakable sound of cannon. The battle of Chancellorsville erupted as smoke and powder filled the air.

Mahone's Brigade made first contact with the enemy and formed a position north of the Orange Turnpike. McLaws hustled his division forward to support them. Semmes' Brigade hustled forward about a mile and moved into position just south of the turnpike with the right of the 51st Georgia next to the road. Semmes' other three Georgia regiments were aligned from right to left: 10th, 53rd, and 50th. Kershaw's Brigade stood in reserve behind Semmes and Mahone.[8]

Semmes' troops moved forward until they reached the edge of the woods. Across an open field stood Major General George Sykes' division of bluecoats arrayed in line of battle. Kershaw's Brigade moved up on Semmes' left, with the 15th South Carolina guarding the 50th Georgia's left flank. Semmes reported: "Soon the enemy's infantry was pushed forward. When within easy range, the order was given to commence firing."[9]

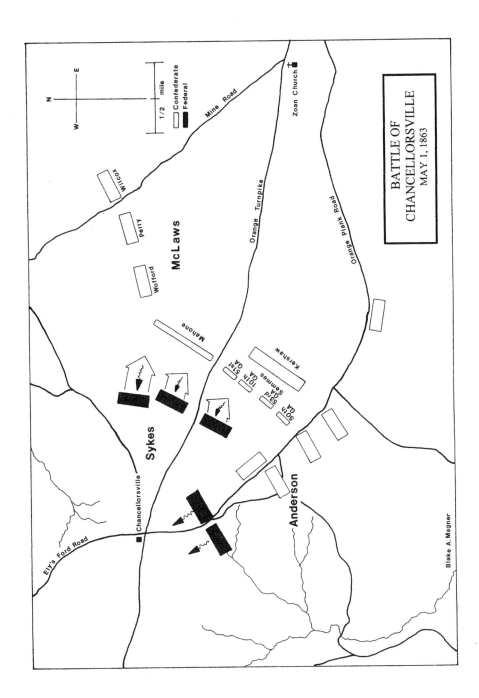

BATTLE OF
CHANCELLORSVILLE
MAY 1, 1863

Confederate
Federal

1/2 mile

N
W — E
S

Mine Road

Zoan Church

Wilcox

Perry

McLaws

Wofford

Orange Turnpike

Orange Plank Road

Mahone

Kershaw

51st GA
10th GA
Semmes
53rd GA
50th GA

Sykes

Chancellorsville

Ely's Ford Road

Anderson

Blake A. Magner

The primary thrust of the enemy attack slammed into the 51st Georgia near the Orange Turnpike. Colonel William M. Slaughter fell with a mortal wound early in the action. Second-in-command Lieutenant Colonel Edward Ball later suffered a serious head wound that took him out of the action.[10]

After heavy fighting on the edge of the dense woods south of the turnpike, Sykes' men fell back a short distance and regrouped. Semmes' Georgians repulsed a second assault by Sykes' regulars with heavy enemy losses. The 10th Georgia then sent a strong line of skirmishers to the left of the 51st Georgia. The 10th and 51st Georgians caught the Federals in a deadly enfilading fire that sent them running to the rear. The Union assault had been broken and the enemy "handsomely driven from the field after a sharp contest of perhaps three-fourths of an hour."[11]

Sergeant William Moore Jones, Company K, suffered a slight knee wound. The Brooks County soldier described his good luck when he wrote: "On this engagement I was wounded by a sharpshooter, in the knee, which would have been serious but for the fact that the ball hit a small hickory bush which deadened the force of the ball." Jones remained with his company during the rest of the battle.[12]

As McLaws and Mahone held the Yankees along the Orange Turnpike, Joseph Hooker's men faced additional Confederate obstacles to the south along the Orange Plank Road. Two divisions from the Union XII Corps advanced on both sides of the road and ran directly into Jackson's column. This stopped the Federal advance.

The strong Rebel offensive caught Hooker off guard, and communication and supply problems compounded his difficulties in the Wilderness. This combination of unexpected events prompted the now-cautious Hooker to cease the advance and withdraw to a better defensive position. About 2:00 p.m., the Federal commander ordered his men to move back toward the Chancellor house. Within two hours, the Union strategy had gone from offense to defense.

Hooker's change of heart played perfectly into Jackson's aggressive nature. The Rebel commander vigorously pressed the attack as soon as he learned of the Union withdrawal. Jackson's column closely pursued Slocum's retreating XII Corps along the Orange Plank Road. At about 4 p.m., McLaws' division pushed the enemy along the Orange Turnpike toward Chancellorsville. General Semmes described the personal effects left by the fleeing Yankees: "The road, the woods, and fields on either side, over which the enemy retired, were strewn with knapsacks, blankets, overcoats, and many other valuable articles."[13]

The Confederates pushed Hooker's army back approximately two miles to its original position at the Chancellorsville crossroads. Heavy skirmishing continued until around 10 p.m. The Federals spent the night building defensive fortifications. "Fighting Joe" Hooker now decided his best opportunity for success would be to invite a Rebel attack. Robert E. Lee would be happy to oblige, on his terms.

McLaws' command received heavy casualties in that first day of fierce fighting, most of them in Semmes' and Mahone's Brigades. The 51st Georgia endured the brunt of the enemy assault and lost an estimated one hundred men, including its top two officers, one of whom was killed. Sykes' Union division lost about the same number as McLaws'. The two opposing commands had slugged it out during the afternoon until the Federals retreated.[14]

That evening, McLaws' troops bivouacked under a bright moonlit night along the ridge to the west of Zoan Church. Semmes' soldiers passed the night with the 53rd Georgia's right resting on the Orange Turnpike while the 50th Georgia anchored the brigade's left flank. Early that evening, Generals Lee and Jackson met by firelight and agreed to split the Confederate forces. Stonewall Jackson would take the majority of Lee's army on a historic flanking movement the following day.[15]

Lee and Jackson conferred for the last time in the chilly predawn dampness on Saturday, May 2. At about sunrise, Stonewall Jackson's entire command silently marched south and then northwest toward the Orange Turnpike on a twelve-mile trek around the unsuspecting Federal right flank. The cool air felt good to the soldiers as they walked in the morning dampness. Later the day would turn very warm, and the rapid pace of the march would cause many of the soldiers to fall out from the heat.

Hooker occupied a six-mile front and waited for Lee to attack. The Union defensive position was strong, except for the right flank, which Oliver O. Howard's XI Corps occupied.

Lee ordered McLaws to create a diversionary action along his lines during the day to keep Federal attention away from Jackson's flanking movement. When Jackson's attack commenced, McLaws would then press strongly against the enemy positions. However, Jackson's maneuver left only McLaws' and Anderson's divisions—about fifteen thousand men— to defend the Confederate lines against the much larger enemy force.

Throughout the morning, McLaws and Anderson skirmished along the lines. Later in the day, McLaws shifted some of his command south toward the Orange Plank Road. Kershaw's men anchored the division left with Semmes and Wofford in order to the right. McLaws increased the pressure on the Federal left to divert attention from Jackson's flanking movement.[16]

Semmes ordered the 10th Georgia skirmishers to periodically move toward the Yankee pickets, to give the appearance of an attack, and then withdraw. The men of the 10th Georgia accomplished their diversionary attacks throughout the day with loss of one man killed and five wounded. One Georgia soldier recalled, "During that day and night and next morning I think we drove in their pickets ten or twelve times."[17]

Thinking themselves safe from attack, many of the soldiers in Howard's XI Corps leisurely cooked supper or lounged about their tents just before sunset. At about 6:00 p.m., Jackson's screaming men burst out of the thick woods just west of the unsuspecting Federals, quickly overwhelming Howard's men. Many threw down their weapons in terror and ran, and hundreds were captured before they could even fire a shot. The rout continued as the Rebels continued to press against the disorganized Yankees. Finally, at about 7:30 p.m., the combination of fading light and exhaustion slowed the Confederate attack.

When word of Jackson's attack reached McLaws, he ordered an advance to keep the Federal skirmishers engaged. The plan worked, and the Federal troops along the Chancellorsville eastern front remained entrenched.

Wanting to exploit his success, Jackson prepared to make another attack. The brilliant commander, along with A. P. Hill and Hill's staff, rode forward ahead of the lines to reconnoiter the area. Rebel pickets fired upon the party in the darkness, mistakenly wounding Jackson, Hill, and others. Stonewall Jackson would die from wound complications several days later.

A shocked and saddened Lee temporarily replaced Jackson with Major General Jeb Stuart. As a result of the confusion, the second Confederate attack of the day was postponed. During the night, Semmes' Brigade remained in position between the Orange Plank Road and the Orange Turnpike.

Lee renewed the Confederate offensive at daylight on Sunday, May 3. The Rebels pressed hard from the west, south, and east. Both sides attacked and counter-attacked with staggering losses. At about 8:00 a.m., General McLaws ordered Semmes' Brigade forward in support of Kershaw's advancing right. The Rebels strongly pressed the easternmost part of Hooker's line, held by Major General Winfield Scott Hancock's division in Couch's II Corps. Hancock's men had the dubious duty of holding back McLaws' advance from the east while keeping open a northern escape corridor for the embattled Federals. As McLaws' relentless troops overran Hancock's defenses, the Union division commander ordered a withdrawal.[18]

Two units on the far right of Hancock's eastern defensive line did not hear the order to retreat. The 27th Connecticut Regiment and part of the 145th Pennsylvania Regiment of Colonel John R. Brooke's 4th Brigade remained in their trenches as Semmes' men poured over the lines. The 10th Georgia, "in conjunction with two regiments of Wofford's brigade," moved behind the hapless Yankees and eliminated their escape route. Lieutenant

Colonel Willis C. Holt reported: "Seeing the hills in rear of the enemy's line carried by a portion of our army, I at once directed a portion of my reserve to pass around their right flank and close upon their rear." Rather than ordering his men to attack at once, Holt decided to ask for the Federals' surrender. The 10th Georgia commander explained: "I thought that they might surrender, knowing them to be entirely cut off, and sent Lieutenant Bailey to them with a flag of truce, demanding their surrender, which demand was complied with." The men of the 10th Georgia seized 340 enemy prisoners - more men than were in the entire Georgia regiment.[19]

The bitter struggle turned in favor of the Confederates by mid-morning. The brigades of Wofford, Kershaw, and Semmes closed in from the southeast. Anderson's division now pushed from the south, and J. E. B. Stuart led Jackson's men from the west. Lee's onrushing soldiers pushed into and captured Chancellorsville as the Federal defenses collapsed. Hooker's fleeing army took up defensive positions near the Bullock House, less than a mile northwest of the area.

At about 10:00 a.m., Semmes marched his brigade in a line of battle through some woods and into a low, marshy, open area within about 150 yards of an enemy position. Yankee sharpshooters raked the ranks of the Georgians, causing them to quickly rush under the cover of a nearby hill. Led by the 50th Georgia, the brigade then moved about one-half mile north, until it reached the Orange Turnpike. At about 11:00 a.m., the brigade halted on the south side of the road.[20]

Salem Church

As Lee prepared to pursue Hooker's retreating army, he received word that Major General Sedgwick's VI Corps had broken through Early's defenses at Fredericksburg. This gave Sedgwick a clear path west along the Orange Plank Road to the rear of the Confederate army some eight to ten miles away. Only Brigadier General Cadmus M. Wilcox's Alabama brigade stood in the way.

Lee ordered McLaws' division to reinforce Wilcox and intercept the Federal advance. The dirty, hungry, bone-tired men of the 50th Georgia fell into formation as they grabbed handfuls of ammunition to fill their cartridge boxes. As the Wiregrass men filed onto the Orange Turnpike and headed east with the rest of Semmes' Brigade, they had no idea that one of their finest hours lay just ahead.[21]

Lieutenant Billy Pendleton recalled that after a few miles he heard the thump of cannon fire and other familiar sounds of battle. After resting a few minutes to catch their breath, the Wiregrass soldiers hurriedly marched out to enter the fray. The men closed their ranks and quickened their pace as they came within sight of Salem Church, which one of them described as "a little country church by the side of the road."[22]

View of Salem Church from Orange Plank Road. After the battle of May 3, the church was turned into a field hospital for wounded men from both sides. Bloodstains can still be seen on the floors. Photo by author.

Wilcox had been fighting a delaying action for several hours. The Alabamians stubbornly fell back to a low ridge at Salem Church. They straddled the Orange Turnpike and awaited the advance of Union brigadier general William T. H. "Bully" Brooks' 1st division. McLaws' division reached the area at about 3:30 p.m., and immediately deployed under a hail of bullets. Semmes' Brigade scrambled into position on Wilcox's left, and Mahone took up a line of battle on Semmes' left. The brigades of Kershaw and Wofford extended the Confederate line on Wilcox's right. The 50th Georgia filled in between the 53rd Georgia on the left and 51st Georgia on the right. The 10th Georgia occupied Semmes' far right, next to the left of Wilcox's 14th Alabama Regiment.[23]

Major Peter McGlashan described the brigade's difficulty in getting into position:

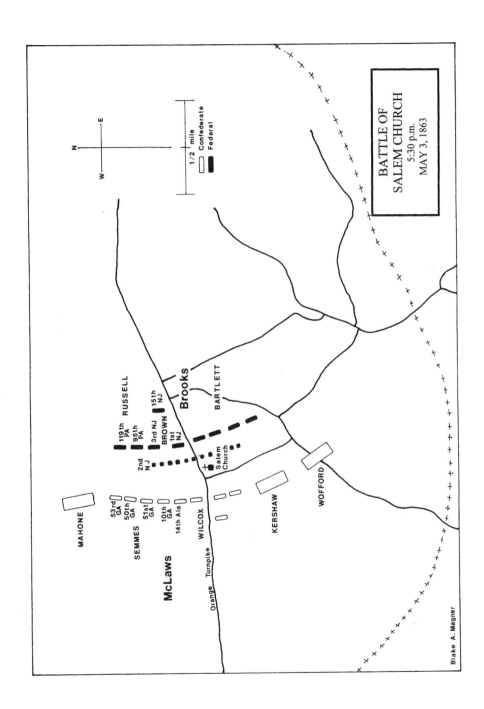

BATTLE OF
SALEM CHURCH
5:30 p.m.
MAY 3, 1863

1/2 mile

▢ Confederate
▮ Federal

N
W — E

Blake A. Magner

The moment was critical; we could scarcely reach our line
before the enemy. There was no time for brigade movements.
Each regiment commander rapidly noted the position his
regiment would occupy and rushed for it by the nearest route
at the double-quick. . . . The 50th Georgia on reaching their
ground found the formation obstructed by a ditch and cedar
wattled fence at the edge of the field. Leaping over that, like
so many deer, the men formed like lightning on the right by
file into line. Receiving a terrible fire from the enemy at 60
yards range, and then, with a wild yell, we charged and drove
the enemy over and beyond the line in confusion and ranged
up alongside the 53rd Georgia to receive their next assault.
We had lost about 15 or 20 men, but a more gallant deed I
never witnessed.[24]

Similarly, Sergeant William Jones of Company K recalled: "We
were attacked by the enemy before we were fully formed and the first man
that I saw killed in the 50th Ga. Regiment was Capt. Richard McLean of
Co. E from Thomas County."[25]

Despite the difficulties in getting into position, Semmes' men took
advantage of the natural protection afforded by the relative high ground of
the ridge. Rebels fired from the protection of embankments, fencing, and
shallow trenches to inflict terrible casualties on the Union troops. Private
John L. G. Wood described the 53rd Georgia Regiment's position—behind
an embankment north of the Orange Turnpike—as "beautiful." The
Georgian continued, "we could load and fire without exposing any thing
except our heads and arms. In shooting our company fired averaging from
15 to 20 rounds apiece at the vandals."[26]

Union troops from Brigadier General Henry W. Brown's 1st
Brigade, Brigadier General Joseph Bartlett's 2nd Brigade, and Brigadier
General W. A. Russell's 3rd Brigade traded point-blank fire with the men
from Semmes' and Wilcox's brigades along a half-mile front. The 95th and
119th Pennsylvania Regiments of Russell's brigade anchored the Federal
far right. Extending from their left to the northern edge of the Orange
Turnpike stood the 3rd and 1st New Jersey Regiments of Brown's brigade.
Brown's 2nd New Jersey Regiment manned the advance skirmish line and
straddled the road on both sides. The 15th New Jersey stood in reserve.
These Pennsylvania and New Jersey soldiers assaulted Semmes' Georgians
and Wilcox's Alabamians for more than two hellish hours.[27]

Smoke obscured the lines as both sides unleashed volley after volley.
The main Federal attack was directed against Semmes' Brigade, primarily the
50th and 53rd Georgia Regiments. Wave after wave slammed against the

steadfast Georgians. As one soldier from the 53rd Georgia recalled, "The struggle became furious." Sergeant Jones, Company K, added: "We repulsed eleven successive lines of battle that came against us."[28]

The stubborn Rebel resistance stymied the enemy advance. Union colonel Henry W. Brown, 1st Brigade commander, reported: "The regiment [3rd New Jersey] advanced gallantly, but was met by an overwhelming fire from the enemy, concealed in some trenches and behind a fence."[29]

Although they were better protected than the Federals, the 50th Georgians continued to suffer a high rate of casualties. Major McGlashan recalled the intensity of the struggle and the heroism of the men:

> We were suffering terribly, three color bearers shot down in succession. Gaps were seen along the line strewn with dead and wounded, the men steadily closing up the gaps, and kneeling, were firing with deliberation. The roar of musketry was incessant and terrific. Still the men cheered and loaded and fired, not a break or waver in the line, although nearly two-thirds of their number lay dead and wounded around them. Rush after rush was made by the enemy and as often vigorously repulsed. Our rifles were leading up so they were useless, the men throwing them away would pick up the rifle of some dead or wounded comrade and resume the fight.[30]

During the fierce fighting, the regiment exhausted almost all of its ammunition. At the height of the battle, McGlashan reported that Lieutenant Colonel Kearse shouted to him, "I shall have no regiment left if this lasts a half hour longer." When informed that the 50th Georgia was running dangerously low on ammunition, General Semmes ordered the regiment to replenish its supply if possible, and if not, to continue the fight until the bullets were gone. The regiment could then retreat some fifty yards to the rear of Mahone's right.[31]

The battle raged nonstop, with both sides charging and countercharging. As the Federal attacks wavered, Wilcox's men rose from their defenses and rushed headlong into the disorganized enemy. Seeing the charge of the Alabamians to his right, General Semmes ordered his brigade to join the attack. The brave commander personally led the 10th Georgia and 51st Georgia Regiments through a skirt of woods after the fleeing Yankees, "a half mile across an open field, shooting them as they ran." As Lieutenant Colonel Willis Holt reported: "General Semmes was with us in the charge, and, as usual, in the front rank. No officer or man with any pride could skulk behind and see his general display such courage as General Semmes displayed in the charge." The 50th Georgia and 53rd Georgia Regiments, unaware of the order to charge, held their hotly contested positions on the left.[32]

Just before the 50th Georgia ran out of ammunition, the enemy line in its front gave way and then collapsed. With a wild Rebel yell, both the 50th and 53rd Regiments joined in the chase and helped drive Sedgwick's shattered force from the field. The 53rd Georgia captured the national colors of the 2nd Rhode Island Regiment. McGlashan described how some of his men grabbed the flag staff of the 43rd New York: "Some of the men made a dash at the colors of the Forty-Sixth [43rd] New York Regiment, but the gallant color bearer tore off the colors and escaped, leaving the staff in our hands." After the fighting stopped, the exhausted remnants of the 50th Georgia retired to a sheltered position, in the rear of Mahone's right, to rest and refill their cartridge boxes.[33]

The results of the struggle could be seen in the enemy casualties opposing Semmes' Georgians and Wilcox's Alabamians. The 95th Pennsylvania Regiment lost almost its entire command structure: its colonel and lieutenant colonel were killed, the major suffered a severe wound, and the adjutant received a mortal wound. The 119th Pennsylvania also lost several officers and many men. The 1st New Jersey Regiment lost its colonel and 105 other men. The 2nd New Jersey suffered 56 casualties. The 3rd New Jersey received ninety-nine casualties, four of whom were commissioned officers. Colonel Henry W. Brown, 1st Brigade commander, reported, "we held them until about 6:30 p.m., when, having been severely wounded, I was carried to the rear."[34]

For the 50th Georgia, the Battle of Salem Church represented one of their finest days of the war. They had routed John Sedgwick's troops, and as a correspondent for the *Richmond Daily Enquirer* reported: "Indeed, this must have been the most sanguinary fight of the week, judging from the number of Yankees dead and wounded left upon the field."[35]

Nevertheless, the 50th Georgia paid a terrible price for its victory. Losses were almost as high as those they had received during the carnage eight months earlier at Fox's Gap. As McGlashan recalled, "The roll was called and of the gallant 316, who gallantly rushed at the enemy three short hours before, 187 were not there to answer to their names. The survivors were sadly dismissed to care for the wounded and bury their dead."[36]

Major McGlashan described a touching encounter with a gruesomely wounded Wiregrass soldier:

Just then a litter-bearer approached me and said, "Colonel, one of your men, badly wounded, desires to see you before he dies!" I went back with him and found, stretched on a litter, a private named John Culpepper, of Company H, from Colquitt County, Ga., a plain pine woods farmer, always present for duty, plain and unobtrusive in his manners. He was terribly wounded: a ball had struck him on the edge of the temple, tearing out both eyes and nose; the very brains seemed coming out. He evidently had not long to live, although quite conscious. "Is the Colonel here?" he said. "Yes," I answered, and I am grieved to find you so sorely hurt. He groped out with his hand. "Colonel, take my hand." I took it in both mine and knelt down beside him.

"Colonel, he whispered, "have I done my duty?" I was thrilled to the heart with the dying hero's devotion. Yes, I said, I can truly testify you have nobly done your duty now and all the time. "Oh, that is all right", he said; "tell my people, when you return home, that John Culpepper died doing his duty." He never spoke again, dying shortly afterward.[37]

Lieutenant Billy Pendleton, whom the men had elected as second lieutenant only the week before, had survived his first real battle. Shortly after the fighting stopped, the young officer reflected on his experience under fire:

It was nearly dark when the battle was over, and I was much surprised that the time had passed so quickly. I was left in command of the company. Lieutenant Whiteford was killed, Lieutenant White wounded, and Captain Bedford wounded, but the latter came back in a few days. It soon got dark, but was a moonlight night. I began thinking of home after the men had finished talking about the battle. All the officers were very kind and praised me highly. Captain Wells later told my father that I, in my first battle, kept saying to the men, "Men, remember that you are Georgians." I went for a walk in a field and thinking over all I had been through, decided to join the Methodist Church.[38]

Semmes' men dug in and prepared for a possible enemy attack. Captain Andrew J. McBride, 10th Georgia, recalled the aftermath of the battle:

It was growing dark, eight or ten men of the Tenth who had been left near the Chancellor house to bury our dead, having finished their sad work, came to where I was and together we came across the field to where our regiment was and found them working like beavers digging trenches. This work kept up nearly all night on both sides. We could hear the axes of the

Yankees quite plain. Some artillery horses had been wounded
near us—their groanings were frightful. We could hear the
wounded calling for help. . . .

We had to be quiet; Sedgewick's men were on the alert and
sent a shower of bullets in our direction if they heard noise or
saw lights. After doing all we could for the wounded, we lay
upon our arms the balance of that dark, chilly, cheerless
Sunday night. Never did I feel more sad or lonely, I had lost so
many loved companions.[39]

The spoils of war belonged to the Rebels. Rueben T. "Tompy"
Roberds, 50th Georgia Adjutant, submitted the regimental casualty report to
a correspondent for the *Savannah Daily Morning News* the next day. In his
report, Roberds briefly described the battle and praised the 50th Georgia:

The regiment formed in line of battle under a heavy fire, and
met the New Jersey boys, whom they drove back, and were
then fought by a regiment of regulars for near two hours,
whom they also drove back, the enemy leaving the battle
ground strewed with dead in the proportion of five to our one.
They must have suffered in wounded and killed at least five
hundred. It was a bloody field, and the well aimed shots of
nine thousand cartridges were expended in rendering the road
to Richmond "a hard road to travel."

The regiment was led into action by two gallant field officers,
Lieut. Colonel F. Kearse and Major P. McGlashan—the first in
command of the right and the latter the left wing.

We are still in line of battle, holding our position, and
I give you this report written upon Yankee paper. The boys of
the 50th are ——ing [passing?] their trophies all around.
Though but few are now left, we still keep up good feelings. . .
.

R. T. Roberds, Adjutant
P.S. – Our regiment captured enough guns, Springfield and
Enfield rifles, to furnish the entire regiment with these latest
improved weapons. We also have the flag staff of the New
Jersey regiment.[40]

The brigade ordnance officer made a detailed inventory of the enemy
arms and materials captured by the regiment. The list included 270 rifles, 50
cartridge boxes, 85 cap pouches, 30 bayonet scabbards, and 65 bayonets.[41]

As McLaws' and Wilcox's men recuperated, General Early's troops managed to regain control of Marye's Heights on the morning of May 4. Early's men now stood in position to attack the flank and rear of Sedgwick's force. Robert E. Lee urged General McLaws to coordinate an attack with Anderson and Early to crush Sedgwick. Although fighting continued off and on all day, McLaws' positions along the Orange Turnpike remained essentially the same as the previous day. Semmes' men built breastworks and remained in position on the north side of the road all day. The exhausted 50th Georgians welcomed the brief opportunity to eat and rest.[42]

General Lee finally maneuvered his forces into position to attack as evening approached. At 5:30 p.m., six brigades from Anderson and Early led the assault against Sedgwick's left and rear. McLaws held his division back in support until the attack began and then sent Kershaw's and Wofford's brigades to his right. Semmes' battered brigade, including the 50th Georgia, remained in reserve. Sedgwick's men fought desperately and repulsed the Confederate assaults. By the end of the day, General Sedgwick withdrew his force north toward Bank's Ford and entrenched with his back to the Rappahannock River. The Union VI Corps began crossing the river after midnight. Sedgwick made his escape and removed the pontoon bridges by daylight on the morning of May 5.[43]

When Lee learned of Sedgwick's withdrawal, he planned an all-out attack for later that day against Hooker's remaining army. The Confederate commander ordered McLaws and Anderson to return to Chancellorsville. McLaws' men spent the morning "burying the dead, attending the wounded, and collecting arms and accouterments." That afternoon, McLaws moved Kershaw's Brigade to relieve General Heth's position near the Rappahannock River and Mine Road junction. Semmes' Brigade joined Kershaw later in the day.[44]

Thunderstorms erupted in the late afternoon and continued to worsen throughout the evening. Rain fell in torrents, and lightening illuminated the darkened sky. Conditions made it practically impossible to move Lee's army into position to attack. Muddy roads were almost impassable, and the men were cold, wet, and exhausted. By sundown, Semmes' men stopped and pitched their tents, most of which had been captured from the Yankees. Lee reluctantly postponed the attack until daylight the next morning.[45]

Under cover of predawn darkness on May 6, General Joseph Hooker pulled his shattered army back across the swollen Rappahannock River and made his escape. The retreating Federals removed the pontoon bridges to keep the pursuing Confederates from crossing to the north side of the river. The scouts and skirmishers of Kershaw and Semmes discovered at daylight that the Federals had crossed the river, and a frustrated Lee called off the attack. His chance to destroy the Army of the Potomac had been lost.

Later that day, McLaws ordered Semmes to return to his former position just west of Fredericksburg, and the Wiregrass men marched back to their old campsite the next day. A few days later, the regiment moved to a new location a short distance away. The exhausted Georgians needed time to rest and regroup after more than half of their comrades had fallen in the recent fighting. [46]

As was the case after any battle, men hurriedly wrote letters home to let their families know they were alive. An unidentified 50th Georgia officer described his miraculous escape from death during the battle of Salem Church:

> I keep in good health; don't know how I escaped. Yankee prisoners say they tried to shoot me down for over an hour, but the terrible close shooting of my men saved me every time. We are back now at our old camp, wearied and worn out by eight days constant marching and fighting. We marched fifteen miles back through the most drenching rain storm I have ever been in; found everything in confusion and disorder, and nearly everything lost in the way of baggage. Thankful to God for my preservation, I have to mourn the loss of many brave officers and men. The 50th has, indeed, done well.[47]

Private William J. Evers, Company E, recounted his harrowing experience to his wife. Evers also expressed his longing to return home to see his family:

> My Dear, I can say to you that we have seen as hard a time as common. We have had a battle hear that lasted 8 days. It has bin an awful time hear. I was struck on my arm though slightly. It did not brake the skin. It deadend my arm and it is sore some yet. We was not in but one fight, that was on sunday eavning. We had 14 wounded and two killed in our company. Our capt. was killed dead on the field and one private. All our officers is absent but one lieutenant. I am happy to think that it is as well with me as it is, for it did not look like any could possibly make their esscape. My Dear, I cant see how I come clare, only through gods kind and tender mercy to me. I know nothing elce could of protected me through such a difaculty but if I can have his kind assistance it will be well with me and I truly hope it may be his good pleasure to stand by and protect me is my prair. I know that he has bin merciful to me and I

intend to do the best I can hoping he will remain my grate friend.

My Dear, I want to see you and my little children verry bad. I hope the lord will be with all. I cant see no prospect of peace but it may be will of god that this war may stop soon and it may not. We poore short sighted mortals can not tell any thing about his dezigns. We can only hope for the best and he is able to help us if it is concistant with his will.

My Dear, I want you to write to me as often as you for I am verry glad to hear from you. It is more satisfaction than any thing elce that I can get.[48]

Two weeks after the battle, Private Malachi Nesmith, Company H, wrote a poignant letter to his wife from a hospital bed in Richmond. Nesmith had been badly wounded at Salem Church.

My Dear Wife,

I know a few lines from me will be acceptable, therefore, I will try and form them as best can. I am at this time in a hospital in Richmond, quite sick and got a severe wound in the late battle at Fredericksburg. My right arm has already been amputated and I am weakened down with loss of blood. I am suffering too with jaundice which has become quite a prevailing disease among the soldiers. I am sorry that I could not write to you sooner, but I know you will excuse my remissiveness when you hear of my situation; think not for a moment my long silence was caused by indifference or forgetfulness. You are still the same loved companion, not time, absence, or distance will ever change my affection for you. I sometimes fear that I shall never see you again and those thoughts are badly distressing. My daily prayer to God is to spare me that I may once more be with you and my little family, but should He otherwise order it, I must bear to the stern decree and endeavor to be prepared to meet Him in peace, my hope and faith in him is strong and I feel that come good or come evil, all will be well. Pray for me my own wife and should we never meet on earth, I hope to join you in a better world—there to be separated no more.

I am blessed in having good attention shown me. My every want and wish is granted almost before I ask and could you be with me I would be content to suffer on. We had upwards of five (or six) thousand man killed and wounded in the last battle and I am sure the enemies must have been three times that number, but kill as many of them as you may, it appears that we don't miss them. I am in a Georgia hospital and it is filled with Georgians, some badly wounded, and others slightly.

You must write as soon as you get this. I am all impatient to hear from you and my boys. Kiss each of them for their father and tell them not to forget him. I must conclude—have nothing else worth stating. Give my love to all and our friends. Farewell—your own,

Malachi NeSmith[49]

Malachi NeSmith died the next day at age thirty, leaving his widow, Susan L. NeSmith, and two young sons, Malley and Matthew.

The remnants of the 50th Georgia remained in camp about two miles from Fredericksburg for the rest of the month. The location was apparently a good one, as referenced in a May 21 letter from Private John G. F. McCall, Company K, to his sister Becky: "We are camped now in a beautiful oak grove on a high hill and good spring water, if we could only stay here til the war ends but I fear it will be a long time before it ends." As the men rested and recuperated their ranks slowly swelled as recuperated soldiers returned from the hospitals.[50]

The Battle of Chancellorsville was the costliest of the war to date for the Federals, with more than 17,000 casualties. The losses were only slightly less for the Confederates, estimated at about 13,000. McLaws' reported a total of 1,889 men killed, wounded or captured from his division. Semmes' Brigade suffered the highest casualty rate in the division, 603, accounting for almost one-third of the total.[51]

The 50th Georgia Regiment had the highest casualty rate in the brigade, with losses of more than 59 percent. The 50th Georgia experienced 187 casualties, almost all of which occurred at Salem Church. Of the total, 20 were killed, 15 were mortally wounded, 150 were wounded, 1 was captured, and 1 was reported missing. Individual company losses are as follows:

Company A (17) – 4 killed, 1 mortally wounded, 12 wounded
Company B (14) – 1 killed, 2 mortally wounded, 11 wounded
Company C (26) – 3 killed, 2 mortally wounded, 21 wounded
Company D (22) – 2 killed, 19 wounded, 1 missing
Company E (16) – 2 killed, 1 mortally wounded, 13 wounded
Company F (11) – 1 mortally wounded, 10 wounded
Company G (18) – 3 killed, 2 mortally wounded, 13 wounded

Company H (31) – 3 killed, 5 mortally wounded, 22 wounded, 1 captured
Company I (16) – 2 killed, 14 wounded
Company K (16) – 1 mortally wounded, 15 wounded[52]

Four of the ten company commanders in the 50th Georgia were casualties. Captain Richard J. McLean, Company E, was killed. Captain Peter B. Bedford, Company B; Captain Jeremiah W. Wells, Company H; and Captain David P. Luke, Company I, received wounds.[53]

Captain Jeremiah Wesley Wells, Company H. Wells was elected captain of the Colquitt Volunteers when the company was organized on March 4, 1862. He was seriously wounded while leading his men at the Battle of Salem Church on May 3, 1863. Wells resigned his commission on December 30, 1863, due to the lingering effects of his wounds and his election to the Georgia State Assembly. Courtesy of the Lowndes County Historical Society and Museum, Valdosta, Georgia.

Privates George Washington Chitty and Neil Peterson, Company D, both suffered wounds during the fierce struggle at Salem Church. Chitty's wound was slight and did not require hospitalization. Peterson's was more severe. The young soldier remained in a Richmond hospital until July 26, when he received a thirty-day furlough to return home to Lowndes County for rest and recuperation. Three other Salem Church casualties were Privates Hillory C. Cone and Charles T. Gandy, Company E, and Private James R. Thomas, Company A. Thomas was killed. Gandy received a severe wound to the left arm that required amputation. Cone's wound was less severe, and he was able to soon return to his company.[54]

Private Hillory C. Cone, Company E. This Thomas County soldier enlisted on March 4, 1862, at Thomasville. Cone was wounded at Salem Church on May 3, 1863. He was promoted to fourth corporal on August 6, 1864, and was home on furlough at the close of the war. Cone died in Thomas County, Georgia, on March 28, 1909. Courtesy of the U.S. Army Military History Institute, Carlisle, Pennsylvania.

Another casualty was Second Lieutenant George E. Fahm. A regimental color bearer at Fox's Gap, Fahm miraculously made it through that battle unscathed. He received a promotion to second lieutenant on April 27 and acted as regimental color bearer at Salem Church. During the battle, he suffered severe wounds to his neck and right lung, thought to be a mortal injury. The Wiregrass officer received transport to a Richmond hospital. Two days after his wounding, he received a promotion to first lieutenant for his bravery at Salem Church. He later recovered and rejoined the regiment.[55]

In less than eight months, the ranks of the 50th Georgia had been decimated in two horrific battles at Fox's Gap and Chancellorsville. Any excitement experienced by the young Wiregrass volunteers fourteen months ago had vanished. The grim reality and horror of war made battle-hardened veterans of the survivors.

The brilliant Confederate victory at Chancellorsville was received with glee in the South and dismay in the North. *New York Times Tribune* editor Horace Greeley reportedly reacted to the news with, "My God. It is horrible—horrible; and to think of it, 130,000 magnificent soldiers so cut to pieces by less than 60,000 half-starved ragamuffins!"[56]

On the heels of perhaps his most spectacular victory, Robert E. Lee had already planned his next campaign. He made the fateful decision to again invade the North. The 50th Georgia had little time to rest. A long hard march into Pennsylvania would be next for the Wiregrass veterans.

Chapter Seven
The Gettysburg Campaign
June 3–August 1, 1863

After his brilliant victory at Chancellorsville, General Robert E. Lee planned another bold move to take the war to the North. Lee's rationale was similar to that he used in 1862. The army needed rations, which were in short supply in central Virginia. The victory at Chancellorsville gained Lee no ground, because the two armies simply returned to their former positions. If Lee moved northward, General Joseph Hooker would have to move his army from Fredericksburg to block Lee's path, thereby removing the current threat to Richmond. Finally, a victory on northern soil might pressure the U.S. Government to entertain a peace settlement. President Jefferson Davis approved the plan, and Lee immediately made preparations to march the Army of Northern Virginia north.

Paul Semmes' Brigade had been badly shot up in the recent battle, and several excellent officers had been lost. The regiments relished the opportunity to take the next four weeks—most of May—to reorganize and replenish their ranks so that they could return to fighting strength.

A few promotions occurred within the 50th Georgia while it camped near Fredericksburg. In Company A, Captain James A. Waters resigned on May 26 due to illness. First Lieutenant Edward M. Ford replaced him, and Second Lieutenant George W. Waldron became first lieutenant. In Company E, First Sergeant John W. Everitt received a promotion to second lieutenant on May 11. John Sirmons became second lieutenant in Company G on May 19.[1]

The relative peace and tranquility of camp life ended on the afternoon of June 2. The army received orders to cook rations and prepare to march. The next morning, McLaws' division started toward Culpeper, Virginia, some thirty miles to the west. The men reached their destination by June 5. William J. Evers, Company E, recounted the long, grueling march in a June 8 letter to his wife: "I take the pleasure of writing you a few lines to let you know that I am as well as common with the exception of my feet being verry sore from the march. We have moved from whare we was up to Culpep. We had to march about 30 miles."[2]

While the regiment camped near Culpeper, the June 9 resignation of Company D Captain James T. Bevill caused a flurry of activity. The men elected First Lieutenant William D. Howell as captain and Augustus H. Lane as first lieutenant. Marion Nelson became second lieutenant and Etheldred Langford moved to junior second lieutenant.[3]

The 50th Georgia remained near Culpeper until June 15. That morning, the regiment marched west and then north along the eastern edge of the Blue Ridge Mountains toward Winchester. Lee had ordered James Longstreet and J. E. B. Stuart to guard the mountain gaps to protect the right and rear of the army as it moved.[4]

The mid-June weather had become dangerously hot, and the hard marching took a toll on the men. Many of Semmes' Georgians fell out from heat exhaustion and sunstroke. Captain William O. Fleming of Company F described the brutal conditions in a letter to his mother: "It has been necessary for us to make forced marches in the hottest weather (& in the heat of the day) that I ever experienced. I never saw so many fainting and sunstroke cases in my life. It became so alarming one day that the Genl had to order a halt or lose nearly his whole force. I have suffered very much and felt sometimes as if I should have to give up but would make up my mind to go a little farther & a little farther until the day's march was over."[5]

On June 19, Longstreet posted McLaws' division in Ashby's Gap. That evening, the 50th Georgia waded across the Shenandoah River near Berry's Ford. Heavy rains from a recent storm had swollen the river and the water was refreshingly cold. Captain Fleming reported: "It came nearly under my arms & the current was so swift that it was with difficulty that I could keep my feet. The men were made to pull off their clothes and carry their cartridge boxes, clothes, etc., on the end of the bayonet. They went in with a shout."[6]

On June 21, Federal cavalry attacked J. E. B. Stuart's troopers and drove them into Ashby's Gap. Longstreet ordered McLaws to recross the river and drive off the enemy. McLaws' men waded across the river and occupied the gap before nightfall. At daylight the next morning, a line of Rebel sharpshooters drove away the enemy cavalry without a fight. The division withdrew across the river later that day. On June 23, Lee ordered Longstreet to march toward Maryland, and the corps moved out at dawn the following morning. The 50th Georgia passed through Berryville and Martinsburg. The Wiregrass men camped near the Potomac River on the night of June 25.[7]

The next morning, Semmes' Brigade eagerly splashed across the wide, swift-flowing Potomac River into Maryland near Williamsport. Private Lucius L. Cochran, Company E, 10th Georgia Regiment, described the crossing:

The river where we crossed was perhaps nearly 200 yards wide and from four to five feet deep. Our passage was characterized by much jollity and merriment. One little bandy-legged fellow of a company in front of ours, who could scarcely keep his nose above the surface, fell down in midstream and lost his gun, and many other mishaps of more or less seriousness befell the unlucky ones on the way. All of which seemed, by some law of compensation, to do about as much good in the amusement afforded the fortunate ones as harm in the discomfiture and dejection of the unfortunate.[8]

The Confederates camped that night near Williamsport, Maryland. On June 27, the division marched through Hagerstown, Maryland, and then Greencastle, Pennsylvania. The 50th Georgia camped for the evening about five miles from Chambersburg, Pennsylvania. The next day, the long, slow-moving column of butternut soldiers marched through Chambersburg, some twenty-four miles west of Gettysburg. The exhausted men rested the next couple of days about one mile out of town. Private Cochran reported, "We spent a night and about half the next day at Chambersburg, testing the qualities of Pennsylvania poultry, which proved to have a very palatable flavor."[9]

During the initial Confederate movements from Fredericksburg, General Joseph Hooker could never quite determine Lee's intentions. By June 25, Hooker learned of the Rebel crossing into Maryland and ordered the Army of the Potomac to move north from Virginia to intercept the Southerners. In the meantime, President Abraham Lincoln had become increasingly dissatisfied with the Union commander's performance. Hooker offered his resignation, and the President accepted it. On June 27, Lincoln appointed Major General George G. Meade as the new commander of the Army of the Potomac.

The next evening, Lee learned that the pursuing Army of the Potomac had moved as far north as the vicinity of Frederick, Maryland. The Confederate commander quickly decided to concentrate his army east of the Blue Ridge Mountains and to block the Federal pursuit. On June 29, General Lee ordered his corps commanders to march toward Gettysburg. Around noon on June 30, the Wiregrass men were interrupted by the beat of the drums calling them to attention. They headed east toward Greenwood, located on the western edge of the mountain range.[10]

Lee's Army of Northern Virginia moved south and east while Meade's Army of the Potomac moved north. The two great armies marched on a collision course toward a little town called Gettysburg.

The Battle of Gettysburg: July 1 – 3

McLaws' division left Greenwood around 7:30 on the morning of July 1 and marched southeast toward Gettysburg. At about this time, forward elements of Major General Henry Heth's division from A. P. Hill's Third Corps engaged Federal pickets on the northwest side of Gettysburg. This skirmishing signaled the beginning of the Battle of Gettysburg. Neither side had sought a fight at this location, but the chance encounter at this small Pennsylvania town would soon result in the largest battle ever fought on American soil.

The fighting on July 1 escalated as both sides poured in reinforcements. By the end of the day, Richard Ewell's Second Corps and Ambrose Hill's Third Corps had pushed the Yankees southeast through town. Although bloody, the first day's fighting had been a solid Confederate success.

Just after dark, McLaws' division finally reached Marsh Creek, about four miles from Gettysburg. The tired and hungry 50th Georgians set up camp for the night. The division had arrived too late to take part in the first day's fighting, but it would more than make up for it the next day.[11]

Major General Joseph Brevard Kershaw was born in Camden, South Carolina. A successful lawyer and state legislator before the war, Kershaw served with distinction throughout the war. He was captured at the Battle of Sailor's Creek on April 6, 1865. After the war, Kershaw returned to the South Carolina Legislature and served as senate president. He was later appointed circuit court judge and served until his death in 1894. Courtesy of the U.S. Army Military History Institute, Carlisle, Pennsylvania.

The division marched from Marsh Creek toward Gettysburg shortly after sunrise on July 2, finally stopping behind Herr's Ridge. Lee met with his generals in the early morning to finalize battle strategy. The plan called for Longstreet's divisions led by McLaws and Hood to move into position on the Confederate far right. McLaws would lead the attack on the Federal left and turn the enemy's left flank. After McLaws became engaged, Hood would attack. The two divisions would then wheel left and fight their way up Emmitsburg Road. Richard H. Anderson's division of Hill's Third Corps would then attack the Union center at Cemetery Ridge. McLaws gave the honor of leading the assault to Brigadier General Joseph B. Kershaw's veteran South Carolina brigade.[12]

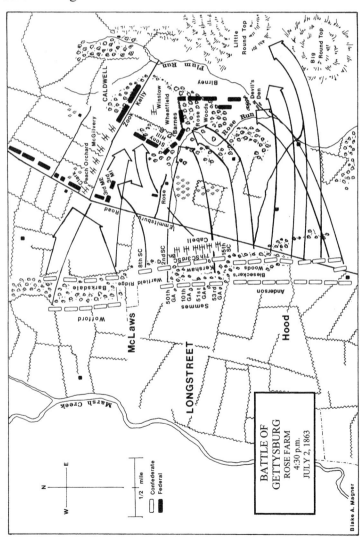

Faulty information and miscommunication hindered Lee's plan of attack and these problems persisted among the Confederate command throughout the day. Precious hours were lost while Longstreet's scouts sought a route that would not be detected by the enemy. McLaws' and Hood's divisions finally began their march after twelve noon.

The July heat became more intense as the day wore on. The men sweltered as they marched and countermarched in the choking dust. Many collapsed from heat exhaustion. By mid-afternoon, McLaws' division finally took position along the tree line on Warfield Ridge. Instead of being aligned opposite the Federal left flank, the division had stopped directly across from Major General Daniel E. Sickles' III Corps and elements of Major General George Sykes' V Corps. Hood's men moved past McLaws and wound up on the Confederate right flank.

Longstreet swapped the roles of the divisions to correct the error. Hood's division would now lead the attack on the Federal left, and McLaws would attack after Hood engaged the enemy. Kershaw's Brigade would then lead McLaws' division to the Emmitsburg Road before shifting north toward the Peach Orchard and aligning on the left of Hood. Brigadier General William Barksdale's Brigade would align on the left of Kershaw. Semmes' Brigade would form a second line behind Kershaw, with Brigadier General William T. Wofford's Brigade falling in behind Barksdale's Brigade. Both Semmes and Wofford would remain about 150 yards behind the lead brigades in reserve. The plan called for precision and timing, commodities in short supply for the Confederates on July 2.

Earlier in the day, only Captain A. Judson Clark's Battery B, New Jersey Light Artillery occupied the Sherfy Peach Orchard, located on a hill less than one-half mile northeast of McLaws' position. Now, five more batteries from the artillery reserve, under the command of Lieutenant Colonel Freeman McGilvery, stood massed near the Peach Orchard. These estimated three-dozen guns would unleash a horrible enfilading fire on the flanks of the Confederates as they marched across the open fields. In addition, Captain George B. Winslow's Battery D, 1st New York Light Artillery had been positioned on a rise in the Wheatfield, a few hundred yards to the east of Rose Farm.[13]

At about 3:30 p.m., Semmes' Brigade formed on the northern edge of Biesecker's Woods along Warfield Ridge. The brigade deployed behind a stone wall about seventy-five yards behind Kershaw's Brigade.[14]

Moments later, enemy artillery at the Peach Orchard opened fire on the Confederate positions. At about 3:50 p.m., Rebel batteries from Colonel Henry G. Cabell's Artillery Battalion returned fire against the Federal guns and pounded the nearby Yankee infantry positions.

A soldier in the 10th Georgia described the tenuous position of the men as they waited to attack: "We had marched and counter marched until the middle of the day. We lay down in a bunch of timber, and remained there for some hours. In our front was an open field, some six or eight hundred yards across. Beyond this, and on our left were hills and mountains, bristling with federal bayonets and cannon. Already the latter had found our range, and were pouring a steady fire of shot and shell into our ranks."[15]

Longstreet's attack finally lurched forward at about 4:30 p.m. Hood's men stepped smartly out of the woods into a hail of Federal shot and shell. Hood and McLaws focused their attack on Major General David B. Birney's 1st division, III Corps. Hood's men moved toward the Devil's Den, Little Round Top, and Big Round Top. McLaws aimed for Rose Farm, the Wheatfield, and the Peach Orchard.

Shortly after Hood's men plowed into the III Corps' left flank, Kershaw's South Carolina Brigade marched out of Biesecker's Woods and into the open fields west of the Emmitsburg Road. The South Carolinians steadily marched toward the Federal positions. General Kershaw described in detail the deadly terrain that lay ahead:

> In my center front was a stone house [John Rose House], and to the left of it a stone barn [Rose Barn], both about 500 yards from our line, and on a line with the crest of the orchard hill [Sherfy Peach Orchard]. Along the front of the orchard, and on the face looking toward the stone house, the enemy's infantry was posted. Two batteries of artillery were in position, the one in rear of the orchard, near the crest of the hill, and the other some 200 yards farther back, in the direction of the rocky mountain. Behind the stone house, on the left, was a morass; on the right a stone wall running parallel with our line of battle. Beyond the morass some 200 yards was a stony hill, covered with heavy timber and thick undergrowth, extending some distance toward the enemy's main line, and inclining to our left, and in rear of the orchard and the batteries described. Beyond the stone wall, and in a line with the stony hill, was a heavy forest, [Rose Woods] extending far to our right. From the morass a small stream [Plum Run/Rose Run] ran through this wood along the base of the mountain toward the right. Between the stony hill and this forest was an interval of about 100 yards, [ravine] which was only sparsely covered with scrubby undergrowth, through which a small road ran in the direction of the mountain. Looking down this road from the stone house, a large wheat-field was seen. In rear of the wheat-field, and between that and the mountain, was the enemy's main line of battle, posted behind a stone wall.[16]

Kershaw's target was Stony Hill. He recalled, "Under my instructions, I determined to move upon the stony hill, so as to strike it with my center, and thus attack the orchard on its left rear. Accordingly, about 4 o'clock, when I received orders to advance, I moved at once in this direction, gradually changing front to the left."[17]

The 50th Georgia awaited orders to advance. Lieutenant Billy Pendleton, Company B, recalled, "About four in the afternoon we formed in line of battle behind a stone fence which was behind a hill. I knew a battle was imminent. Colonel Kearse addressed each company, telling the men to fight and win." At about 5:00 p.m., Semmes ordered his Georgians to advance. The men in Company B marched forward without their water canteens. Pendleton reported, "Before our canteens were filled, - the man that took them did not get back in time, - we were ordered to advance."[18]

The brigade moved out of the woods under galling artillery fire and into the open field. A 10th Georgia soldier recalled the initial movement: "At last came the order to advance; every old soldier knows how hard it was to obey. Yet, the men sprang quickly into line, and the brigade moved steadily forward into the open field, and then 'hell broke loose' from every hill in our

The "stepping off point" from Biesecker's Woods into the field. The brigades of Kershaw and Semmes left the woods near this point and proceeded across some 500 yards of open field toward Rose Farm. Emmitsburg Road is between 150 to 200 yards in front. In the center distance is the Rose House. Federal artillery from the Sherfy Peach Orchard out of the picture to the far left poured a deadly fire into the men as they waited and during their advance. West Confederate Avenue now runs behind this point. Photo by author.

front, and on our left burst such a roar of artillery and such a storm of shot and shell as we had never faced before; it was Malvern Hill all over again, but on a greater scale; it was reported that one charge of grape or canister from up on our left, killed and wounded 27 men in our regiment."[19]

Major Peter McGlashan reported: "As we moved out, we came directly under the fire of 44 guns. They had our range directly, the first shell killing two men on my left." Sergeant William Moore Jones of Company K added, "The enemy seemed to have the situation well in hand, for, as we went to get over a stone fence, the first shell they threw at us exploded in the midst of my company and killed Jim Alderman and Jim Dixon and wounded George Merriman, Jesse Stephens and several others."[20]

Semmes' Brigade soon reached Emmitsburg Road. The men climbed over fences on each side of the road under heavy enemy fire. The Federal artillery in and around the Peach Orchard showered the brigades of Kershaw and Semmes with canister and grape shot as they advanced across the field. A smoky haze obscured vision, and the smell of sulfur filled the nostrils of the men as they moved forward. Private L. L. Cochran, 10th Georgia, remembered the terrifying ordeal: "It did not seem that human nature could stand the storm. Yet on moved that single line of gray as steadily as if on parade; gaps were closed up as fast as made and still the line pressed forward; at last the field is crossed, though at fearful cost and we come to the edge

Private George H. Merriman, Company K. A native of England, Merriman enlisted in the Brooks Volunteers on April 24, 1862, at Quitman. Private Merriman was seriously wounded in the left lung by an artillery shell fragment on July 2 and later captured. He was paroled from David's Island, New York, on August 24, 1863. Merriman returned to his company, although the wound caused breathing difficulties that troubled him for the rest of this life. He was wounded again at the Battle of Cedar Creek on October 19, 1864, and retired to the Invalid Corps the following month. Merriman returned to Brooks County, Georgia, where he lived until 1875. He then moved a short distance south to the small village of Ashville, Florida, and lived the rest of his life as a farmer. George Merriman died in 1889. Courtesy of the U.S. Army Military History Institute, Carlisle, Pennsylvania.

Federal artillery positions in the Peach Orchard. The Federal batteries positioned here near the Wheatfield Road (immediate foreground) rained a torrent of shot and shell on Semmes' Brigade as it advanced across the open field. Most of the 50th Georgia casualties on July 2 were believed to be from artillery fire. Photo by author.

of the woods and foot of the hills; the line was halted for a moment to get breath for the final struggle; we had not struck the infantry yet, and we all knew that the worst was yet to come."[21]

Major McGlashan witnessed some ugly scenes as he led his men across forward. "All along the line I could see great gaps blown through by shells, six, eight or ten men falling in heaps here and there, but the line closing up the gaps moved steadily to the attack in grim silence. Half way across we encountered the enemy's skirmish line, which was instantly driven in, when their artillery changed to canister and grape, and nothing but the rapid movement of our men saved the line from annihilation."[22]

The enemy skirmish lines noted by McGlashan were composed of the 3rd Maine and the 3rd Michigan regiments. The 3rd Maine occupied the area in front of and west of the Peach Orchard, and the 3rd Michigan extended farther east toward Stony Hill and Rose Farm.

As Kershaw's left wing neared the batteries in the Peach Orchard, his right wing reached the Rose Farm buildings. The 3rd and 7th South Carolina regiments wove around the house and barn as they continued their advance toward Stony Hill. By virtue of being on Semmes' far left, the 50th Georgia likely moved behind Kershaw's left wing, composed of the 8th and 2nd South Carolina regiments and the 3rd South Carolina Battalion. Part of Semmes' Brigade likely also followed behind Kershaw's right wing.

In order to attack the enemy artillery, Kershaw's line slowly wheeled left and advanced in a more northerly direction toward the Peach Orchard. Semmes followed about 150 yards to the rear. The 50th Georgia soon reached a lane running east from the Emmitsburg Road through the Rose Farm. The Wiregrass men encountered high board fences on either side of the lane. Climbing the fences under the relentless enemy fire proved to be a challenge for the Georgians. Lieutenant Pendleton recalled, "We came to a road with high fences on both sides; the firing was getting hotter. I wondered if I would ever get across the fences."[23]

Just as Kershaw's left wing prepared to assault the batteries in the Peach Orchard, the Confederate commander ordered his far right wing regiment, the 7th South Carolina, to make a slight adjustment to the right before moving up Stony Hill. Unfortunately, this order was misinterpreted and all units stopped their advance and made a right oblique movement. The results of the delay were devastating. Enemy artillery and infantry fire raked the Confederate lines.

Sergeant William M. Jones remembered the disastrous event, "The line continued to advance until we were about a hundred yards of the battery [possibly Bigelow's Battery], when the line pressed on the left and we were ordered to right oblique." Jones continued, "While in this position I was shot through the right ankle with an iron from a piece of canister shot."[24]

Lieutenant Billy Pendleton recalled, "We were going toward a peach orchard, but were ordered to right oblique. The firing was very heavy and dangerous. Colonel Kearse and Sergeant Hersey were killed. I didn't know it at the time, but both were killed dead." Sergeant Jones also noted the death of Kearse: "We advanced about two hundred yards when Col. Frank Kearse was killed by a grape shot."[25]

Captain William O. Fleming gave the following account of Kearse's death: "A grape shot passed through his left side coming out of the right side shattering his right arm. After receiving such a shot he said—'I am killed— tell Major McGlashan to take command.'" McGlashan then took temporary command of the 50th Georgia and bravely led the regiment during the rest of the bloody struggle.[26]

The enemy quickly took advantage of the momentary confusion in the Rebel ranks. Colonel Edward L. Bailey boldly led his 2nd New Hampshire Infantry Regiment in a headlong charge for Kershaw's startled left wing. Supported by the 3rd Maine, the 141st Pennsylvania, and the 3rd Michigan regiments, Bailey's men threw the Confederate ranks into temporary disarray.

Sergeant William Moore Jones. This Brooks County native enlisted in the Brooks Volunteers on March 3, 1862, at Quitman. Later in the year, Jones received a promotion to sergeant. He received a slight wound at the Battle of Chancellorsville but remained with his company. During the fierce action on July 2, the twenty-one-year-old Wiregrass soldier received a severe wound to his right ankle that required the amputation of his leg. Jones was left in a Williamsport, Maryland, hospital with many other badly wounded soldiers when Lee retreated into Virginia. Jones was imprisoned at Point Lookout, Maryland, until he could be exchanged on March 27, 1864. Courtesy of the Georgia Department of Archives and History, Morrow, Georgia.

Major McGlashan reported the effect of the enemy attack: "As we entered the woods, a dense mass of the enemy, three lines, rose up, delivered a terrible fire right in our faces and then charged down at us with bayonets fixed." The Georgian continued, "The shock was terrible. So swift was the enemy's advance down the hill that they broke our line by sheer impact of weight and numbers. Our front line [Kershaw's] driven back on the second, [Semmes'] was soon inextricably mixed with them. The mass of struggling, fighting troops broken up into groups, all regimental organizations lost, were being slowly driven backwards before the almost irresistible advance of the enemy, and any other troops in existence would have been irremediably broken and scattered by that terrible shock."[28]

As the left wings of Kershaw and Semmes regrouped under cover of a swale below the crest of the hill and near the Rose house and barn, Kershaw's right wing continued up to the base of Stony Hill. Kershaw and George T. "Tige" Anderson's Brigade slowly pushed the enemy off the hill and out of the Wheatfield.

Shortly after occupying Stony Hill, Kershaw spied Federal II Corps reinforcements quickly moving toward him from the north and east across the Wheatfield. Brigadier General Samuel K. Zook's 3rd Brigade and Colonel Patrick Kelly's 2nd Brigade from Brigadier General John C. Caldwell's 1st Division now threatened Kershaw's position. Zook's brigade, containing the 52nd, 57th, and 66th New York and the 140th Pennsylvania regiments, crossed Wheatfield Road and headed for Stony Hill. Kelly's smaller Irish Brigade, consisting of the 28th Massachusetts, 116th Pennsylvania, and 63rd, 69th, and 88th New York regiments, came from the northeast through the Wheatfield and threatened the right flank of the 7th South Carolina.

Rose House, facing north. The 50th Georgia advanced with Semmes' Brigade from the west (left) across the open field under terrible artillery fire. Federal artillery was positioned in the Peach Orchard behind and to the right of the large tree. To the right (east) out of the picture is Stony Hill. The remains of the Rose Barn are just to the left of the smaller tree and house. Rose's Woods are to the immediate right and a little south of the bottom of the picture. The 50th Georgia fought all around the Rose Farm on July 2. Photo by author.

Remains of Rose Barn, facing east. Men from both Kershaw's and Semmes' Brigades took shelter near the stone barn and house during and after the battle on July 2. The copse of trees beyond the remains is Stony Hill. An outbuilding near Rose House is on far right. Photo by author.

General Kershaw hurried back and met with General Semmes, who stood "some 150 yards in my right rear, to bring him up to meet the attack on my right." The South Carolinian urgently requested Semmes to move his brigade to the right to close a gap between the 7th South Carolina and the left of "Tige" Anderson's Brigade. Kershaw reported, "General Semmes promptly responded to my call, and put his brigade in motion towards the right, preparatory to moving to the front."[29]

The lack of any known official reports and few individual accounts from members of the brigade make it difficult to track the movements of individual regiments with certainty. However, it is believed that when Kershaw made his request for assistance, Semmes' regiments were in the same alignment as during the initial assault. The 50th Georgia, now temporarily commanded by Major McGlashan, anchored the left wing and was closest to Stony Hill when the brigade moved to the aid of Kershaw. The 10th Georgia would have been to the right of the 50th Georgia, and likely entered the northwest edge of Rose Woods. The 51st and 53rd Georgians entered the woods farther to the south.

Relentless artillery fire raked the brigade as it shifted into position. By virtue of being on the far left and nearest the enemy guns, the 50th Georgia was being torn apart. Lucius Cochran of the 10th Georgia recalled: "Just at this critical moment one of the regiments on our left [the 50th Georgia] showed signs of wavering." Cochran continued, "General Semmes was standing out in front exhorting them to stand firm: Captain McBride [acting 10th Georgia commander] ordered the writer and Adjutant Strickland to 'run down there and rally those men.' When we reached them they were on the verge of panic; their leaders had been shot down and they were confused." The regiment steadied and fell back into line.[30]

Major McGlashan later recalled the picture of Semmes rallying his men: "Gallant Paul J. Semmes, with a red skull cap on his head, his fighting cap we used to call it, dashed through the line like a maddened tiger, shouting, 'Look to the front, men! Look to the front! Forward! Forward!'"[31]

After conferring with Semmes, Kershaw rushed back to his 7th South Carolina regiment. He wrote:

> just as the enemy, [Kelly's Irish Brigade] having arrived at a
> point about two hundred yards from us, poured in a volley and
> advanced to the charge. The Seventh received him handsomely
> and long kept him in check in their front. One regiment
> [believed to be the 50th Georgia] of Semmes's brigade came at
> a double-quick as far as the ravine in our rear, and for a time
> checked him in their front. There was still an interval of 100
> yards between this regiment and the right of the Seventh, and
> into this the enemy was forcing his way, causing the Seventh to
> swing back more and more.[32]

As he rallied his men, General Semmes went down with a severe wound to the thigh. An artillery fragment apparently nearly severed the femoral artery. Semmes applied a tourniquet that he always carried with him and waited to be carried from the field. Kershaw believed that the Georgia commander "was shot down near that stonewall, in the open field." The field southeast of the Rose House near the western edge of Rose Woods is the likely location. It is situated between the tree line on the east and another stone wall on the west.[33]

Litter bearers carried the brave commander from the field back to the initial point of attack on Warfield Ridge. The loss of Paul Semmes during this critical time in the battle shattered and demoralized the brigade. The men considered him irreplaceable and the epitome of a leader. An ambulance later transported Semmes to a Martinsburg hospital. Complications from the wound eventually proved fatal, and he died on July 10.

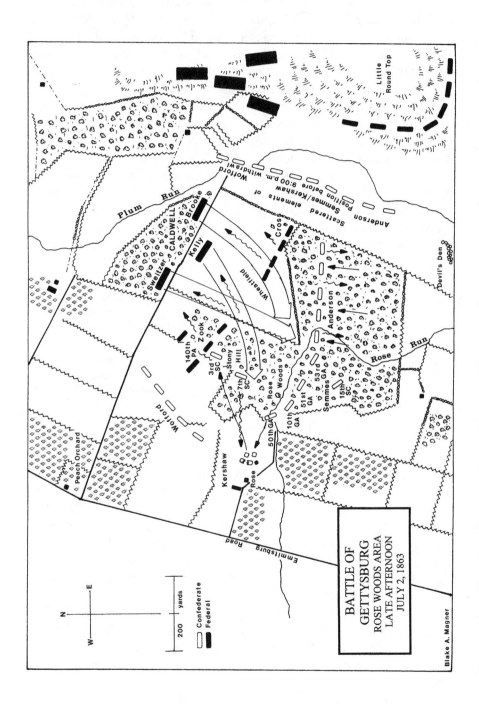

BATTLE OF
GETTYSBURG
ROSE WOODS AREA
LATE AFTERNOON
JULY 2, 1863

Blake A. Magner

It is unclear if anyone assumed temporary command of the brigade during the battle. Some accounts indicate that after the gallant Georgia commander fell, the regiments fought as individual units. No doubt great confusion temporarily occurred in the ranks. Many field officers had already fallen, shattering the continuity of command. The leadership casualties in Semmes' Brigade left a void of official reports, making it unclear who stepped in to untangle the regiments in the wild confusion of battle.[34]

As the struggle intensified, troops from the Irish Brigade pushed their way into the gap between the 7th South Carolina and the 50th Georgia. Eventually, the 7th South Carolina and a portion of the Wiregrass regiment fell back to the stone wall near Rose's house. Kershaw reported: "At length, the Seventh South Carolina gave way, and I directed Colonel Aiken to reform them at the stone wall, some 200 yards in my right rear." Lieutenant Pendleton recalled the withdrawal: "We went down toward a wood and through it. The men in front retreated, and finally our men gave way about two hundred yards." Pendleton also described a grisly scene as he and his

Stone wall near where General Semmes is thought to have fallen. The remains of a stone wall can be seen running northeast from the bottom of the picture. It is believed that Semmes fell while rallying his brigade near the wall in the field to the right. The stone wall and field are to the southeast of Rose House. Federal artillery raked the Confederates from the hill in the far center of the picture. Stony Hill is in the top right. To the far right and out of the picture is the Rose Woods tree line. Photo by author.

men withdrew from the chaos: "We passed a stream [Rose Run] which was bloody from wounded men drinking, but I drank some too."[35]

As the 7th South Carolina and most of the 50th Georgia fell back to the stone wall, Major McGlashan and about forty Wiregrass men peeled off and rushed to the aid of the 3rd South Carolina Regiment on Stony Hill.

Kershaw recalled, "I fell back to the Third Regiment, then hotly engaged on the crest of the stony hill, and gradually swung around its right

Rose Run, facing east. The small stream ran southeast and eventually flowed into the woods to the south. In the left middle is a spring that supplied the Rose family. In the top left is Stony Hill. In the upper center is the Wheatfield. To the upper right is Rose Woods. Thirsty men from both sides drank from the small stream, even though it had been tinged red with the blood of the wounded and dying. Photo by author.

as the enemy made progress around our flank. Semmes' advanced regiment [believed to be the 10th Georgia] had given way. One of his regiments [50th Georgia] mingled with the Third, and, among the rocks and trees, within a few feet of each other, a desperate conflict ensued." Major R. C. Maffett, 3rd South Carolina, also reported on the assistance rendered by the Georgians: "While thus engaged, about 40 men of the Fiftieth Georgia Regiment, under command of its major [McGlashan], came in on our left, and engaged the enemy."[36]

The withdrawal of the 7th South Carolina and most of the 50th Georgia left only the 3rd South Carolina and the small band of Wiregrass men on Stony Hill. Their situation was desperate. Colonel Richard P. Roberts' large 140th Pennsylvania Regiment, part of Zook's brigade, pressed the left of the South Carolinians and Georgians. Elements of the Irish Brigade pressured the right flank. Kershaw described the situation: "Separated from view of my left wing by the hill and wood, all of my staff being with that wing, the position of the Fifteenth Regiment being unknown, and the Seventh being in the rear, I feared the brave men around me would be surrounded by the large force pressing around them, and ordered the Third regiment and the Georgia [50th] regiment with them to fall back to the stone house [Rose house], whither I followed them."[37]

As Kershaw's and Semmes' men were being pushed out of the ravine and off Stony Hill, Caldwell's reserve brigade, commanded by Colonel John R. Brooke, swept across the Wheatfield and into the Rose Woods. The brigade consisted of the 27th Connecticut, 2nd Delaware, 64th New York, and the 53rd and 145th Pennsylvania regiments. Their primary opponent was "Tige" Anderson's Brigade, assisted by part of Semmes' Georgians (probably the 10th, 51st, and 53rd regiments). The two sides slugged it out in the woods until Brooke's men made a bayonet charge to break the Rebel lines. One 10th Georgia soldier recalled, "the order was to retreat and the[y] all retreated back over the fence and ralid again."[38]

Brooke's troops pushed the Georgians out of the northwest portion of Rose's woods. The Rebels fell back all the way past the tree line to the stone wall at the western edge of the field. The Federal advance finally slowed as Brooke's men reached the crest of the hill at the forest's western edge.[39]

Colonel Brooke described the advance of his brigade through the Wheatfield and the woods: "passing the line of Colonel [Edward] Cross at the edge of a wheat-field, I became at once hotly engaged. Pressing forward, firing as we went, we drove back the first line of the enemy, capturing a great number, and then charging the second line, drove it from its almost impregnable position on a rocky crest."[40]

As the exhausted 3rd South Carolina and the small band of 50th Georgians fell back from Stony Hill, General William T. Wofford's Brigade rushed up from the west in support. Kershaw reported: "On emerging from the wood, I saw Wofford coming in in splendid style." The left of Wofford's brigade rested in the Peach Orchard, which by now had been cleared of Yankees by Barksdale's Brigade. Wofford struck the north side of Stony Hill and turned Zook's flank. The Irish Brigade also met stiff resistance as Kershaw's and Semmes' fractured regiments reformed. Anderson's men regrouped and pressured Brooke's left. Part of Semmes' veterans put up strong defense from behind the stone wall west of the field bordering Rose Woods.[41]

Brooke recalled, "I now found my flanks threatened by a strong force of the enemy." Lieutenant Colonel Richards McMichael, 53rd Pennsylvania Regiment, also reported on the increased Confederate threat: "The position was held about fifteen minutes, when it was discovered that the enemy in force was getting in the flank and rear; then I fell back, in accordance with orders from Colonel Brooke." With no reinforcements coming to his aid, Brooke retired back across the Wheatfield.[42]

The hot Confederate fire from several directions forced the troops in John Caldwell's division to fall back. Caldwell rushed Jacob Sweitzer's brigade back into the churning cauldron. Sweitzer hurried his 4th Michigan, 62nd Pennsylvania, and 32nd Massachusetts regiments into the Wheatfield. The brigade moved through the Wheatfield and past Stony Hill toward the edge of Rose Woods. When these Union soldiers reached the stone wall bordering the southern edge of the Wheatfield and the woods, they ran into a hail of lead from three sides. Grasping the hopelessness of their situation, Sweitzer's men soon raced back across the Wheatfield.[43]

Kershaw described the renewed Confederate offensive: "The enemy gave way at Wofford's advance, and, with him, the whole of my left wing

Stony Hill, facing north. This picture, taken in November 2005, shows numerous large rocks and Federal monuments on the hill. The Wheatfield is beyond and to the right. The small band of 50th Georgians would have probably been positioned on the hill to the left. Photo by author.

advanced to the charge, sweeping the enemy before them, without a moment's stand, across the stone wall, beyond the wheat-field, up to the foot of the mountain. At the same time, my Fifteenth Regiment, and part of Semmes' brigade, pressed forward on the right to the same point."[44]

It is unclear which of Semmes' regiments fought on the right with the 15th South Carolina, but some 50th Georgians were involved. Lieutenant Pendleton reported:

> The men rallied in a lane [Rose Lane], I called to them "Let's show we can fight in Pennsylvania as well as in Virginia." When the regiment rallied, Major McGlashan started right for the enemy, but they had retreated. We were now in a thick wood and attacked with Hood's Texas division. We went on with them, following up the enemy. An officer came up who had lost his command—Lieutenant W. A. Tenille, of the Fifteenth Georgia. We got to the edge of the wood, to the right in front were Hood's men. I was behind a fence in the woods. A mile beyond where the enemy had retreated, we reached the top of a hill. At sunset an officer came up to Major McGlashan and asked him for reinforcements. I was sent over in charge of B, C, and H companies and stayed for a while. The firing stopped after dark.[45]

As the Confederates pushed the enemy back toward Little Round Top, Kershaw checked on the 7th South Carolina at the stone wall near his rear. He then went back near the Rose House, where the 3rd South Carolina and the small band of 50th Georgians were waiting. The commander moved the two regiments up to the stone wall with the 7th South Carolina to block any possible enemy advance. Joseph Kershaw then described the painful mission of a commander: "It was now near nightfall, and the operations of the day were over. Gathering all my regiments, with Semmes' brigade, behind the wall, and placing pickets to the front, I commenced the melancholy task of looking up my numerous dead and wounded."[46]

The Southerners appeared to have victory in hand on this part of the battlefield. They had recaptured Stony Hill and Rose Woods, sweeping the Union forces back east across the Wheatfield, Plum Run, and to the base of Little Round Top. Major McGlashan recalled the final Confederate advance: "On reaching the top of the ridge we found the enemy had retreated across the deep ravine that divided the ridge from the superior heights of Little Round Top and were hastily throwing breastworks of rock, commanding our advance, while other lines higher up on the hill were sweeping the crest of the ridge with infantry fire." McGlashan continued, "a hasty survey of our decimated troops discouraged us from a further advance. Regiments that had gone into the action 350 strong could scarce muster 50 men round the colors."[47]

Total exhaustion, lack of reinforcements, and approaching darkness slowed the Confederate offensive. Faced with strong Federal defenses and heavy reinforcements, General Longstreet thought it prudent not to push farther. The First Corps commander hoped to renew the battle in the morning.[48]

At about 9:00 p.m., the Confederates received orders to move back across the Wheatfield to the shelter of Stony Hill and the west end of the Rose Woods. The Southerners quickly withdrew and reformed into defensive positions. There would be no more fighting for the 50th Georgia this day.[49]

The charges and countercharges had left the Peach Orchard, Rose Farm, Stony Hill, Wheatfield, and the nearby woods strewn with more than four thousand dead and wounded. During the battle (from approximately 5 p.m. to 8:30 p.m.), Longstreet's men smashed the III Corps and defeated most of its reinforcements. However, each engagement sapped Confederate strength, ultimately denying General Lee's objective of victory. The estimated total casualties for the day were approximately 6,800 Confederates and 9,000 Federals.

Semmes' Brigade played an active part in the severe and protracted conflict in the Rose Farm area. The brigade also participated in the general advance later in the evening and helped force the enemy out of the woods, through the Wheatfield and across Plum Run Valley. The Georgians paid a heavy price, with about 33 percent casualties, including the loss of its brigade commander, Paul Semmes.[50]

The 50th Georgia Regiment had been in the thickest fighting all afternoon. The regiment had been fractured and many of the officers fell during the conflict, including gallant Lieutenant Colonel Francis Kearse. The Wiregrass veterans slugged it out with components of the Federal II, III, and V Corps, and the next day signaled more fighting.

Lieutenant Billy Pendleton, who had been temporarily detached from the regiment to help reinforce another unit, described the return to his regiment:

> It was a moonlight night. When I went back to my own
> regiment the dead and wounded were lying all around, many
> crying for water. Sergeant [James] Bailey gave some water to
> a Union soldier who assaulted him with his fists. About ten
> o'clock I heard a voice asking what regiment we were. It was
> Lieutenant Colonel Flemming who had not been in the battle.

He had orders to bring the regiment back to the brigade near
the spring [southeast of Rose House]. We started back. I
walked with Flemming and asked about Colonel Kearse.
Captain Bedford of our company had been shot through the
ankle. Captain Ford of Company A had been killed dead. I
said "Colonel, will this war never end?" I was very sad about
my dear friends. We got back to a farm house [Rose] where
we lay all night in line of battle.[51]

During the evening, men wandered the battlefield looking for lost
friends and gathering the wounded. Surgeons worked nonstop throughout
the night and into the next morning, trying to save as many of the suffering
soldiers as possible.

Sergeant William Jones, who had received a severe ankle wound
earlier in the day, could not walk or crawl from the field. Jones later wrote
in his diary:

I lay upon the battle field in the hot, broiling sun the balance
of the day and until eleven o'clock that night, when I heard
the voice of the litter-bearers of my company and called them
to me. The names of the two parties were James Brice and
Clem Humphreys, who took me back to a barn near where we
started to make the charge, and placed me on a pile of wheat
straw and got me a canteen of water, which I drank with great
relish. They then split open my boots and took my feet out of
them. After bathing my broken limb they got me another
canteen of water, and left me to my fate for the balance of the
night.[52]

William Jones apparently remained in the barn until the morning
of July 4. Litter bearers then carried the wounded Brooks County soldier
to a field hospital where he received medical attention. The wound required
the amputation of his right foot, and the brigade surgeon performed the
operation early the next morning.[53]

After the end of the second day's fighting, Colonel Goode Bryan,
commander of the 16th Georgia Regiment from Wofford's Brigade, assumed
temporary command of Semmes' Brigade.

The next morning, General Lee decided that an assault on the
Federal center might turn the tide. The final battle plan for July 3 called for
Major General George Pickett's division to lead the assault on the strongly
entrenched Federal defenses at Cemetery Ridge. McLaws' and Hood's
divisions would remain in support. Lee had earlier considered using
McLaws' and Hood's divisions to lead the attack, but General Longstreet

convinced the Confederate commander that these troops were too used up from the previous day's savage fighting. The two divisions remained in the defensive line in a support role, defending the Confederate right flank and rear. They were also ordered to be ready for a possible Federal counterattack, should Pickett's attack fail.

During the morning of July 3, the 50th Georgia occupied a position east of the Rose Farm and just west of the Wheatfield. Lieutenant Pendleton recalled the sad duty of burying their dead comrades: "The next day we gathered up the dead and buried them. I found a blanket on the field and we buried Colonel Kearse in it. I covered his face with an old shirt. During the burial I heard the battery start firing, so I went back to position after marking Kearse's grave."[54]

After quickly burying their dead, the 50th Georgians moved back across the Emmitsburg Road to Warfield Ridge and the stone wall, where they had first launched their attack the previous day. The men remained at this location for the rest of the day. That afternoon, Lee assaulted the enemy's strongly fortified position farther north on Cemetery Ridge. The disastrous attack, later known as "Pickett's Charge," failed to break the Union lines and resulted in thousands of Confederate casualties. Lee's final attempt at victory had failed.[55]

After Pickett's failed assault, McLaws' division prepared for a Federal counterattack. With the exception of severe skirmishing, however, the division was not engaged. Night fell as the stench of battle and the cries of the wounded permeated the air. The exhausted Confederates awaited a Federal assault the next morning.

During the night, Lee assessed the condition of his army. Short on manpower, ammunition and energy, the Confederate commander decided against another assault. Unless Meade attacked the Confederate positions, the most reasonable option would be to head back to Virginia.

The Rebel lines grimly awaited the anticipated attack as dawn broke on July 4. Rain began falling early and continued all during the day. When General Lee realized there would be no Federal attack, he withdrew his battered army. Thousands of wounded Confederates were loaded into ambulances and wagons for the long trip to Virginia. By mid-afternoon, the procession of wounded departed in the pouring rain and headed west toward Cashtown Gap. The wagon train then turned south, lumbered through Marion and Greencastle, and moved into Maryland. Brigadier General John Imboden commanded the long, slow-moving column over the rough, almost impassable roads toward Williamsport and across the Potomac River.

Heavy rains continued that night and early the next morning, as the remaining exhausted Confederates abandoned their defensive positions and slogged through the mud, away from the horrible battlefield. Lee's retreating army reluctantly left more than four thousand of the most severely wounded soldiers in the care of those surgeons who volunteered to remain behind.

In the early pre-dawn hours of July 5, Colonel Bryan led Semmes' Brigade on the slow, tedious withdrawal west across South Mountain and through Fairfield Gap to Waynesboro. The march then turned south toward Hagerstown, Maryland. The 50th Georgia marched all night in a pouring rain. The ankle-deep mud clung to the soldiers' shoes, making it difficult to put one foot in front of the other. Many men lost their shoes during the march.

An eerie postscript to the battle involved Brigadier General Paul J. Semmes. The brave commander may have had some premonition of his death, or perhaps he was just being prudent. Semmes wrote to a friend a few days before the battle, requesting the friend to renew his life insurance policy. Semmes' mortal wound on July 2, came one day before the policy's expiration date. The Georgian lingered for a week until he was claimed by death on July 10. It is not known if the policy was renewed.[56]

The three days of battle at Gettysburg resulted in more than fifty thousand combined Confederate and Union casualties, the most ever on American soil. The official report of the Army of Northern Virginia's medical director, Surgeon L. Guild, listed a total of 430 killed, wounded, and captured out of some 1,300 men engaged from Semmes' Brigade. The report only listed the number killed and wounded for the following individual regimental regiments, thus the discrepancy in brigade and regimental totals:

> 10th Georgia (86) – 9 killed, 77 wounded
> 50th Georgia (78) – 10 killed, 68 wounded
> 51st Georgia (55) – 8 killed, 47 wounded
> 53rd Georgia (87) – 15 killed, 72 wounded[57]

Between July 1 and July 5, the 50th Georgia lost at least 122 men at Gettysburg, with the vast majority on July 2. Of this number 21 were killed, including Lieutenant Colonel Kearse; 8 were mortally wounded; 43 were wounded; 24 were wounded and captured; and 26 were captured.[58]

The above count includes eleven wounded or sick Wiregrass men captured by the Yankee cavalry on July 4 during an attack on the slow-moving wagon train near Cashtown Gap. Another nineteen severely wounded 50th Georgians fell into enemy hands after being left behind in field hospitals. Two regimental surgeons remained to care for the men, and they also became prisoners. Regimental staff and individual company losses were as follows:

Regimental Staff (3) – 1 killed, 2 captured

Company A (8) – 2 killed, 1 wounded/captured, 5 captured

Company B (6) – 1 killed, 2 wounded, 1 wounded/captured, 2 captured

Company C (8) – 1 killed, 1 mortally wounded, 4 wounded, 2 captured

Company D (12) – 3 killed, 1 mortally wounded, 6 wounded, 1 wounded/captured, 1 captured

Company E (11) – 2 killed, 1 mortally wounded, 4 wounded, 2 wounded/captured, 2 captured

Company F (14) – 1 killed, 3 mortally wounded, 5 wounded, 5 wounded/captured

Company G (14) – 4 killed, 1 wounded, 4 wounded/captured, 5 captured

Company H (13) – 1 killed, 4 wounded, 5 wounded/captured, 3 captured

Company I (16) – 3 killed, 2 mortally wounded, 5 wounded, 3 wounded/captured, 3 captured

Company K (17) – 2 killed, 12 wounded, 2 wounded/captured, 1 captured[59]

The Slow Withdrawal into Virginia: July 5-14

Yankee cavalry harassed General Imboden's lumbering seventeen-mile-long wagon train during the slow-moving retreat, destroying scores of wagons and taking hundreds of prisoners. The remaining wagons reached Williamsport, Maryland, about forty miles from Gettysburg, early on July 6. To his dismay, Imboden learned that Federal cavalry had destroyed the pontoon bridge at Falling Waters, some six miles farther south. Heavy rains raised the normally shallow Potomac River to ten feet above fording, and a small cable ferry at Williamsport provided the only immediate option. The ferry, however, could carry no more than two wagons per trip. Another bridge would have to be built.

During the day, Brigadier General John Buford's Federal cavalry attacked Imboden's stalled column at Williamsport. A brief but deadly firefight ensued. Darkness and Confederate reinforcements ended the fighting, but the wagon train was far from secure. Also on July 6, Lee's cavalry reached Hagerstown. After a heated skirmish with Federal cavalry, the Confederates took control of the town and the immediate area.

General Lee formed his army into a defensive line, with its back to the Williamsport and Falling Waters crossings, until a new pontoon bridge could be constructed at Falling Waters. The Confederate cavalry and infantry took positions in a general north/south line of battle that extended from the Hagerstown area to the Potomac River. For the next several days, while Confederate engineers built strong entrenchments along the eight-mile line, Rebel defenders guarded against an attack. During the delay, most of the buildings in Williamsport were converted into temporary hospitals for the thousands of wounded Southerners.

One of the wounded was Sergeant William Jones of Company K. The Brooks County soldier had been placed in an ambulance shortly after his surgery on July 5. Upon arrival at Williamsport, Imboden decided the cable ferry was not suitable and the wagon train would have to continue south and later cross at Falling Waters, after the completion of the replacement pontoon bridge. For Jones and some of the other wounded soldiers, the bone-jarring trip had already proved too much. They refused to go any farther in the wagons. Jones described his gut-wrenching decision: "A goodly number of us decided that our condition was such that it would be impossible for us to make the trip, and were placed in a hospital and left to the mercy of the citizens of the town." The Wiregrass soldier and many other badly wounded men remained behind in Williamsport when Lee's army crossed back into Virginia. Jones nearly died, but he recovered only to spend the next eight months in prison at Point Lookout, Maryland.[60]

Meanwhile, General George Meade's equally exhausted army moved slowly in its pursuit of the retreating Confederates. Lee's strong defensive positions would be difficult to assault and gave Meade great concern. The Federal commander did not want to jeopardize his earlier great victory with a failed attack.

Captain William O. Fleming, Company F, hurriedly penned a brief letter to his wife as the Southerners waited behind their entrenchments. Fleming described the terrible battle at Gettysburg:

> God has in great mercy has still spared my life to my little family.
>
> On the 2nd of July we were engaged in the most terrific battle of the war, the battle of Gettysburg. The slaughter was tremendous on both sides. At the end of the day we occupied the battlefield & continued to do so on the third & until 4 o'clock P.M. on the 4th.
>
> At this hour we contracted our lines a little. On the night of the 5th we commenced falling back to this place, which we have done with very little annoyance from the enemy.

Our lines are again along the famous Antietam creek. It is not supposed that Gen'l Lee intends to recross the river. He is getting ready it is thought for another advance.

The army has suffered severely but what is left is in good spirits.

Our brigade was engaged in one of the most desperate charges of the war on the 2nd & suffered severely. The grape and canister from about 16 pieces mowed down our men. I give you the casualties in my company which please let those concerned know/I am sorry I have not the time and opportunity to give you a detailed account of all we have passed through.

Lt. Ballard was shot within a few feet of me through the right breast. His wound the Dr. says is mortal. He is no doubt dead ere this. He has died a noble death. An officer could not have acted more gallantly. Lt. Maxwell has already returned to duty. He was struck by a grape shot on the arm which bruised & caused it to swell considerably. It is yet very purple. At the earliest opportunity I will write you a long letter. Another great battle may be fought in a few days. Send this to father as I can not write to him at this time. Kiss over & over again my dear little ones for me.

Yr aff husband

Wm O. Fleming[61]

Skirmish at Funkstown, Maryland – July 10

The Federal cavalry periodically probed the Confederate defenses near the river. On July 9, the enemy appeared in force across Antietam Creek. Longstreet rushed Semmes' and Anderson's Brigades to support J. E. B. Stuart's artillery batteries. Billy Pendleton described the movement of the regiment and the ensuing firefight:

At sundown we turned left, marched two miles, and camped in an apple orchard, on Antietam Creek, near the place of the battle of the year before. Across the creek was Funkstown, Maryland. In the course of the morning we were marched across the creek and through the town, and saw a Confederate battery on a hill. We formed in line of battle and advanced. At the same time both batteries opened up. While advancing Lieutenant Sharp was sent out on skirmish line and soon became engaged with the enemy's skirmish line. My line was in a farm yard, under fire of skirmishers, behind stones and a fence. I saw a hen and some chickens, which made me homesick.

During this time Lieutenant Sharp was fighting bravely, but soon was ordered to retreat to the farmyard. Sharp was angry at being recalled. Then some men started firing but we couldn't see the enemy. I was sitting with Colonel [Major] McGlashan, Captain [Lieutenant] McCalb [McCall], and others. After a while a bullet hit Captain McCalb [McCall] in the cheek, and he had to go to the rear. A little later when I happened to look down the line I saw a man from Thomas County killed dead. He was the only man killed in that place. We stayed there until sundown, and then were withdrawn to the same camp, across the creek in the orchard, where we stayed two days in line of battle, behind a stone wall.[62]

The 50th Georgia suffered at least nine casualties in the heated skirmish, including the death of Private Jeremiah Joyce, Company K. Lieutenant John G. McCall, also of Company K, received a frightful gunshot wound to the face. The ball ripped away three-fourths of McCall's lower right jaw. After being hospitalized for a few weeks in a Richmond hospital, he received a sixty-day furlough and returned home to Quitman, Georgia, to convalesce. The injury would keep McCall from the field for the rest of the war.[63]

After two days, the 50th Georgia moved through Sharpsburg to a new position "down the creek" and camped. Pendleton recalled: "The next morning we went further, formed in line of battle, and built breastworks of logs. We were there for nearly a week. Lee hoped Meade would attack, but he didn't, so there was no more fighting there. While waiting we heard that Vicksburg had fallen on July fourth. I was very much discouraged and thought that if Meade attacked we would be defeated."[64]

A few days after the skirmish at Funkstown, Captain Fleming briefly made reference to it in a letter to his wife: "We had quite a severe fight the 10th at Funktown. J. M. Glover of my Company was slightly wounded in the arm. He has already returned for duty."[65]

Major General George Meade issued orders for his army to attack the Confederate lines at 7 a.m. on July 14. Confederate engineers had fortunately completed a pontoon bridge across the river at Falling Waters the previous day. The ambulances and wagons were the first to cross. The water level had dropped just enough for the men of Ewell's Second Corps to gingerly wade across the chest-high river. Longstreet's First Corps crossed the bridge at Falling Waters into Virginia around daylight on the 14th, closely followed by Hill's Third Corps. Henry Heth's division of Hill's corps served as rear guard as the slow-moving procession of men and wagons crossed the river. Heth's men fought off a Federal cavalry attack just as the last of the army crossed into Virginia.

Lieutenant James Kinchen Hilliard, Company C. Second Lieutenant James Kinchen Hilliard built the first hotel in Douglas, Georgia and was a well-respected member of the community. He also served as clerk of the Superior and Inferior Courts in Coffee County from 1856 to 1860. Hilliard was elected second lieutenant when the Coffee Guards were mustered into service on March 4, 1862. He received a mortal wound at the Battle of Gettysburg on July 2 and died in a Winchester, Virginia, hospital on July 17, 1863. He is buried in Stonewall Confederate Cemetery (Mount Hebron) in Winchester, Virginia. From *Ward's History of Coffee County.*

As the Yankees reached the banks of the Potomac on July 14, they observed numerous Rebel campfires on the other side. Lee had narrowly made his escape. Captain Samuel W. Fiske, a soldier-correspondent in the 14th Connecticut wrote of the Confederate escape: "At daybreak we give the word to advance along our whole line. We 'move upon the enemy's works.' Works are ours. Enemy, sitting on the other side of the river, performing various gyrations with his fingers, thumb on his nose."[66]

The 50th Georgia Regiment lost at least 136 men during the Gettysburg Campaign, with most falling during the fierce fighting on July 2. The rest were primarily a result of the difficult retreat to Virginia, including the skirmish at Funkstown on July 10.[67]

William Ross Stillwell, 53rd Georgia, a courier for General Semmes and later Colonel Bryan, reported in a July 13 letter: "Our brigade and regiment is most all killed and wounded. The brigade has not more than five hundred and fifty or six hundred men. Lost over half. Our Reg has one hundred fifty." Lieutenant J. W. Taylor, 10th Georgia, wrote in a July 18 letter: "Our regiment has only 160 men present, officers and all, but they are as true as the needle to the pine, and will fight as long as there is a man left to fire a gun."[68]

After crossing the Potomac into Virginia at Falling Waters, the bone-tired 50th Georgia survivors stayed about a week in the Shenandoah Valley to rest and recuperate. The Wiregrass men received a surprise during their stay, as described by Billy Pendleton: "We had a wonderful rest and we received some shoes, sent from Richmond. They had come from England, run through the blockade to Wilmington, North Carolina. They were the first pointed shoes I had ever seen."[69]

The 50th Georgia then marched south, passing between Berryville and Winchester and finally reaching Front Royal. From Front Royal the men crossed the Blue Ridge Mountains into Culpeper County. A soldier in the 53rd Georgia Regiment noted in an August 13 letter to his father that the brigade had been camped near the Rapidan River for about one week, "laying still, resting and recruiting." The soldier also reported: "I weigh at present, 122 1/2 lbs. It's from 16 to 20 lbs less, than I weighed last winter. This summers marching to Pa. and Md. has jerked all the flesh off of me." The regiment later continued on to Waller's Tavern, located between Gordonsville and Richmond, where it remained for several weeks.[70]

By the end of July, Colonel Goode Bryan had formally assumed command of the brigade. Colonel John B. Weems recovered from an illness and resumed command of the 10th Georgia; Colonel Edward Ball recuperated from his Chancellorsville wounds and returned to the 51st Georgia; Colonel James P. Simms remained in command of the 53rd Georgia; and Major Peter McGlashan retained temporary command of the 50th Georgia.[71]

Several senior officers in the 50th Georgia advanced in rank. Captain Fleming became a major on July 30 and then less than a month later he moved to lieutenant colonel. Lieutenant Colonel McGlashan was promoted to colonel with an effective date of July 31.[72]

Private William J. Evers, Company E, had received a serious wound on July 2, and yet survived the harrowing wagon trip to Virginia. He wrote a letter to his wife from his Staunton, Virginia hospital bed:

> I write you a few lines to let you know that I am verry feeble at this time but I am better than I have bin. I feel hopefull My Dear that I shall get over my wound. If I could get home so that I could have your attention I would [be] a grate deal better satisfied. I have wrote to uncle to try to get me home and I thought the letters I wrote to him mite fail to go and I would write you a few lines so that you would get some of them. I know that it is a long trip for your father or him to come hear but I want to get home so bad I cant help asking it of them. I ask the doctor if I was to write for some of my people to come after me if he thought I could get a furlow and he said he reconed so and I wrote as soon as I well could. I think if I had some assistance I could get home once moore. I want you to be as well composed about me as you can. Remember that same kind that has protected me all the time is just as able as ever. I feel that the Lord has bin gracious to me and hope he will be with me still. I want to put my trust in him for help so be as well reconciled as you can. I trust that I shall see you again. I am at Stanton general hospital at No 2 Ward C. I must come to a close by saying I remain your loveing husband until death.
> Hospital No 2 Ward C
>
> W. J. Evers
> If no one cant come after me write soon. Direct your letter Stanton general.[73]

The August 27 hospital roll showed Evers as "present." A doctor's note reported, "Evers is improving." There was no further record of William J. Evers, so it was not known if he ever returned home or recovered from his wound.[74]

Although the Army of Northern Virginia suffered a historic defeat at Gettysburg, the spirits of the men of the 50th Georgia still remained relatively high as they rested at Waller's Tavern. The Wiregrass men had performed heroically on the battle's second day. These battle-hardened veterans would soon be called upon again; this time, they would endure some of the war's harshest conditions in the hills of East Tennessee.

Fifty-two-year-old Colonel Goode Bryan was an 1834 graduate of West Point and a Mexican War veteran. He commanded the 16th Georgia Regiment, Wofford's Brigade, at Gettysburg. The day after Paul Semmes' wounding, Bryan assumed temporary command of Semmes' Brigade, and when Semmes died, Goode Bryan became brigade commander. The native Georgian received a promotion to brigadier general on August 29, 1863, and led the brigade through the 1863-64 Tennessee and Overland Campaigns. Bryan's health began to fail in the summer of 1864, and he officially resigned his commission on September 20, 1864. Bryan returned to Georgia. He died in 1885. Courtesy of the U.S. Army Military History Institute, Carlisle, Pennsylvania.

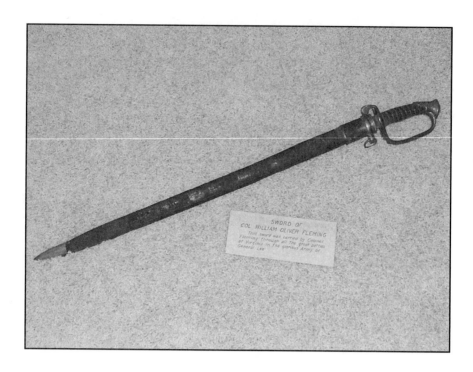

Infantry officer's sword carried by Lt. Colonel William Oliver Fleming while serving in the 50th Georgia Infantry Regiment. Fleming survived the war and became a well-respected judge in the area. Courtesy of William L. Fleming, Sr., great-grandson of William O. Fleming, Bainbridge, Georgia.

T he men of the 50th Georgia enjoyed their brief encampment near
Waller's Tavern, Virginia. Lieutenant William Pendleton recalled: "The
men often went to town to buy things at a store. I saw there a clerk who
was a Jewess, the first woman clerk I had ever seen. It was the middle of
summer and we had watermelons, a great treat."[1]

Although the Wiregrass soldiers were safe from battle for the time
being, deaths from illness and disease continued to plague them. On August
28, Sergeant Arthur Davis, Company C, succumbed to pneumonia in a
Richmond hospital. A few days later, on September 1, Private Wilson Algier,
Company H, died from liver and lung disease at his home in Colquitt County.
One week later, on September 9, Private William Riggs, Company G, died
from typhoid fever in a Richmond hospital.[2]

During this period, two Federal armies stirred up trouble in
Tennessee. Major General Ambrose Burnside's Army of the Ohio captured
Knoxville on September 3. Then, on September 8, Major General William
S. Rosecrans' Army of the Cumberland pushed General Braxton Bragg out
of Chattanooga and into Georgia. If they could keep Bragg out of
Chattanooga, the Federals would control much of Tennessee and disrupt
major Confederate communications and supply routes.

In response to these threats, General Lee detached General James
Longstreet and the divisions of Generals John B. Hood and Lafayette
McLaws to reinforce Bragg in northwest Georgia. The relative tranquility
of camp life at Waller's Tavern came to an end for the 50th Georgia in
early September, when the men received orders to cook rations and prepare
to march. William Pendleton remembered the move: "We marched to
Hanover Junction and got on a train to go to Richmond. It was a freight
train and so crowded inside that I rode on top with Captain Bill Smith
[William A. Smith, Company I] all the way to Richmond, where we arrived
at night. The next day we marched through Richmond, crossed the James
River and camped, then went on to Petersburg on the train.[3]

Captain Andrew J. McBride, 10th Georgia, described an exciting
incident during the trip from Petersburg:

We boarded cars for, we knew not where. We were crowded for standing room on flat cars and inside and on top of box freight cars. As we passed slowly by Salem, N.C., long and continuous cheering was kept up by each company and regiment, and the trains moved slowly past about one hundred college girls, who were standing by the railway waving handkerchiefs and throwing flowers. Miss Mildred Lee, daughter of Robert E. Lee, was near the center of the long line of lovely girls, and was pointed out and named by her companions, and I doubt if [a] human being ever received a tribute of respect and devotion more sincere or heartfelt than was given to that lovely girl by the battle-scarred veterans of the Tenth Georgia regiment that day.[4]

After leaving North Carolina, the train took Goode Bryan's Brigade through Augusta, Georgia. The brigade finally rolled into Atlanta on September 19, four days after leaving Petersburg.

Much of Longstreet's Corps reached Atlanta and headed on to Ringgold, Georgia, before Bryan's Brigade arrived. These troops took part in the bloody Battle of Chickamauga, but Bryan's men did not arrive in time to participate. Captain McBride recalled their good fortune: "My recollection is that we reached Atlanta Saturday, the 19th of September; that we marched up to the courthouse square, now the capitol, and bivouacked for the night. No train being ready to carry us on to Chickamauga, the ladies of Atlanta came in great crowds to see us, bringing flowers and an abundance of eatables."[5]

The brigade left by train for Chickamauga the next day. McBride reported: "The great battle was being fought as we were speeding over the Western and Atlantic railway. Before we left Atlanta, the wounded from Saturday's battle were coming in, and at every station we saw wounded and dying." Upon reaching Ringgold, the men disembarked at a location near the battlefield known as Greenwood's mills. A grim situation greeted them. Hundreds of wounded and dying soldiers lay collected beside the railway, awaiting transport back to Atlanta.[6]

Lieutenant Colonel William O. Fleming penned a brief letter to his wife shortly after the 50th Georgia arrived:

Bivouac 50th ga Regt

Near Ringgold

Sept. 20th 1863

My dear Georgia
    We, that is the Brigade, arrived at this point about an hour ago. The men are now cleaning up their guns & cooking rations preparatory to marching to the front. Our army is about 12 or 15 miles distant.
    Yesterday there was quite a heavy engagement, A number of our wounded took the cars from this point to Atlanta to day.
    I spoke to one of the wounded of the 29th Geo. Regt, Col. Yonge. From his statement the fighting must have been very severe. Col. Yonge & Lt Col Mitchell are both wounded. Rosencrans is falling back before us but I am afraid not so much because [being] driven as to secure a formidable position.
    This has been his tactics heretofore. This Brigade will reach the front I suppose to-morrow & will take part in the fighting.
    The two Brigades of our Division that are ahead have already been engaged. . . .
    I applied for 5 days leave of absence on our way here but it was refused me. If it had been granted I could have been at home two or three days & reached here about the same time the Brig did. There is no telling now, if I live, when I will get home.[7]

The battle had been an overwhelming Confederate victory. Major General William Rosecrans' beaten army retreated toward Chattanooga. On the morning of September 21, the men of the 50th Georgia made their way across the grisly battlefield and joined the rest of McLaws' division in pursuit of the retreating enemy. The men marched all day and camped close to Chattanooga that night. The Confederates resumed their pursuit toward the city early on the morning of September 22.

    Following upon the success at Chickamauga, General Longstreet recommended to General Bragg that the numerically superior Confederate force move north of Chattanooga and cut off the rear of the retreating Federals. Instead, Bragg decided upon a siege of the city. The Southerners took up positions and began entrenching as they reached the outskirts of Chattanooga.

    The Rebel lines stretched about six miles around the city in a semicircle. The lines ran from the base of Lookout Mountain on the left to the Tennessee River on the right. Hood's division, now commanded by Brigadier General Micah Jenkins, occupied the far left. McLaws' division and the division of Brigadier General W. H. T. Walker's moved into position from left to right. Confederate artillery stared down on the city from Lookout Mountain.

Bryan's Brigade defended a position in the center of McLaws' division in Dry Valley, about three miles from Chattanooga and one and one-half miles from Lookout Mountain. The men of the 50th Georgia built breastworks from timber and dirt and then provided support for the artillery batteries. The Confederates laid siege to the city while each side took turns cannonading the other. Billy Pendleton recalled, "We remained in this position about a month. I got sick after a little while. We had nothing to eat except sour cornmeal and bacon. I was not sick enough to be sent to the hospital, but wished I could go home."[8]

Bragg attempted to force a Federal withdrawal from Chattanooga over the next several weeks. The efforts failed, because enemy supplies and reinforcements continued to flow into the city from points beyond the reach of Rebel firepower. The Federal strength grew, and the Confederates lost their earlier numerical advantage.

Private John L. G. Wood, 53rd Georgia Regiment, described the day-to-day monotony of the siege in an October 12 letter to his aunt: "We have cool weather this evening. It sprinkled rain this morning, then cleared off, but looks like rain this evening." Wood continued, "Both sides are in line of battle. There has been some cannonading on our left, this evening. There was considerable cannonading this morning, which sounded as though it was in the yanks rear. It seemed to be a good ways off. We have cannonading on one side or the other every day. We are well fortified here. Our company is at present working on the breastworks. We have a splendid position, and plenty of men and artillery. All we ask them to do, is to attack us."[9]

Other than pulling occasional picket duty, the 50th Georgians avoided significant action during the siege. On October 16, Private Francis M. Boon, Company B, suffered the regiment's only reported battle wound at Chattanooga. The Ware County soldier lost two fingers on his left hand from artillery shell fragments.[10]

Longstreet Heads for Knoxville: November 4 – November 17

On November 3, Bragg ordered Longstreet to take his force of less than twenty thousand men toward Knoxville and drive Major General Ambrose Burnside's Army of the Ohio out of East Tennessee. Burnside commanded a force of about twenty-three thousand, but these soldiers were scattered throughout the region.

The next evening, Bryan's Brigade withdrew from its position near Chattanooga and headed toward Knoxville. On November 5, the 50th Georgia reached Tyner's Station, located a few miles east of Chattanooga, and packed into rail cars for the ride to Sweetwater, which lay northeast of Chattanooga and a little over halfway to Knoxville. The regiment reached Sweetwater the next evening and went into camp. The men rested for the next few days while Longstreet's command waited for supplies and rations.

Chronic delays and bureaucratic bungling prevented supplies and rations from reaching Longstreet's men in a timely fashion. These deficiencies would haunt his command throughout the East Tennessee Campaign and lower the morale of his men. Longstreet's Chief Commissary Officer, Major R. J. Moses, and Assistant Quartermaster, Captain Frank Potts, later sent scathing reports to the Chief Commissary Office detailing numerous examples of poor quality of supplies and a lack of responsiveness to the needs of the army.

Captain Potts reported: "We reached Sweet Water 30 wagons short of the transportation allowed us, while all our supplies were delivered at the railroad terminus 8 miles off." Potts continued, "While we were numerically short of transportation, the condition of what we had was beyond all question the worst I ever saw; wagons frequently breaking down, mules just able in a large proportion of cases to carry their harness, harness much worn, and many teams without collars or saddles."[11]

On November 12, after almost a week at Sweetwater, Longstreet's advance elements reached Loudon, located northeast on the Holston River. The enemy had burned the bridges across the river, so Longstreet ordered his engineers to construct pontoon bridges below Loudon at Huff's Ferry. Early the following morning, Bryan's Brigade arrived near Loudon, and the 50th Georgia soldiers caught some rest as the engineers built the pontoon bridges. By late afternoon, the sky turned dark and stormy. Rain soaked the men, and turned the roads into mud. The soldiers spent a miserable night as they huddled against each other to block the blowing wind and rain. Despite the inclement weather, Longstreet's engineers completed the pontoon bridges by November 15.

Jenkins' command crossed first, followed by McLaws' men. After the 50th Georgia crossed the river, they slowly marched northeast toward Knoxville along a narrow road over high hills. Sucking clay clung to the men's shoes every step of the journey. The next morning, Longstreet ordered McLaws to move his division quickly by the Kingston Road in an attempt to cut off Burnside's withdrawing troops at a crossroads about one mile west of Campbell's Station. If McLaws reached the intersection first, the Confederates could block the enemy before they reached Knoxville, about sixteen miles to the east. The division arrived at the junction just minutes after the main body of Federal troops had passed. Having escaped Longstreet's trap, the Yankees set up strong defensive positions east of the intersection.

Longstreet's lead troops collided with General Burnside's rearguard just east of Campbell's Station. The heated fighting lasted the rest of the afternoon and into the evening. Although exposed to enemy artillery for several hours, Bryan's Brigade held a reserve position and did not actively participate in the engagement. Billy Pendleton recalled the 50th Georgia's limited involvement in the skirmish: "We were formed into line of battle in some woods, so we thought there would be a battle. The firing kept up for some time. We were ordered to advance; we were in a field with a Yankee battery on a hill a quarter of a mile away. We advanced as if we were on dress parade, until the firing was too hot, then we lay down flat in the field, and nobody was killed. It was now about sundown. We lay on the ground until dark, when the enemy withdrew. We then camped all night in the woods."[12]

The attempt to catch Burnside before he reached the safety of Knoxville failed. The only options left were to attack the Federal fortifications or lay siege to the city.

Still undecided, Longstreet headed toward Knoxville the next morning. By late evening, his tired and hungry men arrived about two miles from Fort Loudon. McLaws deployed his division with the right resting on the north bank of the Holston River. Bryan's Brigade formed in reserve on "an open high hill" on the right near the Kingston Road. The brigade remained in this position for the next three days.[13]

The Federal defensive perimeter around Knoxville consisted of fortifications on a series of heights circling the city. Fort Loudon occupied a hill at the northwest corner of the perimeter. The Confederates had designed and partially constructed the earthwork earlier in the war, before it had fallen into Union hands.

On the afternoon of November 18, McLaws ordered Major General Joseph B. Kershaw's Brigade to assault and occupy a troublesome advance line of enemy breastworks, located on a hill about one thousand yards in front of the fort. Brigadier General William P. Sanders, a thirty-year-old Federal cavalry commander, occupied the entrenchments with several hundred troops. After several attacks, Kershaw's men finally drove the stubborn enemy back to the fort from the advance line of breastworks and occupied the vacated position. During the fight, the gallant Sanders received a mortal wound, and the popular Union officer died the next day. In his honor, Burnside changed the name of the fort from Fort Loudon to Fort Sanders.[14]

The removal of the advance Federal entrenchments allowed McLaws to improve his position. Kershaw's Brigade anchored the far right of the line, resting on the north bank of the Holston River. The brigades of Brigadier General

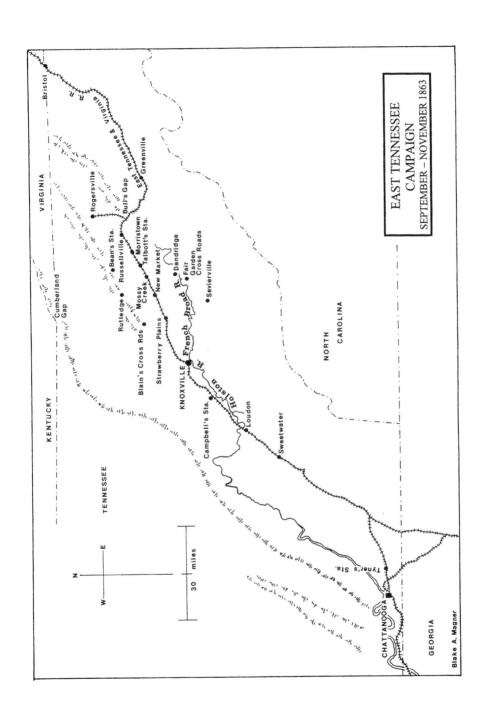

EAST TENNESSEE
CAMPAIGN
SEPTEMBER – NOVEMBER 1863

Blake A. Magner

Benjamin G. Humphreys and Brigadier General William T. Wofford lined to the left. Bryan's Brigade remained in reserve on the right.

Longstreet hoped that Burnside would give up the city and retreat. Over the next few days, both sides attempted to better their positions. Heavy skirmishing occurred, but no major offensive movements took place. On November 20, the 10th Georgia Regiment crossed to the south side of the Holston River on flat boats and drove the enemy from the heights overlooking the river, immediately opposite McLaws' position on the north side. The remainder of Bryan's Brigade crossed the river later that day and occupied the heights. This position gave Bryan's Confederates a commanding view of Fort Sanders. The brigade crossed the river several more times before they rejoined McLaws' division northwest of Fort Sanders on November 27. [15]

Attack on Fort Sanders – November 29

On November 23, General Bragg telegraphed from Chattanooga that he had been attacked and may need assistance. Bragg's urgent message prompted James Longstreet to abandon the time-consuming artillery siege. Instead, he planned an infantry attack to drive the Yankees from Knoxville.

Longstreet decided to concentrate his effort on Fort Sanders. The fortification comprised a salient in the Union defenses. Union engineer Captain Orlando M. Poe described the place as "a bastioned earth-work, built upon an irregular quadrilateral, the sides of which are, respectively, 125 yards southern front, 95 yards western front, 125 yards northern front, and 85 yards eastern front." The walls were originally constructed to a height of six to eight feet. A twelve-foot wide ditch surrounded the works. This ditch barrier was three to four-feet deep. About eighty yards from the northwest bastion, the level ground dropped off into a steep wooded ravine. Shielded from the view of the defenders inside the fort, the drop-off made a perfect staging area for an attack. Longstreet believed his numerically superior forces would quickly overwhelm the fort's small group of defenders. The Confederates could then use Fort Sanders as a base for further attacks to completely drive Burnside from the city. [16]

Burnside also knew that Fort Sanders was a weak link. A week earlier, on November 17, the Union commander ordered Brigadier General Edward W. Ferrero, 1st Division, IX Corps, to prepare the defense of the fort. Ferrero assigned the responsibility to Lieutenant Samuel N. Benjamin, 2nd U.S. Artillery. Lieutenant Benjamin immediately went to work but found the task to be daunting. The fortifications were poor at best. Benjamin reported: "Here a bastion work (square) had been commenced, and was about one-fourth finished on three fronts—fourth front not commenced. It afforded no protection."[17]

For more than a week, Benjamin's men built breastworks and dug two rows of rifle pits between eighty and thirty yards in front of the walls. The line ran from the northwest corner of the fort south to the Holston River and east toward the city. Four "20-pounder Parrotts, four light 12-pounders, and two 3-inch guns" were placed in position to sweep all approaches to the rifle pits. The crafty officer observed, "The northwest bastion was the point to attack, if the rebels could be induced to attack the earth-work instead of the low breastwork or rifle-pit thrown up by the men." Benjamin continued, "I placed the guns so as to sweep thoroughly all approach to the rifle-pits, leaving a large section without fire in front of the salient of the northwest to induce them to assault there."[18]

Yankee pickets crouched in the newly dug outer rifle pits and kept up a lively fire with nearby Rebel sharpshooters in the Confederate lines. Benjamin's men stuck brush along the top of the parapet to shield themselves from view of the deadly snipers. Bags and barrels covered the embrasures to allow the men to see out but not to be seen from the outside. The defenders dug the ditch in front of the fort to a depth of more than eight feet in some locations. The height from the bottom of the ditch to the top of the parapet reached twenty feet in places, including the northwest bastion. The ditch depth and width required planks and scaling ladders to get across and then up the almost sheer vertical walls.

To cap off his defenses, Lieutenant Benjamin constructed an abatis in front of the ditch and stretched telegraph wire between tree stumps about a foot above ground level. Benjamin described his handiwork. "In front of the northwest bastion I made an abatis, concealed from the enemy by a small rise of ground, and inside of the abatis a little entanglement of telegraph wire."[19]

In spite of Benjamin's tireless work, the fortifications remained vulnerable. The garrison was defended by about 125 riflemen from the 79th New York and an equal number of artillerists from Benjamin's battery. They faced four thousand of Longstreet's hardened veterans. Benjamin observed, "The work . . . was very weak, and should have fallen by the ordinary chances of warfare."[20]

Longstreet wavered on the timing of the assault. Over a period of several days he ordered and then rescheduled the attack on several occasions. On November 28, Longstreet ordered the assault for dawn the next morning. The Confederate commander denied a final request by General McLaws to postpone the offensive. Longstreet could not afford any further delays.

McLaws planned for Humphreys' Mississippi Brigade to lead the right flank of the attack while Wofford's Georgians came in on the left. Three regiments from Bryan's Brigade would follow closely behind Humphreys' men in support. Prior to the main assault, a smaller strike force, including the 10th Georgia, would move out ahead to capture and occupy the Yankee rifle pits. Kershaw's Brigade would be held in readiness to advance to the right of the fort as soon as the works were taken.

McLaws believed the attack would be successful against the fort's northwest bastion because the Confederates could assemble under the safety of the wooded ravine and then sprint a short distance to the walls of Fort Sanders. The Confederate commanders did not realize that Lieutenant Benjamin invited an attack against this point. In planning for the assault, the Confederates scouted the fort and observed the Federal defensive preparations. Both Longstreet and his artillery commander, Colonel E. Porter Alexander, viewed the activities from a safe distance. Nevertheless, the Confederate commanders failed to appreciate the critical modifications Union soldiers made to the trench in front of the fort. Longstreet and Alexander concluded that the ditch posed no serious impediment and the works could be taken without the use of ladders. This miscalculation would later prove disastrous.[21]

A cold hard rain fell throughout the day of November 28. Lieutenant Billy Pendleton recalled talking to a friend about the impending battle:

> I was at a little spring with Captain [George W.] Waldron, one
> of my best friends in the war. We were talking about the reports
> of an attack, and Waldron had a feeling that he would be killed.
> I told him to throw off the feeling, but we were both depressed.
> It continued to rain hard all day. My blanket got very wet. At
> sundown the ground was so wet that there was no place to
> sleep, so I took two fence rails, put a tent cloth and the blanket
> over them and slept on the rails. The men built big fires.[22]

That night, at about 11 o'clock, the small Confederate strike force, including the 10th Georgia, rushed forward and captured the Federal pickets in their rifle pits outside the fort. They occupied the rifle pits and waited for the main assault. During the night, temperatures dropped and the wet ground began to freeze. [23]

At about 3 a.m., as the men of the 10th Georgia occupied the enemy rifle pits, the 50th, 51st, and 53rd Georgia Regiments were awakened in preparation for the attack. The men formed into columns of regiments immediately behind Humphreys' Brigade. The capture of the enemy rifle pits had alerted the Federals inside the fort of an impending attack and destroyed any element of surprise. The Yankees strengthened their works in anticipation of the inevitable assault. Union soldiers ingeniously poured buckets of water over the parapets. The water froze, making an icy slick surface along the walls.

The main Confederate force slowly moved toward the point of assault. Men tripped and fell over fallen trees and stumps in the darkness as they struggled to feel their way. In the gloomy pre-dawn dampness, the main force reached the edge of a clearing about two hundred yards from the fort. The men lay or crouched shivering on the cold freezing ground. It was impossible to stay warm without fires. Each man was left to his own thoughts in the eerie silence.

Shortly after 6:30 a.m., just before the silhouette of the fort appeared at first glimmer of light, a brief Confederate artillery barrage commenced to signal the assault. About four thousand freezing, tired, and hungry veterans grimly rose up in the eerie fog and mist. Billy Pendleton recalled, "The order to charge came. 'Order—Forward, guide center'." With a piercing Rebel yell, the Southerners rushed over the icy ground toward the northwest bastion. The sharpshooters in the captured enemy rifle pits fired at the embrasures in the fort to drive away the artillery gunners and to give covering support for the attackers.[24]

Pendleton described the frantic rush toward the fort: "Waldron and I were running along together and he was wounded. I thought he was killed. Just after this we struck telegraph wires that had been laid." Another 50th Georgia officer wrote, "We had to ascend the hill on which the fort stood, encountering obstacles at almost every step, such as abattis, or tops and branches of trees in rows and heaps, and telegraph wires stretched above the ground as nearly as high as the knees. Our progress was necessarily slow, and this gave the enemy time to recover from the suddenness of the attack."[25]

The attackers were exposed to a merciless fire of musketry and canister from the Union defenders. "Many men were in a ditch around the fort," recalled Billy Pendleton, "I saw a Union shell drop into the ditch and explode. The men and I lay down flat behind the ditch, and were under the deadliest fire that I saw in the whole war."[26]

One Wiregrass soldier recalled that "once, in the advance, there was a slight wavering of the line for a moment, as the firing was now heavy, and some of the men began to lie down. Seeing this Gen. Bryan, our brigadier, cried out: 'Forward, forward, forward men! forward!' And adding some words of exhortation which I do not now remember." As Bryan urged the men onward, Adjutant Tompy Roberds "immediately rushed out in front of the line waving his sword, crying: 'General, we will forward! Come on men!' This, as is usual in such cases had quite an inspiriting effect on those who saw it, and we immediately followed him in the rush upon the fort."[27]

The inspirational leadership had limited impact. Roberds soon fell with a severe wound to his right knee, and the attack turned into mass confusion as men continued to jump or fall into the ditch. To their shock, the Rebels found the sides between eight to ten feet deep in places. The icy vertical slopes made climbing out of the ditch almost impossible. The men resorted to standing on one another's shoulders or ramming bayonets into the sides to get a hold to climb out of the ditch and up the walls of the fort. All the while, "the enemy stood on the wall and fired into the struggling mass below. They lighted the fuses of shells, hand grenades and all kinds of infernal appliances and threw them over among the doomed men in the ditch."[28]

The few attackers who clambered out of the ditch and scaled the walls were cut down or captured. The murderous Federal fire pinned down other Confederate units in the open area before they could reach the ditch. It was chaos and terror for the Southerners.

Perhaps spurred on by the exhortations of General Bryan and Lieutenant Roberds, Sergeant-Major James S. Bailey of Company B made it onto the enemy works. Bailey grabbed the 50th Georgia battle flag from its hesitant color bearer, bravely climbed the wall and defiantly waved the flag as balls flew all around him. Miraculously, the shots missed and the defenders captured the Ware County soldier. Although initially thought killed, Sergeant Bailey would soon be on his way to a Union prison.[29]

A 10th Georgia soldier reported on the heroism of Sergeant Bailey and others he witnessed:

> A little after daylight we witnessed the grand assault on Fort
> Loudon, and saw many heroic deeds, our orders being to pick
> off the enemy while the assault was being made. . . . Sergeant
> Bailey, of the Fifty-First [Fiftieth] Georgia, a native of Maine,
> who came to Georgia about 1860, climbed over the shoulders
> of his comrades and hoisted the colors of his regiment on the
> fort, calling to his comrades to join him. Only a few did this,
> among them Adjutant T. W. Cumming, of the Sixteenth
> Georgia, and ten or twelve men entered the fort. The entire
> party was captured.[30]

Although the Southerners fought gallantly, devastating enemy fire forced them to retreat. The ditch trapped many soldiers who were killed, wounded, or captured. As the Rebel offensive collapsed, the retreat proved as deadly as the attack. Enemy musketry and canister raked the men as they ran back across the open field toward the cover of the wooded ravine. Lieutenant Pendleton reported on his narrow escape: "We jumped up and dashed down the hill, then cannon opened up on us. I was caught in the telegraph wire and fell forward down the hill."[31]

As McLaws' troops tumbled back, George T. Anderson's Brigade of Hood's division made a belated attempt to take the works but was quickly dispatched to the rear. After only twenty minutes, Longstreet mercifully called off the assault. The Confederates suffered 813 casualties, including 129 killed, 458 wounded, and 226 captured. Federal losses in the fort were only 13. The attack had been an unmitigated disaster.[32]

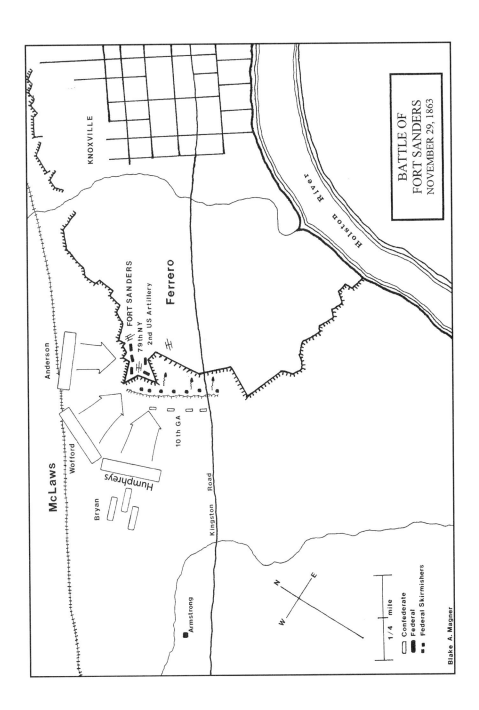

BATTLE OF
FORT SANDERS
NOVEMBER 29, 1863

KNOXVILLE

Holston River

FORT SANDERS

Ferrero

79th NY

2nd US Artillery

Anderson

McLaws

Wofford

10th GA

Humphreys

Bryan

Kingston Road

Armstrong

N
E
W
S

1/4   mile

☐ Confederate
▬ Federal
▪▪ Federal Skirmishers

Blake A. Magner

Billy Pendleton reported that the 50th Georgia survivors "retreated down to a low field, protected from fire, and the firing ceased. We were ordered to build fires and we got breakfast. My blanket was frozen. In an hour or so we were taken back to the position on the hill that we had come from."[33]

Both sides called a truce shortly after the failed attack to collect the dead and wounded, the latter to prevent their freezing to death in the bitter cold. The sight in the ditch was appalling. Rebel dead and wounded were heaped on top of one another. Corporal John Watkins of the 19th Ohio Battery described what he saw as he looked over the parapet into the ditch:

> As soon as the firing stopped I went up and got on the parapet to look at them. And such a sight I never saw before nor do I care about seeing again. The ditch in places was almost full of them piled one on top of the other. . . . They were brave men. Most of them Georgians. I would give one of the wounded a drink as quick as anybody if I had it. That is about the only thing they ask for when first wounded. But at the same time I wished the whole Southern Confederacy was in the ditch in the same predicament.[34]

Andrew McBride of the 10th Georgia recalled, "Between our lines a great many wounded were in danger of freezing to death, and it was a merciful and timely act for General Burnside to call for a truce. We soon had roaring fires between the lines and the surgeons of both armies worked fast and faithfully to alleviate the sufferings of the wounded and dying, and the ambulance corps began to bear away to either side the blue or the gray, the bodies of their dead comrades."[35]

One of the rescued Confederates was Billy Pendleton's friend, George Waldron. The Company A commander survived his wound and remained with the regiment until the end of the war.

After the failed assault, General McLaws recognized Goode Bryan for his leadership and bravery when he wrote, "The conduct of General Bryan during the siege and afterward, and especially at the assault, is worthy of all praise. He led his brigade to the work, and, after seeing that all was done that could be done, was the very last to retire." General Longstreet would later remove McLaws from command for inadequate preparations that resulted in the disastrous assault.[36]

A lack of official reports on the battle from Bryan's regiments makes the specific positions and roles of three of the regiments subject to interpretation. Major John M. Spence temporarily commanded the regiment in place of Colonel McGlashan, who was at home in Thomas County on furlough.[37]

Colonel Edward Ball, 51st Georgia Regiment, filed a brief brigade report on behalf of General Bryan six weeks after the battle. Ball reported:

The assaulting column moved forward about daybreak, and though our advance was obstinately contested by the enemy, we gained the summit of the hill and reached the work with a comparatively small loss; but, owing to the obstructions with which the work was surrounded, it was found impossible with appliances in our possession to carry it, and the troops were therefore withdrawn. A great many men and officers having fallen into the moat in attempting to scale the walls of the work, and being unable to get out again when we retired, were consequently taken by the enemy. The loss in this brigade on that occasion was 8 officers and 19 men killed, 15 officers and 106 men wounded, and 5 officers and 59 men missing, making a total of 28 officers and 184 men, and an aggregate loss of 212 men and officers killed, wounded, and missing.[38]

The 50th Georgia lost at least forty men in the debacle, including seven killed, four mortally wounded, fourteen wounded, twelve captured and one missing. Seven of the wounded were later captured in hospitals or along the withdrawal route from Knoxville. Wiregrass men killed or mortally wounded during the assault included Second Lieutenant Banner Guy, Company A; Sergeant W. C. Ganas and Private O.W. Selman, Company D; Privates Moses I. Guyton, Matthew M. Dukes, and John H. Crosby, Company H; Private William W. Fulford, Company I; First Sergeant William H. McMurray and Privates Sherod Ingram and William G. Newton, Company K; and the popular regimental adjutant, Lieutenant Rueben T. "Tompy" Roberds.[39]

Adjutant Roberds remained on the field after the Rebel withdrawal until enemy litter bearers carried him to a field hospital. A Federal surgeon amputated his leg above the knee. The day after the battle, many of the wounded were exchanged. The Yankee surgeon warned Roberds that he risked death if moved, and the Lowndes County officer decided to remain in the care of the enemy. Sadly, his condition worsened and he died a few days later, on December 3.[40]

In a condolence letter to Roberds' widow three months after the battle, General Goode Bryan recalled his heroic actions and death:

Tis with feelings of the most profound regret, I announce to you the death of your husband Lt & Adj Roberds of the 50th Regt Ga Vols. He received his wound in the attack on the Fort at Knoxville, the morning of the 29th of November last. In the assault no Officer of the Brigade acted more gallantly, cheering the men and nobly leading his regiment to the charge. The last time I saw him was a few moments before he

received his wound. He came to where I was standing, urging
forward some timid men who had laid down, waving his
sword, and his noble bearing accomplished, what my
authority could not affect. For the timid ones caught some
spirit from his enthusiastic bravery, and followed him to the
Fort. No officer in his Regiment can surply [take] his place,
for on the march[,] in the camp and in the battle field he was
a man of mark. Chancellersville, Gettysburg and Funckstown
bear witness to this gallantry and dearing.

May he who Tempers the weather to the shorn lamb
Temper this sad affliction of his providence to your good and
may your life be spared to Tell his child of the gallant deeds
of its lost Father, and teach it to emulate his virtues. [41]

Roberds' widow received a startling letter from a Theo S. Christ a
few months after the war ended. Doctor Christ, formerly head surgeon
with the 45th Pennsylvania Regiment, had amputated her husband's leg.
Because Roberds and the doctor were both Masons, the Federal surgeon
made a promise as a brother Mason to keep Roberds' personal effects and
return them to Mrs. Roberds, if possible. Dr. Christ wrote:

Dear Madam—
At the request of your deceased husband & the trust he
placed in me before he died as a brother Mason—I now fulfil
a promise made to him, to write you as soon as mail
Communications were opened with the South; Such being the
case, it is with a Sympathizing heart I convey to you his last
words—he was wounded through the right knee joint, Nov.
29, 1863 while leading his regiment in making a charge on
Fort Saunders, at Knoxville East Tennessee—he Suffered
excruciating pain when he was brought to my Hospital, upon
examination & consultation with other Surgeons', we found it
necessary to Amputate his leg, which was done just above the
knee, after I had amputated his limb, I placed him in one of
the Wards along with other wounded, the first two days he
done pretty well & said he felt comfortable, but on Dec. 2nd/
63 I found he was failing rapidly & he died on the following
day—Dec. 3rd at 4 A.M. I visited him day & night every few
hours; and all was done for him that Surgical or Medical
attendance could do—reaction never fully took place. When
he was brought to the hospital which was Several hours after
he was wounded he was very pale, & was very unwell, &
Said he had been Sick—he was rational when he died—he
talked of his wife & daughter constantly, & wished he could

See you both once more—he asked me to take charge of his little effects that he had in his pockets, & if I could ever Send them to you to do So—I have carried them with me Since then & have them Still, & will retain them until I hear from you & you give me the directions to Send them to you. Soon after I amputated his limb, I wrote you a letter at his request, & sent it to you by flag of truce from Knoxville, did you receive it—I will await an Answer from you to this & will answer all questions you want to know as far as I can.[42]

Mrs. Roberds had never received the letter Doctor Christ referenced. The two corresponded for some time and the compassionate doctor provided as much information as he could recall about her husband's last hours.

Born near Allendale, South Carolina, in 1834, Reuben Thomason "Tompy" Roberds attended the Citadel. In 1859, he moved to Valdosta, Georgia. In late 1860, the voters elected Roberds as the city's first mayor. When war came he joined the 50th Georgia. He received a promotion to adjutant of the 50th Georgia Regiment in the spring of 1863. On November 29, 1863, Lieutenant Roberds suffered a severe wound to his right knee during the attack on Fort Sanders. Enemy litter bearers carried Roberds from the field to a Federal hospital, where a surgeon amputated his leg above the knee. The Lowndes County soldier died a few days later, on December 3, 1863. He was buried in an unknown grave in Knoxville. Period photograph probably taken just before the war began. Courtesy of the Lowndes County Historical Society and Museum, Valdosta, Georgia.

A few hours after the failed morning assault, Longstreet received a telegram from President Davis advising that Union troops had forced General Bragg from Chattanooga. Davis requested that Longstreet's army attempt to rejoin Bragg. Later that day, Longstreet received word from Bragg that his army had retired to Dalton, Georgia, and that Longstreet's Corps must depend on its own resources. Based on this information, Longstreet decided to remain at Knoxville for the time being.

After the withdrawal from Fort Sanders, Bryan's Brigade, including the 50th Georgia, returned to their position in reserve. Andrew McBride reported that the brigade "went back and occupied position in line near the Armstrong house, about three-quarters of a mile from Fort Sanders, our right resting on the west [north] bank of the Holston River." The exhausted men remained at this location for a few days to recuperate.[43]

On December 1, the Rebels captured an enemy courier. He carried a message to Burnside that three columns of Federal reinforcements advanced to his relief, "one by the south side, under General Sherman: one by Decherd, under General Elliott, and one by Cumberland Gap, under General Foster." This news, coupled with a shortage of ammunition and supplies, convinced Longstreet that he should abandon the siege of Knoxville.[44]

Longstreet concluded, "As our position at Knoxville was somewhat complicated, I determined to abandon the siege and to draw off in the direction of Virginia, with an idea that we might find an opportunity to strike that column of the enemy's forces reported to be advancing by Cumberland Gap." The next day, the Confederate commander ordered a withdrawal toward Virginia.[45]

Bryan's Brigade crossed to the south side of the Holston River on December 3 and held the heights to allow the rest of the army to withdraw. Longstreet's wagons and ambulances, loaded with supplies and wounded soldiers, slowly lumbered away from the city and headed northeast toward Rogersville. Before daybreak the next morning, Bryan's Brigade withdrew from the heights south of the city and crossed back to the north side of the Holston River. That evening, under cover of darkness, the brigade joined the rest of McLaws' division in the withdrawal from Knoxville and headed toward Rogersville. The command moved east over the next few days, passing through Rutledge, Bean's Station and Mooresburg.

When Longstreet withdrew from Knoxville, many sick and wounded had to be left behind in area hospitals or along the withdrawal route. These invalids included at least twenty-two Wiregrass Georgia soldiers who fell into enemy hands. Most would be imprisoned in the newly opened Federal prison at Rock Island, Illinois. Some would never return to their homes.[46]

Of the 50th Georgia men left behind during the withdrawal from Knoxville, three died in Rock Island Prison (Privates John J. Akins, Benjamin Ellis, and Berry Gray of Company I) and five died in Federal hospitals (Private James J. Rewis, Company C; Private J. J. Lewis, Company G; Private John P. Crosby, Company H; and Corporal Kasper G. Duncan and Private Samuel R. Edwards, Company K). Privates Thomas Mack and Dominic McCafferty of Company C took oaths of allegiance to the U.S. Government and were released at Nashville on January 16, 1864.[47]

Longstreet's army spent the next four months marching up and down the hills of East Tennessee. The men faced a lack of adequate supplies and rations combined with miserable weather. Members of the 50th Georgia remembered the winter of 1863-1864 as one of the worst of the war.

McLaws' division arrived near Blevins' farm on December 9, about six miles from Rogersville. The Confederates remained here for several days to forage for much-needed provisions. Federals in the area captured Privates Joshua Ellis and Benjamin F. Hays of Company C along with William J. Pope, Company E. Ellis and Hays spent the rest of the war in Rock Island Prison. Private Pope died in the prison from chronic dysentery on March 22, 1864.[48]

The men constantly suffered from exposure to rain and aching cold, poor rations, and inadequate clothing and shoes. Andrew McBride of the 10th Georgia described the conditions: "The winter of 1863-64 was cold— ice, sleet, and snow all the time; most of the time there was not a tent; the men were thinly clad, poorly shod and were marching and fighting nearly all the time during the months of November, December and January. We spread one oil cloth on the ground, a blanket upon it, two of us would lay down together on them, cover ourselves with a single blanket and oil cloth over it and often be awakened by sleet, rain or snow falling on our heads; we would cover our heads and sleep sound."[49]

Billy Pendleton also recalled the harsh conditions and his narrow escape from the enemy: "My shoes were almost worn out, and Captain [George] Fahm gave me a pair which no one needed. They were very uncomfortable and the ground was frozen. We marched all night and crossed a creek which was terribly cold. The next day Burnside followed us. My shoes hurt me and gave me a bad blister. Captain Fahm gave me his horse, which saved me from being taken prisoner."[50]

General Longstreet described his supply problems in a December telegram to Adjutant and Inspector General Samuel Cooper. The First Corps commander estimated that his corps totaled about twenty thousand, while Burnside's total force amounted to about twenty-seven thousand. The

Federals controlled the railroad and the river from Bean's Station southwest to Knoxville. Longstreet also stressed the hardships for his men, stating: "We are in some distress for want of shoes and other clothing, and are in want of horseshoes, and are a little short of ammunition." The Confederate commander closed with a request for shoes: "I hope that the Quartermaster-General will send us a good supply of shoes at once; about one-half of our troops are without them."[51]

On December 12, Longstreet learned a pursuing enemy column of three brigades of cavalry and one brigade of infantry was located to the west at Bean's Station. He decided to try to capture the smaller Federal force.

The next day, Longstreet ordered Brigadier General Bushrod Johnson to march his division as rapidly as possible toward Bean's Station. Heavy rains fell during the day and into the night and turned to sleet and snow by morning. Although the roads became a muddy mess, Johnson's men labored forward as best they could. At about 2:00 a.m. on December 14, the Confederates caught the unsuspecting Yankees camped near the river. The piercing Rebel yell shattered the still of the pre-dawn morning while fire from the musket flashes illuminated the darkness. The surprised enemy fell back and quickly threw up defenses.

Longstreet ordered the remainder of McLaws' division from their camp west of Rogersville to reinforce the attack. Andrew McBride reported: "The morning we marched from near Rutledge [Rogersville?] to meet the Yankees at Bean's Station we were covered with snow nearly a foot deep when we walked and has [had] rough marching through it all day." Kershaw's Brigade, supported by Bryan's Brigade, hit the enemy's left flank, and the rest of McLaws' division followed in reserve.[52]

The battle lasted all day. By nightfall, the Yankees withdrew southwest to Blain's Cross Roads. The Confederates owned a solid victory and secured the area to supply important forage for Longstreet's hungry men and horses. Bryan's Brigade reported one killed and one wounded. The injured soldier, Private John Bryant of Company H, received wounds in his left side and foot but later returned to his company.[53]

That night, the brigade camped in an open field. The Wiregrass soldiers spent a miserable evening trying to keep warm on the cold, frozen ground. The brigade remained in the area for a day or two, and then crossed to the south side of the Holston River.

On December 16, Longstreet informed General Cooper that, "The enemy have escaped in the direction of Knoxville. We captured sixty-eight of his wagons, about forty loaded with sugar and coffee and other stores. We had a sharp skirmish at this place, losing about 200 men, chiefly from

Johnson's division. . . . We shall be obliged to suspend active operations for want of shoes and clothing."[54]

The lingering effects of the failed assault against Fort Sanders resulted in Longstreet formally removing General Lafayette McLaws from "further duty with this army" and ordered him to "turn over command of the division to the senior brigadier present [Brigadier General Joseph Kershaw]." Longstreet brought charges against McLaws for neglect of duty associated with the disastrous attack against Fort Sanders on November 29. The indignant division commander quickly responded by requesting that the charges be investigated "at an early date by a court of inquiry or court-martial, or they be withdrawn and I restored to duty at once."[55]

In early 1864, a general court-martial found McLaws guilty on one of three charges. The court found the division commander guilty of not providing a means of crossing the ditch or adequately informing his officers of the ditch conditions. However, McLaws was found not guilty of failure to provide adequate supporting fire for the assault force by his sharpshooters and not guilty for failure to designate a select body of men to lead the assault. In May 1864, Adjutant and Inspector General Samuel Cooper overturned the court-martial sentence and ordered that General McLaws be immediately returned to duty with his command. Nevertheless, McLaws would not return to Longstreet's corps, and General Kershaw remained in command of McLaw's former division.[56]

Bryan's Brigade left Bean's Station on December 20 and headed south for Russellville. That day, the enemy captured Privates Peter Hays, Company C, and John Weeks, Company D. Private Hays died of pneumonia the next year in Camp Chase, Ohio Prison. Private Weeks remained in Rock Island Prison until taking an oath of allegiance to the U.S. Government on October 18, 1864.[57]

December 21 brought more changes to the 50th Georgia command structure. Second-in-command Lieutenant Colonel William O. Fleming resigned after being elected to the Georgia Assembly. Major Pliny Sheffield replaced Fleming. Captain John M. Spence, Company C, replaced Sheffield as major. Alfred A. Smith became captain of Company C.[58]

That same day, the brigade crossed the Holston River at Long's Ferry. The men arrived at Russellville two days later and went into winter quarters. Located south of the Holston River and along the East Tennessee and Virginia Railroad, the site offered good forage for the army. Longstreet ordered his cavalry to set up a defensive line between his winter quarters and Knoxville. Lieutenant Pendleton described the 50th Georgia's campsite: "We built huts of logs. It was a fine forest, mostly of chestnut trees. I, and the man who cooked for me [Private John B. Cribb], built one for the two of us." The men remained at this location for the next two months. [59]

The Wiregrass soldiers tried to make the best of another miserable winter. Pendleton recalled Christmas dinner: "Christmas day we had nothing to eat, so three of us got together to see what we could do for dinner. One man had a bacon rind, so we turned our empty flour bags inside out and shook them into water, and put the bacon rind into it to make soup. This was our Christmas dinner, but Lyman Hall a corporal said, 'Well boys, this is right smart better than no eatin.'"[60]

The 50th Georgia Regiment lost another veteran officer on December 30. Captain Jeremiah Wells, Company H commander, had suffered a serious gunshot wound at Chancellorsville. During the Tennessee Campaign, the Colquitt County officer allowed his name to be placed for election to the Georgia Assembly and, like Lieutenant Colonel Fleming, Wells resigned upon learning of his election and returned to Georgia. Lieutenant Lott Townsend succeeded Wells as captain.[61]

The weather became unbearably cold by the end of December as temperatures dropped below zero. The bodies of Rebel and Yankee soldiers killed in skirmishes during that period froze quickly and had to be pried from the icy ground. The temperature reached a record 29 degrees below zero on New Year's Day. Everything froze halting all combat operations. Wagon wheels became anchored to the ground. Men burned every available scrap of wood to try to stay warm. Forage became extremely difficult to find. The deadly temperatures proved exceedingly harsh for many of the already weakened sick and wounded soldiers as well as livestock.[62]

Many men whose shoes had fallen apart wrapped their feet with rags to protect them against frostbite or cuts from rocks and ice. Others created makeshift moccasins from fresh cowhide. Private Daniel I. Walden, 10th Georgia, recalled the harsh conditions and the unique footwear:

> After the repulse at Knoxville we moved on up through east Tennessee towards Bristol. The railroad had been destroyed and we had to live on the country. We went into winter quarters near Russellville about the last of December, 1863. The first of January, 1864, was about as cold a new year as I ever experienced. But we were not allowed to remain long in any one place during the whole of that severe winter. Through mud and rain and snow and ice we were constantly marching and fighting. The men were thinly clad and poorly fed. Many were barefooted. The writer (and he was only one of many) would cut out a piece of fresh beef hide, sew it around the fight [foot] with the hair side in and wear it continually until it wore out.

When it got set to the foot and hardened there was not getting it off except by cutting it off. Sometimes we had something to eat and sometimes we didn't. Sometimes we would get a little corn, dig a hole in a log, but [put] the corn in, pound it with a pestle and make bread and hominy.[63]

The ingenuity of the men to try to keep warm during the terrible winter was remarkable. Private John L. G. Wood, a drummer in the 53rd Georgia, described his living quarters, which may have been more advanced and comfortable than most:

My winter quarters are built on the side of a sloping hill, close to the band and between it and regt., between 12 and 14 feet long, 5 feet wide, and 6 and one half high. It is plenty roomy for two and no more. The part of our shanty up the hill is about one foot in the ground and slopes off to the lower end, which is just on the surface of the ground. Our house and chimney are both built together. The insides of our chimney, including the back, and sides, are dug [out] of the ground. The mantle piece is three feet high. The funnel of our chimney commences a foot from the ground, and extends to 2 or 3 feet of the top of our house. Our house is gabled up, like a common country house, with large saplings and is covered with a good yankey fly. Our door is in the south side of our shanty, in the middle, is two feet wide, By three and one half long. Our mansion is daubed with mud, and is nearly airtight. The chimney forms the west end of our house, draws fine, and throws out more heat then any one I have seen. It is as warm and snug as any house. Our furniture consists of two stools, a wash basin, and two shelves, our cooking utensils of one oven, and 2 or 3 little boilers, or eating utensils, one wooden bowl, one old pocket knife, and two spoons. We have a small cistern to hold water at the north end of our menagerie. It is dug out of a large poplar with an axe. It is arranged so that we catch water in a gutter when it rains, and pours all the water into our cistern. It is covered up to keep from freezing, and has a spout to run the water out. When it runs too full, we have a hole bored in the bottom of it, and a hollow spike drove in it, so that the spike extends from the cistern, to the inside of the house, so when we want a drink of water we can pull the peg out of the end of the spike and draw as much as we want inside of our house. The cistern saves us the trouble of going one half mile for water. Our house has the praise of being the most comfortable one in the brigade. The boys call it the Spotwood House.[64]

While the troops endured the harsh winter, Colonel McGlashan returned from furlough and resumed command. The regiment would occasionally march west toward Knoxville on reconnaissance missions and return. Skirmishing occurred regularly along the lines. Union soldiers captured Privates Stephen G. Hobbs, Company E, and Robert O. Rouse, Company I, on January 5. A terrible wound to the face on November 29 had partially blinded Private Rouse. Both men languished in Rock Island Prison until they were exchanged near the end of the war. A few days later, Captain David P. Luke, Company I commander, resigned due to serious illness. William A. Smith replaced Luke as captain of the Berrien Light Infantry.[65]

On January 28, Longstreet's men decisively routed enemy cavalry southeast of Knoxville in a heated skirmish near Sevierville at Fair Garden Cross Roads. The 50th Georgia did not actively participate in the action. The Federals withdrew toward the city. This engagement effectively ended the fighting in Tennessee for Longstreet's army.

A flurry of promotions occurred within the 50th Georgia in February. In Company B, young Billy Pendleton became first lieutenant and took over command of the company. John L. Wheeler became first lieutenant and William Hudson became first sergeant in Company C. In Company D, George W. Chitty received a promotion to first sergeant. Company E promotions included George E. Fahm, captain; William P. Brown, first lieutenant; Richard W. Baston, second lieutenant; and Charles F. Hudson, first sergeant. In Company H, Andrew McGlashan, brother of Colonel Peter McGlashan, became second lieutenant and replaced Hiram Gay, who had resigned to become captain of the Colquitt County Militia. Company I advancements included Lemuel P. Goodwin, replacing the recently deceased Daniel D. Gaskins as first lieutenant; George M. Clayton, second lieutenant; James H. Kirby, second lieutenant; and Berry J. Connell, first sergeant.[66]

Desertions in Longstreet's army increased during the harsh winter. The desertion rate became a point of concern and authorities took severe measures to reduce the occurrences. A 10th Georgia soldier recalled the fate of one poor deserter:

> I have no distinct recollection of but one of these executions, and I cannot remember the name of command of the victim. The division was formed in kind of a hollow square. A coffin was placed on the open side of the square and a group of men stood near. We were too far away to hear, but could see plainly. A squad of some dozen soldiers marched up and stood in line facing the coffin. The prisoner knelt, blindfolded and with hands tied, near the coffin. Presently, we saw the soldiers aim, a report rang out on the frosty air and the poor fellow fell forward, dead![67]

In mid-February, Longstreet moved his command from Russellville southwest to New Market, near Knoxville. The Rebel infantry pushed to within six miles of Knoxville. The Confederate commander considered another advance on the city, but lack of reinforcements forced him to withdraw up the valley toward Bristol. The army went back into winter quarters southeast of Bean's Station in an area near Bull's Gap.

Private John H. J. Brock of Company E fell into enemy hands on February 21. The Thomas County soldier died of typhoid fever in Camp Chase Prison in Ohio on January 1, 1865.[68]

In late February, General Longstreet marched his command west from Bull's Gap to Morristown. During the march, a sleet storm hit. "I was carrying my company's frying pan," recalled Billy Pendleton, "and put it up to protect my face from sleet."[69]

While at Morristown, three events occurred that left a mark in Pendleton's memory. The first happened while the regiment was on picket duty: "One day my regiment was sent ahead for picket duty near a school house. We had no tent so lay down at night in the open, and woke up the next morning covered with snow. Some of the men had never seen snow before, and that morning the whole regiment started snow ball fights; soon the entire brigade was having a snow battle with another brigade, led by a brigadier-general."[70]

The second event was the receipt of a thirty-day furlough. The excited young officer had not seen his family in a year. While he was away at war, the family had moved from Ware County to a farm near Valdosta, in Lowndes County.

The final event brought no joy to the young soldier. He recalled: "There were two deserters who didn't come back from their furloughs, one of them was in my company. They were tried by court martial and condemned to be shot. There were no mitigating circumstances for the man in my company, but the other man was pardoned, because all the officers signed a petition to Longstreet. My furlough came two or three days before the man was shot. I saw it in the paper on the way home."[71]

The unfortunate deserter from Pendleton's company was Private Isaac Morgan. Sergeant John W. Gaskins of Company I recalled Morgan's execution and that of two other men from the army: "There was three men shot in our army a while back for desertion[.] one belonged to the 21st Miss. Regt. one to the 22th Ga. and one to the 50th Ga. Regt. Co B[.] his name was Isaac Morgan[.] there was twelve guns to each which half of the numbers were loded with lead[.] the men that had to do shoot did not know who had the guns that were loded with lead. A. B. Dixon and Irvin Hendley from my Co. was detailed to shoot Morgan."[72]

It took Pendleton more than a week to reach Lowndes County. Although eagerly awaiting the reunion with his family, the young Company B commander also had the sad duty to inform others of the fates of their loved ones. "I was charged with the news to the families, of the death of the deserter, of the death of Adjutant Roberts [Roberds] in the enemy prison [hospital] in Knoxville, and about Sergeant Bailey who had been taken prisoner."[73]

Billy Pendleton described the joyous occasion when he finally reached home. He first saw his brother Charlie plowing the field, "and at first he didn't know me. I met Father near the house and Charlie ran on to tell the others. Old 'Aunt' Lizzie ran out screaming and threw her arms around my waist. Then came Mother and all the children running out, and I was home!" Pendleton continued, "While at home I went fishing a good deal with my father, and also spent much time telling them about the war. I was much pleased that my two dogs recognized me."[74]

At the end of the month, Longstreet moved the command southeast to Greeneville. The 50th Georgians remained in camp at Greeneville from March 1 to March 27.[75]

A number of promotions took place in the regiment during March. In Company A, Wryon F. Minshew became second lieutenant, and Lewis R. Thomas became first sergeant. In Company B, Hillary W. Cason received a promotion to second lieutenant. In Company C, Parrish Langford became second lieutenant. Simeon B. Lester of Company D received an appointment to second lieutenant. In Company F, Charles H. O'Brien became second lieutenant. Butler W. Leverett of Company K made second lieutenant.[76]

Billy Pendleton returned from his furlough while the regiment was still at Greeneville. He had an amazing bit of good news to share with the men. Pendleton passed through Savannah on his way back to the regiment. "I looked out of the window and there was Bailey [Sergeant James S.]; he had escaped from the enemy on the way to prison." The young lieutenant also received some good news: "Colonel McGlashan sent for me and told me that I was going to be made captain, promoted over Lieutenant [George] White."[77]

Longstreet finally received orders to return to Virginia. On March 27, the command began a northeasterly march from Greeneville toward Bristol. The 50th Georgia trudged along in bitter conditions for the next several days. Heavy snow fell during the march, making travel especially hard for the hungry, poorly equipped Wiregrass troops. The tedious journey continued until March 30, when the men finally reached the vicinity of Bristol and went into camp.[78]

The month of March had been bittersweet for the original 50th Georgia enlistees. As the men marked the beginning of their third year of service they must have wondered what still lay ahead. Most of the young men who had excitedly joined the cause two years earlier were now gone.

The sights and sounds of battle and death had become commonplace. Those who remained were hardened veterans.

A 53rd Georgia soldier expressed what many others were thinking in an April letter home: "It is the general opinion here amongst the troops, that the war will close this year. I hope their judgment is right. If this war was over I think I could content myself at home. I have seen as much of war, and the different parts of the country as I care."[79]

The 50th Georgia Regiment remained in Bristol until April 14. Lieutenant Pendleton recalled that the regiment took a train from Bristol to Lynchburg, Virginia, staying for the night before moving on to Charlottesville. The Wiregrass men camped a few miles from Thomas Jefferson's home at Monticello before marching on toward Gordonsville. They arrived near Gordonsville on April 18 and camped. The regiment remained there for the next few weeks.[80]

Sadly one Wiregrass soldier who did not accompany his 50th Georgia comrades from Lynchburg was Private Joseph Rawls of Company F. The Decatur County native contracted pneumonia and had to be hospitalized in Lynchburg. Rawls' condition deteriorated quickly, and he died on April 29. He was buried in Lynchburg.[81]

Private Joseph Rawls, Company F. Rawls contracted pneumonia on the move from Tennessee back to Virginia in 1864. He was hospitalized in Lynchburg, Va., where he died and was buried. Courtesy of Carolyn Herring Chason, Cairo, Georgia.

A few more changes took place within the 50th Georgia Regiment during April. Andrew McGlashan received a promotion to first lieutenant and adjutant to replace the deceased Tompy Roberds. Aaron Dowling became second lieutenant in Company A; William C. Dodd moved to first lieutenant in Company E; and Sergeant William E. Connell received a discharge upon being elected Judge of Ordinary Court in Berrien County.[82]

The 50th Georgia Regiment lost at least sixty-eight men during the harsh seven-month Tennessee Campaign. More than half (forty) of these casualties came during the disastrous November 29 attack on Fort Sanders. Most of the Georgians seemed happy to be back on familiar soil in Virginia. The good feeling would be short-lived as the conflict moved into its fourth and final year. The Army of Northern Virginia and the soldiers of the 50th Georgia faced their most desperate and brutal campaign of the war. Their next test would be in the tangled hell appropriately called "the Wilderness."[83]

Chapter Nine
The Wilderness
May 4–7, 1864

President Abraham Lincoln made a critical decision in March 1864 that would change the scope of the war in Virginia. Exasperated by previous lackluster commanders, Lincoln appointed Ulysses S. Grant as general-in-chief of all Federal armies. Grant had been successful in the western theater, and Lincoln hoped he would bring a fresh approach to the war in the east. Although Major General George Gordon Meade remained in command of the Army of the Potomac, the new general-in-chief decided to conjoin his headquarters with Meade.

The spring of 1864 opened with the two great armies facing each other across the Rapidan River in Central Virginia. As each side geared up for another campaign, General Robert E. Lee's Army of Northern Virginia continued to face worsening shortages of supplies, rations, and—most critical of all—new recruits. These conditions did not bode well for an army facing a Federal commander who was much more aggressive than his predecessors and who had seemingly limitless resources.

Still recuperating from their brutal winter in Tennessee, the men of the 50th Georgia savored the relative tranquility back in Virginia. On April 22, the regiment moved with Bryan's Brigade and the rest of Longstreet's command to the vicinity of Gordonsville.[1]

Several days later the First Corps camp bristled with excitement as men rushed about, preparing for the April 29 arrival of General Robert E. Lee, who planned to welcome back his "old war horse," James Longstreet. Cannons boomed and bands played to signal Lee's arrival. As their beloved commander rode through the wildly cheering throng, hardened veterans admiringly reached out to touch the rider or his horse, Traveller. Later, the soldiers marched smartly on review during a dress parade. Although many of the men wore tattered uniforms, they still exhibited a fierce pride and reverent bond with their commander.

One of Billy Pendleton's proudest moments occurred during General Lee's review of the 50th Georgia Regiment. The modest young officer simply wrote, "I led the first company. McGlashan was sick, but rode out on his horse. He told me later that I was the only one in the whole division who had

Lieutenant William Frederick Pendleton, Company B. Billy Pendleton had this picture taken in Savannah before returning to Tennessee in early 1864. From *Confederate Memoirs: Early Life and Family History William Frederick Pendleton [and] Mary Lawson Youg Pendleton* edited by Constance Pendleton.

saluted Lee correctly." After the war, Colonel McGlashan provided a more detailed account of the event, noting that he "was on horseback, stationed by General Lee on Traveller, as troops passed in review, when along came the Fiftieth Georgia in battle array, and in front of Company B walked young Captain Pendleton. As he passed, General Lee turned to Colonel McGlashan and asked, 'Who is that boy?' Colonel McGlashan said, 'That's Billie Pendleton.' General Lee answered, 'Well, he knows how to salute his general.'"[2]

Another warmly greeted arrival was Sergeant-Major James S. Bailey, who returned to his regiment after escaping from the enemy. On May 2, Colonel McGlashan wrote a letter to Inspector General Samuel Cooper, recommending that the gallant soldier be promoted to ensign and first lieutenant. McGlashan praised Bailey's courage, especially during the assault of Fort Sanders the previous November. His letter to General Cooper read:

> General,
> I have the honour to recommend for appointment as "Ensign"
> 50th Regt Geo Vols Sergt Major James S. Bailey; for the

following reasons, Viz The present Color Bearer "Elijah Paulk" who had only bore the Colors in <u>one</u> fight, the Assault on Knoxville Nov 29 1863; did <u>not</u> give Satisfaction to that position, on that occasion; Secondly, Sergt Major J. S. Bailey has ever been distinguished for great gallantry in every fight in which the regt has been engaged during the last two years. At the Assault on Knoxville Nov 29 1863, he was the only man of the Brigade who forced his way to the top of Fort Loudon & was there taken prisoner & afterwards escaped from the enemy; he is always "present for Duty" & worthy of the position. if appointed, I would request it to bear date from the 25th March last, when he took the Colors.

Very Respectfully
P. McGlashan Col. Commanding Regt[3]

General Goode Bryan strongly endorsed the request and immediately forwarded it on to Cooper. The well-deserved promotion became effective the following month.

By the beginning of May, the Army of Northern Virginia still remained in their winter camps near Orange Court House, south of the Rapidan River. The position ran in a southwest to northeast line. Lieutenant General Ambrose P. Hill's Third Corps held the left wing near Liberty Mills. Lieutenant General Richard S. Ewell's Second Corps anchored the right wing of the Rebel lines, which stretched eastward past Morton's Ford and west of Mine Run. Longstreet's First Corps remained southwest of the main lines near Gordonsville.

In the cool, pre-dawn darkness of May 4, the Federal vanguard moved out of their winter camps near Culpeper Court House and crossed the Rapidan River at Germanna Ford and Ely's Ford. George Meade's army headed southeast toward Wilderness Tavern. He had to move his army through a densely wooded area the locals called the "Wilderness." Thick stands of second growth trees, tangled underbrush, and briars blanketed this area. The dense foliage made normal military maneuvers impossible and limited cavalry and artillery operations to the few roads that crisscrossed the area. As they moved through the forest, many Yankee soldiers remembered their bad experiences in this infernal region from the Chancellorsville struggle the previous year.

Lee learned of the Federal river crossings by mid-morning. The Confederate commander believed he could negate Meade's nearly two-to-one numerical advantage if he caught the Federals in the tangled forest. Therefore, Ewell and Hill immediately left camp and hurried to intercept the enemy. Ewell's corps took the Orange Turnpike. Hill's men moved along the parallel Orange Plank Road, about two miles to the south.

As Ewell and Hill marched east, Longstreet's corps prepared to march northeast toward Richard's Shop, a small village on the Catharpin Road. The 50th Georgia and the rest of Kershaw's division left the Gordonsville area at 4 p.m. and marched about ten miles. The tired and hungry men bivouacked for the night at Brock's Bridge on the North Anna River.

Many of the soldiers had developed a strong religious faith during the war and often found opportunities for impromptu services. Billy Pendleton recalled such an occurrence that evening: "We camped for dinner in thick woods. . . . I was quite religious by this time. Everyone thought that there was going to be a battle, and at this dinner there were eight or ten of us who were leaders in Revivals. We got together to have a prayer meeting in the woods. One of the men, Norman McCloud, often called on me to pray, and then all would sing."[4]

Meanwhile, as darkness enveloped central Virginia, all of Meade's army had crossed the Rapidan River. However, the Union advance slowed to allow the supply wagons to catch up. Shortly after sunrise on May 5, Meade's troops renewed their march south. This march placed his army on a collision course with Ewell's and Hill's oncoming Rebels. Later that morning, lead elements of the two armies stumbled into one another, and the Battle of the Wilderness erupted in a roar of musketry and cannon. The fighting raged all day and into the evening until darkness put a stop to the struggle. The Confederates held on but desperately needed reinforcements from Longstreet.

Earlier that morning, Longstreet's corps marched out from the North Anna River and covered the sixteen miles to Richard's Shop as the battle raged in the Wilderness. By evening, the dust-covered and foot-sore men of the 50th Georgia fell out and tried to rest though Lee's much-needed reinforcements still had at least ten miles to go before reaching the battlefield.

Captain Andrew J. McBride, 10th Georgia, recalled the march: "On May 5 we made forced march toward the Wilderness. Late in the evening we could hear the ominous thunder of cannon. About 8 o'clock at night we halted and were ordered to cook up rations and be ready to march in two hours. Soon the fires were blazing brightly, lighting up the grand old Virginia forest for miles around us. Hurrying here and there across the long shadows of the majestic oaks which stood around us men were issuing ammunition and rations, others cooking or rubbing up their guns."[5]

Lee anticipated another enemy assault the next morning. Without reinforcements, the depleted Confederate lines could not hold for long. Lee sent urgent word to Longstreet to march as quickly as possible to reinforce Hill's battered and exhausted men. The situation was desperate.

Longstreet put his corps in motion after receiving General Lee's plea. Shortly after midnight, the men hurriedly broke camp, grabbed their gear and quickly marched northeast toward Parker's Store on the Orange Plank Road. The troops covered ten miles in less than five hours. Captain McBride described the grueling march: "about 12:30 o'clock on the morning of May 6th, we were ordered to march in quick time. About 4 o'clock the gray dawn began to break over the eastern hills, the stars to fade, sweet music of singing birds heralded the coming of smiling morn, and the air was laden with the perfume of the flowers of springtime. Boom! Boom! And then one continued long roar of cannon and musketry. Double quick, men! Double quick, and Longstreet's mules with a long and swinging trot went to the battle of the Wilderness."[6]

Before dawn on May 6, Union troops broke through A. P. Hill's beleaguered lines. Hill's men fell back toward the Widow Tapp House, where Lee had set up his headquarters. At about 6 a.m., just as the enemy reached the outskirts of Tapp's Field, Longstreet's men came rushing down Orange Plank Road at the double quick.

The Rebel reinforcements hustled past Parker's Store as they charged toward the fight. Colonel John W. Henagan's Brigade of Kershaw's division led the way on Longstreet's right with Major General John Gregg's Texas brigade of Field's division on the left. Their movement east on Orange Plank Road was slowed by the retreating men of Major General Cadmus Wilcox's and Major General Henry Heth's Third Corps divisions.

Bryan's Brigade, including the 50th Georgia, had some difficulty in getting into the fight. General Bryan reported: "After a rapid march of three hours reached the road and was immediately pushed to the front down the plank road. Some considerable confusion having arisen in a portion of Lieutenant General Hill's corps, the march of the brigade was much obstructed by stragglers from this corps, and was forced from the plank road into the woods in its march to the front." Bryan gave more detail of his difficulties moving his men into position:

> About a mile down the plank road from Parker's Store I was ordered to file to the right of the road and form a line of battle with my left resting on said road. Here again the discipline of the command was severely tried, for while forming line of battle in a dense thicket under a severe fire of the enemy the line was constantly broken through by men hurrying to the rear; but having advanced my sharpshooters, under the command of Lieutenant Strickland, of the Tenth Georgia, to the front, he checked the enemy and allowed me to form line of battle, the men forming quickly, notwithstanding the cry of the stragglers.[7]

The brigades of Henagan and Brigadier General Benjamin G. Humphreys fought the enemy along both sides of Orange Plank Road. Kershaw ordered Bryan to come up on Henagan's right. Kershaw reported: "That officer [Bryan], in obedience to orders, had pushed forward and driven the enemy in his front for some distance through the dense thicket which covered the country to the right of the plank road; but they being heavily re-enforced, forced him back to the line which Humphreys had by this time reached."[8]

Kershaw's three brigades stalled in the face of stiff resistance from Major General David B. Birney's 3rd division brigades commanded by Hobart Ward and Alexander Hays and Brigadier General Gresham Mott's 4th division brigade commanded by Robert McAllister. Kershaw sent an order for Wofford's Brigade to hurry forward. Unable to wait for their arrival, however, he ordered a charge. Kershaw described what happened: "I placed myself at the head of the troops and led in person a charge of the whole command, which drove the enemy to and beyond their original line and occupied their temporary field-works some half mile or more in advance." Kershaw's charge staggered the Federal lines and allowed his left to connect with the right of

The Wilderness area. This dense growth is just west of the Widow Tapp Farm. The Wilderness created havoc with both armies during the battle. The 50th Georgia Regiment fought in these woods on May 6. The trees were younger and the undergrowth thicker at the time of the battle. Photo by author.

Field's division. One continuous Confederate battle line now moved slowly east along each side of Orange Plank Road.[9]

Goode Bryan described his brigade's role in the charge: "At the command forward the gallant fellows sprang forward with a shout, driving back the enemy's first line without firing a gun. The second line of the enemy was behind a line of log breast-works, which checked for a moment our rapid advance, but after a few well-directed volleys the enemy broke from the entrenchments, the command pursuing to the distance of about a mile to a swamp."[10]

Billy Pendleton recalled that the Wiregrass men charged into the thick woods: "We were under heavy fire in a few minutes, and were 'in for it' for two or three hours." Fierce close-range fighting raged all around. Lieutenant Colonel Pliny Sheffield suffered a terrible wound that almost took off his right arm. As he lay on the ground, Sheffield directed two men to make a tourniquet with a handkerchief to slow the loss of blood until stretcher-bearers could carry him to a temporary field hospital. This quick thinking saved the Brooks County officer's life. The severe wound would lead to his resignation from the army in November and cause him great pain for the rest of his life. [11]

Bullets flew in all directions as the 50th Georgians and elements of Hancock's corps fired into one another at almost point-blank range. During a brief lull, Captain Quarterman Staten, Company G Commander, jokingly chided Pendleton, "Lieutenant, I saw you this morning and you smiled." The friendly, young lieutenant's smile from the march earlier in the morning had vanished as the struggle raged.[12]

General Longstreet's determined last-minute counterattack forced Hancock's men back to their original position near the intersection of Orange Plank and Brock Roads. Longstreet's veterans had reversed the battle's momentum and established a new front several hundred yards east of Tapp's Field.

By about 8 a.m., the Confederate counterattack lost momentum after two non-stop hours. Rebels and Yankees poured volley after deadly volley into one another from the thickets and the woods. Smoke from the gunpowder and the burning woods obscured sight as men fired blindly into the haze. The sounds of the struggle prevented the men from hearing orders. The battle became very personal as individual soldiers and small groups desperately fought on their own.

Late in the morning, Bryan's Brigade began to run low on ammunition. Billy Pendleton recalled the situation: "My orderly sergeant came up to me and said, 'My gun's busted.' I said 'Throw it down and pick up another.' Then Jerry Jeffords came and said, 'Our ammunition's out.' I didn't know what to do, but saw one of Longstreet's staff and told him and he said to send a man back. I sent Jerry Jeffords, and I can still see his long legs making for the rear."[13]

Bryan reluctantly ordered his men to withdraw to a better defensive position. The Georgia commander reported: "The enemy being re-enforced and my ammunition being reduced to only 5 rounds, I ordered the command to fall back to the enemy's log breast-works, which I held till relieved by General [Micah] Jenkins."[14]

After he was relieved, Pendleton reported that the exhausted Wiregrass men withdrew to an area in reserve "just out of reach of bullets" to rest and fill their cartridge boxes. The men stayed in the area "for 3 or 4 hours, then we were ordered back to where we had fought, but the battle had stopped. The trees were speckled like smallpox from bullets."[15]

Energized by his early success, Longstreet rode forward with members of his staff to reconnoiter the area in preparation for another all-out assault against Hancock's beleaguered troops. In an incident eerily similar to what had happened to General Stonewall Jackson a year earlier at nearby Chancellorsville, Confederate soldiers mistook the group of officers for Yankees and suddenly opened fire. Longstreet fell from his horse as blood streamed from a severe neck wound, and General Jenkins died immediately from a bullet to the head. The confusion associated with Longstreet's wounding stalled the proposed Confederate attack, and the

Field at western edge of the Widow Tapp Farm. Hancock's II Corps pushed A. P. Hill's men back to this area. On the early morning of May 6, the 50th Georgia arrived near this site with Bryan's Brigade and helped drive the Federals back toward Brock Road. Photo by author.

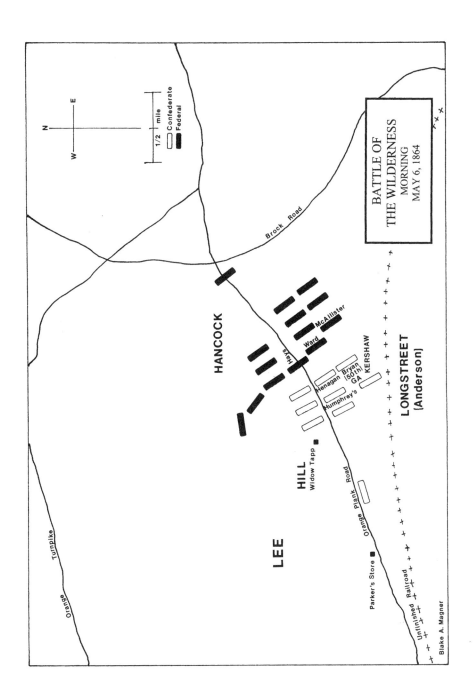

BATTLE OF
THE WILDERNESS
MORNING
MAY 6, 1864

Confederate
Federal

1/2 mile

N
W — E

Brock Road

HANCOCK

McAllister

Ward

Hays

Bryan
50th
GA

Henagan

KERSHAW

Humphrey's

LONGSTREET
(Anderson)

HILL

Widow Tapp

LEE

Parker's Store

Orange Plank Road

Turnpike

Orange

Unfinished Railroad

Blake A. Magner

delay allowed Hancock's forces to regroup and improve their entrenchments along Brock Road.

General Lee appointed General Richard Heron Anderson, a division commander in Hill's Third Corps, to temporarily assume Longstreet's command. Shortly after 4:00 p.m., Anderson launched an attack against Hancock, but the strong Federal works could not be taken. After brief fighting, the Southerners fell back. Bryan's Brigade did not participate in this attack.

The struggle continued until darkness finally forced a halt to the carnage. By about 8 p.m., after more than twelve hours of almost nonstop fighting, the Battle of the Wilderness effectively ended. Both sides were too exhausted and disorganized to mount an effective attack against the other. That night, the two armies camped among the dead and dying soldiers while the burning woods and underbrush crackled. Bryan's Brigade and the 50th Georgia moved to the far right (south) of the Confederate lines and camped near an unfinished railroad corridor.

General Bryan praised his men after the battle. "I cannot speak in too high terms of the bravery manifested by my command under the trying circumstances under which it went into the fights. Each brigade forming separately under a heavy fire; the line constantly being broken through while being formed; the dense character of the woods in which the line was formed rendering it impossible for either men or officers to see the character or numbers of the enemy we were to attack; all these things combined proved that both men and officers acted well and gallantly."[16]

That night, Grant decided that continued fighting at this location would be unproductive. The tangled forest had effectively neutralized his superior numbers. During the following evening, May 7, he began to withdraw his army from the Wilderness. The lead elements moved south along Brock Road toward the crossroads at Spotsylvania Court House, some ten miles away. If undetected, the Federal army could reach Spotsylvania Court House by sunrise the next day before Lee could react. The Confederates would then have to abandon the Wilderness position and fight on open ground. If Lee did not offer battle, Grant's army would have an unobstructed route to Richmond.

Although unsure of Grant's ultimate destination, Lee felt his army must stay between the Union army and the Confederate capital. He ordered the First Corps, now commanded by General Anderson, to march south toward the crossroads at Spotsylvania Court House in an attempt to reach the area before the enemy. Anderson's men withdrew to the rear at around 10 p.m. before heading toward Spotsylvania Court House. A. P. Hill's soldiers moved into the line to replace Anderson's vacated positions.

Because of the noxious smoke and stench, Anderson decided not to rest his men in the Wilderness and instead moved his command completely out of the area. Led by Kershaw's division, the men stumbled and felt their way in the darkness along a temporary trail until they reached Catharpin Road. Finally, the exhausted Rebels rested for about an hour at dawn before continuing the hard march toward Spotsylvania Court House.

The Battle of the Wilderness had no clear-cut victor. Lee's much smaller force had fought Grant to a stalemate, and he could arguably claim a tactical victory. However, Lee felt he lost a great opportunity to halt the Federals in the Wilderness. He might have claimed a clear victory, had it not been for the untimely wounding of General Longstreet and the subsequent loss of Confederate momentum. General Grant had been denied a victory. However, instead of retreating as previous Union commanders had done, Grant retained the initiative and moved toward Spotsylvania Court House.

Bryan's Brigade lost 31 killed and 102 wounded. The 50th Georgia suffered at least 21 casualties during the battle, including 4 killed, 2 mortally wounded, 13 wounded, and 2 captured. Lieutenant Timothy Kirkland, Company C; Private William L. Sellers, Company E; and Privates David J. Brice and John K. Exum, Company K, were killed. Privates Thomas Gill, Company E, and Stephen Williams, Company I, received mortal wounds. Second-in-command Lieutenant Colonel Pliny Sheffield suffered a serious wound that resulted in the amputation of his arm. The losses suffered by the other three regiments in the brigade are unclear. A soldier in the 53rd Georgia reported that his regiment "had 75 killed and wounded."[17]

After the battle, Lieutenant John L. Wheeler, Company C, sent a letter of condolence to Lieutenant Timothy Kirkland's brother:

> It becomes my painful duty to announce to you the sad intelligence that your brother Timothy was shot through the head and died instantly on the 6th inst., while in the front of his company doing his duty as nobly as ever a man did.
>
> I freely offer my sympathy with you and his family, and the entire company mourns his loss, for he was beloved by all. And we trust and hope that God has seen fit to call him to that world where trouble ceases and that he will there meet his brothers and family and friends.
>
> We buried him and his things are in some of the company's hands and as far as I can I will see that they are attended to. He had a one-hundred–dollar certificate that I know of. I do not know how much money he had. I do not think much, but he had some notes.[18]

As the two armies began withdrawing from the Wilderness, hundreds of dead and seriously wounded men remained on the battlefield. Fires continued to burn the woods and brush. Tragically, many of the wounded soldiers burned to death.

The 50th Georgians had little time to mourn their lost comrades as they trudged south. Over the next month, the Wiregrass men would march and fight almost nonstop as the two armies edged slowly toward the Confederate capital of Richmond. The next bloody engagement would be a short distance away at the crossroads of Spotsylvania Court House.

Chapter Ten
From Spotsylvania Court House
to Cold Harbor
May 8–31, 1864

R ichard Anderson's critical decision to march his tired men through the night allowed Lee's army to reach the crossroads at Spotsylvania Court House ahead of Grant. On May 8, Anderson's column reached Catharpin Road in the early morning and angled southwest to Shady Grove Road. The men then turned east on Shady Grove Road toward Spotsylvania Court House. At the same time, Major General Fitzhugh Lee's 3,500-man cavalry division lay barricaded across Brock Road north of the village. Lee's outnumbered cavalrymen blocked Major General Gouverneur K. Warren's V Corps' move to reach the junction before the Confederates. The Rebel troopers made their stand along a ridge, later known as Laurel Hill, opposite the Spindle farmhouse.[1]

The lead brigades of Kershaw's division reached Block House Bridge at the Po River by 7:30 a.m. After marching hard all night, the men of the 50th Georgia stopped about one mile southwest of Fitz Lee's position to catch their breath and eat breakfast. Then the rattle of musketry erupted to the northeast, so the Wiregrass men and the rest of Goode Bryan's Brigade hurriedly gulped down their cold food and prepared to move toward the sound of battle.

As his troopers tried to hold off the Federal V Corps, Fitz Lee pleaded for Richard Anderson to send reinforcements. Brigadier General James H. Wilson's Union cavalry division had already reached Spotsylvania Court House to the southeast, and a column of his horsemen moved north up Brock Road to threaten Fitz Lee's rear. Anderson immediately ordered Kershaw to rush the two brigades of Colonel John W. Henagan and Brigadier General Benjamin G. Humphreys, along with Major John C. Haskell's artillery battalion, to reinforce Lee's embattled position. He then ordered Kershaw's remaining brigades, led by Bryan and Wofford, to move east, circle around, and enter Spotsylvania Court House from the south to surprise the Federal cavalry from their rear.

Charles Field's division arrived on the scene shortly after Bryan and Wofford moved out. Field sent three brigades toward Brock Road north of Spotsylvania Court House to block the enemy cavalry from threatening

Fitz Lee's rear. If Anderson's plan worked, Federal troopers would be caught in a trap between Field's brigades on the north and Kershaw's brigades on the south.

Receiving word of the approaching Rebels, the Yankee column galloped back, heading south along Brock Road to Spotsylvania Court House. They turned left at the junction onto Fredericksburg Road. Wilson's troopers narrowly escaped to the northeast just as Bryan's and Wofford's Brigades caught up to their rear guard.

When the Rebel infantry encountered enemy cavalry, they immediately took positions on both sides of Fredericksburg Road, just east of Brock Road. Bryan's men formed a line on the northwest side of Fredericksburg Road, and Wofford occupied the southeast side. Lieutenant Billy Pendleton recalled that the 50th Georgia "advanced in line of battle, and came to the village of Spotsylvania Court House, marched through it and halted by a large barn. It was still very hot, Colonel McGlashan nearly fainted."[2]

Captain Andrew J. McBride, 10th Georgia, described his regiment's arrival at the crossroads: "We reached Spottsylvania court house about daylight on the 8th and went on picket about half a mile toward Fredericksburg; we had hardly established our line when the Yankees appeared, firing began and the men of the Tenth were in it hot and heavy."[3]

With the Federal cavalry threat eliminated at Spotsylvania Court House, Anderson recalled Kershaw's and Field's men from the crossroads and moved them to strengthen his Laurel Hill defenses. Later that day, the 50th Georgians heard heavy firing coming from that direction. Bryan ordered the regiments to quickly fall in and march toward the sound of battle. The day grew more oppressive as the hot, thirsty men hurried north up Brock Road to join the rest of the division.

Dust caked the Wiregrass soldiers' skin and their sweat-drenched uniforms by the time they reached Laurel Hill. The Confederate defenders had just rejected the assault of Warren's V Corps as Bryan's and Wofford's men reached Kershaw's lines. One 50th Georgian reported: "We went on to some woods and heard heavy firing, but didn't see the enemy. We formed in the woods and built breastworks of logs and fence rails."[4]

By late afternoon, Field's division anchored the left flank of Anderson's Laurel Hill position from Brock Road west to the Po River. Kershaw's division extended east from Brock Road, running through some woods for about one-half mile, then into the open ground of Harrison's farm. Wofford's Brigade rested on the right edge of Brock Road while Bryan, Henagan and Humphreys lined up in order on Wofford's right flank. At about 6 p.m., Richard Ewell's corps arrived and moved into the lines to the right of Humphreys. The Rebel defenses bustled as men worked hurriedly to strengthen the already formidable position.[5]

Union troops launched another attack against Laurel Hill in the late afternoon. The assault concentrated on Ewell's position on Anderson's right, and Ewell's men easily repulsed the Federals. Grant's drive to Spotsylvania Court House had been stopped; Robert E. Lee's men firmly held the crossroads.

Meade did not attack Laurel Hill on May 9, allowing both sides time to fortify their works. A. P. Hill's Third Corps arrived about noon and deployed on Ewell's right, extending south and to the east of Brock Road. Lee's entire army now defended the area around Spotsylvania Court House.

One significant event that may be attributable to Bryan's Brigade happened that morning. Union VI Corps commander General John Sedgwick died from a Rebel sniper's bullet while inspecting his lines, becoming one of the highest-ranking officers killed in the war. Meade appointed Major General Horatio G. Wright as the new VI Corps commander. Reportedly, the man who delivered the fatal shot was from the 10th Georgia. Billy Pendleton recalled the event: "We heard that one of our sharpshooters had killed General Sedgwick at a distance of seven hundred yards."[6]

For the next several days, during miserable weather that brought stifling heat then torrential thunderstorms, Grant attempted to break through Lee's fortifications. Some of the heaviest Federal assaults occurred against Ewell's position, especially the "Mule Shoe" salient, which was given its name because of its shape as it protruded out from the rest of the Rebel line. This location proved to be the weakest portion of the Confederate defenses.

The most horrific fighting occurred during terrible weather conditions on May 12. In the middle of a pouring rain that filled trenches with mud and turned roads into quagmires, Grant hurled the II and IX Corps against Ewell's Mule Shoe in a massive pre-dawn assault. Wave after wave of Yankees crashed against Ewell's defenses all along the salient. During the initial stages of the assault, Bryan's Brigade remained in a support position near Brock Road in the defense of Laurel Hill.

By 7 a.m., about two-and-a-half hours after the initial Federal assault, the fighting on the eastern portion of the salient had reached a stalemate. However, the outcome of the fierce struggle on the western portion remained in doubt. Grant moved in reinforcements. Kershaw rushed elements of Wofford's Brigade to help reinforce Ewell's embattled men. Bryan's Brigade moved about a half-mile from its Brock

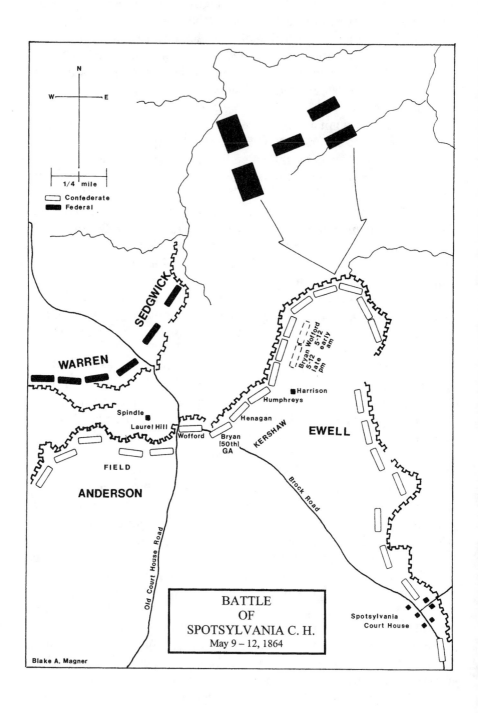

BATTLE
OF
SPOTSYLVANIA C. H.
May 9 – 12, 1864

Blake A. Magner

Road position to near the western edge of the salient, where it occupied breastworks on Wofford's left. The men held their lines all afternoon and throughout the night under a deadly enemy fire.

Captain Andrew McBride, 10th Georgia, described the situation: "On the 12th the Yankees broke through our lines about 200 yards to our right. The regiment next on our right held their line, as did ours, but we suffered terribly. They began to enfilade our position, and many a poor fellow was killed from bullets coming from our right. They kept shooting all night. It was raining and dark."[7]

Lieutenant Pendleton also recalled the ordeal:

> In the morning, there was firing to the right and we moved there about a mile behind the breastworks. Grant fired right down our line, and a cannon ball knocked an oil-cloth cape off the back of a colonel of a Mississippi regiment. He laughed and picked it up again. Another ball knocked off the top of a tree near me and hit a man. We moved nearer the enemy toward the right, into a trench full of mud. The firing kept up all night, and during the night a courier was killed while asleep. It was the most miserable night of the war, —mud, bullets, and rain, no supper, no breakfast.[8]

Lee realized the salient was his weakest link and he gave orders for his men to begin building new defense works about three-quarters of a mile to the rear. Confederate troops worked on the new positions while those at the salient grimly held their spot. The Confederate commander began pulling his exhausted troops back in small groups to the new positions at about 4:00 a.m. on May 13. The fight for the salient finally ended. The nasty struggle had lasted about twenty hours. Many considered this one of the most bloody hand-to-hand engagements of the war. The savage fighting of May 12 cost both sides thousands of casualties.

The 50th Georgia suffered at least seven casualties during the battle. Private Colquitt Stewart, Company A, was killed. Second Lieutenant Hillary W. Cason, Company B, and Privates Alexander Nettles, Company C, and John W. King, Company F, were wounded. Private Wiley Walton, Company D, received gunshot wounds to his thigh and shoulder and was taken prisoner. Also captured were Corporal Calvin Bryant and Private James B. Flowers, Company H.[9]

Enemy skirmishers quickly occupied the vacated Rebel trenches as dawn broke over the grisly battlefield on May 13. As rain continued

Confederate positions at Laurel Hill facing north. Union troops made numerous assaults against these strong Rebel fortifications over three separate days (May 8, 10, and 12). All assaults against Kershaw's and Field's divisions were repulsed with heavy enemy casualties. The 50th Georgia helped man Kershaw's lines throughout the engagements. On May 15, General Lee abandoned the Laurel Hill position and moved the defenders to the southern (right) flank of his lines. Photo by author.

to pour, both sides generally remained in position throughout the day, though some movements occurred. The drenched, mud-covered 50th Georgians shifted their lines to the left into some woods just west of the Old Court House Road.

Grant began moving Warren's V Corps and Sedgwick's VI Corps from the far right to the far left of the Federal lines in preparation for a new assault against Lee's right. Lee became aware of the enemy's movements and shifted Field's division from the left flank at Laurel Hill to the far right of the Confederate lines. Bryan's Brigade, including the 50th Georgia, moved east back across Old Court House Road to their former position near the intersection with Brock Road. As Warren's and Sedgwick's troops withdrew from their positions, Kershaw's men slipped into the vacated VI Corps lines and Field's troops moved into the positions left by the V Corps.

While returning to their original position, the 50th Georgians exchanged heavy fire with enemy skirmishers. Lieutenant Pendleton reported the encounter: "I was leading, on the way back, when we came to a stream, and saw the enemy up the creek. I thought we would be fired at and we were, and my lieutenant was wounded as he jumped across." It was most likely during this skirmish that Privates William D. Curry, Company C, and Thomas Roland, Company H, received fatal gunshot wounds. According to Pendleton, the regiment did not come under heavy fire again while around Spotsylvania Court House.[10]

During a lull in the action, Lieutenant John L. Wheeler, Company C, briefly described the brutal fighting and the casualties in his company: "We have now been fighting eleven days and nights. Tim and Bill Curry have been killed. Harden [Hardy] Joiner and Alex Nettles and William Nipper were wounded. That is all the loss we have sustained as yet. I will write as quick as the fight is over and give you all the news. You must excuse this short letter, for the bomb shells are flying too fast to write."[11]

No serious engagements took place on May 14 or 15. To further strengthen his right flank, Lee pulled Kershaw's division from his left

View of the Mule Shoe Salient/Bloody Angle looking south from Union position toward Confederate lines. During the wet pre-dawn fog and darkness of May 12, thousands of enemy troops from the Union II and VI Corps stormed Ewell's Second Corps position at the "Mule Shoe" salient. For about twenty straight hours, one of the bloodiest hand-to-hand struggles of the war occurred in the western part of the salient at what is known as the "Bloody Angle." The 50th Georgia Regiment held a position a few hundred yards to the south of the fierce fighting. Although not actively engaged at the Bloody Angle, the regiment suffered several casualties from deadly artillery and rifle fire. Photo by author.

and marched it south on Brock Road to a reserve position about a mile behind Field's entrenchments. Pendleton recalled the relief of being placed in reserve: "We had something to eat, - what a luxury it was to rest and feel safe from being killed! We stayed there twenty-four hours, and got one good night's sleep." The stubborn Confederate defensive effort at Laurel Hill had decisively repulsed numerous major enemy assaults. By midnight on May 15, Laurel Hill lay vacant.[12]

The rain continued on the morning of May 16, and the mud made large troop movements almost impossible. Shortly after dawn the next morning, sunshine finally broke through the clouds. Other than a few probes, neither side initiated any significant actions.

During a dense fog that covered the area on May 18, Grant made one last attempt to break Lee's lines. The assault, which began at 4 a.m., covered some of the same ground the Federals crossed on May 12. Decomposing corpses of men and horses were still strewn over the terrain. A devastating Confederate artillery barrage cut down the attackers before they could reach the Rebel lines. Grant called off the futile attack by 9 a.m., finally realizing that further assaults against Lee's fortified lines at Spotsylvania Court House were useless.

The next day, Lee sent Ewell north on a reconnaissance near Fredericksburg Road. That morning, Kershaw's division moved from its reserve position south of Spotsylvania Court House and temporarily filled Ewell's vacated lines. Bryan's Brigade occupied a position south of the Harrison house near the Bloody Angle. The men remained there all day and into the night. When Ewell's exhausted men returned to their lines, Kershaw moved back to his reserve position. This last engagement ended the battles for Spotsylvania Court House.[13]

The 50th Georgia suffered at least thirteen casualties during the twelve days of almost non-stop shelling and fighting around Spotsylvania Court House. Losses included four killed, six wounded, one wounded and captured, and two captured.[14]

Operations Along the North Anna and Pamunkey Rivers and Along Totopotomoy Creek: May 22-31

Grant began withdrawing his army southeast toward Richmond at night on May 20. Lee immediately countered. Over the next twenty-four hours, both armies raced toward the North Anna River. The day had already turned hot by the time Ewell's tired, dusty men reached the river early on the morning of May 22, but Lee had beaten Grant to the North Anna.

Lee crossed the river at Chesterfield Bridge around 8:30 a.m. and moved a little farther south near Hanover Junction. By early

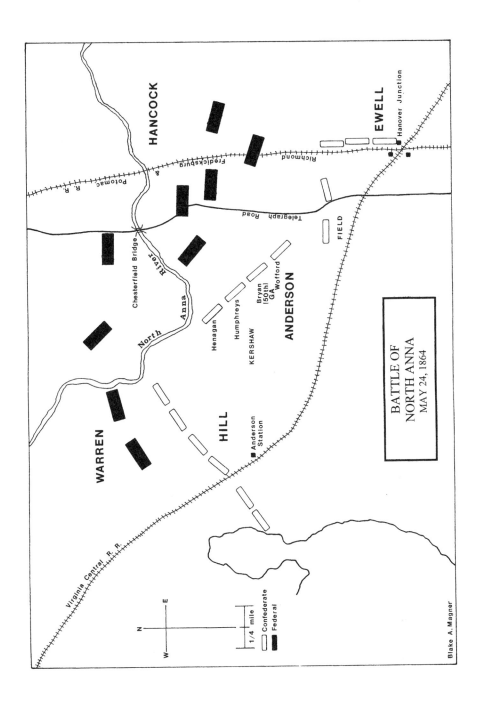

BATTLE OF
NORTH ANNA
MAY 24, 1864

Blake A. Magner

afternoon, the entire Confederate army had reached the south side of the North Anna. The river and the surrounding terrain created one of the most defensible natural barriers between Grant's army and Richmond.

Ewell made camp at Hanover Junction, where the Virginia Central Railroad line crossed the Richmond, Fredericksburg, and Potomac Railroad. Anderson's First Corps moved to Ewell's left flank and manned a defense line on the west side of Telegraph Road just north of the Virginia Central Railroad. A. P. Hill's corps reached the river and camped north of the Virginia Central Railroad and Anderson Station, about three miles northwest of Hanover Junction.

The 50th Georgians were famished and worn out by the time they reached the river. They had marched hard for two days, with little time to rest or eat. The continual fighting and marching over the previous three weeks had taken a toll on the Wiregrass men, but they all knew rest would be short, since the Army of the Potomac followed closely.

Meade's troops reached the northern side of the North Anna a day later, on the morning of May 23. Hancock's II Corps pushed south down Telegraph Road from Mount Carmel Church toward the river. Kershaw positioned Henagan's South Carolina brigade on the north bank of the river at Chesterfield Bridge so that he could delay any Federal attempt to cross at that location.

Hancock's artillery fired on Anderson's position around 5:30 p.m. Anderson deployed Kershaw's division along the heights south of Chesterfield Bridge and Field's division to the east toward the Richmond, Fredericksburg, and Potomac Railroad Bridge. At about 6:30, Major General David B. Birney's 3rd division attacked Henagan's South Carolinians, who were guarding the bridge on the river's north side. The large enemy force captured many of Henagan's men and chased the others across the bridge.

Enemy troops rushed across the bridge to gain a foothold on the south side of the river. A devastating Confederate fire from Kershaw's Rebels on the heights forced a quick withdrawal by the enemy back to the north side. The 50th Georgia suffered one casualty during the scuffle: Corporal Benjamin F. Patterson, Company F, received a gunshot wound to his right arm that sent him to the hospital.[15]

By the end of the day, Hancock's II Corps controlled the river crossings from Telegraph Road east to the Richmond, Fredericksburg, and Potomac Railroad Bridge. Lee suffered another setback for the day when Warren's V Corps routed Hill's men to the west at Jericho Mills and gained a solid foothold south of the river in that sector. During the evening, Lee decided to pull his right and left flanks back to form a line that resembled a wedge, or an inverted V. Hill's corps manned the left wing. Anderson's veterans extended southeast from the apex of the wedge toward Telegraph Road. Ewell's men rested on Anderson's right. Should Grant attack these fortifications, he would have to split his army around the wedge. This would give Lee an excellent opportunity to counterattack Grant's divided force and possibly secure a solid victory.

Around midnight, Captain Andrew J. McBride, 10th Georgia Regiment, received an order to burn Chesterfield Bridge. Captain McBride reported:

> About 12 o'clock that night an order came to me from General
> Kershaw to burn the bridge. The stream was narrow, the north
> bank rose perpendicular to a considerable height; the south bank
> was quite low, and the bridge extended out forty or fifty yards
> over the low ground on the right side. The Yankee pickets lined
> the north bank clearly; the Confederates were some distance back
> from the stream on account of the flat ground. To set fire to that
> bridge was a dangerous job. I am sorry that I can not recall all the
> names of the men who on that night crawled out under the bridge
> shielding themselves like Malcolm at Dunsinane with bushes and
> pine tops as they approached its end.[16]

McBride's men managed to set the bridge on fire, but the enemy quickly drove the small detachment away and extinguished the flames. Meanwhile, the 50th Georgians worked all night building breastworks along the new lines. According to Billy Pendleton, there was only "one shovel to a company." The men used bayonets, cups, and other items to offset the lack of shovels.[17]

The morning of May 24 dawned as another oppressively hot and dusty day. Henagan's Brigade anchored Kershaw's left along the high bluffs at the river. Humphreys rested on Henagan's right while Bryan and Wofford extended farther the line right. The divisions of Field, Rodes, and Early secured the right side of the angle. The Wiregrass men spent the day fortifying their entrenchments.

The withdrawal of the Confederate lines into the wedge mistakenly convinced Grant that Lee intended to retreat to Richmond or to the South Anna River. The aggressive Union commander immediately ordered the Federal troops to advance. Shortly after 8 a.m., Hancock's II Corps began crossing to the south side of the river at Chesterfield Bridge. Kershaw's and Field's sharpshooters laid down a withering fire from the high bluffs and slopes as the enemy crossed.

As the II Corps slowly advanced south of the river, it came under increasingly heavy fire from Confederate troops crouched in entrenchments along the eastern leg of the wedge. At about 3 p.m., Hancock's men made another attempt to move southward, but again ran into the strong Rebel position and fell back. The Yankees met the same resistance when they struck Ewell's lines to the east. Grant realized by evening that Lee's army had not retreated but instead still held very strong positions. The Federal commander called off any further attacks and ordered his divided forces into defensive positions before the Rebels could attack.

The morning of May 25 began with skirmishing along the lines. During the day, Federal artillery crews moved close enough to lob mortar shells into the Rebel trenches. The Wiregrass men dove for cover as enemy rounds dropped all around. Andrew McBride recalled the men "trying to hide from the shells that seemed to be raining down from the clouds." McBride continued, "The Yankees had placed a line of 'brass coehorns's just across the river, and were dropping shells with frightful precision; our works gave us no protection; we scampered out and begged our artillery to blow up the infernal 'coehorns,' but we got little relief till Strickland's sharpshooters made it so hot for the men manning the mortars that they had to fall back over the hill."[18]

The next morning, rain poured from the darkened sky. The Wiregrass men squatted under what little cover they could find in their muddy trenches as water rose around them. The constant rain soaked the men's clothing and made it impossible to find comfort.

Grant cautiously began pulling his troops back across to the north side of the North Anna River. The entire Federal force had withdrawn across the river before daylight on May 27. Grant's army headed southeast toward the Pamunkey River to again try to turn the Confederate right.

The North Anna fight resulted in a stalemate, although both sides claimed a victory. The 50th Georgia suffered at least four casualties during the fighting along the river. In addition to Corporal Patterson's wounding on May 23, Private Timothy Mathis, Company I, fell into enemy hands on May 24 and spent the rest of the war in Elmira Prison in New York. Private Aaron Tison, Company I, suffered a serious knee wound on May 26 that sent him to a Richmond hospital. Lieutenant Pendleton's orderly, Sergeant William A. Byrd, was struck by a spent bullet but remained with the company.[19]

Deadly skirmishing occurred along the lines during the next few days as Grant pressed Lee's army. Billy Pendleton described a close call while in line of battle: "Our skirmishers made piles of fence rails to lie behind. We saw the enemy across the field, but there was no firing for some time. I was just behind the rails, and heard a rifle crack, and a bullet struck a rail right in front of me."[20]

In the pre-dawn hours of May 31, Major General Robert R. Hoke moved his division from south of Richmond to reinforce Lee's army. Before Hoke arrived, Lee learned of Federal movements a few miles southeast of his right flank near Old Cold Harbor. Concerned that Grant may take the crossroads there and threaten his right again, the Confederate commander diverted Brigadier General Thomas L. Clingman, commanding Hoke's lead brigade, to the junction.[21]

Lee dispatched Richard Anderson's First Corps from Totopotomoy Creek later that afternoon to further reinforce the Rebel positions at Cold Harbor. The 50th Georgia fell into line with the rest of Kershaw's division and headed southeast. General Anderson provided a status report to Lee at 7 p.m.: "General Hoke has gotten into position, his right extending a little beyond Cold Harbor and his left a little this side of Beulah Church. There is some skirmishing going on in his front." Anderson continued, "I will push forward a strong force at daylight in the morning on the road from Beulah Church to Mrs. Allen's, on the other side of the Matadequin, and another along the Old Cold Harbor and Old Church road, and find out positively what is before me."[22]

Shortly after Anderson sent his message, Union cavalry pushed Hoke's infantry and Rebel troopers out of Cold Harbor and back about a mile west of the junction. Yankee cavalry controlled the crossroads at the end of the day.

Concerned by the Confederate infantry movements, Grant ordered Major General Horatio G. Wright's VI Corps to reinforce the Federal cavalry at Cold Harbor. About midnight, Wright's men pulled out of their lines on an all-night fifteen-mile march toward the junction.

During the evening of May 31, the Wiregrass men camped a short distance west of Gaines' Mill and caught some much-needed rest. The 50th Georgians had suffered relatively few casualties since the fierce battles in the Wilderness and at Spotsylvania Court House. Although constantly marching and under fire almost daily, they had been fortunate to avoid direct enemy assaults. Their good fortune was about to run out at Cold Harbor.

North Anna River defenses at the wedge. These trenches were constructed by Confederates in the wedge overlooking the North Anna River. Hill's and Anderson's men defended their positions from similar trenches. Photo by author.

Chapter Eleven
Cold Harbor
June 1–June 12, 1864

The steamy early morning dampness of June 1 found both sides hurrying reinforcements toward Cold Harbor. The little crossroads hamlet suddenly became an area of great importance to both Ulysses S. Grant and Robert E. Lee.

The men of Joseph Kershaw's division rose before dawn and marched cross country in a northeasterly direction from Gaines' Mill toward Beulah Church, located about one mile north of Old Cold Harbor. Richard Anderson planned a two-pronged advance to dislodge Major General Philip H. Sheridan's cavalry from Old Cold Harbor. Robert Hoke's men would march northeast along Cold Harbor Road toward Old Cold Harbor. Upon reaching Beulah Church, Kershaw's troops would move southeast from Beulah Church toward the Cold Harbor Road junction. The Federals would be caught between Kershaw and Hoke.

Colonel Lawrence M. Keitt led Kershaw's South Carolina brigade in the advance, followed in reserve by Goode Bryan's Brigade, including the 50th Georgia. As he moved slowly toward Beulah Church, Kershaw assumed Hoke's division marched simultaneously along Cold Harbor Road. Due to miscommunication, Hoke remained in position along the road and never advanced.

Fire from enemy pickets grew more intense as Kershaw's men neared Sheridan's cavalry positions. Kershaw ordered Keitt forward to test the Yankee strength. A barrage of rifle fire from the entrenched enemy troopers met the South Carolinians. Shortly after 8 a.m., Keitt's men reformed and charged across an open field toward the enemy positions in the thick woods. Just before the Confederates reached the wooded area on the other side of the field, Sheridan's troopers unleashed a horrific fire from their Sharps and Spencer repeating rifles. The Union soldiers decimated Keitt's lead regiment, knocking the young commander off his horse with a mortal wound, and the disorganized South Carolinians fell back under fierce enemy fire.[1]

Bryan's Brigade marched toward the sound of battle. The Georgia veterans arrived in time to participate in the latter part of the brief engagement and suffered minimal casualties. Lieutenant Billy Pendleton, Company B, recalled: "I saw a wounded man pass but the bullets did no harm to my regiment. We lay down, and then marched on. I heard a brass band in the midst of the firing." The band Pendleton heard was most likely an enemy cavalry band encouraging the troops.[2]

Anderson called off further assaults as the men withdrew and built breastworks that faced east and ran from north to south. The Georgians hacked at the ground all day and by late afternoon had almost finished their defensive positions. Lieutenant Pendleton remarked, "We worked hard at the breastworks which were made of logs and dirt."[3]

Anderson placed the divisions led by Pickett and Field on Kershaw's left. Kershaw's four brigades manned the line from left to right: Henagan, Humphreys, Bryan, and Wofford. Wofford's right flank ended in a low marshy ravine.[4]

Hoke's division continued the Rebel defensive line to the south. Brigadier General Johnson Hagood's Brigade entrenched on Wofford's right and in front of the marshy ravine area. The left of Brigadier General Thomas L. Clingman's Brigade touched the right of the ravine and stretched south almost to Cold Harbor Road.

The Rebel defenses included advanced rifle pits manned by skirmishers. Several hundred yards behind the rifle pits lay a line of breastworks protected in front with fallen trees and branches. Anderson's infantry and artillery waited behind the breastworks.

Federal VI and XVIII Corps reinforcements poured into Cold Harbor during the hot, dusty morning and early afternoon. Before all the troops had arrived, Meade ordered an attack for late that afternoon against Kershaw's and Hoke's Confederates. Major General Horatio G. Wright's VI Corps arrived first and deployed on the Union left, facing Hoke's lines. Major General William F. "Baldy" Smith's XVIII Corps arrived later and took positions to the right of the VI Corps and generally across from Kershaw's and Major General George E. Pickett's divisions.[5]

Around 4 p.m., Federal artillery began pounding the Confederate breastworks. Rebel artillery responded as Union troops inched closer to the Confederate defenses. At about 6 p.m., thousands of Federal troops rushed out across the no-man's land toward the waiting Rebels. Men from the XVIII Corps divisions of Brigadier General Charles Devens and Brigadier General William T. H. Brooks had to cross an area of cleared ground, which varied in width from three hundred yards to twelve hundred yards. Confederate skirmishers peppered the oncoming enemy until the Yankees forced them back. Rebel canister and musketry then raked the oncoming Federals as they approached the fortified main line defenses. Wave after wave of blueclad troops rushed through the woods toward the Southerners, only to fall back with heavy casualties. It appeared the stubborn butternut lines could not be broken.[6]

The Confederate weak link lay in the wooded marshy ravine area that ran between Kershaw's and Hoke's positions. Just before the Federal assault, Hoke shifted Hagood's Brigade to the southern end of his lines. Inexplicably, Hoke failed to advise either Wofford or Clingman of the move. This unprotected area proved to be an inviting target for the enemy and a disastrous mistake for the Confederates. Enemy troops managed to slip through the marshy ravine during the raging battle and penetrate the unsuspecting flanks of Wofford and Clingman. Yankees poured through the unprotected gap, later named "Bloody Run." Clingman's North Carolinians suddenly began taking fire on their exposed left flank and rear. Caught in deadly fire from three sides, Clingman's lines wavered and then disintegrated.

As Union troops assaulted Wofford's front, they also moved through the gap to fire on the Georgians' exposed right flank and rear. Wofford's veterans finally broke and ran for cover after being overrun by enemy soldiers. When Wofford's men fell back, the right of Bryan's Brigade crumbled against the onrushing enemy. The 53rd Georgia broke on Bryan's far right, then the 51st Georgia fell. Arthur B. Simms, 53rd Georgia, wrote of the regiment's collapse in a letter to his sister: "We ran off in very great disorder and never rallied in an hour or two." Yankee troops captured hundreds of Clingman's, Wofford's and Bryan's men.[7]

Bryan's remaining regiments, the 50th and 10th Georgians, put up a fierce resistance. Companies B, C, and E of the 50th Georgia rushed to aid the regiments on their right as the 10th Georgia held firm. Lieutenant Billy Pendleton, Company B commander, described the desperate situation:

> In the afternoon we were attacked and our skirmishers were driven back to the breastworks. We were all ready to receive the attack, but it didn't reach my regiment. There was, however, a heavy engagement at the right. Suddenly we saw our men over there retreating, all except the regiment next to us. When McGlashan noticed it he acted independently. He gave me the command, "Take companies B, C, and E up the line and hold the enemy in check." We rushed up a hundred yards and found ourselves in the midst of the enemy in the woods. We jumped into the breastworks and fired, the enemy stopped firing and moved toward us. I saw that we would be taken prisoner, so I ordered a retreat.
>
> Colonel McGlashan had formed the regiment at right angles to meet the attack. I went back, behind the hill, with the rest of our regiment. The enemy stopped firing and went toward the breastworks in the woods. The regiment on our left stayed and cheered our regiment, "Hoorah for the Fiftieth," and waved their hats.[8]

    The heroic men of the 50th and 10th Georgia Regiments slowed the enemy break north of the marshy ravine and frantically held on for reinforcements.

    Hoke and Kershaw pleaded for reserves to help close the breach. General Colquitt, whose brigade extended to the right of Clingman, rushed elements of his brigade to Clingman's aid. Henagan pulled Major William Wallace's 2nd South Carolina Regiment and the 3rd South Carolina Battalion out of their positions and hurried them to help Bryan's embattled men.[9]

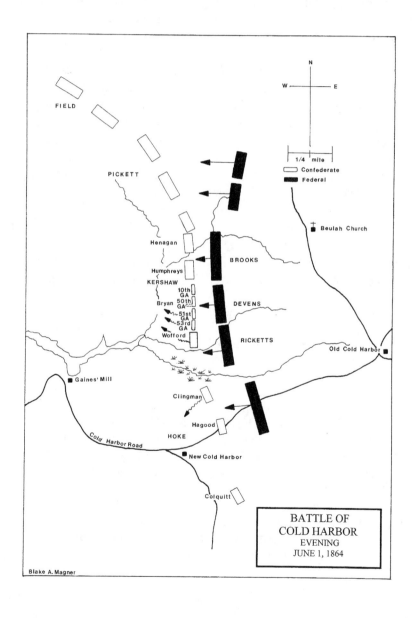

The 50th and 10th Georgia Regiments were locked in a desperate struggle against the enemy brigades of Colonels Jeremiah C. Drake and William B. Barton when Henagan's reinforcements slammed into the startled Yankees and sent them reeling back through the woods with heavy casualties. Pendleton recalled, "I saw a line of battle behind us, it was a South Carolina Regiment coming to our assistance. My regiment cheered them, and then they marched up and called, 'Fiftieth Georgia, forward!' We charged, the enemy gave way, and we took the line again."[10]

Additional Confederate reinforcements pushed the enemy out of the breach as darkness enveloped the battlefield. The break in the Rebel lines had been plugged. Although the Confederates did not retake all their lost ground, they halted Grant's first bloody assault at Cold Harbor.

While many soldiers rested after the hard day's battle, Richard Anderson sent the brigades of Brigadier Generals George T. "Tige" Anderson, Evander Law, and John Gregg of Major General Charles W. Field's division to strengthen Hoke's and Kershaw's lines. Brigadier General Eppa Hunton's Brigade, from Pickett's division, also moved forward to aid the same effort. The Southerners worked through the night to construct new, stronger fortifications.[11]

The Yankees suffered heavy losses in the assaults against Bryan's and Wofford's men. Barton's 1st Brigade lost 224 men, while Drake's 3rd Brigade reported 323 casualties, almost half (153) from the 112th New York Regiment. On the Confederate side, losses in Kershaw's division were estimated in the hundreds, including many who were captured.[12]

The 50th Georgia suffered at least twenty-three casualties during the fighting on June 1. It is unknown how many fell during the morning engagement near Beulah Church; most Wiregrass losses occurred during the savage fighting near the breach in the Confederate line late that afternoon. Private David Dampier, Company D, died on the battlefield. After being wounded, Private James W. Maxwell, Company F, was taken prisoner, and he would spend the rest of the war in Fort Delaware Prison. Nine other Wiregrass men were wounded. Among the casualties were Lieutenant John L. Wheeler, Company C, who received a severe wound to his left arm that required amputation; Private Jacob B. Harnage, Company G, who lost his left leg; Private John J. Norris, Company K, who was shot in the left side of his face and jaw; and Private Joseph M. Hancock, Company K, who received a gunshot wound to his right cheek that cut off the tip of his tongue. Twelve Wiregrass men were captured, and most would spend the rest of the war in prison at Elmira, New York, or Point Lookout, Maryland.[13]

A letter written by a soldier in the trenches shortly after the battle applauded the actions of the 50th Georgia Regiment during the heated engagement of June 1:

Union lines facing west toward Confederate positions. On June 1 and 3, the area between the Union and Confederate lines became a killing field. Rebel defenders fired from fortified entrenchments as Ulysses S. Grant hurled wave after wave of Federal troops against the Southerners. After two days of horrific casualties, Grant finally called off further assaults. The two armies spent the next ten days facing each other from behind entrenchments. Photo by author.

General Bryan's Brigade maintained its reputation during all recent battles, but in the fight of the 1st June, one of its regiments, the 50th Ga., Col. McGlashin, particularly distinguished itself. McLaws' Division [temporarily commanded by Kershaw] was in line of battle, its right resting on what was considered an impassable marsh, about 300 yards wide. The enemy crossed the marsh and attacked the rear and flank, which fell back in some confusion, being unexpectedly and furiously attacked. General Bryan ordered Col. McGlashin to about face and wheel to the right. They were halted, faced about, and held the enemy in check. Major Wallace, with the 2d S.C., joined the gallant 50th Ga., Bryan at once ordered a charge. This was executed according to the style of the Old Division, and the works retaken. No blame can be attached to our troops, either to McLaws' or Hoke's Division —beyond the fact that the marsh should have been more thoroughly tested.[14]

The writer showed his frustration with some of the senior Confederate officers by stating: "Our troops are in fine spirits, and if our corps and division commanders will only take care to guard our flanks and rear, this Old Division will take care of the front."[15]

Although many Union soldiers fell in the first day's failed assault, Meade and Grant planned another attack for the next morning. Hancock's II Corps withdrew that night from its Totopotomoy Creek position to join the VI Corps on the Federal left. Lee recognized the enemy movement to the south and ordered a corresponding shift in his lines to strengthen the Confederate right. Firefights continued throughout the night, as both sides shuffled troops to the south.

The morning of June 2 dawned hot and dusty. Hancock's II Corps failed to move into position in time, forcing Grant to postpone the attack for about twenty-four hours. No significant offensive action occurred along Kershaw's front on June 2, as both sides maneuvered into position. However, accurate enemy sharpshooter fire killed Private Milton J. Glover, Company F, and wounded Sergeant Noah Pittman, Company B.[16]

Later that evening, Goode Bryan temporarily removed himself from brigade command due to illness. Kershaw replaced Bryan with Colonel James P. Simms, the twenty-seven–year-old commander of the 53rd Georgia Regiment. Upon taking over, Kershaw ordered Simms to destroy the earthworks his brigade had constructed and withdraw behind Evander M. Law's Alabama brigade before daylight.[17]

The brigade withdrew a short distance behind a hill to the safety of a deep gorge. The hungry and exhausted Georgians rested and gobbled down their rations. While the others rested, a soldier from each company drew the hazardous assignment of filling the canteens. A Wiregrass soldier described the fate of one of the water bearers: "Prince was sent, he had to run across an exposed place, a bullet hit him, he was taken to the rear, and I never saw him again." Private John Prince of Company K died from a sharpshooter's bullet.[18]

By the early morning of June 3, a solid line of fortifications now stood west of the marshy ravine and connected Kershaw's and Hoke's men. The new position took the shape of a horseshoe and would subject Federal attackers to a three-sided crossfire. Law's Brigade overlooked the ravine's marshy low ground from behind waist-high entrenchments of dirt and logs, and Bryan's Brigade lay in reserve behind the Alabamians.

A light chilling rain fell at 4:30 a.m. as fog and mist covered the ground. At the signal, thousands of blue-clad Yankees rose up and charged the Confederate entrenchments. The Federal commander made another concerted attack all along the Confederate lines, with the II, VI, and XVIII Corps leading the assault. Hancock's II Corps attacked into the devastating fire from Breckinridge and Hoke south of Cold Harbor Road.

North of Cold Harbor Road, General "Baldy" Smith's XVIII Corps' assault centered against Kershaw's fortified lines at the marshy ravine. Colonel

Simms reported: "About the time that the men had stacked arms preparatory to rest an attack was made upon General Law's line. He sent a courier to me

Marshy Ravine. On June 1, Federal troops penetrated a gap in the lines held by Wofford's and Clingman's Brigades. The marshy ravine area is shown in the foreground. This photo was taken facing north from the south side of the marshy area. As Wofford's right flank collapsed, part of Bryan's Brigade crumbled. The 50th and 10th Georgia Regiments held their ground until reinforcements plugged the breach and pushed the enemy back. The open area beyond the marshy ravine is likely where Bryan's Brigade was posted. This area is outside the National Military Park and is privately owned. Photo by author.

asking that I would move up to his assistance, as his works had not been well supplied with ammunition. The brigade was put under arms immediately and moved up to General Law's line through a heavy fire of musketry. The men moved up in gallant style."[19]

The 50th Georgia formed into line of battle and advanced out of the safety of the gorge to the top of the hill. The men sprinted down the hill under a hail of bullets and took cover in a ditch at the bottom. One Wiregrass officer recalled when reaching the ditch, "Just after I got down, lying flat, a man twice my size fell on top of me, - a lieutenant of the Fifty-Third regiment. It hurt me, so I told him to get off, but he seemed so full of fright that I couldn't make him hear. At last I brandished my sword and he slipped off."[20]

A deadly crossfire of Rebel musketry and artillery tore into the ranks of Brigadier General William T. H. Brooks' 1st Division and Brigadier General John H. Martindale's 2nd Division as they charged into the horseshoe. Tige

Anderson's Georgians blasted the oncoming enemy head-on. Law's Alabamians, reinforced by Bryan's Georgians, fired into the writhing blue masses from the northern bank of the marshy ravine. As men of the 15th Alabama Regiment emptied their weapons, they passed them back to Bryan's men. The Georgians reloaded and passed them forward. General Law observed: "the men were in fine spirits, laughing and talking as they fired. It was not war; it was murder."[21]

Martindale's 1st Brigade, under Brigadier General George J. Stannard, marched right into the withering fire from Law's entrenchments. Stannard's regiments, the 55th Pennsylvania and the 23rd, 25th, and 27th Massachusetts were literally shot to pieces. Colonel William C. Oates, 15th Alabama Regiment commander, described the carnage: "The charging column received the most destructive fire I ever saw. They were subjected to a front and flank fire from infantry, at short range, while my piece of artillery poured double charges of canister into them. I could see the dust fog out of a man's clothing in two or three places at once where as many balls would strike him at the same moment." Within a few minutes, Stannard's brigade ceased to exist as a fighting force.[22]

Pendleton noted that after about half an hour, Bryan's Brigade "moved to the right [of Law's Brigade] about one-half mile, and then got into a ditch with the troops there. My regiment was with the Eighth Georgia [regiment in

Remains of Confederate entrenchments. Rebel soldiers poured deadly fire into oncoming Yankees from behind strong earth and wood fortifications during the battle. Sharpshooters from both sides made it a deadly gamble to raise one's head above the entrenchments. Photo by author.

Tige Anderson's Brigade]." Shortly after arriving the Wiregrass men helped repulse another enemy assault. Pendleton noted, "the enemy got only within a hundred yards of the breastworks. They lay down and then retreated, some stayed but mostly only the dead and wounded."[23]

In spite of the slaughter, Grant and Meade continued to feed men into the meat grinder in hopes of breaking the Confederate defenses. Wave after wave from Smith's corps charged against Kershaw's lines. The Southerners rejected each attempt with staggering losses to the enemy divisions of Brooks and Martindale.

The musketry volleys from Kershaw's lines were so intense that entire rows of charging enemy soldiers fell like wheat to a scythe. The assault quickly dissolved into confusion with the surviving attackers caught in a no-man's land. The murderous Rebel fire made it suicide to go forward and just as deadly to retreat. Men were cut down as they tried to run back into the woods while others hugged the ground as canister and musket fire raked the dirt around them. Many Federal soldiers dug shallow depressions with their hands or bayonets. The survivors tried to remain motionless until dark to avoid being picked off by sharpshooters. In some instances, soldiers made shields of their dead comrades.

The disastrous Federal offensive lasted only an hour, and no further assaults were made along these Rebel lines the rest of the morning. Shortly after noon, Grant elected not to launch any further attacks against Lee's impenetrable defenses. Both sides dug in and waited for the other to make a move. In some places the lines stood only fifty yards apart, and the soldiers traded fire with each other throughout the day.

Bryan's fatigued men withdrew that evening to a safe place in reserve. Due to their protected entrenchments, the 50th Georgians suffered only eight confirmed casualties during the brutal fighting. First Lieutenant John J. Sirmons, Company G, and Private William W. Bradford, Company I, were killed. Private Samuel W. Ford, Company I, received a mortal wound and died three days later. Those who received non-fatal wounds included Sergeant Jasper W. Wells, Company A; Corporal Fisher J. Gaskins, Company I; and Privates William Stone, Company C; J. Ellis, Company D; and John B. Wooten, Company F.[24]

In his report to Secretary of War James A. Seddon on the evening of June 3, Robert E. Lee commented, "Repeated attacks were made upon General Anderson's position, chiefly against his right, under General Kershaw. They were met with great steadiness and repulsed in every instance." Lee closed his report with, "Our loss to-day has been small, and our success, under the blessing of God, all that we could expect."[25]

Both sides adjusted their positions and improved breastworks the next day. Before dawn, James Simms shifted his brigade to the right of General Law. Lieutenant Pendleton reported that the 50th Georgia marched to the right and stopped "in some woods with a field in front. Just at dawn, orders came, 'Build breastworks at once for you will probably be fired on at daylight.' Everyone turned in with bayonets and hands, and by daylight when the firing did start we were in ditches. The firing was heavy because Grant was extending his line."[26]

Colonel James Phillip Simms. Born in Covington, Georgia, in 1837, Simms enlisted in the 53rd Georgia Infantry Regiment in 1862. The young soldier quickly moved up in rank. Elected Captain of Company E in May 1862, Simms received a promotion to major one month later, and to colonel in October. The native Georgian led the 53rd Georgia Regiment until he replaced Goode Bryan as brigade commander in August 1864. Simms received a promotion to brigadier general in December 1864. He was captured at Sailor's Creek in April 1865, and imprisoned at Fort Warren, Massachusetts, until July 1865. After the war, Simms served in the Georgia state legislature and practiced law. He died in his hometown of Covington, Georgia, on May 30, 1887. Courtesy of the U.S. Army Military History Institute, Carlisle, Pennsylvania.

The proximity of the Confederate and Federal lines made movements a deadly proposition. Company F suffered two casualties that day. Private John C. Rawls received a wound to his right thigh, and Private Daniel L. Maxwell was captured. The unfortunate Maxwell would spend the rest of the war in Elmira Prison.[27]

The 50th Georgia occupied their position for the remainder of the Cold Harbor Campaign. Despite the danger, only two other Wiregrass soldiers became casualties. On June 10, Private James Clemons, Company G, received a gunshot wound to his collarbone. On June 13, Private Jonathon Walden, Company F, received a hip wound from an artillery canister fragment.[28]

After the Union repulse on June 3, hundreds of enemy dead and wounded lay for days in the boiling summer heat between the opposing lines. By the time Lee and Grant negotiated a truce to remove them, only a handful of the wounded remained alive. With the exception of the deadly sharpshooting, the next several days were relatively quiet.

The lull in the fighting allowed Robert E. Lee to make the following promotions: Major General Joseph Kershaw became permanent commander of Lafayette McLaws' old division, and Richard Anderson and Jubal Early received the rank of lieutenant general to coincide with their new corps commands.[29]

Grant withdrew his army from the area during the night of June 12 and into the next morning. He began a new march southeast around Richmond. Lee again moved south to block the Federals and protect the Confederate capital. Kershaw's division crossed the Chickahominy River at McClellan's Bridge. On the morning of June 14, Bryan's Brigade marched to Frayser's farm, the scene of heavy fighting two years before. The Wiregrass men camped there until June 16.[30]

The 50th Georgia lost at least thirty-eight soldiers during the thirteen days at Cold Harbor, including: five killed; one mortally wounded; eighteen wounded; one wounded/captured; and thirteen captured. Most losses occurred during the Federal attack near the marshy ravine on June 1. Individual company casualties are as follows:

Company A (2) – 1 wounded, 1 captured
Company B (4) – 1 wounded, 3 captured
Company C (2) – 2 wounded
Company D (2) – 1 killed, 1 wounded
Company E (1) – 1 wounded
Company F (13) – 1 killed, 5 wounded, 1 wounded/captured, 6 captured
Company G (5) – 1 killed, 3 wounded, 1 captured
Company H (0) – No reported casualties
Company I (6) – 1 killed, 1 mortally wounded, 2 wounded, 2 captured;
Company K (3) – 1 killed, 2 wounded[31]

Cold Harbor represented an overwhelming victory for Robert E. Lee and an embarrassing defeat for Ulysses S. Grant. The men of the 50th Georgia had endured another savage battle. For the previous six weeks, from May 4 to June 16, the regiment had undergone brutal marches, eaten sporadically, and been exposed to deadly enemy fire almost daily. Many comrades had been left along the way. There would be no time for the weary Wiregrass men to rest. In a few days, they would be called upon to help defend one of the main supply hubs of the Confederacy, the city of Petersburg.

Chapter Twelve
Operations at Petersburg and Deep Bottom
June 18–August 7, 1864

U lysses S. Grant's withdrawal from the trenches at Cold Harbor during the night of June 12 and early morning of June 13 caught Robert E. Lee off guard. Unaware of the planned Federal withdrawal, Lee ordered Jubal Early's Second Corps to the Shenandoah Valley to defend against enemy raids in the area.

The Confederate commander assumed the next Federal movement would be against Richmond, only a few miles to the south. When informed of the Federal withdrawal, Lee quickly ordered Longstreet's First Corps, temporarily commanded by Richard H. Anderson, and A. P. Hill's Third Corps south to block any Federal approach to the Confederate capital. Grant, however, had decided on a different strategy: the important transportation hub of Petersburg would be his next target. Located twenty miles south of Richmond, the city held the key to supplying the Confederate capital and much of the eastern theater. If Petersburg fell, the supplies to Richmond would dry up, and the capital would eventually have to be abandoned. As Lee rushed to defend Richmond, Grant's army looped southeast around the city, crossed the James River to the south, and moved toward Petersburg.

On the evening of June 15, General "Baldy" Smith's XVIII Corps assaulted Petersburg. The initial attack met with some success. The much smaller Confederate force, commanded by Lieutenant General Pierre Gustave Toutant Beauregard, fell back and secured new defensive lines. Over the next two days, Grant's army made several attempts to break Beauregard's line. The outmanned but stubborn Rebel defenders repulsed the enemy each time.

When Beauregard initially requested additional reinforcements, Lee delayed sending troops for fear of weakening his Richmond defenses. By the evening of June 17, however, Lee realized that Grant's current target was Petersburg, not the capital. The Southern commander ordered Major General Joseph Kershaw to hustle his division from the Malvern Hill area to Petersburg and reinforce Beauregard's embattled defenders. Bryan's Brigade, still under the temporary command of Colonel James P. Simms, cooked rations, filled canteens, and moved out with the rest of the division at about 3:00 a.m. in the sultry pre-dawn darkness of June 18. Kershaw's troops crossed the James River near Drewry's Bluff and proceeded toward Petersburg. Major General Charles W. Field's division and Hill's corps soon followed.[1]

After a hard and hot twenty-mile forced march, Kershaw's exhausted division crossed the Appomattox River and entered Petersburg at about 7:30 a.m. By mid-afternoon, Kershaw's men took position on the right of Beauregard's defensive line in support of Major General Bushrod Johnson's division. A few hours later, Field's division arrived and extended the Rebel lines farther to the right.[2]

Just as Kershaw's men filed into the lines, Burnside's IX Corps and Warren's V Corps "came surging across the field" against the Confederate right. The area had very little protection, and the Rebels came under heavy fire as they moved into the unfinished breastworks. In spite of the lack of protection, Kershaw's veterans easily repulsed the uncoordinated Union assaults. By 6:30 p.m., General George Meade called off further attacks for the day.[3]

Bryan's Brigade moved farther to the right of the Confederate lines about dark. One Wiregrass soldier recalled that, upon reaching the new position, "a terrific fire opened on us from the whole line of battle not seventy-five yards away." The men lay behind a small hill until the firing died down and then began building fortifications. First they dug cannon pits for the artillery pieces. Then, to minimize exposure to the deadly enemy fire, they dug out the breastworks from the cannon pits.[4]

The Confederates continued their exhausting work throughout the night despite the constant enemy fire. Colonel Simms described the conditions: "The enemy had thrown up works within sixty yards of ours, and when we were placed there the works were incomplete, and we were compelled to complete them under the incessant fire of musketry and artillery, and on some parts of the line the works were begun without any protection whatever."[5]

Occasionally the Union fire found its mark. During the evening of June 18 and the early morning of June 19, the 50th Georgia lost six men. Corporal Silvester Floyd and Private James Bragg, Company E, and Private Irvine Hendley, Company I, fell with mortal wounds. Sergeant Jonathan B. Ganas, Company D, received a head wound from a shell fragment; Privates James B. Wilcox, Company E, and Jonathon Walden, Company F, went down from gunshot wounds.[6]

Heavy sharpshooting continued on both sides all during the day and into the night. One man acted as a spotter for the sharpshooter. When an enemy head appeared above the lines, the spotter coordinated the location and the sharpshooter fired. The risks for both the spotter and the sniper were great. Enemy snipers killed Rebel spotters Lieutenant Parrish Lankford, Company C, and Sergeant John G. F. McCall, Company K.[7]

John McCall died from a sniper's bullet to the head. The twenty-seven–year-old Brooks County veteran had been promoted only three months earlier. His cousin, Sergeant Major Wilson C. McCall, immediately wrote a letter to the late soldier's father, informing him of his son's death and offering words of comfort:

> Petersburg Va. June 19th 1864
> My Dear Uncle,
>   I have the painful news of writing you that Cousin John was killed a few minutes ago. He was detailed as sergeant of the Sharpshooters and in looking over the breastworks he was shot through the top of the head, he lived a few minutes after he was shot but was not able to speak after being hit. I shall have him buried as decently as possible and have the place marked or I shall have his name cut on the headboard so that if you should wish to have him removed at any time you can do so. We are now near this town and if the telegraph extended to Quitman I would let you know if in a few minutes but as it does not extend all the way you might not get it before you would this, if I thought you would I would start one in a few minutes.
>   Despirate as the time seems it is an old saying that the darkest time is just before day. General Grant has succeeded in getting very close to Petersburg but will have the same obstacle to meet with which he has met with for the past (nearly two months). I think we will have a despirate fight here in a day or two but no one can tell, but Grant has had some successes here before we arrived, he got possession of nearly all our works any distance from the town. The Yankees are close enough to shell the town but General Beauregard has threatened them if they do it, sometimes a shell goes in town anyway.
>   Dear Uncle
>   I shall try and get a coffin to have Cozin John buried, I do not know whether I can procure one or not if it is a possible thing to do so be assured I will have it attended to. I can't tell where we may be by the time you receive this. All his effects are here in the hands of Lt. [Benjamin F.] Whittington. Nothing more at present. If you see any time soon Pa's folks tell them I am well as usual. All the troops are in fine spirits and helped up at the idea that Grant may charge

them soon. No words of consolation can do much good more than to say that John was universally beliked by all who knew him.

Give my love to all and Aunt Vincey, Cozin Becca and except a due portion for yourself.

Write soon.
Your obedient Nephew,
W. C. McCall

P.S. There has been four killed dead this morning and two mortally wounded.[8]

Shortly after writing the letter, Sergeant Major McCall received a slight wound. Fortunately for the Wiregrass soldier, the injury did not require hospitalization, and McCall remained in the line with his company. Lieutenant Whittington, who collected John McCall's personal effects, later received a head wound while spotting for a sharpshooter. Second Lieutenant Joseph Tomlinson of Company G fell with a mortal gunshot wound in the side and died five days later in a Richmond hospital. The Clinch County officer had earlier been recommended for promotion to first lieutenant. Tomlinson's promotion came one week after his death. Enemy fire also killed Lieutenant Jesse Mobley on June 20.[9]

First Sergeant George Washington Chitty, Company D, and Private John Spikes of Company C received gunshot wounds. A minie ball severely damaged Chitty's left hand. The Echols County veteran made his way to a field hospital and received a transfer the next day to Jackson Hospital in Richmond. His wound required the amputation of a portion of his hand, including one finger. On July 24, after a month in the hospital, the sergeant received a thirty-day furlough to recuperate at home. Petersburg would be Chitty's last battle because he lost use of his hand. Chitty spent the rest of the war convalescing at his Echols County home.[10]

Over the next two days, hostile fire killed Corporal Elijah Ellis, Company C, and Private Moses Pittman of Company B. Sergeant A. J. Butler of Company D also went down with a non-fatal gunshot wound.[11]

Bryan's Brigade suffered numerous casualties while occupying this deadly part of the line between June 18 and June 23. Colonel Simms reported: "The number of casualties occurring in the brigade at this place will give some idea of the difficulties which had to be contended against. There were fifteen killed and thirty-one wounded, most of which proved fatal." The vast majority of 50th Georgia casualties at Petersburg occurred during this period. At least seventeen Wiregrass men fell, including four killed, five mortally wounded, and eight wounded.[12]

On June 23, Kershaw pulled the brigade out of the line and placed it in reserve, about three-fourths of a mile in the rear. Billy Pendleton recalled, "The fourth night we went down the trenches to a low valley, to the rear, toward Petersburg, where we stayed for two weeks. Stray shells came there occasionally, but we had a good rest. It was near the Weldon Road. When we got to camp we had a Revival, in which I took an active part. One moonlight

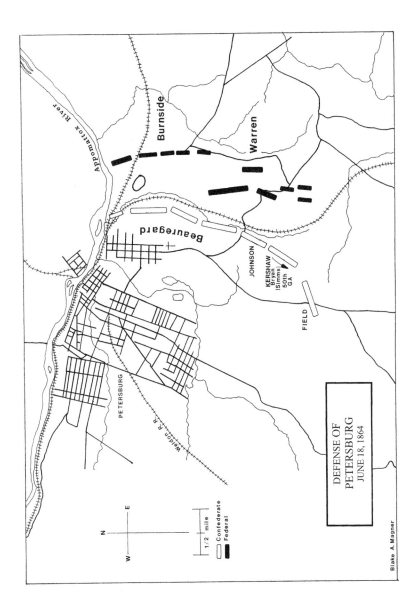

night several of us went off in the woods and had a prayer meeting. While one of the men was praying, a stray bullet fell in the midst of us."[13]

The brigade remained in this area for a month. Both sides continued to improve their entrenchments as the sharpshooters plied their deadly trade both day and night. Colonel Simms recalled: "Here we remained until July 23, during which time nothing occurred worthy of special notice, except an occasional march down the Weldon railroad in quest of the enemy; but failing to find him we returned to our same place of bivouac each time."[14]

On July 1, Private Moses Ellis, Company I, received a severe face wound. After spending almost two months in a Richmond hospital, the wounded soldier obtained a furlough back to Berrien County. However, Ellis never recovered from his wound, and he died at home in December 1864.[15]

The oppressive heat and dry weather continued during June and July. The high temperature, not bullets, felled many soldiers making them unfit for duty. No rain fell for over a month, adding to the misery of the troops on both sides. Any movements caused dust clouds that coated the men. Many small streams and ponds dried up making drinking water scarce. The troops dug shallow wells whenever they stayed in place for any length of time.

Engagements on the north side of the James River near Deep Bottom: July 26-29

During the unsuccessful attempts to take Petersburg, the Yankees established a bridgehead at a bend on the north side of the James River known as Deep Bottom. General Lee became concerned that Union control of this area of the river allowed enemy troops to cross over the pontoon bridges from the south side. Therefore, Lee decided to weaken his Petersburg defenses and send troops to confront the threat along the James River. The Confederate commander ordered Kershaw to move from Petersburg and push the enemy back to the south side of the James. Bryan's Brigade left the trenches with Kershaw's division early on the morning of July 23 and headed toward Chaffin's Bluff, located on the north side of the James River. The division crossed the river by late afternoon, and camped for the night near Chaffin's Bluff.[16]

The next day, Kershaw moved his four brigades east toward the high ground that stood north of Deep Bottom. This area was known as New Market Heights. The Confederate line stretched from west to east overlooking the village of New Market and a small tributary known as Bailey's Run. Bryan's Brigade occupied a position on New Market Road west of Bailey's Run. The brigade received fire from enemy gunboats but did not actively participate in the fighting on July 27. According to

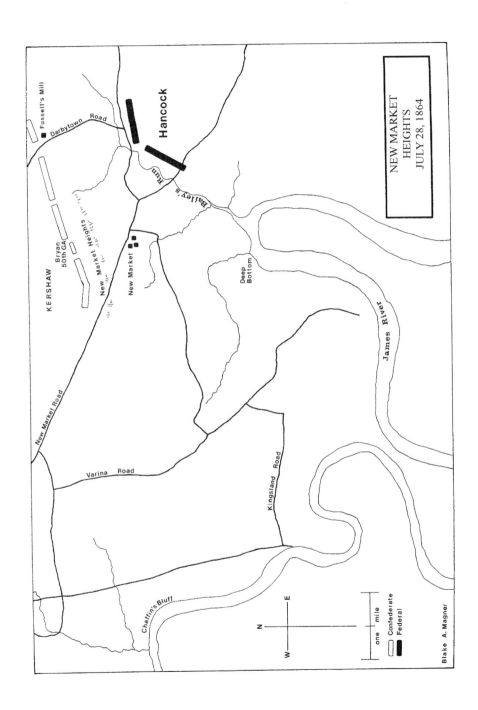

Fussell's Mill

Darbytown Road

Hancock

Bailey's Run

Bryan
50th GA

New Market Heights

KERSHAW

New Market

New Market Road

Varina Road

Chaffin's Bluff

Deep Bottom

James River

Kingsland Road

NEW MARKET
HEIGHTS
JULY 28, 1864

N
W E
S

one mile

☐ Confederate
■ Federal

Blake A. Magner

Lieutenant Pendleton, the brigade moved a short distance that night and camped near an old mill, likely Fussell's Mill.[17]

The 50th Georgia deployed as skirmishers the following day. Pendleton described the action when Yankee skirmishers advanced toward the Rebel lines in front of the brigade: "McGlashan saw the enemy skirmishers advancing on our right and ordered me to take three companies and go to meet them. We ran, fired into their flank, and they retreated. The colonel soon followed, charged into their flank and took twenty prisoners, who were all Germans and couldn't speak English. It is very demoralizing to receive fire on your flank. After they retreated we formed a skirmish line, advanced to the woods and made breastworks of fence rails."[18]

Colonel Simms praised the 50th Georgia commander's actions: "Colonel McGlashan was sent out with the Tenth and Fiftieth Georgia Regiments, with which he attacked their line, and succeeded in capturing the greater part of the enemy's skirmish line, which he had so advanced, and for the skillful manner in which he managed to accomplish this he deserves credit."[19]

The enemy skirmishers retreated across a field to the cover of some woods. The Yankees kept up constant firing all day, which meant that any Georgian who exposed himself took a great risk. In one incident, Pendleton recalled, "McGlashan sent me down the line to Major Spence [John M.], about two hundred shots were fired at me, but they were mostly spent bullets, and I was not hit." That night, the 50th Georgia moved back to their previous position and camped.[20]

No fighting occurred on July 29, and in the evening, the main Yankee force withdrew across the James River toward Petersburg. The inconclusive engagement resulted in several hundred casualties on each side, although the 50th Georgia suffered no confirmed casualties during the Deep Bottom operation.

Bryan's Brigade crossed back to the south side of the James River after the Federal withdrawal. The 50th Georgia camped in some woods near Chester Station on the Telegraph road, about six miles north of Petersburg. Lieutenant Pendleton remembered, "We were at this camp for a short time, but never went back to Petersburg. . . . The officers would sometimes get together at night and sing old songs. I heard the song 'Long, Long ago,' for the first time."[21]

As the men of the 50th Georgia endured the Petersburg Campaign, their thoughts often turned to home and concern for their families. News from Georgia contained depressing stories of hardship and fear, as Major General William T. Sherman's army moved toward Atlanta, less than two hundred miles north of many Wiregrass families.

A letter from a 53rd Georgia soldier to his father reflected the mood of many Rebel soldiers during these trying times:

> My dear Father,
> It is with the greatest anxiety, that I avail myself of this pleasant and good opportunity to drop you a few lines in order to inform you of my welfare. I am doing as well at present, as could be expected and doing well, with the exception of a right smart touch of the rheumatism in my left ankle, and right knee. . . . I would give anything for a letter from home. Just think, I have been from home five months, and oyer [over] and have not received a letter from any one of you. It's really discouraging now, is it not, and I can't help believe you have wrote, but I have not received the letter. You ought to write, at least once ever two or three weeks. . . . I have no news of importance to communicate to you, at present, that will interest you. We are camped on the Richmond and Petersburg, railroad, five miles from Petersburg, and about one mile from the line of battle. . . . I have learned that Gov. Brown has called for every person from 16 to 60. I afraid you will have to go, I hope not. Keep out of the army if you can honorably do so. If the Yankeys come to our house, treat them so as to save your property, but kill them if you can get a sly chance, and to get one by himself, in a good place. Send me a pair of socks, by the first opportunity, as I am nearly without a pair. I must close. Give my love to all the family and receive a portion for your self. I remain, your most devoted Son' until death.
> John L. G. Wood [22]

On August 6, General Anderson ordered Kershaw's Brigade to march to Richmond. The Wiregrass men welcomed any opportunity to leave the deadly trenches and oppressive heat. Between June 18 and August 5, the 50th Georgia suffered at least twenty-one battle related casualties at Petersburg, including four killed, seven mortally wounded, and ten wounded. Another four died from disease.[23]

The next destination for these battle-hardened south Georgians would be the beautiful Shenandoah Valley. While in the Valley they would fight one of their last great battles of the war.

Chapter Thirteen
The Shenandoah Valley
August 7–October 18, 1864

L ieutenant General Jubal A. Early's army enjoyed immediate success after their departure from Cold Harbor for the Shenandoah Valley on June 13. The Southerners ran Major General David Hunter's force out of the Valley in late June and marched to the doorstep of Washington, D.C., in July. Early's success attracted the attention of the North. After meeting with President Lincoln, Grant appointed General Philip H. Sheridan as overall commander of the Army of the Shenandoah on August 1. Sheridan's orders were relatively simple: destroy Early and take back control of the Shenandoah Valley.

Robert E. Lee decided to reinforce Early with troops from the Petersburg/Richmond defenses against the Federal threat. Although this move weakened his lines near the Confederate capital, Lee could not risk losing the Valley's extensive transportation network and food supply. On August 6, the Confederate commander conferred with President Jefferson Davis and Lieutenant General Richard H. Anderson, who had replaced James Longstreet as First Corps commander when Longstreet suffered serious wounds at the Wilderness. After the meeting, Lee ordered Anderson's First Corps, the cavalry division of Major General Fitzhugh Lee, and the artillery battalion of Major Wilfred E. Cutshaw to join Early.

That same day, Anderson ordered Joseph Kershaw to march his division from its encampment at Chester Station to Richmond and board a train to Gordonsville. Lieutenant Billy Pendleton recalled, "When the orders came to march the men did not know where we were going, except that it was in the direction of Richmond. We marched through Manchester, [now a part of Richmond] across the James river, and into Richmond, then the column turned toward the railroad station. The men wondered where we were going. On the train, I had a seat in the passenger car for the first time during the war, always before I had ridden in baggage cars, and generally on top."[1]

The young lieutenant later changed to the top of the car, "as there was better air on top. We saw a lot of children, and Lieutenant [James] Bailey wished we were boys again." The train rattled through Hanover Junction and finally reached Gordonsville. By this point the men believed they were headed to reinforce General Early in the Shenandoah Valley.[2]

The Wiregrass men scrambled off the cramped train at Gordonsville, stretched their legs, and marched northeast toward Culpeper Court House. The troops later crossed the Rapidan River and camped for the night on the old Cedar Run battlefield. General Anderson met the division the next day at Mitchell's Station, just south of Culpeper. The 50th Georgia remained near Mitchell's Station for several days, waiting for the rest of Anderson's command to arrive.[3]

Anderson's corps marched from Mitchell's Station shortly after sunrise on August 12, and halted near Culpeper about midday. Pendleton commented on the changes to the area since he had last seen it: "The whole of Culpeper County was stripped of the beautiful forest which had been there the year before. Grant had been there in winter camp." That afternoon, Kershaw's division marched out of Culpeper, turned left, and headed for the Hazel River. The men camped for the night along the river. Any remaining doubts about their destination had been resolved; the 50th Georgia was headed west toward the Shenandoah Valley.[4]

The troops arrived near Front Royal, at the northern end of the Luray Valley, on the afternoon of August 14. The 50th Georgia camped for a few days on the banks of the Shenandoah River, and the men seized the opportunity to relax and bathe in the cool waters. One Wiregrass soldier recalled, "We had a fine time there and went in swimming every day."[5]

The north and south forks of the Shenandoah River meet at Front Royal and continue their flow to the north. Valley residents commonly referred to any movement northward as "down the valley" and, conversely, any move to the south as "up the valley."

William Wofford's Brigade and supporting cavalry engaged enemy troopers on August 16 along the north side of the river near Cedarville. After a heated exchange, Wofford withdrew with a number of casualties. Upon hearing of the skirmish, Bryan's Brigade hurried toward the fighting. The 50th Georgia marched through the streets of Front Royal as soldiers wounded in the earlier skirmish were brought into town. The enemy cavalry had broken off the fight and withdrawn by the time Bryan's men passed through the town and reached the river. Billy Pendleton noted, "We came to the river but found that Sheridan's cavalry had retreated. The men had expected a battle, but there was none. We camped on the battlefield."[6]

Sheridan withdrew his troops toward Winchester after learning that his cavalry had clashed with infantry from Anderson's corps. The Yankees left a trail of destruction, burning and destroying anything of value to the Southerners as they marched north down the Valley Pike.[7]

Early pursued Sheridan and ordered Anderson to follow. Anderson's corps left Front Royal shortly after daylight on August 18. During the march, Lieutenant Pendleton commented on the handiwork of the Yankees: "The next day we followed Sheridan toward Winchester, and were quite near the enemy. As we went along we found all the barns and mills burning, which made the men very angry and excited."[8]

Kershaw's men arrived within sight of Winchester that evening and camped in the nearby woods by the Berryville Pike. The 50th Georgia remained at this position the next few days. Steady rains blanketed the area, making movements difficult for both forces.[9]

While camped near Winchester, Billy Pendleton took the opportunity to renew his acquaintance with the Burgess family. The Burgesses had befriended Pendleton and his father when both were quite ill during the Maryland Campaign, two years earlier. Billy and Captain William H. Sharpe, Company K, decided to go into town and pay the family a visit. "We arrived at their house just before breakfast, were welcomed by the family and given breakfast." Apparently smitten by one of the daughters, young Pendleton paid several more visits to the Burgess home. "We went to tea on Sunday night and to church. I was with the younger one and offered her my arm, which was a new experience for me, but I saw Captain Sharpe do it first. Going back to camp I spoke of the great pleasure it was to have a young lady on my arm, and never heard the last of it from the officers."[10]

On August 20, General Goode Bryan submitted his resignation. Having been plagued by poor health for several months, the Georgia native finally gave in to the rigors of the campaign. The retiring brigade commander wrote to Secretary of War James A. Seddon recommending Colonel McGlashan as his replacement. Bryan's letter stated: "I have the honor to recommend Col Peter McGlashan, of 50th Ga Regt for Brigadier General, to fill the vacancy caused by my resignation. Col McGlashan is a very gallant officer, a good diciplinarian, a man of education and his appointment would in my opinion be highly satisfactory to the entire Brigade." In the meantime, Kershaw again placed Colonel James P. Simms in temporary command of the brigade.[11]

Skirmish at Summit Point – August 21

At daylight on August 21, Bryan's Brigade, now commanded by James Simms, led Kershaw's division from Winchester along the old Charlestown Road toward Charlestown in search of the enemy. The brigade encountered the advance of Brigadier General James H. Wilson's Federal cavalry division about six miles from Summit Point. Colonel Simms described the action: "After moving some six of [or] eight miles we encountered the cavalry of the enemy. The major-general [Kershaw] ordered me to send forward two

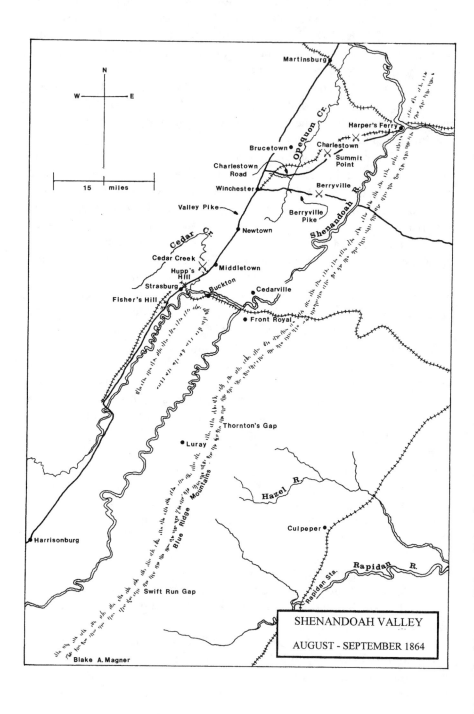

SHENANDOAH VALLEY

AUGUST - SEPTEMBER 1864

regiments to attack, which was done, driving the enemy a short distance, when it was found necessary to re-enforce with another regiment. I suppose we met about one brigade of the enemy's cavalry, driving them about six miles, when they fell back upon a division of their cavalry strongly posted and with artillery. Here I halted [at] the bridge, thinking it not prudent to advance farther, when the major-general brought up the remainder of the division and ordered an advance. By this time the enemy had retreated hastily in the direction of Charlestown. In this affair we lost a few men wounded and one or two killed."[12]

Lieutenant Pendleton recalled being startled by a wounded enemy soldier during the fight. "While charging, I ran ahead and saw a soldier in blue lying in some bushes. I though he was dead, he was badly wounded in the abdomen, but he raised up and said, 'Say, Mister, you won't hurt me, will you?' I didn't take his gun but went on." The brigade advanced about a mile and camped along the road.[13]

Sergeant Jesse King, Company K, and Private Josiah Harrell, Company F, received wounds during the engagement. Sergeant King suffered a serious wound to his right foot, which required amputation of his leg below the knee. King was hospitalized in Winchester. The unfortunate Wiregrass soldier was later taken prisoner and spent the rest of the war in Point Lookout Prison.[14]

The march toward Charlestown resumed at daylight the next morning. After meeting up with General Early, Anderson camped his men along the old Charlestown Road about two and a half miles from town. The troops remained there for the next few days as rain dampened the area.[15]

Skirmish at Charlestown – August 26

On August 25, General Early marched toward Martinsburg. Heavy skirmishing occurred the next day along Anderson's lines near Charlestown. At one point, enemy infantry and cavalry routed the picket line of the 15th South Carolina Regiment, capturing about one hundred men. However, the 50th Georgia and Lieutenant Pendleton held their ground and repulsed a heavy enemy assault. The young officer proudly recalled:

> We had been skirmishing all day. At four in the afternoon
> there appeared a line of battle about three hundred yards
> away. I noticed that our men were going away, but I thought
> it was too soon to retreat. I had two companies behind two
> rail piles, and decided that we ought not to retreat until the
> last minute. I then noticed that the enemy lay down, which
> surprised me, as I felt they would retreat. My men wanted to
> leave but I would not let them. I had to hold one big fellow. I

kept my head above the rail pile and, sure enough, saw the enemy retreat. My men jumped up to charge and gave the rebel yell. Then I saw that all our men had left except the ones with me. I could see the whole Fiftieth regiment retreating. So I ran down across the field and called, "Major," and waved my cap. [Lieutenant Benjamin] Whittington heard me and called to Major Spence, "Billy Pendleton is calling us back." Spence called the same to the men. They all came back and fired into the enemy, killing nine men. It made me quite the hero among our men. One of them said, "It was Billy Pendleton that beat those Yankees." We went on to Winchester. On the way Major Coston, an aide of Kershaw, rode by. I ran out and said, "Major, we repulsed a whole line of battle today." He asked what regiment it was, and said that it was one of his favorite regiments. That evening Major Spence said to me, "Billy, you held your ground today, and I honor you for it."[16]

Anderson's men headed for Winchester at daybreak the next morning. The 50th Georgia marched through Smithfield and remained near Brucetown for the next few days. The men enjoyed a break from the recent warm days as the weather turned pleasantly cool. At daylight on August 31, Bryan's Brigade marched into Winchester to scout for reports Federal movement near the Berryville area. Bryan's men detected no enemy, and by afternoon the rest of Kershaw's division arrived. The Wiregrass soldiers settled into their former camp near the Berryville Pike, just east of Winchester.[17]

The politics surrounding a permanent replacement for Goode Bryan as brigade commander grew intense. Supporters of Colonel James Simms drew up a petition for Secretary of War Seddon. In a September 2 letter, Colonel Simms' brother, Arthur, informed their sister of the petition: "It was signed very nearly unanimous by the brigade with the exception of Colonel McGlashan's regiment, and of course it was expected of them as General Bryan had recommended Colonel McGlashan. Whether Bud [brother] Jim receives the appointment or not—the unanimous petition of the brigade with a very flattering endorsement of General Kershaw—is certainly a compliment worth being proud of. I presume that Lt. General Anderson from what I can learn will also endorse the paper favorably."[18]

Skirmish at Berryville – September 3

Anderson's corps left Winchester about noon on September 3 and marched along the Berryville Pike toward Berryville. Kershaw's division ran into General George Crook's Army of West Virginia outside Berryville just before sunset. Kershaw formed a line of battle and attacked the entrenched 1st Brigade positions of Colonel Rutherford B. Hayes, along with two regiments of Colonel Daniel D. Johnson's 2nd Brigade. A brief but intense fight ensued, resulting in a number of Yankee and Rebel casualties.[19]

Both sides claimed victory. General Sheridan reported, "just before dark, Kershaw's division attacked Crook on the Berryville pike, and was handsomely repulsed, with a loss of 50 prisoners and over 200 killed and wounded."[20]

Colonel James Simms countered Sheridan's account by reporting: "Line of battle was formed by order of the major-general, in conjunction with the other brigades of the division, and an attack made upon their lines. Our men moving forward with great spirit and gallantry, the enemy only held their position long enough to fire one round, then fled precipitately." Simms estimated his casualties at "4 killed and 26 wounded."[21]

Billy Pendleton supported Colonel Simms' version of the engagement. "We charged into some woods and the enemy retreated. We came to where their line had been and I found a full haversack. We went on into a field, and the enemy kept on retreating, but we withdrew as there was danger of an enemy trap. We came back and camped in the woods. . . . The fighting was not serious. When I opened the haversack, I found it full of hardtack, a bag of coffee, and a little sugar. It was quite a treat for us."[22]

The 50th Georgia suffered at least four casualties in the battle: Enemy fire killed Private Isaiah Brunson, Company F; Private Aaron Williams, Company I, fell with a severe wound and died the next day; Private Samuel Griffis, Company G, suffered a wounded right hand that required amputation of a finger; and Private Fleming J. Hall received a gunshot wound to his left hip.[23]

Darkness curtailed further action. The exhausted Wiregrass soldiers slept on the field as a chilling rain fell during the night. The lull in battle allowed Sheridan's men to fortify their lines. More of Early's troops arrived by 10 a.m. the next morning to reinforce Anderson. After probing the Federal defenses, Early determined that the enemy force was too strong to be driven away. Both sides lay across from each another throughout the day and into the evening. Later that night, the Confederates withdrew to their former camp outside Winchester.[24]

Probes and skirmishing occurred over the next week, but neither side mounted a serious offensive. Between fights, the men of both sides rested, caught up on news from home, and awaited the next movement. The lull in action also brought some brigade promotions as Captains William H. Briggs and J. M. Ponder of the 50th Georgia became assistants to the brigade quartermaster.[25]

Sherman's capture of Atlanta on September 2 became a main topic of conversation on both sides. The news was sobering to the Confederates and created great consternation among the Georgians. Not only had their capital fallen, but also the State of Georgia lay open for Sherman's army. A soldier in the 53rd Regiment expressed the concern felt by many Wiregrass men in a letter to his father: "After hearing of the bad news, that has befallen Empire State, and our army at Atlanta, and of the evacuation of it by Hood's [writing faded] I have concluded to drop you a few lines, and send them off before communications are cut off, between here and home, if this has not a ready been done." The soldier continued, "I am afraid they [Yankees] have visited you, but I hope not. I shall be troubled, until I hear from home."[26]

As Sheridan and Early faced each another across the Opequon Creek, plans were made to return Anderson's corps to Petersburg. Robert E. Lee offered to leave Kershaw's division with Early, but "Old Jube" believed his army could hold the area. On September 14, Anderson prepared to move out of the Shenandoah Valley. A cool rain fell most of the day as the weather turned cold.

Kershaw led Anderson's First Corps from Winchester up the Valley Pike at sunrise on September 15. The Southern column slowly trudged south, stopping to camp on the North Fork of the Shenandoah River opposite Buckton. Three days later, the footsore men of the 50th Georgia crossed the Blue Ridge Mountains at Thornton's Gap, turned southeast toward Culpeper Court House and moved out of the Shenandoah Valley.[27]

Sheridan planned an offensive against Early's weakened army as soon as he learned of Anderson's departure. After briefly conferring with Grant and obtaining approval of his plan, the feisty Federal commander launched an assault against the Confederates at Winchester on September 19. At sunrise that day, Anderson's men continued their march away from the Valley, unaware of Sheridan's attack on Early at Winchester. As each hour passed, the First Corps distanced itself farther from Early's beleaguered command.

Anderson's men arrived near Culpeper later in the day. They learned that a Federal raiding party from the 16th New York Cavalry had burned the bridge over the Rapidan River near Rapidan Station. Kershaw ordered Bryan's Brigade to try to intercept the enemy troopers before they escaped. Colonel Simms reported:

> On the 19th the general, having received information that a
> raiding party was in the vicinity, and that they were going
> toward Stevensburg, ordered me with this brigade to a certain
> point on that road to intercept them. The brigade was put in

motion immediately and moved at double-quick for nearly two miles, but upon arriving within about 500 yards the enemy were opposite to us in the road, having proceeded so far as to render it impossible to cut them off. Finding that this was the only opportunity we would have of inflicting damage upon them, I gave the order to fire. We killed and wounded several of them. Our loss was nothing. We recaptured from this party quite a number of horses and mules which they had captured from a Government lot near Rapidan Station.[28]

Anderson reached Rapidan Station the next evening. The Confederates remained there for the next two days awaiting construction of a new bridge over the river. In a letter to his sister, a soldier in the 53rd Georgia Regiment expressed disappointment at leaving the Valley: "Five days steady marching and we are here at the Rapidan River awaiting orders, or probably transportation to Petersburg again. We have spent a pleasant time in the Valley—getting butter, eggs, chickens, and fruit in great quantities and at a very cheap rate to what we have been paying. We have certainly fared well in the eating line, our marches I would suppose would be altogether not exceeding three hundred miles. . . . We reached this place yesterday evening, and have no doubt but that we are 'bound for' Petersburg. I don't like the idea much it is entirely too confining and then we cannot get vegetables and fruit as we could in the valley."[29]

General Early suffered a bitter defeat at the Battle of Third Winchester on September 19 and then another loss at Fisher's Hill on September 22, prompting the a request for reinforcements. The next day, General Lee ordered Anderson to send Kershaw's division and Cutshaw's artillery battalion back to the Shenandoah Valley to reinforce Early. The rest of Anderson's corps continued on to Petersburg.[30]

Kershaw's division left Gordonsville at sunrise on September 24 and headed back toward the Valley. The command marched through Swift Run Gap and rejoined Early's army in the late morning of September 26. The enemy captured Corporal Elias Blun, Company E, near Peak Mountain during the march. Blun later swore allegiance to the U.S. Government and joined the Union service. At least three other Wiregrass men fell into enemy hands while hospitalized at Harrisonburg when Sheridan's troops entered the town on September 24. These men were Private Edward Moore, Company C, along with Privates J. Bailey and Fleming Hall, Company G. Moore and Hall were exchanged a few weeks later. Bailey was transferred to Point Lookout Prison.[31]

Bryan's Brigade, including the 50th Georgia, changed position frequently over the next couple of weeks as they skirmished with the enemy.

A letter from John L. G. Wood of the 53rd Georgia written to his father during this time reflected the common fatigue, homesickness, and desire for an end to the terrible war:

> Once more after waiting to receive a letter from you for some time, I have concluded to drop you a few lines so as to inform you of my welfare. . . . I hope you will excuse me for not writing oftener than I have of late, but the fact is I receive so few letters that I have little or no desire [illegible] ages me to write and receive no answer. It is fine, I can hear from you all through a few friends, that come from home occasionally, but that is by no means like a letter from you all. I seldom ever hear from my dear little brothers and sisters who I think of very often. I have been very uneasy about you all, for fear the Yanks would get down in our settlement and play havoc with you all. You can't imagine how glad I am that they have not visited you. I have been troubled about you for fear you would have to go in reserve and be exposed to camp life. I hope you will not have to go and leave the family as I don't see how Mother and the children will get along without you. I am getting very tired of this war. It looks like it is to be an ever-lasting war[.] if we have got to get our independence. I want us to get it shortly, and if we are to be subjugated, I want it to be shortly done, as I want peace. I want to go home and live where I can see you all and live in peace and harmony. I think I have seen enough of war and of different countrys to satisfy me the rest of my days. I think I will be pleased to live with you and attend to your business. I think we can both live and be happy together the rest of our days, if this cruel war will only cease.[32]

Buoyed by his recent successes, Sheridan decided to destroy what was left of Early's fighting effectiveness by eliminating the remaining Confederate source of food and supplies. Federal troops went on a rampage, burning crops and buildings in the southern end of the Valley between September 26 and October 5. After devastating the area, Sheridan withdrew his army down the Valley. Early's men tracked Sheridan's path of destruction for the next week, looking for an opportunity to catch the enemy off guard. On October 13, the Confederates caught the unsuspecting XIX Corps and General Crook's command at Hupp's Hill near Strasburg. A brief but heated struggle resulted in a Rebel victory. Satisfied that he had shown the enemy that some fight remained in his army, Early withdrew through Strasburg to the former Confederate defenses on Fisher's Hill.

Bryan's Brigade did not become actively engaged at Hupp's Hill. As Colonel Simms reported: "This brigade was held as reserve for his [Brigadier General James Conner's Brigade] support, but that brigade having accomplished the work assigned to it so handsomely it was not thought necessary to bring it into action; therefore the brigade was not engaged, but lost in wounded some eight to ten men." The 50th Georgia reported no casualties in the engagement.[33]

Early's aggressiveness surprised Sheridan and caused him to concentrate his Army of the Shenandoah between Middletown and Cedar Creek. Only minor skirmishing occurred over the next few days. On the evening of October 15, Sheridan left for a meeting in Washington, D.C., with Secretary of War Edwin Stanton and Ulysses Grant to discuss strategies for the next campaign. The Union commander planned to return by October 18 and did not consider Early's army strong enough to create major problems while he was away.

The men of the 50th Georgia welcomed the quiet time. The regiment had marched up and down the Shenandoah Valley for more than two months, participated in numerous skirmishes, and suffered at least fourteen casualties. Little did the Wiregrass men know that they would soon find themselves in the vanguard of one of the fiercest struggles of the war, near a winding little stream called Cedar Creek.

Chapter Fourteen
Cedar Creek
October 19, 1864

G eneral Philip Sheridan returned to Winchester on October 18 after his meeting in Washington, D.C., with Secretary of War Edwin Stanton and General Ulysses Grant. With everything quiet, the Federal commander decided to spend the night in town and ride to Middletown the next morning. Sheridan incorrectly assumed Jubal Early's army was finished as a fighting force. One month earlier, "Old Jube" misjudged Sheridan's caution as a weakness, and it cost his army dearly at the Battle of Third Winchester. Now, "Little Phil" misjudged Early's fighting spirit.

Meanwhile, Jubal Early faced a critical dilemma. Sheridan's troops had laid waste to the Valley, making it impossible for the Rebel army to sustain itself in the area for very long. The Confederate commander must either withdraw his army or drive away the enemy and capture supplies and rations from the abundant Federal stores. Early decided on the latter. He later explained his rationale: "I was compelled to move back for want of provisions and forage, or attack the enemy in his position with the hope of driving him from it, and I determined to attack."[1]

Early and his staff met during the day of October 18 to plan a major offensive. They realized the disparity between the two armies was significant as Federal troop strength exceeded thirty thousand men. The ragged Confederate force was less than half and more likely only one-third the size of Sheridan's army. Estimates range from a high of about seventeen thousand to a low of eighty-five hundred, but the latter estimate was probably more accurate. Therefore, a surprise assault would be the only chance of success for his outnumbered army. Early realized the great risks of such a move, but after making the fateful decision, Old Jube acted quickly.[2]

Early initially considered an assault on the Federal right flank; however, Major General John B. Gordon convinced the Confederate commander that an attack on the enemy's left would have a better chance of success. The plan called for Gordon's Second Corps to move between the base of Massanutten Mountain and the North Fork of the Shenandoah River and attack the Federal left flank. Kershaw's division would cross Cedar Creek at Bowman's Mill Ford and hit Colonel Joseph Thoburn's 1st

Division, VIII Corps of George Crook's Army of West Virginia in the middle of the Federal line. Brigadier General Gabriel C. Wharton's division and the artillery would press the Federal right down the Valley Pike toward Middletown.[3]

General Kershaw gave Bryan's Georgia brigade, commanded by Colonel James P. Simms, the honor of spearheading the assault. The Wiregrass men cooked two day's rations and filled their cartridge boxes with sixty rounds of ammunition. These battle-hardened veterans knew the impending fight would be much more than another skirmish.[4]

While the Georgians prepared their equipment, Colonel Peter McGlashan sat in front of his tent listening to a nearby prayer meeting led by the regimental chaplain. McGlashan saw Colonel Simms approaching and he recalled: "He said, 'Colonel, will you take a walk with me?' Rising to my feet, we went toward the prayer meeting and listened awhile with bowed heads. 'Poor fellows,' said the General [Col. Simms], 'this may be their last meeting, Colonel. We are going to attack the enemy's lines before daybreak, and our brigade has been selected for the post of honor to break the line. Wofford's brigade will support us. Your regiment being on the right, I depend on you to lead the attack. The men must be in line, ready to move at midnight.' We shook hands and parted."[5]

McGlashan further recalled, "I issued the necessary orders, and at midnight, we filed out on the Winchester road, past the waiting columns of troops already there, and took position at the head of the column." The night was cloudy, making it difficult for the Confederates to see ahead, but this also aided the element of surprise. Orders went down the lines to maintain complete silence. The men removed their canteens and anything else that might make noise as they marched.[6]

Early's army quietly moved ahead in the cold darkness toward Sheridan's unsuspecting troops. Simms' Brigade led Kershaw's division from Fisher's Hill and down the Valley Pike to Strasburg. The men finally approached a low range of hills through a gap and arrived near Cedar Creek at about 3:30 a.m. Colonel Simms reported: "Having passed through Strasburg, we left the turnpike and moved upon a little road turnpike to the right, which we followed until we came in sight of the enemy's camp-fires." Shortly after reaching the creek, thick ground fog developed, making vision difficult for both the approaching Rebels and the enemy pickets.[7]

Shortly before 5:00 a.m., the Georgians quietly waded across Cedar Creek at Bowman's Mill Ford. Simms moved his brigade downstream a short distance, faced it left, and formed the men into line of battle. While Simms' men stepped forward into a clump of trees, Kershaw's other three brigades moved into position, as follows: Conner's Brigade, commanded

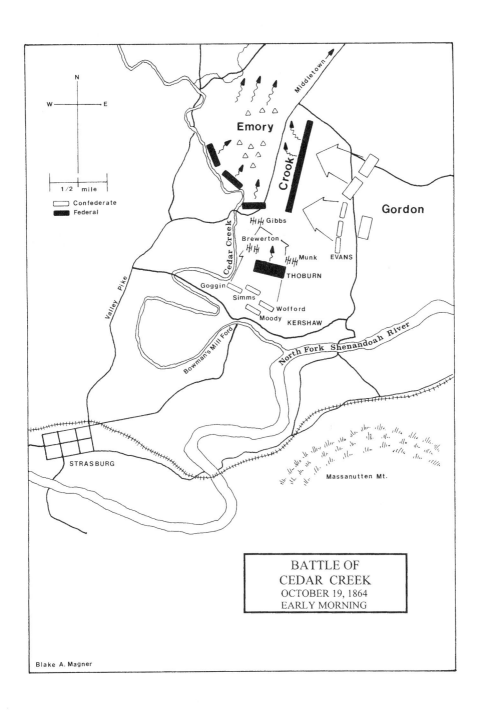

N

W——E

S

1/2 mile

☐ Confederate
■ Federal

Emory

Crook

Middletown

Gordon

Cedar Creek

Gibbs

Brewerton

Munk

EVANS

THOBURN

Goggin

Simms

Wofford

Moody

KERSHAW

Valley Pike

Bowman's Mill Ford

North Fork Shenandoah River

STRASBURG

Massanutten Mt.

BATTLE OF
CEDAR CREEK
OCTOBER 19, 1864
EARLY MORNING

Blake A. Magner

Bowman's Mill Ford facing northeast. The 50th Georgia led Simms' Brigade across the chilly waters of Cedar Creek at this location in the pre-dawn fog of October 19. The brigade surprised and completely routed Union Colonel Joseph Thoburn's 1st Division. Photo by author.

by Major James M. Goggin, on Simms' left; Wofford's Brigade on Simms' right; and Humphreys' Brigade, commanded by Colonel Daniel N. Moody, to Simms' right and rear.[8]

Orders moved down the lines that the men were not to fire, even if fired upon. The 50th Georgia led the brigade through the clump of trees and silently moved up the slope toward the enemy position.[9]

Hidden by the dense fog, Simms' men eased so close to the Federals that they could hear some of the men talking to one another. Colonel McGlashan recalled:

> I soon descried, dotted all along the edge of the woods in
> front, the enemy's pickets. The faded gray uniforms of our
> men were so nearly the color of the October grass they could
> not distinguish us. But we could see their dark blue uniforms
> readily; it was about 4 o'clock a.m.; day had not yet broke,
> yet the pickets were evidently uneasy. They could hear some
> movements in front, but could not see anything. Finally, one
> picket, sharper-eyed than the rest, cried out: "I see them," and
> fired, when Lieut. [George M.] Clayton of the Fiftieth fell
> forward on the grass mortally wounded. A rattling volley
> from the picket line followed and another man fell out of the

ranks. Still the line swept on in utter silence. The whole
picket line, now thoroughly alarmed, broke for the woods,
but were soon halted by their officers, who were cursing the
men for running at a false alarm. They had scarcely formed
line, however, before we were on them. This terrible
approach of a silent line of battle they could not see appalled
them and they fled in terror without firing another shot,
yelling out their alarm to the troops in camp.[10]

Without firing a single shot, the Georgians overwhelmed Captain
Frederick C. Wilkie's 2nd Battalion, 5th New York Heavy Artillery. The
340-man artillery unit, assigned to Captain Henry A. DuPont's artillery
brigade, had been deployed as infantry. Only forty New Yorkers managed
to escape in the confusion. The swarming Rebels captured the rest and sent
them to the rear as prisoners.[11]

As the 50th Georgia emerged from the strip of woods, they saw all
of Thoburn's lines. Ahead of them lay a slight ravine, and on the heights
beyond were entrenchments covered with abatis. The Wiregrass men could
see half-dressed soldiers in camp rushing in all directions. The Rebel line
steadily moved down into the ravine and quietly aligned its ranks.[12]

Colonel Simms barked the order to attack. McGlashan remembered,
"Then ringing through the air came the command: 'Now men, fix bayonets.
Forward, double quick, charge!' With a wild, fierce yell that seemed to rend the
clouds above, the line rushed up the slope and dashed at the intrenchments." The
ghostly silhouettes suddenly appeared out of the fog, and with a thunderous roar
of musketry, the Georgians poured over Thoburn's entrenchments. The 50th
Georgians slammed into the left of Thoburn's division and quickly overran
Lieutenant Colonel Thomas F. Wildes' 1st Brigade and Colonel Thomas M.
Harris's 3rd Brigade.[13]

McGlashan described a unique method used by his Georgians to get
into the enemy's works. "By common consent, it seemed, the men thrust their
bayonets under the abatis and turned it clear over against the earthworks, thus
making it a help instead of an obstacle in getting on top. Then leaping into the
ditch, firing, bayoneting and slashing on every side, they soon cleared it of the
alarmed and terrified enemy."[14]

Within fifteen minutes, Simms' men wrecked Thoburn's command and
sent it in a mad scramble to the rear. Next in line came the rest of Dupont's
artillery emplacements. By the time the artillerymen saw the onrushing Rebels
through the fog, the 50th Georgians were on top of them. Lieutenant William
Munk's Battery D, 1st Pennsylvania Light Artillery, had no chance. The half-
dressed gunners failed to fire off more than a single round before the Wiregrass
men swarmed over them. The Georgians killed, wounded, or captured most of

these enemy artillerists. The other two batteries in the brigade, Lieutenant Henry F. Brewerton's Battery B, 5th United States Artillery, and Captain Frank C. Gibbs' Battery L, 1st Ohio Light, barely escaped the screaming, onrushing Southerners.[15]

Sketch of Simms' Brigade and 50th Georgia overrunning Lieutenant William Munk's Battery D, 1st Pennsylvania Light Artillery during the initial attack through the fog at Cedar Creek. Signal Knob, a prominent point on the north end of Massanutten Mountain looms in the background. Art by Francis Augustín O'Reilly.

As Kershaw's division demolished the right flank of George Crook's Army of West Virginia, Gordon's men made similar work of its left. This rout of Crook's army took less than half an hour to unfold. Early's pre-dawn surprise attack had worked perfectly against the dazed and disorganized Yankees.

Led by the 50th Georgia, Simms' men outpaced Kershaw's other brigades and bore almost the entire struggle against Thoburn's infantry and Dupont's artillery. Simms halted his exhausted soldiers in the abandoned Federal works and waited for the rest of the division to catch up to his position. He reported, "After capturing the works and sweeping through the camp (which was just inside the works), there being no troops either on our right or left, I thought it prudent to fall back to the captured works and await the arrival of other troops."[16]

Colonel McGlashan later described an amusing incident he observed while the Georgians waited for the other brigades:

Right here an absurd incident occurred, which goes to show that no situation may be so terrible or tragic but it may have a comic side to it. In leaping over the earthworks, a young lieutenant discovered a large pot of boiling coffee on one of the camp fires, got ready, doubtless, for some picket's early breakfast. Well, coffee was more than scarce to us. He was excited and thirsty, and the chance to get a good drink of real coffee was a temptation he could not resist, so he sprang over and seized the pot, took a huge swallow and scalded the tongue and roof of his mouth out of his head. Just then, a general officer galloped up and cried: "What regiment is this?" "Hell fire and damnation!" screamed the agonized officer, sputtering out the hot coffee. The general stared, but, taking in the situation, rode off, laughing and saying: "A very good name for your regiment, indeed."[17]

During the pause, the retreating enemy attempted to reform along the ridgeline to the north. Colonel McGlashan turned the captured artillery against the Yankees. The 50th Georgia commander reported, "Seeing the dense mass of the enemy in front and the danger of their re-forming and charging us in turn, I called on my adjutant, [and brother, Andrew McGlashan] . . . an old British artillery officer, to try and turn the captured guns against the enemy. In an incredibly short space of time he had formed six gun squads and was sending shell after shell into their broken ranks, completing their route [rout] and hastening their retreat."[18]

The brigades of Goggin and Moody soon reached Simms. They were joined by Brigadier General Clement A. Evans' division of Gordon's corps. Colonel Wofford's Brigade had drifted off to the northeast and become separated from Kershaw's other brigades. Major General William H. Emory's XIX Corps stood as the next line of Federal defenders in the path of the Confederate onslaught.

Kershaw's three brigades came over the ridge from the southwest, through the smoke and fog, while Evans's troops rushed in from the east. Screaming like banshees, Kershaw's men charged up the ravine and crossed the Valley Pike toward the 156th and 176th New York regiments of Colonel Daniel McCauley's Third Brigade. The 50th Georgia smashed into the left side of the two New York regiments as the 53rd, 51st, and 10th Georgia troops tore into the right side of McCauley's bluecoats.[19]

Hellish fighting occurred along the lines, but nothing could stop the overwhelming Rebel tide. Lieutenant Colonel Alfred Neafie, 156th New York, reported: "A desperate hand-to-hand fight ensued on the left of the brigade line. The enemy had planted their colors on our works and were desperately fighting across them, meeting stubborn resistance, while they swarmed like bees round the battery on our left and rear." The outnumbered New Yorkers put up a heroic struggle but soon broke and ran for the rear. As Simms' men crushed the 156th and 176th New York regiments, Colonel Goggin's South Carolina brigade, to Simms' left, overpowered the 128th New York and 38th Massachusetts regiments.[20]

Current view from north side of Valley Pike looking south. Simms' Brigade and the 50th Georgia rushed up from the southwest and overwhelmed the 156th and 176th New York Regiments of the Union XIX Corps near this area. Photo by author.

Kershaw's and Evans' veterans swamped the XIX Corps defenses. Although General Emory's men put up a tougher struggle than Crook's corps, they were soon pushed back northeast as the Confederates continued their relentless attack. Two Federal corps had been routed in less than two hours, and the retreating Yankees had been swept some five miles, "like chaff before the wind."[21]

Crook's and Emory's troops abandoned thousands of weapons and provisions, plus hundreds of their captured comrades. As the enemy vacated their camps, many of the poorly clad, ill-equipped, thirsty, hungry Confederates stopped their pursuit to plunder the wealth left behind. Colonel McGlashan estimated that almost one-half of the men around him, officers and enlisted men alike, stopped to sample the fruits of victory, albeit prematurely. With tongue-in-cheek, the 50th Georgia commander recalled the ransacking of the enemy quartermaster stores: "These last were so valuable and so badly needed by us that an undue number of our officers and men remained behind to look after them, leaving little over half of the force who remained faithful to the colors to pursue the enemy into the open country."[22]

The final enemy line of defense was Major General Horatio G. Wright's VI Corps. Wright's men hurriedly constructed defenses north of Meadow Brook and tried to rally the other retreating Federals against the oncoming Rebel wave. At about 7:30 a.m., Kershaw's three brigades and Evans' division rushed up the hill and slammed into the Union lines. The sides stood toe-to-toe and fired point blank into one another's faces. The smoke and fog made for an almost surreal picture.

The VI Corps troops put up a fierce resistance and initially repulsed the Rebel advances. However, the Federal line slowly began to waver and break under the relentless Confederate pressure. The Yankees fell back from the hilltop as the line of screaming butternuts moved over the crest. The bluecoats retreated almost a mile northward before they stopped and regrouped in the woods northwest of Middletown.

Around 8 a.m., after three hours of battle, the Confederate attack slowed and became disorganized. The emerging daylight exposed the terrible path of destruction as warmth from the rising sun began to burn off the fog. Hundreds of dead and wounded lay strewn over the battlefield from Cedar Creek to beyond Middletown. Both armies were exhausted from the fierce conflict. As Colonel McGlashan remembered, "The day was advancing, the heat increasing, and the men, under the tremendous exertions they were making, having driven the enemy over six miles over a rough country, were rapidly becoming wearied and faint."[23]

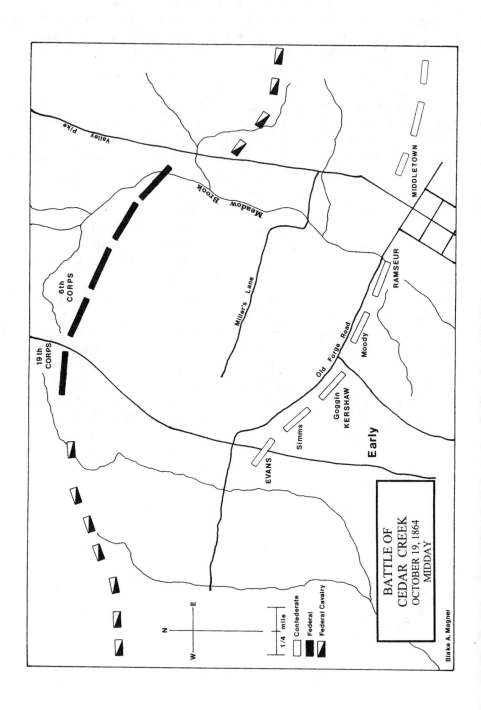

BATTLE OF
CEDAR CREEK
OCTOBER 19, 1864
MIDDAY

Confederate
Federal
Federal Cavalry

1/4 mile

Blake A. Magner

Two hours later, Jubal Early's surprise offensive had stalled. Early first assumed the Federals were in full retreat, but he later feared enemy reinforcements and a possible attack on his right flank by Yankee cavalry. The Confederate commander made a critical decision to hold the ground that had been gained instead of gathering his wayward troops and pushing ahead. In his report after the battle, Early stated, "I determined, therefore, to content myself with trying to hold the advantages I had gained until all my troops had come up and the captured property was secured."[24]

Confederate position along Old Forge Road. Simms' Brigade and the 50th Georgia Regiment faced elements of the Union VI Corps that were located a mile across the field in the woods. About 1:00 p.m., the Confederates probed the Federal defenses and advanced northeast beyond Miller's Lane before being repulsed. At approximately 4:00 p.m., Sheridan launched a fierce counterattack from the woods. Simms' men held their position until the brigades to their left retreated. The Georgians then joined in the disorganized retreat as the Federal counterattack routed Early's army. Photo by author.

Early's smaller Confederate force had pushed the Yankees to a position northwest of Middletown. The Rebel lines stood along the Old Forge Road facing northeast toward the Union lines, which were about one mile away. Joseph Kershaw's division lay between the right of Clement Evans' division and the left of Stephen Ramseur's division. Simms' Georgia brigade anchored Kershaw's left; Goggin's South Carolina brigade occupied the center; and Moody's Mississippi brigade held Kershaw's right.

Little action took place between about 10:00 a.m. and 1:00 p.m. The lull allowed Phil Sheridan to ride from Winchester to rally his disorganized army.

At about 1:00 p.m., Early directed General Gordon to send the divisions of Kershaw, Evans, and Ramseur to probe the VI and XIX Corps positions. By now, the Yankees had regrouped and reinforced their defenses. The unfortunate delay neutralized the earlier element of surprise by the Rebels. The Confederates moved from their position along Old Forge Road to just beyond Miller's Lane. There they ran into heavy Union resistance. The enemy repulsed Early's probe after brief but intense fighting.

At 4:00 p.m., Sheridan's re-energized army launched a fierce counterattack from the woods against the Confederate positions as both lines exploded in musketry. Emory's XIX Corps made up the Federal right, Wright's VI Corps occupied the middle, and Crook's Army of West Virginia held the far left and stood in reserve. The XIX Corps slammed into Evans' lines on the Confederate left. Brigadier General Frank Wheaton's 1st and Colonel Warren Keifer's 3rd divisions of Wright's VI Corps hit Kershaw's position in the middle, while George Getty's 2nd Division attacked Ramseur on the Rebel right.

The fighting became savage as both sides refused to give ground. Firing from behind the cover of a stone wall along Miller's Lane, Kershaw's veterans, including the 50th Georgians, inflicted a murderous toll on Wheaton's and Keifer's men. The Confederates repulsed attack after attack and held their position. After about an hour of brutal combat, however, the Rebel line began to waver. First, Ramseur pulled back his line on Kershaw's right to a better defensive position. Then part of Evans' line to the left of Simms' Brigade began to give way, leaving Kershaw's men in the foremost position.

Simms' Georgians fell back about a quarter-mile and attempted to reform. The brigade held for a short time, but enemy troops soon overran their position. Colonel McGlashan described the desperate situation for the 50th Georgians:

> Evans' brigade on the left, fearing capture, gave way and fell
> back toward us, bring[ing] on a general retreat of the whole
> line to escape the converging lines threatening them. Another
> halt was made, again our flanks were turned and another
> retrograde movement was made; by this time the retreat was
> general, the line was threatened with entire capture and large
> bodies of cavalry could be seen breaking off to our rear and
> riding toward the captured camps. The men, acting by a kind
> of instinct, broke their line formation, and deploying as

skirmishers, managed to cover the whole front of the enemy's advance, thus checking their cavalry, but without power any longer to stop the infantry advance. So the huge line of skirmishers fell back rapidly, fighting as they went, every man for himself. By this time every officer was in his place trying to retrieve the lost honors of the day, but too late. All organization was gone, and the men, marching and fighting for eighteen hours continuously, were utterly exhausted and incapable of further effort.[25]

While attempting to rally his men late in the battle, 50th Georgia commander Colonel Peter McGlashan fell, having been shot through both thighs. McGlashan would be the third of Simms' regimental commanders to fall on the battlefield this day. Nineteen-year-old Lieutenant Billy Pendleton, Company B commander, also went down near the end from a rifle ball to his left temple.[26]

Both McGlashan and Pendleton were initially taken to temporary field hospitals then transported to a hospital in Staunton. On October 24, McGlashan received a furlough to his home in Thomasville, Georgia, to recuperate. Pendleton spent six weeks in the hospital before rejoining his company near Richmond. Fortunately, the ball that struck the young lieutenant was almost spent. Otherwise the wound likely would have been fatal.[27]

Another Wiregrass officer seriously wounded that day was the Company G commander, Captain Quarterman B. Staten. Transported to a hospital near New Market after the battle, Staten was later transferred to a Richmond hospital. On December 30, the Echols County officer received a furlough to his home in Stockton, Georgia, where he spent the rest of the war convalescing.[28]

The disastrous end to Early's brilliant morning offensive came quickly. As thoroughly as the Rebels had routed Sheridan's army in the morning, the Federals did the same to the stunned Confederates in the late afternoon. Sheridan's men pushed the Confederates south of Cedar Creek and Hupp's Hill by 7:00 p.m. The Union cavalry continued to wreak havoc on the retreating Southerners during the evening. The Yankees captured scores of disorganized Confederates, including Private Cornelius Peterson of Company D. One of many Wiregrass soldiers taken prisoner, Peterson spent the rest of the war in Point Lookout Prison. He was finally paroled on June 6, 1865.[29]

The shooting faded away by midnight, leaving a trail of carnage. Dead and wounded men covered the battlefield. One unfortunate Rebel soldier, Sergeant John Wade King of Company F, suffered a mortal wound and died on

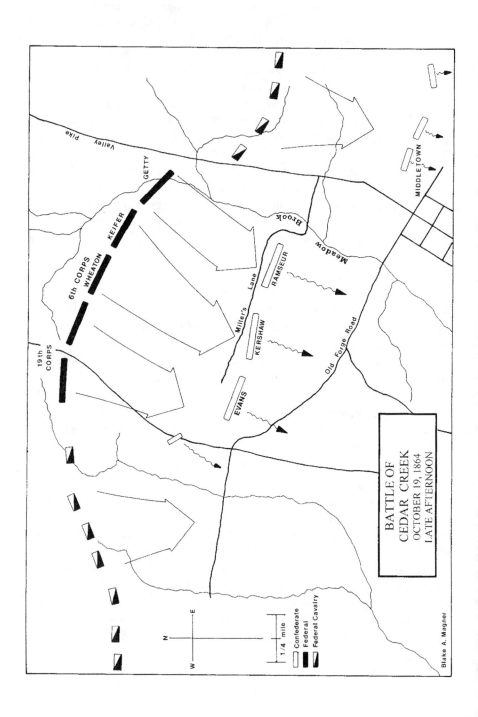

BATTLE OF
CEDAR CREEK
OCTOBER 19, 1864
LATE AFTERNOON

Confederate
Federal
Federal Cavalry

1/4 mile

Blake A. Magner

the battlefield. A comrade collected his personal effects to return to his widow. The items included a letter the Decatur County soldier wrote to his wife four days earlier but had not mailed. In the letter, King described the harsh conditions and his longing to see his family:

> times is pretty hard her[e] at this time. this Division has fought and Marched and Marched and fought ever since I have Bin Back here. Wife I should lie [like] to see you all very mutch though I cant tell when that time will come. . . . I Must close this letter. Wright Soon, give me all the News you have. Wife pray for Me that I May get out of this War safe and return home again. Believe Me to Bee as ever your true Husband
> John W. King
> To Mrs. Arena King
> Tell Thomas I will write to him soon.[30]

After the disaster, the remnants of Early's broken army straggled back and camped near Fisher's Hill. At about 3 a.m. the next day, the exhausted men continued their march. They reached New Market around 4:00 p.m., after a grueling twenty-nine mile trek.[31]

Sergeant John Wade King, Company F. Before the war, this South Carolina native was a farmer in Decatur County. The father of seven children, King enlisted in the Decatur Volunteers on July 8, 1862 at Bainbridge. He received a wound at Spotsylvania Court House on May 12, 1864, and convalesced at his home in Calvary, Georgia. According to family history, the women of his hometown made him five sets of uniforms before he returned to his company. John Wade King fell five months later at the Battle of Cedar Creek. He was thirty-nine. His final resting place is unknown but a Confederate memorial marker was placed near his wife's grave in Piedmont Cemetery, Calvary, Georgia. Photo courtesy of Robert and Annette Harrell, Cairo, Georgia.

The Battle of Cedar Creek was the last large engagement to take place in the Shenandoah Valley. What began as a masterful opportunity for victory ended in a crushing defeat and the end of Confederate military power in the Valley. The official Federal casualty report listed 644 killed, 3,430 wounded and 1,591 missing. Rebel battle reports are scarce, although total Confederate casualties are thought to be about 3,000. General Early estimated about 2,800 casualties. Another report counted 320 killed, 1,540 wounded and 1,050 missing.[32]

Simms' Brigade, led by the 50th Georgia, had been in the vanguard of the initial assault and suffered heavy casualties. Simms reported: "In this battle the brigade had about five hundred and twenty arms bearing men. Of four regimental commanders, three were wounded, two have since died of the wounds —Colonels Ball and Holt. Colonel McGlashan was wounded through both thighs. . . . The loss of the brigade was heavy in officers and men —about two hundred killed and wounded." Many others were captured during the confused retreat. Assuming the total effective strength of the brigade to be between "about 400 muskets," as stated by McGlashan after the war, and "520 arms-bearing men" in Simms' post-battle report, the brigade may have lost more than half of its total effective force.[33]

Casualty reports for the 10th and 51st Georgia Regiments could not be located. One source stated the 53rd Georgia "lost ten killed and 31 wounded." The 50th Georgia suffered at least seventy-four casualties, including fourteen officers. Of the total losses, ten were killed; five mortally wounded; twenty wounded; six wounded/captured; and thirty-three captured. Based on estimated strength going into the battle, the Wiregrass soldiers probably suffered more than 50 percent casualties. Individual company losses are as follows:

> Regimental Staff (2) – 1 wounded, 1 wounded/captured
> Company A (6) – 1 mortally wounded, 1 wounded, 4 captured
> Company B (3) – 3 wounded
> Company C (5) – 1 mortally wounded, 4 captured
> Company D (8) – 1 killed, 3 wounded, 2 wounded/captured, 2 captured
> Company E (8) – 1 mortally wounded, 2 wounded, 5 captured
> Company F (6) – 2 killed, 2 wounded, 2 captured
> Company G (13) – 2 mortally wounded, 2 wounded, 9 captured
> Company H (3) – 1 killed, 1 wounded, 1 captured
> Company I (6) – 3 killed, 1 wounded/captured, 2 captured
> Company K (14) – 3 killed, 5 wounded, 2 wounded/captured, 4 captured.[34]

Stragglers from the battle continued to wander back into camp over the next few weeks. Early's army remained near New Market, regrouping and staging lackluster forays to blunt possible Federal attacks. The shattered army had no strength to mount another offensive.

Robert E. Lee decided to recall Kershaw's division in mid-November to help defend Richmond. The morning of November 15 started out dreary, cold and wet as Kershaw's men slowly marched south out of the Shenandoah Valley. The division reached Waynesborough on November 17. The 50th Georgia boarded a train for Richmond that night and arrived near the Confederate capital the next day.[35]

The Wiregrass veterans had marched up and down the Shenandoah Valley during the previous three months. They participated in numerous skirmishes and small engagements. The 50th Georgia had been in the forefront of what could have been one of the greatest Confederate victories of the war but turned into one of the most devastating defeats. Now the Valley—the breadbasket of the Confederacy—was lost. As the shattered remnants of the regiment settled into the trenches around Richmond, the men must have realized that the end was now just a matter of time.

A fter returning from the Shenandoah Valley on November 18, the 50th Georgia settled into the trenches about four miles southeast of Richmond. Major John M. Spence temporarily commanded the regiment while Colonel Peter McGlashan recuperated from the serious wounds he suffered at Cedar Creek. Brigadier General Joseph Kershaw's division rejoined their old corps commander, James Longstreet. General Lee's "Warhorse" had recovered from the near-fatal wound he received at the Wilderness and had resumed command of the First Corps.[1]

On November 23, the 50th Georgia moved a short distance and took their position on the left of Simms' line, just north of the York River Railroad. The Wiregrass men would remain here for the next month.[2]

Robert E. Lee's ragged Army of Northern Virginia had dwindled to an effective infantry force of fewer than sixty thousand men by the winter of 1864-1865. It faced a well-supplied Federal army of almost twice that size. This winter would be especially harsh on the remnants of Lee's once-powerful army. One Union officer reported: "It was especially so to the Confederate troops with their threadbare, insufficient clothing, and meager food, chiefly corn bread made of the coarsest meal. Meat they had but little of, and their Subsistence Department was actually importing it from abroad. Of coffee or tea and sugar, they had none except in the hospitals."[3]

The razor-thin Confederate lines stretched almost forty miles around Richmond and Petersburg. Lieutenant General Ambrose P. Hill's Third Corps held the Rebel right from Hatcher's Run to Fort Gregg. The troops of Lieutenant General John B. Gordon and Lieutenant General Richard H. Anderson manned the lines from Hill's left to the Appomattox River. Lieutenant General James Longstreet's First Corps anchored the line from the Appomattox River to the Rebel left flank at White Oak Swamp. Lieutenant General Richard S. Ewell commanded the Reserve Corps, including the Department of Richmond forces defending the capital.[4]

By the end of November, Kershaw's division numbered about 3,500 troops—the strength of a single brigade earlier in the war. The effective strength of the division fell each day due to attrition from casualties, sickness, and the increasing number of desertions. The exact numbers for Simms' Brigade are unknown. Even with soldiers replenishing the ranks after the Battle of Cedar Creek, the brigade likely counted only about seven hundred Georgians. The muster roll of the 50th Georgia would most likely have been less than 150 muskets.[5]

Active operations slowed as both sides settled into winter quarters. On December 8, James P. Simms finally received his long-overdue promotion to brigadier general. Simms had commanded the brigade for most of the past six months and provided effective leadership. Another happy event occurred during the month when popular Billy Pendleton rejoined his comrades in Company B. The young lieutenant still bore the scar next to his left eye from his near-fatal Cedar Creek wound.[6]

On December 20, General Lee ordered Major General Robert F. Hoke's 5,600-man division from the Richmond lines to Wilmington, North Carolina, to defend Fort Fisher from an anticipated Federal assault. Over the next two days, Kershaw's men moved down the lines into the positions being vacated by Hoke.[7]

The 50th Georgia moved from its position north of the York River Railroad to a location south of the Darbytown Road to relieve Brigadier General William W. Kirkland's Brigade of Hoke's division. The site was near Chaffin's Farm and the area the regiment had briefly occupied during the Deep Bottom operations in late July. The Wiregrass men would remain in that location until the evacuation of Richmond.[8]

Shortly after occupying Hoke's former position, Longstreet ordered Kershaw to shift two of his regiments farther right, relieving General Ewell's troops on that part of the line. The 50th Georgians remained in their position, but the movement further stretched Kershaw's thin lines.[9]

As the men languished in the trenches, conditions back home continued to weigh heavily on their minds. A soldier in the nearby 18th Georgia Artillery Battalion (Savannah Guards) described the deteriorating conditions and sinking morale in a letter to his father: "The army is in very bad spirits though I feel hopeful the idea of subjugation will not stick in my head. The men continue to desert very fast. Over sixty have left the Battalion. I have no idea of getting home this winter. You must make the best arrangements for Ma & Sis in the future. I never expect to leave the army until circumstances change very much." The soldier continued, "Rations are very scarce. We have been two and three days without a mouthful of meat. Christmas was very dull. I am going to go to town on new years and get one more dinner."[10]

Worsening weather and declining morale continued as the 50th Georgia soldiers marked the New Year huddled in their trenches. Lieutenant

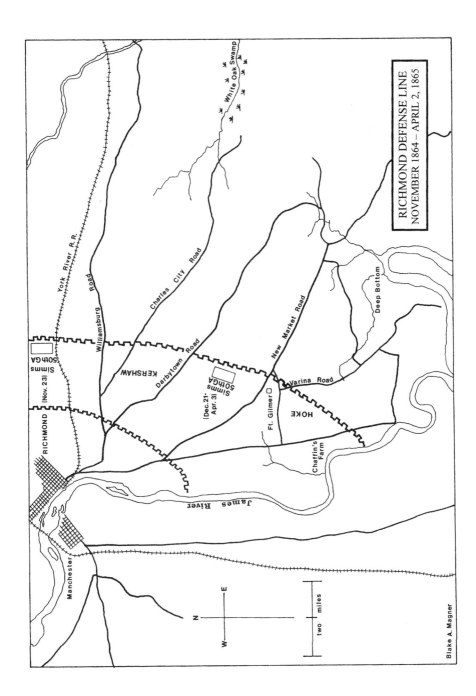

RICHMOND DEFENSE LINE
NOVEMBER 1864 – APRIL 2, 1865

White Oak Swamp

York River R.R.

Williamsburg Road

Charles City Road

Darbytown Road

New Market Road

Deep Bottom

Varina Road

Slms 50th GA
[Nov. 23]

KERSHAW

Simms 50th GA
[Dec. 21-
Apr. 3]

RICHMOND

Ft. Gilmer

HOKE

Chaffin's Farm

James River

Manchester

N
W — E
S

two miles

Blake A. Magner

Billy Pendleton noted: "The Soldiers are in the lowest spirits I have ever seen them." On January 13, Private Hugh O'Neal of Company B could not take the despair any longer. The Ware County soldier left his picket post and walked into the enemy lines. O'Neal swore allegiance to the U.S. Government and received transportation to Baltimore, Maryland.[11]

In January, Brigadier General Simms temporarily relinquished command of the brigade due to illness. Colonel James Dickey of the 51st Georgia Regiment assumed command in Simms' absence. On January 25, Billy Pendleton finally received a promotion to captain, retroactive to January 11. Still two months shy of his twentieth birthday, Pendleton had served as the temporary commander of Company B for the past year.[12]

Weather conditions turned miserable during much of late January and early February. Pendleton recorded in his diary some particularly bad days: "Jan. 21. A good deal of rain today, and it freezes as fast as it falls to the ground. . . . Sun. Jan. 29. Capt. Smith of Co. I, while attempting to skate on some ice, received a severe fall which came very near killing him. . . . Feb. 7. On picket today; the weather is bitter cold; the wind blowing hard."[13]

On February 10, Colonel Peter McGlashan rejoined the regiment, although he had not completely recovered from his Cedar Creek wounds. The popular commander received a warm welcome from the men, as Pendleton described: "Col. McGlashan came in last night a little after dark; whereupon the boys got the 53rd [regiment] band and serenaded him. He made us a speech which gave a very encouraging view of affairs in Georgia; and I think it has had a good effect. I was very glad to see the Col.; he has been a great friend to me."[14]

McGlashan assumed temporary command of the brigade due to General Simms' continued illness. Colonel Dickey returned to the 51st Georgia. Captain George E. Fahm took over the 50th Georgia when Major Spence received a furlough to his home in Ware County.[15]

On February 13, Billy Pendleton left for home on a twenty-four-day furlough. After obtaining transportation in Richmond, the newly promoted captain made his way home to Lowndes County. He had not seen his family in almost a year.[16]

Orders arrived by the end of February transferring Brigadier General James Conner's Brigade to South Carolina. Their departure left Kershaw's division with fewer than 2,000 effective officers and men. Simms' Brigade totaled about 650. As the war slowly ground on toward a predictable end, more and more Southerners simply slipped out of the trenches and either walked into the enemy lines or headed home. For the two-week period from February 23 to March 8, Kershaw's division reported a total of 135 desertions, with 24 from Bryan's (Simms') Brigade.[17]

Sergeant Simeon (Sim) L. Morton, 18th Georgia Artillery Battalion, described the discouragement of the soldiers in a letter to his father. The Georgian gave little hope for victory, stating: "Our men are deserting very fast. I expect it will ruin the army. Exactly one half of our Battalion have deserted. Two from Brooks [county] went a few nights ago. . . . Great many men have gone who were looked upon as men of good standing at home. I am told the 50th Ga. Reg are deserting very fast." Faithful to the end, Morton remained with his battalion and was killed on April 6 at Sailor's Creek.[18]

The Rebel lines continued to grow thinner. Colonel McGlashan recalled, "Our line was so attenuated that had we attempted to man the works in continuous line of battle, the line would have been in single rank and the men ten feet apart. Yet so completely were the enemy kept deceived as to our real strength that when we were strengthening our works with chevaux-de-frise and flooding Deep Bottom with water, their pickets called out to ours to know if we thought they were darned fools to charge such lines as that. So few in numbers were we, that one-half of the entire force had to go on picket every night. The men were ill-fed and poorly clad, but bright and cheerful and hopeful to the last."[19]

Grant's army continued to tighten the noose around Petersburg and Richmond as the situation for the Army of Northern Virginia grew more desperate. In a confidential March 9 letter to Secretary of War John C. Breckinridge, General Robert E. Lee gave his somber assessment of the situation:

> My correspondence with the Department will show the extreme difficulties under which we have labored during the past year to keep this army furnished with necessary supplies. This difficulty is increased, and it seems almost impossible to maintain our present position with the means at the disposal of the Government. . . . Unless the men and animals can be subsisted, the army cannot be kept together, and our present lines must be abandoned. Nor can it be moved to any other position where it can operate to advantage without provisions to enable it to move in a body. . . . While the military situation is not favorable, it is not worse than the superior numbers and resources of the enemy justified us in expecting from the beginning. Indeed, the legitimate military consequences of that superiority have been postponed longer than we had reason to anticipate.[20]

Lee knew that he would have to abandon his defensive lines around Petersburg and Richmond soon. The Confederate commander hoped to join General Joseph E. Johnston's Army of the Tennessee in North Carolina and continue the struggle. Aware of this possibility, General Grant ordered his forces to mount an offensive to turn Lee's right and prevent the Rebels' escape.

On April 1, the enemy broke the Confederate right at Five Forks. Shortly after hearing the news of the Union success, Grant ordered a general assault early on April 2 all along the Petersburg lines. Longstreet hurried Major General Charles W. Field's division south from Richmond to reinforce Lee's right, but kept Kershaw's division in the trenches near the capital. This move placed Kershaw's troops under the temporary command of General Richard Ewell.[21]

Grant's army attacked the weakened Confederate defenses at Petersburg before Lee could plug the gaps. Although the greatly outnumbered Rebels put up a fierce struggle, the overwhelming Federal force broke through the lines. Lee ordered the abandonment of Petersburg and Richmond as his troops fell back in all directions. Later that day, Ewell received the order to evacuate Richmond and destroy the provisions that could not be removed. Ewell ordered Kershaw's division to Richmond. "On the evening of the 2nd," recalled Colonel McGlashan, "we learned that our lines had been broken in front of Petersburg, that Lee was in retreat southward, and that Richmond must be evacuated."[22]

Simms' Brigade silently withdrew its pickets around midnight and filed onto the road toward Richmond. In the city, word spread of the Confederate abandonment. Desperate mobs plundered stores for food and supplies and set fire to buildings. Unable to control the rampaging crowds with local militia, Ewell rushed word to Kershaw, "who was coming up from the lines, to hurry his leading regiment into town." Kershaw recalled, "I detached two battalions to suppress the mob then engaged in sacking the city."[23]

McGlashan described the march of the brigade into the Confederate capital and the tragic scene awaiting the Georgians:

> Concentrating on the road towards Richmond we took up the
> line of march for the alarmed capital, the stern, sad faces of
> the men showed their sense of the gravity of the situation and
> the crisis before them. As we approached Richmond, the
> evidences of alarm, sorrow and despair showed themselves
> on every hand. People wildly rushing about in every
> direction; bands of lawless roughs breaking into and looting
> stores and repositories of government supplies; houses and
> stores on fire and gutted; explosions of fire arms and
> munitions of war, accentuated by the tremendous explosions

of the gunboats on the James, as they were blown up, the
sorrow and despair of the forsaken people and the shouts of
the maddened rabble on the streets, made up a scene of horror
never to be forgotten while life lasts.[24]

Ewell's troops restored some order to the city before they received
evacuation orders. The Confederate commander reported, "By daylight
the riot was subdued, but many buildings which I had carefully directed
should be spared had been fired by the mob." Ewell's troops marched out
of the burning city and crossed the Manchester Bridge over the James River.
By the time Kershaw's division reached the bridge, it was in flames. Colonel
McGlashan recalled the 50th Georgia's narrow escape from the city:
"Thinking the troops had all crossed, the bridge had been fired to check
pursuit, and was burning fiercely in the center. Double-quicking my men
through the flames, we gained the other side, being the last troops to leave
the city."[25]

The Rebels left behind many sick and wounded soldiers when they
abandoned Petersburg and Richmond. At least six Wiregrass soldiers became
prisoners in Richmond area hospitals when Union troops entered the city
on April 3. The unfortunate Georgians were Sergeant O. W. Wells of
Company A; Corporal William B. Bagley of Company B; Privates James
Conner and John C. Parnell of Company E; Sergeant Lewis Bloodworth of
Company H; and Private William H. Harrell of Company K. Private Conner
served as a hospital nurse and elected to remain with his sick comrades.
Corporal Bagley died of chronic diarrhea on April 23.[26]

Over the next two days, the beleaguered Confederate troops trudged
toward Amelia Court House, some thirty miles to the west. General Lee
hoped to gain a day's lead on his pursuers and combine his forces at Amelia
Court House. He intended to provide the famished army with much-needed
rations before moving farther southwest to link up with General Joseph E.
Johnston's army. Heavy rains during the previous week resulted in
overflowing waterways and almost impassable roads that hampered both
the Confederate withdrawal and the Federal pursuit.

Peter McGlashan recalled the agonizing march:

> As we advanced, we saw everywhere the evidences
> of the terrible nature of the retreat of Lee's army. The road
> was lined with dead horses and mules in all states of
> emaciation from want of food; abandoned artillery, half
> covered with earth, for the time could not be spared to
> effectually cover them from the gaze of the enemy; foot-sore
> and half-starved wrecks of soldiers, still clinging to their

bright muskets and striving hard to keep up, cheering us as we passed, defiant and resolute to the last, while all over the country behind us streamed the pursuing legions of Grant.[27]

James Longstreet led Lee's slow-moving column into Amelia Court House by the afternoon of April 4. Gordon's command followed close behind. Other units, including Ewell's, stretched behind for miles. Unfortunately for the hungry troops, the much-anticipated rations had not been delivered to Amelia Court House. The Confederate commander had to either keep moving or stop and forage for rations while waiting for his remaining troops. Lee reluctantly chose to forage. The decision would prove costly.

The combination of Lee's decision to forage for rations and delays by his ragged army allowed the Federals to make up the one-day Confederate lead. The Army of Northern Virginia needed time to distance itself from the enemy pursuers. Unfortunately, that precious commodity had slipped away.

On the rainy afternoon of April 5, Longstreet led the column out of Amelia Court House and headed southwest toward the Burkeville rail crossing. The 50th Georgia and the rest of Ewell's exhausted and hungry troops reached Amelia Court House just as the rear of Longstreet's command marched away in the distance. Anticipating Lee's route, Union infantry and cavalry blocked the Rebel path to Burkeville near Jetersville. Lee then detoured the army on another all-night forced march toward Farmville, more than twenty miles to the west. The Confederate commander hoped that by marching throughout the night, his men might gain some time.

General Longstreet's command, consisting of the First and Third Corps, led the Confederate column, and General Richard Anderson's Corps followed. Ewell's Reserve Corps, including the 50th Georgia and the rest of Kershaw's division, trailed Anderson. The main wagon train followed Ewell, and Gordon's Second Corps brought up the rear.

The organization of Lee's army began to break down. Numbed from the combination of constant marching, lack of proper rations, and relentless Federal pursuit, men who could go no further fell out along the wayside or just gave up and started home.

Little Sailor's (Saylor's) Creek - April 6

On the morning of April 6, the Confederates plodded toward Farmville along the Deatonsville Road. Union cavalry harassed the rear columns and gobbled up stragglers throughout the morning. Just before noon, a small body of Union cavalry skirmished with Richard Anderson's force near Holt's

Corner. Anderson stopped to set up defenses, but Mahone's rearguard of Longstreet's command unknowingly continued moving southwest. This created a two-mile gap in the Rebel column that later allowed the enemy to get between Longstreet and the rest of the trailing Confederate army.

Anderson easily repulsed the enemy cavalry raid and resumed his southwest march to catch up with Longstreet. Unfortunately, about one mile after crossing Little Sailor's Creek, he encountered a much larger body of Federal troopers blocking his path at Marshall's Crossroads.

General Ewell's command followed about a mile to the rear of Anderson's column. By mid-afternoon, Ewell reached Little Sailor's Creek and learned of the large enemy cavalry force blocking Anderson. The Confederate commander detoured the slow-moving wagon train and Gordon's Corps northwest along the Jamestown Road and galloped off to meet with Anderson.[28]

As the two Confederate commanders conferred, Major General Horatio G. Wright's Union VI Corps appeared in Ewell's rear. Meanwhile, three divisions of Major General Wesley Merritt's cavalry corps stood in front of Anderson. Ewell's and Anderson's men were effectively cut off from the rest of the Confederate force. The surrounded Rebels could either try to break through the roadblock to the west, or make a stand at Little Sailor's Creek. The two Confederate generals agreed that Ewell would protect the rear while Anderson attempted to break out of the enemy noose.[29]

Ewell positioned his small two-division command of about 3,500 weary and famished men on a crest overlooking Little Sailor's Creek and the James M. Hillsman farm. The Confederate commander described his defensive alignment: "My line ran across a little ravine which leads nearly at right angles toward Sailor's Creek. . . . All of [Major General G. W. Custis] Lee's and part of Kershaw's division were posted behind a rising ground that afforded some shelter from artillery. The creek was perhaps 300 yards in their front, with brush pines between and cleared field beyond it." The cleared field was part of the Hillsman farm.[30]

The left side of Ewell's line consisted of the Richmond Local Defense Troops under the command of Major General G. W. Custis Lee. Numbering about 1,600 men, the division consisted of a hodgepodge of units, including a small naval battalion placed in the rear as reserve.[31]

Kershaw's command anchored the right of the line. The division, numbering "less than 2,000 effective men," consisted of Brigadier General Benjamin G. Humphreys' Brigade commanded by Colonel William H. FitzGerald and the brigades of Brigadier General James Simms and Brigadier General Dudley M. DuBose. The Confederates constructed fortifications to make a stand against the oncoming Federals.[32]

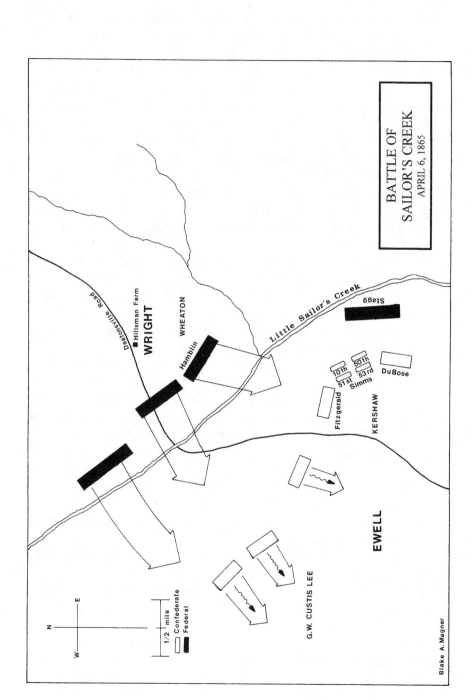

Kershaw initially dispatched Humphreys' Brigade and a battalion of dismounted cavalry to cover his crossing of the creek. He then positioned DuBose's Brigade to anchor his right in the edge of some woods on the Deatonsville Road. Simms' men stood to the left and a little in advance of DuBose. The enemy soon attacked and chased Humphreys' Brigade and the dismounted cavalry back across the creek. The two units formed on Simms's left as he shifted his brigade a little farther to the right.[33]

Colonel Peter McGlashan described the position of Simms' Brigade:

> Crossing the creek we took possession of a low eminence.
> Our line faced to the rear, and overlooking the narrow valley
> in front through which the creek ran. The wagon trains were
> massed on our right, with orders to Commissary [James R.]
> Sheldon to burn if unable to escape. On our left a dense
> thicket of young pines separated us from the position taken
> by the [Savannah] Guards. This thicket was for some reason
> left unoccupied, and became the cause of disaster to the
> Guards. Away to the left stretched the line of Gen. Custis
> Lee's Division and Ewell's line. All the morning the woods
> seemed full of the enemy skirmishers, firing and advancing,
> trying to feel our lines.[34]

Each of Kershaw's brigades formed in two defensive lines. In Simms' Brigade, the 50th Georgia Regiment occupied the right front, and the 10th Georgia took the left. In the rear line, the 53rd Georgia occupied the right, and the 51st Georgia was on the left.[35]

Shortly after 5:00 p.m., the Federal VI Corps opened a strong artillery barrage on Ewell's men. Without their own artillery, Ewell's men could only endure the deadly fire. Thousands of Union VI Corps troops emerged from the woods about a half hour later and moved down the slope toward Little Sailor's Creek.[36]

The enemy artillery fire ceased as the Union infantry advanced. Colonel McGlashan vividly described the enemy attack:

> A beautiful spectacle unrolled itself before us. A line of
> skirmishers sprang out of the woods on the heights above us,
> and, with arms at the trail, came running down the slope to the
> creek, which they tried to cross, when a scattering volley from
> our men checked them, and they threw themselves down in the
> tall grass, awaited the coming of their line of battle. Following
> them in splendid array, with bayonets gleaming and colors
> flying, column after column of infantry defiled out of the woods

and deployed in line of battle for attack, while far away to our
left we could see masses of infantry and cavalry crossing the
road we had just left, and forming for attack on Custis Lee's
Division. It was a magnificent sight. We had no artillery to
hinder their movements, and it looked like a grand field day of
parade. The scene seemed to enchant my men as they gazed at it,
but the low, stern command: "Ready, men! Ready!" broke the
spell, and the men, closing up in line, drew their cartridge boxes to
the front of their belts, capped their guns, and knelt in line and
waited. "Aim low, men; fire as they cross the creek." The enemy
moved steadily to the attack, and as they neared the creek the
command: "Commence firing!" was given. A sheet of flame
leaped from our rifles and the enemy's line, broken and
decimated, staggered back in confusion. It was but a moment,
however. Quickly rallying they leaped the creek and made a rush
up the slope, but the deadly, merciless fire of our men drove them
back again, again and again, with terrible loss, until they retreated
back across the creek, and the men, throwing themselves down in
the grass, refused to advance. I could plainly see their officers
striking their men with the flats of their swords, trying to make
them again face our deadly fire.[37]

The enemy again crossed the creek; this time, they would not be denied.
As the Union VI Corps enveloped Ewell's defenders, Merritt's enemy cavalry
divisions overran Anderson's command near Marshall's Crossroads. In a fierce
but brief struggle, most of Anderson's men surrendered, although Anderson
and a few survivors escaped into the woods during the confusion.

The overwhelming enemy force turned both of Ewell's flanks. Kershaw
described the hopelessness for Simms' and his embattled men: "The enemy
made his appearance in rear of Simms' brigade, at the same time he was engaged
in front and flank. That officer attempted to extricate his command, but found
it impossible to do so without confusion, as he was attacked on all sides." As
Ewell's men fell back, the Yankees continued to press the attack, throwing
new troops into the battle against the overmatched Rebels. Kershaw withdrew
his men about four hundred yards, but soon realized that the enemy surrounded
his command. After brief hand-to-hand combat, the fighting was over. Kershaw
ordered his men and members of his staff "to make their escape in any way
possible."[38]

Colonel McGlashan remembered the last desperate minutes of the
50th Georgia:

The enemy failing to dislodge us with their infantry, brought up
artillery to complete the work. Battery after battery rolled out of

the woods until I counted over twenty guns commanding our position at grape shot range. I knew it was now untenable, and I listened anxiously for news from the left, but the roar of battle had ceased, the Guards [18th Georgia Battalion] was no more, and the men who were falling fast from the constant fire, glanced anxiously at me as the cannon unlimbered in front. Just then a shout from the rear attracted my attention; looking back I saw a staff officer calling to me; going towards him he cried; "Why don't you stop firing? Ewell has surrendered his entire force, and you must cease firing." I was astounded, but soon made up my mind not to surrender my men if I could help myself.

Going back to the line I gave the order to cease firing, in retreat march! The men rose to their feet, faced about, and I marched them back to the low wooded ground in rear, where they were momentarily sheltered from the enemy's fire. There I halted them and faced them to the front, and advancing close to the line, looked keenly at them. They were cool and steady, ready to obey any order. Poor fellows! Originally over eleven hundred strong, only ninety battle-scarred veterans at last faced irremediable defeat. I said, "Men, Gen. Ewell has surrendered his force, we are cut off and surrounded, yet I cannot, will not, surrender you. Bring me the colors." The color guard advanced and placed the colors in my hand. Tearing it off the staff, I broke the staff against the tree, and tearing the flag into fragments, I scattered them in the brush. I then said, "Men, I will dismiss you right here, in the hope you may succeed in escaping and joining the army under Lee. Break ranks, march!" The men looked at me a moment, then the line wavered, broke, and melted in the brush and I was left alone. Suffering from unhealed wounds, I could not accompany them.[39]

Some individual Wiregrass soldiers escaped and continued the struggle for another few days. However, the 50th Georgia Volunteer Infantry Regiment, which had gallantly served for three years of bitter conflict, ceased to exist as a formal fighting unit.

The overwhelming Union force routed the Confederates. The commands of Ewell and Anderson lost between 5,500 and 6,000 men during the battle, most being captured. Ewell reported, "2,800 were taken prisoners, about 150 killed and wounded." Anderson lost another 2,600 men. Eight Confederate generals fell into enemy hands, including Ewell, Kershaw, and Simms. Colonel McGlashan also became a prisoner. This was a final devastating blow to the already decimated Army of Northern Virginia.[40]

View of Little Sailor's Creek Valley facing west. On April 6, 1865, Union troops moved down the slopes toward Little Sailor's Creek, hidden beyond the trees to the west. After being initially repulsed, the much larger Union force overwhelmed and captured most of the 50th Georgia and Richard Ewell's Reserve Corps at the Battle of Sailor's Creek. Photo by author.

The firing ended after nightfall. General Longstreet sent Mahone's division back to help cover the escape of the remaining Confederates. Many of the stragglers were rounded up by Anderson and Mahone and placed in units under Mahone's command. Some individual 50th Georgia survivors likely fell into this group.

At least sixty-five veterans of the 50th Georgia Regiment laid down their weapons at Sailor's Creek. Another fifteen Wiregrass men became prisoners the same day at various other locations in the area, including Amelia Court House (4), Burkeville (1), Farmville (8), and High Bridge (2). Although some may have been left behind during the previous days of grueling forced marches, many likely escaped during the battle and were later taken prisoner. The total casualties for April 6 are listed by individual company, as follows:

Regimental Staff (1) – 1 captured
Company A (8) – 8 captured
Company B (4) – 4 captured
Company C (6) – 6 captured
Company D (8) – 2 wounded/captured, 6 captured
Company E (7) – 7 captured
Company F (17) – 17 captured
Company G (5) – 5 captured
Company H (7) – 7 captured
Company I (10) – 10 captured
Company K (7) – 7 captured[41]

The remnants of the Army of Northern Virginia struggled on for the next few days against insurmountable odds. The end finally came on April 9, at Appomattox Court House. After Robert E. Lee's surrender, the victorious Union army issued rations to the famished Confederates.

Formal surrender ceremonies took place for each of the cavalry, artillery, and infantry branches of service. On April 10, the official surrender for the Confederate cavalry took place, followed by the artillery the next day. April 12 marked the formal surrender ceremony for the Confederate infantry. On this day, the ragged but proud troops, led by General John B. Gordon, marched into the village. Union General Joshua L. Chamberlain, who had been assigned to take charge of the formal surrender ceremony, ordered his men to salute the vanquished foe. Upon seeing the Union salute, General Gordon ordered his men to return the salutation. As the men slowly filed past, they stacked rifles, furled their tattered battle flags, and placed them across the stacks. It was an emotional end for Lee's brave warriors.

After the surrender, the tabular statement of Confederate officers and men paroled at Appomattox Court House listed a total of 12 officers and 178 men from Simms' Brigade. Captain George W. Waldron, formerly of Company A, commanded the brigade due to the capture of General Simms. The last organizational report of General Lee's Army of Northern Virginia listed the 50th Georgia as commanded by Lieutenant Hillery W. Cason, formerly of Company B.[42]

Only twenty-nine 50th Georgia officers and enlisted men remained to stack arms on April 12 (See Appendix C). This list did not include those soldiers hospitalized, imprisoned, detached, or furloughed. The bodies of soldiers from the 50th Georgia lay in the ground from Pennsylvania to Georgia. The proud regiment had participated in more than forty-five engagements, including most of the major battles in the east, and suffered extensive casualties.[43]

Private William W. Griner, Company I. Griner joined the Berrien Light Infantry on March 4, 1862 at Nashville, and he was appointed drummer in October 1864. The Berrien County soldier and most of those left in the 50th Georgia Regiment were captured at the Battle of Sailor's Creek on April 6, 1865. Griner spent the rest of the war at Point Lookout Prison and was released on June 28, 1865. Family records show that after he was paroled, Griner, his cousin, John M. Griner, and other ex-Confederate soldiers were sent by ship from Point Lookout to Savannah, Georgia. The two cousins then walked along railroad tracks from Savannah to their home in Nashville, Georgia. After the war, the Wiregrass soldier farmed, married, and raised ten children. Griner died in 1915, at age 73. Courtesy of the U.S. Army Military History Institute, Carlisle, Pennsylvania.

After the official surrender ceremony concluded, Union officials issued parole slips for the Wiregrass soldiers and allowed them to return to their homes. Men departed on their long journey carrying their parole passes and their meager belongings. Some caught rides along the way. Many walked the entire journey from Virginia to south Georgia.

The remaining Confederate forces surrendered over the days and weeks that followed, bringing an end to the bitter four-year conflict. Although the fighting had ended, many Wiregrass men would endure the hell of Federal prisons until paroled months later. Those soldiers fortunate enough to have survived the war returned to their beloved Georgia only to find homes and families wrecked by the conflict. The men of the 50th Georgia gave their best for a cause in which they believed. Now, these battle-scarred veterans were anxious to put the war years behind them and attempt to resume their lives.

James R. Sheldon, Company E, 50th Georgia Commissary Officer. Born in 1841, Sheldon enlisted as a private in the Thomas County Rangers on March 4, 1862, at Thomasville. In February 1864, Sheldon became ensign/regimental commissary sergeant. Committed to supplying the needs of the soldiers, Sheldon received high praise from the regimental commander, Colonel Peter McGlashan, who stated: "in simple justice to a faithful officer, that we never suffered for want of rations in camp or on the fighting line while Commissary Sheldon could get to us." Sheldon surrendered with the remnants of the 50th Georgia Regiment. After the war he moved to Savannah, and later participated in many Confederate veterans' activities. This postwar photograph shows Sheldon in uniform with what appears to be a badge from a veterans' convention. He died in 1928 at age 88. Courtesy of the U.S. Army Military History Institute, Carlisle, Pennsylvania.

Epilogue

O f the 898 Wiregrass men who enthusiastically volunteered for service on March 4, 1862, only seventeen of the original enlistees remained among the twenty-nine officers and enlisted men present when the Army of Northern Virginia surrendered at Appomattox Court House on April 9, 1865. Many others were in hospitals or Union prisons or had returned home on furlough. About 1,400 men served in the 50th Georgia Infantry Regiment over its three years of existence, and at least 530, more than one of every three, members of the regiment made the ultimate sacrifice.[1]

As the men straggled back to their beloved Georgia over the following weeks and months, they found homes and families devastated by the war. The physical and mental scars from the horrible conflict and the bleak future that awaited them would be difficult to overcome. However, most would resume their civilian lives. Like the hardy wiregrass plant, these veterans shared an innate toughness that saw them through the war and would continue to give them the strength to survive.

Longtime friends Lewis F. Butler and Daniel L. Bryant of Company F, released from Maryland's Point Lookout Prison in June 1865, traveled south to Savannah by ship. They walked from Savannah to the Altamaha River and then caught a train southwest to Thomasville. After getting off at Thomasville, the friends walked the remaining few miles to Decatur County, reaching their homes on July 7, 1865.[2]

After the war, Butler married and began to raise a family of nine children. He purchased more than eighty acres of land and built a home near the Florida border in 1877. After lawmakers adjusted the Georgia/Florida border, the house stood just below the Georgia line in Gadsden County, Florida. Butler died in 1922 and was buried in the family cemetery in front of his house.[3]

Lewis Fennell Butler, Company F. Butler enlisted in the Decatur Infantry on April 8, 1862, at Bainbridge. He was wounded at the Battle of Chancellorsville on May 3, 1863, and later promoted to sergeant. Butler was captured with most of the regiment at Sailor's Creek on April 6, 1865. The Decatur County native was released from Point Lookout Prison on June 24, 1854. Courtesy of Marilee (Mrs. Ermon) Butler, Calvary, Georgia.

After being captured at the Battle of Cedar Creek, Cornelius Peterson spent the next eight months in Point Lookout Prison. Family lore tells that, while traveling back home after his release, the young Wiregrass soldier ran into his brother, Daniel, who was also making his way homeward. They walked back to Lowndes County together. Filthy and covered with lice, when they reached the home place, the brothers refused to enter the house until hot water and clean clothes were left for them on the front porch. Peterson moved to Kilgore, Texas, in 1870, and spent the rest of his life farming. He died in 1930 at age eighty-six.[4]

William W. Douglass, the young soldier whose mother nursed him back to health after his wounding at Fox's Gap, moved to Jacksonville, Florida, after the war. He later married and worked as a printer to support his family. Douglass received a Florida Confederate Service pension from 1907 until his death in 1915, at age seventy-two.[5]

After losing an arm at Chancellorsville, twenty-year-old Charles T. Gandy returned to Thomas County to convalesce. After the war, Gandy farmed and raised a family of eleven children. He was later elected Thomas County coroner and held that post until his death in 1919 at age seventy-seven.

Charles Thomas Gandy, Company E. Gandy lost an arm at the Battle of Chancellorsville. After the war he raised a large family in Thomas County and served as the county coroner until his death in 1919. Courtesy of the U.S. Army Military History Institute, Carlisle, Pennsylvania.

Colonel William R. Manning returned to his large land-holdings in Lowndes County after his resignation as commander of the regiment in 1863. After the war, Manning was mired in debt. The lingering effects of his earlier illness and the strain of financial ruin took a toll on Manning's health, and he died in October 1871.[6]

After resigning in December 1863 to accept a seat in the Georgia Assembly, William O. Fleming briefly returned to military service to help defend against General William T. Sherman's invasion of Georgia. After the war, the Decatur County resident resumed a very successful law practice in Bainbridge. Fleming became solicitor-general of the Albany, Georgia, circuit court in 1876, and superior court judge in 1880. William O. Fleming died in 1881 at the age of forty-six.[7]

When the war ended, Sergeant George Washington Chitty was at home in Echols County on furlough from wounds suffered at Petersburg. Chitty attempted to continue farming, but the loss of the use of his left hand and other health problems made it difficult for him to earn a living for his family of nine children. He applied for and received a Georgia Confederate Service Pension from 1898 until his death. In 1907, the Valdosta Chapter No. 471 of the United Daughters of the Confederacy bestowed the Southern Cross of Honor upon the Company D veteran. He died in 1910 at age seventy-two.[8]

Captain Quarterman Baker Staten was at home in Echols County at the war's end, recuperating from wounds received at Cedar Creek. He served as Clinch County Inferior Court Justice from 1865 to 1868. The former Company G commander died in 1872 at the relatively young age of forty-one.[9]

Colonel Peter Alexander Selkirk McGlashan received a parole from Johnson's Island Prison on August 25, 1865, four and one-half months after his capture at Sailor's Creek. He returned to Thomasville and resumed his saddle and harness business. The voters of the city elected the popular Scotsman as mayor in 1866.[10]

McGlashan moved to Savannah in 1885, where he operated another saddle and harness business. He later held a position in the Savannah city plumbing inspector's office. McGlashan was a popular speaker at veteran's events, and he served as president of the Savannah Confederate Veteran's Association in 1899. He later served a term as the commander of the Georgia Division of the United Confederate Veterans Association.[11]

The former 50th Georgia commander was often introduced as "General McGlashan." His obituary reported that President Davis signed a commission making the colonel a brigadier general just before the fall of Richmond; however, no official record of the promotion has been found. In 1905, the old soldier suffered a stroke that partially paralyzed his left side. Three years later, at age seventy-seven, Peter McGlashan suffered a fatal heart attack while swimming in the river at Isle of Palms near Savannah. He is buried in Laurel Grove Cemetery in Savannah.[12]

Headstone of Colonel Peter Alexander Selkirk McGlashan in Laurel Grove Cemetery, Savannah. Photo by author.

After his furlough ended, Captain William Frederick "Billy" Pendleton made a valiant attempt to rejoin his regiment in March and April 1865. Pendleton's diary reveals that he left home for Virginia on March 24. During his journey, he met up with other Wiregrass soldiers attempting to return to the regiment, including Lieutenants Benjamin Devane, Butler Leverette, and James Waters. On April 18, while just outside of Charlotte, North Carolina, the group learned of General Lee's surrender. Most of the men turned back and headed home. Pendleton and Waters continued to Charlotte, where they received orders to return to Augusta, Georgia. Pendleton's diary entries end on April 22, but other documents reveal that he reached Augusta and received orders on April 27 to proceed to Ware County. The conscientious young officer never made it to Ware County. On May 12, he presented his parole to the Union commander at Macon and was allowed to return home to Lowndes County.[13]

After the war, Billy Pendleton completed his education and taught school for a term in nearby Brooks County. Unhappy with teaching, the twenty-three year-old decided to take up the study of medicine. During this time, Pendleton became increasingly interested in the religious writings of eighteenth-century scientist and theologian Emanuel Swedenborg and the General Church of New Jerusalem, also known as the New Church.[14]

William Pendleton graduated from Savannah Medical College in 1870 and moved to New York to practice medicine. However, his growing interest in the New Church changed the course of his life. He gave up the medical profession and prepared for the ministry.[15]

Pendleton's plans for the ministry were briefly interrupted, however, when his brother's death required him to return home to Lowndes County and help run the family newspaper business. In May 1872, Pendleton married and moved with his new bride to Waltham, Massachusetts, to enter the New Church Theological School. William Pendleton soon began his career as a minister. Pendleton moved to Philadelphia and devoted the rest of his life to the church, never returning to his home in Georgia. He served as president of Bryn Athyn College and Bishop of the Church. In 1927, Bishop Pendleton died at Bryn Athyn, Pennsylvania, at the age of eighty-two.[16]

After being badly wounded and losing a leg at Gettysburg, Sergeant William Moore Jones had to be left in a Williamsport, Maryland, hospital during Lee's retreat to Virginia. In his diary, Jones described the horrible conditions and his near death while awaiting treatment of his amputated limb in a Federal hospital. He and several other wounded Confederates were later transported to Philadelphia, Pennsylvania, in a cattle car. Jones recalled that another wounded Wiregrass soldier, Private Jack Connell of Company I, accompanied him to Point Lookout Prison, where the two became separated after arriving on October 27, 1863.[17]

Jones languished in Point Lookout Prison for five months. He was exchanged with more than one thousand other sick and wounded Confederates at City Point, Virginia, on March 27, 1864. The next day, the men were transferred to Chimborazo Hospital in Richmond. In early April, Jones received a sixty-day furlough home to Brooks County. He soon arrived at Quitman and spent a night with his cousin. The next morning, Jones' cousin accompanied him to his homecoming. The crippled veteran described the event: "We arrived at my father's house about 9 o'clock. No one at home recognized me and talked to me as a stranger. When I revealed myself to them I have never been able to remember whether I got out of the buggy or whether they took me out. The first thing I do remember, I was in my mother's arms. The plantation bell was rung and soon everybody on my father's plantation and Uncle Tommy Denmark's plantation was in my father's yard and that was a day of general rejoicing at home." Jones later received a disability discharge.[18]

Despite his disability, William Jones led a productive life as a farmer and merchant. Jones moved to the nearby Thomas County community of Boston in 1880, where he served a term as postmaster. After a term as county treasurer, the voters elected him judge of the Thomas County Ordinary Court in 1901, an office he held for the next thirty-two years. Jones later moved from Boston to Thomasville. Advancing years finally slowed the old veteran. After a brief illness, Jones died at his home on March 2, 1936. He was six months shy of his 95th birthday.[19]

William Moore Jones may well hold the distinction of being the final surviving member of the regiment. With his death, the last valiant Wiregrass soldier and the 50th Georgia Infantry Regiment passed into history.

Judge William Moore Jones, Company K. Jones' leg had to be amputated after his wounding at Gettysburg. He was left behind at a Williamsport, Maryland hospital resulting in his capture and imprisonment at Point Lookout, Maryland. He was eventually exchanged. After the war he moved to Thomas County where he served in several public positions. He died in 1936, just shy of his ninety-fifth birthday. He was probably the last surviving 50th Georgia veteran. Courtesy of Thomas County Historical Society and Museum, Thomasville, Georgia.

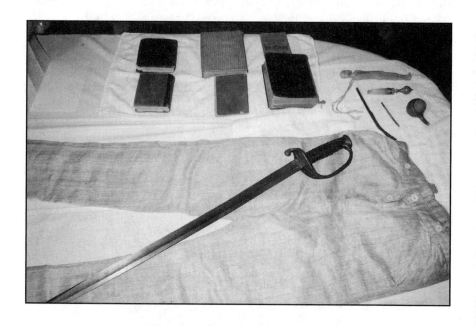

Lt. Frances Lawton Mobley, Company F, wore these trousers and carried this infantry officer's sword during the Battle of Sharpsburg on September 17, 1862. Mobley received a mortal wound and later died in a Winchester, Virginia hospital. The sword was left on the battlefield and is currently owned by a private collector. The trousers were returned to Mobley's widow after his death. Close inspection clearly reveals Mobley's name inscribed on the sword and blood stains on the trousers from his wound. Also shown are children's toys and books in Mobley's possession at the time, including a Bible and daily log. The toys were hand crafted by Mobley for his children. Courtesy of Glenn Hodges, great-great grandson of Frances L. Mobley, Nashville, Georgia.

Appendix A

50th GEORGIA INFANTRY REGIMENT ROSTER

ROSTER ABBREVIATIONS

Adj – Adjutant
ANV – Army of Northern Virginia
Appt – appointed
AWOL – absent without leave
Bde – brigade
Bn – battalion
Bur – buried
C – captured
Cav – Cavalry
Cem – cemetery
Co – company
Col – Colonel
Cpl – Corporal
Cpt – Captain
CSP – Confederate Service Pension
Cty – county
D – died
Des – deserted
Disc – discharged
DW – died of wounds
E – exchanged

Frl – furloughed
Hos – hospital
Inf – infantry
K – killed in action
Lt – Lieutenant
LtC – Lt Colonel
Maj – Major
M – missing in action
NLR – no later record
P – paroled
Prom - promoted
Pvt – private
R – released
Regt - regiment
Res - resigned
Rich – Richmond, Va.
S - surrendered
Sav – Savannah, Ga.
Sgt – sergeant
Trn – transferred
Unk - unknown
W – wounded in action

Most of the men who joined the ten individual companies that would eventually make up the 50th Georgia Infantry Regiment enlisted in March of 1862 in their home counties. The companies would officially become part of the 50th Georgia when the regiment was organized near Savannah in April 1862. The 50th Georgia's rosters constantly changed due to deaths, discharges and new arrivals during the three long years of conflict.

The primary sources of information for the roster include the National Archives' Compiled Service Records, M266, Rolls 505-510; the *Roster of Confederate Soldiers of Georgia, Vol. 3*, compiled by Lillian Henderson; and the microfilm rolls of Pension Applications of Confederate Soldiers and Widows who applied from Georgia and Florida. Other sources include casualty reports, local historical organizations, period newspaper articles, personal diaries, letters and other accounts. I have made every attempt at accuracy. In instances where sources conflict, I have made my best attempt to determine the most accurate source. Unfortunately, it is not always possible in this work to determine ultimate accuracy. I would welcome any documented corrections to the roster.

An observation should be made concerning the regimental muster role entries near the end of the war. Several soldiers were reported as being "Absent Without Leave." Although the muster roll may officially list a soldier as AWOL, there could be extenuating circumstances. For example, many furloughed soldiers simply could not return to their companies in late 1864 and early 1865, because they could not get through the Union lines. Pension records clarify some situations, while others remain unresolved.

The Roster of the Regimental Field & Staff is shown first. Most of these staff members were brought up from the companies during the course of the war. Detailed individual information can be found in the complete regimental roster. Following the Field & Staff roster is the complete regimental roster in alphabetical order by Last Name, Rank, Date of Enlistment, and Significant Actions. The reader is encouraged to research the Compiled Service Records and Confederate Pension Records for further information on a particular soldier of interest.

FIELD AND STAFF ROSTER

Manning, William R., Colonel.
McGlashan, Peter Alexander Selkirk, Colonel.
Kearse, Francis, Lieutenant Colonel.
Fleming, William Oliver, Lieutenant Colonel.
Sheffield, Pliny, Lieutenant Colonel.
Curry, Duncan, Major.
Pendleton, Philip Coleman, Major.
Spence, John M., Major.
Fleming, John Morgan, Adjutant.
Graves, James P., Adjutant.
Roberds, Reuben Thomason, Adjutant.
McGlashan, Andrew, Adjutant.
Mathis, Hiram M., Chaplain.
McCauley, George, Chaplain.
Curry, William L., Chaplain.
Bailey, James S., Sergeant Major.
McCall, William C., Sergeant Major
Briggs, William H., Quartermaster.
Converse, Albert, A., Quartermaster.
Wells, Lyman P. (Lemuel P.), Quartermaster Sergeant.
Smith, William A., Quartermaster Sergeant.
Lawson, Homer L., Surgeon.
Brandon, David S., Surgeon.
Parramore, Henry Jones, Surgeon.
Pue, William H., Assistant Surgeon.
Monroe, Edward (Edmund) D., Assistant Surgeon.
Bethea, J.F., Hospital Steward.
Sheldon, James R. Commissary Sergeant.
Connell, John E., Jr., Commissary Sergeant.
Morgan, Elijah C., Commissary Sergeant.

Colding, Silas M., Assistant Commissary Sergeant.
Parmalee, C.H., Assistant Commissary Sergeant.
McTyre, H.W., Ordnance Sergeant.

ROSTER A

Abbott, Andrew J., Pvt Co. E 3/4/62 – D "disease" Macon, Ga. Hos 4/23/62.
Abbott, J., Pvt Co. F 3/4/62 – D Rich 5/22/62; Bur Hollywood Cem, Rich.
Adams, Vincent, Pvt Co. C 3/4/62 –Roll for 2/65 shows AWOL since 5/10/63; however,
    an undated entry also shows "Discharged on Surgeon's Certification of
    disability; NLR.
Adkinson, Benjamin, Pvt Co. F 3/4/62 – K Fox's Gap 9/14/62.
Akins John J., Pvt Co. I 8/28/62 – W Chancellorsville 5/3/63; C near Knoxville 12/3/63;
    D Rock Is, Ill. 1/22/64.
Albritton, James H., Pvt Co. A 3/4/62 – W Chancellorsville 5/3/63; W (damaged hearing
    – shell burst) Gettysburg 7/2/63; Appt 1st Cpl 3/23/64; Des 3/10/65; took oath of
    allegiance to U.S. Govt. and furnished trans to St. Augustine, Fl.
Alday, Daniel, Pvt Co. F 3/4/62 – W (side) Fredericksburg 12/62; W (hand) Ft. Sanders
    11/29/63; C Sailor's Creek 4/6/65; R Pt. Lookout, Md. 6/23/65; widow filed for
    CSP Decatur Cty, Ga. 1893; pension record says he contracted a disease in
    service, which eventually led to his death in 1866.
Alday, Greene Benjamin, Pvt Co. F 4/30/63 – S Appomattox CH 4/9/65; filed for CSP
    Decatur Cty, Ga. 1913; pension record says he joined the company to be with
    his father.
Alday, Littleton B., Pvt Co. F 3/4/62 – Disc 5/62; NLR.
Alderman, Enoch W., Pvt Co. K 5/13/62 – Detailed as carpenter Whitesville, Ga. Hos
    5/21/62; Disc 12/14/62 due to chronic ulcer of leg; P 1865; widow filed for CSP
    Jackson Cty, Fl. 1905.
Alderman, G.T., Pvt Co. K 3/4/62 – Home without Frl 1862; NLR.
Alderman, I. (J), Pvt Co. K 3/4/62; Appt 3rd Cpl; NLR.
Alderman, James M., Pvt Co. K 3/4/62 - K (artillery shell) Gettysburg 7/2/63.
Alderman, John A., Pvt Co. H 3/4/62 – W (gunshot, l arm) Chancellorsville 5/3/63; Rich
    Hos 5/8/63; P 5/23/65; filed for CSP Colquitt Cty, Ga. 1884.
Alderman, Mitchell J., Pvt Co. H 3/4/62 – W Gettysburg (shoulder-flesh) 7/2/63; C in
    Hos 7/3/63; P Camp David, N.Y. 9/63; Petersburg Hos 9/15/63; roll for 2/65
    shows AWOL since 11/63; P Thomasville, Ga. 5/24/65; filed for CSP Colquitt
    Cty, Ga. 1898; pension record says he was home on W Frl at close of war.
Alderman, William, Pvt Co. K 3/4/62 – D (diphtheria) Camp Davis near Sav 3/30/62;
    widow filed for CSP Brooks Cty, Ga. 1891.
Alderman, William Robertson, Pvt Co. K 3/4/62 – C Fox's Gap 9/14/62; E 10/2/62; Rich
    Hos 10/9/62; Appt 3rd Cpl 10/63; W (r hand – thumb/forefinger shot off)
    Wilderness 5/6/64; roll for 2/65 shows absent at Madison Cty, Fl.; filed for CSP
    Bradford Cty, Fl. 1901; pension record says he was home on Frl at surrender.
Aldswater, J.A., Pvt Co. H 3/4/62 – W Chancellorsville 5/3/63; NLR.
Algier, James R., 1st Sgt Co. H 3/4/62 – D (pneumonia) Rich Hos 12/3/62; Bur
    Oakwood Cem, Rich.
Algier, Vincent, Co. H 3/4/62 – NLR.
Algier (Alger), Wilson L., Pvt Co. H 3/4/62 – Detailed as wagoner 5/62; D at home on
    sick Frl (lung & liver disease) 9/1/63; widow filed for CSP Berrien Cty, Ga. 1891.
Allcox, Jesse H., Pvt Co. G 3/4/62 – D (small pox) Rich Hos 12/5/62; Bur Oakwood
    Cem, Rich.

Allen, George W., Pvt Co. A 3/4/62 – W (l leg) /C Fox's Gap 9/14/62; E City Point, Va. 12/18/62; Petersburg Hos 12/18/62; Appt 4th Cpl 3/23/64; C Wilderness 5/6/64; P Elmira, N.Y. 6/16/65.

Allen, John M., Jr, 2nd Lt Co. A 3/4/62 – D (brain fever) home in Pierce Cty Ga. 5/20/62.

Alligood, Andrew, Pvt Co. H 3/4/62 – Reported K (date Unk).

Alligood, Daniel C., Pvt Co. H 5/3/62 – Appt 3rd Cpl 1/63; W Chancellorsville 5/3/63; Frl 8/63; roll for 2/65 shows AWOL since 10/1/63; P Thomasville, Ga. 5/13/65; filedfor CSP Thomas Cty, Ga. 1911; pension record says he was sent to Rich Hos(typhoid fever) 9/64; later Frl home sick and was home at close of war.

Alligood, David A., Pvt Co. K 8/4/62 – Roll for 2/65 shows AWOL since 4/64; P Thomasville, Ga. 5/10/65.

Alligood, Thomas M., Pvt. Co. H 3/4/62- W Chancellorsville 5/3/63; roll for 2/65 shows AWOL since 8/28/64; P Thomasville, Ga. 5/19/65; pension record says he was Disc 4/6/64.

Allred, Allen, Pvt Co. H 3/4/62 – Disc (disability) 6/15/62.

Allred, Irwin, Pvt Co. H 3/4/62 – W (leg & arms – flesh) Sharpsburg 9/17/62; NLR.

Allred, Jackson A., Pvt Co. H 3/4/62 – W (r thigh) Fox's Gap 9/14/62; Rich Hos 10/15/62; W Chancellorsville 5/3/63; DW Rich 5/22/63; Bur Hollywood Cem, Rich.

Altman, Jasper S., Pvt Co. A 3/4/62 – C Fox's Gap 9/14/62; E 10/2/62; C Cashtown 7/4/63; E Ft Delaware, Del. 7/30/63; C Sailor's Creek 4/6/65; R Pt. Lookout, Md. 6/22/65.

Altman, Samuel, Pvt Co. A 8/11/62 – Enlisted as Pvt Co. K, 5th Regt Ga. State Troops 10/6/61; mustered out 4/62; enlisted in Co. A 50th Ga.; W (head)/C Fox's Gap 9/14/62; DW Phila, Pa. Hos 10/11/62.

Alvis, Charles A., Pvt Co. K 3/4/62 – W (l hand) Petersburg 7/10/64; Rich Hos same day; roll for 2/65 shows absent, sent to Charlottesville Hos 10/28/64; NLR.

Alvis, James, Pvt Co. K 3/4/62 – W (gunshot- l leg) Cedar Creek 10/19/64; roll for 2/24/65 shows detailed as a guard in Lynchburg, Va.; C Sailor's Creek 4/6/65; R Pt. Lookout, Md. 1865; widow filed for CSP Brooks Cty, Ga. 1911.

Alvis, William Robert, Pvt Co. K 4/24/62 – W Gettysburg (hip & heel) 7/2/63; C 7/4/63; P 7/21/63; Rich Hos 8/28/63; C Sailor's Creek 4/6/65; R Pt. Lookout Md. 6/22/65; filed for CSP Madison Cty, Fl. 1892.

Alvis, Willis W., Pvt Co. K 3/4/62 – Left sick Knoxville Hos 12/4/63; C 1/5/64; took oath of allegiance to U.S. Govt. and joined U.S. Army at Rock Island, Ill. 10/31/64.

Anderson, Alfred, Pvt Co. I 3/4/62 – Reported ill 4/7/62 with "brain fevor" by Lt. Francis Mobley at Camp Davis, Ga.; NLR.

Anderson, Bryce, Pvt Co. G 4/27/62 – D in camp near Sav 6/9/62.

Anderson, James, Pvt Co. B 3/4/62 – W Fox's Gap 9/14 62; Rich Hos 9/25/62; roll for 2/65 shows AWOL with 4th Ga. Cav, Ware Cty, Ga.

Anderson, W.L., Pvt Co. B 3/4/62 – Elected Jr 2nd Lt 10/31/62; Res 3/4/63; NLR.

Andrews, George D., Pvt Co. C 3/4/62 – D (typhoid pneumonia) Rich Hos 1/2/63; Bur Hollywood Cem, Rich.

Andrews, John S, 2nd Sgt Co. A 3/4/62 – W (r arm) Chancellorsville 5/3/63; C Cashtown 7/4/63; R Ft. Delaware, Del. 6/10/65; widow filed CSP Bradford Cty, Fl. 1898.

Archibald, Thomas B., 1st Cpl Co. K 3/4/62 – W (leg – flesh) Sharpsburg 9/17/62; roll for 2/65 shows on Frl; NLR.

Arnold, Henry, Pvt Co. G 3/4/62 – D Rich Hos (typhoid fever) 3/17/63; Bur Oakwood Cem, Rich.

Arnold, James Madison, Pvt Co. G 4/27/62 – W (gunshot, 1 side) Chancellorsville 5/3/63; roll for 2/65 shows AWOL since 10/1/64; filed for CSP Volusia Cty Fl. 1902; pension record says he was Disc (disability-typhoid fever) Sulphur Springs, Va. 4/8/65 and home at close of war.

Ashley, Nathan, Pvt Co. C 5/14/62 –Hos roll for 4/63 shows returned to duty from Charlottesville, Va. Hos 4/15/63; NLR.

Austin, William M., 3rd Sgt Co. G 3/4/62 – W Gettysburg (thigh –flesh wound) 7/2/63; C Cashtown 7/4/63; E City Point, Va. 8/28/63; Richmond Hos 8/28/63; Frl 9/4/63; Disc 4/18/64, on having been Appt Clinch Cty, Ga. Tax Collector.

ROSTER B

Bachelor, William Bennett, Pvt Co. F 5/13/62 – W Fox's Gap 9/14/62; W Chancellorsville 5/3/63; DW Rich 5/23/63; Bur Hollywood Cem, Rich.

Bagley, Charles T., Pvt Co. B 3/4/62 – Appt 4th Sgt 1/1/63; roll for 2/28/64 shows AWOL in Ware Cty, Ga.; NLR.

Bagley, William B.(G), Pvt Co. B 3/4/62 – W (abdomen) Chancellorsville 5/3/63; Appt 2nd Cpl 8/5/64; C Rich 4/3/65; D (chronic diarrhea) Rich Hos 4/23/65; Bur Hollywood Cem, Rich.

Bailey, J., Pvt Co. G – C Harrisonburg, Va. 9/24/64; Pt. Lookout, Md. Prison 10/1/64; NLR.

Bailey, James S., 2nd Sgt Co. B 3/4/62 – Appt 1st Sgt 3/22/62; C (sick) Frederick, Md. 9/12/62; E Aikens Landing, Va. 10/19/62; Appt SgtM; W Funkstown (1 shoulder/side/back) 7/10/63; Hos 7/19/63; C Ft. Sanders 11/29/63; escaped enroute to Camp Chase, Md. Prison 12/15/63 and returned to company; Appt Ensign/1st Lt. 6/17/64; W Cedar Creek 10/19/64; escaped C at Sailor's Creek 4/6/65; roll for 2/28/65 shows "wounded furlough, absent without leave since Janry 1"; NLR.

Bailey, Thomas R., 2nd Cpl Co. F 3/4/62 – W (1 hand) Fox's Gap 9/14/62; Rich Hos 9/28/62; reduced to Pvt 10/62; W Chancellorsville 5/36/3; W Gettysburg (gunshot, r shoulder/l lung) 7/2/63; C 7/5/63; P David's Island, N.Y. 8/24/63; Disc (disability) 2/29/64; S Appomattox CH 4/9/65 (parole list shows a "T.R. Burley, Co F"); filed for CSP Mitchell Cty, Ga. 1899; filed for CSP Citrus Cty, Fl. 1917.

Bailey, W.R., Pvt Co. G 4/5/62 – NLR.

Baker, Burrell A., Pvt Co. H 3/4/62 – Appt 5th Sgt 6/62; Appt 3rd Sgt 1/63; K Chancellorsville 5/3/63.

Baker, S.W., Jr. 2nd Lt Co. D 3/4/62 – Res (disability) 6/10/63.

Baker, Thomas P., Pvt Co. H 3/4/62 – W (shoulder – flesh) Sharpsburg 9/17/62; Winchester, Va. Hos 9/18/62; S Appomattox CH 4/9/65.

Baker, William J. (W.), Pvt Co. H 3/4/62 –Roll for 2/65 shows AWOL since 1/20/65; P Thomasville, Ga. 5/20/65; NLR.

Ballard, Thomas A., 3rd Sgt Co. F 3/4/62 – Appt 2nd Sgt 10/62; Elected Jr. 2nd Lt 1/1/63; W Gettysburg (r lung) 7/2/63; DW 7/5/63; Bur Gettysburg; removed 1872 or 1873 to Hollywood Cem, Rich.

Barber, John W., Pvt Co. C 5/12/62 – Application for Trn to Cav forwarded from Rich Hos 11/63; roll for 2/65 shows AWOL since 3/22/63; NLR.

Barden, Simon M., Pvt Co. K 3/4/62 – W Chancellorsville 5/3/63; W Ft. Sanders 11/29/63; C near Knoxville 12/3; E Louisville, Ky. 12/23/63; C Cedar Creek 10/19/64; R Rock Island, Ill. 6/21/65; filed for CSP Brooks Cty, Ga. 1897 (name shown as "Borden".

Bass, A.J., Pvt Co. D 4/26/62 – Roll for 2/63 shows present; K Tn. early 1864.

Bass, Archibald C., Pvt Co. G 3/4/62 – W Fox's Gap 9/14/62; C Cedar Creek 10/19/64; E

Pt. Lookout, Md. 3/17/65; P Thomasville, Ga. 5/11/65; filed for CSP Osceola Cty, Fl. 1907.

Bass, David, Pvt Co. G 3/4/62 – K Fox's Gap 9/14/62.

Baston, Richard W., Pvt Co. E 3/4/62 – W Gettysburg (thigh – flesh) 7/2/63; Elected Jr. 2nd Lt 2/64; home on W Frl 10/31/64; recommended for light duty 11/30/64; roll for 2/28/65 shows AWOL; P Thomasville, Ga. 5/20/65.

Battle, John R., Pvt Co. C 3/4/62 – Appt 1st Cpl 12/63; P Newton, N.C. 4/19/65; filed for CSP Decatur Cty, Ga. 1911.

Baxley, William R., Pvt. Co. G 3/4/62 - W Chancellorsville 5/3/63; C Sailor's Creek, 4/6/65; R Pt. Lookout, Md. 6/24/65; widow filed for CSP Baker Cty, Fl. 1907.

Beasley, Shadrack, Pvt Co. E 8/13/62 – Roll for 8/31/63 shows sick Rich Hos; NLR.

Beckton, Joseph M., Pvt Co. K 3/4/62 – D Sav 7/15/62.

Bedford, Peter B., 1st Lt Co. B 3/4/62 – Elected Cpt 3/22/62; W Chancellorsville 5/3/63; W Gettysburg (r ankle, minie ball – leg amputated) 7/2/63; C Cashtown 7/5/63; E City Point, Va. 5/24/64; retired to Invalid Corps 1/11/65; P Thomasville, Ga. 5/65; filed for CSP Duval Cty, Fl. 1899.

Belote (Belot), James, Pvt Co. G 3/4/62 – Roll for 12/31/62 shows Disc 7/6/62, and turned over to Sav Vol Guards by court of inquiry; Trn to Co A, 18th Bn Ga. Inf 7/5/62; C Sailor's Creek 4/6/65; R 6/12/65.

Benefield, William, Pvt Co. I 11/27/62 – C Cold Harbor 6/1/64; D (pneumonia) Pt. Lookout, Md. 12/15/64; believed Bur Confederate Cem, Pt. Lookout.

Bennett, Henry P., Pvt 3/4/62 – NLR.

Bennett, James, Pvt Co. G 3/4/62 – Roll for 12/31/62 shows "absent. On sick furlough for 30 days dated Oct. 15th"; NLR.

Bennett, James, Pvt Co. B 3/4/62 – Disc 10/9/62.

Bennett, Jesse, 3rd Sgt Co. C 3/4/62 – C Cedar Creek 10/19/64; R Pt. Lookout, Md. 5/12/65.

Bennett, John F., Pvt Co. B 8/25/62 – D (rheumatism) Rich Hos 4/18/63; Bur Oakwood Cem, Rich.

Bennett, John P., Pvt Co. G 3/4/62 – W (l elbow) Fredericksburg 12/13/62; Disc (disability) 4/27/63; filed for CSP Clinch Cty, Ga. 1893.

Bennett, W.B., Pvt – P Thomasville, Ga. 5/19/65.

Bennett, William, Pvt Co. G 3/4/62 – P Thomasville, Ga. 5/11/65.

Berry, W.H., Pvt, Co. F 1862 – NLR.

Bethea, J.F., Regt Hos Steward 3/4/62 – Roll for 12/10/64 shows Trn to Rich as Hos Steward; NLR.

Bevill, James T., Cpt Co. D 3/4/62 – Res commission (disability) 6/9/63; Trn Sav 6/13/63; NLR.

Bird, (Byrd) Alfred, Pvt Co. F 3/4/62 – Appt 3rd Sgt 1/1/63; K Gettysburg 7/2/63; Bur Gettysburg; removed to Laurel Grove Cem, Sav 9/24/1871; Bur Lot 853.

Bishop, James B., Pvt Co. B 3/4/62 – D Sav 6/10/62; Bur Laurel Grove Cem, Sav.

Black, Henry William, Pvt Co. D 8/21/62 – D (typhoid fever) Hanover Junction, Va. Hos 4/23/63.

Blackburn, Martin Ebenezer Lycurgus, Pvt Co. B 3/4/62 – Disc (rejected by surgeon); enlisted as Pvt Co. A, 24th Bn Ga. Cav 9/22/62; Trn to Co. G, 7th Regt Ga. Cav 2/13/64; C Louisa C.H., Va. 6/11/64; D (chronic diarrhea) Elmira, N.Y. 5/29/65.

Blair, John, Pvt Co. K 3/4/62 – Appt Sgt; widow filed for CSP Bradford Cty, Fl. 1903; pension record says he was Disc (sickness) Rich 1864.

Blakely, Clark (Claude), Pvt Co. K 3/4/62 – C Cashtown 7/4/63; E 7/63; D (chronic diarrhea) Petersburg, Va. Hos 8/2/63.

Blakely, John H., Pvt Co. K 3/4/62 – D Winchester, Va. 10/28/62.

Bland, J.J. – Not in CSR; *Register of Confederate Dead* shows D 5/21/63; Bur Hollywood Cem, Rich.
Bloodworth, Lewis, Pvt Co. H 3/4/62 – Appt Sgt; C Rich Hos 4/3/65; R Pt. Lookout, Md. 7/19/65.
Blun, Elias, 4th Cpl Co. E 3/4/62 – Reduced to Pvt 11/1/62; C near Peak Mountain, Va. 9/25/64; R Pt. Lookout, Md. upon joining U.S. service 10/14/64.
Bonan, H.J., Regt Surgeon – C Gettysburg 7/5/63; E City Point, Va. 8/11/63; NLR.
Boon, Francis M., Pvt Co. B 3/4/62 – W near Chattanooga (1 hand – lost 2 fingers) 10/16/63; C Cold Harbor 6/1/64; R Elmira, N.Y. 5/29/65; filed for CSP Ware Cty, Ga. 1892.
Boon, Harley L., Pvt Co. B 3/4/62 – Roll for 2/63 shows present; NLR.
Bostick, Jesse S., Pvt Co. G 3/4/62 – Appt 3rd Sgt 2/64; C Cedar Creek 10/19/64; E James River, Va. 3/30/65; NLR.
Bowen, John L., Pvt Co. H 3/4/62 – W Chancellorsville 5/5/63; C Chambersburg 7/5/63; R Ft. Delaware, Del. 5/11/65; filed for CSP Columbia Cty, Fl. 1903.
Boyd, B.J. Pvt Co. D 1862 – Appeared on 5/11/62 return; NLR.
Boyd, Littleton B., Pvt Co. D 5/11/62 – D (measles) in camp at Ft. Boggs, Ga. 6/20/62; widow filed for CSP Lowndes Cty, Ga. 1891.
Boyett (Boyet), Francis M., Pvt Co. K 3/4/62 – W Chancellorsville 5/3/63; D (typhoid) Rich Hos 6/12/63; Bur Hollywood Cem, Rich.
Boyett, Isaac Jackson, Pvt Co. F 3/4/62 – Sent to Atlanta Hos 9/11/63; roll for 2/65 shows absent sick; NLR.
Boyett (Boyd), John, Pvt Co. K 3/4/62 – W Ft. Sanders 11/29/63; C (sick) Knoxville 12/6/63; Rock Island, Ill. Prison 2/15/64; P 6/16/65.
Boyett, John H., Pvt Co. F 3/4/62 – W Gettysburg (leg – flesh wound) 7/2/63; C in Hos 7/4/63; E David's Island, N.Y. 8/24/63; K Cedar Creek 10/19/64; widow filed for CSP Decatur Cty, Ga. 1891; pension record says he was K by Yankee pickets.
Boyett (Boyet), William Newton, Pvt Co. K 3/4/62 – D Rich 3/24/63; Bur Hollywood Cem, Rich.
Boyett, W.R., Pvt Co. K 5/11/62 – NLR.
Boyett, William H., Pvt Co. I 8/22/62 – Detached as shoemaker Columbus, Ga. 11/17/62 to close of war; P Thomasville, Ga. 5/11/65; widow filed for CSP Lowndes Cty, Ga. 1910.
Boyett, William T., Pvt Co. F 3/22/62 - W Fox's Gap 9/14/62; Rich Hos 9/27/62; Appt 4th Cpl 1/1/63; W Gettysburg (gunshot, r hand – arm amputated below elbow) 7/2/63; C 7/5/63; E 9/63; Petersburg Hos 9/15/63; retired to Invalid Corps 4/13/64; P Bainbridge, Ga. 5/20/65; filed for CSP Decatur, Ga. 1880.
Boyett (Boyet), William W., Pvt Co. K 5/17/62 – D Whitesville, Ga. Hos 6/28/62.
Brack, Augustus, 4th Sgt Co. G 4/1/62 – W Fox's Gap 9/14/62; Rich Hos 10/5/62; W Chancellorsville 5/3/63; Appt 1st Sgt 7/2/63; W Gettysburg (thigh – flesh) 7/2/63; C 7/5/63; E (date Unk); C Cedar Creek 10/19/64; E Harpers Ferry 3/17/65; P Thomasville, Ga. 5/16/65.
Brack, John W., Pvt Co. G 5/13/62 – W Chancellorsville 5/3/63; DW 5/14/63.
Brack, Washington, Pvt Co. G – NLR.
Bradford, Franklin, 2nd Sgt Co. D 3/4/62 – C/P Leesburg, Va. 10/2/62; D Martinsburg, Va. (now W.V.) 10/13/62.
Bradford, John, Pvt Co. D 3/4/62 – W Cedar Creek 10/19/64; P Thomasville, Ga. 5/23/65.
Bradford, John W., Pvt Co. D 3/4/62 – D Hanover Junction, Va. Hos 5/14/63.
Bradford, William, Jr., Pvt Co. D 5/11/62 – Detailed as a nurse Macon, Ga. Hos 12/62; roll for 2/65 shows absent sick; P Thomasville, Ga. 5/23/65; filed for CSP

Lowndes Cty, Ga. 1909; pension record says he was home on sick Frl at close of war.

Bradford, William W., Pvt Co. I 3/4/62 – C/P Warrenton, Va. 9/29/62; W Gettysburg (heel - flesh wound) 7/2/63; C 7/5/63 Cashtown: E City Point, Va. 8/20/63; K Cold Harbor 6/3/64.

Brady, John A., Pvt Co. G 3/4/62 – D in camp near Sav 6/3/62; Bur Laurel Grove Cem, Sav.

Brady, Louis (Lewis) J., Pvt Co. G 3/4/62 – Detailed as wagoner 12/62; roll for 2/3/65 shows AWOL; NLR.

Brady, Robert N., Pvt Co. G 3/4/62 – C Gettysburg 7/2/63; E Elmira, N.Y. 10/29/64; NLR.

Brady, Samuel E., Pvt Co. G 3/4/62 – D near Sav 5/3/62; Bur Laurel Grove Cem, Sav.

Brady, Thomas A. (J.), Pvt Co. G 3/4/62 – Detached as wagoner; S Appomattox CH 4/9/65.

Bragg, James, Pvt Co. E 3/4/62 – W Petersburg 6/18/64; DW 6/20/64.

Branch, David, Pvt Co. B 3/4/62 – Des 4/2/62; roll for 7/62 shows name dropped from rolls 6/62 and reported AWOL; NLR.

Branch, James, Pvt Co. G 3/4/62 – D Rich Hos 3/3/63; Bur Hollywood Cem, Rich.

Brandon, David S., Pvt Co. E 3/4/62 – Appt Regt Surgeon 3/30/62; AWOL 11/29/62; Res 2/7/63.

Braswell, George L., Pvt Co. E 3/4/62 – Appt 3rd Cpl 4/23/62; Reduced to Pvt 11/1/62; D after 1/1/63; roll for 12/64 shows "Died, time unknown"; previously shown AWOL since 9/23/63; NLR.

Brewton, David L., Pvt Co. B 6/6/62 - C (sick) Frederick, Md. 9/12/62; Frederick Hos 9/18/62; E 11/10/62; roll for 2/63 shows present; NLR.

Brice, David J., Pvt Co. K 3/4/62 – K Wilderness 5/6/64.

Brice, Timothy, Pvt Co. K 3/4/62 – Disc 7/17/62; P Thomasville, Ga. 5/26/65.

Briggs, William H., Pvt Co. D 3/4/62 – Appt 2nd Sgt 1862; Appt Ordnance Sgt 6/1/62; C Williamsport, Md. 9/15/62; E Aikens Landing, Va. 10/19/62; Appt Cpt & Regt Quartermaster 1/31/63; Appt Asst to Bde Quartermaster 9/14/64; NLR.

Brock, John H.J., Pvt Co. E 3/4/62 – Appt 2nd Cpl 10/8/62; W (ankle fractured) Ft. Sanders 11/29/63; C near Knoxville 2/21/64; D (typhoid fever) Camp Chase, Oh. 1/5/65; Bur Grave #713 Confederate Cem Camp Chase; widow filed for CSP Lafayette Cty, Fl. 1900.

Brooker, Gilbert, Pvt Co. C 3/4/62 – K Chancellorsville 5/3/63.

Brooker, Harrison, Pvt Co. C 3/4/62 – Disc (disability) 6/13/62.

Brooker, James R., Pvt Co. C 3/4/62 – Appt 3rd Cpl 1/1/63; Appt 4th Sgt 2/64; C Sailor's Creek 4/6/65; R Pt. Lookout, Md. 6/24/65; filed for CSP Clay Cty, Fl. 1901.

Brooker, William H., Pvt Co. C 3/4/62 – W Chancellorsville 5/3/63; roll for 2/65 shows AWOL since 8/64; NLR.

Brown, Hezekiah, Pvt Co. D 3/4/62 – K Fox's Gap 9/14/62.

Brown, J.O., Pvt Co. K 3/4/62 – W Cedar Creek 10/19/64; NLR.

Brown, James, Pvt Co. H 3/4/62 – Appt 4th Sgt 6/62; K Fox's Gap 9/14/62; widow filed for CSP Coweta Cty, Ga. 1891.

Brown, John, Pvt Co. F 3/4/62 – W Summit Point, Va. 8/21/64; C Sailor's Creek 4/6/65; R City Point, Va., 6/24/65; widow filed for CSP Decatur Cty, Ga. 1906.

Brown, John H., Pvt Co. K 3/4/62 – Appt 2nd Sgt 8/62; W Chancellorsville 5/3/63; roll for 2/65 shows AWOL since 1/22/64; widow filed for CSP Brooks Cty, Ga. 1910; pension record says he was W (foot) 1864, and home, disabled and unfit for further duty.

Brown, Robert D., Pvt Co. K 3/4/62 – Enlisted as Pvt in Co. H, 9th Regt Ga. Inf 6/6/61;

Trn to Co. K, 50th Ga.; roll for 2/28/65 shows present; P Macon, Ga. 4/65; filed for CSP Brooks Cty, 1912; pension record says he was cut off from command while on foraging detail near Lynchburg, Va. 3/65; C/P Macon, Ga. 4/65.

Brown, W. P. Pvt Co. K – Appt. 2nd Lt 7/31/63; NLR.

Brown, William Ponder, Pvt Co. E 3/4/62 – Appt Cpl; Appt Sgt; W/C Fox's Gap 9/14/62; Frederick, Md. Hos 9/18/62; E 11/10/62; Elected 2nd Lt 4/3/63; Appt 1st Lt 2/64; W (r thigh) Cedar Creek 10/19/64; Rich Hos; roll for 2/28/65 shows absent with leave; P Thomasville, Ga. 5/19/65; widow filed for CSP Grady Cty, Ga. 1919; pension record says he was at Danville, Va. enroute to command at close of war.

Brown, William Riley, Pvt Co. F 3/4/62 – D Sav 6/30/62.

Brown, William W., Pvt Co. G 4/27/62 – Disc 6/14/62.

Brunson, Isaac (Isaiah), Pvt Co. F 3/4/62 – K near Berryville, Va. 9/3/64.

Bryan, Warren, Pvt Co. A 3/4/62 – NLR.

Bryan, William, Pvt Co. A 3/4/62 – NLR.

Bryant, Calvin, Pvt Co. H 3/4/62 – Appt 2nd Cpl 4/64; C Wilderness 5/7/64; E Pt. Lookout, Md. 3/10/65; P Thomasville, Ga. 5/2565; filed for CSP Colquitt Cty, Ga. 1907; pension record says he arrived in Colquitt Cty 3/31/65, and was home at close of war.

Bryant, Daniel L., Pvt Co. F 4/28/62 – W (both legs)/C Fox's Gap 9/14/62; Frederick, Md. Hos 10/1/62; E 12/62; C Sailor's Creek, Va. 4/6/65; R Pt. Lookout, Md. 6/24/65; filed for CSP Grady Cty, Ga. 1919.

Bryant, H.T., Pvt Co. K 3/4/62 - "hand chopped off since enlisting"; NLR.

Bryant, John, Pvt Co. F 3/4/62– C Sailor's Creek 4/6/65; R Pt. Lookout, Md. 6/24/65.

Bryant, John, Pvt. Co. H 3/4/62- W Gettysburg 7/2/63; W (l side & l foot) at Beans Station, Tn. 12/10/63; C Sailor's Creek 4/6/65; R Pt. Lookout, Md. 6/24/65; filed for CSP Colquitt Cty, Ga. 1892.

Bryant, John W., Pvt Co. F 3/4/62 – K Fox's Gap 9/14/62; widow filed for CSP Thomas Cty, Ga. 1891.

Buckland, M.T., Pvt Co. G - W Fox's Gap 9/14/62; Hos 10/16/62; NLR.

Bullard, Green, Pvt Co. I 3/4/62 – Roll for 2/65 shows sick in Rich Hos; NLR.

Bullock, John M., Pvt Co. E 8/22/62 – D (typhoid pneumonia) Petersburg Hos 2/7/63; widow filed for CSP Thomas Cty, Ga. 1891.

Bullock, Thomas, Pvt Co. F 3/4/62 – C Sailor's Creek 4/6/65; R Pt. Lookout, Md. 6/24/65.

Burgsteiner, Thomas J., Pvt Co. D 3/4/62 – W Chancellorsville 5/3/63; C Cedar Creek 10/19/64; R Pt. Lookout, Md. 4/65; filed for CSP Lowndes Cty, Ga. 1907.

Burkett, Enos, Pvt Co. C 8/28/62 – Disc (disability) 7/12/63.

Burkett, John, Pvt Co. C 3/4/62 – D (pneumonia) Rich Hos 2/7/63; Bur Oakwood Cem, Rich.

Burkett, William B., Pvt Co. C 9/18/62 – D (pneumonia) 3/17/63 Rich Hos; Bur Hollywood Cem, Rich.

Burkhalter, Isaac, 2nd Lt Co. G 3/4/62 – Elected 1st Lt 10/25/62; Cpt 3/20/63; K Gettysburg 7/2/63; Bur Gettysburg; removed to Laurel Grove Cem, Sav 9/24/1871; Bur Lot 853; widow filed for CSP Clinch Cty, Ga. 1891.

Burnett, Richard W., Pvt Co. I 3/4/62 – Disc (disability) 6/12/62.

Burns, Seaborn, Pvt Co F 3/13/62 – Appt 4th Sgt; K Fox's Gap 9/14/62.

Butler, Andrew J., Pvt Co. D 3/4/62. – Appt 4th Cpl 9/14/62; W Chancellorsville 5/3/63; Appt 4th Sgt 12/63; W Petersburg 6/21/64; W (l lung)/C Cedar Creek 10/19/64; E 2/10/65; P Tallahassee, FL 5/10/65.

Butler, Charles Hibern, Pvt Co. F 5/3/62 – Disc (disability) 6/2/62.

Butler, John R., Pvt Co. F 3/4/62 – D Martinsburg, Va. (now W.V.) 9/24/62.

Butler, Lewis Fennell, Pvt Co. F 4/8/62 – W Chancellorsville 5/3/63; Appt Sgt; C
    Sailor's Creek 4/6/65; P Pt. Lookout, Md. 6/24/65; filed for CSP Gadsden
    Cty, Fl. 1909.

Butler, Lucien, Pvt Co. F 3/4/62 – W Gettysburg (leg) 7/2/63; C 7/3/63 (leg amputated);
    DW 8/7/63; Bur Gettysburg; removed 1872 or 1873 to Hollywood Cem, Rich.

Bynum, Joseph, Pvt Co. D 3/4/62 – W/C Fox's Gap 9/14/62; E Aikens Landing, Va.
    9/27/62; C Funkstown 7/12/63; R Pt. Lookout, Md. 6/24/65.

Byrd, Anthony, Pvt Co B 3/4/62 – W (gunshot, l arm – amputated at shoulder)
    Chancellorsville 5/3/63; Disc (disability) 6/2/63; filed for CSP Clinch Cty,
    Ga. 1880.

Byrd, William Arrington, Pvt Co. B 3/4/62 – W (r shoulder & leg) Chancellorsville
    5/3/63; W North Anna River 5/64; Appt 1st Sgt; S Appomattox C.H. 4/9/65;
    filed for CSP Worth Cty, Ga. 1898.

ROSTER C

Caldwell, William G. (C.), Pvt Co. F 11/28/64 –Roll for 2/65 shows present; C
    Farmville, Va. 4/6/65; P 6/10/65.

Calvin, Calvin C., Pvt Co. B 3/4/62 – NLR.

Cannon, Lewis J., Pvt Co. E 8/13/62 – Disc (disability) between 2/63 and 8/31/64.

Carlton, Isaac, Pvt Co. H 3/4/62 – Appt 4th Sgt 8/62; Appt 1st Sgt 1/63; W (shot through
    both jaws) Chancellorsville 5/3/63; Disc 11/15/64 upon being elected
    Ordinary of Colquitt Cty, Ga.; filed for CSP Colquitt Cty, Ga. 1899.

Carr, John T., Pvt Co. E 4/12/62 – D Whitesville, Ga. Hos 5/15/62.

Carter, Alexander, Pvt Co. F 3/4/62 – W (l hand - amputated below elbow)
    Chancellorsville 5/3/63; roll for 2/65 shows absent sick; P Thomasville, Ga.
    5/25/65; filed for CSP Decatur Cty, Ga. 1879.

Carter, David, Pvt Co. B 3/4/62 – Disc on surgeon's recommendation 5/62.

Carter, John J., Pvt Co. F 3/4/62 – W (l hand - amputated below elbow) Cedar Creek
    10/19/64; roll for 2/28/65 shows absent sick; filed for CSP Appling Cty, Ga.
    1888; widow filed for CSP Orange Cty, Fl. 1923.

Carter, Wiley, Pvt Co. D 3/4/62 – D Sav Hos 7/29/62; widow filed for CSP Echols Cty,
    Ga. 1891.

Carter, Willis S., Pvt Co. A 5/13/62 – Roll for 8/31/62 shows present; filed for CSP
    Ware Cty, Ga. 1896; pension record says he contracted rheumatism in right
    leg and hip during service.

Carver, Allen, Pvt Co. C 3/4/62 – Disc 10/21/62.

Carver, James A., Pvt Co. C 3/4/62 – Appt Cpl; W (l arm & side)/C Fox's Gap 9/14/62;
    E Aiken's Landing, Va. 10/19/62; Rich Hos 10/24/62; Disc (disability)11/11/64.

Carver, James .J., Pvt Co. C 3/9/62 – W Fox's Gap 9/14/62; DW Ft. Brown, Ga. 9/28/62.

Carver, Richard, Pvt Co. C 5/3/62 – D Ft. Brown, Ga. 5/19/62; Bur Laurel Grove Cem,
    Sav (headstone incorrectly inscribed "Carter").

Carver, Sampson B., Pvt Co. B 3/4/62 – Roll for 2/65 as AWOL in Ware Cty, Ga.; P
    Thomasville, Ga. 5/27/65; widow filed for CSP Berrien Cty, Ga. 1911;
    pension record says he was home on sick furlough at close of war.

Carver, Sampson, B., Pvt Co. C 3/4/62 – Appt 3rd Cpl 11/1/64; Roll for 2/65 shows
    AWOL since 2/3/65; P 5/24/65.

Carver, Samuel, Pvt Co. C 3/4/62 – Roll for 2/63 shows "left sick at Winchester, Va."; NLR.

Casey, J.W., Pvt Co. D 3/4/62 –Roll for 2/65 shows absent with leave; P 5/15/65.

Cason, D., Pvt Co. C – Only CSR entry shows P 5/16/65.

Cason, Hillery W., 2nd Cpl Co. B 3/4/62 – W Gettysburg (r hip) 7/2/63; Appt 2nd Lt

3/23/64; W (r groin) Spotsylvania C.H. 5/12/64; Appt 1ˢᵗ Lt 1/11/65; commanding Regt when S at Appomattox C.H. 4/9/65; filed for CSP Ware Cty, Ga. 1905.

Cason, McGinty T., Pvt Co. B 3/4/62 – D Hos Shenandoah Cty, Va. 2/63; Bur Mt. Jackson Cem, Mt. Jackson, Va.

Castleberry, Joseph (Jasper), Pvt Co. H 3/4/62 – K Fox's Gap 9/14/62.

Cato, John, Pvt Co. C 3/4/62 – D at home (chronic diarrhea) 11/7/62; widow filed for CSP Coffee Cty, Ga. 1891.

Cato, William R., Pvt Co. C 3/4/62 – W (arm)/C Fox's Gap 9/14/62; E Aikens Landing, Va. 10/19/62; Rich Hos 10/23/62; W Chancellorsville 5/3/63; Rich Hos roll for 4/20/64 shows Frl on 4/20/64 for 30 days; roll for 2/28/65 shows AWOL since 7/25/63; filed for CSP Coffee Cty, Ga. 1895; pension record says he remained until war ended.

Chambers, Hugh C., Pvt Co. I 3/4/62 - C Williamsport, Md. 9/15/62; E Pt. Lookout, Md. 10/62; D (smallpox) Valdosta Ga. 10/14/62; widow filed for CSP Berrien Cty, Ga. 1891.

Chambers, Jacob A., Pvt Co. I 3/4/62 – Disc (under-age - 17) 10/9/62.

Chancey. Jesse P., Pvt Co. F 3/4/62 – Appt 1ˢᵗ Cpl 1/63; W Chancellorsville 5/3/63; Appt 5ᵗʰ Sgt 3/4/64; Last on roll 2/65 as absent sick; NLR.

Chaney, Harrison C., Pvt Co. I 8/28/62 – Roll for 2/65 shows AWOL since 11/6/63; filed for CSP Coffee Cty, Ga. 1904; pension record says in Rich Hos 10/63, then Atlanta Hos; Frl home for 30 days and unable to return before close of war.

Chaney (Chancey), Samuel, Pvt Co. G 3/4/62 – D Sav Hos 6/19/62.

Chapman, Archibald, Pvt Co. E 3/4/62 – D Macon, Ga. Hos 5/15/62.

Chastain, John T., Pvt Co. E 3/4/62 – Detailed as nurse due to poor health Farmville, Va. Hos 9/62; C Farmville 4/6/65; P Farmville between 4/11 and 4/21/65; filed for CSP Thomas Cty, Ga. 1920.

Chism, James E. Pvt Co. I 3/4/62 – Disc (under-age - 17) 10/9/62; enlisted as Pvt in Co. H, 4ᵗʰ Regt Ga. Cav 2/11/63; P Thomasville, Ga. 5/22/65.

Chism, John C., Pvt Co. I 3/4/62 – D Macon, Ga. Hos 6/6/62.

Chitty, George Washington, Pvt Co. D 3/4/62 – W Chancellorsville 5/3/63; Appt 1ˢᵗ Sgt 2/64; W (gunshot, l hand – finger & part of hand amputated) Petersburg 6/20/64; Rich Hos 6/20/64; Frl home 7/24/64; roll for 2/65 shows home on wounded Frl; P Thomasville, Ga. 5/18/65; filed for CSP Echols Cty, Ga. 1885.

Chitty, Stephen B., Pvt Co. D 3/4/62 – D Sav Hos 6/20/62.

Clanton, Daniel D. Pvt Co. K 3/4/62 – Roll for 3/12/63 shows present; NLR.

Clark, Burrell, Pvt Co. H 3/4/62 – Prom 3ʳᵈ Sgt; K Chancellorsville 5/3/63.

Clark, Daniel, Pvt Co. A 5/13/62 – Enlisted as Pvt in Co. K, 5ᵗʰ Regt Ga. State Troops 10/6/61; mustered out 4/62; enlisted in Co. A, 50ᵗʰ Ga.; Appt Color Sgt; K Chancellorsville 5/3/63.

Clark, James C., Pvt Co. I 4/16/63 – Substitute for Dennis Williams; W Chancellorsville 5/3/63; roll for 2/65 shows AWOL since 11/1/64; NLR.

Clark, John W., Pvt Co. E 3/4/62 – W Chancellorsville 5/3/63; Appt 3ʳᵈ Sgt 2/64; Des 2/11/65; took oath of allegiance to U.S. Govt. City Point, Va. & furnished trans to Sav 2/12/65.

Clark, Samuel, Pvt Co. A 3/4/62 – W Chancellorsville 5/3/63; Roll for 2/65 shows AWOL since 1/1/65; P Tallahassee, Fl. 5/15/65.

Clayton, George M., 2ⁿᵈ Sgt Co. I 3/4/62 – Appt 1ˢᵗ Sgt 1/1/63; 2ⁿᵈ Lt 2/64; K Cedar Creek 10/19/64.

Clemons, James, Pvt Co. G 3/4/62 – W (gunshot, r upper arm) Fox's Gap 9/14/62; Rich Hos 9/26/62; detailed as wagoner 12/28/62; W (gunshot, l collar bone) Cold

Harbor 6/10/64; S Appomattox C.H. 4/9/65; filed for CSP Bradford Cty, Fl. 1902.

Clifton, John S., Pvt Co. D 3/4/62 – D (measles) Sav Hos 5/12/62; Bur Lot 860, Laurel Grove Cem, Sav; widow filed for CSP Bulloch Cty, Ga. 1891.

Cloud, Martin L., Pvt Co. F 3/4/62 – C Fox's Gap 9/14/62; E 11/10/62; Appt 2nd Cpl 1/1/63; left sick Bristol, Tn. 1/64; D early 1864 Bristol, Tn.; Bur Grave #154, Emory & Henry Holston Conference Cem, Washington Cty, Va.

Cloud, Peter M., Pvt Co. F 5/13/62 – W Fox's Gap 9/14/62; Rich Hos 9/26/62; W Chancellorsville 5/3/63; roll for 2/65 shows absent sick; P Bainbridge, Ga. 5/20/65.

Cobb, Robert C., Pvt Co. F 3/4/62 – Rich Hos (pneumonia) 2/27/65; register shows Frl 3/20/65; P Tallahassee, Fl. 5/19/65.

Cobb, Turner B. Pvt Co. B 3/4/62 – D 10/12/62.

Cobb, William, Pvt Co. F 3/4/62 – D 4/26/62. Cohen, Adolphus (Adolph) M., Pvt Co. B 3/4/62 – Roll for 12/31/62 shows Trn to Co. C 5/5/62; NLR.

Coker (Croker), Andrew Jackson, Pvt Co. H 3/4/62 – D (typhoid fever) Rich Hos 5/19/63; Bur Oakwood Cem, Rich; widow filed for CSP Berrien Cty, Ga. 1891.

Colding, Silas M., Asst Commissary Sgt 3/10/62 – Roster for 51st Ga. Inf Regt Field and Staff shows "Assistant Commissary Sergeant April 1, 1862. Dropped August 2, 1862. Restored August 4, 1862"; entry for 50th Ga. at Sav dated 7/1/64 shows a forage requisition for horse; NLR.

Coleman, Bernard, Pvt Co. D 3/4/62 – C Fox's Gap 9/14/62; P 9/27/62; C 12/64; roll for 2/65 shows absent POW; NLR.

Coleman, Thomas, Pvt Co. D 3/4/62 – D Rich 7/7/63.

Collier, George M., Pvt Co. G 3/4/62 – Detailed as wagoner; roll for 2/63 shows sent to Winchester, Va. Hos sick 10/13/62; NLR.

Collier, John T., Pvt Co. E 8/13/62 – D (typhoid fever) Gordonsville, Va. 11/19/62.

Collier, Talbot A., Pvt Co. G 6/30/62 – C Winchester, Va. 12/2/62; P Winchester 12/4/62; D 1/16/63.

Collins, George W., Pvt Co. A 3/4/62 – W Fox's Gap 9/14/62; Rich Hos 9/27/62; C Sailor's Creek 4/6/65; R Pt. Lookout, Md. 6/26/65; filed for CSP Madison Cty, Fl. 1898.

Collins, J., Pvt Co. B – C Gettysburg 7/3/63; Ft. Delaware, Del. Prison 7/63; NLR.

Collins, John W., Pvt Co. D 5/10/62 – Substitute for Jesse Byrd Hightower; S Appomattox C.H. 4/9/65.

Cone, Hillory C., Pvt Co. E 3/4/62 – W Chancellorsville 5/3/63; Appt 4th Cpl 8/6/64; on Frl from 2/65 to close of war; filed for CSP Thomas Cty, Ga. 1904.

Cone, John C., Pvt Co. E 5/15/62 – D (typhoid fever) Rich Hos 10/28/62; Bur Oakwood Cem, Rich.

Cone, Moses B., Pvt Co. E 3/4/62 – D Thomas Cty, Ga. 6/23/62.

Connell, Berry J., Pvt Co. I 3/4/62 – Appt 4th Sgt 6/10/62; 3rd Sgt 10/8/62; W Chancellorsville 5/3/63; Appt 1st Sgt 2/64; C Sailor's Creek 4/6/65; R Pt. Lookout, Md. 6/24/65.

Connell, J.I.G., Pvt Co. I 8/23/62 – Roll for 2/28/65 shows AWOL since 2/1/65; P Thomasville, Ga. 5/22/65; widow filed for CSP Berrien Cty, Ga. 1891; pension record says he contracted consumption while in service and died on 12/10/66.

Connell, John E., Jr., Pvt Co. I 3/4/62 – Appt 3rd Sgt; Commissary Sgt; W (1 arm – amputated below shoulder) Gettysburg 7/2/63; left at Williamsport, Md./C 7/14/63; P Pt. Lookout, Md. 10/27/63; roll for 2/28/65 shows absent sick; P Thomasville, Ga. 5/22/65; filed for CSP Berrien Cty, Ga. 1879.

Connell, Richard P., Pvt Co. I 3/4/62 – K Sharpsburg 9/17/62; Bur Elmwood Cem Shepherdstown, Va. (now WV).

Connell, Simon P, Pvt Co. H 3/4/62 – Roll for 8/31/62 shows Trn to Co. E, 17th Regt Ga. Inf 7/15/62.

Connell, William E., Pvt Co. I 8/22/62 – Appt Sgt; W Gettysburg 7/2/63; Disc 4/10/64 upon being elected Judge of Ordinary Court, Berrien Cty, Ga.; widow filed for CSP Berrien Cty 1910.

Conner, James O., Pvt Co. E 4/22/62 – Detailed as nurse Camp Lee, Va. Hos near Rich 2/65; C Camp Lee 4/3/65; NLR.

Conner, T.W., Pvt Co. I 9/4/62 – C Ft. Sanders 11/29/63; took oath of allegiance to U.S. Govt. and joined U.S. Navy at Rock Island, Ill. 1/25/64.

Conners, Benjamin F., Pvt Co. I – C Burkeville, Va. 4/6/65; R City Point, Va. 6/24/65.

Converse, Albert, Regt Quartermaster 3/20/62 – Last entry for pay voucher 11/62; roll for 51st Inf Regt shows dropped 10/25/62; NLR.

Cooper, Elijah, Pvt Co. F 3/4/62 – D (smallpox) Rich Hos 12/22/62; Bur Oakwood Cem, Rich.

Cook, Jasper John, Pvt Co. I 3/4/62 – Roll for 2/65 shows AWOL since 9/16/64; P Thomasville, Ga. 5/24/65; filed for CSP Berrien Cty, Ga. 1911; pension record says he was granted sick Frl on 1/1/65 and too ill to return.

Cook, John, Pvt Co. K 5/13/62 – D (pneumonia) Rich 4/21/63; Bur Hollywood Cem, Rich; widow filed for CSP Brooks Cty, Ga. 1910.

Cooper, Jesse H., Pvt Co. E 3/4/62 – W (hand shot off)/C Fox's Gap 9/14/62; Frederick, Md. Hos 9/19/62; P 9/27/62; Disc, disability 2/11/63.

Cooperman, William, Pvt Co. E 3/4/62 – Disc, furnished John McGlynn as substitute, 5/14/62.

Cope, Pembroke G., Pvt Co. D 3/4/62 – Joined Co. C, 1st Regt Ga. Inf "without Permission"; NLR.

Copeland, Daniel G., Pvt Co. D 5/7/62 – Enlisted in Sav Guards 1861; mustered out and enlisted in Co D; W Fox's Gap 9/14/62; Appt 5th Sgt 10/62; W Chancellorsville 5/3/63; Appt 3rd Sgt 10/63; C Ft. Sanders 11/29/63; R Rock Island, Ill. 6/18/65; filed for CSP Lowndes Cty, Ga. 1909.

Copeland, David S., Pvt Co. D 3/4/62 – Enlisted as Pvt in Co. I, 12th Regt Ga. Inf 6/14/61;Trn to Co. D, 50th Ga. after 9/63; roll for 2/28/65 shows AWOL since 1/15/65; widow filed for CSP Berrien Cty, Ga. 1937; pension record says he was home on sick Frl 3/65 at close of war.

Copeland, Henry, Pvt Co. E 3/4/62 – Disc (disability) Cedar Hill, Va. 5/31/62; P Thomasville, Ga. 5/16/65.

Coppage, George Washington, Pvt Co. I 3/4/62 – Roll for 12/64 shows Trn to Co. C, 18th Ga. Bn 12/22/64; P Manchester, Va. 4/21/65; filed for CSP Lowndes Cty, Ga. 1899.

Corbett, John B., Sr., Pvt Co. D 3/4/62 – Roll for 2/63 shows home sick Frl; roll for 2/65 shows AWOL since 12/25/63; filed for CSP Echols Cty, Ga. 1911; pension record says he was C "Sharpsburg" 10/64 (must have meant "Strasburg") and sent to Pt. Lookout, Md.; Trn to Sav for E 11/64; sent home on sick Frl; home sick at close of war.

Corbitt (Corbett), Manning, Pvt Co. G 3/4/62 – W/C Fox's Gap 9/14/62; DW Frederick, Md. Hos 10/1/62; Bur Mt Olivet Cem, Frederick.

Corbitt, Martin S., Pvt Co. G 5/5/62 – W Fox's Gap 9/14/62; Frl home 1/28/64 due to chronic diarrhea; roll for 2/65 shows AWOL since 3/10/64; widow filed for CSP Atkinson Cty, Ga. 1938; pension record says he was home sick from 1/28/64 to close of war.

Corbitt, William B., 3rd Cpl Co. G 5/3/62 – W (head) Fox's Gap 9/14/62; Rich Hos 9/27/62; Appt 1st Sgt 1/1/63; D (pneumonia) Rich Hos 4/14/63; Bur Oakwood Cem, Rich.

Corbitt, William H., Pvt Co. G 3/4/62 – K (head) Sharpsburg 9/17 62.

Cornelius, Edward H., Pvt Co. G 4/27/62 – Roll for 12/31/62 shows Disc (disability) Rich Hos 5/30/62; enlisted as Pvt in Co. I, 4th Regt Ga. Cav 1/2/63; Trn to Clinch's Battery Ga. Light Artillery; D "in service."

Cornelius, George, Pvt Co. G 4/27/62 – Roll for 2/65 shows detailed as nurse at Ft. Gaines, Ga. Hos 8/64; P Thomasville, Ga. 5/16/65; widow filed for CSP Clinch Cty, Ga. 1910; pension record says he was with command "at the surrender."

Cornwallis, J., Pvt – Only CSR entry is P 5/15/65.

Cothran (Cothren), William Jasper, Pvt Co. C 5/9/62 – C Cedar Creek 10/19/64; E James River, Va. 3/30/65; widow filed for CSP Appling Cty, Ga. 1901.

Cowart, Kindred C., Pvt Co. G 3/4/62 – W Gettysburg (gunshot, l thigh) 7/2/63; C 7/5/63; E City Pt., Va. 1/12/64; P Thomasville, Ga. 5/16/65; filed for CSP Coffee Cty, Ga. 1888; pension record says he was sent home and unable to return.

Cowart, Manning, Pvt Co. G 3/4/62 – Roll for 2/63 shows absent sick Frl for 60 days from 11/13/62; Rich Hos register shows Trn to Sav 7/10/63; NLR.

Crapps, Jesse, Pvt Co. C 5/9/62 – Roll for 2/63 shows absent sick in Hos; NLR.

Creech, Benjamin, Pvt Co. F 3/4/62 – Disc (disability) 6/1/62.

Creede, Eli, Pvt Co. H 3/4/62 – D Macon, Ga. 5/4/62.

Creede, Jacob, Pvt Co. H 3/4/62 – W Chancellorsville 5/3/63; D (dysentery) Rich 7/27/64; Bur Hollywood Cem, Rich.

Creede, Paul, Pvt Co. H 3/4/62 – NLR.

Creed, Paul M.J., Pvt Co. E 3/4/62 – W/C Fox's Gap 9/14/62; E 10/62; W Chancellorsville 5/3/63; C Sailor's Creek 4/6/65; D Pt. Lookout, Md. 1865; Believed Bur Confederate Cem, Pt. Lookout; widow filed for CSP Decatur Cty, Ga. 1912.

Crews, Alexander, Pvt Co. G 3/4/62 – W/C Funkstown 7/10/63; roll for 2/65 shows absent POW; NLR; reported to have D in prison.

Crews, Bryant, Pvt Co. A 3/4/62 – Roll for 2/63 shows absent, sent to Hos 9/2/62; NLR.

Crews, C.C., Pvt Co. B 3/4/62 – NLR.

Crews, Thomas, Pvt Co. A 3/4/62 – C/P Leesburg, Va. 10/2/62; roll for 2/65 shows AWOL since 6/9/64; NLR.

Cribb, John B. Pvt Co. B 5/5/62 – C Amelia C.H., Va. 4/6/65; D Pt. Lookout, Md. 6/16/65; believed Bur in Confederate Cem, Pt. Lookout.

Croft, Jacob H., Pvt Co. H 3/4/62– W (gunshot, l knee – leg amputated) Chancellorsville 5/3/63; Frl from Rich Hos 7/3/63 for 60 days; roll for 2/65 shows AWOL since 8/13/63; filed for CSP Brooks Cty, Ga. 1879 (name shown as "Craft").

Croft, Leroy, Pvt Co. H 3/4/62 – "Served until 1862"; Roll for 2/65 shows AWOL; NLR.

Crosby, Adam Joshua, Pvt Co. I 3/4/62 – Appt 4th Cpl 10/28/62; W (r leg)/C Ft. Sanders 11/29/63; leg amp below knee U.S. Hos 12/63; R Pt. Lookout, Md. 6/6/65; filed for CSP Brooks Cty, Ga. 1899.

Crosby, Henry Washington, Pvt Co. K 3/4/62 – W (leg)/C Cedar Creek 10/19/64; E Pt. Lookout, Md. 3/17/65; widow filed for CSP Brooks Cty, Ga. 1901; pension record says he was home on W Frl at close of war.

Crosby, John P., Pvt Co. H 3/4/62 – W (l arm) Ft. Sanders 11/29/63; C near Knoxville 12/5/63; DW Middle Brook Hos, Knoxville 1863 or 1864; Bur near Knoxville.

Crosby, Paul, 1st Cpl Co. I 3/4/62 – C Sailor's Creek 4/6/65; R Pt. Lookout, Md. 6/24/65; widow filed for CSP Cook Cty, Ga. 1919.

Crosby, Peter B., Pvt Co. I 3/4/62 – D Rich Hos 4/1/63; Bur Oakwood Cem, Rich.

Cross, J.D. Pvt Co. E – Not in CSR; Bur Stonewall (Mount Hebron) Cem, Winchester, Va., marker #144; Cem register reads "J.D. Cross, Co. E, 50th Ga. Died Oct. 16, 1862."

Crowley (Croley), John R., Pvt Co. I 6/18/62 – Substitute for William DeVane; W Gettysburg (arm – amputated) 7/2/63; DW 7/31/63; widow filed for CSP Lowndes Cty, Ga. 1891.

Crum, Benjamin H., Pvt Co. I 3/4/62 – W Gettysburg 7/2/63; C Cedar Creek 10/19/64; R Pt. Lookout, Md. 6/24/65; filed for CSP Tift Cty, Ga. 1919.

Crum, George W., 3rd Cpl Co. I 6/10/62 – D Rich Hos 2/5/63; Bur Oakwood Cem, Rich.

Crum, J.W.T., Pvt Co. I 8/22/62 – C Cedar Creek 10/19/64; D Pt. Lookout, Md. 1/15/65; believed Bur Confederate Cem, Pt. Lookout; widow filed for CSP Berrien Cty, Ga. 1893.

Culpepper, J. (John) B., Pvt Co. H 3/4/62 – NLR.

Culpepper, David (Daniel) C., Pvt Co. H 9/11/62 – W (head – both eyes shot out) Chancellorsville 5/3/63; Frl home from Hos 5/22/63; widow filed for CSP Worth Cty, Ga. 1891; pension record says his brother, J.B. Culpeper brought him home to Mitchell Cty, Ga. from the Hos, where he DW 6/23/63.

Curies, A.I., Pvt Co. H 3/4/62 – NLR.

Curry, Charles W., 2nd Sgt Co. G 3/4/62 – W (gunshot)/C Fox's Gap 9/14/62; Wash D.C. Hos 9/27/62; E 10/62; Rich Hos 10/6/62; Appt 4th Sgt 2/64; P Lynchburg, Va. 4/65; filed for CSP Clinch Cty, Ga. 1907; pension record says he was with command at close of war.

Curry, Duncan, Cpt, Co. F 3/4/62 – W (breast - slight) 2nd Manassas Campaign 8/23/62; Elected Maj 10/8/62; Res (ill health) 2/24/63; P Bainbridge, Ga. 6/2/65.

Curry, William D., Pvt Co. C 3/4/62 – K Spotsylvania CH 5/14/64.

Curry, William L., Chaplain, 9/1/62 – C Cedar Creek 10/19/64; roll for 3/65 shows absent Frl; P Camp Hamilton, Va. 6/6/65.

Cutner, Hyman, Pvt Co. D 3/4/62 – Des 3/20/65; took oath of allegiance to U.S. Govt. and furnished trans to Sav.

ROSTER D

Dailey, Daniel, Pvt Co. K 3/4/62 – C Fox's Gap 9/14/62; E 10/17/62; W Chancellorsville 5/3/63; roll for 2/65 shows absent POW; P Thomasville, Ga. 5/19/65.

Dailey, Dennis, Pvt Co. K 4/24/62 – W Chancellorsville 5/3/63; roll for 2/65 shows sent to Hos 11/1/64; P Thomasville, Ga. 5/18/65; filed for CSP Brooks Cty, Ga. 1912; pension record says he received a 60 day sick Frl 1/65, and was home sick at close of war.

Dailey, James, Pvt Co. K – Only CSR entry shows sick in Sav Hos 6/62; NLR.

Dampier, David (Daniel), Pvt Co. D 3/4/62 – K Cold Harbor 6/1/64.

Dampier, G.W., Pvt Co. D – Entry for 7/62 shows "detailed to cleanup convalescent camp near Whitesville, GA"; P Thomasville, Ga. 5/19/65.

Dampier, Henry W., Pvt Co. K 4/20/62 – D (measles) at home Brooks Cty, Ga. 12/25/62; widow filed for CSP Brooks Cty, Ga. 1891.

Dampier, John H., Pvt Co. D 3/4/62 – W (head) Chancellorsville 5/3/63; Trn to Co. I, 12th Regt Ga. Inf 1863; C Spotsylvania C.H. 5/64; R Elmira, N.Y. 6/27/65; filed for CSP in Alachua Cty, Fl. 1903.

Daniels, C., Pvt Co. F 11/28/64 – Des 5/26/65.

Daniels, William, Pvt Co. I 1/9/63 - Trn from Co. E 5th Ga. Regt; NLR.

David, William J., Surgeon – NLR.

Davidson, Gideon C., Pvt Co. F 3/4/62 – C Fox's Gap 9/14/62; E Aikens Landing, Va. 10/62; Rich Hos 10/14/62; W Gettysburg (thigh) 7/2/63; NLR.

Davis, Arthur, Pvt Co. C 3/4/62 – D (pneumonia) Rich Hos 8/26/63; Bur Oakwood Cem, Rich.

Davis, Charlton S., Pvt Co. A 3/4/62 – W (gunshot, r elbow) Wilderness 5/6/64; roll for 2/28/65 shows absent sick; P Thomasville, Ga. 5/18/65; filed for CSP Pierce Cty, Ga. 1888; pension record claims he was disabled from the wound and home at close of the war.

Davis, Daniel D., Pvt Co. G 3/4/62 – Original muster roll shows "Volunteered & stayed at home"; roll for 2/65 shows AWOL since 8/1/62; NLR.

Davis, Elisha, Pvt Co. H 5/14/62 – D Sav 7/18/62; Bur Laurel Grove Cem, Sav.

Davis, Glen, Pvt Co. A – W Chancellorsville 5/3/63; NLR.

Davis, James L., Pvt Co. A 3/4/62 – D (typhoid fever) Rich Hos 5/23/63; Bur Hollywood Cem, Rich; widow filed for CSP Wayne Cty, Ga. 1891.

Davis, Jasper N., Pvt Co. E 8/22/62 – D (pneumonia) Rich Hos 12/24/62; Bur Oakwood Cem, Rich.

Davis, John H., Pvt Co. A 3/4/62 – Roll for 2/28/65 shows AWOL since 11/13/63; NLR.

Davis, John W., Pvt Co. E 3/4/62 – D (typhoid pneumonia) Jordan Springs, Va. Hos 10/3/62 (near Winchester); widow filed for CSP Thomas Cty, Ga. 1891; pension record says he was left along the roadside during withdrawal from Sharpsburg in an exhausted condition.

Davis, Mark, Pvt Co. C 9/5/62 – D (pneumonia) Rich Hos 6/18/63; Bur Oakwood Cem, Rich; widow filed for CSP Coffee Cty, Ga. 1891.

Davis, R., Pvt Co. G – K Gettysburg 7/2/63.

Davis, Simon (Simeon), Pvt Co. C 9/5/62 – D Fredericksburg, Va. 12/14/62.

Davis, William D., Pvt Co. E 3/4/62 – Disc (chronic rheumatism & bronchitis) 12/15/62.

Davis, William P., Pvt Co. F 3/4/62 – Arrested 8/64; roll for 10/31/64 shows under arrest, court martial; roll for 2/65 shows present; C Farmville, Va. 4/6/65; P Pt. Lookout, Md. 6/26/65.

Deen, John, Pvt Co. A 3/4/62 – Trn from Co. B; D 4/25/62.

Dekle, William G., Jr. 2nd Lt Co. F 3/4/62 – Elected 2nd Lt 6/29/62; K Fox's Gap 9/14/62; widow filed for CSP Grady Cty, Ga. 1910.

Delk, John W., Pvt Co. K 3/4/62 – D (bronchitis) Rich Hos 1/24/63; Bur Oakwood Cem, Rich.

DeLoach, Edmund, Pvt Co. D 3/4/62 – D Rich Hos 4/29/63; Bur Oakwood Cem, Rich.

DeLoach, John, Pvt Co. D 3/4/62 – W (hip) Funkstown 7/10/63; C 7/20/63; U.S. Hos Winchester, Va.; E 1863; Staunton, Va. Hos 11/8/63; roll for 2/65 shows absent sick; P Thomasville, Ga. 5/10/65; filed for CSP Lowndes Cty, Ga. 1897; pension record says Disc (disability).

DeLoach, Riley, Pvt Co. D 4/26/62 – Prom 4th Cpl 1/63; W Gettysburg (hand) 7/2/63; W (l leg)/C Sailor's Creek 4/6/65; R Wash, D.C. 6/14/65.

Denman, William, 1st Cpl Co. H 3/4/62 – Appt 4th Sgt 1864; roll for 2/65 shows "Des March 22-64"; NLR.

Denmark, James M., Pvt Co. A 3/4/62 – C Gettysburg 7/2/63; E Pt. Lookout, Md. 11/1/64; roll for 2/28/65 shows absent sick; P Thomasville, Ga. 5/19/65.

Denmark, James W., Pvt Co. A 3/4/62 - Roll for 2/63 shows "absent left at Burkeville about 4 October not since heard from"; D 11/2/62; Bur Stonewall (Mount Hebron) Cem, Winchester, Va., marker #208.

Dent, John A., 2nd Cpl Co. C 3/4/62 – C Fox's Gap 9/14/62; E 12/18/62; Petersburg Hos (typhoid fever) 12/18/62; K Chancellorsville 5/3/63.

Denton, John, Pvt Co. C 5/9/62 – Roll for 2/28/65 shows present; widow filed for CSP

Jeff Davis Cty, Ga. 1910; pension record says he was with his command at the surrender on 4/9/65, but not on parolee list with 50th Ga. Regt.

Denton, Joshua T., Pvt Co. C 10/17/62 – D 5/11/63; widow filed for CSP Coffee Cty, Ga. 1910.

Denton, William M., Pvt Co. C 5/9/62 – Entry for 5/62 shows "enlisted Ft. Brown, Ga." 5/9/62; Trn to Co. F, 4th Regt Ga. Cav 11/21/63; filed for CSP Ware Cty, Ga. 1924; pension record says was on courier duty in Tattnall County, Ga. when his cavalry command S in Screven Cty, Ga. 4/65.

Devane, Benjamin Mitchell, Pvt Co. I 5/9/62 – Detailed Whitesville, Ga. Hos 6/62; Appt 2nd Lt 1/4/64; roll for 2/28/65 shows "leave of absence Genl Lee" on 2/12/65: enroute to command at close of the war.

Devane, Patrick, Pvt Co. I 8/14/62 – Fell out on march near Culpeper, Va. 11/18/62; D (probably bronchitis) Scottsville, Va. 12/13/62.

DeVane, William, Pvt Co. I 3/4/62 – Disc 6/18/62, furnishing J.R. Croley as substitute.

Dial, John, Pvt Co. D 3/4/62 – C near Hagerstown, Md. 7/7/63; E Pt. Lookout, Md. 4/27/64; D Rich 3/21/65; Bur Hollywood Cem, Rich.

Dickey, J.E., Pvt Co. D - Only CSR entry shows P Thomasville, Ga. 5/15/65.

Dillard, Meredith, 2nd Cpl Co. E 3/4/62 – Prom 4th Sgt 9/14/62; reduced to Pvt; Des 3/14/65, furnished trans to Jacksonville, Fl.

Dixon, Absalom B., Pvt Co. I 3/4/62 – W (gunshot, r thigh)/C Cedar Creek 10/19/64; E City Point, Va. 10/29/64; P Thomasville, Ga. 5/23/65.

Dixon, B., Cpl Co. D – Only CSR entry shows P Thomasville, Ga. 5/15/65.

Dixon, James J., Pvt Co. A 3/4/62 – NLR.

Dixon, James M., Pvt Co. K 5/13/62– K (artillery shell) Gettysburg 7/2/63.

Dixon (Dickson), Malachi, Pvt Co. A 3/4/62 – K Chancellorsville 5/3/63.

Dixon, Moses, Pvt Co. K 5/13/62 – D Sav Hos 6/23/62.

Dixon, Pleasant W., Pvt Co. K 5/13/62 – D (pneumonia) Rich Hos 4/23/63; Bur Oakwood Cem, Rich.

Dobson, Andrew, 4th Cpl Co. I 3/4/62 – Roll for 8/31/62 shows left at Sulphur Springs, Va. 8/25/62; D (typhoid fever) Raleigh, N.C. 10/28/62; widow filed for CSP Berrien Cty, Ga. 1891; pension record says he died on the way home on sick Frl.

Dodd, William C. Pvt Co. E 3/4/62 – Appt 3rd Sgt 5/5/62; Elected Jr. 2nd Lt of Co. H 4/27/63; Appt 1st Lt 4/25/64; W (r hip) Wilderness 5/6/64; W (thigh) 10/13/64; Trn from Harrisonburg, Va. Hos to Rich Hos 11/8/64; Frl from Rich Hos 12/14/64; roll for 2/28/65 shows leave expired 2/15/65; P Albany, Ga. 5/15/65 widow filed for CSP Sumter Cty, Ga. 1902; pension record says he was home on W Frl at close of war.

Dollar, Simeon, Pvt Co. F 3/4/62 – D (smallpox) Rich Hos 1/28/63; Bur Oakwood Cem, Rich.

Dollar, Thomas J., Pvt Co. F 5/13/62 – Appt 4th Corp 8/29/64; C High Bridge, Va. 4/6/65; P Newton, N.C. 4/19/65; widow filed for CSP Decatur Cty, Ga. 1901.

Donaldson, Aaron J., Pvt Co. E 3/4/62 – W/C Fox's Gap 9/14/62; Wash D.C. Hos 9/21/62; E 10/62; Rich Hos 10/24/62; detailed in Bde Quartermaster Dept. 10/64; S Appomattox CH 4/9/65; filed for CSP Grady Cty, Ga. 1908.

Dopson, William J., Pvt Co. A 3/4/62 – NLR.

Dorsett, Alfred M., Pvt Co. K 3/4/62 – Appt 1st Sgt 3/23/64; W Wilderness 5/6/64; roll for 2/65 shows present sick; NLR.

Douglass, Hezekiah, Pvt Co. B 3/4/62 – Rolls from 8/31/64 to 2/28/65 shows "absent sick left on march"; P Thomasville, Ga. 5/26/65.

Douglass, James, 1st Sgt Co. G 3/4/62 – W (both thighs) Fox's Gap 9/14/62; C 10/6/62; E Aikens Landing, Va. 10/13/62; Rich Hos 10/23/62; Elected Jr. 2nd Lt 3/2/63; Appt 1st Lt 7/2/63; K Gettysburg 7/2/63.

Douglas, James R., Pvt Co. H 3/4/62 – D (small pox) Rich Hos 1/25/63; Bur Oakwood Cem, Rich.

Douglass, William W., Pvt Co. E 3/4/62 – W (head & hip) Fox's Gap 9/14/62; Rich Hos 9/28/62; Trn Sav Hos 10/62; Disc, disability 1/12/63; worked in Commissary Dept.; filed for CSP in Duval Cty Fl. 7/22/1907.

Dover, J.A., Pvt Co. F 3/4/62 – Disc 1864.

Dowling, Aaron, 2nd Lt Co. A 3/4/62 – W/C Fox's Gap 9/14/62; E 10/6/62; Rich Hos 10/8/62; Appt 1st Lt 12/31/62; Res as 1st Lt 1/31/63; Appt 2nd Lt 4/64; S Appomattox CH 4/9/65; filed for CSP Charlton Cty, Ga. 1900.

Dowling, Darling Wesley, Pvt Co. A 3/4/62 – C Sailor's Creek 4/6/65; R Pt. Lookout, Md. 6/26/65; filed for CSP Pierce Cty, Ga.1910.

Dowling, David L., Pvt Co. A 3/4/62 – C (sick) Frederick, Md. 9/12/62; Frederick Hos 9/19/62; E 10/19/62; Rich Hos 10/22/62; roll for 2/63 shows AWOL since 12/1/62; NLR.

Dowling, Jabez Jackson, Pvt Co. A 3/4/62 – Appt 3rd Cpl 3/23/64; W Petersburg 7/64; Frl home from Hos 8/64; roll for 2/65 shows AWOL since 10/11/64; filed for CSP Pierce Cty, Ga. 1902; pension record says he contracted typhoid fever while in Hos and received sick Frl home; home sick at close of war.

Dowling, John H., Pvt Co. A 3/4/62 – Roll for 2/65 shows AWOL since 5/4/63; filed for CSP Bradford Cty, Fl. 1907; pension record says he was home sick on extended Frl with typhoid fever and unable to return.

Dowling, Lazarus, 4th Cpl Co. A 3/4/62 – Injured (1 leg disabled) Harpers Ferry 9/15 or Sharpsburg 9/17/62; Rich Hos; Disc 3/5/63; filed for CSP Pierce Cty, Ga. 1890; pension record says while tearing up railroad tracks, a rail fell on his l knee, causing loss of use of the leg.

Downing, George W., Pvt Co. D 3/4/62 – W (gunshot, head - loss of sight 1 eye) Chancellorsville 5/3/63; roll for 2/65 shows absent sick; P Thomasville, Ga. 5/24/65; filed for CSP Lowndes Cty, Ga. 1889.

Drew, Josiah, 3rd Sgt Co. E 3//4/62 – D Sav Hos 5/4/62.

Driggers, James J., Pvt Co. C 9/18/62 – W Chancellorsville 5/3/63; D Gordonsville, Va. Hos 6/18/63.

Dryden, Benjamin, Pvt Co. G 3/4/62 – Roll for 2/65 shows AWOL since 3/10/63; NLR.

Duffie, James, Pvt Co. I 3/4/62 – W (back) Spotsylvania C.H. 5/12/64; Charlottesville Hos 5/12/64; Frl 60 days from Rich Hos 7/12/64; roll for 2/65 shows AWOL since 2/1/65 ; NLR.

Duke, B.D., Pvt – Only CSR entry shows S Tallahassee, Fl. 5/10/65; P Bainbridge, Ga. 5/20/65.

Dukes, James W., 3rd Sgt Co. H 3/4/62 –D Camp Davis, Ga. 4/4/62; widow filed for CSP Colquitt Cty, Ga. 1891.

Dukes, Matthew Miles, Pvt Co. H 5/13/62 – W Chancellorsville 5/3/63; W (knee) Ft. Sanders 11/29/63; DW 11/29/63.

Dukes, Wyatt (Wiatt), Pvt Co. H 3/4/62 – D (measles) Sav 7/62.

Dukes, Z., Pvt Co. H 3/12/64 – D 1864 or 1865.

Dunaway, G.W., Pvt Co. H 3/4/62 – Disc 12/64.

Dunbar, Timothy S., Pvt Co. E 3/4/62– W (hand) Fox's Gap 9/14/62; W (same hand) Gettysburg 7/2/63; Appt 5th Sgt 1/65; roll for 2/65 shows present; filed for CSP Hillsborough Cty Fl. 5/2/1904.

Duncan, Kasper G., 3rd Cpl Co. K 3/4/62 – W Chancellorsville 5/3/63; W Gettysburg (foot) 7/2/63: W (hip) Ft. Sanders 11/29; C Knoxville 12/5/63; D Middle Brook Hos, Knoxville 1863 or 1864; Bur near Knoxville.

Dunlap, William B., Pvt Co. F 3/4/62 – W (r leg - amputated) Fox's Gap 9/14/62; C

South Mtn. 10/4; P Ft. McHenry, Md. 11/6/62; Disc (disability) Rich Hos
    12/17/62; filed for CSP Thomas Cty, Ga. 1879.
Dupriest, J.B., Pvt Co. K 9/63 – Supposed to have been K 11/64.
Durham, George W., Pvt Co. C 3/4/62 – W Chancellorsville 5/3/63; C Cedar Creek
    10/19/64; D Pt. Lookout, Md. 2/2/65.
Dyess, Josiah, Pvt Co. A 3/4/62 – D (pneumonia) Lynchburg, Va. 2/3/63; Bur Lot 191,
    Confederate Cem, Lynchburg.
Dykes, George, Pvt Co. A 3/4/62 – NLR.
Dyson, John M., Pvt Co. E 3/4/62 – Disc (disability) 10/27/63.

ROSTER E

Eady, S., Pvt Co. C – Detailed as nurse Macon, Ga. Hos 5/62; NLR.
Earnest, Thomas J., Pvt Co. F 5/13/62 – D (typhoid fever) Rich Hos 12/7/62; Bur
    Oakwood Cem, Rich.
Easters, J.H., Pvt Co. D 5/9/62 – W Chancellorsville 5/3/63; K Gettysburg 7/2/63.
Eaves, J, Pvt – Not in CSR; Bur Stonewall (Mount Hebron) Cem, Winchester, Va.,
    marker # 182; Cem register reads "—Eaves, 50th Ga. Died October 30, 1862";
    (could be Seaborn Edwards, who D same date at Winchester Hos).
Echols, Floyd, Pvt Co. C 3/4/62 – Disc (under-age) 10/8/62; NLR.
Edenfield, William, Pvt Co. A 3/4/62 – C Middletown, Va. 9/14/62; E Aikens Landing,
    Va. 10/19/62; K Chancellorsville 5/3/63.
Eddy, William F., Pvt Co. C 5/6/62 – K Fox's Gap 9/14/62.
Edmonds, J.S. Pvt Co. K – D (date Unk); not in CSR; Bur Stonewall (Mount Hebron)
    Cem, Winchester, Va., marker #184; Cem register reads "J.S. Edmunds, Co. K
    50th Ga" (could be James Edmondson, Co. K).
Edmondson, David, Pvt Co. K 3/4/62 – NLR.
Edmondson, James, Pvt Co. K 4/20/62 – Only entry in CSR; (could be the "J.S.
Edmunds" Bur in Stonewall (Mount Hebron) Cem, Winchester, Va.).
Edmondson, William R., Pvt Co. I 5/9/62 – D (pneumonia) Rich Hos 2/23/63; Bur
    Hollywood Cem, Rich.
Edwards, George A., Pvt Co. K 3/4/62 – D Augusta, Ga. 5/21/62.
Edwards, George S., Pvt Co. K 4/24/62 – C (sick pneumonia) Frederick, Md. 9/15/62; E
    9/62; Rich Hos 10/1/62; Disc 10/23/62; filed for CSP Lafayette Cty Fl. 1897.
Edwards, John G.M., Pvt Co. F 11/17/64 – C Sailor's Creek 4/6/65; R Pt. Lookout, Md.
    6/26/65.
Edwards, Samuel R., Pvt Co. K 3/4/62 – C Middle Brook Hos near Knoxville 12/5/63;
    D Middle Brook Hos 1/1/64.
Edwards, Seaborn A., Pvt Co. K 3/4/62 - W/C Fox's Gap 9/14/62; P 9/25/62; Rich Hos
    10/1/62; DW Winchester, Va. Hos 10/30/62 (could be "—Eaves" Bur in
    Stonewall (Mount Hebron) Cem, Winchester, who D same date.
Ellis, Benjamin A.H., 2nd Cpl Co. I 3/4/62 – C near Knoxville 12/3/63; D Rock Island,
    Ill. 3/25/64.
Ellis, Elijah, Pvt Co. C 3/4/62 – Appt 4th Cpl 1/1/63; K Petersburg 6/21/64.
Ellis, Hiram, Pvt Co. C 5/9/62 – D Danville, Va. Hos 3/31/63; widow filed for CSP
    Coffee Cty, Ga. 1891.
Ellis, J., Pvt Co. D 3/4/62 – W Cold Harbor 6/6/64; Rich Hos 6/8; roll for 2/65 shows
    AWOL since 8/1/64; NLR.
Ellis, Joshua, Pvt Co. C 3/4/62 – W Chancellorsville 5/3/63; C near Knoxville 12/7/63; R
    Rock Island, Ill. 6/17/65; filed for CSP Coffee Cty, Ga. 1895.
Ellis, Moses L., Pvt Co. I 3/4/62 – C Gettysburg 7/2/63; Chester, Pa. Hos; E City Point,

Va. 9/23/63; W (face) Petersburg 7/1/64; Frl 30 days 8/12/64; roll for 8/31/64 shows absent wounded; D at home Berrien Cty, Ga. 12/64.

Ellis, William, Pvt Co. C 5/9/62 – D (pneumonia) Lynchburg, Va. Hos 11/11/62; Bur Lot 181, Confederate Cem, Lynchburg.

Ellis, William A., 1st Cpl Co. F 3/4/62 – Reduced to Pvt 10/62; Appt 2nd Cpl 2/64;W Spotsylvania C.H. 5/10/64 (1 hand – 3 fingers amputated); Hos 5/9/64; S Appomattox C.H. 4/9/65.

Elmore, John W., Pvt Co. D 3/4/62 – Disc, underage (16) 6/62; re-enlisted; C Sailor's Creek 4/6/65; R 6/65; widow filed for CSP Lowndes Cty, Ga. 1904.

Eunice, A. Pvt Co. A 3/10/62 – Filed for CSP Worth Cty, Ga. 1910; pension record says he was C in Tn. 1863, sent to Rock Island, Ill. Prison and R 5/16/65.

Evans, George W., Pvt Co. H 3/4/62 – Disc (disability) 10/29/62.

Evans, J.B., Pvt Co. H 3/4/62 – D Macon, Ga. Hos 5/1/62.

Everett, A. Dempsey, Pvt Co. C 3/4/62 – W Chancellorsville 5/3/63; W Cedar Creek 10/19/64; DW Mt. Jackson, Va. Hos 10/20/64; widow filed for CSP Clinch Cty, Ga. 1891.

Everitt, John W., Pvt Co. E 3/4/62 – Appt 5th Sgt 9/14/62; Appt 1st Sgt 1/1/63; Elected 2nd Lt 5/11//63; W (r hip) Cedar Creek 10/19/64; roll for 2/65 shows present; P Thomasville, Ga. 5/10/65.

Evers, William J., Pvt Co. E 8/13/62 – W Gettysburg 7/2/63; Staunton, Va. Hos 7/30/63; Hos roll for 8/27/63 shows present; doctor's note "Evers is improving"; NLR.

Exom (Exum), John Kinchen, Pvt Co. K 7/18/62 - K (gunshot – thigh) Wilderness 5/6/64; widow filed for CSP Brooks Cty, Ga. 1895.

ROSTER F

Fahm, George E., Pvt Co. E 3/4/62 – Appt 3rd Sgt 8/1/62; W (hip – slight) Sharpsburg 9/17/62; Elected Jr. 2nd Lt 4/27/63; W (neck/right lung) Chancellorsville 5/3/ 63; Appt 1st Lt 5/5/63; Rich Hos 5/7/63; Appt Cpt 2/64; tendered Res as Cpt 2/22/65; C Sailor's Creek 4/6/65; R Johnson's Island, Oh. 6/18/65; filed for CSP Glynn Cty, Ga. 1910.

Fails, C.C. Pvt Co. B 3/4/62 – NLR.

Fain (Fane), John T., Pvt Co. F 11/17/64 – C Farmville 4/6/65; R Pt. Lookout, Md. 6/26/65.

Fender, George W., Pvt Co. D 3/4/62 – D Macon, Ga. 5/6/62.

Fender, Riley R., Pvt Co. D 3/4/62 – Disc (disability - contracted measles, resulting in total blindness 4/62); filed for CSP Lowndes Cty, Ga. 1889.

Fields, Elijah, Pvt Co. H 3/4/62 – Detailed as wagoner 5/62; C Farmville 4/6/65; R Pt. Lookout, Md. 6/26/65.

Finch, Hilliard J., Pvt Co. K 3/4/62 – C Ft. Sanders 11/29/63; R Rock Island, Ill. 6/17/65; filed for CSP Duval Cty, Fl 1910.

Finch, James B., 2nd Lt Co. K 3/4/62 – W (shell fragment - lost 1 eye) Fox's Gap 9/14/62; Res (disability) 7/27/63; filed for CSP Brooks Cty, Ga. 1889.

Finch, Jimpsey, C., Pvt Co. K 5/11/62 – C Fox's Gap 9/14/62; E 10/2/62; Rich Hos 10/8/62; roll for 2/63 shows AWOL since 12/20/62; NLR.

Fleming, John Morgan, Regt Adj 3/30/62 – D Mechanicsville, Va. 3/23/63.

Fleming, William Oliver, 1st Lt Co. F 3/4/62 – Elected Jr. 2nd Lt. Co. G, 1st Regt Ga. Inf 3/18/61; Res 1/2/62; enlisted in Co F, 50th Ga. Inf Regt; Elected Cpt 10/8/62; Appt Maj 7/30/63; LtC 8/24/63, effective 7/31/63; Res 12/21/63, upon being elected to Ga. State Assembly.

Fletcher, John W., Pvt Co. A 3/4/62 – W Fox's Gap 9/14/62; roll for 2/63 shows "sent to hospital Sept 14, 1862-not since heard from"; NLR.

Flowers, George W., Pvt Co. I 3/4/62 – W Gettysburg 7/2/63; C near Knoxville, Tn. 12/3/63; E Rock Island, Ill. 3/2/65; Rich Hos 3/7/65; Frl for 60 days 3/21/65.

Flowers, James B., Pvt Co. H 3/4/62 – W Fox's Gap 9/14/62; Rich Hos 9/26/62; W Gettysburg 7/2/63; C Spotsylvania C.H. 5/12/64; E Belle Plain, Va. 9/18/64; NLR.

Flowers, O. Nathan, Pvt Co. H 3/4/62 – W Fox's Gap 9/14/62; W (l hand – thumb "shot off" & r elbow) Chancellorsville 5/3/63; roll for 2/65 shows present; P 4/65; filed for CSP Colquitt Cty, Ga. 1897.

Floyd, Reubin Perry, Pvt Co. C 3/4/62 – Roll for 2/65 shows AWOL since 8/21/62; P Thomasville, Ga. 5/25/65; widow filed for CSP Coffee Cty, Ga. 1917; pension record says he was at surrender on 4/9/65, but not on list of parolees for 50th Ga. Regt.

Floyd, Sylvester H., Pvt Co. E 3/4/62 – Appt Cpl; W (l arm) Petersburg 6/18/64; Rich Hos 6/22/64 (arm amputated); DW Rich Hos 7/17/64; Bur Hollywood Cem, Rich.

Floyd, Thomas, Pvt Co. B 3/4/62 – NLR.

Folsom, H.V, Pvt Co. H 5/15/62 – Disc, upon furnishing John D. Henley as substitute 6/11/62.

Ford, E.C., Sgt Co. F – Only CSR entry shows P Thomasville, Ga. 5/10/65.

Ford, Edward M. Pvt Co. A 3/4/62 – Elected 3rd Lt 8/31/62; W Chancellorsville 5/3/63; Appt Cpt 5/26/63; K (gunshot - head) Gettysburg 7/2/63; Bur Gettysburg; removed to Laurel Grove Cem, Sav 9/24/1871; Bur Lot 853.

Ford, Samuel, Pvt Co. G 3/4/62 – D Rich 7/5/64; Bur Hollywood Cem, Rich.

Ford, Samuel, Pvt Co. I 3/4/62 – W Chancellorsville 5/3/63; W (breast) Cold Harbor 6/3/64; DW 6/6/64.

Ford, William D., Pvt Co. I 3/4/62 – D Winchester, Va. Hos 10/26/62; Bur Stonewall (Mount Hebron) Cem, Winchester, marker 187; widow filed for CSP Berrien Cty, Ga. 1891; pension record says he gave out from exhaustion on the march and was carried to the Hos where he died.

Frank, Pvt Co. E – CSR entry for 5/62 shows re-enlisted near Ft. Brown 5/16/62; NLR.

Franklin, George W., Pvt Co. E 3/4/62 – W Gettysburg (l thigh - leg amputated) 7/2/63; C 7/5/63; DW 8/10/63 U.S. Hos Gettysburg.

Franklin, W.W., Pvt Co. H 3/4/62 – C Ft. Sanders 11/29/63; E Rock Island, Ill. 3/2/65; NLR.

Fulford, William Warren, Pvt Co. I 3/4/62 – K Ft. Sanders 11/29/63; widow filed for CSP Berrien Cty, Ga. 1910.

Fulwood, Daniel Archibald, Pvt Co. K 3/4/62 – W (gunshot - l thigh)/C Sharpsburg 9/17/62; leg amputated near hip; E 9/27/62; C Shepherdstown, Va. (now W.V.) 11/25/62; E City Point, Va. 2/2/63; Petersburg, Va. Hos 3/12/63; detailed as Conscript Officer in Ga. 1864; filed for CSP Houston Cty, Ga. 1879.

Fulwood, John W., 3rd Cpl Co. E 3/4/62 – D Macon, Ga. 4/23/62.

Fulwood, William A., Pvt Co. K 3/4/62 – Roll for 1/23/65 shows on detail Macon, Ga. Hos with chronic rheumatism; NLR.

ROSTER G

Gainey, I., Pvt Co. H 3/4/62 – NLR.

Gainey, Robert S., Pvt Co. H 8/13/62 – D in camp near Fredericksburg, Va. 2/28/63.

Ganas, Jonathon B., Pvt Co. D 5/13/62 – Appt 2nd Sgt 10/8/62; W (head) Petersburg 6/18/64; Rich Hos 6/23/64; C Sailor's Creek 4/6/65; R Pt. Lookout, Md.

6/27/65; filed for CSP Clinch Cty, Ga. 1907.

Ganas, W.C., Pvt Co. D 5/13/62 – W Chancellorsville 5/3/63; W Ft. Sanders 11/29/63; DW Knoxville Hos late 1863.

Gandy, Charles Thomas, Sr., Pvt Co. E 7/31/62 – W (1 arm) Chancellorsville 5/3/63; Rich Hos (arm amputated) 5/27/63; Disc (disability) 1/12/64; P Thomasville, Ga. 1865; filed for CSP Thomas Cty, Ga. 1879.

Gandy, Francis M., Pvt Co. E 5/15/62 – W (shoulder – severe) Sharpsburg 9/17/62; Rich Hos 9/30/62; Petersburg Hos 10/10/62; Frl home Thomasville, Ga.; Charlottesville Hos 10/31/64; retired to Invalid Corps 1/18/65; roll for 2/65 shows "absent detached Lynchburg, Va."; S Lynchburg, Va. 4/13/65 widow filed for CSP in Al.

Gandy, Jared I., Pvt Co. E 5/15/62 – W (shoulder – slight) Sharpsburg 9/17/62; Appt 2nd Cpl 2/64; C Sailors Creek, Va. 4/6/65; R Newport News, Va. 6/25/65; widow filed for CSP Grady Cty, Ga. 1911.

Gandy, John Matthews, Pvt Co. E 5/15/62 – W (1 wrist) Sharpsburg 9/17/62; Disc (disability) 5/21/63; widow filed for CSP Thomas Cty, Ga. 1937.

Gandy, Nathaniel Worthy, Pvt Co. E 8/13/62 – Enlisted as Pvt in Co. D, 2nd Regt, 1st Bde, Ga. State Troops 10/8/61; mustered out 4/62; enlisted in Co E, 50th Ga.: roll for 2/65 shows AWOL since 11/1/64; P Thomasville, Ga. 5/12/65.

Gandy, Samuel, Pvt Co. E 3/4/62 – K Fox's Gap 9/14/62.

Gandy, W.H.H., Pvt Co. E 8/22/62 – Roll for 2/63 shows present; D Rich 1863 or early 1864; death claim filed 3/24/64; NLR.

Garland, Nathaniel, Pvt Co. F 5/19/62 – Enlisted as Pvt in Co. K, 1st Regt, 1st Bde, Ga. State Troops 10/8/61; mustered out 4/8/62; enlisted in Co. F, 50th Ga.; W/C Fox's Gap 9/14/62; P 9/25/62; DW 9/30/62.

Garrett, William H., Pvt Co. I 3/4/62 – C Cold Harbor 6/1/64; P Pt. Lookout, Md. 3/17/65; last CSR entry 3/25/65 shows sick in Rich Hos; NLR.

Gaskins, Archibald S., Pvt Co. I 3/4/62 – W (abdomen) Wilderness 5/6/64; Rich Hos 5/15/64; roll for 2/65 shows AWOL since 9/28/64; filed for CSP Berrien Cty, Ga. 1919; pension record says he was Frl home 6/64, and on duty with enrolling officer at close of war.

Gaskins, Daniel David, Pvt Co. I 3/4/62 – Elected Jr. 2nd Lt 6/18/62; W Fox's Gap 9/14/62; Elected 2nd Lt 10/18/62; 1st Lt 4/14/63; D 11/30/63.

Gaskins, Fisher W., Pvt Co. I 3/4/62 – Disc, under age 10/14/62.

Gaskins, Fisher Jackson, Pvt Co. I 5/2/62 – Appt 3rd Cpl 1/5/63; W (hip – flesh) Gettysburg 7/2/63; C Gettysburg 7/5/63; E 9/63; W (breast) Cold Harbor 6/3/64; Rich Hos 6/4/64; Frl for 30 days 6/16/64; roll for 2/65 shows AWOL since 1/1/65; NLR.

Gaskins, Harmon, Jr., Pvt Co. I 5/2/62 – D Ft Brown, Ga. 6/13/62.

Gaskins, J., Pvt Co. I – W Chancellorsville 5/3/63; NLR.

Gaskins, James, Pvt Co. K 10/21/62 – D (pneumonia) Rich Hos 12/7/62; Bur Hollywood Cem, Rich.

Gaskins, John W., Pvt Co. I 8/22/62 – Appt 5th Sgt 1/1/63; C Sailor's Creek 4/6/65; R Pt. Lookout, Md. 6/28/65; widow filed for CSP Berrien Cty, Ga. 1920.

Gaskins, Jordan, Pvt Co. I 5/2/62 – D Sav Hos 7/5/62.

Gaskins, Joseph L., Pvt Co. I 5/2/62 – Roll for 2/28/65 shows AWOL since 2/25/65; pension record says he received a 30-day Frl from Rich 2/10/65.

Gaskins, Lemuel Elam, Pvt Co. I 3/4/62 - W/C Fox's Gap 9/14/62; E 10/2/62; Rich Hos 10/15/62; DW Rich Hos 10/26/62; Bur Hollywood Cem, Rich.

Gaskins, Richard, Pvt Co. I 3/4/62 – NLR.

Gaskins, William Henry, Pvt Co. I 3/4/62 – NLR.

Gaston, D.M., Pvt Co. G – W (abdomen)/C 9/64; U.S. Field Hos, Winchester, Va. 9/19/64; D Winchester Hos 11/17/64.

Gay, Hiram, Pvt Co. H 3/4/62 – Appt 3rd Sgt 11/1/62; 2nd Sgt 1/63; Elected 2nd Lt 4/27/63; AWOL near Bristol, Tn. 2/3/64; tendered Res 2/11/64; Elected Cpt Colquitt Cty, Ga. militia 3/5/64; dropped from 50th Ga. rolls 4/26/64; W near Atlanta 7/22/64; DW 11/22/64; widow filed for CSP Colquitt Cty 1891.

Gay, Matthew, Pvt Co. H 3/4/62 – W Fox's Gap 9/14/62; Appt 1st Sgt; W (shell fragment, head & gunshot, 1 arm) Wilderness 5/6/64; Macon, Ga. Hos 12/22/64; roll for 2/65, shows "absent sick- wounded"; P Thomasville, Ga. 5/25/65; filed for CSP Worth Cty, Ga. 1889.

Giddens, Jimpsey B., Pvt Co. I 8/22/62 – Detailed as shoemaker Columbus, Ga. 11/17/62- 4/65; filed for CSP Berrien Cty, Ga. 1905.

Giddens, John M., Pvt Co. B 5/7/62 – Sav Hos 6/62; Convalescent Camp Whitesville, Ga. 7/17/62; roll for 12/64 shows "absent sent to hospital in Nov 1862. Not heard from since. Supposed to be dead"; NLR.

Giddens, Patrick F., Pvt Co. B 3/4/62 – Roll for 2/63 shows present; NLR.

Giddens (Giddings), Virgil A., Pvt Co. K 5/6/62 – W Gettysburg 7/2/63; W Cold Harbor 6/1/64; K Cedar Creek 10/19/64.

Gigmillit, G.W., Cpl Co. G – Only CSR entry shows P Thomasville, Ga. 5/16/65; NLR.

Giles, David A., Pvt. Co. H 3/4/62– W (1 hand) Fox's Gap 9/14/62; Winchester, Va. Hos same day; Disc (disability) 4/20/63; enlisted in Co. C, 11th Cav Ga. State Guards 8/63; filed for CSP Thomas Cty, Ga. 1907.

Gill, J.D., Pvt Co. F 11/28/64 – Des 2/26/65; took oath of allegiance to U.S. Govt. and furnished trans to Cairo, Ill.

Gill, Thomas, Pvt Co. E 3/4/62 – Detailed as wagoner 7/25/62; C Fox's Gap 9/14/62; U.S. Hos Frederick, Md. 9/19/62; E 10/2/62; Rich Hos 10/6/62; W Chancellorsville 5/3/63; W Ft. Sanders 11/29/63; W (1 hand - amputated) Wilderness 5/6/64; DW (erysipelas) Petersburg Hos 7/5/64.

Gill, William John, Pvt Co. C 3/4/62 – C Sailor's Creek 4/6/65; R Pt. Lookout, Md. 6/27/65; filed for CSP Ware Cty, Ga. 1910.

Glover, Elisha M., Pvt Co. F 3/4/62 - W Gettysburg (slight) 7/2/63; C Cedar Creek 10/19/64; R 1865.

Glover, J. Milton, Pvt Co. F 3/4/62 – W (arm – slight) Funkstown 7/10/63; K Cold Harbor 6/2/64.

Godwin, Jacob, Pvt Co. A 3/4/62 – Only CSR entry; NLR.

Godwin, John, Pvt Co. A 3/4/62 – Only CSR entry; NLR.

Goethee, George, Pvt Co. B 3/4/62 – On sick leave 5/4/62; NLR.

Goldberg, Louis, Pvt Co. E 3/4/62 – Disc, upon furnishing Henry McPherson as substitute 5/15/62.

Gooding, William H., Pvt Co. A 3/4/62 - W Fox's Gap 9/14/62; roll for 2/65 shows absent sick (chronic diarrhea); filed for CSP Emanuel Cty, Ga. 1915; pension record says he was sent to Sav Hos 10/64, and C at Sav 12/64; R Port Royal, Va. after 4/65.

Goodwin, Lemuel P., Cpl Co. I 3/4/62 – Appt 1st Sgt 9/62; reduced to Pvt 1/1/63; Elected 2nd Lt 4/27/63; W Gettysburg 7/2/63; Appt 1st Lt 2/64; roll for 2/65 shows "absent with leave. Genl Lee as of 2/18/65"; P Albany, Ga. 5/17/65; filed for CSP Berrien Cty, Ga. 1900; pension record says he was in Macon, Ga. on the way back to command at the close of the war.

Grantham, Elijah T., Pvt Co. F 3/4/62 - Appt 2nd Cpl 1862; K Fox's Gap 9/14/62.

Grantham, Jackson, Pvt Co. C 8/28/62 – Des 11/28/62; W Chancellorsville 5/3/63; C

Gettysburg 7/2/63; P Pt. Lookout, Md. 2/18/65; E Camp Lee, Va. 2/21/65: filed for CSP of war.

Graves, James P., Adj 3/23/63 – Served as Adj, 51ˢᵗ Ga. 7/12/62; Trn to 50ᵗʰ Ga. 3/63; Res 9/17/63.

Gray, Berry, Pvt Co. I 3/4/62 – C near Knoxville, Tn. 12/3/63; D Rock Island, Ill. 4/20/65; Bur Rock Island.

Greaves, Thomas, Pvt Co. I 5/2/62 – D (pneumonia) Rich Hos 12/31/62; Bur Oakwood Cem, Rich.

Green, Early O., Pvt Co. H 3/4/62 – D (measles) Macon, Ga. Hos 4/29/62; widow filed for CSP Colquitt Cty, Ga. 1891.

Green, Jack (John), Pvt Co. H 3/4/62 – D "in service" (date Unk).

Griffin, Enoch, Pvt Co. G 3/4/62 – Original muster roll shows "Volunteered and stayed at home"; roll for 12/62 shows Disc and turned over to the Sav Guards 7/6/62, by court of inquiry; Trn to Co. A, 18ᵗʰ Bn Ga. Inf 7/5/62; C Sailor's Creek 4/6/65; R 1865.

Griffin, John Jackson, Pvt Co. I 8/22/62 – W (l knee – gunshot)/C Gettysburg 7/2/63; U.S. Hos Gettysburg (leg amputated above knee) 7/5/63; Baltimore, Md. Hos 11/3/63; E City Point, Va. 11/12/63; P Thomasville, Ga. 5/23/65; filed for CSP Berrien Cty, Ga. 1879.

Griffin, Sion Dixon, Pvt Co. I 4/5/62 – C Sailor's Creek 4/6/65; R Pt. Lookout, Md.6/28/65.

Griffis, B., Pvt Co. G – P Thomasville, Ga. 5/23/65.

Griffis, Charles, Pvt Co. G 5/6/62 – D Sav Hos 6/10/62.

Griffis, Eli, Pvt Co. G 3/4/62 – D Sav Hos 5/31/62; Bur Laurel Grove Cem, Sav.

Griffis, Samuel, Pvt Co. B 3/4/62 – Trn to Co. G; W (r hand – 2 fingers amputated) Berryville, Va. 9/3/64; Charlottesville, Va. Hos 9/22/64; roll for 2/65 shows AWOL since 10/10/64; P Thomasville, Ga. 5/23/65; filed for CSP Clinch Cty, Ga. 1889; pension record says he was with his command at surrender.

Griffis, William, Pvt Co. G 5/15/62 – Disc 6/10/62; enlisted as Pvt in Co. I, 4ᵗʰ Regt Ga. Cav 1/2/63; C in Fl. 4/64; R Ft. Delaware, Del. 6/16/65.

Griner, Charles J., Pvt Co. I 3/4/62 – Disc (disability) 6/3/62.

Griner, Daniel J. Pvt Co. I 3/4/62 – D near Fredericksburg 11/21/62.

Griner, John Martin, Pvt Co. I 5/20/62 – W Chancellorsville 5/3/63; Frl Rich Hos home 8/14/64; roll for 2/65 shows AWOL since 9/10/64; filed for CSP Irwin Cty, Ga. 1929; pension record says he was home on sick Frl at close of war.

Griner, Martin J., Pvt Co. I 3/4/62 – Roll for 2/65 shows AWOL since 2/27/65; filed for CSP Berrien Cty, Ga. 1913; pension record says he contracted jaundice while on way home with Frl and sent to Albany, Ga. Hos, unable to return.

Griner, Thomas J., Pvt Co. I 3/4/62 – Disc (disability-heart) 6/13/62; widow filed for CSP Berrien Cty, Ga. 1920; application disapproved because soldier served for less than six months.

Griner, William W., Pvt Co. I 3/4/62 – Appt drummer 10/64; C Sailor's Creek 4/6/65; R Pt. Lookout, Md. 6/28/65; widow filed for CSP Berrien Cty, Ga. 1915.

Groover, James Abner, 4ᵗʰ Cpl Co. K 3/4/62 – C Sailor's Creek 4/6/65; R Pt. Lookout, Md. 6/4/65; widow filed for CSP Thomas Cty, Ga. 1920.

Gully, James N., Pvt Co. K 12/15/63 – Roll for 2/65 shows AWOL since 3/28/64; NLR.

Gunn, Donald, Pvt Co. F 3/4/62 – D (typhoid pneumonia) Scottsville, Va. 1/15/63.

Guthery, William James, Pvt Co. G 3/4/62 – K Fox's Gap 9/14/62.

Guy, Banner, 5ᵗʰ Sgt Co. A 3/4/62 – Appt Orderly Sgt 12/31/62; W Chancellorsville 5/3/63; Appt Jr. 2ⁿᵈ Lt; K Ft. Sanders 11/29/63.

Guyton, Moses J. (I), Pvt Co. H 3/4/62 – K Ft. Sanders 11/29/63.

ROSTER H

Hainson, James M. Pvt Co. F 3/4/62 – NLR.

Hall, Fleming J., Pvt Co. G 3/4/62 – W (1 hip-minie ball) Berryville, Va. 9/3/64; C Harrisonburg, Va. 9/25/64; U.S. Hos Winchester, Va. 10/6/64; E Pt. Lookout, Md. 10/29/64; S Tallahassee, Fl. 5/10/65; P Thomasville, Ga. 5/24/65; widow filed for CSP Suwannee Cty Fl. 1909; pension record says he was home at close of war.

Hall, Henry Harrison, Pvt Co. D 3/4/62 – W Chancellorsville 5/3/63; C Sailor's Creek 4/6/65; R Pt. Lookout, Md. 6/28/65; widow filed for CSP Lowndes Cty, Ga. 1910.

Hall, Littleton, Pvt Co. D 3/4/62 – K Chancellorsville 5/3/63.

Hall, Lyman, Pvt Co. K 3/4/62 –Roll for 2/65 shows present; widow filed for CSP Madison Cty, Fl. 1909; Brooks Cty, Ga. 1926; pension record says he S Appomattox C.H. 4/9/65, but not on the list of parolees with the 50th Ga. Regt.

Hall, William, Pvt Co. H 3/4/62 – Detailed as nurse Whitesville, Ga. Hos 6/21/62; K Cedar Creek 10/19/64.

Hales, John J., Pvt Co. E 3/4/62 – Disc (disability-hernia) Charlottesville, Va. Hos 2/19/63.

Halvey, Moses, Pvt Co. G – C Gettysburg 7/2/63; U.S. Hos Ft. McHenry, Md. 7/6/63; "returned to post" 8/11/63; NLR.

Hancock, General Harrison, Pvt Co. H 3/4/62 – K Fox's Gap 9/14/62.

Hancock, Hardin, Pvt Co. H 3/4/62 – Dropped out on march 9/14/62 near South Mtn; C 9/62; P Sharpsburg, Md. 9/21/62; roll for 2/65 shows AWOL since 12/62; P Albany, Ga. 5/19/65; filed for CSP Colquitt Cty, Ga. 1905; pension record says he received Frl home from Staunton, Va. Hos 11/62, and remained home sick for rest of war.

Hancock, Henry W., 4th Cpl Co. H 3/4/62 – Appt 2nd Cpl 1/63; W Gettysburg 7/2/63; Appt 3rd Sgt 1863 or 1864; roll for 2/65 shows "absent, extra duty. Detached as Enrolling Officer of Colquitt County, GA"; P Albany, Ga. 5/20/65.

Hancock, James M., Pvt Co. F – W Cold Harbor 6/1/64; NLR.

Hancock, Jeremiah T., 3rd Cpl Co. H 3/4/62 – K Fox's Gap 9/14/62; widow filed for CSP Colquitt Cty, Ga. 1910.

Hancock, John, Pvt Co. H 3/4/62 – Roll for 2/65 shows absent sick since 9/6/64; S Appomattox C.H. 4/9/65; filed for CSP Putnam Cty, Fl. 1907.

Hancock, Joseph M. (N), Pvt Co. K 3/4/62 – Detailed as nurse Macon, Ga. Hos 4/13/62; W (r cheek – cut off tip of tongue) Cold Harbor 6/1/64; retired from service 3/24/65; P Thomasville, Ga. 5/19/65.

Hancock, M. Watts, Pvt Co. H 3/4/62 – D Sav Hos 7/14/62.

Hardee, J.T., Pvt Co. D 3/4/62 – D Winchester, Va. 10/11/62; Bur Stonewall (Mount Hebron) Cem, Winchester, marker #138.

Hardee, Jesse A., Pvt Co. D 3/4/62 – C Fox's Gap 9/14/62; E Aikens Landing, Va. 11/10/62; W 1864; roll for 8/31/64 shows absent on W Frl; C Sailor's Creek 4/6/65; R Pt. Lookout, Md. 6/28/65; filed for CSP Lowndes Cty, Ga. 1913.

Harden, John, Pvt Co. E – M Fox's Gap 9/14/62; NLR.

Harden, Lewis, Pvt Co. E 3/4/62 – Roll for 2/63 shows "absent without leave in Thomas County, Ga."; NLR.

Harding, D., Pvt Co. K – C Fox's Gap 9/14/62; E Aikens Landing, Va. 11/10/62; NLR.

Hardwick, James A., Pvt Co. H 5/13/62 – Roll for 2/65 shows AWOL since 1/23/65; P Thomasville, Ga. 5/24/65.

Hardy, Bythel, Pvt Co. E 3/4/62 – K Fox's Gap 9/14/62.

Hargraves, Christopher C., Pvt Co. C 3/4/62 – W Fox's Gap 9/14/62; C Williamsport,

Md.9/15/62; E Aikens Landing, Va. 10/19/62; roll for 2/65 shows AWOL since 10/2/64; NLR.

Hargraves, (Hargroves) James R., Pvt Co. G 3/4/62 – W Fox's Gap 9/14/62; Frl home 10/11/62; W Cold Harbor 6/1/64; roll for 2/65 shows AWOL; NLR.

Harnage, George A., Pvt Co. G 5/1/62 – Roll for 2/65 shows AWOL since 3/21/64; P Thomasville, Ga. 5/19/65; widow filed for CSP Cook Cty, Ga. 1923; pension record says he was sick in Hos at close of war.

Harnage, Jacob B., Pvt Co. G 5/1/62 – W (1 leg - amputated below knee) Cold Harbor 6/1/64; roll for 2/65 shows AWOL since 10/10/64; filed for CSP Clinch Cty, Ga. 1880; widow filed for CSP Bradford Cty, Fl. 1899.

Harnage, Jeremiah C., Pvt Co. G 4/27/62 – Des and joined Cpt Bryan's Co. in Fl. 10/21/62; D (pneumonia) Rich Hos 6/15/63; Bur Oakwood Cem, Rich; widow filed for CSP Clinch Cty, Ga. 1910.

Harper, B., Pvt Co. B – Detailed as nurse to accompany wounded William B. Dunlap home after Dunlap's Disc from Rich Hos 12/17/62; NLR.

Harper, Joseph W.S., Pvt Co. F 3/4/62 – C Cold Harbor 6/1/64; E Elmira, N.Y. 3/14/65; P Tallahassee, Fl 5/18/65; widow filed for CSP Suwannee Cty, Fl. 1897; pension record says he S at Appomattox C.H. 4/9/65; not on list of parolees with 50th Ga. Regt.

Harper, Light R., Pvt Co. C 8/29/62 – D (measles) Rich Hos 11/23/62; Bur Oakwood Cem, Rich.

Harper, Moses, Pvt Co. C 8/28/62 – Des 11/23/62; D Rich Hos 2/20/63; Bur Oakwood Cem, Rich.

Harrell, Benjamin D., Co. K 5/13/62 - W (shell frag) Sharpsburg 9/17/62; Winchester, Va. Hos 9/30/62; detailed in Ordnance Dept., Macon, Ga. Arsenal 64/65; P Thomasville, Ga. 5/24/65; filed for CSP Suwannee Cty, Fl. 1903; pension record says he was home on Frl at close of war.

Harrell, Joseph, Pvt Co. F 3/4/62 – Roll for 10/31/64 shows absent W; roll for 2/65 shows AWOL since 1/24/65; NLR.

Harrell, Josiah, Pvt Co. F 3/4/62 – W Summit Point, Va. 8/21/64 [now W.Va.]; Hos 8/64; P Bainbridge, Ga. 5/20/65; widow filed for CSP Decatur Cty, Ga. 1907; pension record says he was sent to Hos at Quincy, Fl., due to disability, and remained there until close of the war.

Harrell, Lewis, Pvt Co. I 3/4/62 – Left sick near Leesburg, Va. 9/3/62; D 9/15/62.

Harrell, Moses, Pvt Co. K 5/11/62 – CSR entry for 5/62 shows enlisted at Ft. Brown 5/11/62; NLR.

Harrell, Newton J., Pvt Co. F 3/4/62 – Entry for 5/62 shows D 5/1/62.

Harrell, Samuel J., Pvt Co. K 5/13/62 – W (collar bone) Cedar Creek 10/19/64; roll for 2/65 shows absent sick; P Thomasville, Ga. 5/19/65; widow filed for CSP Brooks Cty, Ga. 1911; pension record says he was home on W Frl at close of war.

Harrell, William, Pvt Co. C 3/4/62 – D Sav 5/2/62; Bur Lot 861, Laurel Grove Cem, Sav.

Harrell, William H. Pvt Co. K 3/7/62 – Detailed to help build Hos Whitesville, Ga. 5/13/62; C Rich Hos 4/3/65; P Tallahassee, Fl 5/15/65; widow filed for CSP Madison Cty, Fl. 1897.

Harrell, William W., Pvt Co. F 3/4/62 – Enlisted as Pvt in Co. G, 1st Regt Ga. Inf 3/18/61; Disc (disability) 11/12/61; enlisted in Co. F, 50th Ga.; D 5/2/62.

Harrington, J.C., Pvt Co. I 11/64 – P 1865.

Harris, Dred, Pvt Co. H 3/4/62 – NLR.

Harris, Ebenezer, Pvt Co. A 3/4/62 – Left at Sav Hos 7/19/62; D Sav Hos 12/3/62.

Harris, John, Pvt Co. A 3/10/62 – Widow filed for CSP Pierce Cty, Ga. 1910; pension record says he was taken sick and D (Pneumonia) in Va. 7/63.

Harris, Lazarus J. S., Pvt Co. A 3/4/62 – D 9/4/62.

Harris, Robertson, Pvt Co. A 3/4/62 – D 12/2/62.

Harris, William J., 3rd Cpl Co. A 3/4/62 – D in camp 2/5/65.

Harrison, Joseph M., Pvt Co. F 3/4/62 - W/C Fox's Gap 9/14/62; Wash D.C. Hos 9/21/62; E 11/10/62; D Hanover Junction, Va. 9/10/63.

Hart, Allen T., Pvt Co. H 5/13/62 – W (hand - finger amputated) Chancellorsville 5/3/63; Rich Hos 5/9/63; Trn from Rich Hos to Huguenot Springs, Va. Hos 6/14/63; DW 1863.

Hart, Berrien, Pvt Co. G 3/4/62 – Left sick Rapidan Station, Va. 8/13/62; C Cedar Creek 10/19/64; R 1865.

Hart, Simon, Pvt Co. H 3/4/62 – D (measles) Winchester, Va. Hos 10/23/62; Bur Stonewall (Mount Hebron) Cem, Winchester, marker #159; widow filed for CSP Mitchell Cty, Ga. 1891.

Hartley, William H., Pvt Co. I 3/4/62 – K Fox's Gap 9/14/62.

Hatton, John, Pvt Co. A 3/4/62 – C Hagerstown 7/12/63; R Pt. Lookout, Md. upon taking oath of allegiance and joining U.S. Army 2/1/64.

Hays (Hayes), Benjamin F., Pvt Co. C 3/4/62 – W Chancellorsville 5/3/63; C near Knoxville 12/7/63; R Rock Island, Ill. 5/18/65; filed for CSP Coffee Cty, Ga. 1906.

Hayes, (Hays) Bryant, Pvt Co. C 8/29/62 – W Chancellorsville 5/3/63; C Sailor's Creek 4/6/65; R Pt. Lookout, Md. 6/28/65.

Hayes, (Hays) Peter, Pvt Co. C 8/29/62 – CSR shows C near Knoxville 12/20/63; D (pneumonia) Camp Chase, Oh. 1864; widow filed for CSP Pierce Cty, Ga. 1891; pension record says he D (pneumonia) near Fredericksburg, Va. about 2/13/63; inconsistency between CSR and CSP.

Hecks, James, Pvt Co. E – M Fox's Gap 9/14/62; NLR.

Henderson, Mark F., Pvt Co. G 5/1/62 - C Williamsport, Md. 9/15/62; E Aikens Landing, Va. 10/2/62; Appt 5th Sgt; 1/1/63; W (abdomen/thigh) Chancellorsville 5/3/63; Rich Hos 5/12/63; DW Rich Hos 5/22/63; Bur Hollywood Cem, Rich.

Henderson, William LaFayette, Pvt Co. B 3/4/62 – Appt 4th Sgt 8/15/62; Elected 2nd Lt 1/63; Res as 2nd Lt 3/4/63; W (l shoulder & r wrist) Gettysburg 7/2/63; W Ft. Sanders 11/29; C near Knoxville 12/3/63; R Camp Chase, Oh. 6/13/65; filed for CSP Ware Cty, Ga. 1889; pension record says W Gettysburg.

Hendley, Irvin, Pvt Co. I 3/4/62 – W Petersburg 6/18/64; DW Petersburg 6/20/64.

Hendley, James, Pvt Co. I 8/22/62 – D near Fredericksburg 1/15/63.

Hendley, John Daniel, Pvt Co. H 6/10/62 – Substitute for H.V. Folsom; roll for 2/65 shows AWOL since 3/4/64; NLR.

Hendley, Matthew, Pvt Co. I 3/4/62 – K Fox's Gap 9/14/62; widow filed for CSP Berrien Cty, Ga. 1891.

Hendricks, G.W., Pvt Co. I 4/63 – NLR.

Hennessy, Michael, Pvt Co. A 3/4/62 – Left on march from Centreville, Va. to Frederick Md. 9/2/62; NLR.

Herndon, Daniel, Pvt Co. A 3/4/62 – NLR.

Herndon, George W., Pvt Co. D 3/4/62 – W Fox's Gap 9/14/62; W Gettysburg (breast – slight) 7/2/63; Appt 3rd Cpl 10/63; D Gordonsville, Va. 11/18/64.

Herndon, John, Pvt Co. D 3/4/62 – K Chancellorsville 5/3/63.

Herren, John, Co. A 3/4/62 – Not in CSR; widow filed for CSP Marion Cty, Fl. 1903; pension record says he was taken sick 7/64 and sent to Hos; received sick Frl home 9/64, and was home sick at close of war.

Herring, Edward, Pvt Co. F – CSR entry for 7/62 shows in Raleigh, N.C. Hos 7/62; NLR.

Herring, Elisha D. (B.) Pvt Co. I 3/4/62 – K Fox's Gap 9/14/62; widow filed for CSP Dooley Cty, Ga. 1891.

Herring, John W., Pvt Co. A 3/4/62 – W Chancellorsville 5/3/63; roll for 2/65 shows AWOL since 10/11/64; NLR.

Herring, Levi, Pvt Co. I 2/4/63 – Substitute for Elijah Vickers; W Chancellorsville 5/3/63; roll for 2/65 shows AWOL since 1/1/65; NLR.

Hersey (Hursey), John Thomas, Pvt Co. C 3/13/62 – D (measles) near Rappahannock River, Va. 9/15/62; widow filed for CSP Coffee Cty, Ga. 1891.

Hersey (Hursey), William R., Sgt Co B 4/62 – K Gettysburg 7/2/63; widow filed for CSP Bradford Cty, Fl. 1901.

Hicks, James W., Pvt Co. K 5/11/62 – Detailed as wagoner 6/62; D 1/10/63.

Hicks, Moses, Pvt Co. E 3/4/62 – K Fox's Gap 9/14/62.

Hicks, Newton, Pvt Co. F 3/4/62 – W (arm) Fox's Gap 9/14/62; Rich Hos 10/23/62; W Gettysburg (severe) 7/2/63; S Appomattox CH 4/9/65; filed for CSP Echols Cty, Ga. 1901.

Hiers, David Daniel, Pvt Co. K 3/4/62 – D Rich Hos (chronic diarrhea) 1/16/63; Bur Oakwood Cem, Rich.

Hiers, W.M., Pvt Co. E "Spring" 1864 – Filed for CSP Colquitt Cty, Ga. 1919; pension record says he was C Ft. McAlister 12/13/64; R Pt. Lookout, Md. 7/2/65.

Higdon, J.P.Y., Pvt Co. A 3/4/62 – NLR.

Higgs, James J.A., Pvt Co. A 3/4/62 – C Ft. Sanders 11/29/63; P Knoxville upon taking oath of allegiance to U.S. Govt. 1/25/64.

Highsmith, John M., Pvt Co. A 3/4/62 – D (typhoid pneumonia) Rich Hos 1/29/63; Bur Oakwood Cem, Rich.

Hightower, Jesse Byrd, Sr., Pvt Co. D 3/4/62 – Disc upon furnishing John W. Collins as substitute 5/10/62.

Hill, Green T, Pvt Co. K 3/4/62 – Macon, Ga. Hos 4/15/63; D Macon Hos 1863.

Hill, Henry B., Pvt Co. G 3/4/62 – On original Muster Roll as "refuses to come"; NLR.

Hill, J.G., Pvt – D Sav Hos 5/3/63; Bur Lot 853, Laurel Grove Cem, Sav; marker reads "JG Hill, 50 GA REGT CSA MAY 3, 1863."

Hill, Joseph L., 2nd Cpl Co. K 3/4/62 – Appt 3rd Sgt 8/62; W (l groin & shoulder) Fox's Gap 9/14/62; C Sharpsburg 9/62; E 11/10/62 Aikens Landing, Va.; Frl from Rich Hos 10/25/62; roll for 12/31/62 shows absent Frl from Hos to Brooks Cty, Ga."; filed for CSP Bradford Cty, Fl. 1905; pension record says he was retired from service due to wounds suffered at Fox's Gap.

Hilliard, James Kinchen, 2nd Lt Co. C 3/21/62 – W Gettysburg 7/2/63; DW Winchester, Va. Hos 7/17/63; Bur Stonewall Cem Winchester, marker #241; Cem register incorrectly reads "Lt. J.R. Hillerd, 58th Ga."

Hines, Daniel, Co. H 9/26/62 – Disc (disability-hernia) 4/27/63; filed for CSP Hillsborough Cty, Fl. 1909; pension record says he was at Albany, Ga. at close of war.

Hines, James G., Pvt Co. F 3/4/62 – Trn to Co. C 51st Ga. Inf Regt 7/63; filed for CSP Decatur Cty, Ga. 1903; pension record says C near Frazier's Farm 4/6/65; R Pt. Lookout, Md. 7/2/65.

Hitchcock, F.T., Pvt Co. A – Not in CSR; Bur Stonewall Cem, Winchester, Va., marker #170; Cem register reads " F.T. Hitchcock, Co. A, 50th Ga. Died Oct. 24, 1862"; marker inscribed "F.F. Hichcock."

Hobbs, Gilbert, Pvt Co. E 3/5/62 – Roll for 8/62 shows "Dropped out sick on march near Gordonsville, Va."; Disc (disability) 10/24/62.

Hobbs, Stephen G., Pvt Co. E 3/4/62 – W Ft. Sanders 11/29/63; C near Knoxville 1/5/64; Rock Island, Ill. Prison; E James River, Va. 3/27/65; P Thomasville, Ga. 5/10/65;

widow filed for CSP Thomas Cty, Ga. 1901.

Holland, Redding, Pvt Co. G 5/5/62– Returned to duty from Danville, Va. Hos 1/30/63; W Chancellorsville 5/3/63; NLR.

Hollingsworth, George Washington, Pvt Co. H 5/13/62 – W Gettysburg (face, severe) 7/2/63; C 7/5/63; Frederick, Md. Hos 7/21/63; E David's Island, N.Y. 1863; Petersburg Hos 9/18/63; C Sailor's Creek 4/6/65; R 6/27/65 Pt. Lookout, Md.

Hollingsworth, I., Pvt Co. H 5/13/62 – D Lynchburg, Va. Hos 9/4/62; Bur Lot 178, Confederate Cem, Lynchburg.

Hollingsworth, Jesse, Pvt Co. H 5/13/62 – W Chancellorsville 5/3/63; Frl from Rich Hos for 30 days 6/23/63; NLR.

Hollingsworth, John H., Pvt Co. H 5/13/62 – W (face - teeth, jaw, part of tongue and nose shot off) Chancellorsville 5/3/63; roll for 2/65 shows AWOL since 8/20/63; filed for CSP Lowndes Cty, Ga. 1898; pension record says he was Disc (disability).

Honeywell, William C., Pvt Co. K 5/13/62– D Rich Hos (pneumonia) 2/15/63; Bur Oakwood Cem, Rich.

Hood, J.B. Pvt Co. H 3/4/62 – K Gettysburg 7/2/63.

Hood, James A., Pvt Co. H 3/4/62 – Appt 3rd Cpl 1862; K Fox's Gap 9/14/62; widow filed for CSP Colquitt Cty, Ga. 1891; pension record says K Sharpsburg 9/17/62.

Horn, John (James) M., Pvt Co. F 3/4/62 – K Fox's Gap 9/14/62.

Horne, James J., Pvt Co. H 5/62 – Enlisted as Pvt in Co. E, 17th Ga. Inf Regt 8/12/61; Trn to Co. H, 50th Ga.; S Appomattox CH 4/9/65; filed for CSP Mitchell Cty, Ga. 1901.

Howard, Moses W., Pvt Co. A 3/4/62 – Disc (disease) 1863; D 3/9/64; widow filed for CSP Charlton Cty Ga. 1891.

Howell, George W., Pvt Co. D 3/4/62 – Detached as blacksmith in Rich 7/63; rejoined Co 7/13/64; appt Sgt; W (gunshot, l leg)/C Sailor's Creek 4/6/65; R Wash, D.C. 7/18/65; widow filed for CSP Hillsborough Cty, Fl. 1898.

Howell, Elijah, Pvt Co. B 3/4/62 – Left sick on the march 7/63; C Manassas Gap 7/23/63; sent to Union Hos 10/63; D (chronic diarrhea) Pt. Lookout, Md. Hos 10/16/63; believed Bur Confederate Cem, Pt. Lookout; widow filed for CSP Pierce Cty, Ga. 1891.

Howell, J., Pvt Co. B 3/4/62 – Roll for 3/4/62 shows absent; NLR.

Howell, James O.A., Pvt Co. D 3/4/62 – Disc, upon furnishing John W. Taylor as substitute 5/9/62.

Howell, Lewis, Pvt Co. H – C/P Leesburg, Va. 10/2/62; NLR.

Howell, William D., 1st Lt Co. D 3/4/62 – Res 4/2/63, upon election to Ga. State Assembly; elected Cpt 6/9/63; NLR.

Howreek, W.H., Cpl Co. H – W Chancellorsville 5/3/63.

Hudson, Calvin H., Pvt Co. E 8/13/62 – D (consumption) Rich Hos 12/12/62.

Hudson, Charles Franklin, Pvt Co. E 6/1/62 – Substitute for James A. McClendon; Appt 1st Sgt 2/64; roll for 2/65 shows AWOL; P Tallahassee, Fl. 5/19/65.

Hudson (Hutson), William, Pvt Co. C 3/4/62 – Appt 5th Sgt 1/1/63; 1st Sgt 2/64; roll for 2/28/65 shows AWOL since 2/24/65; NLR.

Hughes, Elbert, Pvt Co. D 4/2/62 – W Fox's Gap 9/14/62; D Rich Hos (typhoid fever) 1/19/63; Bur Oakwood Cem, Rich.

Hughes, Isaac, Pvt Co. G 4/27/62 –D Rich Hos (chronic diarrhea) 11/25/62; Bur Oakwood Cem, Rich.

Hughes, James Thomas, Pvt Co. D 3/4/62 – W Sharpsburg 9/17/62; W (gunshot, r arm – amputated at shoulder) Chancellorsville 5/3/63; roll for 2/65 shows "absent disabled"; P Tallahassee, Fl. 5/15/65; filed for CSP Echols Cty, Ga. 1880.

Hughes, R. Perry, Pvt Co. D 4/2/62 – Appt Cpl 1862; W (compound fracture) Fox's Gap 9/14/62; C Sharpsburg 9/17/62; DW Frederick, Md. Hos 11/25/62; Bur Mt. Olivet Cem, Frederick.

Humphreys, Clement T., Pvt Co. K 3/4/62 – Detailed as nurse in Macon, Ga. Hos 4/13/62; detailed as ambulance driver 63-65; P Thomasville, Ga. 5/19/65; widow filed for CSP Thomas Cty, Ga. 1911; pension record says he was detailed as an ambulance driver because of a bad foot and was with that detachment at the surrender.

Humphries (Humphreys), Lewis W., Pvt Co. H 3/4/62 – W (contusion, ankle & thigh) Gettysburg 7/2/63; C 7/5/63; P Pt. Lookout, Md. 2/18/65; P Thomasville, Ga. 5/10/65.

Hunter, James Madison, Pvt Co. G 3/4/62 – D in camp near Rich 7/28/62.

Hurst, William E., Pvt Co. E 3/4/62 – C Frederick, Md. 9/12/62; E City Point, Va. 11/10/62; D (pneumonia) Lynchburg, Va. Hos 12/30/62; Bur Lot 101, Confederate Cem, Lynchburg.

Hutchinson, Thomas A., Pvt Co. E 5/15/62 – W Cedar Creek 10/19/64; DW Lynchburg, Va. Hos 11/11/64; Bur Lot 198, Confederate Cem Lynchburg.

ROSTER I

Ingram, John, Pvt Co. K 3/4/62 – Roll for 2/65 shows "sick in Brooks County, Ga."; P Thomasville, Ga. 5/26/65.

Ingram, John L., Pvt Co. K 3/4/62 – W Sharpsburg 9/17/62; roll for 1/2/65 shows sick in Sav Hos since 8/31/64 (chronic rheumatism); filed for CSP Berrien Cty, Ga. 1910; pension record says he was on 30 days sick Frl from 3/15/65 at close of war.

Ingram, Sherod (Sherrard) J., Pvt Co. K 3/4/62 – C Sharpsburg 9/17/62; E 10/17/62; K Ft. Sanders 11/29/63.

ROSTER J

Jackson, James W., Pvt Co. D 3/4/62 – Disc (disability-asthma) 6/1/62.

Jeffords, Alexander G., 4th Sgt Co. B 3/4/62 – Appt 3rd Sgt 3/22/62; D near Ft. Brown, Ga. 7/4/62.

Jeffords, Daniel J., Jr. 2nd Lt Co. B 3/4/62 – Elected 2nd Lt 3/22/62; Res after suspended by Board of Examiners 3/4/63; D Rich Hos 4/21/63; Bur Hollywood Cem, Rich; widow filed for CSP Coffee Cty, Ga. 1891.

Jeffords, Jeremiah M., Pvt Co. B 3/4/62 – W Chancellorsville 5/3/63; Des 3/2/65; took oath of allegiance to U.S. Govt. and furnished trans to Pa.

Jenkins, William W., Pvt Co. A 3/4/62 – D in camp near Fredericksburg 2/24/63.

Jerger, Adolph, Pvt Co. E 5/16/62 – Enlisted as Pvt in Co. D, 2nd Regt, 1st Bde, Ga. State Troops 11/4/61; mustered out 4/62; enlisted in Co. E, 50th Ga.; C Gettysburg 7/2/63; R Ft. Delaware 5/10/65.

Jerger, Louis, Pvt Co. E 1862 – Entry for 6/62 shows sent to Macon, Ga. Hos 4/15/62; NLR.

Jewel, Reuben, Pvt Co. G 5/6/62 – Sick furlough 8/10/62; roll for 2/65 shows AWOL since 12/23/63; NLR.

Johns, Jeremiah E., 2nd Cpl Co. A 3/4/62 – Appt 2nd Sgt 3/23/64; C 12/24/64; D (chronic diarrhea) Fed Hos, Sav 1/28/65.

Johnson, John, Pvt Co. G 3/4/62 – Des and joined Co. D, 9th Fl. Regt 10/10/62; D Atlanta, Ga. Hos 10/6/63.

Johnson, Jonathan J., 1ˢᵗ Lt Co. H 3/4/62 – Roll for 7/62 shows "present near Chafin Farm, Va."; requisitioned shoes and a pick ax at Winchester 10/4/62; roll for 2/63 shows "not stated" for whether present or absent; NLR.

Johnson, Lott W., 5th Sgt Co. E 3/4/62 – Prom 3ʳᵈ Sgt 10/20/62; C Ft. Sanders 11/29/63; took oath of allegiance to U.S. Govt. at Rock Island, Ill. 5/64; Trn to U.S. Navy 5/23/64.

Johnson, Riley, Pvt Co. G 4/27/62 – Disc, under age (17) 10/30/62; enlisted as Pvt in Co. I, 4ᵗʰ Ga. Inf Regt 1/2/63.

Johnson, Thomas, Pvt Co. G 4/27/62 – C/P Winchester, Va. 12/2/62; C Winchester 12/22/62; P Ft. Monroe, Va. early 1863; W (left shoulder) Chancellorsville 5/3/63; C Gettysburg 7/4/63; P City Point, Va. 8/22/63; roll for 2/65 shows absent sick since 10/19/64; P Thomasville, Ga. 5/10/65; filed for CSP Osceola Cty, Fl. 1903; pension record says he was in Hos at close of the war.

Johnson, William A.P., Pvt Co. G 3/4/62 – Des & joined Co. D, 9ᵗʰ Fl. Regt 10/10/62; later rejoined Co. G; W (gunshot, l shoulder) Chancellorsville 5/3/63; Des 3/2/65; took oath of allegiance to U.S. Govt. and furnished trans to Jacksonville, Fl.; filed for CSP Clinch Cty, Ga. 1903; widow filed for CSP Dixie Cty, Fl. 1937; pension record says he was sick in Rich Hos at time of surrender.

Johnson, William S., Pvt Co. G 3/4/62 – Des & joined Co. D, 9ᵗʰ Fl. Regt 10/21/62; later rejoined Co. G; W (gunshot) 5/64; DW Staunton, Va. Hos 5/22/64.

Joiner, Jacob, 4ᵗʰ Cpl Co. C 3/4/62 – W/M Fox's Gap 9/14/62; NLR.

Joiner, Hardy, Sr., Pvt Co. C 3/4/62 – W/C Fox's Gap 9/14/62; E Aikens Landing, 11/10/62; Appt 4ᵗʰ Cpl 12/63; W (r elbow) Wilderness or Spotsylvania C.H. 5/64; on Liberty, Va. Hos roll 5/20/64; roll for 2/28/65 shows present; filed for CSP Coffee Cty, Ga. 1907; pension record says he got lost from command the night before surrender.

Joiner, W.F., Pvt Co. K – W Fox's Gap 9/14/62; NLR.

Jones, Aaron, Pvt Co. G 3/4/62 – NLR.

Jones, Abner, Pvt Co. G 4/27/62 – W Fox's Gap 9/14/62; DW 9/15/62.

Jones, Daniel I. (J.), Pvt Co. D 3/4/62 – Appt 4ᵗʰ Sgt 3/62; Disc, upon furnishing George Plankinhand as substitute 6/12/62.

Jones, Henry, Pvt Co. I 5/2/62 – D (small pox) between 11/21/62 and 12/62.

Jones, Irwin, Pvt Co. I 8/22/62 – Assigned to commissary; K Gettysburg 7/2/63.

Jones, Isaac F., Pvt Co. K 3/4/62 – K (head) Sharpsburg 9/17/62; Bur Elmwood Cem Shepherdstown, Va. (now W.V.).

Jones, John A., Pvt Co. K 3/4/62 – Roll for 12/31/62 shows "left sick on march near Bunker Hill Sept 26"; NLR.

Jones, John F., Pvt Co. I 3/4/62 – K Gettysburg 7/2/63.

Jones, Joshua M., Pvt Co. E 6/1/63 – C Sailor's Creek 4/6/65; R Pt. Lookout, Md. 5/14/65.

Jones, Malachi Frank (Francis), Pvt Co. K 5/13/62 – W Fox's Gap 9/14/62; Rich Hos 10/5/62; C Sailor's Creek 4/6/65; R Pt. Lookout, Md. 6/28/65; filed for CSP Brooks Cty, Ga. 1908.

Jones, Nedham, Pvt Co. B 3/4/62 – Roll for 3/4/62 shows "Assigned to my command. Absent."; NLR.

Jones, W.H., Pvt Co. I 5/9/62 – Detailed to work on floating battery at Sav 5/12/62; roll for 2/65 shows detached at Sav Navy Yard; NLR.

Jones, William Moore, Pvt Co. K 3/4/62 – Appt 5ᵗʰ Sgt 9/62; W (slight) Chancellorsville 5/3/63; W (r ankle – artillery canister) Gettysburg 7/2/63; leg amputated 7/5/63; C Williamsport, Md. 7/13/63; E City Point, Va. 3/20/64;

retired to Invalid Corps 10/25/64; roll for 2/65 shows "sick in Brooks County, Ga."; P Tallahassee, Fl 5/20/65; filed for CSP Thomas Cty, Ga. 1879.

Jordan, Elijah, Pvt Co. B 3/4/62 – NLR.

Jowers, Eli, Pvt Co. C 3/4/62 – Detailed as wagoner 62-63; Appt 3rd Cpl 12/63; 2nd Sgt 11/1/64; roll for 2/65 shows present; NLR.

Joyce, Jeremiah Walter, Pvt Co. K 3/4/62 – W Chancellorsville 5/3/63; K Funkstown 7/10/63.

Joyce, Tarlton B., Pvt Co. K 3/20/62 – W (thigh-flesh) Gettysburg 7/2/63; C 7/4/63; P David's Island, N.Y. 8/23/63; Appt 4th Sgt 3/23/64; W (r leg-flesh)/C Cedar Creek 10/19/64; R Pt. Lookout, Md. 6/28/65; filed for CSP Brooks Cty, Ga.1905.

ROSTER K

Kearse, Francis, Pvt Co. E 3/4/62 – Elected LtC 3/22/62; Appt temporary Regt commander 3/63; K Gettysburg (grape shot - side) 7/2/63; Bur Gettysburg; removed to Laurel Grove Cem, Sav 9/24/1871; Bur Lot 853.

Kelly, James M., Pvt Co. K 3/4/62 – W Gettysburg 7/2/63; C Amelia C.H. 4/6/65; R Pt. Lookout, Md. 6/28/65; widow filed for CSP Madison Cty, Fl. 1899.

Kelly, James P., Pvt Co. A 3/4/62 – Roll for 2/65 shows AWOL since 10/11/64; filed for CSP Wayne Cty, Ga. 1908; pension record says he was Frl at Petersburg, Va. 7/17/64 and enroute to command at close of war.

Kendrick, James G., Pvt Co. D 8/7/62 – Detailed as a teamster 1862-65; W 1/63; roll for 2/65 shows "Brigade Wagoner extra duty"; P Thomasville, Ga. 5/24/65; filed for CSP Lowndes Cty, Ga. 1902; pension record says he had left Rich about 4/1 for N.C. to get provisions and was in N.C. at surrender on 4/9/65.

Kennedy, John J., Pvt Co. E 3/4/62 – Disc (disability) Rich Hos 9/27/62.

Kight, (Kite) William, Pvt Co. B 3/4/62 – D Rich Hos 2/14/63; Bur Hollywood Cem, Rich.

Kinard, Jacob, Pvt Co. H 3/4/62 – C Fox's Gap 9/14/62; E Aikens Landing, Va. 10/62; D (smallpox) Valdosta, Ga. 11/15/62.

King, Jesse, Pvt Co. K 3/4/62 – Appt 2nd Cpl 1862; W Chancellorsville 5/3/63; Appt 2nd Sgt 8/3/64; W (gunshot, lower r leg) Summit Point, Va. 8/21/64; sent to Winchester, Va. Hos (r leg amputated below knee); C Winchester Hos 9/19/64; U.S. Hos Baltimore, Md. 11/23/64; R Pt. Lookout, Md. 6/4/65; filed for CSP Brooks Cty, Ga. 1880.

King, John H., Pvt Co. K 5/11/62 – W Gettysburg 7/2/63; W (gunshot - l forearm) Ft. Sanders 11/29/63; roll for 2/65 shows "absent sick in Lowndes Co, Ga."; filed for CSP Berrien Cty, Ga. 1890.

King, John Wade, Pvt Co. F 7/8/62 – Enlisted as Pvt in Co. G, 1st Regt Ga. Inf 9/1/61; mustered out 3/18/62; enlisted in Co. F. 50th Ga.; Appt 2nd Sgt 9/63; W Spotsylvania CH 5/12/64; K Cedar Creek 10/19/64.

King, William H., Pvt Co. B 3/4/62 – Rich Hos register for 9/26/62 shows FRL for 30 days on 9/23; roll for 2/63 shows AWOL since 10/23/62; widow filed for CSP Ware Cty, Ga. 1891; pension record says he D (pneumonia) at home on sick Frl 2/9/63.

Kirby, James H., 5th Sgt Co. I 3/4/62 – Appt 4th Sgt 1/1/63; 2nd Lt 2/64; Res as 2nd Lt 3/18/64; Disc upon being elected to civil office 7/6/64; apparently returned to command in 64; Frl for 24 days 1/4/65; roll for 2/28/65 shows AWOL since 2/3/65; P Thomasville, Ga. 5/24/65; widow filed for CSP Berrien Cty, Ga. 1910; pension record says he was at Albany, Ga., attempting to return to command from Frl at close of war.

Kirby, John F.M., Pvt Co. I 8/22/62 – D (pneumonia) Rich Hos 12/14/62; Bur Oakwood Cem, Rich; widow filed for CSP Berrien Cty, Ga. 1891.

Kirby (Kerby), William, Pvt Co. G 3/4/62 – W (thigh) Chancellorsville 5/3/63; roll for 2/65 shows AWOL since 7/27/64; NLR.

Kirby, William M., Pvt Co. I 5/2/62 – D Winchester, Va. 10/26/62.

Kirkland, A.C., Sgt Co. K – Only CSR entry shows P 5/16/65; NLR.

Kirkland, H. Pvt Co. K –June 62 entry shows "sent to Macon hospital 15th April"; NLR.

Kirkland, Harrison J., Pvt Co. C 5/3/62– D Rich Hos (typhoid fever) 9/5/62; Bur Hollywood Cem, Rich.

Kirkland, Richard G., Pvt Co. C 5/3/62 – D Rich Hos (typhoid fever) 3/2/63; Bur Oakwood Cem, Rich.

Kirkland, Timothy, Pvt Co. C 3/4/62 – Detailed as wagoner 3/62; K (head) Wilderness 5/6/64.

Kirkland, Willett F. (L.) M., Pvt Co. K 5/13/62 – D Rich Hos (pneumonia) 1/27/63; Bur Oakwood Cem, Rich.

Kirkland, Zean William, Pvt Co. C 3/4/62 – W (r leg)/C Fox's Gap 9/14/62; Frederick [Md.] Hos 10/22/62; E Ft. Monroe, Va. 1/31/63; sent to Petersburg, Va. Hos; Frl home 2/63; roll for 2/65 shows absent sick; widow filed for CSP Coffee Cty, Ga. 1908; pension record says he was home on W Frl at close of war.

Kirktona, H., Pvt Co. C – C Fox's Gap 9/14/62; E Aikens Landing, Va. 11/10/62; NLR.

Knight, Jesse Carter, Pvt Co. D 5/13/62 – D Rich Hos (pneumonia) 12/16/62; Bur Oakwood Cem, Rich.

Knight, Matthew A. Pvt Co. D 3/4/62 – W (arm-artillery shell) Fredericksburg 12/12/62; W/C Funkstown 7/10/63; roll for 2/65 shows "prisoner of war since 10 July 63"; NLR.

Knox, Franklin, Pvt Co. A 3/4/62 – D 6/30/62.

Kornegay, G.W., Pvt Co. D 3/4/62 – D Rich Hos (typhoid fever) 4/25/63; Bur Oakwood Cem, Rich.

Kubitshek, Isaac, Pvt Co. E 4/15/62 – Disc, upon furnishing James O'Rourke as substitute 5/10/62.

ROSTER L

Lackison, Robert, Pvt Co. F – C Salisbury, N.C. 4/12/65; POW roll shows received at Camp Chase, Oh. from Louisville, Ky. 5/4/65; NLR.

Lamb, B., 1st Lt Co. K – C Cedar Creek 10/19/64; POW roll shows received at Ft. Delaware, Del. from Harpers Ferry, Va. 10/27/64; NLR.

Lamb, Thomas L., Pvt Co. I 3/4/62 – NLR.

Lane, Augustus Harding, 2nd Lt Co. D 3/4/62 – Elected 1st Lt 6/9/63; Cpt later in 1863; Res 12/30/63; NLR.

Langdale, John R., Pvt Co. I 10/7/62 – Enlisted as Pvt in Co C, 29th Ga. Regt 8/22/61; Disc 8/18/62; enlisted in Co I, 50th Ga. as substitute for D.L. Sutton; D (pneumonia) in camp near Fredericksburg 3/2/63; widow filed for CSP Lowndes Cty, Ga. 1891.

Langdale, Noah H., Pvt Co. A 3/4/62 – D 5/20/62.

Langford, Ethelred, 4th Sgt Co. D 3/4/62 – Appt 3rd Sgt 1/1/63; Elected 2nd Lt 4/22/63; K Gettysburg 7/2/63; widow filed for CSP Berrien Cty, Ga. 1891.

Langford, Hardy, Pvt Co. C 9/5/62 – D Rich Hos (typhoid fever) 12/3/62; Bur Hollywood Cem, Rich; widow filed for CSP Coffee Cty, Ga. 1911.

Lankford, Parrish, Pvt Co. C 3/4/62 – Appt 1st Cpl 1863; W Gettysburg 7/2/63; Appt 5th Sgt 1/21/64; Jr. 2nd Lt 3/23/64; K Petersburg 6/19/64.

Lankford, Tarlton, Pvt Co. C 3/4/62 – D Winchester, Va. 10/7/62.

Lastinger, David M., Pvt Co. G 3/4/62 – M Fox's Gap 9/14/62; C Middletown 9/17/62; E

10/62; W (r lung)/C Cedar Creek 10/19/64; Federal Hos Winchester, Va. 10/23/64; DW 11/17/64; Bur Stonewall (Mount Hebron) Cem, Winchester, marker #254.

Lastinger, G.C., Pvt Co. G 1862 – NLR.

Lastinger, Guilford T., Pvt Co. G 3/4/62 – Appt 2nd Cpl 1/1/63; W (r forearm) Chancellorsville 5/3/63; W (r hip) Petersburg 6/20/64; roll for 2/65 shows AWOL since 10/10/64; P Thomasville, Ga. 5/11/65; filed for CSP Lowndes Cty, Ga. 1915; pension record says he was home on W Frl at close of war.

Lawson, Homer L. (U.), Regt. Surgeon 4/16/62 – Res 12/2/62.

Law, John, Pvt Co. F 3/4/62 – NLR; P 4/65.

Lebrette, Adolph, Pvt Co. E 7/1/62 – Substitute for Thomas.J. Young; "Dropped out on march near Rapidan" 8/22/62; Des 9/12/62; roll for 8/31/64 shows Des; NLR.

Lee, Francis Marion, Pvt Co. H 3/4/62 – D Lynchburg, Va. Hos 6/6/64; Bur Lot 201, Confederate Cem, Lynchburg.

Lee, Friar, Pvt Co. B 3/4/62 – Roll for 2/63 shows present; NLR.

Lee, George, Pvt Co. B 3/4/62 – W Fox's Gap 9/14/62; Appt 3rd Cpl 2/14/63; 1st Cpl 2/64; C Sailor's Creek 4/6/65; R Pt. Lookout, Md. 6/30/65; filed for CSP Pierce Cty, Ga. 1911.

Lee, Marion, 1st Cpl, Co. H 3/4/62 – Roll for 2/65 shows "absent sent to hospital May 2, 1864; NLR .

Leggett, E.G., Pvt – S Tallahassee, Fl. 5/10/65; P Thomasville, Ga. 5/18/65.

Leggett, George W., Pvt Co. G 3/4/62 – Detailed as teamster 2/64; roll for 2/65 shows AWOL since 7/27/64; P Thomasville, Ga. 5/11/65; filed for CSP Berrien Cty, Ga. 1900; pension record says he was granted leave of absence in 1864, and still sick at Dupont, Ga. at close of war.

Lenny, W.M. Pvt Co. E – Not in CSR; included in list of 50th Ga. parolees that S Appomattox C.H. 4/9/65.

Lester, Simeon B., Pvt Co. D 3/4/62 – C Frederick, Md. 9/12/62; E Aikens Landing, Va. 11/10/62; Elected Jr. 2nd Lt 3/24/64; roll for 2/65 shows "present In arrest"; C 4/65; P Libby Prison, Rich between 4/3/65 - 4/24/65.

Leverett, Butler W., Pvt Co. K 3/4/62 – W Fox's Gap 9/14/62 or Sharpsburg 9/17/62; Appt Jr. 2nd Lt 3/23/64; Frl 24 days on 1/16/65; roll for 2/65 shows AWOL since 2/20/65; NLR.

Lewis, Jesse C., Pvt Co. E 3/4/62 – Appt 3rd Cpl 11/1/62; Appt 5th Sgt 1/1/63; W (l hand – 2 fingers amputated) Chancellorsville 5/3/63; Appt 4th Sgt 2/64; 3rd Sgt 1/65; roll for 2/65 shows absent with leave; P Thomasville, Ga. 5/10/65; filed for CSP Thomas Cty, Ga. 1890; pension record says he received a 60 day Frl 2/9/65 and was home at close of war.

Lewis, J.J., Pvt Co. C – C 12/20/63 near Knoxville; D Knoxville Hos 1/13/64.

Lightsey, Jacob S., Jr. 2nd Lt Co. G 3/4/62 – Elected 2nd Lt 10/25/62; Res 3/2/63.

Lindsey, Thomas D., Pvt Co. I 3/4/62 – C Sailor's Creek 4/6/65; R 6/28/65 Pt. Lookout, Md.

Lindsley, James, Pvt – Only CSR entry shows Des 2/20/65; NLR.

Little, Absalom Granberry, Pvt Co. F 4/28/62 – Detached as teamster 1862; C Cold Harbor 6/1/64; E Pt. Lookout, Md. 3/14/65; P Thomasville, Ga. 5/19/65; widow filed for CSP Habersham Cty, Ga. 1901.

Little, Miles G.V., Pvt Co. F 3/4/62 – Roll for 2/65 shows AWOL since 2/10/65; P 5/20/65.

Little, Urastus B., Pvt Co. F 3/4/62 – Disc (disability) Sav 6/1/64; P Thomasville, Ga. 5/19/65; filed for CSP Sumter Cty, Ga. 1898.

Lodge, Malcomb M., Pvt Co. F 5/5/62 – Appt 2nd Sgt 1/1/63; 2nd Lt. 3/23/64; W (r

shoulder/face) Cedar Creek 10/19/64; Charlottesville, Va. Hos 10/24/64; roll
for 2/65 shows absent sick; filed for CSP Mitchell Cty, Ga. 1895; pension
record says he was in Hos at close of war.

Love (Lowe), John, Pvt Co. H 3/4/62 – S Tallahassee, Fl. 5/10/65; P Quincy, Fl 5/24/65.

Love, (Lowe) John W., Pvt Co. E 3/4/62 – M Ft. Sanders 11/29/63; C 12/3/63 near
Knoxville; Trn from Rock Island, Ill. for E 3/2/65; P Thomasville, Ga. 5/23/65.

Lott, Richard, Pvt Co. C 5/62 – D (measles) in camp near Sav 5/20/62; widow filed for
CSP Coffee Cty, Ga. 1891.

Lovett, Joshua W., Pvt Co. I 3/4/62 – Disc (disability) (date Unk).

Lovett, Robert, Pvt Co. K 3/4/62 – D Macon, Ga. 5/29/62.

Lowrey, C.B., Pvt – Only CSR entry shows P Thomasville, Ga. 5/15/65.

Luke, A.J., Pvt Co. I 5/2/62 – D Sav Hos 7/14/62.

Luke, Daniel F. (J.), Pvt Co. K 3/4/62 – S Appomattox CH 4/9/65.

Luke, David Perry, 2nd Lt Co. I 3/4/62 – Elected 1st Lt 6/17/62; Cpt 4/14/63; W
Chancellorsville 5/3/63; Res (disability-prostate cancer) 12/3/63, eff. 1/8/64;
filed for CSP Berrien Cty, Ga. 1911.

ROSTER M

Mack (Myck), Thomas, Pvt Co. C 3/4/62 – Appt 2nd Cpl 1/1/63; W Chancellorsville
5/3/63; C near Knoxville 12/7/63; P upon taking oath of allegiance to U.S.
Govt. at Nashville, Tn. 1/16/64.

Mallard, George R. (J.R.), Pvt Co. F 3/4/62 – K Fox's Gap 9/14/62.

Maloney, John, Pvt Co. E 8/25/62 – Substitute for Columbus M.D. Stewart; roll for
12/31/62 shows Des 8/26/62 "while on the march to Manassas"; NLR.

Maloy, Stephen E., Pvt Co. F 3/4/62 – Appt 1st Cpl 1/1/63; 4th Sgt 1864; C Farmville
4/6/65; R Pt. Lookout, Md. 6/29/65.

Manning, Lewis P, Pvt Co. A 3/4/62 –Roll for 2/65 shows absent sick; P Thomasville,
Ga. 5/23/65.

Manning, William R., Col 3/4/62 – Elected Regt Commander 3/22/62; W (thigh – flesh)
Fox's Gap 9/14/62; Rich Hos 2/26/63; Trn Columbia, S.C. Hos 5/6/63; Res,
illness (chronic hepatitis), effective 7/31/63.

Marshall, John, Pvt Co. K 3/4/62 – D (typhoid fever) Staunton, Va. Hos 12/1/62.

Marshall, Lewis W., Pvt Co. I 3/4/62 – K Fox's Gap 9/14/62.

Martin, Alonzo C., 1st Sgt Co. A 3/4/62 – Elected Jr. 2nd Lt 6/18/62; Res (disability)
11/7/62; filed for CSP Fulton Cty, Ga. 1889; pension record says he joined
Co. K, 12th Ga. Militia Cav 1864, and was home on Frl at close of the war.

Martin, R.G., Pvt Co. E – Entry for 7/62 shows detailed as wagoner 7/25/62; NLR.

Martin, Seth L., Cpl Co. D 3/4/62 – Appt 3rd Sgt 6/11/62; C/P Leesburg, Va. 10/2/62;
Appt 2nd Sgt 1/1/63; W (gunshot, l hand - forefinger amputated)
Chancellorsville 5/3/63; Appt 1st Sgt 9/1/63; reduced to Pvt 10/64; S
Appomattox CH 4/9/65; filed for CSP Lowndes Cty, Ga. 1889.

Mashburn, Henry D., Pvt Co. K 3/4/62 – Detailed as nurse Sav Hos 10/62; C Sav Hos
12/21/64; R Ft. Delaware, Del. 6/18/65; widow filed for CSP Coffee Cty, Ga.
1901; pension record he was detailed to Hos because of deafness.

Massey, J.S., Pvt – S Tallahassee, Fl. 5/10/65; P Thomasville, Ga. 5/19/65.

Mathis, Henry M., Pvt Co. I 8/23/62 – D (pneumonia) Rich Hos 2/8/63; Bur Hollywood
Cem, Rich.

Mathis, Hiram M., Chaplain 3/30/62 – Trn to 51st Ga. 4/1/62; Res 7/29/62; NLR.

Mathis, Hiram M., 1st Sgt Co. I 3/4/62 – NLR.

Mathis, John, Pvt Co. I 5/9/62 – D (pneumonia) Rich Hos 12/10/62; Bur Hollywood

Cem, Rich; widow filed for CSP Clinch Cty, Ga. 1891; pension record says he D 12/10/64, but believed to be in error.

Mathis, Mahlon, Pvt Co. I 5/9/62 – Roll for 12/62 shows "Left near Shepherdstown sick Sept 19"; D Shepherdstown, Va. (now W.V.) Hos 9/19/62; Bur Elmwood Cem, Shepherdstown.

Mathis, Timothy, Pvt Co. I 5/14/62 – C Hanover Junction, Va. 5/24/64; R Elmira, N.Y. 6/21/65.

Maxfield, James F. – Des 2/20/65; NLR.

Maxwell, Daniel L., Pvt Co. F 4/28/62 – W (l hip) Chancellorsville 5/3/63; C Cold Harbor 6/1/64; R Elmira N.Y. 6/23/65; filed for CSP Gadsden Cty, Fl. 1907.

Maxwell, James W., 3rd Cpl Co. F 3/4/62 – Appt 3rd Sgt 10/62; Elected 2nd Lt 1/1/63; 1st Lt 2/24/63; W Gettysburg (arm, slight - grapeshot) 7/2/63; W/C Cold Harbor 6/1/64; R Ft. Delaware, Del. 6/17/65; widow filed for CSP Grady Cty, Ga. 1914.

Maxwell, John Robert, Jr., Pvt Co. F 4/28/62 – Appt 4th Sgt 1/1/63; W (shell burst to face - loss of sight r eye) Ft. Sanders 11/29/63; Appt 1st Sgt; C Cold Harbor 6/1/64; E Aikens Landing, Va. 3/11/65; filed for CSP Decatur Cty, Ga. 1888.

Maxwell, William F., Pvt Co. F 3/4/62 – Appt 3rd Cpl 10/62; W/C Fox's Gap 9/14/62; E Aikens Landing, Va. 11/10/62; Appt 3rd Sgt 1864; C Cold Harbor 6/1/64; E James River, Va. 2/65 or 3/65; Rich Hos 3/4/65; NLR.

McArthur, Nathaniel, Pvt Co. E 3/4/62 – Detailed as Supt., St Johns Hos Sav 6/1/62; D (Erysipelas) Sav Hos 3/6/63; Bur Laurel Grove Cem, Sav.

McCafferty, Dominic, Pvt Co. C 4/10/62 – C Fox's Gap 9/15/62; E Aikens Landing, Va. 10/19/62; Appt 2nd Sgt 1/1/63; W Gettysburg 7/2/63; C Knoxville 12/7/63; R upon taking oath of allegiance to U.S. Govt. at Nashville, Tn. 1/16/64.

McCall, John Goldwire, 1st Lt Co. K 3/4/62 - W Funkstown (face – 3/4 of lower jaw, teeth removed) 7/10/63; Frl from Hos for 60 days 7/27/63; Appt Cpt 7/31/63; detailed as Enrolling Officer in Ga.; retired 12/2/64; P Thomasville, Ga. 5/26/65; filed for CSP Brooks Cty, Ga. 1914.

McCall, John G. F., Pvt Co. K 3/4/62 – W Gettysburg 7/2/63; W Funkstown 7/10/63; Appt 2nd Sgt 3/23/64; K (head) Petersburg 6/19/64.

McCall, Wilson C., 4th Sgt Co. K 3/4/62 – W (slight) Fox's Gap 9/14/62; W (leg - flesh) Sharpsburg 9/17/62; Rich Hos 9/26/62; Appt 2nd Sgt 3/23/63; W Chancellorsville 5/3/63; Appt SgtM 1863 or 1864; W Petersburg 6/19/64; C Sailor's Creek 4/6/65; reportedly escaped without surrendering 4/9/65.

McCauley, George, Chaplain 6/12/62 – C (date Unk); NLR.

McClendon (McLendon), James A., 2nd Sgt Co. E 3/4/62 – Disc, upon furnishing Charles Franklin Hudson as substitute 6/1/62.

McConnell, Larkin Jefferson, Pvt Co. D 4/26/62 – Detached as wagoner 64; C Sailor's Creek 4/6/65; R Pt. Lookout, Md. 6/29/65; filed for CSP Lowndes Cty, Ga.1905.

McConnell, W.F., Pvt Co. D 4/10/62 – Appt 4th Cpl 6/11/62; K Fox's Gap 9/14/62.

McCord, John, Pvt Co. G 3/4/62 – Roll for 2/63 shows at Sav Hos when Regt left for Rich on 7/19/62; NLR.

McCoy, John M., Pvt Co. E 3/4/62 – Appt Sgt 9/9/62; K Fox's Gap 9/14/62.

McCullers, Elijah Seth Allen, Pvt Co. F 6/20/64 – W (r leg) 1864: roll for 2/65 shows present; filed for CSP DeSoto Cty, Fl. 1904; pension record says he was about twelve miles west of Appomattox C.H. at S on 4/9/65; P Spartanburg, S. 4/20/65.

McCranie, Josiah, Pvt Co. I 3/4/62 - C Williamsport, Md. 9/15/62; E Aikens Landing, Va. 10/62; D Rich Hos 1/1/63 (pneumonia & small pox); Bur Oakwood Cem, Rich; widow filed for CSP Berrien Cty, Ga. 1891.

McCreary (McCrary), Asa W., Pvt Co. E 3/4/62 – D (chronic diarrhea) at home Thomas Cty, Ga. 12/26/62.

McCutcheon, Jasper, Pvt Co. I 3/4/62 – Detailed as Hos steward; C Gettysburg 7/3/63; P

Baltimore, Md. 9/25/63; Rich Hos 9/28/63; roll for 2/65 shows AWOL since 2/10/65; P Thomasville, Ga. 5/24/65.

McDaniel, A.J., Pvt Co. D 3/4/62 – W Chancellorsville 5/3/63; P Albany, Ga. 5/24/65.

McDonald, Kenneth M., 1st Cpl Co. E 3/4/62 – Appt 4th Sgt 7/1/62; 1st Sgt 9/14/62; Elected Jr. 2nd Lt 10/20/62; 1st Lt 4/3/63; W Chancellorsville 5/3/63; DW Rich Hos 5/21/63

McElhany, John T., Pvt Co. A 3/4/62 – K Fox's Gap 9/14/62.

McGlashan, Andrew M., Co. H – Was 1st Sgt in Co. A 4th Cav Bn when Appt 2nd Lt of Co. H 2/17/64; Appt Regt Adj to replace T. Roberds 4/12/64; W/C Cedar Creek 10/19/64; R Ft. Delaware, Del. 7/65.

McGlashan, Peter Alexander Selkirk, 1st Lt Co. E 3/4/62– Elected Cpt 10/1/62; Prom Maj 5/63; Col/Regt commander to replace LtC Kearse 9/16/63, retroactive to 7/31/63; recommended for appt to brig gen/Bde commander by Gen Goode Bryan 8/20/64, but not selected; W Cedar Creek 10/19/64; Frl home from Staunton, Va. Hos 10/22/64; rejoined Regt 2/10/65; C Sailor's Creek 4/6/65; R Johnson's Island, Oh. 7/25/65.

McGlynn, John, Pvt Co. E 5/14/62 – Substitute for William Cooperman; C Fox's Gap 9/14/62; E Aikens Landing, Va. 10/19/62; C Cedar Creek 10/19/64; R Pt. Lookout, Md. 5/14/65.

McHargue, John, Pvt Co. G 3/4/62 – Initial Clinch Cty muster roll shows "Volunteered & refused to come."; NLR.

McKinnon, Charles, Pvt Co. D 3/4/62 – D Valdosta, Ga. 7/13/62.

McKinnon, Daniel J., Pvt Co. E 5/13/62 – Appt 4th Cpl 1/1/63; D (typhoid fever) Rich Hos 2/16/63; Bur Hollywood Cem, Rich.

McKinnon, Duncan Neal, Pvt Co. E 3/4/62 –Roll for 2/65 shows absent sick in Thomas Cty since 4/10/62; NLR.

McKinnon, John N., 2nd Lt Co. E 3/4/62 – Elected 1st Lt 10/1/62; Res (disability-chronic illness) 4/3/63.

McLean, Richard J., Jr. 2nd Lt Co. E 3/4/62 – Elected 2nd Lt 10/1/62; Cpt 4/3/63; K Chancellorsville 5/3/63.

McLendon (McLindon), Thomas C., Pvt Co. H 3/4/62 – Appt 3rd Sgt 5/1/62; D Sav Hos 6/29/62.

McLenney (McClenny), William C., Pvt Co. E 3/4/62 – W Chancellorsville 5/3/63; detailed in Bde QM Dept. 9/64; S Appomattox CH 4/9/65.

McLeod, Norman, Pvt Co. K 3/4/62 – K Cedar Creek 10/19/64.

McLinn, Robert J., Pvt Co. E 5/15/62 – D (typhoid fever) Amissville, Va. 8/30/62; widow filed for CSP Thomas Cty, Ga. 1891; pension record says he became ill with fever on the march toward Md. and D shortly thereafter.

McMath, G.W., Pvt Co. I 3/65 – NLR.

McMillan, Andrew J., Pvt Co. E 5/7/62 – D Sav Hos 6/21/62.

McMillan, Archibald C., Pvt Co. I 3/4/62 – W Chancellorsville 5/3/63; C Sailor's Creek 4/6/65; R Pt. Lookout, Md. 6/29/65.

McMillan, Daniel N., Pvt Co. I 8/28/62 – D (typhoid fever) Farmville, Va. Hos 4/1/63; Bur Farmville; widow filed for CSP Coffee Cty, Ga. 1906.

McMillan, John C., 1st Lt Co. I 3/4/62 – Res (disability), effective 5/23/62; enlisted as Pvt in Co. H, 4th Ga. Cav 7/23/63; S Doctortown, Ga. 1865.

McMillan, Randall, Pvt Co. I 3/4/62 – W (thigh) Fox's Gap 9/14/62; Rich Hos 10/7/62; Rich Hos 4/14/63 (pneumonia and typhoid fever); Frl home 4/23/63; roll for 2/65 shows AWOL since 2/10/64; widow filed for CSP Cook Cty, Ga. 1924; pension record says he was never able to return and home sick at close of war.

McMullan (McMillan), James, Pvt Co. H 3/4/62 – Disc (disability) 1/9/63; D 2/18/63.

McMullen, John M., Pvt Co. E 3/4/62 – Appt 1st Cpl 7/4/62; D Rich Hos (chronic diarrhea) 10/28/62; Bur Oakwood Cem, Rich.

McMurray, William H., 1st Sgt Co. K 3/4/62 – Appt 2nd Lt.; K Ft Sanders 11/29/63; widow filed for CSP Brooks Cty, Ga. 1891.

McNabb, John J., Pvt Co. I 3/4/62 – Roll for 2/65 shows AWOL since 7/17/64; filed for CSP Berrien Cty, Ga. 1911; pension record says he was sent from Cold Harbor to Hos 6/2/64 sick with fever and Frl for 60 days; also says he was home on detail "getting up deserters" at close of war.

McNair, James M., Pvt Co. F 4/28/62; Trn to Co. D, 17th Ga. Regt 8/11/62; D Winchester, Va. Hos 10/14/62.

McPherson, David, Pvt Co. E 4/13/62 – K Chancellorsville 5/3/63.

McPherson, Henry, Pvt Co. E 5/15/62 – Substitute for Louis Goldberg; Disc (under-age) 10/25/62.

McPherson, Wyatt H., Pvt Co. E 5/15/62 – Enlisted as Pvt in Co. D, 2nd Regt, 1st Bde, Ga. State Troops 11/6/61; mustered out 4/62; enlisted in Co. E, 50th Ga.; W Fox's Gap 9/14/62; C Sharpsburg 9/17/62; leg amputated Frederick, Md. Hos; DW 10/27/62; Bur Mount Olivet Cem, Frederick.

McRae, Phillip, W.C., Pvt Co. K 4/20/62 – Roll for 8/31/64 shows absent sent to Hos Spotsylvania C.H. 5/15/64; roll for 2/65 shows still in the Hos; NLR.

McSwain, John, Pvt Co. A 3/4/62 – CSR entry dated 10/21/62 references a court martial; C Gettysburg 7/2/63; E (date Unk); C Cedar Creek 10/19/64; roll for 2/65 shows "absent prisoner of war"; NLR.

McTyre, Henry W., Ord Sgt Co. F – C Boonsboro 9/15/62; E Aikens Landing, Va. 10/19/62; S Appomattox CH 4/9/65.

Mercer, James, Pvt Co. H 5/16/62 – W (head – lost r eye) Chancellorsville 5/3/63; Disc (disability) 10/9/63; P Macon, Ga. 1865; filed for CSP Brooks Cty, Ga. 1894; widow filed for CSP Sumter Cty, Fl. 1929; pension record says he was home sick at close of war.

Mercer, John, Pvt Co. H 5/15/62 – W Fox's Gap 9/14/62; Rich Hos 10/29/62; W (gunshot l lung, skull, both legs - l leg amputated) Gettysburg 7/2/63; C 7/4/63; E 1863; roll for 2/65 shows AWOL since 9/10/63; P Thomasville, Ga. 5/20/65; filed for CSP Brooks Cty, Ga. 1888; pension record says wound caused paralysis.

Mercer, Malichi, Pvt Co. B 3/4/62 – Roll for 2/63 shows present; NLR.

Mercer, Saul, Pvt Co. H 3/4/62 – W (gunshot - both legs) Cedar Creek 10/19/64; retired to Invalid Corps and assigned light duties as result of wounds and age (51) 3/29/65; S Appomattox C.H. 4/9/65; widow filed for CSP Colquitt Cty, Ga. 1921.

Merriman, George Henry, Pvt Co. K 4/24/62 – W (l lung – shell fragment)/C Gettysburg 7/2/63; P David's Island, N.Y. 8/24/63; W Cedar Creek 10/19/64; retired to Invalid Corps 11/22/64; P Madison, Fl 5/20/65; filed for CSP Jefferson Cty, Fl. 1888.

Merritt, Alexander, Pvt Co. C 3/4/62 - W Sharpsburg 9/17/62; W Chancellorsville 5/3/63; S Appomattox C.H. 4/9/65.

Merritt, Benjamin, Pvt Co. C 3/4/62 – K Fox's Gap 9/14/62.

Merritt, Frederick, Pvt Co. C 5/13/62 – D Winchester, Va. Hos 11/13/62; Bur Stonewall (Mount Hebron) Cem, Winchester, marker #214.

Merritt, Sloan, Pvt Co. C 3/4/62 – Disc (disability-rheumatism) 6/1/62; widow filed for CSP Coffee Cty, Ga. 1909.

Metcalf, Benjamin F., Pvt Co. F 3/4/62 – W (r leg)/ C Fox's Gap 9/14/62; P 9/25/62; Rich Hos 10/1/62; retired to Invalid Corps 3/29/65; S Appomattox CH 4/9/65.

Miller, Hagen, Pvt Co. K 5/13/62 - W Chancellorsville 5/3/63; NLR.

Miller, William M., 3rd Cpl Co. C 3/4/62 – K Fox's Gap 9/14/62.

Millirons, James, Pvt Co. D – C Ringold, Ga. 11/25/63; P Rock Island, Ill., upon taking oath of allegiance to U.S. Govt. 3/18/64; enlisted in U.S. Army for "frontier service" 10/14/64.

Mills, Benjamin J., Pvt. Co. E 3/4/62 – Appt Sgt 3/62 or 4/62; D Sav Hos 5/3/62.

Minshew, Jacob, Pvt Co. G 3/4/62 – W Gettysburg (l thigh) 7/2/63; C 7/5/63 (l leg amputated above knee); P City Point, Va. 11/17/63; retired to Invalid Corps 10/27/64; filed for CSP Ware Cty, Ga. 1889.

Minshew (Minchew), John J., Pvt. Co. B 3/4/62– C Cold Harbor 6/1/64; R Elmira, N.Y. 5/19/65; filed for CSP Charlton Cty, Ga. 1898.

Minchew (Minshew), Wryan F., 3rd Sgt Co. A 3/4/62 – C Fox's Gap 9/14/62; E Aikens Landing, Va. 10/19/62; Appt 2nd Sgt 12/31/62; 1st Sgt 3/1/64; elected Bvt 2nd Lt 3/23/64; W (l lung)/C Cedar Creek 10/19/64; DW Fed Hos Winchester, Va. 10/24/64; Bur Stonewall (Mount Hebron) Cem, Winchester, marker #286; (marker reads "Lt. W. Manshaw").

Mitchell, Thomas H., Pvt Co. G 3/4/62 – Appt Sgt and SgtM 1862; CSR entry for 2/28/63 shows receiving pay; NLR.

Mitchell, William N., Pvt Co. K 3/4/62 – D (pneumonia) Gordonsville, Va. 2/13/63.

Mizell, William, Pvt Co. G 4/27/62 – D Liberty, Va. Hos 3/26/63; Bur Blk 1, Lot A, Space 94, Longwood Cem, Liberty (now Bedford), Va.

Mobley, Francis L., Jr. 2nd Lt Co. I 3/4/62 – Elected 2nd Lt 6/17/62; W (head - slight) Fox's Gap 9/14/62; W (r breast) Sharpsburg 9/17/62; DW Winchester, Va. Hos 10/9/62; Bur Stonewall (Mount Hebron) Cem, Winchester, marker #121.

Mobley, Jesse, Pvt Co. C 3/4/62 – Elected 1st Sgt 1863; 2nd Lt 12/21/63; K Petersburg 6/20/64.

Money, James O., Pvt Co. I 8/22/62 – D (typhoid fever) Gordonsville, Va. Hos 3/24/63.

Monroe, Edward D., Asst. Regt. Surgeon 7/16/64 – NLR.

Moody, Isaac, Pvt Co. G 3/4/62 – K Chancellorsville 5/3/63.

Moore, Edward H., 1st Sgt Co. C 3/4/62 – W/C Fox's Gap 9/14/62; P 9/25/62; reduced to Pvt 1/1/63; C Harrisonburg, Va. 9/25/64; received for E Harper's Ferry, Va. 10/4/64; C near Fisher's Hill, Va. 10/22/64; R Pt. Lookout, Md. 5/14/65.

Moore, Franklin, Pvt Co. I 1862 – Disc (disability - imbecility) 10/10/62.

Moore, J.H., Pvt Co. E – Not in CSR; Bur Stonewall (Mount Hebron) Cem, Winchester, Va., marker #242; Cem register reads "J.H. Moore, Co. E, 50th Ga. Died Sept. 2, 1864."

Moore, William N., Pvt Co. K 3/4/62 – W Chancellorsville 5/3/63; W Funkstown 7/10/63; C High Bridge, Va. 4/6/65; R Pt. Lookout, Md. 6/29/65; widow filed for CSP Clinch Cty, Ga. 1919.

Morgan, Elijah C., Cpt Co. I 3/4/62 – Res (disability) 4/14/63; enlisted as Pvt in Co. H, 4th Regt Ga. Cav 9/1/63; Appt Commissary Sgt 10/18/63; Disc 1/9/64.

Morgan, Evans W., Pvt Co. B 3/4/62 – Only CSR entry shows "Rejected by Surgeons"; NLR.

Morgan, Isaac, Pvt Co. B 3/4/62 – M Fox's Gap 9/14/62; C Hagerstown, Md. 9/15/62; E Aikens Landing, Va. 10/19/62; executed in Tn. as a deserter 2/64 or 3/64.

Morgan, Jacob, Pvt Co. B 3/4/62 – W (wrist – amputated above elbow) Chancellorsville 5/3/63; roll for 2/65 shows AWOL in Ware Cty, Ga.; filed for CSP Clinch Cty, Ga. 1879.

Morgan, William L., 3rd Cpl Co. D 3/4/62 – C Gettysburg 7/2/63; P Pt. Lookout, Md. 8/22/63; Appt 1st Cpl 10/63; in Rich Hos 3/10/64; widow filed for CSP Fulton Cty, Ga. 1919; pension record says he was on sick Frl at close of war.

Morrison, John J., Sgt Co. I 3/4/62 – D (measles) Valdosta, Ga. 4/18/62; widow filed
for CSP Berrien Cty, Ga. 1891; pension record says he D on way home on
sick Frl.

Muner, D.G., Pvt – S Tallahassee, Fl. 5/10/65; P Thomasville, Ga. 5/18/65; NLR.

Mounds (Muns), William, Pvt Co. C 3/4/62 – NLR.

Mullis, Madison, Pvt Co. I 3/4/62 – Enlisted as Pvt in Co. K, 5th Regt Ga. State Troops
10/6/61; Disc (disability) 10/27/61; enlisted in Co. I, 50th Ga.: Disc
(disability) (date Unk).

Munsy, J., Pvt Co. B – CSR entry for 7/62 shows sent to convalescent camp located
near Whitesville, Ga. 7/17; NLR.

Murphy, David, Pvt Co. E 7/12/64 – W (r hand – lost middle finger) Shenandoah Valley
8/64; Charlottesville, Va. Hos 9/1/64; Rich Hos register for 9/11/64 shows Frl
60 days; roll for 2/65 shows AWOL; P Thomasville, Ga. 5/11/65; filed for
CSP Colquitt Cty, Ga. 1899; pension record says he was home on W Frl at
close of war.

Murphey, David Wright, Pvt Co. H 8/1/62 – W Chancellorsville 5/3/63; S Appomattox
CH 4/9/65; filed for CSP Thomas Cty, Ga. 1913.

Murphey, James N., Pvt Co. E 5/15/62 – K Fox's Gap 9/14/62.

Murphey, Kilby, Pvt Co. E 5/15/62 – C Falling Waters, Va. [WVa.] 7/14/63; P
Washington, D.C., upon taking oath of allegiance to U.S. Govt. 12/13/63, and
"sent north."

Murphey, Timothy, Pvt Co. E 5/15/62 – Roll for 12/31/62 shows Des to Thomas Cty, Ga.
7/19/62; P Thomasville, Ga. 5/11/65.

Murphey, William H., Pvt Co. F 3/4/62 – Trn to Co. E 5/15/62; roll for 12/31/62 shows
Des to Thomas Cty, Ga. 11/25/62; D (typhoid fever) Rich Hos 8/12/64; Bur
Hollywood Cem, Rich.

Murray, James M., Pvt Co. B 3/4/62 – Roll for 12/64 shows "absent sent to hospital in
November 1862 not since heard from supposed to be dead"; NLR.

Music, Abram, Pvt Co. B 3/4/62 – W (left side - lost 3 ribs) Chancellorsville 5/3/63;
roll for 10/64 shows AWOL in Ware Cty, Ga.; filed for CSP Ware Cty 1896;
pension record says he spent several months in Hos after being W and was
sent home on sick Frl; was home due to wounds at close of war.

Music, Mills, Pvt. Co. B 3/4/62– W (elbow) C Fox's Gap 9/14/62; P Ft. McHenry, Md.
12/14/62; DW "on his way from Fort Delaware" 12/16/62.

ROSTER N

Nellums, James N. (M.), Pvt Co. G 3/4/62 –Initial Clinch Cty muster roll shows "at
home refused to come"; NLR.

Nelson, Isaiah, Pvt Co. C 5/3/62 – Des 7/18/62; court-martialed 3/17/63; D (dropsy)
Rich Hos 4/25/63.

Nelson, John B., Pvt Co. K 3/4/62 – NLR.

Nelson, Marion, Pvt Co. D 3/4/62 – Elected 2nd Lt. 6/9/63; W (below chest-flesh)
Gettysburg 7/2/63; Appt 1st Lt 7/9/63; W (l foot) Wilderness 5/6/64; Frl from
Hos 6/23/64 for 60 days; roll for 2/65 shows AWOL since 8/16/64; C near
Macon, Ga. 4/20/65 or 4/21/65.

Nelson, William J., Sr., Pvt Co. D 3/4/62 – W (r foot – great toe amputated) Fox's Gap
9/14/62; C Boonsboro 9/15/62; P 10/3/62; Rich Hos 10/24/62; filed for CSP
Lowndes Cty, Ga. 1889; pension record says he was sent to Petersburg, Va.
Hos (chronic dysentery) 7/64 and Frl home; was home on sick Frl at close of
war; P 1865.

Nesmith, Elijah, Pvt Co. F 3/4/62 – K Fox's Gap 9/14/62.

Nesmith, Linton C., Pvt Co. K 3/4/62 – D (pneumonia) Rich Hos 4/17/63; Bur Oakwood Cem, Rich.

Nesmith, Malachi, Pvt Co. H 3/4/62 – W (l arm) Chancellorsville 5/3/63; DW Rich Hos 5/18/63; Bur Oakwood Cem, Rich; widow filed for CSP Colquitt Cty, Ga. 1891.

Nesmith, Nathaniel M., Pvt Co. F 5/13/62 – Enlisted as Pvt in Co. K, 1st Regt, 1st Bde Ga. State Troops 10/8/61; mustered out 4/8/62; enlisted in Co. F, 50th Ga.; C Sailor's Creek 4/6/65; R Pt. Lookout, Md. 6/29/65; filed for CSP Decatur Cty, Ga. 1904.

Nettles, Alexander, Pvt Co. C 3/4/62 – W (gunshot, head – lost eyesight l eye) Fox's Gap 9/14/62; W (l hand) Chancellorsville 5/3/63; W (l hand) Wilderness 5/6/64; roll for 2/65 shows absent sick; filed for CSP Clay Cty, Fl. 1889; pension record says he was home on Frl at close of war.

Nettles, Benjamin W., Pvt Co. C 3/4/62 – Disc (disability-chronic dysentery and under age) 11/2/62; filed for CSP Volusia Cty, Fl. 1904; pension record he was home at close of war.

Nettles, Jeremiah F., Pvt Co. A 3/4/62 – Roll for 2/63 shows present; widow filed for CSP Alachua Cty, Fl. 1903; pension record says he D (pneumonia) Fredericksburg, Va. 4/3/63.

Nettles, Samuel Perry, Pvt Co. C 3/4/62 – Disc (disability-rheumatism) 7/1/62.

Newburn, Etheldred, Pvt Co. I 3/4/62 – Des 3/2/65; took oath of allegiance to U.S. Govt. and furnished transportation to Newville, Pa; witnessed for Elijah Paulk CSP application and stated that he (Newburn) was present at the surrender.

Newiss, A., Cpl Co. A – C near Knoxville, Tn. 12/3/63; on Rock Island, Ill. POW roll 1/10/64; NLR.

Newman, Andrew J., Pvt Co. D 3/4/62 – M Fox's Gap 9/14/62; rolls from 8/64 - 2/65 show absent sick; NLR.

Newman, George H., Pvt Co. K – W Gettysburg 7/2/63; NLR.

Newman, Theodore B., Pvt Co. B 3/4/62 – Disc (under age) 10/16/62.

Newsom, Asa, Pvt Co. D 8/23/62 – Disc (disability-hernia, both sides) 11/10/62.

Newton, Ezra P., Pvt Co. A 5/2/62 – Appt Cpl 1863; K Gettysburg 7/2/63; Bur Gettysburg; removed to Laurel Grove Cem, Sav 9/24/1871; Bur Lot 853.

Newton, James H., Pvt Co. K 3/4/62 – Only CSR entry shows; P Thomasville, Ga. 5/19/65; widow filed for CSP Lowndes Cty, Ga. 1912; pension record says he was W (l hand) 1864 (believed to be Cedar Creek 10/19/64), and home on W Frl at close of war.

Newton, William George, Pvt Co. K 3/4/62 –K Ft. Sanders 11/29/63.

Nipper, Ben, Pvt Co. C 3/62 – NLR; widow filed for CSP Coffee Cty, Ga. 1910; pension record he D "while in service at Savannah, Ga. about the first of November 1862."

Nipper, Hiram, Pvt Co. G 3/4/62 – Roll for 2/65 shows AWOL since 4/29/64; S Tallahassee, Fl. 5/10/65; P Tallahassee 5/15/65; widow filed for CSP Baker Cty, Fl. 1903.

Nipper, Ivey, Pvt Co. G 3/4/62 – D (pneumonia) Lynchburg, Va. Hos 12/21/62.

Nipper, J.D., Pvt Co. G 1862 – D Lynchburg, Va. Hos 12/20/62; Bur Lot 123, Confederate Cem Lynchburg.

Nipper, John J. (G), Pvt Co. G 5/13/62 – K Chancellorsville 5/3/63

Nipper Joel, Pvt Co. G 3/4/62 – K Chancellorsville 5/3/63.

Nipper, John, Pvt Co. C 3/4/62 – NLR.

Nipper, William, Pvt Co. C 3/4/62 – Appt 2nd Cpl 12/15/63; W (leg-gunshot) Spotsylvania C.H. 5/10/64; Rich Hos 5/10/64; Trn to Columbia, S.C. Hos

5/27/64; S Appomattox CH 4/9/65.

Nix, Clayton, Pvt Co. F 5/5/62 – Enlisted as Pvt in Co. K, 1st Regt, 1st Bde Ga. State Troops 10/8/61; mustered out 4/8/62; enlisted in Co. F, 50th Ga.; K Fox's Gap 9/14/62.

Nix, John T., Pvt Co. F 5/5/62 – Enlisted as Pvt in Co. K, 1st Regt, 1st Bde Ga. State Troops 10/8/61; mustered out 4/8/62; enlisted in Co. F, 50th Ga.; W (gunshot) Fox's Gap 9/14/62; C Sharpsburg 9/17/62; DW Frederick, Md. Hos 10/14/62; Bur Mount Olivet Cem, Frederick.

Nix, Larkin J., Pvt Co. F 3/4/62 – W (gunshot, r leg)/C Ft. Sanders 11/29/63; E same day; roll for 2/28/65 shows AWOL since 2/1/65; filed for CSP Grady Cty, Ga. 1910; pension record says he was home sick (typhoid fever) at close of war.

Nix, Monroe, Pvt Co. F 5/5/62 – Enlisted as Pvt in Co. K, 1st Regt, 1st Bde Ga. State Troops 10/8/61; mustered out 4/8/62; enlisted in Co. F, 50th Ga.; D in camp near Fredericksburg 12/10/62.

Nix, Newton, Pvt Co. F 3/4/62 – W Fox's Gap 9/14/62; D Atlanta, Ga. Hos 10/23/62 Bur Oakland Cem, Atlanta.

Norman, J.C., Pvt – S Tallahassee, Fl. 5/10/65; P Thomasville, Ga. 5/23/65; NLR.

Norman, Joel Samuel, Pvt Co. H 5/13/62 – W (gunshot, r shoulder, spine & lung) Ft. Sanders 11/29/63; roll for 2/65 shows AWOL since 7/21/64; P Thomasville, Ga. 5/24/65; filed for CSP Colquitt Cty, Ga. 1888; pension record says W caused partial paralysis of r arm.

Norman, Joseph J., Pvt Co. H 3/4/62 – Detailed as shoemaker in Rich and Columbus, Ga. 12/62 to 10/63; roll for 2/65 shows AWOL since 4/1/64; P Thomasville, Ga. 5/24/65; filed for CSP Colquitt Cty, Ga. 1906; pension record says he received Frl home after being elected Colquitt Cty Tax Collector.

Norman, William H.H., Pvt Co. H 3/4/62 – W (l leg/r thigh) Gettysburg 7/2/63; C 7/5 (l leg amputated below knee); E City Point, Va. 11/17/63; Rich Hos 11/18/63; Frl from Macon, Ga. Hos 7/12/64; P Thomasville, Ga. 5/24/65; filed for CSP Colquitt Cty, Ga. 1889.

Norris, John J., Pvt. Co. I 9/4/62 - W (l hip/head) Chancellorsville 5/3/63; W (gunshot, face – l side & jaw) Cold Harbor 6/1/64; roll for 2/65 shows absent sick; filed for CSP Hamilton Cty, Fl. 1901; pension record says he was Disc (disability) 1864.

Norwood, John T., Pvt Co. H 3/4/62 – D Augusta, Ga. Hos 5/22/62.

Norwood, Joseph, Pvt Co. H 3/4/62 – Last CSR entry shows at Macon, Ga. Hos 11/26/63; reported D at home 1864; NLR.

Norwood, Lorenza A., Pvt Co. K 3/4/62 – Roll for 6/62 shows sent to Macon, Ga. Hos 4/15/62; NLR.

Nunez, Alexander, Pvt Co. A 3/4/62 – C near Knoxville 12/3/63; R Rock Island, Ill. 5/16/65.

Nunez, Daniel G., Pvt Co. C 3/4/62 – Trn to Co A 1/1/63; W Chancellorsville 5/3/63; W (r leg – amputated below knee) Cedar Creek 10/19/64; roll for 2/65 shows absent sick; P Thomasville, Ga. 5/16/65; filed for CSP Ware Cty, Ga. 1880.

ROSTER O

O'Berry, Robert G., Pvt Co. A 5/19/62 – Enlisted as Pvt in Co. K, 5th Regt Ga. State Troops 10/1/61; mustered out 4/9/62; enlisted in Co. A, 50th Ga.; W Fox's Gap 9/14/62; Appt 3rd Sgt 3/23/64; roll for 2/65 shows present; filed for CSP Pierce Cty, Ga. 1909; pension record says he commanded some sharpshooters

at Sailor's Creek 4/6/65; he escaped capture and S at Appomattox C.H. 4/9/
65; parolee list does not include him with the Regt.

O'Brien (or O'Bryan), Charles H., Pvt Co. F 3/4/62 – Appt 5th Sgt 1/1/63; Jr. 2nd Lt
3/23/64; K Cedar Creek 10/19/64.

Odom, James B., Pvt Co. K 3/4/62 – D (meningitis) Lynchburg, Va. Hos 12/27/62; Bur
Lot 101, Confederate Cem Lynchburg 12/27/62.

Ogden, Elias W., Pvt Co. C 9/5/62 - D (phlebitis – r thigh) Rich Hos 11/9/62; Bur
Oakwood Cem, Rich.

Oliver, A.J., Pvt Co. D 3/4/62 – NLR.

O'Neill (O'Neal), Hugh, Pvt Co. B 3/4/62 – W Chancellorsville 5/3/63; Des 1/14/65;
took oath of allegiance to U.S. Govt. and furnished transportation to
Baltimore, Md. 1/18/65.

O'Rourke, James, Pvt Co. E 5/15/62 – Substitute for Issac Kubitshek; K Fox's Gap 9/14/62.

O'Steen, John Riley, Cpt Co. G 3/4/62 – W/C Fox's Gap 9/14/62; DW Frederick, Md.
Hos 9/23/62; Bur Mount Olivet Cem, Frederick.

O'Steen, William B., Pvt Co. G 4/27/62 – D at home in Clinch Cty, Ga. 12/14/62.

Overstreet, William H., Pvt Co. G 3/4/62 – Original muster roll shows "Volunteered
and refused to come"; NLR.

Owen, James T., Pvt Co. E 3/4/62 – W (gunshot, l ankle – leg amputated below knee)
Chancellorsville 5/3/63; roll for 2/65 shows absent sick; P Thomasville, Ga.
5/20/65; filed for CSP Mitchell Cty, Ga. 1879.

Owens, John, Pvt Co. H 3/4/62 – NLR.

Owens, Peter, Pvt Co. H 3/4/62 – Disc, (date Unk); NLR.

ROSTER P

Pafford, James Marion, Pvt Co. G 5/15/62 –Most muster rolls for 1862/63 show absent
on sick Frl; roll for 2/65 shows AWOL since 10/10/64; NLR.

Palmer, John Milton, Pvt Co. F 3/4/62 – D Macon, Ga. 4/26/62.

Parmalee, C.H., Asst Commissary Sgt 6/12/62 – Dropped 2/5/63; NLR.

Parnell, John Cullen, Pvt Co. E 3/4/62 – W Chancellorsville 5/3/63; Appt 4th Cpl 1864;
reduced to Pvt 8/6/64; C Rich 4/3/65; R Pt. Lookout, Md. 6/16/65; widow
filed for CSP Decatur Cty, Ga. 1937.

Parramore, Henry Jones, Asst. Surgeon 3/30/62 – C Gettysburg 7/5/63; E City Point,
Va. 11/63; Appt Regt Surgeon 7/16/64; S Appomattox Court House 4/9/65.

Parrish, A.J., Pvt Co. I 5/9/62 – W/M Fox's Gap 9/14/62; NLR.

Parrish, Absalom J, Pvt Co. I 8/22/62 – Appt 3rd Sgt 4/1/64; roll for 8/31/64 shows
"absent sick (wounded)"; roll for 2/65 shows absent sick; widow filed for
CSP Polk Cty, Fl. 1932.

Parrish, Ezekiel, 4th Sgt Co. I 3/4/62 – Detached as carpenter on Guyton Hos,
Whitesville, Ga. 5/62; D Guyton Hos 6/5/62.

Parrish, Matthew A., Pvt Co. I 3/4/62 – Detached as carpenter on Guyton Hos,
Whitesville, Ga. 5/21/62; D (typhoid pneumonia) at home in Berrien Cty, Ga.
10/21/62; widow filed for CSP Berrien Cty, Ga. 1891.

Partin, Joseph W., Pvt Co. B 3/4/62 – NLR.

Passmore, Alexander, Pvt Co. C 3/4/62 – W Chancellorsville 5/3/63; retired to Invalid
Corps 7/26/64; NLR.

Passmore, John, Pvt Co. C 3/4/62 – Granted 30 day Frl home 7/30/64; roll for 2/65
shows AWOL since 8/6/64; NLR.

Passmore, Nathan, Pvt Co. C 3/4/62 – K Fox's Gap 9/14/62.

Patterson, Benjamin F., Pvt Co. F 4/26/62 – W Chancellorsville 5/3/63; Appt 3rd Cpl

2/64; W (gunshot - r arm) North Anna River 5/23/64; Rich Hos 5/25/64; C
Amelia C.H. 4/6/65; R Pt. Lookout, Md. 6/17/65.

Patterson, Malcomb M., Pvt Co. I 8/23/62 – D (typhoid fever) Rich Hos 1/4/63; Bur
Oakwood Cem, Rich.

Patterson, W.A., Pvt Co. F 11/18/64 –Roll for 2/65 shows present; NLR.

Paulk, Daniel (David) C., Pvt Co. I 8/29/62 – D (measles) Winchester, Va. 11/2/62; Bur
Stonewall (Mount Hebron) Cem, Winchester, marker #206; widow filed for
CSP Irwin Cty, Ga. 1893.

Paulk, Elijah Eli, Pvt Co. I 8/28/62 – Appt 4th Sgt 4/64; roll for 2/65 shows present;
NLR; filed for CSP Atkinson Cty, Ga. 1919; pension record says he was with
the ambulance corps, sick with rheumatism when command surrendered.

Paulk, K.E., Pvt Co. I 8/22/62 – NLR.

Paulk, R. Henry, Pvt Co. I 8/29/62 –Roll for 2/65 shows AWOL since 9/11/64; NLR.

Peacock, James T., Pvt Co. A 3/4/62 – CSR shows D (debilitas) Rich Hos 9/14/62; Bur
Hollywood Cem, Rich.

Pendleton, Philip Coleman, Cpt Co. B 3/4/62 – Elected Maj 3/22/62; Res (disability
- chronic diarrhea) 10/8/62.

Pendleton, William Frederick, Pvt Co. B 3/4/62 – Appt 3rd Sgt 1862; Disc (under age-17)
10/9/62; reenlisted 3/25/63; Elected 2nd Lt 4/27/63; Appt 1st Lt 2/64; W (head)
Cedar Creek 10/19/64; Appt Cpt 1/11/65; granted Frl 2/14/65; enroute to Regt
at close of war; P Ga. 4 or 5/65.

Perry (Percy), James, Pvt Co. K 3/4/62 – Disc (disability-spinal injury) 7/18/62.

Peters, Isham H., Cpl Co. D 3/4/62 – Appt 5th Sgt 6/11/62; W Sharpsburg 9/17/62; Rich
Hos 11/8/62; Appt 4th Sgt 10/62; Disc upon election as Lowndes Cty, Ga.
Sheriff 7/19/64; filed for CSP Calhoun Cty, Fl. 1902.

Peters, S.F., Pvt Co. D 4/26/62 – W (head) Fox's Gap 9/14/62; C Sharpsburg 9/17/62;
Wash D.C. Hos 9/29/62; P Wash, D.C. 10/62; Rich Hos 10/9/62; DW at
home in Lowndes Cty, Ga. 11/4/62.

Peters, S.J., Pvt Co. D 3/4/62 –Roll for 2/65 shows present; NLR.

Peters, Solomon M., Pvt Co. D 3/4/62 – NLR; widow filed for CSP Dade Cty, Fl. 1908;
pension record says he S Appomattox C.H. 4/9/65, but not on list of parolees
with 50th Ga. Regt.

Peters, William J., 2nd Cpl Co. D 4/2/62 – Enlisted as Pvt Co. B, 18th Ga. Bn 1861;
mustered out early 1862; enlisted in Co D., 50th Ga.; reduced to Pvt 8/62; roll
for 2/65 shows absent on Frl; P Thomasville, Ga. 5/23/65; filed for CSP Lowndes
Cty, Ga. 1909; pension record says he was home on Frl at close of war.

Peters, William Lott, Pvt Co. D 3/4/62 – Roll for 2/65 shows "absent with leave on
furlough; widow filed for CSP Berrien Cty, Ga. 1918; pension record says this
was his first Frl of the war.

Peterson, Neil, Pvt Co. D 3/4/62 – W (head) Chancellorsville 5/3/63; Rich Hos; C Cedar
Creek 10/19/64; R Pt. Lookout, Md. 6/16/65; filed for CSP Rusk Cty, Tx. 1912.

Phillips, Gordon J. (Warren) Pvt Co. B 3/4/62 – W (head)/C Fox's Gap 914/62; Phil., Pa.
Hos 9/27/62; E Ft Monroe, Va. 12/15/62; Appt 2nd Cpl 2/14/63; W
Chancellorsville 5/3/63; Appt 3rd Sgt 1863; M Gettysburg 7/2/63; C Cashtown
7/4/63; R Pt. Lookout, Md. on taking oath of allegiance and joining U.S. service
1/24/64.

Phillips, Hiram C., Pvt Co. D – NLR.

Phillips, Jackson, Pvt Co. F 3/4/62 – W 8/64; roll for 10/31/64 shows absent W; C
Sailor's Creek 4/6/65; R Pt. Lookout, Md. 6/17/65; pension record says he S at
Appomattox C.H., but not on list of parolees with 50th Ga. Regt.

Phillips, John N., Pvt Co. H 3/4/62 – CSR entry shows he never joined the company and remained home in Colquitt Cty, Ga.; roll for 2/65 shows AWOL since 3/4/62; reported to have joined Co. C, 11ᵗʰ Ga. State Guards Cav 8/4/63; NLR.

Phillips, John R., Pvt Co. A 3/4/62 – Appt 2ⁿᵈ Cpl 3/23/64; C Cold Harbor 6/1/64; R Elmira, N.Y. 7/7/65.

Phillips, Joshua G., Pvt Co. E 3/4/62 – K Fox's Gap 9/14/62.

Phillips, Nelson P., Pvt Co. H 3/4/62 – Only CSR entry shows absent with leave at Macon, Ga. 5/62; NLR.

Pierce (Pearce), William Brown, Pvt Co. E 5/15/62 –Roll for 2/63 shows, AWOL in Thomas Co, Ga."; NLR.

Pittman, Arthur, Pvt Co. B 3/4/62 – NLR.

Pittman, John, Pvt Co. B 1862 – Disc by surgeon 5/62.

Pittman, Moses (N.), Pvt Co. B 5/15/62 – W Petersburg 6/21/64; DW Rich Hos 6/64; May 22, 1866 Savannah Daily News and Herald list of "Confederates buried in a field on the north bank of the Appomattox, a short distance from the village of Ellricks, and a mile from Petersburg," includes an "N P Pittman, 50ᵗʰ Ga."

Pittman, Noah, 3rd Sgt Co. B 3/4/62 – Appt 2ⁿᵈ Sgt 3/22/62; W Fox's Gap 9/14/62; Rich Hos 10/14/62; W Cold Harbor 6/2/64; roll for 2/65 shows AWOL at Ware Co, Ga."; NLR.

Pitts, James H., Pvt Co. A 3/4/62 – Roll for 2/65 shows "absent sick, has been absent without leave from Dec 1 1862 to Oct 15, 1864"; NLR.

Pitts, John, Pvt Co. A – Only CSR entry shows "sent sick to hospital at Savh 30ᵗʰ June"; NLR.

Plankinhorn (Plankinhand), George, Pvt Co. D 6/12/62 – Substitute for Daniel I. Jones; detailed as cook at Springfield, Ga. Hos 6/62; roll for 2/65 shows "detailed Whitesville, Ga."; NLR.

Platt, George W., 4ᵗʰ Sgt Co. E 3/4/62 – D Sav Hos 4/24/62.

Platt, Thomas, Pvt Co. E 3/4/62 – Appt 1ˢᵗ Cpl 2/64; rolls from 9/64 to 2/65 show absent sick; P Tallahassee, Fl 5/18/65.

Plymeal, Jacob, Pvt Co. H 3/4/62 – D Springfield, Ga. Hos (Pneumonia) 9/17/62; widow filed for CSP Thomas Cty, Ga. 1893.

Plymeal, Zion, Pvt Co. E 3/4/62 – Dropped out on march near Amissville, Va. 8/62; W (r upper thigh) Wilderness 5/6/64; roll for 2/65 shows absent sick; filed for CSP Colquitt Cty, Ga. 1896.

Plymeal, James C., Pvt, Co. E 3/4/62 – Only CSR entry of 7/62 shows "sick in hospital at Savh"; NLR.

Pope, William J., Pvt Co. E 3/4/62 – C Knoxville, Tn. 12/10/63; D (chronic diarrhea) Rock Island, Ill. 3/22/64; Bur Rock Island.

Powell, James G., 4ᵗʰ Cpl Co. F 3/4/62 – D (chronic dysentery) Lynchburg, Va. Hos 9/1/62; Bur Lot 178, Confederate Cem Lynchburg.

Powell, Jesse H., Pvt Co. F 5/14/62 – C Fox's Gap 9/14/62; E Aikens Landing, Va. 11/10/62; W Gettysburg (shoulder-flesh)/C 7/2/63; E David's Island, N.Y. 7/63; Petersburg Hos 9/15/63; disabled from field service and sent home to gather conscripts; roll for 2/65 shows absent sick; P Macon, Ga. 1865.

Powell, John J., Pvt Co. F 5/5/62 – Only CSR entry; NLR.

Powell, Orrin, Pvt Co. B – C Sailor's Creek 4/6/65; R Pt. Lookout, Md. 6/16/65.

Powell, William, 2ⁿᵈ Lt Co. F 3/4/62 – Res (disability) 6/29/62, effective 7/8/62.

Powell, William J., Pvt Co. F 3/4/62 – K Fox's Gap 9/14/62.

Powers, George, Pvt Co. A 3/4/62 – W Chancellorsville 5/3/63; DW Rich Hos 6/5/63; Bur Hollywood Cem, Rich.

Powers, William, Pvt Co. D 3/4/62 – S Appomattox Court House 4/9/65.

Preston, Thomas T. (P.), Pvt Co. E 3/4/62 – Appt Sgt 3/63; C Cashtown 7/4/63; D (chronic diarrhea) Pt. Lookout, Md. Hos 12/9/63; believed Bur Confederate Cem, Pt. Lookout, and later moved.

Price, William A., Regt Surg – NLR.

Price, Willis, Pvt Co. H 3/4/62 – W Fox's Gap 9/14/62; DW Danville, Va. 9/28/62.

Prince, John, Pvt Co. K 3/4/62 – C/P Warrenton, Va. 9/29/62; W (gunshot - l shoulder) Chancellorsville 5/3/63; K Cold Harbor 6/2/64.

Privett, Irvin, 4th Cpl Co. B 3/4/62 – W Chancellorsville 5/3/63; Appt 2nd Sgt 8/5/64; roll for 2/65 shows present; C Sailor's Creek 4/6/65; P Pt. Lookout, Md. 6/16/65; filed for CSP Charlton Cty, Ga. 1903.

Pue, William H., Asst Regt Surgeon 2/28/64 – S Appomattox Court House 4/9/65; P Richmond 5/15/65.

Purvis, Andrew J., Pvt Co. I 5/9/62 - K Fox's Gap 9/14/62.

Pyles, Francis M., Pvt. Co. E 8/22/62– W (hip) Gettysburg 7/2/63; C in Hos 7/5/63; E City Point, Va. 8/28/63; C Cedar Creek 10/19/64; R Pt. Lookout, Md. 6/16/65.

Pyles, Thomas J., Pvt Co. E 3/4/62 – W Gettysburg 7/2; C in Hos 7/5/63; E City Point, Va. 8/28/63; W (gunshot, l elbow) Cold Harbor 6/1/64; roll for 2/65 shows absent sick; filed for CSP Thomas Cty, Ga. 1889.

ROSTER Q, R

Radney, Henry G., Pvt Co. E 3/4/62 – M Fox's Gap 9/14/62; C 9/15/62; E Aikens Landing, Va. 10/6/62; Rich Hos 10/14/62; Appt Cpl; K Gettysburg 7/2/63; widow filed for CSP Calhoun Cty, Ga. 1911.

Radney (Radley), W.H., Pvt Co. K – S Tallahassee, Fl. 5/10/65; P Madison, Fl 5/20/65.

Rainey, Felix E., Pvt Co. K 5/13/62 –Roll for 2/65 shows present; P Thomasville, Ga. 5/16/65; widow filed for CSP Jefferson Cty, Fl. 1903.

Rambo, Thomas W., Pvt Co. K 3/4/62 – W (l shoulder, side & r arm)/C Fox's Gap 9/14/62; Frederick, Md. Hos 10/1/62; E City Point, Va. 4/12/63; Williamsburg, Va. Hos 4/12/63; roll for 2/65 shows "absent sick in Brooks Co, Ga."; filed for CSP Brooks Cty, Ga. 1889.

Raney, John R., Pvt Co. G 11/27/62 – W Chancellorsville 5/3/63; K Gettysburg 7/2/63.

Rawls, David P., Pvt Co. F 3/4/62 – Disc (disability) Sav 7/22/62.

Rawls, John C., Pvt Co. F 3/4/62 – W (gunshot - r thigh) Cold Harbor 6/1/64; Rich Hos 6/5/64; C Sailor's Creek 4/6/65; R Pt. Lookout, Md. 6/17/65.

Rawls, Joseph, Pvt Co. F 4/28/62 – Detailed as wagoner 5/62; D (pneumonia) Lynchburg, Va. Hos 4/29/64; Bur Lot 189, Confederate Cem, Lynchburg; widow filed for CSP Decatur Cty, Ga. 1891.

Rawls, T.J., Pvt Co. E 8/13/62 – D Winchester, Va. Hos 10/22/62; Bur Stonewall (Mount Hebron) Cem, Winchester, marker #157; marker reads "J.T. Roules."

Ray, Franklin, Pvt Co. I 8/23/62 – W (r arm – amputated) Chancellorsville 5/3/63; roll for 2/65 shows absent sick; widow filed for CSP Berrien Cty, Ga. 1911; pension record says he received Disc after loss of arm.

Ray, John, Pvt Co. I 9/4/62 – K Chancellorsville 5/3/63.

Redd, James J. Pvt. Co. H 3/4/62– Detailed to work on floating battery Sav 5/6/62; W (gunshot, r leg) Chancellorsville 5/3/63; on detached non-field service in 1864; Macon, Ga. Hos roll for 2/20/65 shows "on detail"; filed for CSP Macon Cty, Ga. 1896; pension record says he "was discharged at close of the war."

Reeves, Henry S., 2nd Sgt Co. F 3/4/62 – Elected Jr. 2nd Lt 7/18/62; W (slight – canister fragment to foot) 2nd Manassas Campaign 8/23/62; Elected 1st Lt 10/8/62; Appt Cpt 8/18/63; W (r elbow) 9/64 or 10/64; Charlottesville, Va. Hos 10/5/64;

Rich Hos 10/7/64; Res (disability), retired to Invalid Corps 12/23/64; S Macon, Ga. 4/20 or 4/21/65.

Register, Guilford A., Pvt Co. G 3/4/62 – Appt Cpl; C Cedar Creek 10/19/64; R Pt. Lookout, Md. 6/17/65.

Register, John F., Pvt Co. G 5/1/62 – Widow filed for CSP Cook Cty, Ga. 1938; pension record says he received a sick Frl about 1864 and was home sick at close of war.

Register, John Thomas, Pvt Co. G 5/1/62 – W (neck) Fox's Gap 9/14/62; Rich Hos 9/27/62; Appt 3rd Cpl 2/64; C Sailor's Creek 4/6/65; R Pt. Lookout, Md. 6/17/65; widow filed for CSP Clinch Cty, Ga. 1919.

Register, Miles, Pvt Co. G 3/4/62 – D Leesburg, Va. 9/23/62.

Register, Samuel W., Pvt Co. G 3/4/62 – W (hand - 3 fingers amputated) Second Manassas 8/30/62; detailed at Bde Hqs 1864; retired to Invalid Corps 10/11/64; detached with supply train, Army of Tennessee, at Catawba Bridge, S.C.; C 1865; R Charlotte, N.C. 5/3/65; filed for CSP Clinch Cty, Ga. 1889.

Reneau, Russell Ramsey, Pvt Co. E 3/4/62 – Appt 2nd Sgt 6/1/62; K Fox's Gap 9/14/62.

Rewis (Ruis), Calvin, Pvt Co. C 9/5/62 – D 1/16/63.

Rewis (Ruiss), Jackson J., Pvt Co. C 3/4/62 –D near Fredericksburg, Va. early 1863; widow filed for CSP Coffee Cty, Ga. 1891; pension record says he D as a result of exposure.

Rewis, James Jackson, Pvt Co. C 3/4/62 – W Fox's Gap 9/14/62; W Chancellorsville 5/3/63; W (gunshot – arm) Gettysburg 7/2/63; Danville, Va. Hos 7/17/63; C near Knoxville, Tn. 12/7/63; D (pneumonia) Knoxville Hos 1/13/64; Bur City Cemetery, Knoxville.

Rewis, (Ruis) John, Pvt Co. C 3/4/62 – D Winchester, Va. Hos 5/10/63.

Rewis, John, Pvt Co. G 4/27/62 – Roll for 2/63 shows absent, sent to Winchester, Va. sick 10/18/62; NLR; believed to be the "John Ruis" listed in the Stonewall (Mount Hebron) Cem register who D 10/31/62.

Rewis (Ruis), Malachi, Pvt Co. B 3/4/62 – D (Measles) Rich Hos 1/24/63; Bur Hollywood Cem, Rich.

Rewis (Ruis), Manning, Pvt Co. B 3/4/62 –Roll for 2/65 shows AWOL in Ware Cty, Ga.; NLR.

Reynolds, John C., Ord Sgt Co. E 3/4/62 – Disc, upon furnishing Joseph R. Shelton as Substitute, 9/9/62.

Reynolds, William H., Pvt Co. F 3/4/62 – D Winchester, Va. Hos 10/17/62; Bur Stonewall (Mount Hebron) Cem, Winchester, marker #150.

Rich, Isaac, Pvt Co. F 5/4/62 – D Gordonsville, Va. Hos prior to 7/63.

Rich, James E., Pvt Co. F 3/4/62 – W (gunshot - head) Spotsylvania C.H. between 5/10 and 5/15/64; Rich Hos 5/15/64; C Sailor's Creek 4/6/65; R Pt. Lookout, Md. 6/3/65.

Rich, Jordan G., Pvt Co. F 5/13/62 – D at home in Decatur Cty, Ga. 4/20/63.

Rich, Washington, Pvt Co. F 3/4/62 –Roll for 2/63 shows "absent Left on the road while on the march to Maryland. Not heard from since"; NLR.

Richardson, Francis M., Pvt Co. I 5/14/62 – D (chronic diarrhea) Staunton, Va. Hos 10/29/62; Bur Thornrose Cem, Staunton; widow filed for CSP Berrien Cty, Ga. 1891; pension record says he dropped out sick on the march into Md. in 1862.

Richardson, William H., Pvt Co. I 3/4/62 –Roll for 12/31/62 shows "absent left at Bull Run sick Aug 31st"; roll for 2/63 shows absent sick; widow filed for CSP Berrien Cty, Ga. 1891; pension record says he D on 8/31/62 at "Bull Run".

Ricketson, Ivey, Pvt Co. C 3/4/62 – K Fox's Gap 9/14/62; widow filed for CSP Coffee Cty, Ga. 1891.

Ricketson, James, Pvt Co. C 3/4/62 –Roll for 12/31/62 shows "absent. Left at

Thoroughfare Gap Aug 28"; C between 8/28/62 - 10/2/62; P Leesburg, Va. 10/2/62; NLR.

Ricks, Aaron G., Pvt Co. C 3/4/62 – Roll for 12/31/62 shows "absent. Left sick near Rapidan River"; 60 day Frl from Gordonsville, Va. Hos for "extreme debility from pneumonia" 3/3/63; NLR.

Ricks, James W., Pvt Co. F 3/4/62 – C Fox's Gap 9/14/62; E Aikens Landing, Va. 10/62; Rich Hos 10/9/62; W (hip & 1 hand – finger "shot off") Ft. Sanders 11/29/63; C 12/3 Knoxville, Tn.; R Rock Island, Ill. 6/19/65; filed for CSP Mitchell Cty, Ga. 1897.

Ricks, John, Pvt Co. C 3/4/62 – K Gettysburg 7/2/63.

Ricks, Samuel, Pvt Co. F 3/4/62 – D 4/23/62.

Riggins, William W., Pvt Co. A 3/4/62 – Disc (disability) 6/9/62; widow filed for CSP Pierce Cty, Ga. 1908; pension record says he enlisted in Co. G, 4th Regt. Ga. Cav 1862, and Disc (disability) 5/63.

Riggs, William, Pvt Co. G 3/4/62 – D (typhoid fever) Rich 9/9/63; Bur Hollywood Cem, Rich.

Roberds, Reuben Thomason "Tompy", 1st Sgt Co. D 3/4/62 – Appt Regt Adj 3/63; W (r knee)/C Ft. Sanders 11/29/63; (r leg amputated above knee); DW Knoxville, Tn. Hos 12/3/63; Bur (unknown grave) Knoxville.

Roberts, Daniel (David) P., Pvt Co. C 3/4/62 –Roll for 2/65 shows AWOL since 8/10/64; widow filed for CSP Coffee Cty, Ga. 1911; pension record says he came home on sick Frl in 1864, with liver and kidney disease and was home at close of war.

Roberts, Henry J., Pvt Co. E 3/4/62 – Disc (under age-16) 12/16/62; NLR.

Roberts, Henry M., Pvt Co. F 3/4/62 – C Cold Harbor 6/1/64; E Aikens Landing, Va. 3/14/65; P Quincy, Fl. 5/11/65; filed for CSP Miller Cty, Ga. 1903; pension record says he was paroled 3/65 and sent home.

Roberts, Isham, Pvt Co. G 3/4/62 - Appt 4th Cpl 2/64; W (slight)/C Cedar Creek 10/19/64; R Pt. Lookout, Md. 6/17/65; widow filed for CSP Clinch Cty, Ga. 1918.

Roberts, John, Pvt. Co. G 4/27/62 – K Fox's Gap 9/14/62; widow filed for CSP Coffee Cty, Ga. 1891.

Roberts, John L., Pvt Co. A 3/4/62 – W (side & arm) Chancellorsville 5/3/63; DW Rich Hos 5/27/63.

Roberts, Mark, Pvt Co. G 4/27/62 – C Cedar Creek 10/19/64; reportedly D "in service"; NLR.

Roberts, Moses, Pvt Co. G 3/4/62 – W Fox's Gap 9/14/62; Frl home 30 days Rich Hos 10/3/62.

Roberts, William, Pvt Co. D 3/4/62 – Detailed as wagoner 5-6/62; W (1 leg – flesh)/C Cedar Creek 10/19/64; roll for 2/65 shows absent wounded; P Madison, Fl. 5/20/65; filed for CSP Franklin Cty, Fl. 1902; pension record says he was P Chatham Cty, Ga. 12/24/64; S Tallahassee, Fl. 5/10/65.

Roberts, William T., 4th Cpl Co. G 3/4/62 – W Fox's Gap 9/14/62; Elected 2nd Lt (date Unk); D 5/14/64.

Robinson, James J., Pvt Co. H 3/4/62 – M Gettysburg 7/2/63; C 7/3/63; D (chronic diarrhea) Ft. Delaware, Del. 10/25/63; Bur Ft. Delaware.

Robinson, John N. (A.), Pvt Co. B 3/4/62 – Entry for 3/4/62 roll shows "Assigned to my command. Absent."; NLR.

Rodgers, Francis M., Pvt Co. E 4/22/62 – D Rich Hos (chronic diarrhea) 3/1/63; Bur Oakwood Cem, Rich.

Roe, Ezekiel, Pvt Co. I 3/4/62 – Des 3/2/65; took oath of allegiance to U.S. Govt. and furnished trans to Jacksonville, Fl.

Roe, John, Pvt Co. I 3/4/62 – D 5/25/62.

Roe, Jordan, Pvt Co. I 3/4/62 – D Culpeper, Va. Hos 9/1/62.

Roe, Josiah, Pvt Co. I 3/4/62 – D (pneumonia) in Ga. 1/1/64; widow filed for CSP Irwin Cty, Ga. 1891.

Roe, Matthew, Pvt Co. I 3/4/62 – C Sailor's Creek 4/6/65; R Pt. Lookout, Md. 6/30/65; filed for CSP Berrien Cty, Ga. 1910.

Roe, Samuel B., Pvt Co. E 3/4/62 – Des 2/10/65; took oath of allegiance to U.S. Govt. and furnished trans to Pittsburgh, Pa. 2/12/65.

Rogers, Thomas J., Pvt Co. D 3/4/62 –W (l arm, r leg) Gettysburg 7/2/63; Hos (r leg amputated) 7/3/63; C in Hos 7/5/63; E City Point, Va. 3/16/64; Rich Hos 3/20/64; roll for 2/65 shows "absent-disabled"; P Thomasville, Ga. 5/26/65; filed for CSP Chatham Cty, Ga. 1879; pension record says that while placing obstructions in Sav River he contracted a disease, which resulted in loss of l eye.

Roland (Rollins), Thomas, Pvt Co. H 3/4/62 – K Spotsylvania C.H. 5/13/64.

Rouse, Robert O., Pvt Co. I 8/23/62 – W (face, both cheek bones - damaged eyesight) Ft. Sanders 11/29/63; C near Knoxville, Tn. 1/5/64; E James River, Va. 3/27/65; filed for CSP Berrien Cty, Ga. 1901.

Rowland (Roland), Richard, Pvt Co. B 3/4/62 – D Rich Hos 10/30/62; Bur Hollywood Cem, Rich.

Rowland (Roland), Richard L., Pvt Co. B 3/4/62 – W Fox's Gap 9/14/62; D (typhoid fever) Staunton, Va. Hos 10/31/62; Bur Thornrose Cem, Staunton.

Rowland (Roland), Robert Perry, Sr., Pvt Co. B 5/12/62 – D Rich Hos 6/19/64; Bur Hollywood Cem, Rich.

Rowland (Roland), Thomas, Pvt Co. H 5/13/62 –Roll for 2/63 shows "Absent. Sent to hospital Nov 25th 1862"; NLR; reported to have D.

Rowland (Roland), William N., Pvt Co. B 3/4/62 – W Fox's Gap 9/14/62; Hos 10/62; W Chancellorsville 5/3/63; DW Rich Hos 5/26/63; Bur Hollywood Cem, Rich.

Royal, Robert, Pvt. Co. H 3/4/62– K Chancellorsville 5/3/63.

Ruis, John, Pvt Co. I – Not in CSR; Bur Stonewall (Mount Hebron) Cem, Winchester, Va., marker #190; Cem register reads "John Ruis, Co. I, 50th Ga. Died Oct. 31, 1862"; believed to be the same as "John Rewis", Co. G, who was sent to Winchester Hos sick 10/18/62, and D 10/31/62.

Royal, Thomas A., Pvt Co. H 3/4/62 – D Whitesville, Ga. Hos 7/7/62.

Rutherford, Babel Jackson, Pvt Co. I 8/23/62 – Detailed as Bde wagoner 62; detached as shoemaker in Columbus, Ga. 11/30/63 – 1/2/64; S Appomattox CH 4/9/65.

Ryals (Ryalls), William, Pvt Co. G 3/4/62 – C Gettysburg 7/3/63; E City Point, Va. 4/27/64; C Cedar Creek 10/19/64; D Pt. Lookout, Md. 6/11/65; believed Bur Confederate Cem, Pt. Lookout.

Ryan, William (W.M.), Pvt Co. B 7/15/62 – Substitute for Peter Shone; detailed to Div Provost Guard in 64/65; Des 4/14/65; took oath of allegiance to U.S. Govt. and furnished trans to Philadelphia, Pa.

ROSTER S

Sapp, Homer, Pvt Co. F 3/4/62 – W Chancellorsville 5/3/63; C Sailor's Creek 4/6/65; R Pt. Lookout, Md. 6/19/65; widow filed for CSP Decatur Cty, Ga. 1922.

Sargent, J.W., Pvt – Des 2/10/65.

Sears, Burrell, Pvt Co. C 8/28/62 – Roll for 2/63 shows present; NLR.

Sears, Hiram, Pvt Co. G 3/4/62 – W (gunshot, head – r jawbone shot in two) Fox's Gap 9/14/62; roll for 2/65 shows AWOL since 10/15/63; filed for CSP Hillsborough Cty, Fl. 1906; pension record says he was home on sick Frl at close of war.

Sears, James, Pvt Co. G 3/4/62 – W (chin) Fox's Gap 9/14/62; Rich Hos 9/27/62; NLR.

Sears, Marion, Pvt Co. C 8/28/62 – D 11/19/62.

Sego, John T., Pvt Co. D 3/4/62 – Appt 2nd Cpl 8/62; W (shoulder) Chancellorsville 5/3/63; Appt 5th Sgt 10/63; W (knee)/C Wilderness 5/6/64; R Elmira, N.Y. 6/19/65; filed for CSP Orange Cty, Fl. 1902.

Selph (Self), Samuel, Pvt Co. 1862 – S Tallahassee, Fl. 5/10/65; P Thomasville, Ga. 5/22/65.

Sellers, William L, Pvt Co. E 8/12/62 – K Wilderness 5/6/64.

Selman, O.W., Pvt Co. D 3/4/62 – Detailed as wagoner 5-6/62; K (gunshot – forehead) Ft. Sanders 11/29/63; widow filed for CSP Banks Cty, Ga. 1891.

Senterfit, Levi, Pvt Co. D 3/4/62 – W Chancellorsville 5/3/63; W (1 arm torn off below elbow-artillery) Gettysburg 7/2/63; W Cedar Creek 10/19/64; roll for 2/65 shows absent-disabled; P Thomasville, Ga. 5/10/65; filed for CSP Lafayette Cty, Fl. 1899.

Senterfit, S.L., Pvt Co. D 3/4/62 – Not in CSR; disabled 3/64.

Senterfit, Samuel S., Pvt Co. D 3/4/62 – W Chancellorsville 5/3/63; W (r hand – lost little finger & part of hand) near Berryville, Va. 9/18/64; roll for 2/65 show AWOL; P Thomasville, Ga. 5/10/65; reported to be home on W Frl at close of war.

Shanks, James, Pvt Co. D 3/4/62 – D 11/11/62.

Sharpe, William H., Pvt Co. K 3/4/62 – Elected 2nd Lt 6/18/62; Appt 1st Lt 7/30/63; W (shell fragment, r thigh) Ft. Sanders 11/29/63; C Cedar Creek 10/19/64; R Ft. Delaware, Del. 6/17/65; filed for CSP Brevard Cty, Fl. 1907.

Sheffield, Pliny, Cpt Co. K 3/4/62 – Appt Maj 9/16/63, effective 7/31/63; Appt LtC 12/21/63; W (gunshot r arm – amputated at shoulder) Wilderness 5/6/64; Res (disability) 9/24/64, effective 11/28/64; filed for CSP Brooks Cty, Ga. 1879.

Sheffield, Simeon B., Pvt Co. E 3/4/62 – W/C Fox's Gap 9/14/62; took oath of allegiance to U.S. Govt. 9/62.

Sheldon, James Rodes, Sr., Pvt Co. E 3/4/62 – Detached as Regt Commissary Sgt 2/64; S Appomattox C.H. 4/9/65.

Shelton, Joseph R., Pvt Co. E 9/9/62 – Substitute for John C. Reynolds; Des 9/10/62 Frederick, Md.

Shepherd, F. (E.) H., Pvt Co. I 8/29/62 – Detailed as Bde wagoner 6/64-8/64; P Greensboro, N.C. 5/1/65.

Shone, Peter, Pvt Co. B 3/4/62 – Disc upon furnishing William Ryan as substitute7/15/62.

Shone, William J., 1st Sgt Co. B 3/4/62 – Elected 2nd Lt 3/22/62; Res (disability)10/31/62.

Shuman, Andrew, Pvt Co. E – Not in CSR; D Frederick, Md. Hos 9/25/62; Bur Mount Olivet Cem, Frederick; marker reads "PVT Andrew Shuman Co G 50 GA INF CSA SEP 25, 1862."

Shuman, Emanuel, Pvt Co. E 3/4/62 – W (gunshot)/C Fox's Gap 9/14/62; DW Frederick, Md. Hos 9/24/62; Bur Mount Olivet Cem, Frederick.

Shuman, George H., Pvt Co. E 3/4/62 – D Sav Hos 11/1/62.

Simpson, John, Pvt Co. H 5/16/62 – Appt 4th Sgt 1/63; NLR.

Simpson, Joseph Pvt Co. H 5/16/62 – Appt 5th Sgt 1863; C Sailor's Creek 4/6/65; R Pt. Lookout, Md. 6/20/65; filed for CSP Thomas Cty, Ga. 1901; pension record says he S at Appomattox C.H., but not on list of parolees with 50th Ga. Regt.

Sineath, Henry J., Pvt Co. I 8/23/62 – D Rich Hos 5/17/63; Bur Hollywood Cem, Rich.

Sirmans, John, Pvt Co. G 4/27/62 – D Sav 6/21/62.

Sirmons, John J., 1st Cpl Co. G 3/4/62 – Elected 2nd Lt 5/12/63; Appt 1st Lt 5/25/64; K Cold Harbor 6/3/64.

Sirmans, Lewis, Pvt Co. G – Reported to have D; NLR.

Sirmans, Lyman A. Pvt Co. G 4/27/62 – K Fox's Gap 9/14/62.

Skinner, Randall Pvt Co. G 3/4/62 – Des 3/19/62.

Skipper, Joel, Pvt Co. D 5/9/62 – D (bronchitis) Rich Hos 12/5/62; Bur Hollywood
    Cem, Rich.

Skipper, Stephen, Pvt Co. D 3/4/62 – W Chancellorsville 5/3/63; W (r thigh)
    Gettysburg 7/2/63; W (arm – amputated above elbow) Wilderness 5/6/64; roll
    for 2/65 shows absent-disabled; filed for CSP Coffee Cty, Ga. 1880.

Slave, J. Pvt – Not in CSR; Bur Stonewall (Mount Hebron) Cem, Winchester, Va.,
    marker #203; Cem register reads "J. Slave, 50th Ga. Died Nov. 2, 1862."

Sloan, David, Pvt Co. F 3/4/62 – W/C Fox's Gap 9/14/62; DW Frederick, Md. Hos
    9/27/62; Bur Mount Olivet Cem, Frederick.

Slots, J., Pvt Co. K – W Chancellorsville 5/3/63; NLR.

Smith, Allen Nichols, Pvt Co. G 3/4/62 – Enlisted in militia 5/61; enlisted in Co. G;
    furnished substitute (date Unk); widow filed for CSP Pierce Cty, Ga. 1920;
    pension record says he served with Regt about eight months.

Smith, Albert C., Pvt Co. B 3/4/62 – K Chancellorsville 5/3/63.

Smith, Alfred A., 1st Lt Co. C 3/4/62 – Elected Cpt 12/21/63; C Cedar Creek 10/19/64; R
    Ft. Delaware, Del. 6/17/65.

Smith, Alfred (Allred), Pvt Co. H 3/4/62 – D Macon, Ga. Hos 5/2/62.

Smith, Benjamin F., Pvt Co. F 3/4/62 – K Fox's Gap 9/14/62.

Smith, Berrien, Pvt Co. C 3/4/62 – D Macon, Ga. 5/1/62.

Smith, Henry, Pvt Co. C 3/4/62 – K Fox's Gap 9/14/62.

Smith, Hiram D., Pvt Co. C 3/4/62 – NLR.

Smith, Isham M., Pvt Co. E – Appt 1st Cpl 9/14/62; 2nd Sgt 2/64; 1st Sgt 1864; C
    Farmville 4/6/65; R Pt. Lookout, Md. 6/19/65.

Smith, J.R.S., Pvt Co. I – NLR; filed for CSP Al.

Smith, J. W., Cpl Co. E – W Gettysburg 7/2/63; NLR.

Smith, Joel, Pvt Co. B 3/4/62 – Disc (disability-mental) 7/10/62.

Smith, John W., Pvt Co. G 3/4/62 – C/P Warrenton, Va. 9/29/62; Appt 1st Cpl 6/63; C
    Ft. Sanders 11/29/63; E Rock Island, Ill. 3/13/65; Rich Hos 3/25/65; Frl 60
    days 3/30/65; at home on Frl at close of war; filed for CSP Berrien Cty, Ga.
    1903.

Smith, Simeon J., Pvt Co. G 4/27/62 – D near Ft. Brown, Ga. 6/25/62.

Smith, William, Pvt Co. C 3/4/62 – W Fox's Gap 9/14/62; Rich Hos 10/7/62; roll for
    2/65 shows present; widow filed for CSP Coffee Cty, Ga. 1911.

Smith, William A., Pvt Co. I 5/14/62 – Appt QM Sgt 6/19/62; Elected Jr. 2nd Lt 10/20/62;
    Appt Cpt 2/64; C Sailor's Creek 4/6/65; R Johnson's Island, Oh. 6/20/65.

Smith, William N., Pvt Co. B 5/3/62 – Roll for 12/64 shows "absent left sick on the
    March in Sept 62. Supposed to have died"; widow filed for CSP Coffee Cty,
    Ga. 1891; pension record says he was W in 1862, sent to the Richmond Hos
    and "never heard of after and supposed to be dead."

Solomon, James, Pvt Co. I 3/4/62 – D (typhoid fever) Rich Hos 12/7/62; Bur
    Hollywood Cem, Rich.

Spears, John A., Pvt Co. E 8/22/62 – Detailed in Div Provost Guard 1864-65; S
    Appomattox CH 4/9/65 (parole list shows a "Jas. Speers").

Spell, Lewis Franklin, Pvt Co. B 3/4/62 – W (r breast & lung) Cedar Creek 10/19/64;
    roll for 2/65 shows AWOL in Appling Cty, Ga."; NLR.

Spence, John Middleton, Cpt Co. C 3/4/62 – Appt Maj 12/21/63; roll for 2/28/65 shows
    "leave of absence Gen. Lee"; enroute to command at close of war; widow
    filed for CSP Nassau Cty, Fl. 1911.

Spikes, Benjamin S., Pvt Co. G 3/4/62 – D (smallpox) Danville, Va. 2/14/63; Bur
    Confederate Cem, Spotsylvania, Va.

Spikes, Isaac, Pvt Co. G 3/4/62 – Left at Leesburg, Va. Hos on march to Md. 9/1/62; C

10/2/62; P Leesburg 10/2/62; NLR.

Spikes, John, Sr., Pvt Co. C 8/28/62 – W (r arm) Chancellorsville 5/3/63; roll for 2/65 shows AWOL since 2/2/64; earlier rolls show disabled; filed for CSP Coffee Cty, Ga. 1896; pension record says W Petersburg 6/20/64 and Disc (disability) 1864.

Spivey, Matthew, 4th Sgt Co. C 3/4/62 – Appt 2nd Sgt 2/64; reduced to Pvt 11/1/64; C Sailor's Creek 4/6/65; R Pt. Lookout, Md. 6/19/65.

Stallings, Timothy W., Pvt Co. K 3/20/62 – W (gunshot, r elbow) Cedar Creek 10/19/64; on W Frl at end of the war; P Thomasville, Ga. 5/26/65; filed for CSP Lowndes Cty, Ga.1887.

Stalvey, Moses, Pvt Co. G 11/26/62 – C Gettysburg 7/3/63; R Pt. Lookout, Md. upon taking oath of allegiance and joining U.S. service 1/30/64; widow filed for CSP Hillsborough Cty Fl. 1909.

Stanfield, Allen J., Pvt Co. B 3/4/62 – Appt 5th Sgt 1/1/63; D (pneumonia) Lynchburg, Va. Hos 11/2/62; Bur Lot 182, Confederate Cem Lynchburg.

Stanfill (Stanfield), Joseph J. Pvt Co. E 3/4/62 – Detailed as nurse Sav Hos 5/62 or 6/62; W (head) Fox's Gap/C 9/14/62; Frederick, Md. Hos 9/17/62; P Wash., D.C. 9/29/62; C Ft. Sanders 11/29/63; D (pneumonia) Rock Island, Ill. 5/21/64.

Starling, James Thomas Tharpe, Pvt Co. G 3/4/62 – D (pneumonia) Rich Hos 1/5/63; Bur Hollywood Cem, Rich.

Starling, Raymond H.M., Pvt Co. G 3/4/62 – Sav Hos 7/62; roll for 2/63 shows sick Frl 7/21/62; roll for 2/65 shows AWOL since 10/10/62; NLR.

Staten, Quarterman Baker, 1st Lt Co. G 3/4/62 – Elected Cpt after death of Cpt O'Steen 10/25/62; Res commission due to illness (typhoid fever) 3/20/63; Elected 2nd Lt 4/9/63; 1st Lt 4/27/63; Appt Cpt after death of Cpt Burkhalter 7/31/63; W Cedar Creek 10/19/64; Staunton, Va. Hos 10/19/64; 12/30/64 Hos report shows "Sent to Hospital wounded by Brig. Surg. Furloughed from there to Stockton, Ga."; roll for 2/28/65 shows "absent without leave P.O. Clinch Co., Ga. Name reported to Conscript Bureau"; P Ga. 1865.

Stephens, George Washington, Pvt Co. I 3/4/62 – W (foot) Gettysburg 7/2/63; C 7/3/63; Ft. Delaware, Del. Prison 8/22/63; E James River, Va. 2/21/65; NLR.

Stephens, James E., Pvt Co. C 8/28/62 – W (1 arm – amputated above elbow) Chancellorsville 5/3/63; Frl home to Quitman, Ga. 60 days 6/6/63; roll for 12/64 shows "absent without leave since 26 Feb 1864. Disabled"; filed for CSP Coffee Cty, Ga. 1879.

Stephens, Jesse N., Pvt Co. K 3/4/62 – W (head, shell fragment – lost sight 1 eye) Gettysburg 7/2/63; detailed as nurse Rich Hos 8/24/64; P Thomasville, Ga. 5/21/65; filed for CSP Suwannee Cty, Fl. 1896; pension record says he was Disc Petersburg, Va. 1865.

Stephenson, David, Pvt Co. E 8/13/62 – W (gunshot, lower groin - both hips) Chancellorsville 5/3/63; detailed in Bde QM Dept. 1864; S Appomattox C.H. 4/9/65; filed for CSP Lafayette Cty, Fl. 1890.

Stephenson, Ezekiel, Pvt Co. E 7/31/62 – D (pneumonia) "in camp" 11/22/62.

Stewart, Colquitt, Pvt Co. A 3/4/62 – K Spotsylvania C.H. 5/12/64.

Stewart, Columbus M.D., Pvt Co. E 3/4/62 – Disc upon furnishing John Maloney as substitute 8/25/62.

Stewart, James, Pvt Co. A 3/4/62 – D Fernandina, Fl 1862; Bur Fernandina, Fl.

Stewart, Orren, Pvt Co. F 3/4/62 – D Thomas Cty, Ga. 6/29/62.

Stewart, Thomas J., Pvt Co. F 3/4/62 – W (severe concussion - artillery shell) Gettysburg 7/2/63; C in Hos 7/5/63; E Pt. Lookout, Md. 2/18/65; P Tallahassee, Fl. 5/18/65.

Stokes (Stocks), F.L., Pvt Co. D 3/4/62 – D Sav 6/11/62.

Stokes (Stocks), Lewis A., Pvt Co. B 3/4/62 – Entry on roll for 3/4/62 shows "Assigned to my command. Absent."; NLR.

Stone, George R., Pvt Co. A 3/4/62 – K Fox's Gap 9/14/62.

Stone, James J., Pvt Co. C 3/4/62– W Gettysburg 7/2/63; roll for 2/65 shows AWOL since 2/26/65; P Thomasville, Ga. 5/17/65; filed for CSP Coffee Cty, Ga. 1904; pension record says he was home on sick Frl at close of war.

Stone, John W., Pvt Co. G 8/10/62 – C Ft. Sanders 11/29/63; P Rock Island, Ill. upon taking oath of allegiance to U.S. Govt. and joining U.S. Navy 1/6/64.

Stone, William, Pvt Co. C 3/4/62 – C/P Leesburg, Va. 9/62; W (head) Chancellorsville 5/3/63; W Cold Harbor 6/3/64; Danville, Va. Hos 6/4/64; Frl 6/17/64; P Lynchburg, Va. 4/13/65; filed for CSP Coffee Cty, Ga. 1905; pension record says he was "with wagons" at the surrender.

Stone, William H., Pvt Co. A 5/22/62 – Enlisted as Pvt in Co. K, 5th Regt Ga. State Troops 10/6/61; Disc (disability) 12/25/61; enlisted in Co. A, 50th Ga.; W/C Fox's Gap 9/14/62; E Aikens Landing, Va. 11/10/62; Appt 3rd Sgt 12/31/62; W (1 ankle & side) Gettysburg 7/2/63; C in Hos 7/5; P David's Island, N.Y. 9/63; C Cedar Creek 10/19/64; R Pt. Lookout, Md. 6/19/65; filed for CSP Baker Cty, Fl. 1907.

Stout, Allen, Pvt Co. F 3/4/62 – D Strasburg, Va. 11/30/62.

Strange, Edward (Edmond), Pvt Co. F 3/4/62 – W Chancellorsville 5/3/63; C Ft. Sanders 11/29/63; sent to Camp Chase, Oh. 12/15/63; roll for 2/65 shows "absent prisoner of war"; NLR.

Strickland, Abraham, Pvt Co. A 3/4/62 – Des 3/10/65; took oath of allegiance to U.S. Govt. and furnished trans to St Augustine, Fl. 3/18/65.

Strickland, Charles W., Pvt Co. G 3/4/62 – Frl from Danville, Va. Hos 7/19/63 (debilitas) roll for 2/65 shows AWOL since 10/15/63; NLR.

Strickland, Henry H., Pvt Co. K 3/4/62 – W Gettysburg 7/2/63; Frl from Rich Hos for 30 days (pneumonia) 7/14/64; roll for 2/65 shows AWOL since 8/14/64; S Tallahassee, Fl. 5/10/65; P Thomasville, Ga. 5/18/65.

Strickland, Joel P., Pvt Co. K 3/4/62 – W Chancellorsville 5/3/63; C Sailor's Creek 4/6/65; R Pt. Lookout, Md. 6/19/65; filed for CSP Levy Cty, Fl. 1902.

Strickland, Martin R., Pvt Co. G 3/4/62 – D (pneumonia) Rich Hos 3/22/63; Bur Hollywood Cem, Rich.

Strickland, Matthew T., Pvt Co. G 3/4/62 – W (compound fracture-gunshot)/C Fox's Gap 9/14/62; DW Frederick, Md. Hos 12/4/62; Bur Mount Olivet Cem, Frederick.

Strickland, Reddin Simpson, Pvt Co. K 3/4/62 – D (typhoid fever) Rich Hos 11/5/62; Bur Hollywood Cem, Rich; widow filed for CSP Berrien Cty, Ga. 1897.

Studstill, John, Pvt Co. I 3/4/62 – Disc (illness) 6/30/64.

Studstill, William A. (R.), 1st Cpl Co. K 3/4/62 – D Camp Davis, Ga. 4/2/62.

Suber, George T., Pvt Co. H 3/4/62 – Detailed as wagoner 7/25/62; roll for 2/65 shows absent sick since 8/24/64; NLR.

Summerall, Elhannon, Pvt Co. B 3/4/62 – Disc (disability-paralysis of lower extremity) 2/28/63.

Summerall, J.M., Pvt Co G – Not in CSR; D Frederick, Md. Hos 9/19/62; Bur Mount Olivet Cem, Frederick; marker reads "PVT J M Summerall Co G 50 GA INF CSA SEP 19, 1862."

Sutton, J.L., Pvt Co. I 8/23/62 – Disc upon furnishing John R. Langdale as substitute 10/7/62; widow filed for CSP Cook Cty, Ga. 1926; pension record says failing health resulted in his Disc.

Swatts (Swartz), Glen B., Pvt Co. F 3/4/62 – W Ft. Sanders 11/29/63; C near Knoxville 12/5/63; P New Orleans, La. 5/23/65.

Sweat, Nathan F., Pvt Co. B 3/4/62 – W 1862; DW Rich Hos 12/30/62; Bur Oakwood Cem, Rich.

Sweet, William B. (D.) A., Pvt Co. F 3/4/62 – NLR.

Swilley, Francis M., Pvt Co. D 5/11/62 – W (gunshot, face – 1 eye shot out) Chancellorsville 5/3/63; C Sailor's Creek 4/6/65; R Pt. Lookout, Md. 6/19/65; filed for CSP Lowndes Cty, Ga. 1888.

Swilley, Jack, Pvt Co. D 5/11/62 – W Fox's Gap 9/14/62; W Chancellorsville 5/3/63; K Gettysburg 7/2/63; widow filed for CSP Lowndes Cty, Ga. 1905.

Swin, J., Pvt Co. C – W Chancellorsville 5/3/63; NLR.

ROSTER T

Taff, Jasper J., Pvt Co. C 3/4/62 – C near Appomattox 4/8/65; P Burkeville Junction, Va. between 4/14 and 4/17/65; filed for CSP Coffee Cty, Ga. 1904; pension record says he was C "a few hours before the surrender."

Taff, Robert, Pvt Co. C 3/4/62 – Roll for 2/65 shows AWOL; NLR.

Talbot, A.J., Pvt Co. C – NLR; may have joined 18th Ga. Inf.

Tanner, Green, Pvt Co. C 3/4/62 – NLR.

Tanner, John B., Pvt Co. C 5/3/62 – NLR.

Tanner, Mitchell, Pvt Co. C 8/29/62 – Admitted to general Hos, Farmville, Va. with tuberculosis 11/15/62; Hos roll for 5/9/63 shows "Furlough 30 days to rep. here"; NLR.

Taylor, Eaton, Pvt Co. B 3/4/62 – NLR.

Taylor, J.N., Pvt Co. E – C Fox's Gap 9/14/62; E Aiken's Landing, Va. 11/10/62; NLR.

Taylor, John, Pvt Co. C 10/17/62 – Roll for 2/63 shows present; widow filed for CSP Ware Cty, Ga.1891; pension record says he D (measles) Dalton, Ga. Hos 1/7/63.

Taylor, John W., Pvt Co. D 5/9/62 – Substitute for James O.A. Howell; C Fox's Gap 9/14/62; E Aikens Landing, Va. 10/6/62; detailed as ambulance driver & wagoner 1863; roll for 2/65 shows "present. Brigade wagoner – extra duty"; NLR.

Taylor, Seaborn, Pvt Co. I 3/4/62 – NLR.

Taylor, Thomas L., Pvt Co. I 3/4/62 – P Thomasville, Ga. 5/24/65; filed for CSP Berrien Cty, Ga. 1919; pension record says he was Disc (disability) Rich 2/63.

Taylor, William, Pvt Co. C 3/4/62 – K Chancellorsville 5/3/63.

Teston, Henry J. (G.), Pvt Co. C 3/4/62 – W Fox's Gap 9/14/62; Rich Hos 10/18/62; W Chancellorsville 5/3/63; C Gettysburg 7/3/63; E Aikens Landing, Va. 2/24/65; Frl 30 days Rich Hos 3/6/65; NLR.

Teston, James, Pvt Co. C 5/9/62 – W (face-gunshot) Fox's Gap 9/14/62; C Sharpsburg 9/28/62; P Aikens Landing, Va. 10/12/62; Rich Hos 10/17/62; roll for 2/65 shows "absent. Detailed in Hospital in Richmond July 1863"; filed for CSP Appling Cty, Ga. 1897; pension record says he received Frl 3/6/65 and was home at S.

Teston, Ruel Benjamin, Pvt Co. C 5/9/62 – On ten day sick Frl 8/19/62; roll for 2/65 shows AWOL since 8/22/62; filed for CSP Sumter Cty, Fl. 1903; pension record says he was ruptured while working on blockade in Sav River 1862; Disc (disability) Macon, Ga. 8/12/64.

Thigpen, Stafford G., Pvt Co. C 5/9/62 – K Fox's Gap 9/14/62.

Thomas, Benjamin, Pvt Co. C 3/4/62 – D 1863 or 1864; roll for 2/63 shows "absent. Sick in hospital"; Register of Deceased Soldiers shows receipt filed in 1864.

Thomas, Colin (Colan), Pvt Co. G 3/4/62 – W/C Fox's Gap 9/14/62; E Aikens Landing, Va. 10/6/62; Rich Hos 11/62; W (gunshot - r thigh) Cedar Creek 10/19/64; Charlottesville Hos 10/24/64; Des 1/18/65; took oath of allegiance to U.S. Govt. and furnished trans to Jacksonville, Fl. 1/24/65.

Thomas, Edmund, 4th Sgt Co. A 3/4/62 –C Frederick, Md. 9/12/62; D Ft. Delaware, Del. 9/25/62.

Thomas, Edward T., Pvt Co. C 3/4/62 – D 3/4/63; Rich Hos Surgeon report shows "Brought from the cars dead."

Thomas, Hardy, Pvt Co. D 4/10/62 –Roll for 2/65 shows present; filed for CSP Hillsborough Cty, Fl. 1902; pension record says W (gunshot, l side) (date Unk) and S Appomattox C.H. 4/9/65, but not on list of parolees with 50th Ga. Regt.

Thomas, Jackson, Pvt Co. A 3/4/62 - C Frederick, Md. 9/19/62; E Aikens Landing, Va. 10/6/62; D Rich Hos 10/8/62; Bur Hollywood Cem, Rich; widow filed for CSP Pierce Cty, Ga. 1891; pension record says he D (typhoid fever).

Thomas, James F., Pvt Co. A 3/4/62 – K Fox's Gap 9/14/62.

Thomas, James R., Pvt Co. A 3/4/62 – K Chancellorsville 5/3/63; Bur Lot 188, Confederate Cem, Lynchburg, Va.

Thomas, John L., Pvt Co. A 3/4/62 – NLR.

Thomas, Lewis R., Pvt Co. A 3/4/62 – W Fox's Gap 9/14/62; Rich Hos 9/27/62; Appt 4thSgt 12/31/62; 1st Sgt 3/23/64; C Farmville, Va. 4/6/65; R Pt. Lookout, Md. 6/21/65; filed for CSP Alachua Cty, Fl. 1909.

Thomas, William, Pvt Co. B 3/4/62 – NLR.

Thompson, A.M., Pvt Co. H 3/4/62 – D Rich 7/4/64; Bur Hollywood Cem, Rich.

Thompson, Calvin, Pvt Co. B 3/4/62 –Entry on original 3/4/62 muster roll as, "Assigned to my command. Absent."; NLR.

Thompson, James L., Pvt Co. H 5/13/62 – Detailed in Division Commissary Dept. 8/64; C Cedar Creek 10/19/64; D (chronic diarrhea) Pt. Lookout, Md. 1/9/65.

Thompson, Richard A., Pvt Co. B 3/4/62 – D Macon, Ga. 6/9/62.

Thompson, W.A., Pvt – P Tallahassee, Fl. 5/15/65.

Thornton, P.P., Pvt – Only CSR entry shows C; R Elmira, N.Y. 6/21/65.

Thrift, John, Pvt Co. B 3/4/62 – D (pneumonia) Charlottesville, Va. Hos 11/20/62; Bur Confederate Cem, Charlottesville.

Tillman, Albert (Elbert) R., Pvt Co. H 5/13/62 – D (measles) Camp Brown, Ga. 6/16/62; widow filed for CSP Berrien Cty, Ga. 1913.

Tillman, Benjamin J., Pvt Co. H 3/4/62 – W Chancellorsville 5/3/63; DW 5/15/63; Bur Hollywood Cem, Rich.

Tillman, Brock, Pvt Co. H 3/4/62 – D "in service" (date Unk).

Tillman, Elijah, 2nd Lt Co. H 3/4/62 – W "early 1863"; Res (disability – kidney disease) 4/8/63; filed for CSP Colquitt Cty, Ga. 1901; pension record says he joined Co. C, 11th Ga. State Guards Cav as Cpt 8/4/63, and served until close of war.

Tillman, James Harrison, Pvt Co. H 3/4/62 – C Sailor's Creek 4/6/65; R Pt. Lookout, Md. 6/21/65; filed for CSP Lowndes Cty, Ga. 1902.

Tillman, John A. (F.), Pvt Co. H 5/13/62 – W Chancellorsville 5/3/63; Appt 2nd Sgt 11/63; C Sailor's Creek 4/6/65; R Pt. Lookout, Md. 6/21/65.

Tillman, Jordan Joshua, Pvt Co. H 3/4/62 – Appt 2nd Lt 4/26/64; Des 3/14/65; took oath of allegiance to U.S. Govt. and furnished trans to Jacksonville, Fl. 3/24/65; widow filed for CSP Colquitt Cty, Ga. 1911; pension record says he S at Appomattox C.H., but not on list of parolees with 50th Ga. Regt.

Tillman, Mitchell, Pvt Co. H 5/13/62 – D Camp Brown, Ga. 6/16/62; widow filed for CSP Hillsborough Cty, Fl. 1904.

Tillman, Thomas, Pvt Co. H 3/4/62 – D in camp near Fredericksburg 3/6/63.

Tippett, J.B., Pvt Co. D 3/4/62 – Appt 3rd Sgt 1862; D (pneumonia) Rich Hos 12/12/62; Bur Hollywood Cem, Rich.

Tippins, James T., Pvt Co. A 3/4/62 – W Fox's Gap 9/14/62; C Gettysburg 7/4/63; R Ft. Delaware, Del. 5/11/65; filed for CSP Gwinnett Cty, Ga. 1913.

Tison, Aaron, Pvt Co. I 3/4/62 – W Chancellorsville 5/3/63; W (r knee) North Anna River 5/26/64; Rich Hos 5/27/64; Frl for 60 days 5/29/64; roll for 2/65 shows AWOL since 7/22/64; NLR.

Tison, James H., Pvt Co. I 3/4/62 – K Fox's Gap 9/14/62.

Tomlinson, Enoch, Pvt Co. G 4/27/62 – Appt 3rd Cpl 1/1/63; 3rd Sgt 7/63; W (slight) Gettysburg 7/2/63; W (r elbow) 10/64; Ret to Invalid Corps 11/3/64; detailed to Charlottesville, Va. Hos 11/17/64; P Thomasville, Ga. 5/21/65.

Tomlinson, Harris, Pvt Co. G 3/4/62 – W Chancellorsville 5/3/63; roll for 2/65 shows AWOL since 1/2/65; P Thomasville, Ga. 5/14/65; widow filed for CSP Clinch Cty, Ga. 1911; pension record says he received a sick Frl 3/10/65, and was home at close of war.

Tomlinson, Joseph, Pvt Co. G 4/27/62 – Appt 2nd Lt; W (gunshot - r side & back) Petersburg 6/18/64; DW Rich Hos 6/23/64; Appt 1st Lt 6/30/64 (posthumously).

Tomlinson, Needham, 2nd Cpl Co. G 3/4/62 – Roll for 12/31/62 shows left sick at White Plains, Va. 9/6/62; NLR.

Tomlinson, Thomas, Pvt Co. G 3/4/62 – W (gunshot – r thigh) Wilderness or Spotsylvania C.H. 5/64; Rich Hos 5/10/64; roll for 2/65 shows AWOL since 8/10/64; P 1865; filed for CSP Clinch Cty, Ga. 1897; pension record says he "Served up to the surrender."

Townsend, Lott, 2nd Sgt Co. H 3/4/62 – Appt 1st Sgt 10/1/62; Elected 2nd Lt 1/15/63; 1st Lt 4/63; W Chancellorsville 5/3/63; W Gettysburg (1 forearm - minie ball) 7/2/63; Appt Cpt 1/64; C Sailor's Creek 4/6/65; R Johnson's Island, Oh. 6/20/65; filed for CSP Lafayette Cty, Fl. 1892.

Trawick, Isaac, Pvt Co. F 3/4/62 – W Fox's Gap 9/14/62; D (typhoid fever) Rich Hos 6/2/63; Bur Oakwood Cem, Rich.

Trawick, Orthenald, Pvt Co. F 5/13/62 – W (thigh – leg amputated)/C Fox's Gap 9/14/62; DW Frederick, Md. Hos 9/28/62; Bur Mount Olivet Cem, Frederick.

Trowell, John W., Pvt Co. I 8/28/62 – K Chancellorsville 5/3/63.

Trulock, Charles, Pvt Co. F 4/28/62 – W Fox's Gap 9/14/62; C Sharpsburg 9/17/62; Frederick, Md. Hos 9/17/62; D (typhoid fever) 9/27/62; Bur Mount Olivet Cem, Frederick.

Trulock, Gordon Bryan, Pvt Co. F 5/15/62 – Enlisted as Pvt in Co. G, 1st Regt Ga. Inf; Disc 2/9/62; enlisted in Co. F, 50th Ga.; Disc (disability-hemorrhoids) 2/17/63; widow filed for CSP, Grady Cty, Ga. 1937; pension record says he enlisted as Pvt in Co. F, 29th Bn Ga. Cav 11/7/63, and P at Bainbridge, Ga. 5/10/65.

Trulock, Zimmerman, 5th Sgt Co. F 3/4/62 – Reduced to Pvt 10/62; W Gettysburg 7/2/63; C in Hos 7/5/63; P Pt. Lookout, Md. 5/3/64; C Sailor's Creek 4/6/65; R Pt. Lookout, Md. 6/21/65.

Tucker, A., Sgt Co. H – W Chancellorsville 5/3/63; NLR.

Tucker, Elijah, Pvt Co. I 3/4/62 – Filed for CSP Berrien Cty, Ga. 1911; pension record says he received Frl 9/18/62, but no reference to any later record.

Tucker, Henry Sapp, 4th Sgt Co. H 3/4/62 – Disc (illness) 6/13/62; D Sav 6/28/62.

Tucker, John, Sr., Jr. 2nd Lt Co. H 3/4/62 – Res (disability) 5/28/62; filed for CSP Colquitt Cty, Ga. 1899; pension record says he enlisted in Co. C, 11th Regt Ga. State Guards Cav 1863, and served until close of war.

Tucker, John W., Pvt Co. E 8/22/62 – Enlisted as Pvt in Co. D, 2nd Regt, 1st Bde, Ga. State Troops 10/12/61; mustered out 4/62; enlisted in Co. E, 50th Ga.; Appt 3rd

Cpl 8/6/64; C Sailor's Creek 4/6/65; R Pt. Lookout, Md. 6/20/65.

Tucker, Richard M., Pvt Co. H 3/4/62 – Left sick at Leesburg, Va. Hos 9/8/62; Appt Sgt 1862 or 1863; W (l heel) Chancellorsville 5/3/63; roll for 2/65 shows AWOL since 1/20/65; P Thomasville, Ga. 5/19/65; filed for CSP Colquitt Cty, Ga. 1898; pension record says he was Disc in 1863 as result of the wound

Tucker, William J., Pvt Co. E 8/22/62 – NLR.

Turner, John W., Pvt Co. I 3/4/62 – K Cedar Creek 10/19/64.

Tweedle, James A., Pvt Co. D 3/4/62 – Detailed as carpenter on Whitesville, Ga. Hos 5/62; W (gunshot - l knee)/C Cedar Creek 10/19/64; U.S. Hos Baltimore, Md. 10/25/64; R Pt. Lookout, Md. 6/6/65; U.S. Hos Sav (diarrhea) 6/20/65; R 6/28/65.

ROSTER U, V

Vann, Andrew J., Pvt. Co. E 3/4/62 – Appt 5th Sgt 1/1/63; W Chancellorsville 5/3/63; Appt 4th Sgt 1864; C Cedar Creek 10/19/64; R Pt. Lookout, Md. 6/8/65; U.S. Hos Pt Lookout (scurvy) 6/28/65; R 7/9/65; filed for CSP Thomas Cty, Ga. 1913.

Vann, John, Pvt Co. E 5/12/63 – K Fox's Gap 9/14/62.

Varnedoe, Henry J. Pvt Co. H 3/4/62 – D (pneumonia) Rich Hos 11/29/62; Bur Oakwood Cem, Rich.

Venchell, John, Pvt Co. K 1862 – D (typhoid fever) 12/1/62; Bur Thornrose Cem Staunton,Va.

Vick, Demboriah, W., Pvt Co. C 3/4/62 – Injured (scalp) 5/5/63; Frl 30 days from Rich Hos to Douglas, Ga. 6/6/63; roll for 2/65 shows AWOL since 7/18/63; NLR.

Vickers, Andrew (Drew), Pvt Co. D 5/9/62 – Sent to Staunton, Va. Hos 8/62 or 9/62; roll for 2/63 shows "absent. In Hospital"; D 10/3/62; Bur Stonewall (Mount Hebron) Cem, Winchester, Va., marker #104; marker incorrectly reads "D. Bucker"; widow filed for CSP Berrien Cty, Ga. 1891; pension record says he was left on the march into Md. and later "Died from exhaustion."

Vickers (Vickery), Elijah, Pvt Co. I 3/4/62 – Disc, upon furnishing Levi Herring as substitute 2/4/63.

Vickers, H., Pvt Co. D 3/4/62 – D (pneumonia) Rich Hos 6/11/64; Bur Oakwood Cem, Rich.

Vickers, John Jackson, Pvt Co. D 3/4/62 – K Fox's Gap 9/14/62.

Vickers, J.W., Pvt Co. G – Only CSR entry shows P U.S. Hos Charlotte, N.C. 5/65.

Vickers, Matthew, Pvt Co. D 3/4/62 – K Fox's Gap 9/14/62.

Vickery, Hezekiah, Pvt Co. I 3/4/62 – Sent home on sick Frl 4/11/62; roll for 2/63 shows AWOL since 12/5/62; P Thomasville, Ga. 5/24/65; pension record says he was injured by falling tree at Fredericksburg and Disc (disability) 4/1/63.

Vickery, Richard, Pvt Co. B 3/20/62 – W Chancellorsville 5/3/63; D (typhoid fever) Lynchburg, Va. Hos 6/1/64; Bur Lot 197, Confederate Cem, Lynchburg; widow filed for CSP Charlton Cty, Ga. 1891.

Vickery, William, Pvt Co. K 3/4/62 – C Fox's Gap 9/14/62; E Aiken's Landing, Va. 10/19/62; last CSR entry shows receiving pay Kingston, Tn. 11/27/63; NLR.

Vining, James, Pvt Co. G 4/7/62 - C Fox's Gap 9/14/62; E Aiken's Landing, Va. 10/19/62; C Cedar Creek 10/19/64; R Pt. Lookout, Md. 5/14/65; filed for CSP Coffee Cty, Ga. 1900.

Vining, Jasper H., Pvt Co. G 3/4/62 – C Fox's Gap 9/14/62; E 10/62; NLR.

ROSTER W

Wade, Hezekiah, Pvt Co. F 5/5/62 – D (measles) Sav 6/21/62; widow filed for CSP Decatur Cty, Ga. 1891.

Wainwright, John E., Pvt Co. B 3/4/62 – Entry on roll for 3/4/62 shows "Assigned to my command. Absent."; NLR.

Wainwright, William R., Pvt Co. B 3/4/62 – Entry on roll for 3/4/62 shows "Assigned to my command. Absent."; NLR.

Walden, Jonathan, Pvt Co. F 3/4/62 – W (shell - hip) Petersburg 6/18/64; Frl Rich Hos 30 days 6/29/64; C Sailor's Creek 4/6/65; R Pt. Lookout, Md. 6/22/65; widow filed for CSP Calhoun Cty, Fl. 1915.

Waldron, Benjamin D., Pvt Co. A 7/18/62 – Substitute for Randal D. Waldron; W (1 shoulder & r ear)/C Fox's Gap 9/14/62; E Aikens Landing, Va. 10/19/62; Rich Hos 10/23/62; C Sailor's Creek, Va. 4/6/65; R Pt. Lookout, Md. 6/22/65; filed for CSP Wayne Cty, Ga. 1903.

Waldron, George W., Co. A 5/15/62 – Elected 1ˢᵗ Sgt 6/18/62; 2ⁿᵈ Lt 12/31/62; 1ˢᵗ Lt 5/26/63; Cpt 7/3/63; W (mouth) Ft. Sanders 11/29/63; commanding Simms' Bde at S Appomattox C.H. 4/9/65; widow filed for CSP Columbia Cty, Fl. 1899.

Waldron, Oliver, Pvt Co. B 3/4/62 – D Macon, Ga. Hos 5/15/62; widow filed for CSP Jeff Davis Cty, Ga. 1910.

Waldron, Randal (Randall) D., Pvt Co. A 4/30/62 – Enlisted as Pvt in Co. N, 26ᵗʰ Regt Ga. Inf 10/21/61; mustered out 3/31/62; enlisted in Co. A, 50ᵗʰ Ga.; Disc upon furnishing Benjamin Waldron as substitute 7/18/62; filed for CSP Fulton Cty, Ga. 1910; pension record says he enlisted as Pvt in Co. A, 24ᵗʰ Bn Ga. Cav 9/22/62; Trn to Co. G, 7ᵗʰ Ga. Cav 2/13/64; C 6/11/64; R Elmira, N.Y. 6/16/65.

Walker, G.G., Pvt Co. D 5/9/62 – NLR.

Walker, Henry Clay, Pvt Co. D 5/9/62 – W Gettysburg (shell fragment, r foot – gunshot, r hand – one finger shot off) 7/2/63; roll for 2/65 shows present; P 5/4/65; filed for CSP Taylor Cty, Fl. 1902.

Walker, Isham, Pvt Co. A 3/4/62 – D Macon, Ga. Hos 5/26/62.

Walker, J., Pvt Co. D 5/9/62 - W Fox's Gap 9/14/62; D (pneumonia) Lynchburg, Va. Hos 11/17/62; Bur Lot 144, Confederate Cem, Lynchburg.

Walker, James J., Pvt Co. K 3/4/62 – Roll for 12/64 shows present; roll for 2/65 shows "Not Stated"; P Thomasville, Ga. 5/18/65; filed for CSP Brooks Cty, Ga. 1907; pension record says he was home on Frl at close of war.

Walker, Jasper, Pvt Co. A – Only CSR entry of 7/62 shows "Sick in hospital at Savh, Ga"; NLR.

Walker, Joel, 3ʳᵈ Cpl Co. B 3/4/62 - W/C Fox's Gap 9/14/62; E Aikens Landing, Va. 10/6/62; D 1/20/63.

Walker, John, Pvt Co. A – D 5/28/62.

Walker, Joseph, Pvt Co. G – NLR.

Walker, Love, Pvt Co. B 3/4/62 – Disc (disability) 5/27/63; widow filed for CSP Ware Cty, Ga. 1893; pension record says he was Disc after contracting consumption.

Walker, Richard H., Pvt Co. C 3/4/62 – Disc (disability) 1/4/63.

Wall, William B., Pvt Co. C 3/4/62 – NLR.

Walters, John, Pvt Co. F – C Fox's Gap 9/14/62; E Aikens Landing, Va. 10/6/62; NLR.

Walton, Wiley, Pvt Co. D – W (gunshot - thigh & shoulder)/C Spotsylvania C.H. 5/12/64; U.S. Hos Fredericksburg, Va. 5/23/64; P Elmira N.Y. 10/29/64; received Sav River 11/15/64; NLR.

Ward, Benjamin, Pvt Co. C 3/4/62 – D Sav 6/25/62.

Ward, Calvin A. (E.), Pvt Co. C 5/9/62 – D (pneumonia) Danville, Va. Hos 3/1/63.

Ward, John E., Pvt Co. C 5/9/62 – W (gunshot, r shoulder) Chancellorsville 5/3/63; roll
for 12/64 shows "Retired"; filed for CSP Coffee Cty, Ga. 1905; pension
record says he was Disc in 1863 as result of the wound.

Ward, John F., Pvt Co. C 5/9/62 – W (face/shoulder) Fox's Gap 9/14/62; Rich Hos
9/27/62; Appt 1st Cpl 1/1/63; D (pneumonia) in camp near Fredericksburg
3/20/63; widow filed for CSP Coffee Cty, Ga. 1891.

Ward, Lewis J., Pvt Co. E 3/4/62 – Appt 4th Cpl 11/1/62; W Chancellorsville 5/3/63; C
(date Unk); received Louisville, Ky. Prison 5/65; NLR.

Ward, Stafford G., Pvt Co. C 5/9/62 – Roll for 2/65 shows AWOL since 10/15/64;
widow filed for CSP Coffee Cty, Ga. 1911; pension record says he was with
command at surrender.

Warren, Jackson, Pvt Co. B 3/4/62 – NLR.

Waters, James A., 1st Lt Co. A 3/4/62 – Elected Cpt 1/1/63; Res commission 5/12/63;
roll for 2/28/65 shows "absent with leave Gen. Lee."; NLR.

Waters, James B., Pvt Co. G 3/4/62 – C/P Leesburg, Va. 10/2/62; C Sailor's Creek
4/6/65; R Pt. Lookout, Md. 6/22/65; filed for CSP Brooks Cty, Ga. 1902.

Waters, James F., Pvt Co. A 3/4/62 – Roll for 2/65 shows "Absent. Sent to Hospital
May 7-63. Not since heard from."; widow filed for CSP Coffee Cty, Ga.
1893; pension record says he was W and "he was started to the Hospital – but
was never heard of again. Suppose he died in 1863."

Waters, Matthew M., Pvt Co. G 3/4/62 – C/P Leesburg, Va. 10/2/62; W Chancellorsville
5/3/63; C Sailor's Creek 4/6/65; R Pt. Lookout, Md. 6/22/65.

Waters, Washington W., Pvt Co. A 5/2/62 – W Chancellorsville 5/3/63; C Cedar Creek
10/19/64; E Camp Lee, Va. 2/17/65; NLR.

Watson, John, Pvt Co. G 3/4/62 – Last shown on Rich Hos roll as Frl 60 days 6/11/63
(hepatitis); NLR.

Wattles, Alexander E., Pvt Co. E 3/4/62 – Detailed as Col. Manning's orderly 5/62-7/62;
Disc (under-age) 10/10/62; widow filed for CSP Putnam Cty, Fl. 1909;
pension record says he enlisted in Co. I, 12th Ga. Inf in late 1862 and
remained until close of war.

Wattles, William S., Pvt Co. E 4/22/62 – C Cedar Creek 10/19/64; R Pt. Lookout, Md.
5/14/65.

Weatherington, Ivan, Pvt – NLR; P Tallahassee, Fl. 5/15/65.

Weaver, Isaac Soloman, Pvt Co. I 8/23/62 – Enlisted as Pvt in Co. K, 5th Regt Ga. State
Troops 12/20/61; Disc (disability) 1/27/62; enlisted in Co. I, 50th Ga.; C near
Knoxville, Tn. 12/3/63; E Rock Island, Ill. 3/2/65; filed for CSP Berrien Cty,
Ga. 1909; pension record says he was home on Frl at close of war.

Weaver, Peter, Pvt Co. G 3/4/62 – W Chancellorsville 5/3/63; C Cold Harbor 6/1/64; R
Elmira, N.Y. 5/19/65.

Weekly, J.D., Pvt Co. I 8/28/62 – W (l hand) Funkstown 7/10/63; roll for 8/31/64 shows
detailed as ordnance guard; Des 12/2/64; NLR.

Weekly, John T., Pvt Co. I 3/4/62 – W (r thumb shot off) Sharpsburg 9/17/62; Rich Hos
12/9/62; K Gettysburg 7/2/63; Bur Gettysburg; removed to Laurel Hill Cem,
Sav 9/24/1871; Bur Lot 853.

Weeks, Charles Pinkney, Pvt Co. H 3/4/62 – W Chancellorsville 5/3/63; Des 3/14/65;
took oath of allegiance to U.S. Govt. and furnished trans to Jacksonville, Fl.
3/24/65; filed for CSP Colquitt Cty, Ga. 1895; pension record says he served
"Until the surrender."

Weeks, James, Pvt Co. H 3/4/62 – D Sav 4/16/62.

Weeks, John, Pvt Co. D 3/4/62 – C near Knoxville, Tn. 12/20/63; P Rock Island, Ill.
upon taking oath of allegiance to U.S. Govt. 10/18/64.

Wells, James C., Pvt Co. K 3/4/62 – Disc (disability) 6/2/62.

Wells, Jasper W., Pvt Co. A 3/4/62 - Appt 4th Sgt 3/23/64; W (gunshot - r hip) Cold
    Harbor 6/3/64; Rich Hos (chronic dysentery) 3/22/65; P Rich 4/29/65; filed
    for CSP Telfair Cty, Ga. 1901.

Wells, Jeremiah Wesley, Cpt Co. H 3/4/62 – W (gunshot) Chancellorsville 5/3/63; Res
    due to disability and election to Ga. State Assembly 12/30/63; filed for CSP
    Bradford Cty, Fl. 1908; pension record says he was home at close of war.

Wells, John W., 2nd Cpl Co. H 3/4/62 – D (pneumonia) Rich Hos 1/20/63; Bur Oakwood
    Cem, Rich.

Wells, Lyman (Lemuel) P. Quartermaster Sgt 3/22/62 – S Appomattox C.H. 4/9/65.

Wells, Newton R., Pvt Co. A 5/7/62 – Enlisted as Pvt in Co. K, 2nd Regt, 1st Bde, Ga.
State Troops 10/6/61; mustered out 4/62; enlisted in Co. A, 50th Ga.; Appt 5th Sgt 12/
    31/62; W (hand) Ft. Sanders 11/29/63; reduced to Pvt 1864; C Sailor's Creek
    4/6/65; filed for CSP Telfair Cty, Ga. 1902; pension record says he was
    detailed as a sharpshooter when C at Sailor's Creek; P Danville, Va. 1865.

Wells, O.W., Sgt Co. A – C Rich 4/3/65; escaped from Hos 5/1/65; NLR.

Westberry, John S., Pvt Co. D 3/4/62 – NLR.

Wetherington, J.B., Pvt Co. D 3/4/62 – Disc (disability – rheumatism, l leg) 1/21/63;
    filed for CSP Hillsborough Cty, Fl. 1898.

Wheeler, John L., Pvt Co. C 3/4/62 – Appt 2nd Sgt 1862; 1st Sgt 1/1/63; Elected 1st Lt
    2/64; W (l arm - amputated) Cold Harbor 6/1/64; applied for retirement 7/2/64;
    roll for 2/28/65 shows "Disabled. Has applied for retirement"; NLR.

Whidden, Patrick K., Pvt Co. E 8/13/62 – K Gettysburg 7/2/63

White, F.G., Pvt Co. E – C/P Winchester, Va. 12/2/62; NLR

White, George Washington, 1st Cpl Co. B 3/4/62 - C Fox's Gap 9/14/62; E Aikens
    Landing, Va. 11/10/62; Elected 2nd Lt 4/27/63; W Chancellorsville 5/3/63;
    dropped for incompetence 5/24/64; C Cold Harbor 6/1/64; R Ft. Delaware,
    Del. 6/17/65.

White, J.R., Pvt, Co. I – K Gettysburg 7/2/63; Bur Gettysburg; removed to Laurel
    Grove Cem, Sav 9/24/1871; Bur Lot 853.

White, Joseph G. (E.), Pvt Co. E 8/13/62 – Roll for 10/64 shows AWOL 10/20/64; roll
    for 2/65 shows AWOL; P Thomasville, Ga. 5/19/65.

White, James L., 4th Sgt Co. G 3/4/62 – Reduced to Pvt 1862; Des 7/20/62; NLR.

White, Mathew, Pvt Co. E 7/12/62 – C Cedar Creek 10/19/64; D (chronic diarrhea) Pt.
    Lookout, Md 2/11/65; believed Bur Confederate Cem, Pt. Lookout.

White, Thomas George, Jr 2nd Lt Co. B 3/4/62 – W (gunshot - knee) Chancellorsville
    5/3/63; Rich Hos 5/6/63; Frl 30 days 5/16/63; filed for CSP Walton Cty, Ga.
    1897; pension record says he Res (disability) 9/4/63 due to wounds.

White, Van A., Pvt Co. B 3/4/62 – Roll for 12/64 shows "Absent. Left sick on the
    march in September 1862. Supposed to have died."; NLR.

Whiteford, William Thomas, 2nd Lt Co. B 3/4/62 – Elected 1st Lt 3/22/62; W
    Chancellorsville 5/3/63; DW Rich Hos 5/11/63; Bur Hollywood Cem, Rich.

Whitehurst, Andrew Jackson, Pvt Co. G 3/4/62 – W (gunshot – l breast & l arm)
    Chancellorsville 5/3/63; Frl 60 days 6/6/63; Trn to Cpt Parker's Co., Va. Light
    Artillery 12/11/63; W 1864; widow filed for CSP Berrien Cty, Ga. 1913;
    pension record says he was never able to return to command due to wounds.

Whittington, Benjamin Franklin, Pvt Co. K 5/9/62 – Elected 2nd Lt 5/28/63; W
    Petersburg 6/19 (head); roll for 2/65 shows "Leave of absence Gen. Lee.
    Expired Feb 17, 1865 Albany, Ga."; P Albany, Ga. 5/20/65; filed for CSP
    Lowndes Cty 1919:pension record says he was Frl home for 30 days in March
    and was home at close of war.

Whittington, J.M., Co. K - W Gettysburg 7/2/63; left at Williamsport, Md.; C 7/13/63; NLR.

Wilcox, James Bryant, Pvt Co. E 3/4/62 – W (abdomen) Petersburg 6/18/64; roll for 2/65 shows present; P Thomasville, Ga. 5/65; widow filed for CSP Brooks Cty, Ga.1902.

Wilder, Henry H., Pvt Co. F 3/4/62 – W Cold Harbor 6/1/64; roll for 2/65 shows absent sick; C Va. 4/65; NLR.

Wiley, (Weyley) William R., Pvt Co. F – W/C Fox's Gap 9/14/62; DW Frederick, Md. Hos 9/23/62; Bur Mount Olivet Cem, Frederick.

Wilkerson, Pvt Co. A 3/4/62 – Disc on Surgeon's certification 3/4/62.

Williams, Aaron, Pvt Co. I 3/4/62 – W Chancellorsville 5/3/63; W Berryville 9/3/64; DW 9/4/64.

Williams, Berry L., Pvt Co. K 3/4/62 – Appt 2nd Cpl 3/23/64; roll for 2/65 shows present; P Thomasville, Ga. 5/18/65; filed for CSP Brooks Cty, Ga. 1908; pension record says he was with the command at the surrender.

Williams, Butler, Pvt Co. H 3/4/62 – C Gettysburg 7/4/63; D U.S. Hos Gettysburg9/20/63.

Williams, Dennis, Pvt Co. E 8/22/62 – Trn to Co. I 1/9/63; W between 1/63-3/63; sent to Hos; Disc, upon furnishing James Clarke as substitute 4/16/63.

Williams, Isaac, Pvt Co. F 4/28/62 – Disc (disability-hiatal hernia) 10/23/62.

Williams, Nathan B., Pvt Co. F 3/13/62 – D Macon, Ga. 5/62.

Williams, Onzelow, Pvt Co. F 4/28/62 – D (typhoid pneumonia) Rich Hos 6/1/63; Bur Oakwood Cem, Rich.

Williams, Redding G., Pvt Co. C 3/4/62 – C Sailor's Creek 4/6/65; filed for CSP Coffee Cty, Ga. 1906.

Williams, Stephen, Pvt Co. I 3/4/62 – W Wilderness 5/6/64; DW Lynchburg, Va. Hos 5/22/64; Bur Lot 193, Confederate Cem, Lynchburg.

Williams, William, Pvt Co. E 3/4/62 – D Whitesville, Ga. Hos 4/24/62.

Williams, William, Pvt Co. I – D 7/1/63; Bur Gettysburg; removed to Laurel Grove Cem, Sav 9/24/1871; Bur Lot 853.

Williams, William H., Pvt Co. F 3/4/62 – C Fox's Gap 9/14/62; E Aikens Landing, Va. 10/19/62; NLR.

Williams, William M., Pvt Co. C 5/9/62 – D (typhoid fever) Lynchburg, Va Hos 11/28/62; Bur Confederate Cem, Lynchburg, Lot 78.

Willis, Alfred, Pvt Co. F 3/4/62 – D (pneumonia) Rich Hos 3/24/63; Bur Oakwood Cem, Rich.

Wilson, Alderman, Pvt Co. E 5/15/62 – Enlisted as Pvt in Co. D, 2nd Regt, 1st Bde, Ga. State Troops 10/25/61; mustered out 4/62; enlisted in Co. E, 50th Ga.; Des to Thomas Cty, Ga. 11/25/62; Des 1/9/65; took oath of allegiance to U.S. Govt. and furnished trans to Sav 1/16/65.

Wilson, Ezekiel, Pvt Co. A 3/4/62 – Roll for 2/65 shows AWOL since 6/1/64; NLR; P Thomasville, Ga. 5/23/65.

Wilson, John T., Cpt Co. A 3/4/62 – W Fox's Gap 9/14/62; DW 1862 (death claim filed by widow 1/19/63).

Wilson, Robert, Pvt Co. C 3/4/62 – W (l shoulder) Chancellorsville 5/3/63; widow filed for CSP Ware Cty, Ga. 1901; pension record says he was crippled (r foot) Cold Harbor 6/64 and received a sick Frl home; was home at close of war.

Wilson, Thomas, Pvt Co. I – C Fox's Gap 9/14/62; E Aikens Landing 11/10/62; NLR.

Wilson, William, Pvt Co. D – W Fox's Gap 9/14/62; NLR.

Wing, Peter O., Pvt Co. H 3/4/62 – Disc (disability) 4/23/63.

Winters, Leonard, Pvt Co. K 5/8/62 – W Gettysburg 7/2/63; C Falling Waters, Va. [WVa.] 7/14/63; D (pneumonia) U.S. Hos Chester, Pa. 9/30/63; Bur Chester., Pa.

Winters, Solomon, Pvt Co. K 3/4/62 – Roll for 12/31/62 shows sent to Hos 12/15/62; roll for 3/12/63 shows D.

Winters, William J., Pvt Co. K 4/24/62 – W Ft. Sanders 11/29/63; roll for 2/65 shows absent W; P Thomasville, Ga. 5/18/65.

Wisenbaker, James C., Pvt Co. D 5/4/62 – Roll for 2/63 shows "Absent. Sick Furlough Valdosta, Ga."; Trn to Co. H, 4th Regt Ga. Cav 2/1/64; P Thomasville, Ga. 5/65; filed for CSP Lowndes Cty, Ga. 1906; pension record says he was sick in Thomasville, Ga. Hos at close of war.

Wisenbaker, William H., 1st Cpl Co. D 3/4/62 – W (breast - slight) Sharpsburg 9/17/62; D (typhoid fever) Rich Hos 5/18/63; Bur Oakwood Cem, Rich.

Witherington (Wetherington), Jesse W., Pvt Co. D 3/4/62 – K Cedar Creek 10/19/64.

Witherington (Wetherington), Matthew, Pvt Co. D 3/4/62 – W Gettysburg (foot shot off) 7/2/63; C Williamsport, Md. 7/14/63; DW U.S. Hos Harrisburg, Pa. 10/17/63; Bur Harrisburg.

Witherington (Wetherington), Perry, Pvt Co. D 3/4/62 – Disc by medical board (date Unk); NLR.

Wood, Eben J., 2nd Lt Co. K 3/4/62 – D (consumption) Staunton, Va. Hos 11/1/62; Bur Thornrose Cem, Staunton.

Woods, Edward C., Pvt Co. A 3/4/62 – C Sailor's Creek 4/6/65; R Pt. Lookout, Md. 6/22/65; widow filed for CSP Volusia Cty, Fl. 1927.

Woods, George W., Pvt Co. A 6/21/62 – W (l hand/r side) Chancellorsville 5/3/63; roll for 2/65 shows AWOL since 6/3/63; S Tallahassee, Fl. 5/10/65; P Thomasville, Ga. 5/16/65; filed for CSP Bradford Cty, Fl. 1907; pension record says he received W Frl home to Appling Cty, Ga. 1863, was home at close of war.

Woods, N.C., Pvt Co. A – C Sailor's Creek, Va. 4/6/65; R Pt. Lookout, Md. 6/22/65.

Woods, William R., 1st Cpl Co. A 3/4/62 – W Chancellorsville 5/3/63; reduced to Pvt; roll for 2/65 shows AWOL since 12/14/63; P Thomasville, Ga. 5/16/65.

Wooten, F.L., Pvt Co. C – Only CSR entry of 5/62 shows "Detailed as company cook"; NLR.

Wooten, J.D., Pvt Co. F – Last CSR entry shows receiving pay on 6/8/64; NLR.

Wooten, Joel W., Pvt Co. C 3/4/62 – W/C Fox's Gap 9/14/62; E Aikens Landing, Va. 10/19/62; Rich Hos 10/62; Appt 5th Sgt 2/64; Des 1/18/65; took oath of allegiance to U.S. Govt. and furnished trans to Jacksonville, Fl. 1/24/65.

Wooten, John B., Pvt Co. F 3/4/62 – W Chancellorsville 5/3/63; W (l hand – finger amputated) Cold Harbor 6/3/64; roll for 2/65 shows AWOL since 8/4/64; P Bainbridge, Ga. 5/20/65; filed for CSP Decatur Cty, Ga. 1904; pension record says he received 60 day Frl home 2/65, and was home at close of the war.

Wooten, Simon L., Pvt Co. C 5/9/63 – C Sharpsburg 9/17/62; E Aikens Landing, Va. 10/19/62; Rich Hos 10/62; Des 1/18/65; took oath of allegiance to U.S. Govt. and furnished trans to Jacksonville, Fl. 1/24/65.

Wooten, William J. Pvt Co. C 3/4/62 – D 4/15/62.

Wright, James Madison. Pvt Co. D 3/4/62 – Trn to Co. A, 18th Bn. Ga. Inf. 6/1/62; Des 2/23/65; took oath of allegiance to U.S. Govt. and furnished trans to Jacksonville, Fl 2/27/65.

Wright, Mitchell, Pvt Co. C 3/4/62 – Roll for 2/65 shows AWOL since 10/4/63; P Thomasville, Ga. 5/24/65.

Wright, R., Pvt Co. I 3/4/62 – NLR.

Wright, Rial, 1st Sgt Co. C 3/4/62 – C (sick) Sharpsburg 9/18/62; U.S. Hos Philadelphia, Pa. 9/27/62; E 8/64; P Thomasville, Ga. 5/24/65; filed for CSP Coffee Cty, Ga. 1911; pension record says he was E and sent to Tn. in 1864, then Frl home and remained there until close of war.

Wright, William, Pvt Co. B 3/4/62 – Last CSR entry of June 62 shows "Sent to Macon Hospital 13th April"; NLR.

ROSTER X,Y, Z

Yates, Morgan G., 2nd Sgt Co. K 3/4/62 – D Winchester, Va. Hos 10/15/62; Bur Stonewall (Mount Hebron) Cem, Winchester, marker #265; marker reads "N.G. Yates."

Yates, Owen, 3rd Sgt Co. K 3/4/62 – C Cedar Creek 10/19/64; R Pt. Lookout, Md. 6/15/65; filed for CSP Hamilton Cty, Fl. 1901.

Yawn (Yann), Irwin, Pvt Co. C 8/28/62 – D (pneumonia) Rich Hos 2/28/63; Bur Oakwood Cem, Rich; widow filed for CSP Coffee Cty, Ga. 1891.

Youmans, W.D., Pvt Co. A 3/4/62 – Disc on Surgeon's certification 3/4/62.

Young, Cicero Holt, Cpt Co. E 3/4/62 –Res (illness) 6/16/62; D (typhoid pneumonia) Winchester, Va. Hos 10/1/62; Bur Stonewall (Mount Hebron) Cem, Winchester.

Young, Francis E., 5th Sgt Co. K 3/4/62 – Reduced to Pvt 8/62; Disc (disability-chronic diarrhea) 7/27/63.

Young, Henry B., Cpl Co. K 3/4/62 – Roll for 2/65 shows "Absent. Sick in Brooks County, Ga."; P Thomasville, Ga. 5/24/65; filed for CSP Berrien Cty, Ga. 1907; pension record says he was on detached service as a steward in Sav Hos from 11/62 to close or war.

Young, John J., Pvt Co. I 3/4/62 – Detailed as teamster 10/63-12/63; detailed as division pioneer 1/1/63-1/1/64; roll for 2/65 shows AWOL since 2/25/65; P Thomasville, Ga. 5/18/65.

Young, Lovick M., Pvt Co. I 3/4/62 – W Chancellorsville 5/3/63; K Cedar Creek 10/19/64; Bur Stonewall (Mount Hebron) Cem, Winchester, Va., marker #75; marker reads "S.M. Young"; widow filed for CSP Berrien Cty, Ga. 1893.

Young, Thomas Jefferson, Pvt Co. E 3/4/62 – Appt 4th Sgt 4/24/62; Disc upon furnishing Adolph Lebrette as substitute 7/1/62.

Zweifel (Zweitsfels), J. Frederick, Pvt Co. E 5/16/62 – Enlisted as Pvt in Co. D, 2nd Regt, 1st Bde, Ga. State Troops 11/4/61; mustered out 4/62; enlisted in Co. E; Des Hagerstown, Md. 9/12/62; NLR.

Appendix B

50th GEORGIA INFANTRY REGIMENT CASUALTIES

OOver fourteen hundred men served in the 50th Georgia Infantry Regiment between March 1862 and April 1865. At least five hundred-thirty soldiers, or one in three, died during this three-year period. The following listing represents the number of Wiregrass soldiers who made the ultimate sacrifice, including battle-related deaths and those who succumbed to illness. Some of the deaths attributed to illness were likely the results of complications from battle wounds. I have made every attempt at accuracy, including review of pension and service records, newspaper casualty lists, letters, diaries, and other sources. In some instances, there are conflicts among the sources. I have made my best attempt to determine the most accurate source.

Breakdown of Battle or Illness Related Deaths by Regiment and Company.

50th Georgia Infantry Regiment

Total members—1404
Death by battle—195
Death by illness—335
Total deaths—530
Percentage of deaths by battle—13.88%
Percentage of deaths by illness—23.86%
Percentage of total deaths—37.74%

Regimental Field and Staff:
    Death by battle—2
    Death by illness—1

Company A, Pierce County (Satilla Rangers):
    Total members—109
    Death by battle—17
    Death by illness—24
    Total deaths—41
    Death percentage—37.61%

Company B, Ware County (Ware Volunteers):
    Total members—103
    Death by battle—8

Death by illness—25
Total deaths—33
Death percentage—32.03%

Company C, Coffee County (Coffee Guards):
Total members—146
Death by battle—21
Death by illness—42
Total deaths—63
Death percentage—43.15%

Company D, Lowndes County (Valdosta Guards):
Total members—124
Death by battle—17
Death by illness—25
Total deaths—42
Death percentage—33.87%

Company E, Thomas County (Thomas County Rangers):
Total members—153
Death by battle—22
Death by illness—37
Total deaths—59
Death percentage—38.56%

Company F, Decatur County (Decatur Infantry):
Total members—141
Death by battle—25
Death by illness—30
Total deaths—55
Death percentage—39.00%

Company G, Clinch and Echols Counties (Clinch Volunteers):
Total members—147
Death by battle—22
Death by illness—34
Total deaths—56
Death percentage—38.09%

Company H, Colquitt County (Colquitt Marksmen):
Total members—136
Death by battle—21
Death by illness—38
Total deaths—59
Death percentage—43.38%

Company I, Berrien County (Berrien Light Infantry):
Total members—164
Death by battle—25
Death by illness—45
Total deaths—70

Death percentage—42.68%

Company K, Brooks County (Brooks Volunteers):
    Total members—141
    Death by battle—15
    Death by illness—34
    Total deaths—49
    Death percentage—34.75%

Unknown company affiliation:
    Total number—22
    Death by battle—0
    Death by illness—4
    Total deaths—4
    Death percentage—18.18%

Appendix C

50th GEORGIA INFANTRY REGIMENT
APPOMATTOX PAROLE LIST

Only a handful of haggard Wiregrass men remained when the 50th Georgia Regiment and the rest of Simms' Brigade surrendered at Appomattox Court House on April 9, 1865. Most of the regiment had been captured three days earlier at Sailor's Creek. Other members were either sick or wounded in hospitals, on assigned duties elsewhere, or on furlough at the time of surrender.

Some of the 50th Georgia field and staff were temporarily assigned to the brigade level due to attrition. The following are those Wiregrass soldiers included in the list of parolees:

Brigade/Regimental Field and Staff:

George W. Waldron, Cpt., Commanding Simms' Brigade
C.H. Parmalee, Maj., Commissary
Henry J. Parramore, Surgeon, 50th Ga. Regiment
William H. Price, Surgeon, 50th Ga. Regiment
Hillery W. Cason, Lt., Commanding 50th Ga. Regiment
Aaron Dowling, 2d Lt., Co. A, 50th Ga. Regiment
James R. Sheldon, Commissary Sgt.
Henry W. McTyre, Ordnance Sgt. (Shown as "H.W.M. Tyn" on parole list).
Lyman P. Wells, Q. M. Sgt.

Company A (Pierce County)
    None

Company B (Ware County)
    Sgt. William A. Byrd, Pvt. (Shown as "W.A. Bird" on parole list)

Company C (Coffee County)
    Alexander Merritt, Pvt. (Shown as "A. Merrit" on parole list).
    William Nipper, Pvt.

Company D (Lowndes County)
    John W. Collins, Pvt.
    Seth Martin, Pvt.

Company E (Thomas County)
    Aaron J. Donaldson, Pvt. (Shown as "A.J. Duroldson on parole list).
    W.M. Lenny, Pvt.
    John A. Spears, Pvt. (Shown as "Jas. Speers" on parole list).
    David Stephenson, Pvt.

Company F (Decatur County)
    Greene B. Alday, Pvt.
    Thomas R. Bailey, Pvt. (Shown as "T.R. Burley" on parole list).
    William A. Ellis, Cpl.
    Newton Hicks, Pvt.
    Benjamin F. Metcalf, Pvt.

Company G (Clinch County)
    James Clemmons, Pvt.

Company H (Colquitt County)
    Thomas P. Baker, Pvt. (Shown as "T.B. Baker" on parole list).
    John Hancock, Pvt.
    James J. Horne, Pvt.
    David W. Murphy, Pvt.
    Saul Mercer, Pvt.

Company I (Berrien County)
    Babel J. Rutherford, Pvt. (Shown as "G.J. Relliford" on parole list).

Company K (Brooks County)
    Daniel Luke, Pvt.

Above list from Paroles of the Army of Northern Virginia, *Southern Society Historical Papers*, Vol. XV, 1887, p. 170, 183.

Appendix D

50th GEORGIA BATTLE FLAG

A Confederate battle flag identified as that carried by the 50th Georgia Infantry is currently housed in the Georgia Capitol Archives and included in the publication, *Hallowed Banners*. A photograph of the flag also graces the cover of this book. The flag in question was captured by Corporal John Keough of the 67th Pennsylvania Volunteers, who received the Medal of Honor for his heroic action at the Battle of Sailor's Creek, Virginia, on April 6, 1865. The flag was returned to the State of Georgia by the U.S. War Department in 1905.

Georgia Capitol Museum, Office of Secretary of State, Atlanta, Georgia

The unit identification of the flag housed at the Georgia Capitol Archives has come into question as the result of a post-war account of the Battle of Sailor's Creek by the 50th Georgia Commander, Colonel Peter A.S. McGlashan. According to an 1895 address given by McGlashan before the Confederate Veteran's Association of Savannah, Georgia, he personally removed the flag from the flagstaff, tore it into fragments and threw them into the brush to avoid capture by the Yankees.

In December 2005, Mr. Timothy Frilingos, curator of exhibits, graciously allowed the author to view and photograph the flag stored in the Georgia Capitol Archives. The honors displayed on the flag correctly identify the major engagements in which the 50th Georgia fought, except for one. "Charlotsville" is incorrectly displayed as a battle honor. The 50th Georgia never fought at Charlottesville, but covered itself with glory in the Battle of Chancellorsville. It is doubtful that these proud warriors would have gone into battle with a flag that bore such a grievous error. The battle honors were most likely placed on the flag after the war, but when and by whom?

If the flag at the Georgia Capitol Archives is authentic, and if Colonel McGlashan tore up the flag at Sailor's Creek, did the 50th Georgia carry more than one flag into the battle? Did Corporal Keough capture the battle flag of another regiment and erroneously receive credit for capture of the 50th Georgia colors?

It is not known if Colonel McGlashan was ever asked to confirm the authenticity of the flag returned to the State of Georgia in 1905. Although in poor health at the time the flag was returned, McGlashan did not die until 1908.

The author contacted two well-respected Georgia flag historians, Keith Bohannon and Greg Biggs, in an effort to resolve the issue. After much deliberation, no definite conclusions were reached. The actual fate of the flag remains a mystery.

Appendix E

FINAL RESTING PLACES

Headstone of Sergeant
Alfred Bird

Headstone of Private
James Bishop

Headstone of Private
John A. Brady

Headstone of Private
Samuel E. Brady

Headstone of Private
Richard Carver

Headstone of Private
John S. Clifton

See Headstone information on pages 351 - 354

Headstone of Private
Richard P. Connell

Headstone of Private
Manning Corbitt

Headstone of Private
Elisha Davis

Headstone of Private
James W. Denmark

Headstone of Captain
Edward M. Ford

Headstone of Private
William D. Ford

Headstone of Private
Eli Griffis

Headstone of Private
J.T. Hardee

Headstone of Private
William Harrell

See Headstone information on pages 351 - 354

Headstone of Private
Simon Hart

Headstone of Lieutenant
James Kinchen Hilliard

Headstone of Private
I. Hollingsworth

Headstone of Corporal
R. Perry Hughes

Headstone of Lt. Colonel
Francis Kearse

Headstone of Private
David Lastinger

Headstone of Dr.
Nathaniel McArthur

Headstone of Private
Wyatt H. McPherson

Headstone of Private
Frederick Merritt

See Headstone information on pages 351 - 354

Headstone of Lieutenant
Wryan Minshew

Headstone of
Second Lieutenant
Francis L. Mobley

Headstone of Private
Ezra Newton

Headstone of Private
John T. Nix

Headstone of Captain
John Riley O'Steen

Headstone of Private
Daniel C. Paulk

Headstone of Corporal
J.G. Powell

Headstone of Private
T. J. Rawls

Headstone of Private
William H. Reynolds

See Headstone information on pages 351 - 354

Headstone of Private
John Rewis (Ruis)

Headstone of Private
Emanuel Shuman

Headstone of Private
David Sloan

Headstone of Private
Matthew T. Strickland

Headstone of Private
Orthenald Trawick

Headstone of Private
Charles Trulock

Headstone of Private
Andrew "Drew" Vickers

Headstone of Private
John T. Weekly

Headstone of Private
J.R. White

See Headstone information on pages 351 - 354

Headstone of Private
William R. Wiley

Headstone of Private
Morgan G. Yates

Headstone of Captain
Cicero Holt Young

Headstone of Private
Lovick M. Young

See Headstone information on pages 351 - 354

Headstone of Sergeant Alfred Bird, Company F. Killed at Gettysburg on July 2, 1863, and buried at Gettysburg. He was later removed to Laurel Grove Cemetery at Savannah, Ga. in 1871.

Headstone of Private James Bishop, Company B. Died from disease in Savannah on June 10, 1862, and is buried in Laurel Grove Cemetery at Savannah, Ga.

Headstone of Private John A. Brady, Company G. Died from disease at Fort Brown on June 3, 1862, exactly one month after the death of his brother, Samuel. He is buried near his brother in Laurel Grove Cemetery at Savannah, Ga.

Headstone of Private Samuel E. Brady, Company G. Brady died of disease near Savannah on May 3, 1862, and is buried in Laurel Grove Cemetery at Savannah, Ga.
Photo by author

Headstone of Private Richard Carver, Company C. Died from disease at Fort Brown on May 19, 1862, and is buried in Laurel Grove Cemetery at Savannah, Ga. His marker is incorrectly inscribed as "Carter."

Headstone of Private John S. Clifton, Company D. Died from disease in Savannah's St. John's Hospital on May 12, 1862, and is buried in Laurel Grove Cemetery at Savannah, Ga.

Headstone of Private Richard P. Connell, Company I. Killed at the Battle of Sharpsburg on September 17, 1862, and is buried in the Confederate Section of Elmwood Cemetery at Shepherdstown, W.V.

Headstone of Private Manning Corbitt, Co. G. Wounded and captured at Fox's Gap on September 14, 1862. Corbitt died on October 1, 1862, and is buried in Mount Olivet Cemetery at Frederick, Md. His name was misspelled ("Corbert") on the marker.

Headstone of Private Elisha Davis, Company H. Died from disease at Savannah on July 18, 1862, and is buried in Laurel Grove Cemetery at Savannah, Ga. His marker is inscribed "E. Davis."

Headstone of Private James W. Denmark, Co. A. Died from disease on November 2, 1862, and is buried in Stonewall Confederate Cemetery (Mount Hebron) at Winchester, Va. Denmark's marker is incorrectly inscribed as "J.W. Derrett."

Headstone of Captain Edward M. Ford, Company A. The Company A commander was killed at Gettysburg on July 2, 1863, and buried at Gettysburg. He was later removed to Laurel Grove Cemetery at Savannah, Ga. in 1871.

Headstone of Private William D. Ford, Co. I. Died from disease in a Winchester hospital on October 26, 1862, and is buried at Stonewall Confederate Cemetery (Mount Hebron) at Winchester, Va. Ford's marker is inscribed "W.M. Ford."

Headstone of Private Eli Griffis, Company G. The twenty-one year-old died from disease in a Savannah hospital on May 2, 1862, and is buried in Laurel Grove Cemetery at Savannah, Ga.

Headstone of Private J.T. Hardee, Co. D. Died from disease in a Winchester hospital on October 11, 1862, and is buried in Stonewall Confederate Cemetery (Mount Hebron) at Winchester, Va. Hardee's marker is incorrectly inscribed "J.F. Hardle."

Headstone of Private William Harrell, Company C. Died from disease at Savannah on May 2, 1862, and is buried in Laurel Grove Cemetery at Savannah, Ga.

Headstone of Private Simon Hart, Co. H. Died from disease in a Winchester hospital on October 23, 1862, and is buried in Stonewall Confederate Cemetery (Mount Hebron) at Winchester, Va. Hart's marker is incorrectly inscribed "T. Heart."

Headstone of Lieutenant James Kinchen Hilliard, Company C. Wounded at Gettysburg on July 2, 1863. He died on July 17, and is buried in Stonewall Confederate Cemetery (Mount Hebron) at Winchester, Va. Hilliard's marker is incorrectly inscribed "J. K. Hillerd."

Headstone of Private I. Hollingsworth, Company H. Died from disease in a Lynchburg hospital on September 4, 1862, and is buried in the Confederate Cemetery at Lynchburg, Va.

Headstone of Corporal R. Perry Hughes, Co. D. Wounded at Fox's Gap on September 14, 1862, and later captured at Sharpsburg on September 17. Hughes died on November 25, 1862, and is buried in Mount Olivet Cemetery at Frederick, Md. His name is misspelled ("Hughs") and date of death ("Nov 5") is incorrect on the marker.

Headstone of Lt. Colonel Francis Kearse, Commander, 50th Georgia Regiment. Killed at Gettysburg on July 2, 1863, and buried at Gettysburg. He was removed to Laurel Grove Cemetery at Savannah, Ga. in 1871.

Headstone of Private David Lastinger, Company G. Wounded at Cedar Creek on October 19, 1864, and died in a Winchester hospital on November 17. He is buried in Stonewall Confederate Cemetery (Mount Hebron) at Winchester, Va. His marker is incorrectly inscribed "Lastenger."

Headstone of Dr. Nathaniel McArthur, Superintendent, St. Johns Hos., Savannah, Ga. This Thomas County soldier was detailed as Superintendent of St. Johns Hospital at Savannah on June 1, 1862. McArthur died from disease on March 3, 1863, and is buried in Laurel Grove Cemetery at Savannah, Ga. His headstone reads "In memory of Dr. N. McArthur, Aged 39, 50th Reg. Ga. Vol. A native of North Carolina. A good soldier of Jesus Christ he died from disease contracted in the General Hospital while ministering to his sick comrades."
Photo by author

Headstone of Private Wyatt H. McPherson, Co. E. Wounded at Fox's Gap on September 14, 1862, and later captured at Sharpsburg on September 17. He died on October 27, 1862, and is buried in Mount Olivet Cemetery at Frederick, Md. His first name is misspelled ("Wyat") on the marker.

Headstone of Private Frederick Merritt, Co. C. Died from disease in a Winchester hospital on November 13, 1862, and is buried at Stonewall Confederate Cemetery (Mount Hebron) at Winchester, Va. His marker is incorrectly inscribed "F. Merett."

Headstone of Lieutenant Wryan Minshew, Company A. Wounded at Cedar Creek on October 19, 1864. He died in a Federal hospital at Winchester on October 24, and is buried in Stonewall Confederate Cemetery (Mount Hebron) at Winchester, Va. His marker is incorrectly inscribed "Menshaw."

Headstone of Second Lieutenant Francis L. Mobley, Company I. Wounded at Sharpsburg on September 17, 1862. He died in a Winchester hospital on October 9, and is buried in Stonewall Confederate Cemetery (Mount Hebron) at Winchester, Va.

Headstone of Private Ezra Newton, Co. A. Killed at Gettysburg on July 2, 1863, and buried at Gettysburg. He was later removed to Laurel Grove Cemetery at Savannah, Ga. in 1871.

Headstone of Private John T. Nix, Co. F. Wounded at Fox's Gap on September 14, 1862, and later captured at Sharpsburg on September 17. He died on October 14, and is buried in Mount Olivet Cemetery at Frederick, Md. His date of death on the marker ("Oct 4") is incorrect.

Headstone of Captain John Riley O'Steen, Company G. Wounded and captured at Fox's Gap on September 14, 1862. He died on September 23, 1862, and is buried in Mount Olivet Cemetery at Frederick, Md.

Headstone of Private Daniel C. Paulk, Co. I. Died from disease in a Winchester hospital on November 2, 1862, and is buried in Stonewall Confederate Cemetery (Mount Hebron) at Winchester, Va. Paulk's marker is incorrectly inscribed "D. Paril."

Headstone of Corporal J.G. Powell, Company F. Died from disease in a Lynchburg hospital on September 1, 1862, and is buried in the Confederate Cemetery at Lynchburg, Va.

Headstone of Private T. J. Rawls, Company E. Died from disease in a Winchester hospital on October 20, 1862, and is buried in Stonewall Confederate Cemetery (Mount Hebron) at Winchester, Va. His marker is incorrectly inscribed "J. T. Roules 157."

Headstone of Private William H. Reynolds, Company F. Died from disease in a Winchester hospital on October 17, 1862, and is buried in Stonewall Confederate Cemetery (Mount Hebron) at Winchester, Va. His marker is inscribed "W. H. Reynolds 151."

Headstone of Private John Rewis (Ruis), Company I. Died from disease in a Winchester hospital on October 31, 1862, and is buried in Stonewall Confederate Cemetery (Mount Hebron) at Winchester, Va. The marker inscription is "John Ruis 190."

Headstone of Private Emanuel Shuman, Co. E. Wounded and captured at Fox's Gap on September 14, 1862. He died on September 24, and is buried in Mount Olivet Cemetery at Frederick, Md.

Headstone of Private David Sloan, Co. F. Wounded and captured at Fox's Gap on September 14, 1862. The Decatur County soldier died on September 27, 1862, and is buried in Mount Olivet Cemetery at Frederick, Md.

Headstone of Private Matthew T. Strickland, Co. G. Wounded and captured at Fox's Gap on September 14, 1862. He died on December 4, 1862, and is buried in Mount Olivet Cemetery at Frederick, Md.

Private Orthenald Trawick, Company F. Wounded and captured at Fox's Gap on September 14, 1862. He died on September 28, and is buried in Mount Olivet Cemetery at Frederick, Md. His first name was misspelled ("Orthnold") on the marker.

Headstone of Private Charles Trulock, Co. F. Wounded at Fox's Gap on September 14, 1862, and later captured at Sharpsburg on September 17. He died on September 27, and is buried in Mount Olivet Cemetery at Frederick, Md.

Headstone of Private Andrew "Drew" Vickers, Company D. Died from disease in a Winchester hospital on October 3, 1862, and is buried in Stonewall Confederate Cemetery (Mount Hebron) at Winchester, Va. His marker is incorrectly inscribed "D. Bucker 104."

Headstone of Private John T. Weekly, Company I. Killed at Gettysburg on July 2, 1863, and buried at Gettysburg. He was later removed to Laurel Grove Cemetery at Savannah, Ga. in 1871.

Headstone of Private J.R. White, Company I. Killed at Gettysburg on July 2, 1863, and buried at Gettysburg. He was later removed to Laurel Grove Cemetery at Savannah, Ga. in 1871.

Headstone of Private William R. Wiley, Co. F. Wounded and captured at Fox's Gap on September 14, 1862. He died on September 23, 1862, and is buried in Mount Olivet Cemetery at Frederick, Md.

Headstone of Private Morgan G. Yates, Company K. Died from disease in a Winchester hospital on October 15, 1862, and is buried in Stonewall Confederate Cemetery (Mount Hebron) at Winchester, Va. His marker is incorrectly inscribed "N. G. Yates 265."

Headstone of Captain Cicero Holt Young, Company E. Died from disease on October 1, 1862, and is buried in Stonewall Confederate Cemetery (Mount Hebron) at Winchester, Va. His marker inscription reads, "In Memory of C. H. Young of Thomasville, Ga., Capt. 50th Regt. Ga. Vol. who died in Winchester, Va. Oct. 1st 1862 in the 40th year of his age."

Headstone of Private Lovick M. Young, Company I. Killed at Cedar Creek on October 19, 1864, and is buried in Stonewall Confederate Cemetery (Mount Hebron) at Winchester, Va. The marker is incorrectly inscribed "S. M. Young."

Notes

Abbreviations

CSP - Confederate Service Pension Records.

CSR - "Compiled Service Records of Confederate Soldiers Who Served in Organizations from the State of Georgia," Fiftieth Infantry Regiment (National Archives Microfilm Publication M266, Rolls 505-510), National Archives Building, Washington, D.C.

GDAH - Georgia Division of Archives and History, Morrow, Ga.

OR - *War of the Rebellion: A Compilation of the Official Records of the Union and Confederate Armies*. 130 Vols.

SHSP - *Southern Historical Society Papers*

Chapter One - Defending the Homeland: Organization and Early Camp Life

1. Lillian Henderson, *Roster of the Confederate Soldiers of Georgia 1861-1865, Vol. V*, (Hapeville, Ga.: Longino & Porter, 1960) p.289-303; Dean Broome, *History of Pierce County, Georgia*, Vol. I, (Blackshear, Ga., 1973) p.264-267; CSR.

2. Henderson, p.297-303; CSR.

3. Henderson, p.303-312; CSR.

4. Henderson, p.313-321; CSR.

5. *Savannah Republican*, Savannah, Ga., April 14, 1862, Lowndes County Historical   Society & Museum, Valdosta, Ga.

6. Henderson, p.321-332; *Original Muster Roll of Thomas County Rangers, March 4, 1862*, Thomas County Historical Society and Museum, Thomasville, Ga.

7. Copy of document appointing Duncan Curry as captain of the Decatur Infantry Militia dated March 4, 1862, and signed by Duncan Curry on March 17, 1862, *Major Duncan Curry Letters & Civil War Papers 1862-1865*, microfilm, Curry Hill Plantation Collection, Southwest Georgia Regional Library, Bainbridge, Ga.; Henderson, p.332-339; CSR.

8. Henderson, p.339-347; *Original Clinch County Muster Roll March 4, 1862*, GDAH; Folks Huxford, *History of Clinch County, Georgia* (Macon, Ga., 1916. reprinted 1992) p.61-62; CSR.

9. Folks Huxford, *Pioneers of Wiregrass Georgia*, Vol. IV, (Pearson, Ga., 1960) p.278.

10. *Ibid.*, p. 279

11. Henderson, p.347-354; *Confederate Soldiers in Colquitt County, Georgia*, MoultrieMcNeill Chapter 661, United Daughters of the Confederacy, (Moultrie, Ga.,

1980. reprinted 2003) p.16; W. A. Covington, *History of Colquitt County* (1937. reprinted Genealogical Publishing Co., Inc., Baltimore, Md., 1997) p.31-32; CSR.

12. Moultrie McNeill Chapter 661, United Daughters of the Confederacy, Moultrie, Ga., p.9.

13. Henderson, p.355-363; L. E. Lastinger, *The Confederate War, A compilation of the Confederate Soldiers going from Berrien County, Georgia. When they enlisted—and whether or not they survived the war*, (Nashville, Ga., 1928. reprinted 1975) p.15-20.

14. Henderson, p.363-370; Folks Huxford, *The History of Brooks County Georgia 1858-1948* (1948. reprinted Spartanburg, SC, 1978) p.97, 99-100, 119-123.

15. William S. Smedlund, *Camp Fires of Georgia's Troops, 1861-1865.* (Kennesaw, Ga. 1994) p.162, Letter of E. C. Corbett to "Col. Wm. T. Thompson from Whitesville, No. 3, C.R.R."

16. *OR*, Vol.14, p.487.

17. Huxford, *Pioneers of Wiregrass Georgia*, Vol. IV, p.191.

18. Henderson, p.331; *Charleston Mercury*, Charleston, S.C., August 3, 1863, "Death of Colonel F. Kearse."; CSR.)

19. Constance Pendleton, *Confederate Memoirs, Early Life and Family History William Frederick Pendleton [and] Mary Lawson Pendleton*, (Bryn Athyn, Pa., 1958), p.11-12, 19-21.

20. Letter of J. G. F. McCall to "Dear Father from Camp Davis Geo. March 20th 1862," *Confederate Letters, Diaries and Reminiscences 1860-1865*, Vol. X, 1946, Georgia Division United Daughters of the Confederacy, p.233, GDAH.

21. Letter of Duncan Curry to "Dear Wife from Camp Davis March the 22", Curry Hill Plantation Collection; Lori Nash-Cosgrove, *North-South Trader Civil War*, Vol. XXXVII, No. 2 "There is no half way ground." p.25, Letter of Francis L. Mobley to "Mrs. F.L. Mobley from Camp Davis March 23rd 1862."; Francis L. Mobley Collection, in the possession of Mobley's great-great grandson, Glenn Hodges of Nashville, Georgia. The author is deeply indebted to Glenn Hodges for permission to use Mobley's letters. Excerpts from these letters were used in Nash-Cosgrove's article.

22. Letter of W. A. Studstill to "Dear Father Mother & Sisters March 23rd 1862," Civil War Miscellany, Microfilm Drawer 150, GDAH.

23. Letter of J. G. F. McCall to "Dear Sister from Camp Davis, Guyton Ga. April 1st –62," *Confederate Letters, Diaries and Reminiscences 1860-1865,* Vol. X, 1946, Georgia Division United Daughters of the Confederacy, p.234, GDAH.

24. McCall letter; CSR.

25. Letter of Francis L. Mobley to "Dear Wife from Camp Davis April 2 1862," Francis L. Mobley Collection.

26. Nash-Cosgrove, p.25, Letter of Francis L. Mobley to "Dear wife from Camp Davis April 7th 1862 Eight O'Clock P.M."; Francis L. Mobley Collection.

27. Letter of Francis L. Mobley to "Mr. Harmon Gaskins hi[gh]ly esteemed father from Camp Davis April 16th/ '62," Francis L. Mobley Collection.

28. Letter of J. A. Hardee to "Dear Sir from Camp Davis April 14 1862," *Confederate Reminiscences and Letters 1861-1865*, Vol. X, 1999, Georgia Division United Daughters of the Confederacy, p.251, GDAH.

29. Letter of Francis L. Mobley to "Dear wife from Camp Davis April 7th 1862 Eight O'Clock P.M." Francis L. Mobley Collection.

30. CSR; Letter of Duncan Curry to "Dear Wife from Camp Davis April 14th 62," Curry Hill Plantation Collection.

31. Smedlund, p.81-82; Nash–Cosgrove, p.30, Letter of Francis Mobley to "Mr. Harmon Gaskins from Camp Brown May 3, 1862." ; Francis L. Mobley Collection.

32. CSR.

33. Letter of Duncan Curry to "Dear Mary from Camp near Fort Boggs May the 26th 62," Curry Hill Plantation Collection.

34. Letter of J. G. F. McCall to "Dear Sister from Savannah Ga. May the 29th 1862," *Confederate Letters, Diaries and Reminiscences 1860-1865*, Vol. X, 1946, Georgia Division United Daughters of the Confederacy, p.236, GDAH.

35. Smedlund, p.456; CSR; Letter of Duncan Curry to "Dear Wife from Battery Walker June the 23rd 62," Curry Hill Plantation Collection.

36. Curry letter, June 23, 1862.

37. Letter of Francis L. Mobley to his wife from "Ft. Brown June 10th [1862]," Francis L. Mobley Collection; CSR; Letter of Duncan Curry to "Dear Wife from Battery Walker June the 30th 62," Curry Hill Plantation Collection.

38. Letter of S.L. Morton to "Dear Sister from Savannah July 3rd 1862," *Confederate Reminiscences and Letters 1861-1865*, Vol. XV, 2000, Georgia Division United Daughters of the Confederacy, p.172, GDAH.

39. Folks Huxford, *Pioneers of Wiregrass Georgia*, Vol. 5, (Waycross, Ga. 1967) p.65 66; CSR.

40. Letter of Duncan Curry to "Dear Wife from Battery Walker July the 19th 62," Curry Hill Plantation Collection; CSR.

41. Pendleton, p.24.

42. Henderson, p.289-370; CSR.

43. *OR*, Vol.14, p. 586-588.

Chapter Two - *Second Manassas Campaign*

1. *OR*, Vol.14, p.586, 587.

2. CSR.

3. Constance Pendleton, *Confederate Memoirs: Early Life and Family William Frederick Pendleton [and] Mary Lawson Young Pendleton*. Pendleton, (Bryn Athyn, Pa., 1958) p. 24.

4. *OR, Vol.12, Pt.2, p.552.*

5. *CSR.*

6. *OR, Vol.12, Pt.3, p.928, 929.*

7. Letter of William O. Fleming to "My dear Georgia, Camps 6 miles from Gordonsville, Va., August 16, 1862," William Oliver Fleming Papers, #2292-z, Southern Historical Collection, Manuscripts Department, Wilson Library, The University of North Carolina at Chapel Hill, Chapel Hill, NC.

8. *OR*, Vol.12, Pt.2, p.552; Pt.3, p.940, 941.

9. *Ibid.*, Vol.12, Pt.2, p.729.

10. *Savannah Republican*, Savannah, Ga., October 16, 1862, "The Fiftieth Georgia Regiment in Virginia and Maryland," Letter of Peter McGlashan to "Mr. Editor: from Bivouac Army of Northern Va. Near Winchester, Oct. 5, 1862."; Pendleton, p.25; OR., Vol.12, Pt.2, p.552.

11. *OR*, Vol.12, Pt.2, p.552-553, 563.

12. Ibid., *p.553, 564, 569, 578; Pendleton, p.25.*

13. Letter of Duncan Curry to "Dear wife from Rappahannock river August the 23rd 62," Major Duncan Curry Letters & Civil War Papers 1862-1865, Curry Hill Plantation Collection, Southwest Georgia Regional Library, Bainbridge, Ga.; CSR.

14. *OR,* Vol.12, Pt.2, p.564, 579.

15. *Ibid.,* p.555, 564.

16. *Savannah Republican,* October 16, 1862.

17. *OR,* Vol.12, Pt.2, p.564, 579.

18. *Ibid.,* p.555-556, 564, 579; *Savannah Republican*, October 16, 1862.

19. *OR.,* Vol.12, Pt.2, p. 556, 579; CSR.

20. *OR,* Vol.12, Pt.2, p. 556, 564, 579; Pendleton, p.26.

21. *OR,* Vol.12, Pt.2, p.556, 565, 579.

22. *Ibid.,* p.557, 565, 579.

23. *Ibid., p.579;* *Savannah Republican,* October 16, 1862.

24. *OR,* Vol.12, Pt.2, p.557, 566.

25. *Ibid.,* p.579, 580.

26. *Savannah Republican,* October 16, 1862.

27. *OR,* Vol.12, Pt.2, p.557, 580; CSR.

28. Pendleton, *p.26.*

29. *OR,* Vol.12, Pt.2, p.558, 566, 580.

30. *Ibid.,* p.558, 566.

31. *Ibid.,* p.566.

32. *Ibid.,* p.568; CSR.

33. *Richmond Daily Dispatch*, Richmond, Va., September 16, 1862, "A flag of truce visit to the battle-field of Manassas."

34. *Ibid.*

35. *Savannah Republican,* October 16, 1862.

Chapter Three - Into Maryland: Fox's Gap

1. *OR*, Vol.19, Pt.1, p.144, 885.

2. Daniel H. Hill, Address at the Reunion of the Virginia Division Army of Northern Virginia Association, October 22, 1885, *SHSP*, Vol. XIII, p.271.

3. *Savannah Republican*, Savannah, Ga., September 20, 1862, V.A.S.P. Letter to "Mr. Editor from Near Frederick, Md., Sept. 7, 1862."

4. Constance Pendleton, *Confederate Memoirs Early Life and Family History William Frederick Pendleton [and] Mary Lawson Young Pendleton.* (Bryn Athyn, Pa., 1958) p.28.

5. Pendleton, p.28-29.

6. *Savannah Republican*, October 16, 1862, "The Fiftieth Georgia Regiment in Virginia and Maryland," Letter of Peter McGlashan to "Mr. Editor: from Bivouac Army of Northern Va. Near Winchester, Oct. 5, 1862." ; SHSP, Vol. XIII, p. 271, October 22, 1885.

7. *Savannah Republican*, October 16, 1862.

8. Diary of J. Evans Edings, Edward Willis Papers, Library of Congress, Washington, D.C.

9. *OR*, Vol.19, Pt.1, p.885; *Savannah Republican*, September 22, 1862, Peter W. Alexander Letter from "In Front of Fredericktown, Md., Sept 8th, 1862."

10. Letter of Francis L. Mobley to "Dear Lady love from [Savannah] Tuesday eavning Aug 26, 1862," Francis L. Mobley Collection, in the possession of Mr. Glenn Hodges, Nashville, Ga. Excerpts from these letters were used in Lori-Nash Cosgrove's article; Lori Nash-Cosgrove, *North-South Trader Civil War*, Vol. XXXVII, No.2 "There is no half way ground," p.30, Letter from Francis L. Mobley to "Dear Lady love from Maryland near Fredericksburg [Frederick, Md.] Sept. 8th 1862."

11. *OR*, Vol.19, Pt.1, p.145.

12. *Ibid.*

13. *Ibid.*, p.145, 885.

14. *Ibid.*, p.145.

15. CSR.

16. *OR*, Vol.19, Pt.1, p.1019, 145, 885; *Savannah Republican*, October 16, 1862.

17. *OR*, Vol. 19, Pt.1, p.1019; Daniel H. Hill, "The Battle of South Mountain, or Boonsboro, Fighting for Time at Turner's and Fox's Gaps," *Battles and Leaders of the Civil War*, Vol. 2 (New York, 1884-1887) p.564.

18. *OR*, Vol.19, Pt.1, p.1019, 1022.

19. *Ibid.*, p.1020.

20. *Ibid.*, p.1020, 908, 1031; SHSP, Vol.XIII, p.268, October 22, 1885.

21. *Ibid.*, p.885, 1020, 908, 1032.

22. *OR*, Vol.19, Pt.1, p.1020, 908, 1032.

23. *OR*, Vol.19, Pt.1, p. 908, 1032, *Savannah Republican*, October 16, 1862.

24. *Savannah Republican*, October 11, 1862, Letter of William O. Fleming regarding the battles of Fox's Gap and Sharpsburg.

25. *Ibid.*

26. CSR.

27. *Savannah Republican*, October 16, 1862; Nash-Cosgrove, p.31, Letter from Francis L. Mobley to "My Dear Wife from Winchester Va Sept 25th 1862."; Francis L. Mobley Collection.

28. *Savannah Republican*, October 11, 1862.

29. *Ibid*; CSR.

30. *Savannah Republican*, October 16, 1862.

31. Ronald G. Watson, ed., *From Ashby to Andersonville, The Civil War Diary and Reminiscences of Private George A. Hitchcock, 21st Massachusetts Infantry* (Campbell, Ca., 1997), p.18-19.

32. "Civil War Diary of Sergeant Henry W. Tisdale, Company I, Thirty-Fifth Regiment, Massachusetts Volunteers, 1862-1865," Copyright 2001. Mark F. Farrell,

great-grandson of Henry W. Tisdale was kind enough to allow the author to use excerpts from Sergeant Tisdale's diary.

33. *Ibid.*

34. George E. Fahm, "Reminiscences of the Sixties (By George E. Fahm) Capt. Co E 50th Ga," Margaret Davis Cate Collection, typeset copy, Brunswick Public Library, Brunswick, Ga.

35. *OR*, Vol.19, Pt.1, p.147.

36. *Ibid.*

37. CSR.

38. *OR*, Vol.19, Pt.1, p.811; Edings diary; *Savannah Republican*, October 16, 1862.

39. *Savannah Republican*, October 1, 1862, "Casualties of the 50th Georgia Regiment—Conduct of the Regiment in the Affairs of Sunday and Wednesday—Lawton's Brigade—Casualties in the Seventeenth," Letter from V.A.S.P. to "Mr. Editor from Bivouac In The Field, Va., September 22d, 1862." ; *Augusta Constitutionalist*, Augusta, Ga., October 9, 1862, "List of Casualties in the 50th Georgia Regiment in the fight near Boonsboro, Sunday, Sept. 14th, 1862, From the Savannah Republican Oct 1." (The article repeats the October 1, 1862, *Savannah Republican* 50th Georgia casualty list from both the Battles of Fox's Gap and Sharpsburg); CSR.

40. Mary Ann Douglass Diary, Thomasville Historical Society, Thomasville, Ga.

41. *Ibid.*

42. *Ibid.*

43. *Ibid.*

44. *Ibid.*

Chapter Four - Sharpsburg and Operations in Virginia

1. *OR*, Vol.19, Pt.1, p.886.

2. *OR*, Vol.19, Pt.1, p.148. In addition to being known as the Rohrbach Bridge and the Lower Bridge, after the battle, the structure also became known as the "Burnside Bridge."

3. *OR*, Vol.19, Pt.1, p.886, 889.

4. *Ibid.*; CSR; *Savannah Republican*, Savannah, Ga., October 16, 1862, "The Fiftieth Georgia Regiment in Virginia and Maryland," Letter of Peter McGlashan to "Mr. Editor: from Bivouac Army of Northern Va. Near Winchester, Oct. 5, 1862."

5. *OR*, Vol.19, Pt.1, p.889, 890.

6. *Ibid.*, p.889.

7. *Ibid.*, p.890, 419; Jerry W. Holsworth, "Friends To The Death," *Civil War Times*, Vol. XLV, No.7 (September 2006) p.40-45.

8. *OR*, Vol.19, Pt.1, p. 419.

9. *Savannah Republican*, October 16, 1862.

10. *OR*, Vol.19, Pt.1, p. 451, 453.

11. *Savannah Republican*, October 16, 1862.

12. *OR*, Vol.19, Pt.1, p.890.

13. *Ibid.*, p.890-891.

14. *Savannah Republican*, October 16, 1862; *OR*, Vol. 19, Pt.1, p.891.

15. *Ibid.*, p.886, 890-891.

16. *Ibid.*, p.840; *Savannah Republican*, October 11, 1862, Letter of William O. Fleming regarding the battles of Fox's Gap and Sharpsburg.

17. *Savannah Republican*, October 11, 1862

18. *OR*, Vol.19, Pt.1, p. 887, 891.

19. *Ibid.*, p.150, 453-454.

20. *Ibid.*, p.150, 840-841, 887, 891; *Savannah Republican*, October 11, 1862.

21. *OR*, Vol.41, Pt.1, p.166-167; Vol.19, Pt.1, p.887, 892

22. *Savannah Republican*, October 16, 1862.

23. *Savannah Republican*, October 11, 1862.

24. Lori Nash-Cosgrove, *North-South Trader Civil War*, Vol.XXVII, No.2 "There is no half way ground," p.30, Letter of Francis Mobley Letter to "My Dear Wife, from Winchester Va Sept 25th 1862."; Francis L. Mobley Collection.

25. *OR*, Vol. 19, Pt.1, p. 887, 151.

26. *Savannah Republican*, October 16, 1862.

27. *OR*, Vol.19, Pt.1, p.887.

28. CSR; *Savannah Republican*, October 1, 1862, "Casualties of the 50th Georgia Regiment—Conduct of the Regiment in the Affairs of Sunday and Wednesday—Lawton's Brigade—Casualties in the Seventeenth," Letter of V. A. S. P. to "Mr. Editor: from Bivouac In The Field, Va. September 22d, 1862."

29. *Savannah Republican*, October 15, 1862, "The Fiftieth Georgia at Sharpsburg," Letter of Wm. R. Manning to "Mr. Editor: from Valdosta, Ga., Oct. 12th, 1862."

30. *Ibid*; *Savannah Republican*, October 1, 1862.

31. *Savannah Republican*, October 15, 1862.

32. *Ibid.*

33. *OR*, Vol.19, Pt.1, p.152; J. Evans Edings Diary, Edward Willis Papers, Manuscript Division, Box 4, "1862 MMC 3182, Confederate Pamphlets," Library of Congress, Washington, D.C.; *Savannah Republican*, October 16, 1862.

34. CSR.

35. Nash-Cosgrove, p.30; Francis L. Mobley Collection.

36. CSR

37. *Savannah Republican,* October 11, 1862.

38. William J. Evers' Letter to "Dear wife from Savannah Georgia Aug. the 11th 1862," *Confederate Reminiscences and Letters*, Vol. VI, 1992, Georgia Division United Daughters of the Confederacy, p.204, GDAH.

39. CSR.

40. William O. Fleming letter to "My dear Georgia from Camp near Winchester, Oct 7th 1862", William Oliver Fleming Papers [#2292-z], Southern Historical Collection, Manuscripts Department, Wilson Library, The University of North Carolina at Chapel Hill, NC.

41. CSR.

42. Nash-Cosgrove, p.31, Letter of David P. Luke to "Mrs. F.L. Mobley from Camp near Bruiceville Oct. 14th 1862."; Francis L. Mobley Collection.

43. CSR.

44. Duncan Curry Letter to "Dear wife from Camp near Harpers Ferry Oct the 23rd 62", Curry Hill Plantation Collection, Major Duncan Curry Letters & Civil War Papers 1862-1865, Southwest Georgia Regional Library, Bainbridge, Ga.

45. *Ibid.*

46. CSR.

47. *Ibid.*

48. Duncan Curry Letter to "Dear wife Near Culpepper Courthouse, Nov the 4th 62." This was the only allegation made against Drayton related to drinking that was found during the research for this book.

Chapter Five - Fredericksburg: The Battle and the Harsh Winter

1. *OR*, Vol.21, Pt.1, p.1016.

2. *Ibid.*

3. *Ibid.*, p.1015-1016.

4. CSR.

5. *OR*, Vol.21, Pt.1, p.1029-1030.

6. *Ibid.*, p.1033.

7. Andrew J. McBride, *Atlanta Journal*, Atlanta, Ga., September 14, 1901, "10th Georgia Captures 27th Connecticut."

8. *OR*, Vol.21, Pt.1, p.538.

9. *Ibid.*, p.568-569, 578.

10. *Ibid.*, p.1041.

11. John G. F. McCall Letter to "My Dear Sister from Camp near Fredericksburg Va. December 3rd 1862," *Confederate Letters, Diaries and Reminiscences 1860-1865*, Vol. X, 1946, Georgia Division United Daughters of the Confederacy, p.237, GDAH.

12. Duncan Curry Letter to "Dear wife from near Fredericksburg Dec the 6th 62," *Major Duncan Curry Letters & Civil War Papers 1862-1865*, microfilm, Curry Hill Plantation Collection, Southwest Georgia Regional Library, Bainbridge, Ga.

13. *OR*, Vol.21, Pt.1, p.569, 578.

14. *Ibid.*, p.569, 579.

15. John L. G. Wood Letter to "Dear Father from Camp near Fredericksburg, Va. This Dec. the 18th 1862," John L. G. Wood Letters, Microfilm Drawer 194, Box 3, GDAH.

16. A. J. McBride, *Atlanta Journal*, May 4, 1901, "Banner Battle of the War, The Tenth Georgia on Lee's Hill, Northern Lady Searching for the Body of Her Husband."

17. *OR*, Vol.21, Pt.1, p.547, 554-555, 570-571, 580-581.

18. William Moore Jones, "War Service and Diary of Sergeant William Moore Jones, Company K, 50th Georgia Infantry," *Confederate Reminiscences and Letters*, Vol. V, 1997, Georgia Division United Daughters of the Confederacy, p.117, GDAH.

19. *OR*, Vol.21, Pt.1, p.581, 607; McBride, *Atlanta Journal*, May 4, 1901.

20. McBride, *Atlanta Journal*, May 4, 1901; John L. G. Wood letter December 18, 1862.

21. John L. G. Wood letter December 18, 1862.

22. *OR*, Vol.21, Pt.1, p.555.

23. *OR*, Vol.21, Pt.1, p.583; CSR.

24. *OR*, Vol.21, Pt.1, p.582.

25. CSR.

26. William O. Fleming letter to "My dear Georgia from Camp 50th Ga Regt, Jan 22nd 1863," William Oliver Fleming Papers [#2292-z], Southern Historical Collection, Manuscripts Department, Wilson Library, The University of North Carolina at Chapel Hill, NC.

27. CSR.

28. *Ibid.*

29. *Ibid.*

30. *Ibid.*

31. *Ibid.*

32. *Ibid.*

33. *Ibid.*; R. T. Roberds Letter to "My Own Dear Wife from Camp near Fredericksburg Va April 1, 1863," R. Tompy Roberds Collection, Civil War Miscellany-Personal Papers, Microfilm Roll 283/38, GDAH.

34. Roberds letter, April 1, 1863.

35. CSR.

36. *OR*, Vol.21, Pt.1, p.687.

37. Constance Pendleton, *Confederate Memoirs: Early Life and Family History, William Frederick Pendleton [and] Mary Lawson Young Pendleton.* (Bryn Athyn, Pa., 1958) p.30.

38. CSR.

39. *Ibid.*; Pendleton, p.30.

Chapter Six – The Chancellorsville Campaign

1. Edwin Taliaferro Papers, RG 109, Box 1, Entry 134, PI 101, National Archives, Washington, D.C. Date of report unknown, but believed to be the winter of 1862-1863.

2. *OR*, Vol.25, Pt.1, p.833.

3. *The Daily Richmond Enquirer*, Richmond Va., May 11, 1863, "The Battles Around Fredericksburg (Special Correspondence of the Enquirer) from In Camp Near Fredericksburg May 8th, 1863."

4. *OR*, Vol.25, Pt.1, p. 833, 837.

5. *Ibid*; *OR*, Vol.25, Pt.2, p.762; *Savannah Daily Morning News*, Savannah, Ga., May 30, 1863, "(Correspondence of the *Savannah Morning News*) From Gen. Semmes's Brigade," Letter to "Editor Daily Morning News: from Camp Near Fredericksburg, Va., May 14th, 1863."

6. *OR*, Vol.25, Pt.1, p.824; OR., Vol.25, Pt.2, p.762; *The Daily Richmond Enquirer*, May 11, 1863.

7. *OR*, Vol.25, Pt.1, p.797, 825.

8. *Ibid*, p.825, 833.

9. *Ibid*, p.825, 833-834.

10. *Ibid.*, p.834.

11. *Ibid.*, p.833-834, 837.

12. William Moore Jones, "War Service and Diary of Sergeant William Moore Jones, Company K, 50th Georgia Infantry," *Confederate Reminiscences and Letters*, Vol. V, 1997, Georgia Division United Daughters of the Confederacy, p.117, GDAH.

13. *OR*, Vol.25, Pt.2, p.764; *OR*, Vol.25, Pt.1, p.825, 834.

14. *OR*, Vol.25, Pt.1, p.825, 834; John L. G. Wood Letter to "Dear Aunt from New Camp, 8 miles from Fredericksburg This May the 10th 1863," John L. G. Wood Letters, Microfilm Drawer 194, Box 3, GDAH.

15. *OR*, Vol.25, Pt.1, p.797, 825, 834.

16. *Ibid.*

17. *Ibid*, p. 826, 834, 838; Andrew J. McBride, *Atlanta Journal*, Atlanta, Ga., August 31, 1901, "The Tenth Georgia at Zoar Church and Chancellorsville."

18. *OR*, Vol.25, Pt.1, p.826, 834-835.

19. *Ibid*, p.835, 838.

20. Wood letter, May 10, 1863.

21. *OR*, Vol.25, Pt.1, p.826, 835.

22. Constance Pendleton, *Confederate Memoirs: Early Life and Family History William Frederick Pendleton [and] Mary Lawson Young Pendleton*, (Bryn Athyn, Pa., 1958) p.32; Peter McGlashan, "Battle of Salem Church, May 3, 1863," The Confederate Veterans Association of Savannah, Ga., April 18, 1893, Georgia Historical Society, Savannah, Ga.

23. *OR*, Vol.25, Pt.1, p.827, 835; *Savannah Daily Morning News*, May 30, 1863.

24. McGlashan.

25. Jones, p.118.

26. Wood letter, May 10, 1863.

27. *OR*, Vol.25, Pt.1, p.568, 570-571.

28. *Ibid*, p.570-572, 574-582, 586, 835; Wood letter, May 10, 1863; Jones, p.118.

29. *OR*, Vol.25, Pt.1, p.571.

30. McGlashan.

31. *Ibid.*; *OR*, Vol.25, Pt.1, p.836.

32. *OR*, Vol.25, Pt.1, p.827, 835-836, 838-839; Andrew J. McBride, *Atlanta Journal*, September 14, 1901, "10th Georgia Captures 27th Connecticut"; *Savannah Daily Morning News*, May 30, 1863.

33. *OR*, Vol.25, Pt.1, p.836-837; McGlashan.

34. *OR*, Vol.25, Pt.1, p.568, 576-578, 592-593.

35. *The Daily Richmond Enquirer*, May 11, 1863.

36. McGlashan.

37. *Ibid.*; The reference to McGlashan as "Colonel" is in error. Lieutenant Colonel Francis Kearse commanded the regiment. Peter McGlashan had recently assumed the rank of major. He did not receive a promotion to colonel until after Gettysburg. In researching the compiled service records, two Culpepper brothers from Company H were found in the 50th Georgia Regiment. Private David C. Culpepper suffered a horrible head wound at the Battle of Salem Church on May 3, 1863. Henderson's Roster of Confederate Soldiers, Vol. V, and a pension application by Culpepper's widow reference the loss of both eyes. This must have been the soldier McGlashan described. According to his widow's

pension application, his brother, Private J. (John) B. Culpepper brought him home from the hospital to Mitchell County, Georgia, where he died on June 23, 1863.

38. Pendleton, p.32-33.

39. *Atlanta Journal*, September 14, 1901.

40. *Savannah Daily Morning News*, May 16, 1863, R. T. Roberds Letter to "Mr. Editor from Battlefield Near Fredericksburg, May 4th, 1863."

41. Taliaferro Papers.

42. *OR*, Vol.25, Pt.1, p.801, 827.

43. *Ibid*, p.802, 827-829.

44. *Ibid*, Pt.1, p.829.

45. *Ibid*; Wood letter May 10, 1863.

46. *OR*, Vol.25, Pt.1, p.829; *Atlanta Journal*, September 14, 1901; Pendleton, p.33.

47. *Savannah Republican*, May 18, 1863, letter from unidentified 50th Georgia officer (believed to be Adjutant R.T. Roberds) to "Dear ___ from Headq'rs 50th Regiment Near Fredericksburg, May 8, 1863."

48. William J. Evers Letter to "Dear wife from Camp near Fred[ericksburg] Va. May the 9th 1863," *Confederate Reminiscences and Letters 1860-1865*, Vol. VI, 1997, Georgia Division United Daughters of the Confederacy, p. 215-216, GDAH.

49. Malachi NeSmith Letter to "My Dear Wife from Richmond, Virginia May 18, 1863, The Museum of Colquitt County History, Moultrie, Ga.; CSR.

50. John G. F. McCall Letter to "Dear Sister from Camp near Fre-Burg [Fredericksburg]Va. May 21st 1863," *Confederate Letters, Diaries and Reminiscences 1860-1865*, Vol. X, Ga. Division, UDC, GDAH.

51. *OR*, Vol.25, Pt.1, p.829.

52. *Savannah Daily Morning News*, May 16, 1863; CSR; Regimental casualty rate percentage based on number of casualties (187) divided by McGlashan's May 3 morning muster roll report showing 316 men.

53. CSR.

54. *Ibid*.

55. *Ibid*; Jones, p.118.

56. Gary W. Gallagher, *The Battle of Chancellorsville*, National Parks Civil War Series, (1995) p. 51.

Chapter Seven - The Gettysburg Campaign

1. CSR.

2. *OR*, Vol.27, Pt.1, p.293; William J. Evers Letter to "Dear wife from Camp near Culpep[er] Va. June the 8th/63," *Confederate Reminiscences and Letters*, Vol.VI, 1997, Georgia Division, United Daughters of the Confederacy, p.216, GADH.

3. CSR.

4. *OR*, Vol.27, Pt.2, p.357.

5. William O. Fleming Letter to "Dear Mother, from Ashbys Gap 14 Miles from Winchester Va June 23rd 1863," William Oliver Fleming Papers [#2292-z], Southern Historical Collection, Manuscripts Department, Wilson Library, The University of North Carolina at Chapel Hill, N.C.

6. *OR*, Vol.27, Pt.2, p.357; Fleming Letter, June 23, 1863.

7. *OR*, Vol.27, Pt.2, p.357-358.

8. L.L. Cochran, *Atlanta Journal*, Atlanta, Ga., February 23, 1901, "The Tenth Georgia Regiment at Gettysburg."

9. *OR*, Vol.27, Pt.2, p.357, 366; Unidentified 10th Georgia Soldier, *Atlanta Journal*, August 31, 1901, "Some Incidents of the March to Gettysburg."

10. *OR*, Vol.27, Pt.2, p. 297-298, 358; *Atlanta Journal*, August 31, 1901.

11. *OR*, Vol.27, Pt.1, p.358.

12. *OR*, Vol.27, Pt.2, p.366-367.

13. *OR*, Vol.27, Pt.1, p.881.

14. Battlefield historian John B. Bachelder's map for July 2, published a few years after the battle, depicts the order of Semmes' Brigade, from left to right, as: 50th, 10th, 51st and 53rd. His source for this alignment is unknown by the author. Other modern sources also place the 50th Georgia on the far left. There is much less consensus on the location of the other three regiments. Without evidence to the contrary, the author believes that the initial alignment of the regiments to be as Bachelder depicted. Once engaged, the brigades of Kershaw and Semmes became commingled. There are no known reports from Semmes' Brigade on the battle. Therefore, the locations of individual regiments during the fog of battle are based on reports from other brigades, individual soldier accounts, and conjecture.

15. *Atlanta Journal*, February 23, 1901.

16. OR, Vol.27, Pt.2, p.367-368.

17. *Ibid.*, p.368.

18. Constance Pendleton, *Confederate Memoirs: Early Life and Family History, William Frederick Pendleton [and] Mary Lawson Young Pendleton*, (Bryn Athyn, Pa., 1958) p.35.

19. *Atlanta Journal*, February 23, 1901.

20. *Savannah Morning News Print*, Savannah, Ga., 1902, "Longstreet's Charge At Gettysburg – July 2, 1863," Address by Peter A. S. McGlashan to Confederate Veterans Association of Savannah, May 1899; William Moore Jones, "War Service and Diary of Sergeant William Moore Jones, Company K, 50th Georgia Infantry," *Confederate Reminiscences and Letters*, Vol.V, 1997, Georgia Division, United Daughters of the Confederacy, p.118, GDAH.

21. *Atlanta Journal*, February 23, 1901.

22. *Savannah Morning News Print*, 1902.

23. Pendleton, p.35.

24. Jones, p.118.

25. Pendleton, p.35; Jones, p.118. Lt. Col. Kearse was reportedly buried the next day in the Rose orchard near the springhouse. This location is consistent with the Bachelder map of the July 2 battle, which depicted Semmes' Brigade just southeast of the Rose House at about 5:40 in the afternoon. Kearse likely would have fallen near this area.

26. William O. Fleming Letter to "My dear Georgia from Funkstown Md July 18th 1863."

27. *OR*, Vol.27, Pt.1, p.574, 505.

28. *Savannah Morning News Print*, 1902.

29. *OR*, Vol.27, Pt.2, p.368.

30. *Atlanta Journal,* February 23, 1901; *Savannah Morning News Print,* 1902. McGlashan reported that thirteen officers in the 50th Georgia had been killed. Many more officers and non-commissioned officers were wounded.

31. *Savannah Morning News Print,* 1902.

32. *OR,* Vol.27, Pt.2, p.368.

33. Letter of Joseph B. Kershaw to John B. Bachelder, April 6, 1876. John B. Bachelder Papers, New Hampshire Historical Society, Concord, New Hampshire. The most reliable account of where General Semmes received his mortal wound would appear to be that of General Kershaw. In his April 6, 1876, letter to battlefield historian John B. Bachelder, the Confederate commander recalled that Semmes fell near a stone wall in an open field. A short time earlier, Kershaw had met with Semmes and urged him to bring his men up on Kershaw's right.

34. *Savannah Morning News Print,* 1902; McGlashan reported that at one point in the battle "the mass of struggling, fighting troops broken up into groups, all regimental organizations lost, were being slowly driven backwards before the almost irresistible advance of the enemy. . . ." He also mentioned the troops "gallantly rallying by squads and groups."

35. *OR,* Vol.27, Pt.2, p.369; Pendleton, p.35.

36. *OR,* Vol.27, Pt.2, p.369, 372.

37. *OR,* Vol.27, Pt.1, p.394; *OR.,* Vol.27, Pt.2, p.369.

38. *OR,* Vol.27, Pt.1, p.400, 410; Letter of William W. Howell, 10th Georgia Regiment, Drawer 283, Box 28, GDAH, Morrow, Ga.

39. *OR,* Vol.27, Pt.1, p.400, 410.

40. *Ibid,* p.400-401, 403.

41. *OR,* Vol.27, Pt.2, p.369.

42. *OR,* Vol.27, Pt.1, p.400, 410.

43. *Ibid.,* p.611-612.

44. *OR,* Vol.27, Pt.2, p.369.

45. Pendleton, p.35. Pendleton was apparently mistaken about Lt. Tenille's regiment. No W. A. Tenille could be found in the 15th Georgia roster. However, the 9th Georgia Regiment did contain a Lt. W. A. Tenille.

46. *OR,* Vol.27, Pt.2, p.369.

47. *Savannah Morning News Print,* 1902.

48. *OR,* Vol.27, Pt.2, p.359.

49. *Savannah Morning News Print,* 1902.

50. *OR,* Vol.27, Pt.2, p.338-339; Casualty rate based on Surgeon L. Guild's report of 430 killed, wounded or captured out of an estimated 1,300 men engaged.

51. Pendleton, p.36. Pendleton's comment that Fleming "had not been in the battle" appears to be in error. In a letter to his wife a week after the battle, Fleming mentioned, "Lt. [Thomas A.] Ballard was shot within a few feet of me through his right breast." Fleming also mentioned the wounding of Lieutenant (James W.) Maxwell. The regiment had been scattered during the fighting and it appears that Fleming (Company F) did not participate in the later Confederate advance with Pendleton (Company B). Pendleton also incorrectly mentioned Fleming's rank as "Lieutenant Colonel." Fleming's promotion to Lieutenant Colonel occurred after the battle.

52. Jones, p.118-119.

53. *Ibid.*, p.119.

54. Pendleton, p.36.

55. *Ibid.*

56. Gary Kross, "Gettysburg Vignettes To Die Like Soldiers The Retreat from Sickles's Front, July 2, 1863, Vignette #2 The Wheatfield," *Blue & Gray Magazine*, Vol. XV, Issue 5, June 1998, p.21.

57. *OR*, Vol.27, Pt.2, p.338-339.

58. CSR; Casualty List for the Fiftieth Georgia Regiment, *Daily Chronicle and Sentinel*, Augusta, Georgia, July 31, 1863; "Sick and Wounded Confederate Soldiers at Hagerstown and Williamsport," SHSP, Vol. XVII, 1899, p.241-250.

59. CSR.

60. Jones, p.119.

61. William O. Fleming letter to "My dear Georgia from Funkstown Md July 10th 1863."

62. Pendleton, p.38.

63. CSR.

64. Pendleton, p.39.

65. William O. Fleming Letter to " My Dear Georgia from near Williamsport, Md. July 13 1863."

66. Samuel W. Fiske Letter to *Springfield Republican*, Springfield, Mass., July 14, 1863 located in *Mr. Dunn Browne's Experiences in the War: The Civil War Letters of Samuel W. Fiske*, Stephen W. Sears, editor (New York, 1998) p.122-123.

67. CSR; Casualty List for the Fiftieth Georgia Regiment, *Daily Chronicle and Sentinel*, Augusta, Georgia, July 31, 1863; "Sick and Wounded Confederate Soldiers at Hagerstown and Williamsport," SHSP, Vol. XVII, 1899, p.241-250.

68. William Ross Stillwell Letter to "My Dear and Beloved Mollie from Camp near Hagerstown, Maryland July 13, 1863," William Ross Stillwell Letters, GDAH; *Daily Chronicle & Sentinel*, Augusta, Georgia, July 23, 1863, "From the Tenth Georgia Regiment," J. W. Taylor Letter to "Dear ___ from Camp 10th GA. Regiment, Three miles from Williamsport, Md., July 13th, 1863."

69. Pendleton, p.39-40.

70. Pendleton, p.40-41; John L. G. Wood Letter to "Dear Father from Camp near the Rapidan River, in Orange County, this Aug. 13th 1863," John L. G. Wood Letters, Microfilm Drawer 194, Box 3, GDAH.

71. CSR.

72. *Ibid.*

73. William J. Evers Letter to "Dear wife from Stanton, Va. August the 4th/63," *Confederate Reminiscences and Letters*, Vol.VI, 1997, Georgia Division, United Daughters of the Confederacy, p. 217-218, GDAH.

74. CSR.

Chapter Eight - The East Tennessee Campaign

1. Constance Pendleton, *Confederate Memoirs: Early Life and Family History, William Frederick Pendleton [and] Mary Lawson Young Pendleton*, (Bryn Athyn, PA, 1958) p.41.

2. CSR.

3. Pendleton, p 41.

4. Andrew J. McBride, *Atlanta Journal*, Atlanta, Ga., March 9, 1901, "The Tenth Georgia in Atlanta: A Military Execution at Chattanooga."

5. *Ibid.*

6. *Ibid.*

7. Letter of William O. Fleming to "My dear Georgia from Bivouac 50th Ga Regt Near Ringold Sept 20th 1863", William Oliver Fleming Papers (#2292-z), Southern Historical Collection, Manuscripts Department, Wilson Library, The University of North Carolina at Chapel Hill, NC.

8. Pendleton, p.44

9. Letter of John L. G. Wood to "My Dear Aunt, Camp in line of battle in Dry Valley 3 miles from Chattanooga This Oct. the 12th 1863," John L. G. Wood Letters, Microfilm Drawer 194, Box 3, GDAH.

10. CSR.

11. *OR*, Vol.31, Pt.1, p.476.

12. Pendleton, p.46

13. *Ibid.*

14. The Confederates continued to call the fortification Fort Loudon during the war.

15. *OR*, Vol.31, Pt.1, p.523.

16. *Ibid.*, p.309.

17. *Ibid.*, p.342.

18. *Ibid.*

19. *Ibid.*, p 343.

20. *Ibid.*, p.342, 343.

21. *Ibid.*, p.487-489.

22. Pendleton, p.47.

23. McBride, *Atlanta Journal*, March 9, 1901.

24. Pendleton, p.47.

25. *Ibid.*, p. 48; *Valdosta Times*, Valdosta, Georgia, "Death of Mrs. Tompy Roberds," Civil War Miscellany, R. Tompy Roberds Letters, Microfilm Drawer 283, Box 38, GDAH. The author unsuccessfully attempted to obtain the date the obituary appeared in the *Times*. Apparently this particular edition did not survive for future microfilming. Mrs. Roberds died on May 29, 1885, and it is presumed that the obituary would have followed shortly thereafter, most likely in early June.

26. Pendleton, p. 48.

27. *Valdosta Times*.

28. Daniel I. Walden, *Atlanta Journal*, January 11, 1902, "Tenth Georgia at Knoxville."

29. *Ibid.*; McBride, *Atlanta Journal*, March 9, 1901; Pendleton, p. 54; CSR; Letter of P. McGlashan to "General, from HdQrs 50th Regt Geo Vols May 2nd 1864." It does not appear that the 50th Georgia flag was captured with Bailey as there are no reports that mention its loss. Union troops apparently captured 3 other flags during the fight with one Union report mentioning that the captured flags came from the 16th Georgia, 17th Mississippi and 13th Mississippi.

30. *Atlanta Journal*, March 9, 1901. Andrew J. McBride erroneously reported that Sergeant Bailey was a member of the 51st Georgia Regiment, when in fact he was a member of the 50th Georgia.

31. Pendleton, p.48.

32. *OR*, Vol.31, Pt.1, p.461, 475-476, 344.

33. Pendleton, p.48.

34. Letter of John Watkins to friend John Probert from "Knoxville Tennessee Dec 15th/63," MS-1161, John Watkins Papers, The Special Collections Library of the University of Tennessee, Knoxville, Tn.

35. *Atlanta Journal*, March 9, 1901.

36. *OR*, Vol.31, Pt.1, p.495.

37. Pendleton, p.49.

38. *OR*, Vol.31, Pt.1, p.524.

39. CSR.

40. *Valdosta Times*.

41. Letter of General Goode Bryan to "Madam from Hdqrs Bryan's Brigade February 25th 1864," Civil War Miscellany, R. Tompy Roberds, Drawer 283, Box 38, GDAH.

42. Letter of Dr. Theo S. Christ to "Dear Madam from Chester, Aug. 21st 1865," Civil War Miscellany, R. Tompy Roberds, Drawer 283, Box 38, GDAH.

43. Andrew J. McBride, *Atlanta Journal*, June 29, 1901, "From the Chuckee To the Wilderness."

44. *OR*, Vol.31, Pt.1, p.462.

45. *Ibid.*

46. CSR; Built in mid-1863, Rock Island Prison had not been finished when prisoners began arriving in December 1863. The first Confederate prisoners received were from the battles around Chattanooga and Knoxville.

47. CSR.

48. *Ibid*; Confederate Pension Records of Georgia, GDAH.

49. *Atlanta Journal*, June 29, 1901.

50. Pendleton, p.49.

51. *OR*, Vol.31, Pt.3, p.817-818.

52. *Atlanta Journal*, June 29, 1901.

53. Confederate Pension Records of Georgia, GDAH.

54. *OR*, Vol.31, Pt.3, p.838.

55. *Ibid.*, p.497, 503.

56. *Ibid.*, p.505-506.

57. CSR.

58. *Ibid.*

59. Pendleton, p.50.

60. *Ibid.*

61. CSR.

62. David C. Smith, *The Battle That History Lost* (Rogersville, Tn., 1982) p. 27-28.

63. *Atlanta Journal*, January 11, 1902.

64. Letter of John L. G. Wood to "Dear Father, Camp near Russellville, Tenn. This Jan 3rd, 1864."

65. CSR.

66. *Ibid.*

67. *Atlanta Journal*, January 11, 1902.

68. CSR.

69. Pendleton, p.51.

70. *Ibid.*

71. *Ibid.*

72. Letter of John W. Gaskins to "Dear Cousin from East Tennessee Camps Near Greenville, Mis. [Tennessee] March 2nd, 1864, Francis L. Mobley Collection.

73. Pendleton., p.52

74. *Ibid.*, p.52-53.

75. CSR, Company I Record of Events for "Feb 29 to Aug 31, 1864 from Winchester, Virginia."

76. CSR.

77. Pendleton, p.54.

78. *Ibid.*; CSR, Company I Record of Events for "Feb 29 to Aug 31, 1864."

79. John L. G. Wood letter to "My Dear Father, Camp Near Bristol, Tenn.-This April the 8th, 1864."

80. Pendleton, p.54; CSR, Company I Record of Events for "Feb 29 to Aug 31, 1864."

81. CSR; Marilee (Mrs. Ermon) Butler, *A Book of Butlers* (Tallahassee, FL; 1985) p.125.

82. CSR.

83. *Ibid.*

Chapter Nine – The Wilderness

1. *OR*, Vol.36, Pt.1, p.1054. Longstreet's report mentioned that they marched to a place called Mechanicsville and camped. This place is apparently south of Gordonsville and was such a small hamlet that it does not appear on period maps. The place is <u>not</u> the same Mechanicsville located near Richmond where a major battle was fought in 1862.

2. Constance Pendleton, *Confederate Memoirs: Early Life and Family History, William Frederick Pendleton [and] Mary Lawson Young Pendleton* (Bryn Athyn, Pa., 1958), p.55, 150-151.

3. CSR., Letter of P.McGlashan to "General, from HdQrs 50th Regt Geo Vols May 2nd 1864."

4. Pendleton, p.55.

5. Andrew J. McBride, *Atlanta Journal*, Atlanta, Ga., June 29, 1901, "From the Chuckee to the Wilderness."

6. *Atlanta Journal*, June 29, 1901.

7. *OR*, Vol.36, Pt.1, p.1063.

8. *Ibid.*, p.1061.

9. *Ibid.*

10. *Ibid.*, p.1063.

11. Pendleton, p.56; Rosalind Sheffield (Mrs. J. M.) Heath, "Co. Pliny Sheffield, 1859-1908, *Confederate Reminiscences and Letters 1861-1865*, Vol. II, 1996, Georgia Division, United Daughters of the Confederacy, p. 45, GDAH.

12. Pendleton, p.57.

13. *Ibid.*

14. *OR*, Vol.36, Pt.1, p.1063.

15. Pendleton, p.57.

16. *OR*, Vol.36, Pt.1, p.1064.

17. *Ibid.*; CSR; Letter from John L. G. Wood to "Dear Father, Camp near Hanover Junction, This May 25th, 1864," John L. G. Wood Letters, Microfilm Drawer 194, Box 3, GDAH.

18. Letter of John L. Wheeler to "M. J. Kirkland, from The Line of Battle, Spottsylvania Court House, May 14, 1864," Moses J. Kirkland Papers, Special Collections, Microfilm Box 348, The Robert W. Woodruff Library, Emory University, Atlanta, Ga.

Chapter Ten – From Spotsylvania Court House to Cold Harbor

1. The location for the Confederate position is widely known as "Laurel Hill." However, some historians also refer to the location as "Spindle Farm."

2. Constance Pendleton, *Confederate Memoirs: Early Life and Family History, William Frederick Pendleton [and] Mary Lawson Young Pendleton*, (Bryn Athyn, Pa., 1958), p.58.

3. Andrew J. McBride, *Atlanta Journal*, Atlanta, Ga., June 29, 1901, "From the Chuckee To the Wilderness."

4. Pendleton, p.58.

5. Andrew J. Humphreys, *The Virginia Campaign of 1864 and 1865*. (originally published by Charles Scribner's Sons, 1883. Reprinted Castle Books, Edison, N.J., 2002) p.73.

6. Pendleton, p.59; It should be noted that numerous claims have been made by others as to the identity of the shooter.

7. *Atlanta Journal*, July 20, 1901.

8. Pendleton, p.58-59.

9. CSR.

10. Pendleton, p.59; CSR.

11. Letter of John L. Wheeler to "M. J. Kirkland, May 14, 1864", Moses J. Kirkland Papers, Special Collections, Microfilm Box #348, Robert W. Woodruff Library, Emory University, Atlanta, Ga.

12. Pendleton, p.59.

13. *OR*, Vol.36, Pt.1, p.1058; Pendleton, p.59.

14. CSR.

15. *Ibid.*

16. *Atlanta Journal*, July 20, 1901.

17. Pendleton, p.61.

18. *Atlanta Journal*, July 20, 1901.

19. CSR; Pendleton, p.61.

20. *Ibid.*, p.62.

21. Maps designate the crossroads as "Old Cold Harbor." A little over one mile to the southwest is another junction identified as "New Cold Harbor." Both locations were named for taverns. The "Battle of Cold Harbor" actually occurred between Old Cold Harbor and New Cold Harbor.

22. *OR*, Vol.51, Pt.2, (Supplements) p.974.

Chapter Eleven – Cold Harbor

1. *OR*, Vol.36, Pt.1, p.1059.

2. Constance Pendleto*n, Confederate Memoirs: Early Life and Family History, William Frederick Pendleton [and] Mary Lawson Young Pendleton*, (Bryn Athyn, Pa. 1958), p.63.

3. *Ibid.*

4. Some sources have Humphreys' Brigade anchoring Kershaw's left wing prior to the Union assault on June 1. Richmond National Battlefield Park Historian Robert E. L. Krick advised the author that he believes Henagan's Brigade occupied the far left when the Union assault began during the afternoon of June 1. A portion of Henagan's Brigade rushed around Humphreys' Brigade to support Bryan and Wofford during the Union breakthrough. Some of Henagan's units remained between Humphreys and Bryan on June 2, possibly creating the confusion.

5. *OR*, Vol.36, Pt.1, p.999-1000.

6. *Ibid.*, p.1000.

7. *Ibid.*, p.1059; Letter of A. B. Simms to "Dear Sister Near Richmond Va. June 4th 1864," Jane Bonner Peacock, ed. "A Georgian's View of the War in Virginia: The Civil War Letters of A. B. Simms," *Atlanta Historical Journal*, Vol. XXIII, No.2, Summer 1979, p.107; OR., Vol.36, Pt.1, p.726.

8. Letter of Eugene A. Thompson to "Mr & Mrs R. J. Thompson Near Gaines Mills Va June 4th 1864," typescript copy, Bound Vol. #15, Richmond National Battlefield Park Library, Richmond, Va.; Pendleton, p.63.

9. *OR*, Vol.36, Pt.1, p.1059.

10. Pendleton, p.63-64.

11. *OR*, Vol.36, Pt.1, p.1059.

12. *Ibid.*, p.1019; *OR*, Vol.51, Pt.1 (Supplements) p.1267.

13. CSR.

14. *Augusta Daily Constitutionalist*, Augusta, Ga., June 16, 1864, "Letter from McLaws' Old Division."

15. *Ibid.*

16. CSR.

17. *OR*, Vol.36, Pt.1, p.1064.

18. Pendleton, p.64; CSR.

19. *OR*, Vol.36, Pt.1, p.1064.

20. Pendleton, p.64-65.

21. E. M. Law, "From the Wilderness to Cold Harbor," *Battles and Leaders of the Civil War*, Vol.4 (New York, 1887) p.141.

22. William C. Oates, *The War Between the Union and the Confederacy and Its Lost Opportunities, with a History of the 15th Alabama Regiment and the Forty-eight Battles in Which It Was Engaged* (New York, 1905) p.366-67.

23. Pendleton, p.65.

24. CSR.

25. *OR*, Vol.36, Pt.1, p.869.

26. *Ibid.*, p.1065; Pendleton, p.65. Pendleton mentions in his memoirs that the brigade marched "two or three miles to the right." This had to be an error because the brigade remained in the immediate area with Kershaw's division.

27. CSR.

28. *Ibid.*

29. *OR*, Vol.36, Pt.3, p.873.

30. *OR*, Vol.36, Pt.1, p.1059-1060, 1065; Pendleton, p.66.

31. CSR.

Chapter Twelve – Operations at Petersburg and Deep Bottom

1. *OR,* Vol.40, Pt.1, p.755, 760-761.

2. *OR,* Vol.40, Pt.2, p.668.

3. *OR*, Vol.40, Pt.1, p.761; Constance Pendleton, *Confederate Memoirs: Early Life and Family History William Frederick Pendleton [and] Mary Lawson Young Pendleton,* (Bryn Athyn, Pa., 1958), p.67.

4. Pendleton.

5. *OR,* Vol.40, Pt. 1, p.768.

6. CSR.

7. Pendleton, p.68; *CSR.*

8. Letter of Wilson C. McCall to "My Dear Uncle from Petersburg, VA June 19th 1864," *Confederate Letters, Diaries and Reminiscences 1860–1865,* Vol. X, 1946, Georgia Division United Daughters of the Confederacy, p.242, GDAH.

9. Pendleton, p.68; CSR.

10. CSR.; 1895 Georgia Confederate Soldier Pension Application of George W. Chitty, microfilm, GDAH.

11. CSR.

12. *OR,* Vol.40, Pt.1, p.768; CSR.

13. *OR,* Vol.40, Pt.1, p.768; Pendleton, p.69.

14. *OR,* Vol.40, pt.1, p.768.

15. CSR.

16. *OR,* Vol.40, Pt.1. p.762, 768; Pendleton, p.69.

17. Pendleton, *p.70.*

18. *Ibid.*

19. *OR,* Vol.40, Pt.1, p.768.

20. Pendleton, p.70.

21. *OR,* Vol.40, Pt.1, p. 768; Pendleton, p. 72.

22. Letter of John L. G. Wood to "My dear Father, Camp Near Petersburg. This Aug. the 5th. 1864," John L. G. Wood Letters, Microfilm Drawer 194, Box 3, GDAH.

23. CSR.

Chapter Thirteen – The Shenandoah Valley

1. Constance Pendleton, *Confederate Memoirs: Early Life and Family History, William Frederick Pendleton [and] Mary Lawson Young Pendleton*, (Bryn Athyn, Pa., 1958), p.72.

2. *Ibid.*

3. *Ibid.*, p.72-73; *OR,* Vol.42, Pt.1, p.873.

4. *OR,* Vol.42, Pt.1, p.873; Pendleton, p.73.

5. *OR,* Vol.42, Pt.1, p.873; Pendleton, p.73.

6. *OR,* Vol.42, Pt.1, p.873; Pendleton, p.74.

7. *OR,* Vol.42, Pt.1, p.873.

8. *Ibid.*, p. 874; Pendleton, p.74.

9. *OR,* Vol.42, Pt.1, p.874; *OR,* Vol.43, Pt.1, p.568.

10. Pendleton, p.74.

11. CSR of Col. McGlashan, Letter of Goode Bryan to "Hon. A.H. [should have been James A.] Seddon Sec of War from Hd Qrs Bryans Brigade August 20th 1864," ; Letter of A. B. Simms to "Dear Sister from Near Charlestown, Virginia August 23rd 1864," Jane Bonner Peacock, ed., "A Georgian's View of the War in Virginia: The Civil War Letters of A. B. Simms," *Atlanta Historical Journal*, Vol. XXIII, No.2, Summer 1979, p.119.

12. *OR,* Vol.42, Pt.1, p. 874; *OR,* Vol.43, Pt.1, p.589.

13. CSR; Pendleton, p.76.

14. CSR.

15. *OR,* Vol.42, Pt.1, p.874.

16. Pendleton, p. 76-77.

17. *OR,* Vol.42, Pt.1, p.874.

18. Letter of A. B. Simms to "Dear Sister, from Near Winchester, Virginia September 2nd 1864." p. 120.

19. *OR,* Vol.42, Pt.1, p.875; *OR,* Vol.43, Pt.1, p.405, 590.

20. *OR,* Vol. 43, Pt.1, p.405.

21. *Ibid.*

22. Pendleton, p.75.

23. CSR.

24. *OR,* Vol.42, Pt.1, p.875; *OR,* Vol.43, Pt.1, p.590.

25. *OR,* Vol.42, Pt.1, p.1250.

26. Letter of John L. G. Wood to "My Dear Father, from Camp At Winchester, Va. This Sept. the 9th. 1864," John L. G. Wood Letters, Microfilm Drawer 194, Box 3, GDAH.

27. *OR*, Vol.42, Pt.1, p.875.

28. *Ibid.*; *OR*, Vol.43, Pt. 1, p.590.

29. Letter of A. B. Simms to "Dear Sister from Rapidan Station Sep. 21ˢᵗ, 1864," p.122.

30. *OR*, Vol.43, Pt.2, p.878.

31. *OR*, Vol.42, Pt.1, p.875; *OR*, Vol.43, Pt.1, p.590; CSR.

32. Letter of John L. G. Wood to "Dear Father, from Camp near Waynesborough Sept. 29th. 1864."

33. *OR*, Vol.43, Pt.1, p.590; CSR.

Chapter Fourteen – Cedar Creek

1. Jubal A. Early, *Autobiographical Sketch and Narrative of the War Between the States*, (Philadelphia, Pa. 1912) p. 438.

2. Jubal A. Early, "Winchester, Fisher's Hill, and Cedar Creek," *Battles and Leaders of the Civil War*, Vol.4 (New York, 1884 – 1887) p.530; OR., Vol.42, Pt.2, p.1213; Peter A.S. McGlashan, "The Battle of Cedar Creek," November 1, 1892, *Addresses Delivered Before the Confederate Veterans Association of Savannah, Georgia*, Vol.1, Savannah, Ga.; OR., Vol.43, pt.1, p.591; Constance Pendleton, *Confederate Memoirs Early Life and Family History William Frederick Pendleton [and] Mary Lawson Young Pendleton*, (Bryn Athyn, Pa., 1958), p.78). Early stated, "I went into this battle with about 8,500 muskets." Kershaw's division arrived in the Shenandoah Valley in mid-August with about 3,800 men. Attrition from casualties, sickness and desertions over the past two months had probably reduced it to around 3,500 effectives before the battle. Colonel McGlashan later stated the Rebel strength to be 7,000 infantry and about 1,200 to 1,500 cavalry and about twenty-four field guns. McGlashan also reported, "Many regiments, originally 1,000 to 1,200 strong, were reduced to, in many cases, less than 100 muskets." Colonel Simms reported that his brigade went into the battle with 520 men. McGlashan stated that the brigade only "mustered about 400 muskets." William Pendleton recalled in a letter to his brother after the war that, "The Battle of Cedar Creek took place near the end of the war and numbers were very much reduced. My company at the time had in it hardly more than ten or twelve men." If the rest of the Wiregrass companies were similarly depleted, the total 50th Georgia strength could not have exceeded 120 to 150 men. If the other three regiments contained similar numbers, the brigade strength reported by Simms would seem to be accurate.

3. *OR*, Vol.43, Pt.1, p.580; Army of the Valley commander Jubal Early assigned temporary command of the Second Corps to Major General John B. Gordon. Brigadier General Clement J. Evans temporarily commanded Gordon's division during the battle.

4. *Ibid.*, p.590-591; McGlashan.

5. McGlashan.

6. *Ibid.*

7. *OR*, Vol.43, Pt.1, p.591.

8. *Ibid.*; It should be noted that Major James M. Goggin commanded Conner's Brigade after Conner received serious wounds at Hupp's Hill on October 13. Colonel

Daniel N. Moody commanded Humphreys' Brigade after Humphreys suffered wounds near Berryville in September.

9. McGlashan.

10. *Ibid*. The other Wiregrass soldier mentioned by McGlashan may have been Private John H. Boyett of Company F. The 1896 pension application filed by his widow stated he was killed by Yankee pickets at Cedar Creek.

11. *OR*, Vol.43, Pt.1, p.382-383.

12. McGlashan.

13. *Ibid*.

14. *Ibid*.

15. *OR*, Vol.43, Pt.1, p.414; McGlashan.

16. *OR*, Vol.43, Pt.1, p.591.

17. McGlashan.

18. *Ibid*.

19. *OR*, Vol.43, Pt.1, p.341-342.

20. *Ibid*., p.342.

21. *Ibid*., p.591.

22. McGlashan.

23. *Ibid*.

24. *OR*, Vol.43, Pt.1., p.562.

25. McGlashan.

26. *Ibid*; Pendleton, p.79.

27. CSR.; Pendleton, p.79.

28. CSR.

29. *Ibid*.

30. Letter of John Wade King to "My Dear Wife, from Line of Battle Nr Fishers Hill Northern Va. Oct 15th 1864," *Confederate Reminiscences and Letters 1861-1865*, Vol.XIII, Georgia Division United Daughters of the Confederacy, 2000, p.259, GDAH.

31. Letter of Arthur B. Simms to "Dear Sister from New Market, Virginia October 21st 1864," Jane Bonner Peacock, ed., "A Georgian's View of the War in Virginia: The Civil War Letters of A.B. Simms," *Atlanta Historical Journal*, Vol. XXIII, No.2, Summer 1979, p.124-125.

32. *OR*, Vol.43, Pt.1, p.137; Early, *Battles and Leaders of the Civil War*, Vol.4, p.529; Jeffery Wert, *From Winchester to Cedar Creek* (Mechanicsburg, Pa.,1997) p.246.

33. *OR*, Vol.43, Pt.1, p.591-592; McGlashan.

34. Simms letter, October 21st 1864; CSR.

35. *OR*, Vol.43, Pt.1., p.584; CSR, Company I Record of Events for "Nov & Dec 1864 near Richmond, Va." Waynesborough now spells the city name, Waynesboro.

Chapter Fifteen – The Final Desperate Months

1. CSR; *OR*, Vol.42, Pt.3, p.1364; Andrew A. Humphreys, *The Virginia Campaign of 1864 and 1865* (1883. Reprinted Castle Books, Edison, N.J. 2002) p.304-305.

2. CSR, Company I Record of Events for "Nov & Dec 1864 near Richmond, Va."

3. Humphreys, p. 308, 311.

4. *Ibid.*, p.310.

5. *OR*, Vol.42, Pt.3, p.1237; Confederate reports show Kershaw's division strength slowly fell from about 3,500 to 3,200 between November 30, 1864, and February 20, 1865. Individual brigade strengths are not shown until the report for February 24 — March 1, 1865. By that time, Conner's Brigade had been transferred to South Carolina, reducing the division strength to 1,922. Bryan's (Simms') Brigade numbered 655 officers and men, Humphrey's Brigade counted 449, and Wofford's Brigade showed 805.

6. CSR; Constance Pendleton, *Confederate Memoirs: Early Life and Family History, William Frederick Pendleton [and] Mary Lawson Young Pendleton*, (Bryn Athyn, Pa., 1958), p.79.

7. *OR*, Vol.42, Pt.3, p.1280-1281; *OR*, Vol.42, Pt.1, p.1287.

8. CSR.

9. *OR*, Vol.42, Pt.3, p.1288.

10. Letter of S. L. Morton to "Dear Father, from Chaffins Farm Decem 28th" [1864], *Confederate Reminiscences and Letters*, Vol. XV, Georgia Division United Daughters of the Confederacy, 2000, p.194, GDAH.

11. Constance Pendleton, *Confederate Diary Capt. W. F. Pendleton January to April 1865* (Bryn Athyn, Pa., 1957), p.7; CSR.

12. *OR*, Vol.46, Pt.2, p.1179; Pendleton, *Confederate Diary...*, p.8.

13. Pendleton, *Confederate Diary...*, p. 8-10.

14. *Ibid.*, p.11.

15. *OR*, Vol.46, Pt.2, p.1268.

16. Pendleton, *Confederate Diary...*, p.11.

17. *OR*, Vol.46, Pt.1, p. 388; *OR*, Vol.46, Pt.2, p.1296.

18. Letter of Simeon L. Morton to "Dear Father from Chaffins Bluff March 2nd 1865," *Confederate Reminiscences and Letters*, Vol XV, Georgia Division, United Daughters of the Confederacy, 2000, p.195-196, GDAH.

19. Peter A. S. McGlashan, "Our Last Retreat," Address to the Confederate Veteran's Association of Savannah, Ga., December 5, 1894. Typeset copy, Georgia Historical Society, Savannah, Ga., p.57-65, 1895.

20. *OR*, Vol.46, Pt.2, p.1295.

21. *OR*, Vol.46, Pt.1, p.1293.

22. *Ibid.*; McGlashan.

23. McGlashan; *OR*, Vol.46, Pt.1, p.1293, 1283.

24. McGlashan.

25. *OR*, Vol.46, Pt.1, p.1293-1294, 1283; McGlashan.

26. CSR.

27. McGlashan.

28. *OR*, Vol.46, Pt.1, p.1294.

29. *Ibid.*

30. Humphreys, p.383-384; *OR*, Vol.46, Pt.1, p.1295.

31. *OR*, Vol.46, Pt.1, p.1295; Humphreys, p.384.

32. *OR*, Vol.46, Pt.1., p.1295, 1284.

33. *Ibid.*, p.1284.

34. McGlashan.

35. Positions of Semmes' regiments based on map by Civil War Preservation Trust, "Battle of Sailor's Creek, Va., Hillsman Farm —April 6, 1865," Map by Steven Stanley.

36. *OR*, Vol.46, Pt.1. p.1295

37. McGlashan.

38. *OR*, Vol.46, Pt.1, p.1284.

39. McGlashan. See also Appendix D for more info on regimental battle flag.

40. Humphreys, p.384; *OR*, Vol.46, Pt.1, p.1295. Simms must have returned in March from his illness to take over command of the brigade.

41. CSR.

42. *OR*, Vol.46, Pt.1, p.1269.

43. *SHSP*, "Paroles of the Army of Northern Virginia Surrendered at Appomattox C. H., Va., April 9, 1865," Vol. XV, 1887, p. 170-171, 183.

Epilogue

1. CSR; *SHSP*, "Paroles of the Army of Northern Virginia Surrendered at Appomattox C.H., Va. April 9, 1865," Vol. XV, 1887, p.170-171, 183; Personal research also included review of casualty lists, period newspaper articles, local historical documents and other sources.

2. Marilee (Mrs. Ermon) Butler, *A Book of Butlers* (Tallahassee, Fl., 1985) *p.126.*

3. *Ibid, p.122.*

4. CSR; Dorothy Peterson Neisen, great-niece of Cornelius Peterson, Lake Park, Ga.; Texas CSP.

5. Florida CSP.

6. Folks Huxford, *Pioneers of Wiregrass Georgia,* Vol. IV, (Pearson, Ga., 1960) p.191.

7. *The Bainbridge Democrat,* Bainbridge, Ga., January 19, 1882, "Death Of Judge William O. Fleming."

8. CSR; Folks Huxford, *Pioneers of Wiregrass Georgia,* Vol. V, (Waycross, Ga., 1967) p.65-66; Georgia CSP.

9. CSR; Huxford, Vol. IV, p. 278-279.

10. CSR; *Savannah Morning News,* Savannah, Ga., June 14, 1908, "Heart Failed While In Water."

11. *Savannah Morning News,* Savannah, Ga., June 14, 1908.

12. *Ibid.*

13. Constance Pendleton, *Confederate Diary Capt W. F. Pendleton January to April 1865* (Bryn Athyn, Pa., 1958) p.13-21.

14. Pendleton, *Confederate Memoirs: Early Life and Family History William Frederick Pendleton [and] Mary Lawson Young Pendleton* (Bryn Athyn, Pa., 1958) p.85, 87, 97, 101.

15. *Ibid.*, p.109.

16. *Ibid.*, p.140, 144-146; additional information has been graciously provided by descendants of W. F. Pendleton.

17. William Moore Jones, "War Service and Diary of Sergeant William Moore Jones, Company K, 50th Georgia Infantry," *Confederate Reminiscences and Letters, 1861-1865*, Vol. V, 1997. Collected by Georgia Division United Daughters of the Confederacy, p. 119, GDAH. Commissary Sergeant Connell lost an arm at Gettysburg. He was later exchanged and returned to his home in Berrien County, Georgia; CSR.

18. *Ibid.*, p.120-121.

19. Georgia CSP; *Thomasville Times Enterprise Semi-Weekly,* Thomasville, Ga., March 15, 1936, "Judge Jones Passes."

Bibliography

MANUSCRIPTS

BRUNSWICK PUBLIC LIBRARY, Brunswick, Georgia.
Fahm, George E., "Reminiscences of the Sixties by George E. Fahm, Capt. Co E 50th Ga." [Taken from the Margaret Davis Cate Collection, which is in possession of Fort Frederica National Monument, St. Simons Island, Georgia, National Park Service, United States Department of the Interior]

EMORY UNIVERSITY, The Robert W. Woodruff Library, Atlanta, Georgia.
Kirkland, Moses J., Confederate Correspondence, 1862-1864. Collection #348, microfilm, Special Collections Department.

John L. Wheeler Letter. 5/14/1864. Moses J. Kirkland Confederate Correspondence, 1862-1864. Collection #348, microfilm. Special Collections Department.

GEORGIA DIVISION OF ARCHIVES AND HISTORY, Morrow, Georgia.
Confederate Pension Records of Georgia.

William J. Evers Letters, *Confederate Reminiscences and Letters 1861-1865*, Vol. VI, 1992. Collected by Georgia Division United Daughters of the Confederacy.

James A. Hardee Letter, Co. D, 50th Ga., 4/14/1862. *Confederate Reminiscences and Letters 1861-1865*, Vol. X, 1999. Collected by Georgia Division United Daughters of the Confederacy.

Sergeant William Moore Jones Diary, Company K, 50th Georgia Infantry, *Confederate Reminiscences and Letters, 1861-1865*, Vol. V, 1997. Collected by Georgia Division United Daughters of the Confederacy.

John Wade King Letter, Co. F, 50th Ga., 10/15/1864. *Confederate Reminiscences and Letters 1861-1865*, Vol. XIII, 2000. Collected by Georgia Division United Daughters of the Confederacy.

John G.F. McCall Letters, *Confederate Letters, Diaries and Reminiscences 1861-1865*. Vol. X, 1946. Collected by Georgia Division United Daughters of the Confederacy.

Wilson C. McCall Letter, Co. K, 50th Ga. *Confederate Letters, Diaries and Reminiscences 1861-1865*, Vol. X, 1946. Collected by Georgia Division United Daughters of the Confederacy.

Simeon M. Morton Letters. *Confederate Reminiscences and Letters 1861-1865*, Vol.XV 2000. Collected by Georgia Division United Daughters of the Confederacy.

"Original Muster Roll of Company G, Clinch Volunteers."

R.T. Roberds Letters, Alfred Holt Colquitt Chapter, United Daughters of the Confederacy, Civil War Miscellany, microfilm.

William Ross Stillwell Civil War Letters 1860-1933, AC 1940-0102M.

W.A. Studstill Letter, Co. K, 50th Ga., 3/23/1862. Civil War Miscellany, microfilm.

John L.G. Wood Letters, microfilm.

Cicero H. Young Letter, Co. E, 50th Ga. 4/14/1862. Civil War Miscellany-Personal Papers, microfilm.

GEORGIA HISTORICAL SOCIETY, Savannah, Georgia
Laurel Grove Cemetery Keeper's Record Books.

LIBRARY OF CONGRESS, Washington, D.C.
J. Evans Edings Diary, Edward Willis Papers, Manuscript Division, Box 4, "1862, MMC 3182, Confederate Pamphlets," Library of Congress, Washington, D.C.

LOWNDES COUNTY HISTORICAL SOCIETY & MUSEUM, Valdosta, Georgia.
"Presentation of a Flag." *Savannah Republican*. April 14, 1862. Savannah, Ga.

MUSEUM OF COLQUITT COUNTY HISTORY, Moultrie, Georgia.
Malachi NeSmith Letter, Co. H, 50th Ga. 5/18/1863.

NATIONAL ARCHIVES, Washington, D.C.
Compiled Service Records of Confederate Soldiers Who Served In Organizations From the State of Georgia.

Company I, 50th Ga. Record of Events. Compiled Military Service Records – Captions and Records of Events.

General Goode Bryan Letter. 8/20/1864. Compiled Service Records of Confederate Soldiers Who Served In Organizations From the State of Georgia.

P. McGlashan Letter. 5/2/1864. Compiled Service Records of Confederate Soldiers Who Served In Organizations From the State of Georgia.

PRIVATE COLLECTIONS
John W. Gaskins Letter, Co. I, 50th Ga. 2/2/1864. Copy in possession of Glenn Hodges, Nashville, Ga.

Francis L. Mobley Letters, Co. I, 50th Georgia. Copies in possession of Glenn Hodges, Nashville, Ga.

Neisen, Dorothy Peterson. "Short Sketch of Cornelius Peterson." 2005.

Civil War Diary of Sergeant Henry W. Tisdale, Company I, 25ᵗʰ Regiment,
    Massachusetts Volunteers, 1862-1865. Copyright 2001, by Mark F. Farrell.

RICHMOND NATIONAL BATTLEFIELD PARK LIBRARY, Richmond, Virginia.
Eugene A. Thompson Letter, Co C, 10ᵗʰ Ga. 6/4/1864. Typescript copy. Bound Vol.15.

SOUTHWEST GEORGIA REGIONAL LIBRARY, Bainbridge, Georgia.
"Major Duncan Curry Letters & Civil War Papers 1862-1865." microfilm. Curry Hill
    Plantation Collection.

THOMAS COUNTY HISTORICAL SOCIETY AND MUSEUM, Thomasville, Georgia.
Mary Ann Douglass Diary.

"Original Muster Roll of Company E, Thomas County Rangers."

THORNROSE CEMETERY, Staunton, Virginia
Thornrose Cemetery Keeper's Record Books, Staunton, Va.

UNIVERSITY OF NORTH CAROLINA AT CHAPEL HILL, Wilson Library, Chapel
Hill, North Carolina.
William Oliver Fleming Papers, #2292-z, Southern Historical Collection, Manuscripts
    Department.

UNIVERSITY OF TENNESSEE, The Special Collections Library, Knoxville, Tennessee
John Watkins Letter. 12/15/1863. John Watkins Papers 1862-1958, MS-1161.

PUBLISHED PRIMARY SOURCES

Early, Jubal Anderson. *General Jubal A. Early: Autobiographical Sketch and Narrative
    of the War Between the States*. Philadelphia: J.B. Lippincott and Co., 1912.

—"Winchester, Fisher's Hill and Cedar Creek." *Battles and Leaders of the Civil War*.
    Vol. IV. Robert U. Johnson & Clarence C. Buel, editors. New York: The
    Century Company, 1884-1887.

Hill, Daniel Harvey, "The Battle of South Mountain, or Boonsboro Fighting For Time
    At Turner's and Fox's Gaps." *Battles and Leaders of the Civil War*. eds.
    Robert U. Johnson & Clarence C. Buel, editors. Vol. II, New York: The
    Century Company, 1884-1887.

Hitchcock, George A., *From Ashby to Andersonville, The Civil War Diary and
    Reminiscences of Private George A. Hitchcock, 21ˢᵗ Massachusetts Infantry
    1862-1865*. Ronald G. Watson, ed. Campbell, Ca.: Savas Publishing Co.,
    1997.

Humphreys, Andrew A., *The Virginia Campaign of 1864 and 1865*. Campaigns of the
    Civil War. Vol. XII, Edison, NJ: Castle Books, 2002.

Kershaw, Joseph B., "Kershaw's Brigade at Gettysburg." *Battles and Leaders of the
    Civil War*. Robert U. Johnson & Clarence C. Buel, editors. Vol. III New York:
    The Century Company, 1884-1887.

Law, Evander M., "From the Wilderness to Cold Harbor." *Battles and Leaders of the Civil War*. Robert U. Johnson & Clarence C. Buel, editors. Vol. IV New York: The Century Company, 1884-1887.

Oates, William C., *The War Between the Union and the Confederacy and Its Lost Opportunities, with a History of the 15th Alabama Regiment and the Forty-eight Battles in Which It Was Engaged*. New York: Neale, 1905.

Pendleton, Constance, ed., *Confederate Memoirs: Early Life and Family History William Frederick Pendleton [and] Mary Lawson Young Pendleton*. Bryn Athyn, Pa., 1958.

—*Confederate Diary Capt. W.F. Pendleton, (January to April 1865)*, Bryn Athyn, Pa.: Pendle House. 1957.

Southern Historical Society Papers. Vol. XIII 1885. p.259-271.

—Vol. XV 1887. p.170-171, 183.

—Vol. XVII 1899. p.241-250.

U.S. War Department., *War of the Rebellion: A Compilation of the Official Records of the Union and Confederate Armies*. 130 Vols. Washington, D.C.: Government Printing Office. 1880-1901.

PUBLISHED SECONDARY SOURCES

Baltz, Louis J., III. *The Battle of Cold Harbor – May 27-June 13, 1864*. Lynchburg, Va.: H.E. Howard, Inc., 1994.

Brooks County Genealogical Society. *Brooks County, Echoes of Its People*. Madison, Fl.: Jim Bob Printing, Inc., 1993.

Broome, Dean. *History of Pierce County, Georgia*. Vol. 1, Blackshear, Ga.: Dean Broome, 1973.

Busey, John W. and Martin, David G., *Regimental Strengths and Losses at Gettysburg*. Hightstown, NJ; Longstreet House, 1994.

Calkins, Chris M., *The Appomattox Campaign – March 29-April 9, 1865*. Conshohocken, Pa.: Combined Books, Inc., 1997.

Cannan, John. *Burnside's Bridge: Antietam*. Conshohocken, Pa.: Combined Publishing, 2001.

Catton, Bruce., *Gettysburg: The Final Fury*. Garden City, NJ: Doubleday & Company, Inc., 1974.

Covington, W.A., *History of Colquitt County*. Clearfield Company, Inc. 1937. reprinted Baltimore, Md.: Genealogical Publishing Co., 1997.

Crute, Joseph H., *Units of the Confederate States Army*. Midlothian, Va.: Derwent Books, 1987.

Davis, William C., ed. *The Confederate General*. Vol. 5, National Historical Society. 1991.

Ferguson, Chris L., *Southerners at Rest: Confederate Dead at Hollywood Cemetery.* Winchester, Va.: Angle Valley Press, 2008.

Furgurson, Ernest B., *Not War But Murder: Cold Harbor 1864*. New York: Alfred A. Knopf, 2000.

Griffin, John A., *Warriors of the Wiregrass – Histories of Selected Georgia Regiments in the War for Southern Independence*. Moultrie, Ga.: Sons of Confederate Veterans Camp #674, 2000.

Henderson, Lillian. *Roster of the Confederate Soldiers of Georgia 1861-1865. Vol. 5* Hapeville, Ga.: Longino & Porter. 1960.

Hennessy, John. J*., Return to Bull Run*. New York, NY: Simon & Schuster, 1993.

Hodges, Mrs. Fred H., Sr., comp. *History of Lowndes County, Georgia 1825-1941*. Valdosta, Ga.: General James Jackson Chapter NSDAR, 1995.

Horn, John. *The Petersburg Campaign: June 1864-April 1865*. Conshohocken, Pa.: Combined Publishing, 2000.

Howe, Thomas J., *Wasted Valor: The Petersburg Campaign – June 15-18, 1864*. Lynchburg, Va.: H.E. Howard, Inc., 1988.

Huxford, Folks, *History of Clinch County, Georgia*. Macon, Ga.: The H.J. Burke Co., 1916.

——*The History of Brooks County, Georgia 1858-1948*. Spartanburg, S.C.: The Reprint Company, 1978.

——*Pioneers of Wiregrass Georgia*. Vol. III Pearson, Ga.: Cooper Press, Inc., 1957.

——*Pioneers of Wiregrass Georgia*. Vol. IV Pearson, Ga.: Atkinson County Citizen, 1960.

——*Pioneers of Wiregrass Georgia*. Vol. V Waycross, Ga.: Herrin's Print Shop. 1967.

Jones, Frank S., *History of Decatur County, Georgia*. Spartanburg, SC.: The Reprint Company, 1996.

Krick, Robert K., *Lee's Colonels: A Biographical Register of the Field Officers of the Army of Northern Virginia*, Dayton, Oh: Press of Morningside Bookshop, 1979.

Lastinger, L.E., *A Compilation of the Confederate Soldiers Going From Berrien County, Georgia. When they enlisted–and whether or not they survived the war*. Nashville, Ga.: The Berrien Press, 1928.

Lewis, Thomas A., *The Guns of Cedar Creek*. New York: Dell Publishing, 1988.

Mahr, Theodore C., *The Battle of Cedar Creek: Showdown in the Shenandoah, October 1-30, 1864*. Lynchburg, Va.: H.E. Howard, Inc., 1992.

National Park Civil War Series. *The Battle of Chancellorsville*. Conshohocken, Pa.: Eastern National, 1995.

—*The Battle of Gettysburg*. Conshohocken, Pa.: Eastern National, 1994.

—*The Battles of Wilderness & Spotsylvania*. Conshohocken, Pa.: Eastern National, 1995.

Pfanz, Harry W., *Gettysburg – The First Day*. Chapel Hill, NC: The University of North Carolina Press, 2001.

—*Gettysburg: The Second Day*. Chapel Hill, NC: The University of North Carolina Press, 1987.

Priest, John M., *Antietam: The Soldier's Battle*. New York: Oxford University Press, 1989.

Rhea, Gordon C., *The Battle of the Wilderness - May 5-6, 1864*. Baton Rouge, La.: Louisiana State University Press, 1994.

—*The Battles for Spotsylvania Court House and the Road to Yellow Tavern – May 7-12, 1864*. Baton Rouge, La.: Louisiana State University Press, 1997.

—*To the North Anna River: Grant and Lee – May 13-25, 1864*. Baton Rouge, La.: Louisiana State University Press, 2000.

—*Cold Harbor: Grant and Lee – May 26-June 3, 1864*. Baton Rouge, La.: Louisiana State University Press, 2002.

Rogers, William Warren. *Thomas County during the Civil War*. Tallahassee, Fl.: The Florida State University, 1964.

Sears, Stephen W., *Landscape Turned Red – The Battle of Antietam*. New York: Houghton Mifflin Co., 1983.

—*Chancellorsville*. Boston: Houghton Mifflin Co., 1996.

—ed. *Mr. Dunn Browne's Experiences in the War: The Civil War Letters of Samuel W. Fiske*. New York: Fordham University Press, 1998.

—*Gettysburg*. New York: Houghton Mifflin Company, 2003.

Smedlund, William S., *Camp Fires of Georgia's Troops, 1861-1865*. Kennesaw, Ga.: Kennesaw Mountain Press, 1994.

Smith, David C., *The Battle That History Lost*. Rogersville, Tn.: East Tennessee Printing Co., Inc., 1982.

Trudeau, Noah A., *Bloody Roads South – The Wilderness To Cold Harbor.* Boston: Little, Brown & Co., 1989.

——*The Last Citadel: Petersburg, Virginia – June 1864-April 1865*. Baton Rouge, La.: Louisiana State University Press. 1993.

——*Gettysburg: A Testing of Courage*. New York, NY: Harper Collins Publishers, Inc., 2002.

Tucker, Phillip Thomas. *Burnside's Bridge: The Climactic Struggle of the 2nd and 20th Georgia at Antietam Creek.* Mechanicsburg, Pa.: Stackpole Books, 2000.

United Daughters of the Confederacy, Moultrie McNeill Chapter No. 661. *Confederate Soldiers in Colquitt County, Georgia.* Moultrie, Ga.: Moultrie McNeill Chapter No. 661, 1980.

Ward, Warren P., *Ward's History of Coffee County*. Spartanburg, SC.: The Reprint Company Publishers, 1985.

Wert, Jeffry D., *From Winchester to Cedar Creek*. Carlisle, Pa.: South Mountain Press Inc., 1987.

—— *Gettysburg – Day Three*. New York: Simon & Schuster, 2001.

White, Virgil P., *Index to Georgia Civil War Confederate Pension Files*, Waynesboro, Tn.; The National Historical Publishing Co., 1996.

Whitehorne, Joseph W.A., *The Battle of Belle Grove or Cedar Creek – Self Guided Tour*. Strasburg, Va.: The Wayside Museum of American History and Arts, 1991.

Wiley, Bell Irvin. *The Life of Johnny Reb*. Baton Rouge, LA.: Louisiana University Press, 2000.

ARTICLES/ESSAYS/NEWSPAPERS/MAPS

"A Flag of Truce to the Battle-field of Manassas." *Richmond Daily Dispatch* Richmond, Va. September 16, 1862.

Alexander, Peter W., "In Front of Fredericktown, Md. Sept 8th, 1862." *Savannah Republican*, Savannah, Ga. September 22, 1862.

Atlanta Journal, Atlanta, Ga. 1901-1902.

Brock, R.A. "Paroles of the Army of Northern Virginia Surrendered at Appomattox C.H., Va., April 9, 1865." *Southern Historical Society Papers*. Vol. XV, 1887.

Civil War Preservation Trust. "Battle of Sailor's Creek, VA., Hillsman Farm – April 6, 1865." Map by Steven Stanley.

Cochran, L.L., "The Tenth Georgia Regiment at Gettysburg." *Atlanta Journal.* February 23, 1901.

Cosgrove, Lori-Nash, "There is no half way ground." *North-South Trader Civil War,* Vol. XXXVII, No.2.

Daily Chronicle & Sentinel, Augusta, Ga. 1863-1864.

"Death of Colonel F. Kearse." *Charleston Mercury.* August 8, 1863.

Fleming, William O. Letter, *Savannah Republican.* Savannah, Ga. October 11, 1862.

"From Semmes' Brigade." Unidentified Letter. *Savannah Daily Morning News.* May 30, 1863.

Graham, Kurt. "Death of a Brigade: Drayton's Brigade at Fox's Gap, September 14, 1862." *News from Fox's Gap Newsletter.* Vol. 1, Issue 9. June 1, 2000.

Holsworth, Jerry W. "Friends To The Death." *Civil War Times,* Vol. XLV #7, September 2006. p.40-45.

Kross, Gary. "Gettysburg Vignettes To Die Like Soldiers, The Retreat from Sickles' Front, July 2, 1863, Vignette #2 The Wheatfield." *Blue & Gray Magazine,* Vol. XV, Issue 5. June 1998, p.21.

"List of Casualties In The 50th Georgia Regiment In The Fight Near Boonsboro, Sunday, Sept. 14th, 1862." *Augusta Daily Constitutionalist.* Augusta, Ga. October 9, 1862.

Manning, William R., "The Fiftieth Georgia at Sharpsburg." *Savannah Republican.* October 15, 1862.

McBride, Andrew J., "Banner Battle of the War." *Atlanta Journal.* May 4, 1901.

—"From the Chuckee to the Wilderness." *Atlanta Journal.* June 29, 1901.

—"Some Warm War Experiences of Colonel A.J. McBride." *Atlanta Journal.* February 26, 1901.

—"10th Georgia Captures 27th Connecticut." *Atlanta Journal.* September 14, 1901.

—"Tenth Georgia at Spottsylvania." *Atlanta Journal.* July 20, 1901.

McGlashan, Peter A.S. "Battle of Salem Church, May 3, 1863." Address to the Confederate Veterans Association of Savannah, Ga. 1893. *Addresses Delivered Before the Confederate Veterans Association of Savannah, Georgia.* The Confederate Veterans Association of Savannah, Ga.: Braid & Hutton Printers, 1893.

—"Longstreet's Charge At Gettysburg - July 2, 1863." Address to the Confederate Veterans Association of Savannah, Ga. May 1899. *Savannah Morning News Print*. 1902.

—"Our Last Retreat." Address to the Confederate Veterans Association of Savannah, Ga. December 5, 1894. *Addresses Delivered Before the Confederate Veterans Association of Savannah, Georgia.* The Confederate Veterans Association of Savannah, Ga.: Braid & Hutton Printers. P. 57-65. 1895.

—"The Battle of Cedar Creek." Address to the Confederate Veterans Association of Savannah, Ga. November 1, 1892. *Addresses Delivered Before the Confederate Veterans Association of Savannah, Georgia.* Vol.1 Savannah: The Confederate Veteran's Association of Savannah, Ga.: Braid & Hutton Printers, 1893.

—"The Fiftieth Georgia Regiment in Virginia and Maryland." *Savannah Republican.* October 16, 1862.

"Letter from McLaws' Old Division." *Augusta Daily Constitutionalist.* June 16, 1864.

Mertz, Gregory A. "Upton's Attack and the Defense of Dole's Salient." *Blue & Gray Magazine.* Vol. XVIII, Issue 6. August 2001.

—"General Gouverneur K. Warren and the Fighting at Laurel Hill." *Blue & Gray Magazine.* Vol. XXI, Issue 4. Summer 2004.

O'Reilly, Frank A. "Battle of Chancellorsville." Map Series 1-12. Eastern National, 1998

—"Battle of Spotsylvania Court House." Map Series 1-24. Eastern National, 2000.

—"Battle of Fredericksburg." Map Series 1-5. Eastern National, 2001.

—"Battle of The Wilderness." Map Series 1-6. Eastern National, 2003.

Parks, Virgil A.S. Letter to "Mr. Editor from Near Frederick, Md., Sept. 7, 1862." *Savannah Republican*, September 20, 1862.

—Letter to "Mr. Editor from Bivouac In The Field, Va. September 22d, 1862." *Savannah Republican.* October 1, 1862.

Peacock, Jane Bonner, ed., "A Georgian's View of the War in Virginia: The Civil War Letters of A.B. Simms." *Atlanta Historical Journal.* Vol. XXIII, No. 2, Summer 1979.

Richards, David L. "Kershaw and Semmes Attack at the Rose Farm." *Blue & Gray Magazine.* Vol. XX, Issue 2. Holiday 2002.

Roberds, R.T., "Chancellorsville Battle Casualty Report." *Savannah Daily Morning News.* May 16, 1863.

—Letter to "Mr. Editor from Battlefield Near Fredericksburg, May 4th 1863." *Savannah Republican*, May 16, 1862.

"Sketch in the Life of Maj. P.C. Pendleton." *Bainbridge Argus*. July 3, 1869.

Savannah Republican, Savannah, Ga. 1862-1865.

Savannah Morning News Print, Savannah, Ga. 1902.

Suderow, Bryce. "Glory Denied: The First Battle of Deep Bottom." *North & South Magazine*. Vol. 3, #7, p.17-32. September 2000.

Taylor, J.W. Letter to "Dear ___ from Camp 10th Ga. Regiment Three miles from Williamsport, Md. July 13th, 1863." *Augusta Chronicle & Sentinel*. Augusta, Ga. July 1863.

"The assault on Knoxville – a Confederate account." *Richmond Daily Dispatch*. December 24, 1863.

"The Fiftieth Georgia in the Late Battles." *Savannah Republican*. May 18, 1863.

Unidentified 10th Georgia soldier. "Some Incidents of the March to Gettysburg." *Atlanta Journal*. August 31, 1901.

Valdosta Times. Valdosta, Ga. June 1885.

Walden, Daniel, "Tenth Georgia at Knoxville." *Atlanta Journal*. January 11, 1902.

Index

Bloodworth, Lewis, 253
Bloody Lane, 46
Blue Ridge Mountains, 7, 35, 108, 109, 137, 224
Blun, Elias, 225
Bondurant, J. W., artillery battery, C.S., 41
Boon, Francis M., 144
Boonsboro, Md., 37-40
Boston, Ga., 271
Boteler's Ford, 63
Bowman's Mill Ford, 229-230, 232
Bradford, William W., 204
Brady, John A., 345 photo, 351
Brady, Samuel E., 345 photo, 351
Bragg, Braxton, 141, 143-144, 148, 158
Bragg, James, 208
Breckinridge, John C., division, C.S. 201
  Secretary of War, C.S., 251
Brewerton, Henry F., battery, U.S. , 234
Brewton, David L., 38
Brice, David J., 179
Brice, James, 129, 179
Briggs, William H., 50, 223
Bristol, Tn., 162, 165-167
Brock, John H.J., 165
Brock Road, 175-176, 178, 181-183, 186, 188
Brock's Bridge, 172
Brooke, John R., brigade, U.S., 7, 92, 125-126
Brooks County, Ga., 5, 6, 7, 9, 13, 90,
  115, 118, 129, 133, 175, 209, 269,
  270, 342
Brooks Volunteers, 9, 11, 12, 115, 118, 339
  see also, Company K, 50th Georgia
Brooks, William T. H. "Bully", division
  U.S., 94, 196, 202
Brown, Henry W., brigade, U.S., 96-98
Brown, Joseph E., 1, 7, 215
Brown, William P., 164
Brucetown, Va., 65, 68, 70, 222
Brunson, Isaiah, 223
Bryan, Goode, 129, 131, 137, 139 photo, 151,
  152, 154, 155, 171, 173-176, 178, 181
  191, 196, 200-201, 205, 219, 222, 373n
  brigade, C.S., 142, 144-146, 148-149,
  154, 158, 160-161, 169, 173, 175-
  176, 178-179, 181-183, 186, 188,
  195, 197-200, 201-204, 206-208,
  210, 212, 214, 218-219, 222, 224,
  225, 227, 230, 250, 378n
Bryant, Calvin, 185
Bryant, Daniel L., 265
Bryant, John, 160
Bryn Athyn College, 269
Buckeystown, Md., 36
Buckton, Va., 224

Buford, John, 132
Bull Run, 27-28, 31, 33
Bull Run, Battle of, *see* Manassas, Battle
  of Second
Bull Run Mountains, 27
Bullock House, 93
Bull's Gap, Tn., 165
Burgess family [Winchester], 219
Burkeville, Va., 254, 260
Burkhalter, Isaac, 4, 5, 8, 70, 82
Burnside, Ambrose, corps and army, U.S.,
  4, 5, 6, 71-72, 78, 79, 81, 85, 144,
  146, 148, 154, 158-159
  resignation from army command, 81
Burnside's Bridge, *see* Rohrbach Bridge
Butler, A.J., 210
Butler, Lewis F., 265-266 photo
Butts County, Ga., 10
Byrd, William A., 192, 341

Cabell, Henry G., artillery battalion, C.S., 112
Caldwell, John C., division, U.S., 119, 126
Camp Chase Prison, 161, 165
Camp Davis, 3, 6, 7, 9, 11, 12, 15, 18
Camp Lee, 23
Camp Randolph, 66-67
Carver, Richard, 354 photo, 351
Cashtown Gap, 130-131
Cason, Hillary W., 166, 185, 261, 341
Catharpin Road, 172, 179, 181
Cedar Creek, 227, 229-232, 234, 237, 241, 247
Cedar Creek, Battle of, 6, 115, 230-244,
  248, 250, 266, 268, 376n, 377n
Cedar Mountain [Run], Battle of, 23, 218
Cedarville, Va., 218
Cemetery Hill, 58
Cemetery Ridge, 111, 129-130
Centreville, Va., 30, 32
Chaffin's Bluff, 212
Chaffin's Farm, 18, 23, 248
Chambers, Hugh C., 50
Chamberlain, Joshua L., division, U.S., 261
Chambersburg, Pa., 7, 38, 109
Chancellor house, 90, 99
Chancellorsville, Battle of, 7, 85, 88, 104,
  118, 266, 267, 344
  see also Salem Church, Battle of
Chancellorsville, Va., 7, 85-93, 95, 97, 99,
  101, 103-107, 118, 137, 162, 171, 176,
  266, 267, 344
Chantilly, Va. 3, 31, 33
Charleston, S.C., 2, 10, 16, 23
Charlestown Road, 219, 221

Author's Biography

James W. Parrish was born in Quitman, Georgia, but grew up in Greenville, Florida, a small rural community just below the Georgia border. He received a BA in History from Florida State University and an MA in Political Science from the University of South Florida. Parrish served in local government administration for over twenty years, including Administrator of Leon County, Florida, before starting his own business. He and his wife lived in the St. Petersburg, Florida area for thirteen years, but have resided for the past twenty-eight years in Tallahassee, Florida.